To Cliff Goldsmith
With warm best wishes
George W Ball,
May 31, 1982

Books by GEORGE W. BALL

Diplomacy for a Crowded World
The Discipline of Power
The Past Has Another Pattern

George W. Ball. Portrait by Everett Raymond Kinstler, 1973

The Past
Has Another
Pattern

MEMOIRS

George W. Ball

W · W · NORTON & COMPANY · *NEW YORK* · *LONDON*

Unless otherwise credited, photographs are from author's personal file.

FIRST EDITION

The text of this book is composed in photocomposition Baskerville. The typeface used for display is Typositor Deepdene. Composition and manufacturing are by the Maple-Vail Book Manufacturing Group.

BOOK DESIGN BY MARJORIE J. FLOCK

Library of Congress Cataloging in Publication Data
Ball, George W.
   The past has another pattern.
   Includes bibliographical references and index.
   1. Ball, George W. 2. United States—Foreign
relations—1945–   3. United States—Foreign
relations—1933–1945. 4. Statesmen—United States—
Biography. I. Title.
E840.8.B32A36 1982   973.9   81–18924
                       AACR2

ISBN 0-393-01481-9

W. W. Norton & Company, Inc. 500 Fifth Avenue, New York, N.Y. 10110
W. W. Norton & Company Ltd. 37 Great Russell Street, London WC1B 3NU

1 2 3 4 5 6 7 8 9 0

To my brother,
STUART S. BALL,
who knows much of this story
better than I

Contents

ILLUSTRATIONS *follow page 234*

MAPS *on pages 223 and 339*

Preface

More than a half-century has passed since I first read T. E. Lawrence's *Seven Pillars of Wisdom,* yet I can still recall his vignettes of the personalities he encountered. I remember particularly his assessment of Sir Ronald Storrs, then the Oriental Secretary of the Residency in Cairo, whom Lawrence described as "the most brilliant Englishman in the Near East." Storrs, he said, was "subtly efficient," but he could have been far more so "had he not spread his energies over a wide spectrum of . . . interests"—or, in other words, "had he been able to deny himself the world. . . ."

I mentioned this comment one afternoon when Jean Monnet and I were working together in his country house at Houjarray, a few kilometers from Paris. "Of course, Lawrence was right," he observed, "and you should take it to heart. You ought to deny yourself the world far more than you do. You shouldn't diffuse your energies, let so many things light up your imagination. You should find yourself a single theme, a single cause, and devote your life to it. That's the only way you'll ever move mountains."

Though Monnet's advice was no doubt right, he knew that I would not follow it. As this book discloses, I could never muster the discipline to concentrate exclusively on a single well-defined objective or—to put it another way—to hold any job very long. Monnet was not the only one to chide me about this. When, in 1968, under relentless pressure from President Lyndon Johnson, I undertook a brief stint as United States ambassador to the United Nations, my old friend John Kenneth Galbraith wrote anxiously to record his bafflement at my "curious career pattern."

A book of memoirs is by definition an exercise in self-indulgence, yet to undertake such a task implies some acknowledgment of fading ambition. I recall a story about Bertrand Russell, who, when urged in his eighties to write his memoirs, replied, "Who can say that it's not premature? Some day I may be the President of Mexico."

Well, I have looked out across the Rio Grande without seeing a single favorable whiff of smoke, so I am now reconciled. I know I shall never be President of Mexico.

Hence, this book.

Acknowledgments

It was James A. (Scotty) Reston who first proposed this book. I could, he suggested, expose my prejudices more effectively through memoirs than through the casual short pieces I was then writing for newspapers and magazines. But that was the extent of his culpability; he is in no way responsible for the content of these pages, and I hope his role as instigator will not trouble his Calvinist conscience.

I have benefitted from the help and advice of many. John Kenneth Galbraith read the manuscript with his legendary fortitude and provided much wise and friendly counsel. Barbara Wendell Kerr cleared away vast amounts of the underbrush strangling my prose, to the extent that I can now understand most of what I have written. George Springsteen, an old comrade in arms on the State Department barricades, supplemented my faulty memory and provided much sound advice. Elinor Green spent hours reviewing manuscripts and expanding and checking bits and pieces of the story.

Yoma Ullman devoted many months assembling, organizing, and interpreting huge dunes of documents I had untidily accumulated over many years; it was a lonely, tedious task performed with patience, high skill, dedication—and good humor. Dr. Larissa Onyshkevych completed that research, held me firmly to the record, and provided much of the documentation found in the footnotes.

I owe a special vote of thanks to Helen T. Vahey, my resourceful assistant for thirteen years. She approached this book with the same impressive energy, dedication, and acute judgment she had displayed during all my other enterprises; the book could not have been completed, even on a long-deferred deadline, without her deep commitment. Mary E. Koester also provided invaluable assistance, patiently transforming my love affair with a tape recorder into pages of elegant typescript and faithfully pointing out when I was talking nonsense. Lee Good Hurford combined patience and tolerance with the magic of word processing to produce the finished product, while Carol Plum proved valiant in time of need.

I express my profound gratitude to Evan W. Thomas, my stern but understanding editor at Norton, whose expert guidance was indispensable. I accepted his advice almost invariably, not from cowardice but because he was right. In addition, I greatly benefitted from the counsel and encouragment of Donald S. Lamm, president of Norton, whose comments were incisive and always helpful.

My thanks, as always, to Ruth M. Ball, who has for a half-century been my most patient but forgiving critic. My historian son, Dr. Douglas B. Ball, proved a sound adviser on times past. My son John C. Ball was a constant source of encouragement. My brother, Stuart S. Ball, also read the book and remembered much I had forgotten or never known. And finally, Alfred and Margarita Ramirez provided the environment conducive to intensive writing.

It seems, as one becomes older,
That the past has another pattern, and ceases to be a mere sequence—
Or even development: the latter a partial fallacy,
Encouraged by superficial notions of evolution,
Which becomes, in the popular mind, a means of disowning the past.
The moments of happiness—not the sense of well-being,
Fruition, fulfillment, security or affection,
Or even a very good dinner, but the sudden illumination—
We had the experience but missed the meaning, . . .

—T. S. Eliot, *The Dry Salvages*

PART I

Years before Pearl Harbor

1. *The First Eighteen Years Are the Easiest*

"Autobiography," wrote Lord Vansittart, "would be easier had we all eccentric parents." Though my own parents lacked that distinction, my paternal grandfather was eccentric enough to make up for the deficiency.

Born in Cornwall in 1849 (which enabled him, when he lived in California many years later, to refer to himself as a "forty-niner"), Amos Ball, Sr., grew up on the island of Jersey, where his father, Isaac Ball, was a gardener on the estate of Charles Tennyson—brother of the poet. Apprenticed to a baker, he was reputed by family legend to have delivered bread to Victor Hugo, then living in exile; indeed, improved by time and retelling, the story even had Hugo hiring him to read the French classics aloud. Since, as I have now discovered, my grandfather was only five years old when Hugo lived in Jersey, I would attribute these claims more to the exuberance of family chroniclers than to his dubious precocity.

On June 24, 1874, my grandfather married Selina Scoble, a lady's maid to a family recently arrived from Devon. It was a marriage of opposites. My grandfather was a small, dark-complexioned Cornishman, with a black beard, mischievous eyes, and a volatile temper; she was a tall, large-boned, handsome girl, compassionate and unselfish. Her indefatigable common sense compensated for my grandfather's irresponsibility.

They were married by the dean of Jersey, the father of Lily Langtry—the "Jersey Lily" who later became famous not only as a beauty and an actress but also as the mistress of Edward VII. Though I doubt my grandfather ever actually met Lily, he talked about her as though she were an old friend, just as he spoke of his acquaintance with the Pre-Raphaelite painter Sir John Millais, who had helped him when he fell from his baker's wagon. In sum, my grandfather was a name-dropper—a trait he passed on to many of his descendants. I suspect also that his desire to associate himself with the famous reflected caste-consciousness. Intellectually contemptuous of almost everyone, he could not conceal his deference toward the "upper classes"—a fine, old-fashioned phrase he used reverentially.

Soon after their marriage, my grandparents moved to Devon to be near my grandmother's family. Settled for a while at Kingswear on the River Dart, they then moved some miles northeast to Highweek, just up the hill from Newton Abbot, where my father, Amos Ball, Jr., was born May 3, 1877.

Five years later, when my grandfather's bakery went bankrupt, he decided—no doubt at his wife's urging—to leave England. He had at the time three children: my father and two daughters, one older and one younger than my father. Another child was on the way. (Years later, my uncle John Ball, the youngest of what had by then become a family of nine children, was accustomed to excuse his own delinquencies by explaining, "What could you expect of anyone born behind the eight Ball?")

My grandfather was encouraged to go to America by his wife's sister, Sarah Parkhouse (known as "Sally"), whose husband, caught poaching and forced to flee England, had invested his earnings from illegal veni-son in farm land near the village of Toledo, Iowa. From there, my great-aunt Sally supplied her kinfolk in the Old Country with a weekly chron-icle of her life in the idyllic Iowa countryside, which combined, she implied, the best features of the Garden of Eden with "England's green and pleasant land."

Impressed, though skeptical, my grandfather set out to see for him-self, arranging with my grandmother that, after their fourth child was born, she should sell their household possessions and join him. Just why he left when his wife was in advanced pregnancy and why he went first to Canada when his ultimate destination was Toledo, Iowa, remains wrapped in mystery—though he did have a penchant for bad planning. In any event, soon after he had left, the baby was born, and some weeks later, my grandfather wrote to ask my grandmother if she felt able to bring the young family to America by herself. If so, she should come; if not, he would return to England and escort them.

Hardheaded as usual, my grandmother knew that, in the month required for a reply to reach her husband, she could already be across the water. So, with her four young children, she set sail for Canada only to find that her husband had impetuously sailed on a ship that had passed hers in the mid-Atlantic. Thus my father's first home in the New World was an immigrant shed in Quebec, where my grandmother and her brood slept until my grandfather could work his way back to Canada as a stoker. It was, my father told me, a shock for a small boy to see his mother embrace a filthy, besooted man who suddenly appeared at their door.

Life with my grandfather was a badly written serial, replete with pratfalls and belly laughs. When the family finally reached Toledo, my grandfather found nothing that resembled Aunt Sally's descriptions. It took him several days to discover that they were in Toledo, Ohio, and not Toledo, Iowa, some five hundred miles away.

Nor did they find a land of milk and honey at their destination. Aunt Sally's husband had become a shiftless drunk, mistreating his wife and neglecting the farm, and her dithyrambic bulletins had been merely an escape from sordid reality—early examples of the modern real estate brochure.

Life in an Iowa village in the 1880s was awkward and precarious for an immigrant family—the poorest in town—looked down on by the natives in spite of my grandfather's belief in the God-ordained superiority of Englishmen. Though his efforts to preach as a lay Wesleyan minister no doubt nourished his soul, they provided no food for the family, which, during their chilly first winter, lived largely on the gift of frozen potatoes. A pumpkin donated by a kindly neighbor proved a disaster; unfamiliar with that exotic vegetable, my grandmother made everyone ill by cooking it whole, including the seeds.

In time, my grandfather established a hay and feed store, which he later expanded to include groceries and general merchandise, and it was in the rooms behind the store that my father grew up. With some help from his younger brother George (for whom I was named), my father kept the faltering business going, while the senior Amos Ball conducted a nonstop seminar in theology for cronies sprawled in perpetual session around the wood stove and spittoon. With his black beard fiercely wagging, he was a certified eccentric in a small midwestern village where, a hundred years ago, eccentrics were a dime a dozen. Wearing an old felt hat, indoors and out, he would elaborately greet any actual or potential customers who might enter the store. When, many years later, his sons installed a telephone, he would cautiously pick up the receiver as though it were about to explode, then lift his hat if a woman's voice answered.

Much to my father's disgust, my grandfather's business practices were idiosyncratic. Since he felt it beneath his dignity to ask the name of a customer, substantial credits might be entered on his books to "the gray beard from north of Tama" or to "the little saddler." But behind his eccentricity lay a shrewd sense of self-survival and a canny stratagem for avoiding work. Though his own father and grandfather had both lived to ninety, he announced in his early fifties that he had only a few more years of life left to him. Even while his beard was still jet black, he would intone lugubriously, "My days are in the sere, the yellow leaf"—a sentiment he repeated incessantly for more than three decades until he finally died at eighty-five. I remember him well in his last years when he came from his home in California to visit us in Des Moines on the excuse of a church convocation. He was still spry and smugly pleased with his own virtuosity. A gifted actor, he could go in and out of character in an instant. After poking cruel fun at the professional ecclesiastics (he never gave up his amateur status), he would, as though on cue, assume that posture of "querulous serenity" perfected by Jane Austen's Mrs. Bennet. For the benefit of his elderly sister, who looked after him, he could give a bravura impersonation of a saint so convincing as to leave her with permanent suspension of disbelief. But piety, as my father pointed out, demanded something more than homiletics and a cunning smile, especially when the old man was sadistically exploiting his sister's sentimentality for his own comfort. It was the first time I had ever witnessed cynicism in action, and as a child I felt confused and uneasy. Later, when I read that at his wife's funeral, Theobald, in *The Way of All Flesh,* "buried his face in his handkerchief to conceal his want of grief," I was reminded of my grandfather.

My Father

With erratic paternal assistance—or, more frequently, obstruction—my father worked fourteen-hour days to keep the small, shaky general store from going under. Though he had to leave school at the age of nine and received a total of only about four years of formal schooling during his entire life, he still became, by any standard, a well-, though unevenly, educated man. He read every book he could borrow. He developed an ear for the beauty of words and the cadence of speech by immersing himself not only in the King James version of the Bible but also in the writings of Sir Thomas Browne, Macaulay, De Quincey, Milton, and Gibbon. For self-discipline and from a love of language, he learned by heart the first five books of *Paradise Lost*—large passages of which he could still recite sixty years later. With his sister's help, he taught himself Pitman shorthand and became such an expert typist that the Remington Typewriter Company once tried to hire him as a speed demonstrator.

When he was nineteen, a traveling salesman offered my father a job with the Standard Oil Company in Marshalltown, Iowa, a larger town eighteen miles away from Toledo. Feeling his heavy responsibility for a fey family, he hesitated to leave until his mother pushed him out of the nest. Scraping together a few dollars she had squirreled away unbeknownst to her husband, she handed my father the railroad fare to Marshalltown and a few days' living expenses. There was, she insisted, no future for him in Toledo, and, much as she wanted him near her, he was destined to do great things.

In Marshalltown, he was first put to work driving a tankwagon, then promoted to a clerk's job where, in addition to sweeping the floor, he could use his stenographic proficiency. Practicing a disciplined frugality, he would walk two miles every night rather than spend five cents for a street car. He always carried a nickel with him but, as he told me later, he took satisfaction in finding it still in his pocket at the end of the day. Those evening excursions were principally to call on a vivacious young country schoolteacher named Edna Wildman, whom he had met some years after arriving in Marshalltown. Only four feet eleven—a tiny partner for a six-foot Englishman—she was not deterred by her diminutive dimensions from spunkily disciplining her farm-boy students, many of whom were as old as she and twice her size.

In time, my father's hard work and intelligence won him a promotion to the divisional office of his company in Des Moines, some seventy miles away; a year later he and Edna Wildman were married. Since the Wildman family was a closed ecosystem, it was a giant step for my mother to leave her parents and move so far away, and, though she finally came to call Des Moines her home, she never felt completely happy away from Marshalltown and the company of her brothers and sisters.

What made her exile bearable was the arrival of a family. My brother Stuart was born in 1905 and my brother Ralph in 1907. I appeared on the scene four days before Christmas in 1909—a far from quiet time. All over the world people and nations were being beastly to one another in imaginative ways. Within a few months before or after my birth, the Shah of Persia was deposed; the Prime Minister of Egypt was assassinated; Italy started a war to acquire Tripoli and Cyrenaica; the British gained control of the four northern states of the Malay Peninsula; Germany and France engaged in a quarrel over dominance in Morocco which was settled by the International Court at The Hague; the Union of South Africa came into existence; the Manchu Dynasty fell; Japan annexed Korea; King Leopold II died in Belgium; Bethmann-Hollweg replaced Prince Bernhard von Bülow as Chancellor of Germany; a radical government under Clemenceau and Briand destroyed the Left Coalition in France; and Britain faced a major constitutional crisis over the 1909 budget.

In spite of these events—which perhaps reflect no more than the world's usual portion of turmoil—most wise men of the West still accepted the nineteenth century's favorable prognosis for the human species. They believed in the idea of progress, reinforced by the Darwinian hypothesis and an abiding faith in the perfectibility of man. Few would have predicted that Europe was moving pell-mell toward the first of those two cataclysmic civil wars—as Dean Acheson later called them—that, within my lifetime, were to change the face of the world.

Early Years

My childhood was a happy time—with few disturbing incidents, except that, for whatever the psychoanalysts may make of it, I was chased by an angry mother swan when I was three years old.* Because two of my mother's uncles had been drowned, I was not allowed to swim—and I have never learned more than a rudimentary stroke. Nor had I any taste for the manly art of murdering animals, though, given an air rifle by an indulgent uncle, I once shot absentmindedly at a robin, confident I could never hit it. When the unaccommodating bird fell dead, I hid my remorse in the darkness of my room. Later an enterprising teacher named Miss Dobson briefly interested me in birdwatching, but—though I am still fond of birds—I can hardly tell a chicken hawk from a chicken.

During my first eleven years, I attended public schools in Des Moines, but, on balance, I probably learned more from arguing with my father and my brother Stuart, both of whom read avidly and were endowed with almost total recall. Since we all held strong views—or, more properly, strong prejudices—the family dinner table was the scene of a continuing dispute about history, literature, and politics; in fact, few meals were ever finished without one of us leaving the table to try to prove a point from Chambers's *Encyclopedic Dictionary.*

My brother Stuart had a weapon that gave him what I regarded as an unfair advantage. Fascinated from an early age by genealogy, he printed in a minute script huge genealogical tables. Inscribed on the reverse side of leftover rolls of wallpaper, his tables ran the full length of each roll, and if one roll were not enough, he pasted two together. Often he would settle an argument by flinging one of his huge rolls dramatically on the floor, giving it a kick, and letting it publish its learning the length of two rooms. His particular delight was to document the illegitimacy that blemished the family trees of noble families, and many years later the idea still seemed to please him. When, as a State Department official, I would introduce him to political figures from Great Britain or the Continent who had titles printed in Burke's or the *Almanach de Gotha,* he would delight in telling me of the bars sinister in their families, going back eight or nine hundred years to prove his point.

Those forays around the dining table were field days for everyone

---

*For reasons I do not understand, I apparently have an irritating effect on swans, since I was pecked at by another such monster in 1961 at a geisha picnic near Kyoto. I got my own back that time by stepping on its bill, but I am sure my more imaginative critics can—and will—draw dark inferences from my odd involvement with a creature so scandalously thought of by both Freud and the ancient Greeks.

but my mother and my brother Ralph, who was the quiet one. My mother came from a gentle, unadventurous family in which conversation was limited to the minutiae of the day. The merest breath of controversy was an ill wind that blew no one any good; argument for the Wildmans was the immoral equivalent of war and they were dialectical pacifists. In sharp contrast to the senior Amos Ball, my maternal grandfather, John Wildman, was a quiet, courteous gentleman whose amiability belied his record as a soldier. Though he abhorred crossing swords at the dinner table, he looked back on his four years in the Union Army (taken prisoner and later exchanged) as the epic experience that drained the rest of his life of drama and color. My early recollections of him consist largely of his Civil War stories; for him, everything after Appomattox was anti-climax. He had married my grandmother—after her first husband failed, either through choice or mortality, to return from the war—and, thereafter, had held a succession of small state or county jobs (deputy sheriff, state oil inspector, and so on), committing only the minimum effort to any assignment. His interests were concentrated in the Grand Army of the Republic, the veteran's organization influential at that time, together with the Masonic Order, in which he played an enthusiastic, if unobtrusive, role.

Since the serene inconsequence of her family household left my mother unprepared for coexistence with a whole zoo of assertive males, she frequently sat defenseless, while unguided missiles whizzed merrily by. It was only after my wife, Ruth, had joined the family that my mother acquired an intrepid ally. Refusing to be cowed, Ruth rose and stood at the table until silence abruptly descended. That happened only once or twice; the lesson was learned, and women were granted the right to be heard. It was the first insidious intrusion of women's lib that the Ball family experienced.

In the evening and on Sundays, my father regularly read aloud from his favorite authors, taking obvious pleasure in the beauty of words and phrases. When he was not reading to us, we were most often reading to ourselves. Each Saturday we followed a ritual. After lunch the whole family walked a half-mile down the hill to the public library, where we spent the afternoon, each pursuing his or her own lines of interest; then, in the evening, we formed a stylized procession back up the hill—the tall man, his short wife, and three sons graduated in height like the downward curve of a disastrous stock market. Each carried a suitcase appropriate to his or her size and station, containing the books borrowed for consumption during the next seven days. It was a weekly adventure to which we all looked forward.

With the advent of World War I, my brother Stuart taught Ralph and me the military drills he was learning in school; we then re-fought the current battles with armies of spools deployed about the attic floor, trying to reconstruct from newspaper descriptions the maneuvering of each side, as well as its strategy and tactics. My mother helped us procure the spools from her neighbors, and we had a vast number. Even greater reality was given to our wartime exertions when my father's much younger brother, John Ball, who lived with us from time to time, went off to the army. Taking naturally to soldiering, he was soon commissioned, and, since he was for a time stationed near Des Moines, his appearance in uniform gave the family a certain distinction. Later, when he sailed for France, we felt near the heart of the conflict.

On November 11, 1918, the guns fell silent and we all went downtown to share in the excitement, thus inadvertently encouraging the spread of the flu then raging. As our troops returned, I principally recall the sight of soldiers embracing whatever girls happened to be wandering by; there was a galvanizing gaiety in the air, and our local heroes all seemed twelve feet tall. I shall never forget when General Pershing came to our school and I actually shook his hand—though I concealed from my parents the dismaying fact that he was wearing a glove. Those scenes came back to my mind twenty-seven years later on V-E Day in Paris.

During my early years, life was not without perils, though I was protected from them as much as possible. In order to shelter his growing family, my father made plans for a larger house to be built on a vacant lot next to the cottage where I was born. To economize, he dug the basement alone at night and on Sundays. During the summer, while our new house was under construction, the family slept in a tent so we could rent the cottage. Though disguised as an outing, that economy measure proved disastrous; exhausted from overwork and exposure to inclement weather, my father contracted lobar pneumonia. For a time it was touch and go whether he would live.

Had he not survived, my life would have followed quite a different course; as it was, he continued his diligent upward climb through the hierarchical layers of the Standard Oil management until finally he became a vice-president and director. As the youngest member of the family, I benefited the most, not only from the rising level of family income, but also from the increasingly liberal view my parents gained from exposure to a wider world. My brother Stuart had the far more difficult task of breaking new ground. Apart from my wife, Ruth, my father takes prime place among those who did most to shape my own attitudes. I absorbed his love of literature, his detachment, and his sense of the ridiculous.

Although my father established a formidable business reputation, his work gave him few intellectual satisfactions or rewarding companions. Respected by colleagues and feared by competitors, he was still regarded as formal and reserved, definitely not one of the boys. It was an attitude he could never shake off, although I think at times he wanted to. He was constrained by shyness, the defensive habits of self-containment acquired in his youth, and the inner knowledge that he differed from his business associates in taste and intellectual interests. So, although—or, to some extent, because—he had an incorrigible sense of the absurd, he was never fully at ease with his fellow businessmen. Withdrawn to the point where he sometimes seemed stiff, he was in awe of those who wore their Doctorates of Philosophy as badges of omniscience. Like several other men I was to know later in life—including one President of the United States— he could not forget the inadequacy of his formal education. Never hesitant to assert his views—no Ball ever had an unexpressed thought—he yet remained to his death excessively deferential toward academics.

In 1922, when I was twelve years old, my father was promoted to the head office of the Standard Oil Company in Chicago, as assistant general manager of marketing. At my mother's urging, the family was established in Evanston, Illinois, the home of Northwestern University, which, she had decreed, her sons would attend. Determined to keep the family intact as long as possible, she saw no reason why any of us should leave home for college if home could be located near college.

The Dolors of Adolescence

Our departure from Des Moines marked the end of my childhood and the beginning of a less tranquil adolescence. That I had a felicitous, albeit confining, childhood seeems self-evident. The more I have seen of the strains and problems in other families, the more I appreciate the affection and solidarity that prevailed in ours. As a family, we were a tight microcosm. My mother saw no reason why her sons should play with any other children, and, indeed, we played together quite happily. Yet all three sons paid some price for it, as we tried clumsily to adjust to a larger social arena.

Evanston Township High School had quite a different quality from the schools I had known in Des Moines and, for a boy of eleven, the transition presented more than the usual problems of adjustment. Although the school now has the shape and appearance of a large, bureaucratized institution, it was then still small, with a curriculum heavy in Latin and Greek. Standards were high, and I had to work far harder than before; but the academic fare was solid, and I found it exhilarating. The physical embodiment of the school's meaning, as it appeared to me, was an impressive Mr. Chips named George Whipple. He had total confidence in his own culture and standard of values. Latin, as he taught it, was far more vivid than any modern tongue, while the ringing plains of Troy became as familiar as our school playing fields. I suppose that in many ways he was the first truly civilized man I had known, and I never forgot him. He was distinctly of the old school—a gallant specimen of a rapidly vanishing species. Like the passenger pigeon, his kind will not be seen again, and so much the worse for all of us.

While I could adapt to Professor Whipple with easy gratification because I was not expected to deal with him on a level of equality, relations with my classmates were difficult. Evanston was still a small town dominated by a group of rich families, far more worldly and experienced than those I had known in my innocent years in Des Moines ("sophisticated" was the word I used to myself without being very sure what it meant). In the summer, the established families went off to Europe or to smart resorts or to vacation houses in the country. During the school years, there were parties and dances accessible only to those in the local social register. But what increasingly set the elite apart was their constant chatter of the future. Those whom I most envied and admired talked in vibrant anticipation of Eastern colleges, where their names had been inscribed from childhood. I made few friends. By nature gregarious, I was forced in on myself more than I would have wished. But within a few days of entering Northwestern University, I met the first (after my father) of a small number of individuals who critically affected the course of my thought and, indeed, the pattern of my life.

The De Voto Influence

Bernard De Voto ("Benny" as we all called him) was not in any sense an overpowering personality, but, pursued by devils of self-doubt and insecurity, he instinctively understood my adolescent awkwardness and could teach me the defenses by which he sustained his own vulnerable ego. Since my brother Stuart, who preceded me at Northwestern, had already worked with Benny, I was overjoyed when—within a fortnight after the opening of school—I was assigned to an experimental English class over which De Voto presided. We were a specially anointed group of eighteen or twenty students and we revelled in that knowledge, exhibiting a cockiness that De Voto first sought to demolish and then to direct toward appropriate targets. Though he was then only twenty-nine years old and had been a mere four years at Northwestern, Benny was already widely known not merely as an outrageously irreverent young instructor but also—it was grudgingly admitted—as a writer of promise.

More than a writer, he was also a gifted teacher—at least for those who were charmed by his provocative manner and were eager to read and talk. The studied unorthodoxy of his teaching methods first shocked us to attention; then, as the rich resources of his reading and perception became evident, we developed mounting respect. De Voto's classroom manner—when he held formal classes at all—was light-hearted and taunting. Perched on the edge of his desk, he began by insulting his students. Most of us would not, he said, be interested in what he would teach and were incapable of learning it; if anyone wanted to avoid his sessions, so much the better. Then he would walk up and down the room, conducting colloquies with individual students, teasing the girls—particularly the prettiest ones—berating the Rotarian spirit that then afflicted the university, and denouncing contemporary tastes and mores.

Yet Benny took a warm interest in the private problems of students who responded to him. The fact that he once or twice adjourned class so that he and I could play tennis, or that I could talk with him at almost any time during the day, gave me the sense that I was, after all, thought worthy of interest by the most interesting man in the university. Too young and preoccupied with my own small problems, I did not suspect that my new mentor had even more agonizing doubts and fears of his own. What I acquired from Benny is hard to assess even after all this time. It was, I suppose, what General de Gaulle referred to as an *idée certaine* of myself and my relation to the rest of the world. As to the immediate scene, he confirmed my belief that Northwestern, at that moment in its history, was something less than my romanticised view of what a great university should be—a comforting excuse for my involuntary aloofness.

Benny turned my personal awkwardness and lack of public acceptance into virtues, transforming me in the process into an obnoxious little intellectual snob. Then, at the end of my first year, he departed, refusing the assistant professorship he had been offered and opting for a life in New England untrammeled by institutional obligations. Yet he did not abandon me entirely but arranged before leaving to pass me on to his closest friend on the faculty, Garrett Mattingly, a man of intellect and sensitivity who later made a distinguished reputation as a historian with his books *Renaissance Diplomacy, Catherine of Aragon,* and *The Armada.* Mattingly was at all times sympathetic and generous with his time.

During my last two academic years, I took an honors course in literature. It ranged ambitiously from the classics through the Middle Ages and into modern times. My tutor managed to convey particularly the intellectual excitement of his own period of specialization, the eighteenth century. I had by then read a bit of Francis Bacon, Hobbes, John Locke, and the other English philosophers, but Voltaire captured my imagination as no one else had done, and I felt myself a citizen of the Age of Reason.

The preeminent attraction of Voltaire was his wit, which sharply distinguished him from the cheerless Rousseau. Since I then believed—and still do—that the only acceptable working hypothesis for a self-respecting man is optimism, it seemed sensible to regard the human condition as fundamentally comic. The long-faced literary types, I thought, had got it backwards. Dramas and novels should not be lugubrious with occasional comic relief, but funny with tragic interludes. That was before the erudite hacks' preoccupation with self had become such a literary bore.

In the summer of 1929, after my junior year at Northwestern, my brothers and I departed for Europe on a Middle-Western interpretation of the eighteenth-century Grand Tour. That we should undertake this pilgrimage had long been an ambition of my mother, who looked on crossing the ocean—which presumably one did only once in a lifetime—as the capstone to an elegant education.

We sailed on a small Cunard liner with an ill-assorted collection of students and vacationing school teachers, and for me, at nineteen, the New Freedom suddenly became more than a slogan. We landed at Le Havre, took the boat-train to Paris, and the next night set off to explore the more innocent fleshpots. Paired off more or less by chance with three girls, we began staidly enough at the opera, then paid tribute to a succession of small Montmartre animals—dead rats, agile rabbits, and the like. Finally, sometime in the latter morning hours, we arrived at a Russian *boîte* (Paris was still filled with them) called the Kazbek. Two or three hours later, we found ourselves at war with an angry *patron*. There were charges and counter-charges, feints and abortive strategems. We maintained stoutly that the management had been caching empty champagne bottles in our ice buckets and counting them on the bill; the *patron* counterattacked by insisting that the girls to whom he had given souvenir silver mugs had, in fact, stolen them. I was never clear about the facts, except that the mugs were certainly not silver and the *patron* was indubitably trying to swindle us. In the end we decided on a tactical withdrawal, and my elder brother and I were led off by a convoy of *flics* to the nearest police station.

I shall never forget my exhilaration walking down the Montmartre streets dressed in a dinner jacket and singing songs, while our blue-coated escorts genially entered into the fun. To a very young man who thought in literary terms, Fitzgerald, Hemingway, and other expatriate heroes were walking by my side. I suppose it was about eight in the morning. Workmen were just debouching from cafés after their matutinal rum or calvados had braced them for the day's labors, and some joined the procession just for the hell of it. My joy was unbounded; if this could happen to a nineteen-year-old lad from Iowa on his second night in Paris, think what potential the place had!

Quite as Hemingway would have written it, the police station was filled with whores of all ages, on hand for the morning inspection. They greeted our entrance with cries of delight. Smiles and cigarettes were exchanged; we were comrades against the exploiters.

Yet slowly but inexorably, doubt intruded. The police magistrate, or whoever he was, flagrantly favored the *patron,* and it was clear to my fledgling lawyer brother that we were outgunned. Since we did not want to become an item in the *Chicago Tribune,* which was then publishing a Paris edition, prudence called for a settlement. Negotiating under duress, Stuart made a deal slightly to the windward side of capitulation. We then retraced our steps soberly—and with considerably fewer travelers' checks—to our hotel. Under the illusion that our companions in revelry might be anxious about our welfare, my always considerate brother telephoned their hotel and spoke to the girl I had been with the previous evening. Obviously, she had not thought well of young Middle Westerners who ended up in the Bastille. "I just wanted to let you know," my brother blithely reported, "that we got out of jail." "Who?" my future wife replied. It had been, as she said later, "a hell of a way to attend the opera!"

Ruth Murdoch

Her name was Ruth Murdoch; she lived in Pittsburgh and, having finished college, was studying painting at Carnegie Tech. I saw her the next night in Paris; then we arranged to meet in Nice, where I made more progress. This time I did not get arrested, and the softness of the Mediterranean night was environmentally helpful. Finally, when we met in Rome, the casual became serious. We wandered over the Pincian Hill, mutually enchanted with the sculptures scattered through the garden that surrounded an open-air cabaret. Letter writing commenced at a frenetic pace until we could meet again in London. Then—through an adroit rearrangement of schedules—we returned to New York on the same ship.

The voyage home enriched what had so far been only tentative feelings. Ruth and I practiced togetherness; Ralph had a girl of his own; while my brother Stuart, who was engaged to a girl at home (one reason for my mother's eagerness to push us off to Europe), spent the entire voyage reading Eddington and Sir James Jeans. Though Stuart could understand scientists turned philosophers, I never could. But I did smuggle in a copy of Joyce's *Ulysses,* which, in those artless days, was regarded as a daring enterprise.

My last undergraduate year in Evanston was anticlimactic. I was too bemused by my summer's adventures to find the campus exciting. Although I became president of the university poetry society and the first editor of a new literary magazine named *MS,* the latter was a dismal effort. The title was not of my choosing; I had wanted to call it "The Ass's Jaw Bone" and dedicate it to the slaying of Philistines, but no one else thought that desirable or even amusing.

My four undergraduate years were not all wasted, but I learned only a little chemistry, even less physics, no biology or anthropology, and no mathematics beyond integral calculus. I should have asked myself then, as Henry Adams had done thirty years before, how I could possibly hope to understand the twentieth century without submitting myself to the hard discipline of the physical sciences, but I was too narrowly concerned with the arts of expression to know how little I had to express. That realization came later. Yet even today I temper my regret with the consoling thought that at least I did not waste my time on the soft social studies (I cannot call them sciences) that mislabel the obvious as arcane by smothering simple thoughts in nonce words or in neologisms that should have been strangled at birth.

What impresses me in looking back is the narrowness of view of my generation. Growing up during the twenties, we cared little for the world unfolding around us. Though we had, as children, lived through the First World War, my friends and I thought of that first cruel blow to Western values largely in terms of the poetry of disillusion that had succeeded the overripe chauvinism of Rupert Brooke. We read Robert Graves, Siegfried Sassoon, Wilfred Owen, Sacheverell Sitwell, and the lot, and were sad that a whole generation of England's finest young men had been decimated, but our thinking seems to have stopped at that point.

We all sympathized vaguely with Sacco and Vanzetti largely because of the poetic quality of the speech that the illiterate "poor fishmonger," Bartolomeo Vanzetti, gave after his sentencing. "If it had not been for this thing, I might have to live out my life talking at street corners to scorning men. I would have died, unmarked, unknown, a failure. Now we are not a failure. This is our career and our triumph. Never in our full life could we hope to do such work for tolerance, for justice, for man's understanding of man as now we do by accident. Our words—our lives—our pains—nothing! This last moment belongs to us—that agony is our triumph."[1]

To an impressionable student in his teens, such words rendered objective evidence unnecessary and the facts irrelevant. What business did society have stilling such a voice? Or who could believe that a man capable of such a noble speech could be guilty of payroll robbery? Justice blindfolded was behaving vindictively. It was my first experience with the liberal fallacy, and it took me a long time to get over it; nor have I ever fully done so in spite of my years at the law. Even today, I have no opinion as to whether Judge Thayer and the jury were right on the facts, but I cannot help feeling sad that we killed the two poor radicals. Having seen how viciously the excesses of the McCarthy years corrupted human judgment, I am no longer confident of justice when society catches rabies from a mad dog.

Meanwhile, of course, there was sex with a literary emphasis. Havelock Ellis's *Dance of Life* was a prelude to bootleg copies of *Ulysses* and *Lady Chatterley;* I even read D. H. Lawrence straight through without experiencing, in Chesterton's phrase, the "emetic ecstasy" that such an overripe diet would induce today. But, over and above (or beyond) sex, was my first encounter with Spengler. I accepted *The Decline of the West* as though inscribed on clay tablets and was haunted for days by the sad lament of Paul Valéry, which I ploddingly read in French: *"Nous autres civilisations, nous savons maintenant que nous sommes mortelles."* "Elam, Nineveh, Babylon," Valéry wrote, "were vague and beautiful names, and the total ruin of these words has as little meaning for us as their very existence. But France, England and Russia—these will also be beautiful names. Lusitania is a pretty name. . . . We see now that the abyss of history is large enough for everyone. We sense now that a civilization is just as fragile as a life."[2]

Though I now find it hard to believe, most of my student days were during the Harding-Coolidge era, more than half a century ago. It was a time of mindless complacency, when few foresaw that America's jerry-built prosperity was nearly over or that, within a decade, the West would find itself at Armageddon. The sky was lit by a Panglossian *ignis fatuus;* messenger boys were getting rich on margined stock; and bank tellers were expanding their garages to fulfill the Hooverian prophecy of a second family car. Had my undergraduate experience been delayed even three years, I would have been subjected to a different environment and I might now see the world in more sharply contrasting shades and colors. I might even have been bitten by the germ of social consciousness just beginning to infect the campuses—or I might not, since it is curious how the depression influenced many students to concentrate on getting jobs rather than converting paving stones into barricades. But since even Northwestern eventually shed much of its Babbitt spirit, my attention would, without doubt, have been differently focused.

What few, if any, of us foresaw in 1929 was that the locusts had been busily eating the years, and a smug America was about to receive its comeuppance. By the time my brothers and I had returned from Europe, in September, the omens were everywhere, though not many people read them properly. The stock market had taken its first premonitory tumble, and during the next three years, the country slipped relentlessly into economic misery. I spent the worst of those depression years at Northwestern Law School, where—partially because the competition was more serious—we absorbed ourselves in our studies, taking little interest in politics. The Hoover Administration was, we thought, a platitudinous bore; no doubt we would have felt more excitement had the New Deal already begun.

Law School and Marriage

My decision to study law had not reflected any basic yearning of mine to be called to the bar. I toyed with the thought of taking a doctorate in English and settling down on a small campus, but, in the end, the bar prevailed, and I never looked back. Not only did I find the law intrinsically interesting, but it also furnished me with a trade union card and a passport that, throughout my working life, has enabled me to move easily back and forth across that prickly border between the public and private sectors.

At law school, I was no longer an outsider, even though many of my classmates had spent the four preceding years in Eastern universities. Some I had known in high school; others I met for the first time. But our different undergraduate backgrounds no longer kept us apart; law school provided a community of interest, with all of us concentrating on a single subject matter. Moreover, we were older; my companions and I were better read than we had been four years before, and most of us took our studies seriously, since we were training for what would presumably be a lifetime career.

During the winter of 1931, as the economy continued on its inexorable downward course and hardship and suffering became increasingly conspicuous, Ruth left her art studies in Pittsburgh and signed up as a social worker. Though untrained for the specific task, she came equipped with compassion and intelligence compounded with hard, common sense. Later she wrote in her family journal,

> My duties were to call on families in their homes, investigate conditions and work records, have the sick admitted to hospitals, the insane to institutions, relief supplied if that appeared to be the last resort, and argue with real estate companies who intended to evict families or seize their furniture.
>
> I would be so tired by the end of the day, after climbing all over the hills of Pittsburgh's slums, that it was all I could do to write my letter to George and get early to bed. . . .

On September 16, 1932, we were married and went off to Bermuda on a wedding trip. In her family history, Ruth describes an episode that tells something about the way we then approached life.

> I found that my new husband was no fritterer of time or opportunity. We were in Bermuda, therefore we should see the place. The best way to do this was to ride a bike. And if your bride had never learned how, this was the time to begin.
>
> Our ship docked at noon. We had lunch. . . . We engaged two English Hercules bicycles with hand brakes. And by mid-afternoon, when I had picked myself up out of the gutter at least twenty times, I could pedal a wobbly course from one hill to the next and dismount on my feet instead of my face.
>
> The next day we cycled around Harrington Sound—a mere matter of thirty miles. . . . Arriving back at our cottage by the Inverurie Hotel, we decided there was just about time enough before dark to pedal across to Coral Beach for a . . . swim. It hurried us a little getting into dinner clothes afterward, but late-comers were still being served.

I returned to law school well after the beginning of the term, leaving Ruth in Pittsburgh to pack up her belongings while I found a place for us to live. With trepidation, I rented an apartment in Evanston without her seeing it. Fortunately she fell in love with the place, and during the months that followed I found the twin vocations of student and husband combining felicitously. My law school comrades repeatedly—and often unexpectedly—dropped by for meals and talk. Ruth bore with exemplary fortitude the fact that I spent most evenings studying and she became a favorite among my classmates, for whom she provided food, drink, and a warm welcome. From indolence or obstinacy or other motives scarcely commendable, I refused to take notes during law school lectures, rationalizing my self-indulgence with the unproven theory that I could remember information best by listening intently while others scribbled. That system, however, assumed that my friends would take careful notes; fortunately, they did.

Employment prospects for a young lawyer were anything but bright in the spring of 1933. Since I had an adequate academic record (law review board and grades near the top of my class), I could be assured of a job with a good Chicago law firm, although at a salary of not more than one hundred dollars a month. By chance, however, another avenue opened that had a major influence on the shape of my future life.

At the outset of his administration, President Roosevelt had asked his Hyde Park neighbor, Henry Morgenthau, Jr., to preside over a new agency, the Farm Credit Administration, which was a consolidation of several bureaus engaged in making loans to farmers. Morgenthau asked Professor Herman Oliphant to assist him by organizing a general counsel's office. Oliphant got in touch with the deans of several law schools, including Dean Green of Northwestern, who nominated me. Ruth and I thought well of the project, and I accepted. I arrived in Washington in May, 1933, prior to my law school graduation in June. Ruth was to follow a week later after she had disposed of our apartment and settled our meager affairs. This time she would be able to play the decisive role in selecting our residence—a small cottage across the river in Virginia.

2. From Depression to War, Ploughs, and "Habbakuks"

Washington was swarming with young lawyers, economists, bankers, and professors-in-exile, all bent on reorganizing the cosmos, rearranging the stars and planets. Programmed like a computer with bits and tags of literature, I mouthed Wordsworth's famous apostrophe to the early weeks of the French Revolution: "Bliss was it in that dawn to be alive,/But to be young was very heaven!"

The times were ebullient, and yeast was in the air. Each morning we awoke to read with excitement of Roosevelt's latest outrageous move. It was *épater les bourgeois* in political and economic terms or—more precisely for us—it was *épater les vieillards,* a form of exercise that inevitably lifts the hearts of anyone under thirty. The old order had discredited itself; we would conjure up a new and better one in its place. Certain lines from Wordsworth's *Prelude* expressed what we thought we were up to, for it did indeed seem to us a time

> In which the meager, stale, forbidding ways
> Of custom, law and statute, took at once
> The attraction of a country in romance!
> When Reason seemed the most to assert her rights . . .

We were, so we thought at the time, not so much interested in smashing pillars and pulling down temples as in designing the shape and form of our New Jerusalem. Discussion might circle for a time—sometimes it seemed to circle for long alcoholic hours—but it invariably settled on the architecture of that refulgent city.

No doubt because the actors in the drama were relatively older—lawyers and young Ph.D.'s in economics rather than undergraduates—the reaction bore no resemblance to the later disorder of the sixties, when "trashing" seemed an end in itself. Though we had read some history, no one thought himself a young Robespierre. Perhaps also because the New Deal was a fresh experience for America (though not for Europe), with government for the first time giving explicit meaning to the welfare clause, we felt hope in the air. Later, in the sixties, much of the new welfare legislation served the bureaucracy more than the commonweal, but in those days of unlimited expectations our basic credo was simple: Nothing that had been done till then was good enough nor was there anything we could not do if we set our minds to it.

To be sure, I was little more than a spear-carrier with few speaking lines. Unlike many of the leading actors, I had, at that time, not even met Felix Frankfurter, let alone clerked for Holmes or Brandeis. Most of the problems with which the New Deal was grappling were for me matters of first impression; I was, by any rational standard, spectacularly ill-equipped. Although assigned to work on developing credit facilities for the farmers, I had never, in spite of my Iowa background, spent a night on a working farm—but then neither had my colleagues, including, I suspect, Henry Morgenthau. That, however, did not deter us. In the atmosphere of New Deal Washington, inexperience was no impediment; one learned fast and improvised boldly. Even professionally, I could not have been more of a neophyte; I had never so much as written a contract to sell a fifty-dollar dog! Yet one of my first professional tasks was to draft and help negotiate a contract for the sale of $75 million worth of Federal Farm Board cotton. It was such a formidable document—seventy or eighty pages in length and replete with intricate internal brokerage arrangements—that, in retrospect, I am amazed that I was not terrified by the assignment. But I took it in stride, as we all did in those days. We were young and nothing was impossible.

Two or three times during those early months I played handball at the old Hotel Ambassador with a lawyer who was later to become a close friend. Dean Acheson, then thirty-eight, was Acting Secretary of the Treasury while Secretary William Woodin lay dying. Shortly afterwards, in November 1933, he resigned over an issue of principle. Franklin Roosevelt, bemused by some dubious advice from Professor George F. Warren, had forbidden the private holding of gold and sought to increase the gold price of the dollar by having the government make large gold purchases. Acheson, quite sensibly opposing the move, responded by resigning. Yet, abhorring vainglorious gestures, he rejected the temptation of a public row with the President that would have won him momentary acclaim in many quarters and contented himself with a graceful letter of resignation.[1]

When, on a later occasion, Roosevelt was to rebuke another under secretary for his flamboyant resignation, he said, ". . . tell him to ask Dean Acheson how a gentleman resigns." That remark impressed me at the time, and I was to recall it during the dispute over Vietnam that I shall recount in a later chapter.

With Acheson's departure from the Treasury, Roosevelt named Morgenthau to succeed him. Morgenthau took Oliphant to be his legal adviser and I went along with the package. It was, I quickly found, a fortunate move, since Morgenthau, a highly suspicious man, knew almost no one in the Treasury except Oliphant and me. Oliphant provided me with far greater traffic with the Secretary than would otherwise have been the case. He was the type of genius *manqué* of whom I seem to have met more than my share. Imaginative and intellectually resourceful, he was unconstrained by any practical experience. Spinning elaborate theories on only the briefest exposure to new situations, he disdained facts that undercut his hypotheses. But while Oliphant was not a man of disciplined judgment, he was enormously stimulating to a young apprentice engaged in on-the-job training as an intellectual freebooter; besides, he was kind to me.

Thus the months that followed were effervescent. While my job with the Farm Credit Administration had brought me into geographical propinquity with the New Deal, my work at the Treasury touched major phases of New Deal policy. I had a dogsbody role in preparing the briefs supporting Roosevelt's devaluation of the dollar by upholding the power of Congress to require holders of government bonds denominated in gold to accept legal tender instead. I worked on peripheral aspects of the Chase Bank loan to the Soviet Union and revised the basic conceptual memorandum that outlined what later emerged as the Internal Revenue Act of 1936—the so-called Undistributed Profits Tax. That was revolutionary legislation. Inspired by a proposal by Professor Gardiner Means, an old friend of Oliphant's, its underlying theory was that the flagging economy could be more rapidly galvanized by increasing purchasing power than by expanding investment in production goods when existing capacity was only partially utilized. (It was the negation of supply-side economics.) Thus, the tax was designed to increase the flow of money into consumers' hands by providing an incentive for corporations to distribute profits to shareholders.[2]

I can only partially recreate my state of mind at the time. Astonished to find myself engaged even tangentially in large affairs, I felt more nearly omniscient than I ever have since. (In fact, a full appreciation of how little I know has come to me only gradually.) Still, I could not avoid a troubling dubiety. The supercharged atmosphere of Washington was unreal; if I were ever to master my profession of the law, I had better get back to the Middle West and touch the earth.

So, in April 1935, Ruth and I headed for Chicago. Departure was not easy because, apart from the stimulus of my work, we had had glorious weekends exploring obscure nooks and crannies in Virginia and Maryland. For the first time, we had lived in our own house—complete with fox terrier, fireplace, and backyard, where Ruth, an ardent gardener, had conducted experiments with floriculture and grown fresh vegetables.

Law Practice in Chicago

The Chicago law firm I chose had little to offer. Though it had once contained giants of the Chicago bar, I found it then in decline. For several months, I was given nothing useful to do, which, after the hyperthyroid activity of Washington, was agonizing. (Ruth considers it the most unhappy period of my life.) Then, gradually, I began to take court assignments from the docket clerk each morning. Since these were given out just as court sessions were beginning, there was no chance for preparation. Frequently the only instruction I received was to see that the other side's motion—whatever it might be—was denied.

It was a travesty of serious law practice. For the first few weeks I did not know the names of our regular clients and, hence, could not tell for whom I was acting until counsel for the other side had spoken. Then, wildly improvising an argument to counter what he had said, I would make an eloquent protest. For one who had envisaged himself shaping history in Washington—if only in fantasy—it was a humbling and discouraging assignment. Yet, in the process I suppose I did learn how to think on my feet and invent arguments—a talent that was to prove useful on later occasions.

I spent a little more than three years with that firm, during half of which I served as a tax lawyer. Since tax law involved the dissection of language, the juggling of concepts, and the manipulation of logic, I enjoyed its casuistical challenge. But, though I became reasonably adept at standing language on its head, I felt the lack of Jesuit or Talmudic training—either of which is ideal preparation for a tax lawyer.

By 1939 I had had enough. With the help of my close friend Carl Spaeth (later dean of the Stanford Law School), I moved to a more active and prestigious law firm, then known as Sidley, McPherson, Austin and Harper. Not only did it provide a more congenial environment, but my new work, which involved the reorganization of railroads, gave me greater scope. Soon I discovered kindred spirits among the partners. One was Paul Harper, the son of William Rainey Harper, the famous president of the University of Chicago. Another was a young junior partner named Adlai E. Stevenson, whom I had known slightly in Washington and with whom I formed a close friendship that continued until his death thirty-five years later.

It was during this period that I first turned my attention to foreign policy. With the world in turmoil, literature, history—and even the law—lost much of their meaning. After the arguments that culminated in the Neutrality Act of 1935 and the beginning of the Spanish Civil War in 1936, one could not ignore mounting evidence that the world was on a pell-mell slide toward a deepening crisis. How could anyone espouse isolationism, which, I thought, was both cowardly and irresponsible? Economic depression in Germany, with one out of eight men unemployed, had helped create the conditions for Hitler's seizure of power. Now Western weakness and myopia were encouraging the destructive demagoguery to which he gave the ultimate expression.

Throughout this period, my wife and I faithfully attended the Friday lunches of the Chicago Council on Foreign Relations, where the chairman, Adlai Stevenson, was gaining respectful attention for his grace, wit, and informed views. His introductions (on which he worked hard) were polished gems, and some of us suspected that quite as many came to hear Adlai as to hear the featured speaker, though the director of the council, the late Clifton Utley, played impresario to a succession of personalities who were either participants in large affairs or at least well-informed observers.

Europe on the Eve of War

Ever since we had left Washington in 1935, Ruth and I had each year taken a holiday in Latin America or the Caribbean—first in Mexico, then

Guatemala, the Virgin Islands, Haiti, and Puerto Rico. But in 1938 we were eager to get back to Europe and, though it meant leaving our two-year-old son, John, with my parents, we sailed cabin class on the *Europa*. That crossing made a lasting impression on us both. Not only were we repelled by the sterile Bauhaus décor of the ship, but we loathed even more the prevalence of swastikas and "Heil Hitler" salutes, while the stiff, heel-clicking arrogance of the ship's officers was a caricature of Prussian militarism. Through some connection we were invited to the captain's quarters for a drink. But when I asked to have a look at the bridge, I was treated almost as a spy and told sternly that all the ship's instruments were secrets no American could possibly see.

Nor did the North German Lloyd line show subtlety in indoctrinating its captive passengers with the gospel according to Dr. Goebbels. The ship's newspaper, the *Lloyd Post,* was each morning filled with blood-curdling accounts of how the belligerent Czechs were threatening the poor, defenseless Germans. In the issue of May 22, for example, a story with a Prague dateline announced that the border had been closed "after the shedding of German blood plunged this republic into the gravest crisis since its birth and after the World War."

On the *Europa* we met George Gamov, a brilliant astrophysicist, who, in 1926 at the age of twenty-four, had propounded an important theory concerning the behavior of alpha rays. Traveling with him was a German astrophysicist named Dr. Karl Wilhelm Meissner. Formerly professor at the University of Frankfurt, he had been forced to retire in his early forties (he was then forty-six) because he had a Jewish wife and was a friend of Einstein's. Gamov was on his way to a scientific conference in Paris under League of Nations auspices; Meissner was en route to Warsaw, also to deliver a paper.

Meissner was the prototype of the kindly, thoughtful, infinitely patient professor. In collaboration with Gamov, he taught Ruth to cut Möbius strips and when we were on deck always insisted on lighting her cigarettes with a magnifying glass to celebrate the energy of the sun.[3]

Another memorable passenger—a young Austrian girl from Salzburg in her early twenties—had left her homeland before the Anschluss for two years of study at the University of Minnesota and now, about to return to a country under Nazi domination, was so filled with fury and apprehension that she could not speak of it without crying. Finally, there were a young Belgian assistant of August Picard, the balloonist, and a young Englishman then in the British civil service in Khartoum, who belonged to the cadet branch of a great noble family and had some hope (never realized) of succeeding to an earldom.

Each evening after dinner, the group gathered to exchange anecdotes out of their pasts and to talk obsessively of the coming war. Our cabin was chosen for these meetings because, being American, we could be trusted. Since it was the first time I had found myself in an environment of brooding apprehension, I was astonished at our friends' fear that their own cabins might be bugged by the Gestapo. On that crossing, I first dimly perceived the cruel visage of the coming war. It was three months before Munich.

Once arrived in London, we hired a small Singer automobile and traveled to Land's End, calling en route on distant cousins in Devon, then through the Midlands to Glasgow and Edinburgh, and as far north as Inverness. Except for the weather—it was a typically wet summer—the United Kingdom was a garden of quiet beauty and repose. The people were, as always, wonderfully warm and hospitable; both Ruth and I felt then, as we have always felt since, that the civility suffusing the whole of British society sets that country apart from any other. Still, it was strangely disquieting to move from the dark menace of the *Europa*—our "Ship of Fools," as I was later to think of it, with its hovering omnipresence of inevitable war—to the apparently relaxed and gracious English countryside, where one found little visible concern at the prospect of impending conflict.

Lacking friends in more sophisticated English circles, I did not then know of the anxiety among the enlightened few in the British government or of the frantic efforts of valiant individuals to prepare the country for a Nazi assault. Nevertheless, when I returned to the United States, I was convinced that Europe was heading for Armageddon and that the United States had better stand on the Lord's side; otherwise, Western civilization would go down before the barbarians in Berlin.

America Enters the War

In September 1938 came Munich and the beginning of a public argument in the United States. Those who were for preserving American isolationism at all costs had organized the so-called America First Committee; others felt, as I did, that sooner or later, Western civilization would be saved only by a united effort and that we Western peoples had better act together while we could still mobilize our full strength. This latter view was advanced by the Committee to Defend America by Aiding the Allies (popularly called the William Allen White Committee), in which Adlai Stevenson played a leading role in Chicago while I carried a spear in the supporting cast. The fall of France left me numb and dismayed; why were we not moving immediately to join with Britain? Holding those views, I was deeply troubled by the attack on Pearl Harbor on December 7, 1941. Would it galvanize America into action in Europe, or would Americans insist that their only enemy was Japan? Would we concentrate on the war in the Pacific, while Western Europe and Britain were pushed against the wall? By declaring war on the United States on

December 11, Hitler resolved not only America's predicament but mine as well. America was now fighting Hitler, and there could be no more business as usual. My days as a Chicago lawyer were over.

As was our custom, Ruth and I spent Christmas at our family home in Florida, returning early in January by way of Washington so I could talk with Adlai, who had by this time become an assistant to Frank Knox, the Secretary of the Navy. He could, he said, arrange a commission for me in the navy if I wanted one, but he urged me not to enter military service; I should instead try to put my Washington experience to some use. A brilliant young lawyer named Oscar Cox was on a continual lookout for able lawyers to assist him in the General Counsel's office of the Lend-Lease Administration. Since Cox also worked closely with Harry Hopkins, as well as with Ben Cohen and Isador Lubin in the White House, Stevenson was sure I would find scope for my energies.

After one interview with Cox, I arranged to leave Chicago for my second tour of duty in Washington. Oscar Cox, my new chief, had many titles: General Counsel of the Lend-Lease Administration, counsel for Harry Hopkins's office in the White House, Assistant Solicitor General (responsible for preparing legal opinions for the President), and—for some months—counsel for Vannevar Bush, then head of the Office of Scientific Research and Development. To carry out his manifold assignments, Cox had gathered about him a collection of young and exuberant lawyers, including Philip Graham (later publisher of the *Washington Post*), Joseph Rauh, Eugene Rostow, John Connor, Lloyd Cutler, and Daniel Boorstin (later to become a distinguished social historian and librarian of Congress).

During my first months with Cox, my own assignments varied from normal Lend-Lease business to investigating the synthetic rubber program and keeping eccentric scientists out of trouble at the request of the White House. What gave a unifying distinction to our small band of activists was not merely our reflexive skepticism of the conventional wisdom but also an uncritical commitment to our own version of unconventional wisdom. We accepted as immutable principle that our military leaders would instinctively try to fight the current war with the weapons of the last, which led us automatically to that other shopworn aphorism (invented by Talleyrand, attributed to Clemenceau, and quoted by Briand) that war was too serious a business to be left to generals. We were determined not to leave our war to the soldiers.

Pyke's Projects

Only three months after I arrived in Washington, Oscar Cox put Eugene Rostow and me in touch with a bearded British intellectual named Geoffrey Pyke, who exceeded even British standards of eccentricity.

Although still known only to a few, he had already lived a full, varied, and eventful life, having been at one time or another a foreign correspondent, the hero of a brilliant prison escape during the First World War, an advertising agent, a commodity speculator, a pioneer in public opinion polls, an experimental educator, a journalist, an organizer of charities, an inventor, a self-styled economist, and a military tactician at least as innovative as that other famous amateur, T. E. Lawrence.

Pyke was given the title of Programme Director by Admiral Mountbatten, then Chief of Combined Operations, and he shared the famous backroom with Professor J. D. Bernal, a highly gifted Cambridge physicist (a Marxist in politics), and the zoologist, Solly Zuckerman (now Lord Zuckerman), later to become the scientific adviser to the Prime Minister. Rostow and I were told to visit Pyke because the Plough Project—his most important proposal to date—was in deep trouble.

The central idea of the Plough Project, as Pyke conceived it, was that in struggling for command of the land, sea, and air, the Allies had ignored the potential advantage of commanding the snows. Pyke envisaged landing bombers on a glacier in Norway and debouching specially designed snow vehicles manned by small crews that could move quickly about the country, destroying bridges, tunnels, railroad tracks, hydro-electric installations, and other vital facilities. He devised not only the requirements and guidelines for the snow vehicle and the composition of the force but also an elaborate set of tactics for delivering the force and vehicle on target. In addition, he designed special demolition weapons, such as explosive "snakes" to be injected in the flumes of hydro-electric stations.

For reasons of greater security and resources, Churchill and Roosevelt had agreed that the Plough Project should be developed in America. But from the moment of his first arrival in America, Pyke's arrogance and impatience had critically prejudiced the project's success. Pyke could not write or talk without skyrocketing wit, interlarded with quotations from Shaw, Churchill, Tolstoy, the Bible, or whatever apt epigram he might dredge from his vast arsenal; it did not endear him to the soldiers.

In the latter part of June, Rostow and I were requested by Cox to get Pyke's snow project back on the track. Our essential role was to serve as a neutralizing element while, at the same time, trying to bring about those procedural changes necessary to make Pyke's advice available and effective.

In a memorandum we prepared for Cox to send to Harry Hopkins on July 4, we pointed out the lamentable condition of the project, emphasizing the failure to develop an adequate vehicle, since the machine then being built ignored the requirements of the central strategy. Moreover, there had been too little research and overall planning essential to an effective tactical operation. Because of the prevailing ignorance about snow and the terrain to be encountered in Norway (no maps of gradients had yet been prepared for the potential area of maneuver), we urged that America should move forward with the design and development of several possible types of vehicle—leaving the final selection to the latest date production could begin. Meanwhile, snow studies should go urgently forward. We recounted the history of the project, including arbitrary decisions that had been made to adapt the design of the amphibious jeep to a snow vehicle, a whole month lost in experimenting with an over-weight amphibious design that could not be steered, the failure to undertake snow research when new snow was available in North America in May, and so on.

Though the new snow machine (later known as the Weasel) was never used in snow, it proved a vital instrument for enabling Allied troops to move through the mud when, during their last convulsion, the Germans flooded the Ardennes Forest, and it turned out to be the only conveyance that could cross the mangrove swamps in Southeast Asia.

Pyke's imagination worked at full steam, but none of his plans was on such a grand scale or offered so much promise as "Operation Habbakuk."[4] The scheme had its genesis in Pyke's discovery that when small particles of foreign substance are frozen in water, the reinforced ice has qualities quite different from those of pure frozen water. "Pykrete," as his proposed material was called, would be made from particles of wood suspended in water and frozen into ice. It would have not only a crush resistance greater than ice by a factor of two to twelve, but it would also have more stability at high temperatures because the wood pulp would insulate the Pykrete after the outer surface of the material had thawed.

In the Habbakuk Project, Pykrete would be used to construct giant aircraft carriers, each of which would be two thousand feet long with a forty-foot-thick hull and a displacement of two million tons. These ships would be unsinkable not merely because of the strength and mass of the construction material, but also because, equipped with their own refrigerating machines, they could, like living organisms, regenerate themselves by freezing more ice to fill any crater made by shell, bomb, or torpedo. With thick Pykrete decks, they could conceal fighter planes in their hollow interiors safe from enemy attack. The ships would have the outward appearance not of floating icebergs but of conventional vessels, for their hulls and flight decks would be sheathed in timber. Several feet of insulation would separate this wooden skin from the Pykrete. With their capacity for regeneration, they would not require new timbers to encase craters, even in case of severe explosive damage—except, of course, on the flight deck.

Once Mountbatten had persuaded Prime Minister Churchill to float a piece of Pykrete in his bath and observe its resistance to melting, Churchill enlisted Roosevelt's enthusiastic support for the project. Thereafter, Pykrete was involved in a now legendary incident at the Quebec Conference in the summer of 1943, when the Allied chiefs of staff engaged in a bitter dispute over the conduct of the war. To give time for tempers to cool, the junior officers were sent out of the room; Lord Mountbatten seized the occasion to demonstrate to the top Allied command the virtues of his favorite material. Two carts were rolled into the room, one containing a cube of pure ice and the other of Pykrete. General "Hap" Arnold, then Chief of Staff of the United States Army Air Corps, was handed a chopper with which he split the block of ice; when he tried to split the Pykrete, the chopper bounced off, wrenching Arnold's arm. Lord Mountbatten then shattered the untreated ice with a pistol shot but, when he fired at the Pykrete block, the bullet ricocheted, causing both Lord Portal and Admiral King to duck.

An anecdote has emerged from this conference. A junior officer in the anteroom, sensitive to the bitter feelings momentarily displayed by the Allied chiefs, exclaimed with alarm, "First they argue, then they begin hitting each other, now they've started shooting."

A one-thousand-ton pilot model was built on a Canadian lake; the experts decreed that the project was feasible, and a contract was let for the design of the first huge vessel.[5] But before a full-size ship could be constructed, a deal had been made with Portugal to use the Azores as a mid-ocean air base; the "Mulberry" artificial harbors had been devised for the invasion of Normandy; and the American campaign in the Pacific had moved beyond the point where Habbakuk might be needed. Today, of course, the development of nuclear weapons has rendered such a project valueless.

My own relation with Operation Habbakuk was marginal. For a time I knew only that Pyke had another, even more grandiose, project, and it was some months before I learned its character. I did, however, assist Pyke whenever he or his people sent up a distress flare, recklessly using the machinery of Lend-Lease credentials. The problem occasionally became sticky—one particular expert Pyke requested was an enemy alien and another a declared Communist—but the importance of the objective justified a considerable indiscretion. Meanwhile, Eugene Rostow maintained closer touch with the project at a time when I was concentrating on other matters.

Although Pyke was a man who incited strong antipathies from many, he inspired unflinching loyalty from a select few. Among those most deeply committed to him was "Sandy" Wedderburn, a young British commando officer who had been on raids in Normandy and was fully trained in the art of strangulation with thin wires and other more silent and subtle means of eliminating intruders. At times his absorbing passion to win the war posed an awkward problem for Rostow and me. Whenever a particularly obtuse soldier or civilian jeopardized either of

Pyke's enterprises by insensitive opposition or foot-dragging, Wedderburn would quietly offer to remove the obstacle neatly and quietly, leaving no incriminating evidence. He seemed disappointed at our negative response. Though Rostow and I both prided ourselves on skill at bureaucratic combat, we used the word "infighting" in a metaphorical sense; Wedderburn's approach was too literal for our taste.

Still later, I was informed that Wedderburn had been killed falling through a stairwell onto a marble floor of a palazzo in which he had been billeted in Naples—which, if the report was correct, seemed an unlikely fate for a skilled mountain climber. Trained as a writer-to-the-signet (a class of Scottish lawyer) in Edinburgh, Wedderburn was a young man of exceptional qualities. A tribute to him in the *Times* of March 13, 1945, pointed out that he had physical problems of which I was totally unaware: ". . . at Trinity Hall, Cambridge, . . . he was President of the Cambridge University Mountaineering Club. During one meet he severely strained his heart helping to rescue a climber from another club. This began a disability from which he suffered considerably in later years. . . . All his energy was devoted to whatever tasks confronted him, and he accomplished them by sheer 'guts.' How many students at the school in Iceland or the troops of both the Navy and Army who were at some period under his command realized that the apparently fit and tireless officer was suffering from a weak heart, severe asthma and a gastric ulcer which periodically necessitated his living on bread and milk?"

I heard that Pyke had been shattered by Wedderburn's death and it may have contributed to his own suicide on January 22, 1945. That event evoked an impressive obituary in the *Times* that spoke of Pyke as "one of the most original, if unrecognized, figures of the present century."

That the world needs more Geoffrey Pykes seems clear, particularly now, when transient intellectual fads increasingly tend to dominate thought. Yet pestiferous characters such as Pyke and Socrates are understandably unwelcome. It is damned annoying to have impertinent questions asked and comforting assumptions undercut—particularly by someone armed with both logic and corrosive wit. Is not the human condition sufficiently absurd without anyone pointing it out through satirical comment? And does that not assure that hemlock, which has been used literally and metaphorically for at least two thousand years, will remain in society's *materia medica* for the next thousand?

PART II

The War Years

3. Lend-Lease and the Avoidance of War Debts

Apart from such marginal activities as looking after stray British intellectuals and doing chores for the White House, my regular assignment during 1942 and 1943 was to serve as operating head of the General Counsel's office of the Lend-Lease Administration, and thus legal adviser to the Administrator of Lend-Lease, Edward R. Stettinius. The handsome son of a Morgan partner, Stettinius had held impressive titles with both General Motors and United States Steel, but, as I quickly discovered, his primary corporate role had been ornamental. A man of good will, he was ill-equipped to cope with the subtle and complex difficulties inherent in supply arrangements with allies bedevilled by their own problems.

Stettinius wanted things to look right no matter how much disarray might lie beneath the surface. Once, when he and I were in the Senate gallery during a debate on one of the Lend-Lease extension bills, I mentioned a press rumor then current that the President might choose him as his running mate for Vice-President. His face lit up and he said with rapture in his voice, "George, if I ever did get to be Vice-President and preside over the Senate, do you know what I'd do first? Look at the shape this place is in; I'd have it painted." Nor did he ever waver in that instinct; the first thing he did when he later became Under Secretary of State was to subject the old State Department building to a thorough cleaning and repainting.

Stettinius had surrounded himself with decent and agreeable men, several of whom had come with him from his private endeavors, and they shared his view of our task as an exercise in public relations. Because of Stettinius's premature white hair, which gave him an appearance of distinction, it is not surprising that when he later took several of these old friends with him to the State Department, the entourage was promptly nicknamed "Snow White and the Seven Dwarfs." That the Lend-Lease Administration lacked strong leadership was unfortunate, since the issues were important. Had the top management been sufficiently aware of the substantive problems in Lend-Lease, my lawyer colleagues and I would have felt less of a mission to shape policy from the side.

The Problem of Definition

Prior to the Lend-Lease Act, all procurement had been handled under the so-called cash-and-carry system; thus, by the time the act was passed on March 22, 1941, Britain's gold and dollar reserves had been reduced to $12 million.[1] With the new legislation, our Allies no longer needed to deplete their meager foreign exchange; supplies would be regularly forthcoming, with accounts ultimately to be settled by "payment or repayment in payments of property or any other direct or indirect benefit which the President deemed satisfactory." Such language shifted the authority to decide the repayment question from the Congress to the President. But, until there was common agreement on fundamental principles, the shape of a future settlement remained a brooding concern of the recipient countries. President Roosevelt had thought little beyond his analogy of the fire hose. If your neighbor's house catches fire and you know that the fire will spread to your own house unless it is put out, will you not, asked the President, lend your hose to your neighbor?

But that parable, though useful, evaded the hard issues. What if the fire hose were consumed in the blaze? Would the neighbor have to pay for it? That was a legitimate question when the act was drafted and passed; then the United States was not at war with Germany. But once we were at war, our house was as much on fire as Britain's, and our neighbor was using our hose to fight a common conflagration. Thus there was now a compelling reason to redefine relationships. What our common predicament required was that each Ally join in the common effort and do all it could. If the United States was contributing the most in material, Britain had contributed far more in the loss of its young men and the destruction of its property. In the final analysis, what difference did it make whether an American tank was used by British, Australian, or our own forces, so long as it was used effectively against the common enemy?

Rostow and I agreed early that the situation needed a clearly enunciated concept of "pooling," but was America prepared for it? Even as late as February 1942, a national poll showed that 75 percent of Americans thought Britain should pay for the war materials we supplied under

Lend-Lease. By July, when the question was asked differently, only 39 percent felt that Britain should pay for *all* the materials while 43 percent wanted payment for *part*.[2] Unhappily, the top officials of the Lend-Lease Administration showed even less comprehension of basic issues than the public. With experience limited to commercial banking and industry, they thought of Lend-Lease in the same terms as the loans J. P. Morgan had arranged for the Allied powers during the First World War. Some of them were, as I saw it, quite capable of repeating Calvin Coolidge's fatuous comment: "They hired the money, didn't they?"

The Politics of a Lend-Lease Settlement

More sophisticated officials elsewhere in the government displayed a different bias. They saw Lend-Lease as a lever that could help them shape a postwar economic environment free of the restrictive commercial policies of the between-wars period that had turned the trading world into a jungle.

America and its European Allies had made a dreadful mess following the First World War. At the Versailles Conference, the economic fate of the world had been left to pompous men with the mentality of money changers. Now wiser heads were not only drawing blueprints for a universal organization to keep the peace (which took final shape in the United Nations Charter), but were also seeking to create a regime of liberal finance and nondiscriminatory multilateral trade. Unhappily, pressure for liberalization collided with the British system of empire preferences provided by the Ottawa agreements that had been created in response to America's high tariffs.

This collision produced severe tensions during the formulation of our Lend-Lease settlement arrangements with the United Kingdom. Even farsighted British who felt time running out on the empire hoped to keep together a Commonwealth that could mobilize and focus the combined resources of the former colonies under London's benign direction. President Roosevelt, on the other hand, foresaw—and desired—the end of the colonial era. Not only did he dislike the great systems of power by which European nations held sway over vast areas and populations around the world, he instinctively knew that those systems could not survive the two world wars that had undercut the metropolitan bases of power and crumbled the social and economic structures that made colonialism possible.

There was thus little patience in the Roosevelt Administration with maintaining preferential commercial arrangements just to help keep the Commonwealth together. They were, as we saw it, incompatible with the nondiscriminatory multilateral trade that Americans considered indispensable to a prosperous world economy.

Parallel with the issue of liberal trade was that of a liberal financial regime. The Nazis, under the tutelage of Dr. Horace Greely Hjalmar Schacht, had utilized not only discriminatory trading practices but also tight monetary controls, blocked accounts, and complex bilateral arrangements to advance their own selfish purposes. Our effort to liberalize trade must, therefore, be paralleled by institutions that would make possible the free movement of capital. Yet that, again, was easier for some nations than for others. Emerging from the war as the dominant economic and financial power, America was amply equipped to flourish in an environment of free trade and liberal finance, yet our principal Allies—and that included Great Britain, with whom most of the common planning was being done—were deeply in debt and facing vast problems of reconstruction. Obviously, they were strongly tempted by import restrictions and bilateral deals.

The element needed to resolve this problem was, as we saw it, some assurance that America would forgo a material *quid pro quo* in settling Lend-Lease accounts. In addition, we needed to make clear our intention to provide ample help to our Allies in the postwar period so they could make the adjustments and survive the pressures and dislocations entailed in the move toward a liberal trading and monetary regime.

But few were willing to discuss the problems of the settlement and of postwar assistance until after we had beaten the Germans. For the moment, major effort was concentrated on assuring that the great trading nations would not again pursue "beggar-thy-neighbor" tactics but would opt for liberal trading and financial policies. Thus, on February 23, 1942, the United States concluded an agreement with the British government that, in Article VII, tied the broad principles of a Lend-Lease settlement to an agreement on multilateralism. There should be, it provided, agreed upon action by the United States and Great Britain "directed . . . to the elimination of all forms of discriminatory treatment in international commerce, and to the reduction of tariffs and other trade barriers." By way of inducement, the United States also agreed that the benefits to be received as compensation by the United States should be "such as not to burden commerce between the two countries but to promote mutually advantageous economic relations between them and the betterment of worldwide economic relations." The negotiation of Article VII was handled by the Department of State, with Assistant Secretary of State for Economic Affairs Dean Acheson taking the lead.

Consistent with our agreement with Britain (which was the pattern for agreements with other Lend-Lease recipients), my lawyer colleagues and I in the Lend-Lease Administration wanted a clear definition of the Lend-Lease concept that would make bookkeeping largely irrelevant. To achieve this, we depended heavily on the most effective instrument available to us: the reports that the Lend-Lease Administration was required to send Congress every ninety days, which were transmitted by Presidential letter. Because we lawyers drafted those reports, we could use them to gain legitimacy for positions and approaches we might be advocating at the time.

Attempt at a Statement of Policy

The first time we achieved an expression of major policy was on June 11, 1942, in the "Fifth Lend-Lease Report"; Eugene Rostow, as the principal draftsman, lucidly spelled out the concept of pooling and the equality of effort. The report stated that "If each country devotes roughly the same part of its national production to the war, then the financial burden of war is distributed equally among the United Nations in accordance with their ability to pay."

This point was emphasized further in the President's transmittal letter, which Rostow also drafted. "Each United Nation is contributing to the ultimate victory not merely its dollars, pounds, or rubles but the full measure of its men, its weapons, and its productive capacity."

The principles enunciated in the "Fifth Lend-Lease Report" were, it seemed to us, fundamental. Yet we still wanted a more explicit statement from the President regarding the repayment issue, since both Congress and the American people were in sore need of education and British anxieties about their postwar situation needed to be allayed in the interest of rational planning.

Our most pressing worry, after all, was to make sure that—once the war was won—we would not repeat the mistakes of the 1920s, draining Europe of resources on the holy principle of the sanctity of debt. For us, the most instructive book—ignored at the time in Washington—was Keynes's brilliant and prophetic essay *The Economic Consequences of the Peace,* which had accurately predicted the disastrous results of Western Europe's insistence on reparations and America's demand for debt repayment. In fact, I recently came across a notebook I used during that period, on the front cover of which I had pasted Keynes's words: "The existence of the great war debt is a menace to financial stability everywhere. . . . We shall never be able to move again, unless we can free our limbs from those paper shackles. A general bonfire is so great a necessity that unless we can make it an orderly and good-tempered affair in which no serious injustice is done to anyone, it will, when it comes to the last, grow into a conflagration that may destroy much else as well."[3]

But if Keynes's dark, prophetic work was our Bible, it was by no means the sacred book of others in the Lend-Lease Administration. When I mentioned his work to my business colleagues, most of them had never heard of it. Because of this pervasive ignorance of what then seemed the transcendental realities, I thought I should try to use the President's letter transmitting the "Eleventh Lend-Lease Report" to condition Congress and the American people not to expect repayment. I therefore asked my deputy, Alfred E. Davidson, to prepare a draft of the report making this point, as well as a proposed letter of transmittal. After noting that the Allies were growing stronger because each was contributing to the common struggle in accordance with its ability and its resources, our transmittal letter continued, "Everything that all of us have is dedicated to victory over the Axis powers. The Congress, in passing and extending the Lend-Lease Act, made it plain that the United States wants no new war debts to jeopardize the coming peace. *Victory and a secure peace are the only coin in which we can be repaid.*" (Italics added.) If the President accepted this language, it would, I thought, sharply focus the issue; if the President rejected it, at least we would have tried.

With these thoughts in mind, I passed our draft briefly by Stettinius, who, perhaps not understanding its implications, sent it on to the White House. There, Isador Lubin, Harry Hopkins's assistant, flagged the key passage and forwarded it to Hopkins, who was at that time with President Roosevelt at the Quebec Conference. Since Hopkins did not react against it, the message was forwarded to the Congress. For the moment, I felt elated to have put the Administration on record that we would not treat Lend-Lease obligations as war debts, and I did not anticipate the storm that followed. Hopkins had apparently not taken specific note of the language and had failed to mention it to the President. Roosevelt, when he learned of it, was furious.

Our original letter, bearing the President's signature, had gone forward on August 25, 1943. In a press conference on September 7, the President publicly repudiated the two sentences on which we had put the most value. A mistake had, he said, been made for which he was apologizing. While he had been in Quebec, he told the press, several drafts of a letter of transmittal were prepared "and on one of the drafts somebody said I approved it. As a matter of fact, I hadn't seen any of the drafts, and the verbal statement that I had approved it—which I hadn't—went into type, and in type as "Franklin D. Roosevelt," not a signature. And as such it was sent to the Clerk of the Senate and the Clerk of the House and released." When he did see it, he went on, there were only two sentences he objected to. They were: "The Congress, in passing and extending the Lend-Lease Act, made it plain that the United States wants no new war debts to jeopardize the coming peace. Victory and a secure peace are the only coin in which we can be repaid."

The President acknowledged that there was "a very large element of truth" in the sentences, but said he took them out because they contained only a condensation of the truth that might be widely misconstrued. He went on,

For instance, "new war debts to jeopardize the coming peace." What is a debt? Is it money, or is it goods, or is it some other benefit? And the way it's put here, it doesn't do justice to the whole situation. It is perfectly true that in . . . the narrow technical sense we want no new war debts, but at the same time the . . . Lend Lease Act does mean that other nations operating with us in its administration will repay us as far as they possibly can. Now that doesn't mean necessarily *dollars,* because there are all kinds of other repayments which can be made. Therefore, the sentence is not . . . clear.

The same way, "Victory and a secure peace are the only coin in which we can be repaid." Well, a great many people in this country think of a coin as something that you will jangle in your . . . pocket, and of course in the large sense there are all kinds of coins. I wouldn't have put it that way if I had had a chance to see it before it was printed.

Now, that's . . . literally all that happened. . . . They thought I had approved it—I never saw it—so it was printed.[4]

Following that statement, on September 24, the President sent Congress a revised version of his letter, with the two offending sentences deleted. It was perhaps the first time in history that the White House had withdrawn a Presidential letter. Such is the background of this curious incident, which, so far as I know, has never been publicly explained. At the time, it was taken for granted in journalistic and political circles that Roosevelt had launched a trial balloon that he had shot down when he found it would not fly past Capitol Hill. Thus history is writ.

As might be expected, the President's action in withdrawing the controversial language did not pass unnoticed by our Allies. The *Economist* of September 11, 1943, interpreted it as meaning that

The President of the United States has made a little-noticed concession to Congress which may, conceivably, have large implications—in view of the drift of American politics from the President's earlier ideas. . . . The comment that it is a matter of strategic accident, and therefore a poor basis for financial reckoning, whether munitions made by one Ally are employed in battle by its own forces or those of another country might possibly be dismissed as special pleading—or restricted perhaps in its application to the 21 months during which the United States has been itself a belligerent. . . .

Memories are still vivid of the way in which world trade and the international exchanges were bedeviled after the last war by war debts—and by the high American tariff, which, in the last resort, made repayment impossible, however good the will. The United States has to show that, this time, it will be possible for its debtors to acquire the dollars, or to sell the goods, required to balance the account when it is finally reckoned.

In retrospect, I do not regret our attempt to clarify American policy—only that we failed. There is ample evidence that the deleted sentences would have been useful. Only a few months earlier, in March

1943, Professor Eugene Staley had written a perceptive article in the *American Economic Review* in which he had concluded: "It would be a wise action if the President, acting under the broad powers delegated to him in the Lend-Lease Act, were to wipe the slate clean of obligations for repayment on account of Lend-Lease deliveries, including those made before Pearl Harbor. This he could do by proclaiming that effective use of Lend-Lease supplies in ways which contribute to defeat of the Axis will be deemed a sufficient 'benefit' to the United States."[5]

I had not seen Staley's article at the time we made the aborted attempt to accomplish exactly what he recommended. That Davidson and I were right is confirmed by Professor (later, Ambassador) Richard N. Gardner in his definitive history of the period, *Sterling-Dollar Diplomacy*. Writing about the event, he says with respect to the payment for articles consumed in the war, "The Lend-Lease Act, it may be recalled, had been deliberately vague on this point. Once the United States entered the war, full acceptance of the pooling concept should have prompted a declaration that no bill would ever be tendered for the provision of war supplies. In fact, abortive attempts were made to do this." He then cited our letter and continued, that it was ". . . the last time during the course of the war that the Administration sought to make a direct approach to the repayment question. Accordingly, the United Kingdom and other countries had no assurance in planning their postwar trade policies that they would be entirely free from the burden of war debts owing to the United States."[6]

In speculating about why the President hesitated to clarify the repayment question, Professor Gardner suggests two influences. The first is that leading figures in the State and Treasury Departments were reluctant to surrender the bargaining power of Lend-Lease indebtedness in persuading the United Kingdom to embrace a policy of multilateral trade. Yet the British had already gone far toward the acceptance of the principles we were urging, and we outraged many in the United Kingdom by linking the acceptance of those principles to the Lend-Lease settlement.

Professor Gardner's second point is more speculative. The President, he suggests, feared the reaction of Congress, particularly after the conservative trend in the Congressional elections of 1942, and was not prepared at the time to bring the issue of repayment to a head. That may well be; yet it may simply have been that the President never wished to give away any leverage he might later find useful.

Varied Lend-Lease Duties

The question of settlement was, of course, only one of many matters that occupied our small enclave of lawyers. Apart from the often exotic assignments that fell our way because Oscar Cox wore so many hats, guiding the Lend-Lease program involved many activities. We had a hand, for example, in drafting, negotiating, and interpreting the Soviet protocols and in helping to resolve the multitude of difficulties that arose in our always prickly relations with the Soviet Union. One of the more delicate of those problems, as I recall, was an attempted extortion by the agents of an important American shipping line, which, against strong cautionary advice, we insisted on exposing.

We also provided arguments to be used when the Lend-Lease Administration acted as advocate for our Allies before the various allocation agencies: the War Production Board, army, navy, Maritime Commission, Agriculture Department, and Treasury. We helped plan a special currency for use during the post-occupation period. We helped devise the patent interchange agreements required when intricate equipment and machinery were transferred from one Ally to another—a chore of monumental complexity. We developed what were known as "knock-for-knock" agreements to make it possible for ship repair services to be provided on a reciprocal basis to American ships by the United Kingdom and to United Kingdom ships by the United States. We largely invented the concept of reverse Lend-Lease, under which Australia and the United Kingdom provided goods and services to the United States on the same basis as our assistance to them.

The Foreign Economic Administration

Yet we worked not so much as part of the Lend-Lease Administration as through and around it. Our small cabal of lawyers was convinced that the management of the agency was beyond redemption; the only way to bring our Lend-Lease activities within the framework of a coherent foreign economic policy was, as we saw it, to abolish the Lend-Lease Administration as then constituted. Since the Office (formerly Board) of Economic Warfare was also in a state of disarray, why not combine the two agencies? The Office of Economic Warfare concentrated on such matters as preemptive buying in order to deny key products and materials to the enemy, while the Lend-Lease Administration screened procurement requisitions for Lend-Lease products and generally formulated Lend-Lease policy. Both agencies needed to be operated with a common strategy, while savings and efficiencies could be achieved by combining various service functions.

So we quietly conspired with friends in the Budget Bureau, which was responsible for the structure of wartime agencies, and, in collaboration with them, evolved a plan for a merged organization to be known as the Foreign Economic Administration. What we could not control was the selection of a leader for the new entity. Since Stettinius had already gone to the State Department as Under Secretary, leaving the Lend-Lease post to a caretaker, we very much hoped the President would install someone of competence with whom we could work effectively.

I well remember my sense of profound shock, therefore, when it was announced that Leo T. Crowley would head the new Foreign Economic Administration. Although Crowley was spectacularly unequipped by training, comprehension, or temperament for the job, Roosevelt (no doubt in a puckish mood) described him as "the best administrator in or out of government." With his limited background—a small-town banker and politician in Wisconsin—Crowley knew nothing about the economic needs of our Allies and seemed quite indifferent to their problems so long as he avoided trouble with Congress. I well recall his initial testimony before the House Foreign Affairs Committee under the chairmanship of the colorful Sol Bloom. He began his opening statement in the customary way: "My name is Leo T. Crowley, and I am the chairman of the *Federal* Economic Administration." While those of us accompanying him cringed, he continued quite unaware of his mistake, mumbling through the remarks we had carefully prepared, in which the name was properly written, yet still repeating *"Federal* Economic Administration." At the end, casting his statement aside, he made his apologia to the committee. "No doubt this agency has made a lot of mistakes," he said, "but you've got to remember one thing—it's impossible to get first-rate people to work on these matters while the war's going on"—an inspiring contribution to the morale of his staff and colleagues.

At that point, those of us who had been arranging the hearing resorted to a heavy-handed maneuver. I had told Chairman Bloom at the outset of the hearing that we wanted the committee to hear a special witness who was based in London and was in Washington only for the day. But to have the benefit of his testimony the committee would have to go into executive session, since his testimony would be highly sensitive. Normally, the suggestion that his committee was about to hear something secret would have been an enticement, but not on the first day of the annual Lend-Lease hearings. The press was present in full force, and Bloom was counting on the headlines, which, with his background in show business, he particularly relished. After all, the annual Lend-Lease authorization was then the principal business to come before the Foreign Affairs Committee, and he wished to make the most of it.

But we did not dare let the committee have a free go at Leo Crowley. He knew nothing about Lend-Lease, had no comprehension of its underlying philosophy, and would almost certainly make comments that would cause us trouble in the future. Thus, as soon as Crowley had finished his statement, I asked that the committee go into executive session, enormously inflating the importance and interest of the secret testimony that would, I insisted, be available only on that day.

Grumbling and irritated, Chairman Bloom finally complied, but what followed was a disaster. Though the surprise witness had, I thought, been fully coached, he either misunderstood our tactic or was not sympathetic with it. Rather than telling the committee anything secret, he gave them a bland, rather halting and thoroughly uninteresting description of his activities. The committee asked him a few half-hearted questions, and that was the end of it. It was a lamentably bad show. I paid a high cost for the maneuver in terms of my relations with Chairman Bloom and the committee, but it was still worth it. By the time our secret witness had finished, the press had grown tired of waiting, while during our witness's dull statement, various committee members had themselves drifted off. When the committee next resumed, we put on a witness more experienced than Crowley.

Among those of us close to the situation during that curious period, "Crowley stories" are a cherished legacy, including the day he mistook George S. Messersmith, the American ambassador to Mexico, for the Mexican ambassador to the United States. While laboring under that misapprehension, he spoke to Messersmith in extravagant praise of the cooperation we were receiving from Mexico and the Mexican government; once the mistake was called to his attention, he turned to Messersmith and denounced the Mexicans and their government in scatological terms.

Cuban Mission

In spite of Crowley's inadequacies as a manager, much less a leader, the consolidation of the two wartime agencies had an inherent logic. Moreover, responsibility for the legal problems of the combined institution greatly expanded my own scope of action. One particularly memorable episode was a mission to Havana. It marked the first time I had ever participated in a full-dress negotiation with a foreign government in its own capital, and it gave me a thoroughly mistaken idea of what international diplomacy was all about.

The mission came about in December 1943, because Justice James A. Byrnes (who had resigned from the Supreme Court on October 3, 1942, to become Director of Economic Stabilization) was disturbed at the lack of progress of the synthetic rubber program. What was needed, he decided, was a forceful effort to stop the Cubans from converting molasses into bad gin; instead, they should turn it into alcohol for producing rubber tires.

A team was, therefore, appointed to negotiate with the Cuban government, and I was sent along as counsel and chief adviser. Since Sidney Scheuer, the chairman of our mission, had spent his life in the textile business, his manners and methods had been shaped in a specialized milieu. Although bright, ingenious, and capable of whimsical charm, he had little respect for diplomatic protocol and approached the task as though he were raising money for a charity drive. His game plan was anything but subtle. "I'm goin' to do a hand-painted job on those Cuban bastards," he told me on the flight to Havana. "They're goin' to know they didn't get no bargain." And he kept his word. In a grandiloquent opening speech to the Cuban negotiators, headed by the Prime Minister, he declaimed, "All of you know there's a war on and we're in it together and you've got to do your share. You've got to give till it hurts, and I've come to see that you do."

Although by diplomatic standards the language was unusual, my leader had such a guileless manner that no Cuban took offense, and only the younger members of the American delegation showed even the trace of a smile. Indeed, once the Cubans had adjusted to a Seventh Avenue rather than a Foggy Bottom style of diplomacy, they seemed vaguely embarrassed by their own flamboyant brand of Hispanic rhetoric. In any event, we soon settled down to the kind of protracted haggle that came naturally to both the Cubans and my colorful leader. Although everyone enjoyed the bazaarlike atmosphere that pervaded our proceedings (I indulged in the fantasy that the green baize table had by some miraculous transmogrification become a counter in a small souk), we still made painfully little progress. By the end of the second day, it was clear that the Cubans were playing games, quite unconvinced that the United States was serious about the harsh sanctions that, we implied, would be imposed if they did not come round to our position. Some further element of persuasion was plainly needed.

Our ambassador to Cuba, a seasoned operator named Spruille Braden, had cautioned us when we first arrived not to place or receive any telephone calls through the switchboard of the Hotel Nacional since they would be intercepted and promptly turned over to the Cuban negotiators. That gave me an idea. When our negotiations approached a dead end, I began to fly each evening to Miami. Once there, I would telephone Stettinius or Cox over an untapped line and dictate a message Stettinius should give me in a telephone call to the Hotel Nacional at the appointed hour the next day.

"We're getting damned angry," I would have him say. "Make it clear we're not fooling and we're going to get really tough if those ungrateful Cuban bastards won't help with the war. If you don't get anywhere in the next forty-eight hours, I'm going to pull you all back; you're not going to enjoy it, but the goddamned Cubans are going to hate it even worse." That was the theme he would repeat with mounting emphasis each day, sometimes adding for special effect, "I talked with the President this morning, and he's furious. He's irritated with you for being chicken, and I've never seen him more angry at another government."

Having arranged for my daily message, I would get a good night's sleep, then fly back to Havana in the morning. To explain my curious nocturnal departures, I dropped vague hints of a girl in Miami and even showed one of the Cubans a photograph that not only improved the respect with which I was treated but gave my story verisimilitude with our Latin antagonists.

Time vindicated my petty stratagem. Each day as we appeared with studiously worried faces, the Cubans seemed increasingly upset. The pace of progress materially improved, and they finally gave us the concessions we wanted. That they had gotten the word I know, for I asked one of the leaders of the Cuban negotiating team about it many years later, when he was an émigré living in New York—after Castro had taken over. "You mean," he asked in a shocked voice, "that those messages were arranged? My God, they scared the hell out of us; they almost brought the government down!"

The lesson to be drawn, for purposes of this morality play, is that gentlemen do not always profit from "reading one another's mail," as Henry L. Stimson described the interception of messages when he shut down the American Black Chamber in 1929.[7] Had the Cubans not been deflected from their original instinct of standing firm, they could no doubt have continued to coin money by flooding America with filthy tasting gin; I doubt they would have suffered for it. As for myself, well, I had two motives for stopping the traffic: patriotism and a respect for good liquor.

Departure for England

The Cuban mission was one of the last chores I undertook for the Foreign Economic Administration. Although Crowley was always courteous to me, I became convinced that I could not work with him in good conscience; on August 21, 1944, I resigned. General "Hap" Arnold, the commanding general of the United States Air Force, had asked me to serve as the civilian member of the board of air force officers being established in London to study the effectiveness of the Allied air offensive. That invitation had been arranged by Fowler Hamilton, a brilliant young lawyer whom I had met some years earlier and who, together with the distinguished New York lawyer, Elihu Root, Jr., had helped the air force select bombing targets.

No doubt my decision was influenced by self-indulgence. My options were either to go into uniform, where, as I saw it, I could have provided little more than another pair of hands for a rifle (although I could have arranged a commission had I chosen), or to undertake a civilian job for the air force that would take me directly to the European theater, where I might apply my experience with useful results. Either choice was, of course, difficult for my family, which then consisted of Ruth and two young sons, John (age eight) and Douglas (age five). Still, I was eager to be closer to the war—more, I suspect, from curiosity than patriotism, although motives are hard to sort out—and I knew enough of the philosophy of strategic bombing to believe that I could help make an objective appraisal of what it had accomplished.

4. The Bombing Survey

I left for London on September 4, 1944, shortly after the liberation of Paris, to join my fellow members of the Air Force Evaluation Board, under the chairmanship of Major General Jacob Fickel. Fickel, then sixty-one years old, had been drawn out of retirement by the war. His principal claim to fame was that he had been the first to shoot a firearm from an airplane in flight. With pride, he handed me a picture of that historic event; it showed a young junior officer, wearing a hunting cap and aiming a deer rifle from the lower wing of an early biplane. He was a pleasant and courteous man, but his major value to the Air Force Evaluation Board was his right to a Packard automobile and the access to high places available to one of his rank. Nor were the other board members much better equipped for the task.

The Evaluation Board was then camping out in a once elegant Edwardian townhouse on the south side of Grosvenor Square—"Eisenhower Platz," as it was then called by the British, since it had become the center of American activities. That was, however, only a temporary location, since the Board had already decided to move to the outskirts of Paris, closer to where our side had actually dropped bombs. The relocation seemed essential to the other Board members, whose concern was largely limited to measuring bomb craters so as to ascertain the detonating effect of various types of explosives; they seemed little interested in the effect of bombing on the enemy economy.

The focus of the study came as a shock to me. I had assumed that the Board would try to assess the damage our bombing had inflicted on the enemy's total war-making capacity, which would obviously entail an exhaustive study of how the Germans mobilized their industry and society for war and how they had adjusted to our attacks. But that was light years beyond the capabilities of the feeble organization I found floundering about in London. The kinds of specialists I had envisaged (first-class economists, engineers, industrialists, statisticians, public opinion experts, scientists, and so on) could never have been recruited to serve under such a Board, and even if they had been assembled, the Board, as constituted, would have had not the vaguest idea what to do with them.

Another problem was that, in the nature of things, the air force could not appraise its own achievements objectively. The central object of our study, as I saw it, was to determine whether America had judiciously allocated its resources. Could we have won the war more quickly by committing more or less effort and material to the air offensive at the expense, or to the benefit, of our ground or naval forces?

Annoyed that I had blundered into such a frustrating situation, I told my new colleagues that I would remain in London for a week while they went on to the Continent. Meanwhile, I intended to determine as well as possible what shape a serious study should take and how it could be organized. Remaining with me was a young captain, a statistician in civilian life, who had been with the Board since its inception and shared my perceptions of its total inadequacy. With his help and the advice of other friends then in London, I drew up an elaborate organization chart to show how to put together a competent study, responsible not to the air force but to the Secretary of War and staffed with experts capable of assessing the behavior under bombing of all aspects of the German economy.

I crossed the channel on an LST, then accompanied a convoy of jeeps to Paris—displaying my disdain for military customs by staying in hotels along the way. After first checking in with my colleagues, who were uncomfortably ensconced in temporary offices in the stables (Les Grandes Ecuries) of the Versailles Palace, I obtained permission from General "Tooey" Spaatz, the commanding general of the United States Strategic Air Forces, to return to Washington. Apart from my hope of promoting a serious strategic survey, I planned, so I told General Fickel, to recruit a few civilian experts for an Evaluation Board survey of the effect of Allied bombing on the French railroads.

That seemed an appropriate study for the Board to undertake. It was limited in scope, and with a few well-trained civilian experts we might help resolve what had been a highly disputed issue. In the early months of 1944, a fierce argument had taken place between the Eighth Air Force and the Royal Air Force (RAF) as to whether our large bombers should be deployed to assist the pre-invasion bombing effort (beginning D-minus-60) by destroying the rail system of northern France or be used in a concentrated attack on German oil production.[1]

Back in Washington, I promptly got in touch with my old friend Fowler Hamilton and other friends in the War Department. I showed them my chart for a large-scale civilian study and emphasized that the Evaluation Board was quite incompetent to conduct the kind of comprehensive survey that could help us shape our continuing air attack on Germany and later on Japan. Much to my surprise, I was pushing against an open door; several able men in the Department had independently come to the same view. Thus, after a few weeks of discussion, we put together a new proposal for what was ultimately to be called the United States Strategic Bombing Survey, and I began helping recruit experts to man it.

The United States Strategic Bombing Survey

When the Survey was finally organized, Secretary Stimson installed as its nominal leader Franklin D'Olier, the president of the Prudential Insurance Company. As vice-chairman, he chose Henry Clay Alexander, a young Morgan partner who was later to become head of the Morgan Bank and to oversee the merger that produced the present institution of the Morgan Guaranty Bank. Although remaining a member of the Evaluation Board, I was also made a director of the Strategic Bombing Survey and was able to bring into the organization as co-directors two old friends of mine: Paul Nitze, with whom I had worked in the Foreign Economic Administration, and John Kenneth Galbraith, who had been a colleague during the latter days of the Lend-Lease Administration.

Since I was to have two jobs, I needed a deputy, so I turned to Adlai Stevenson, who had returned to our old·law firm in Chicago, where I was sure he was languishing in boredom. I telephoned him on Thursday, November 2, asking if he could come to Washington and go with me foi a tour of duty in Paris. He hesitated for only a moment, then said that he could, provided he would be home for Christmas "because of Ellen" (his wife). When did he have to be in Washington? I told him to get there the next day if possible; we would be flying on Saturday. An hour later, he rang me back: "What the hell will we be doing in London?" I explained that I could not answer that question over the telephone but would fill him in completely when we met.

Flying in an Air Force C-54 to London on November 4, the newly constituted directors of the Strategic Bombing Survey set about turning a blueprint into an organization. My first task was to negotiate a division of tasks between the Evaluation Board and the Bombing Survey. With Henry Alexander's skillful help, we worked out a satisfactory treaty. The Bombing Survey, on its part, would appraise the whole strategic air offensive, which included the effect of bombing on every aspect of the German war effort: munitions production, oil, aircraft, transportation, public utilities, morale, and civilian defense. The Evaluation Board would concentrate on appraising the achievements of the tactical air effort in France that had been conducted by the British and our Ninth Air Force, in connection with the Normandy invasion.

I knew that the controversy over the most effective means of providing air support to Operation Overlord (the Allied assault on Normandy) had acquired a religious intensity. The RAF had wanted to concentrate air power as early as March 1, 1944, to destroy the railway network in northern France and the Low Countries. That, it was argued, would create a "railway desert," which would prevent the enemy from moving reserves into the assault area or from shifting troops and supplies behind its own lines. Railway marshalling yards, locomotive repair facilities, bridges, and the like were to be prime targets. The American Air Force, under General Spaatz, violently disagreed. The best way to assure air superiority, they argued, was to defeat the German Air Force by attacking its fuel supply, especially the synthetic oil refineries. Those targets, they contended, were far more important than the French railway system. Since the Germans could not risk the destruction of this vital resource, such attacks would not only cut down the training of German air crews, but also force the German Air Force into the air so it could be destroyed in air battles by Allied airmen, who, at that stage of the war, were being given far more effective training.

The intellectual underpinning for the American plan had been provided largely by a group headed by Professor Charles Kindleberger, an old friend of mine from Washington, while the intellectual champion of the "railway desert" concept was Solly Zuckerman, then scientific adviser to Combined Operations of the RAF.[2]

After hearing the arguments of both sides, General Eisenhower had opted for the British "rail plan" rather than the American "oil plan." But the American planners still regarded Zuckerman with dark suspicion as a shrewd conniver who exercised a kind of Svengali hold over Air Marshal Tedder. Thus, they looked darkly at the Bombing Analysis Unit, which the British had established at about the same time as the founding of our Evaluation Board and which was largely duplicating the Board's work. Its primary purpose—some snide Americans thought—was to vindicate Zuckerman's original theory; the theological overtones of bombing strategy, as I quickly found, turned experts into bigots.

I had had no part in the argument and was interested only in making as objective an assessment as possible. In the course of our work, I came to know Solly Zuckerman quite well, and we remain friends to this day. I made clear at our first talk early in November that I, for one, had no axe to grind and wanted merely to clear up past misunderstandings. I lunched with him at his house in Oxford, and we met again to compare notes when we were both working in France. As a result, our two groups arranged to hold weekly meetings with our French colleagues with all primary data made freely available both to the British Bombing Analysis Unit and the American Air Force Evaluation Board.

Working with Adlai

As soon as the Evaluation Board's jurisdiction had been defined, I flew with Stevenson to Paris to install him as my deputy. He and I were assigned a spacious floor in a run-down villa in St. Germain-en-Laye. It was to be his living quarters, but we would share it during my visits to France. The villa had just been evacuated by the top command of the German Veterinary Corps, and signs of hasty retreat were everywhere—the rooms still strewn with German newspapers and even some official documents. Stevenson, whose olfactory sensitivities were particularly acute, complained that the veterinary corps must have used our rooms to house their horses. Still, the villa would have been quite comfortable save for the fact that it was a cold November and we had neither central heating nor fuel for the fireplace. Since an American general on a lower floor had been amply supplied with both coal and wood from quarter-master sources, we dined with him the first night and spent the evening basking in the warmth of his fire. However, at Stevenson's insistence we left early, and as we struggled back up to our own cold quarters, he issued a solemn pronunciamento: "No more evenings with that old bastard. I'd rather be frozen to death than bored to death."

That led us to an alternative solution. Each evening, after returning from dinner at an officers' mess, we would put a bottle of gin on the table, don our overcoats, mix the gin with water purified with halazone tablets, and drink until, having emptied the bottle, we each felt warm enough to go to bed. Since there was nothing to do but talk and since we both faced futures we could not clearly foresee, we rambled on with unguarded candor of our postwar hopes and intentions. Adlai was invariably interested in other people, and he probed my own unformulated plans with concern and sympathy. He, himself, was bored with law practice—he had never regarded our law firm as more than a base of operations—and he had set his heart on buying the *Chicago Daily News* from the estate of Frank Knox. The group he headed had, however, been outbid, and he was now thinking of running for Senator or Governor of Illinois, although, he lamented, "Ellen hated all of that." The Chicago Democratic boss, Jacob Arvey, had put out vague feelers that could conceivably lead to something.

Fond and admiring as I was of Adlai, I thought his political ambitions little more than wishful talk. He was, as I saw him, a brilliant, engaging amateur but far too fastidious to wield an effective pick on the grim coal face of politics. Besides, his lusty feeling for the comic quality of life would clearly be an obstacle in political campaigning. How could he kiss babies without laughing? His pride as well as his sense of the absurd would inhibit him from playing the political mendicant, while the mindless hyperbole and oversimplifications of a political campaign would bore and repel him.

As with everything else he did, Stevenson approached the work of the Evaluation Board conscientiously and with seriousness of purpose. Within a relatively few days he had filled legal-size yellow pages with innumerable notes of interviews that contributed substantially to the findings of the Board. Then, on Thanksgiving Day, November 23, he arranged a trip to the front as far as Luxembourg, where he discussed tactical bombing with Professor, now Major, Charles Kindleberger. The next day, he went on to Metz, saw General Patton, and returned to St. Germain-en-Laye on the twenty-sixth. I came over from London to find out how Stevenson was progressing, and one night we had dinner with a colleague in a rather poor café in Montmartre. We had worked until late, and it was 2:30 A.M. when we started to walk back from Montmartre to a small hotel just off the Rue de Rivoli where we were staying. As I later described the incident,

We were walking in the vicinity of the Place Vendôme—appropriately enough, as Adlai observed, on the rue Casanova—when we encountered American military police raiding an off-limits house. Field- and Company-grade officers were debouching into the street in maximum disarray, protesting with spleen and outraged innocence at the affront to their dignity.

Adlai and I, although civilians, were in uniform (we each had the assimilated rank of colonel) and hence were indistinguishable from the culprits. This created a situation of some hazard, for Adlai was enchanted with the spectacle of so many chagrined and choleric officers "whose expectations and consummations," as he said, had been abruptly interrupted. He insisted on seeing the show, and at least twice his curiosity led him so far into the crowd that he found himself shoved into a paddy wagon. It took all the advocacy my colleague and I could muster to establish Stevenson as a noncombatant and save him from the indiscriminate sanctions of military justice.

It was the kind of absurd situation he thoroughly enjoyed. Thereafter in my presence on several occasions he repeated the story with imaginative embellishment—generously substituting me for himself as the epic figure rescued from incarceration.

It gives me no comfort to have the last word.[3]

Stevenson returned to the front on December 10 for a few days and proceeded on to Aachen, where he conferred with General Terry Allen, who was attacking from a forward command post in the basement of a bank. He met with General Omar Bradley and the other top brass, toured radar installations, and watched an experiment in blind bombing by automatic radar release. Then he went to Brussels and conferred with SHAEF officers about the Bombing Survey. Returning home after Christmas, he immediately tried to get in touch with Ruth and found her in a hospital. On December 28, I received a message that he had sent through our London embassy: "Ruth very ill, urge you return Washington soonest. Adlai." A telegram arrived from my father almost simultaneously. Ruth, it advised, had had a serious operation.

Arranging a priority passage home, I found her in a hospital slowly recuperating from painful surgery. Although happy to see me, she had not wanted me to learn of her troubles. A sturdy Scot, she had concealed her predicament out of reluctance to worry me and pride in her own self-reliance. It was a kind of self-denial I did not possess and I could not help but contrast her role with mine. An American civilian in Europe with even moderate rank and substantial command of his own time could hardly help but find life absorbing. Though my work required effort and concentration, I had freedom of movement and was surrounded by amiable and interesting companions. Not so with Ruth, who was taking care of our two small sons and maintaining a household with little money and inadequate help. Her mobility was severely restricted since gasoline was rationed. Meanwhile, she was painfully ill.

She had told me none of this in her letters, and I would have known nothing had Stevenson not searched her out in a Washington hospital. Unimpressed by her plea for silence, he telephoned my parents in Evanston and cabled me through the embassy. I stayed in Washington for ten days, as Ruth began a slow recuperation, then returned to London. Two and a half months later my father telegraphed me that she faced a second serious operation—this time for the removal of a kidney.

Returning to Washington the second time, I knew I should stay there. The war would be won without my being on hand to supervise it, and my duties as a husband and parent clearly outweighed the marginal tasks that the government had entrusted to me. Yet, with what seems in retrospect inexcusable self-indulgence, I yielded willingly to the hollow argument that I could not leave a job half-finished and returned to England. I do not regard that as my finest hour.

Return to London

Life in London offered the piquancy of the unexpected. The first V-2 had landed only a week before I first arrived in England, and I soon earned the almost obligatory accolade of a near miss. Billeted at the Mount Royal Hotel, across Oxford Street from Marble Arch, I rose early one Sunday morning with a mild hangover. Ordinarily I would have omitted breakfast—which I have never regarded as an essential meal—but, no doubt moved by contrition for the previous night's indulgence, I resolved to abjure my morning bath and walk down past Marble Arch along Park Lane to the senior officers' mess in the Grosvenor House. When I was half dressed, virtue deserted me. To hell with breakfast, I thought; huge English bath tubs are a delight to anyone over six feet tall, while powdered eggs are no Lucullan delight.

Ten minutes later, just when I was well covered with soap, the sky fell in. My bathroom had a casement window I had left ajar; it was blown wide open with an explosive thud that seriously strained my ear drums. Seconds later, as the debris that had been blown skyward began to crash,

I heard people running compulsively up and down the hall, shouting and laughing idiotically. My first thought was of an air burst, but when I opened the bathroom door, the floor, the bed, the entire living room were covered with shattered glass, while the casement windows hung limply like Daliesque watches, swinging slowly back and forth.

A V-2 had fallen a hundred yards away within a few feet of the Marble Arch. Had I not altered course while dressing, I would have formed part (or parts) of the debris blown wildly into the air—as, indeed, happened to one poor fellow, various pieces of whose anatomy decorated surrounding trees and bushes. Thereafter, I religiously took a long bath every morning. Cleanliness was clearly to be preferred to premature godliness—or even to breakfast.

On to Bad Nauheim

In April 1945, Kenneth Galbraith and I decided that we could carry on our work more efficiently by moving our base of operations to Germany. Bad Nauheim was assigned as our headquarters. In a spa called the Park Hotel, we established offices and billets for the staffs we were then supervising, while Galbraith and I took over a small private hotel served by a German domestic staff of seven.

Each director of the Survey, in addition to his collective responsibility for the management of the whole enterprise, had certain specific supervisory tasks. My special responsibilities were for two broad areas. The first was to assess the effectiveness of area bombing, by which was meant the massive British night raids on cities. Like everything else connected with bombing, their relative efficacy was a subject of major controversy. The United States Air Force, which was dedicated to daytime raids on precision targets, was highly skeptical of the effectiveness of the bombing of cities—the only targets large enough for inaccurate night bombing. The Survey needed to determine exactly what had happened in cities under attack, how fast urban life was restored, and how serious was the effect on the war economy when a major city was knocked out. In addition, I also supervised a detailed study of the effect of bombing on German transportation—another controversial subject.

Ken Galbraith, whose assignment was to pull together the data assembled by the specialized sector divisions and to assess the overall economic effects of the air offensive, had gathered around him a brilliant staff of academics temporarily in uniform—economists, statisticians, and historians—as well as civilian experts recruited directly from America or Great Britain.

Life in Bad Nauheim was stimulating not only because of the intrinsic fascination of the data we were gathering and the exotic means by which we collected it, but also because of the intellectual ferment generated by the gifted men we had brought together. One of the inter-rogators in our psychological effects division was W. H. Auden, the poet, who dined with us drunk on several occasions. Since we both knew a large number of people in the Office of Strategic Services (OSS), located only sixty kilometers away in Biebrich, there was a great deal of visiting back and forth with friends such as Arthur Schlesinger, Jr., Emile Despres, Charles Hatch, and Sherman Kent.

Paris on V-E Day

Winter wore into spring, and, quite by chance, I was in Paris on V-E Day, the undeserving beneficiary of undiscriminating good feeling. How could the *midinettes* know that, far from being an authentic hero, I was merely the "Captain of Köpenick"—a brash intruder on other people's deserved and private ecstasy? The hour belonged to the Parisians, not to a civilian in paramilitary uniform who had never felt the brutality of SS bullies or even heard a shot fired in anger. But, though I tried to retain intellectual detachment—bemused by the conceit that if I held aloof from the public exultation, I could resist the prevailing euphoria—objectivity was quite impossible. Genuine as might be my reservations about the future, they were irrelevant to the moment and incapable of surviving in the Paris streets on that day of victory.

From the balcony of an office building on the Champs Elysées, we looked down on fighter planes that curved over the obelisk in the Place de la Concorde, streaked just above the heads of the masses churning in the street, then jerked abruptly upward to clear the Arc de Triomphe. No one raised a cautionary eyebrow; madness was endemic to the moment. At the liberation of Paris, eight months previously, an American general is said to have announced, "Any GI who sleeps alone tonight is a goddamned exhibitionist." That *mot* was quite as appropriate for V-E night.

Accompanied by one of the Survey's young German-Jewish scholars in uniform, I set out to find his elderly mother, who had hidden for four years in the working-class suburb of Billancourt. Installing her in one of the Survey's jeeps, we drove through uproarious crowds to the top of Montmartre so she could, like Saint Genevieve, look down on Paris. With gleeful youths perched in layers all over my jeep, I made a slow descent, steering by remote control.

Last Days of the Third Reich

The next day was business as usual—or, more than usual. With the Third Reich now a kitchen midden, the people and records we needed had become available, so I rushed back to our London headquarters to catch up on the news. There I learned that the Nazis, in a final convulsive effort to keep control, had split into two parts like an amoeba. A small group of staff officers had gone south to Berchtesgaden; a more important group had found their way to the north. On May 2, 1945, Admiral Doenitz had announced over the Hamburg radio that Hitler was dead and that he was Hitler's heir. Then, as the north German ports fell successively to Field Marshal Montgomery, the group had rendezvoused at Flensburg in Schleswig-Holstein, just five kilometers south of the Danish border. On May 7, the Flensburg radio had carried Doenitz's message of defeat and announced the formation of what he hoped the Allies would recognize as an established government. With a blackmailer's insolence, he insisted that only that "government" could prevent chaos during the period of surrender.

The Bombing Survey had no professional interest in most of the Flensburg group: Admiral Doenitz; Colonel General Jodl; Count von Krosigk, the German finance minister; Backer, the minister of agriculture; Seldte, the doddering and neglected minister of labor; and old Dorpmueller, head of the Reichsbahn. Those were fodder for specialists with a different mission. What excited us was a report from Major Sidney Spivak, our liaison officer with the Twenty-First Army Group, that one of our wandering intelligence teams had found Albert Speer.

Speer was the man we most wished to see. As the czar of German war production ever since the spring of 1942, he, above all others, could, if willing, confirm many of our speculations. But though he was the Survey's number one target, we knew little about him—not much more than what appeared in German publications at a time when censorship was rigorous. I alerted Ken Galbraith and Paul Nitze, who were in the field, and they promptly joined me. Loading a plane with interpreters, we took off across the flooded fields of northern Holland, where the dikes had been bombed or sabotaged, which we still instinctively thought of as enemy territory.

Flensburg airport was crowded with Luftwaffe planes in various stages of disrepair and with Luftwaffe officers still quite intact. Soldiers with swastikas on their caps were pursuing a busy routine as though Germany had never surrendered, while the small cadre of British officers commanding the handful of Allied troops at the field seemed uncertain whether they were conquerors or guests. They were trying hard to avoid diplomatic *gaffes* but had only the vaguest of instructions.

To our disgust, no ground transport was visible. We stood about awkwardly, blinking in the cold morning air. An RAF squadron leader approached with two men in gray uniforms and we shook hands all around; only when the two men responded in German gutterals did we note the insignia on their caps. Though we felt foolish, the squadron leader seemed not to notice; in the three days he had been running the field, the bizarre had become commonplace. Still, he offered little encouragement.

"There are a couple of German divisions between you and those top Nazi bastards. I don't know what's going on in town; that's not my problem. But I'm bloody sure it makes no sense!"

He cranked the field telephone vigorously to put us through to the SHAEF Control Party, but communications worked no better than usual. We were still standing about, cursing Major Spivak, when a caravan wound slowly toward our plane. It consisted of four conscripted cars with German drivers led by a curious kind of gypsy wagon, which I recognized as the major's jeep, long a legend in the area. In his movements throughout the Twenty-First Army Group, the major carried a fantastic inventory of merchandise that he turned over with a velocity to put Macy's and Gimbels in awe. Those trade goods, constantly replenished, were contained in four captured ammunition cases welded on the sides and back of the jeep. It was the least military-looking vehicle in the theater.

The major was both disarming and reassuring. He had arranged lunch and billets for us on the *Patria,* an old Hamburg-America liner anchored in the Flensburg Fjord, where the SHAEF Control Party was stationed. Yes, of course, Speer was available. One of our sergeants had been talking with him for two days.

The *Patria*'s billeting officer was a harried but heroic young captain with protocol problems that would have overwhelmed any foreign office. He could have taken in stride the *protocolaire* complexities of providing cabin space for American army and navy officers of various ranks, but there were also British officers, American civilians, and German naval personnel. A Russian mission was expected in a day or two, and Robert Murphy, who held ambassadorial rank, was coming with a party of diplomats. Added to all this was the vestigial caste system of the liner's tourist days. Since he would not have enough first-class cabins, could one give second-class accommodations to first-class generals?

Frenetically reviewing his resources, the captain assigned us cabins adequate for sleeping, if not for working. A few minutes later, I looked through binoculars (liberated an hour before from a Nazi vice-admiral) at the technicolor blue of the Flensburg Fjord and at its crowded shoreline. First was the Submarine School, then—a mile up the shore through a confusion of Nazi transports, minesweepers, and E-Boats—I saw the Marine and Signal School, which served as the headquarters of the so-called German general staff.

Packed in the Flensburg enclave were several thousand enlisted men with several hundred field-grade officers. Impenitently arrogant, the officers added a carnival air to the promenade along the waterfront; they included infantry colonels and majors from panzer divisions, pilots and navigators from the Luftwaffe, and submarine commanders who looked like commercial travelers costumed for a lodge convention. With their immaculate uniforms and well-burnished medals, they reminded me of a crowd of Hollywood extras loafing during lunch hour. I expected to hear a whistle any moment and to see them all stampede back to the set.

Even after a week in Flensburg, I could not walk past a Luger-bearing Erich von Stroheim without a sense of unreality. Never before had I seen a representative of the Wehrmacht, except in a prisoner of war camp or on a movie screen. Now I was on the receiving end of correct and emphatic salutes from several thousand still fully armed Nazis.

5. Albert Speer on a Grade-B Movie Set

After lunch, we set out for Glücksburg, where Speer was living in a schloss belonging to the Duke of Holstein. The road took us past the offices of the *Oberkommando Wehrmacht* (the German general staff) and through two barricades that the make-believe Flensburg government had erected, more to assert its dignity than to safeguard its personnel or documents. Those barricades were like railroad-crossing gates; stationed beside each were two SS guards with Sten guns. Approaching cars were required to stop for recognition.

Our vehicle was an oversized Mercedes-Benz, on which no one had yet bothered to paint American Army identification; it was driven by a young Jewish lieutenant who would interpret for us during interrogations. Having fled Germany eight years before and been dropped as a paratrooper in Normandy on D-Day-minus-one, he cherished a well-deserved hatred for Nazis. Without advance notice, he introduced me to a game he had invented: he would bear down on the barricades at fifty miles an hour, put his head out of the front window, and shout in angry German, "Out of the way, you swine." The SS guards would raise their Sten guns and advance toward the middle of the road, while I speculated in a detached way whether we would crash into the gates before the bullets crashed into us. But, with the implausible timing of a Pearl White movie serial, the guards would recognize our American uniforms just in time to leap to the side and jerk up the gates as our car scraped under. In the days that followed, I came to suspect that our lieutenant rehearsed the routine with them while off duty.

The castle of the Duke of Holstein, known as Schloss Glücksburg, is a picturesque sixteenth-century chateau, complete with tower, turrets, a moat, and, at that time, a complement of SS guards. Wearing a dark brown uniform, Speer met us in the Great Hall, friendly and self-consciously affable. Only forty years old, he looked, Galbraith remarked, like a young college professor and "like any professor, he enjoyed an audience."

"I'm glad you've come," he said. "I was afraid I'd been forgotten." Later, he asked us if we could arrange to have him arrested; he was, he said, embarrassed to be part of the *opéra bouffe* government on the Flensburg Wilhelmstrasse.

Speer in Close Up

During an afternoon's talk, we organized a pattern for the following week. Each morning, Speer, as minister of economics and production in the Flensburg government, would attend the ten o'clock cabinet meeting on the Wilhelmstrasse. At two in the afternoon, we would arrive for what he referred to as our "bombing high school"—five hours of interrogation, while Speer's frightened but competent stenographers took a verbatim transcript of the testimony. In the evenings, Speer would do his homework, preparing monographs on subjects in which we expressed interest, digging out facts and dates from his files, making lists of the evacuation repositories, and giving us addresses and letters of introduction to his key assistants.

In the six days that followed, we discovered that Speer had a story he was anxious to tell. He gave us detailed information for which our field teams had been searching and which our analysts had been painfully trying to piece together out of bits and pieces of fact, gossip, and rumor. It was like stumbling on the page of answers after one had worked on a puzzle for months.

After one session, Speer motioned us toward a corner, saying he had something important to give us. From under a table, he produced ten or twelve volumes of photocover—pictures, he said, of every hydro-electric installation in the western part of the Soviet Union. Speer had had the pictures taken to be used in an air attack by pick-a-back planes, but Herman Goering had stopped the project out of bureaucratic jealousy. "I give you this," Speer said, "because, sooner or later, you're going to have to fight the Communists. It's too bad we Germans couldn't have made common cause with you. The Russians are the enemy of us both." It was a theme to which he repeatedly recurred—though not at Nuremberg, where Soviet judges were sitting on the bench.

When we arrived back at the *Patria* with the photocover in our car, the British billeting officer seemed upset. He had to give cabins on our deck to a high-ranking Soviet military and naval mission that had just arrived. Though Galbraith, Paul Nitze, and I could stay where we were, our staff had been shifted to the lower reaches of the ship surrounded by Russians. We put a round-the-clock guard on the photocover until we could ship it back to London the next day.

As the week drew to a close, the Flensburg farce was clearly nearing the end of its run. The exclusion of the press meant not only that the outside world was insulated from Flensburg but also that Flensburg was insulated from the outside world. We knew the critics had been writing consistently bad notices of the ham performance in the local Wilhelmstrasse but, thought we were sure the engagement was limited, we were not clear when the sheriff might arrive with an attachment for the scenery and a summons for the cast.

That afternoon, I told Robert Murphy, Eisenhower's political adviser and an old friend of mine from Washington, about our interviews and asked him if he had any specific questions for Speer. "Yes, we'd like to know what happened to Hitler's political will. You'd better find out tonight, since we're pulling in the whole gang tomorrow morning." So we sent a car to bring Speer to a house we had requisitioned on the outer fringes of Flensburg. Galbraith, Nitze, and I were waiting when he arrived at about ten o'clock, and we had with us two majors and a lieutenant from the Survey staff. After six days of interrogation and intensive homework, Speer seemed under strain but was still voluble. In violation of the fraternization regulations, we put a bottle of whisky on the dining-room table; at four-thirty the next morning Speer was groggy but still talking.

Through a Lens Darkly

During our regular interrogations, we had confined ourselves to the Survey's specific frame of reference—the effect of our air offensive on the German economy. Now Speer was encouraged to talk in a much broader context. What had happened just prior to the collapse? What had produced the collapse? How did he characterize the gang Adolf Hitler had gathered about him? How did he, himself, appraise Hitler?

Rather than being put off by this line of questioning, Speer seemed grateful for the opportunity to unburden himself without the constraints of our more technical discussions. Though I took detailed notes of the story that he told, I will not repeat them here, for the story has been completely set down in Speer's own memoirs, as well as in a dozen interviews he gave after his release from prison.

At the time, however, it was all fresh. We were the first on the Allied side to hear the story that he told with at least the illusion of detachment—as though he were talking about other people in another country. His primary emphasis was on the corruption and degraded character of his Nazi colleagues. Goering was a contemptible morphine addict with unlimited greed. Goebbels, who posed as an intellectual, was a sycophantic schemer. Himmler was a fool who dreamed bizarre fantasies about the future glory of the party, while dabbling in astrology and Oriental nonsense. Bormann was a brutal extortionist who kept on Hitler's good side by bribery.

Cunning as he was, Hitler had brought the Third Reich down by his own blunders. He need not have started the war. He had proved he could get power and territory without it. Arrogance had led him to attack Russia, since, after the defeat of France, he thought everything else would be easy. His most stupid mistake was to declare war on the United States. It was a thoughtless act taken in appalling ignorance, since neither he nor his entourage knew anything about America. Nor would he believe any of the statistics he was given.

Toward the end, Hitler retired to the bunker under the Reichschancellery in Berlin. There he lived isolated from the real world and surrounded by toadies who told him only what he wanted to hear. Particularly after the Gestapo massacred or silenced the junior officers involved in the July 20 attempt on Hitler's life, decisions were made in a vacuum. War maps showed divisions that were only skeletal forces, while Hitler compulsively ordered the deployment of troop units that no longer existed.

The constant game was a search for scapegoats, with everyone blaming everyone else. In the end, the grotesque gang in the bunker united in spewing their venom at the German people, calling for a scorched-earth policy, the climactic orgasm of a *Götterdämmerung*. Speer had personally frustrated that policy, first by argument and, when that failed, by sabotage at the risk of his life.

Though in harsh disfavor, Speer returned to the bunker for Hitler's birthday on April 20 to witness the rats leaving the sinking ship. Goering announced he was going south to organize defenses. Others made excuses to leave Berlin on official business when they had not had any official business outside Berlin in years. The decision was then made to split the ministries into two parts: one government to go north, and the other south. Speer left the next day to set up the northern branch of his ministry. But in Hamburg he recorded a radio speech announcing that the war was lost and urging all Germans to cooperate with the conquerors to preserve the means of survival. That speech was to be played immediately after Hitler's death.

On April 23, Speer returned to Berlin to see Hitler one last time and to say goodbye. It was an unnecessary and foolhardy trip, dictated only by sentiment. The bunker was almost empty. Only a few had remained loyal—Bormann, Goebbels with his wife and six children, and Eva Braun, together with some army officers. He stayed until four o'clock in the morning of April 24 to have a second talk with Hitler. He found him cold and empty, though curiously composed because he knew his life was over. He seemed primarily obsessed by thoughts of what would happen to his corpse; he had been horrified by the desecration of Mussolini's body. Then, following the long night, on the morning of Tuesday, April 24, Speer returned to Hamburg.

That was the essence of Speer's long soliloquy. I listened with fascination but almost guiltily, as though I had accidentally tuned in on a sordid and intimate drama I was not meant to hear. It was shot through with a macabre element we found hard to associate with this cultivated, intelligent man who despised his Nazi colleagues as a loathsome breed. He had shown the greatest emotion when, during the course of his long exposition, one of us had asked the important question: "What do you know about the treatment of Jews in the extermination camps?"

He had grimaced with distaste. "I know frightful things have been happening," he said, "but that's all I know. A friend of mine from party circles came to see me some time ago and said in great anguish: 'Never accept an invitation to visit a particular concentration camp in Upper Silesia. What is going on there, you would never believe.' I never went, nor did I ever try to find out what he meant. But I was sick at heart. My sense of guilt has stayed with me; I've thought about that conversation many times. I deliberately avoided discovering things that would have compelled me to take action. I've consoled myself with the thought that, once the war was over—once there were no more shooting and strain— we could get rid of the brutality and turn our talents to constructive tasks."

When Speer stopped talking, it was as though the reel had run out, and for a moment we sat silent. The entire scene was outlandish—much too bizarre even for a bad movie.

Here we were—Galbraith, Nitze, and I—sitting in an ugly bourgeois German house in the middle of the night surrounded by several thousand armed Nazi troops, who would have killed us automatically two weeks before. We were listening to a top Nazi conjure up Hitler—dead just twenty-two days—as a living, ominous presence, talking in a conversational tone of weird events in that house of madmen, the underground bunker.

I thought of Marlow, the narrator in Joseph Conrad's novel *Lord Jim,* who had spun his tale through chapter after chapter; it would have taken him, someone had once pointed out, twenty-six hours to recount the whole story. Now it was not Marlow but Lord Jim himself talking—the flawed man who had made a fatal error of judgment and would have to live with it or die for it. I did not know which. And the tale he was telling was not *Lord Jim* but *The Heart of Darkness*—the Gothic saga of a madman obsessed by power.

My musing stopped abruptly. What about the commission Ambassador Murphy had given me? What had happened to Hitler's will? It had, Speer said, been entrusted to Major Willi Johannmeier on April 28 or 29, after Berlin was surrounded—or all but surrounded—by the Russians. Johannmeier was to board a reconnaissance plane on a golf course near Wannsee.[1] Bormann sent a radiogram on April 30 informing Doenitz that he headed the succession under the will. Another radiogram from Bormann to Doenitz on May 1 said the will was in effect.

An item of minor interest missing from my notes was recorded by Mr. James P. O'Donnell in an article in the *New York Times Magazine* of October 26, 1969.

In May 1945 ... such knowledgeable Americans as George Ball and John Kenneth Galbraith bird-dogged their way through the ruins to Albert Speer. They found him in Schleswig-Holstein, with Admiral Doenitz' rump government. For hundreds of hours Speer was bombarded with questions. Finally, Ball ... asked: "By the way, what was Eva Braun really like?"

Speer's discreet answer, then as now, "For future historians, Eva is bound to be a shattering disappointment. When people first met the Fuehrer's mistress— and not many ever met her—she struck them as nippy and lofty-nosed. That was, however, a front for her shyness and unhappiness. She was no great beauty, rather pert, with very attractive legs—the romantic Bavarian shopgirl type. She had limpid, porcelain blue eyes and wore cheap costume jewelry from Gablonz that her lover gave her every Christmas. She loved to kick up her heels on the dance floor, to ski, to smoke and drink. Hitler loathed these four pursuits but tolerated them. She had no interest in politics."

It had been a long night. Knowing Speer was to be picked up by military police at eight o'clock, we sent him back to his castle and returned to the *Patria*. When arrested in his pajamas, Speer looked, according to the *New York Times*'s correspondent, "unhappy and tired."

We awoke in a greatly constricted world. Everyone would be confined to billets for the next hour. During the night, units of the British Second Army had moved into town, and a regiment of Churchill tanks and two infantry battalions from the 159th Brigade of the 11th Armored Division were rounding up the Wehrmacht. Indignant and bewildered groups were being herded together in vacant lots or marched in reluctant columns toward POW camps.

I could find no trace of Major Spivak. He had, he told me later, been supervising the capitulation. The public rooms of the *Patria* were small; its designers had obviously not had in mind the surrender of the Wehrmacht. But, as Galbraith pointed out, if a railroad coach in Compiègne could be the scene of two great surrenders, the first-class bar of the *Patria* was an adequate setting for the final act of the Flensburg farce.

The Regurgitation of the Master Race

During our days in Flensburg, we had spent our afternoons interviewing Speer and the mornings and late evenings preparing material for the next day's interrogations. Three or four times after returning from Schloss Glücksburg, we drove across the Danish border, which lay only a few kilometers to the north. To anyone who had been for a year in other parts of Europe, Denmark that spring was the flared end of the cornucopia—the hypothetical never-never-land of the classical economists, the perfect illustration of the interplay of supply and demand. In the cafés, one could order not one, but two, steak dinners with the Danish equivalent of smorgasbord. One could consume unlimited quantities of butter and cream and cheese. In the hardware stores, one could find pots and pans; in the bookshops, books. But nowhere could one buy tea or Scotch whisky or cigarettes.

Major Spivak had not been in Denmark since before the war, but he had an unerring instinct for scarcity. Somewhere in his recent travels he had obtained fifty pounds of tea, wrapped in one-pound packages and stowed away in one of his bottomless ammunition cases, which could also yield half a dozen bottles of Scotch and at least a dozen cartons of Chesterfields. The Chesterfields had never seen a PX; through some dubious channel, they had come directly from the United States and were tax-paid, so they were available for use as wampum without violating army regulations.

Our nightly excursions to Denmark were an amiable diversion. The Danes were demonstratively friendly; they had seen few American uniforms, and they behaved toward us as the French had done in the first weeks after the liberation. Americans felt imprisoned in Germany by the restrictions on responding to friendliness; in Denmark, there were no non-fraternization rules.

Traveling north across the border gave me a feeling of going the wrong way on a one-way street, as we constantly pushed through flocks of homing Nazis. Norway and Denmark were regurgitating the master race. The Wehrmacht was on the move again, but this time toward Germany; the occupation armies had brought their women and children with them, and now they were taking them home. Some were tired, ill, underfed, and in rags, but this was not like the migration down the roads of France five years before; the Stukas were not overhead, and there was no strafing.

Hitler's legions resembled an eighteenth-century army as they straggled under untidy packs, pulled nondescript carts, or pushed baby carriages, squeaking and swaying under bed rolls. A few soldiers had managed to salvage bicycles and a rare horse was seen, always bearing a Luftwaffe officer—probably, so Galbraith observed, the only occasion in history when airmen were glad to impersonate cavalry. The general effect was a viscous and slowly moving outpouring of humanity containing an occasional small unit that had preserved its discipline, marching in a well-formed column with a stern martinet in command. The individual men in these disciplined columns looked strikingly different from their dispirited comrades; they had retained a kind of desperate dignity. But most of the amorphous stream reminded me of pictures I remembered having brooded over as a boy, dramatic paintings of the retreat from Moscow or the Confederate Army after Appomattox, and it occurred to me that armies in defeat are indistinguishable.

Our Danish excursions were merely a fleeting break in the serious business of the Survey, and, as soon as Speer had been arrested, we flew back to London to begin sorting out the vast amount of material he had provided. Among other things, he had given us details as to where key members of his staff had taken cover in Germany and where important documents were cached. It was thus relatively easy for us to send out teams to pick up individuals with their papers and return them to our working quarters in the spa hotel at Bad Nauheim, one wing of which we transformed into a kind of genteel concentration camp.

I did not, however, stay in Europe long, since at the end of May I was ordered to return to Washington with Henry Alexander, Paul Nitze, and General Orville Anderson. Two of our other directors, J. Fred Searls, Jr., who was in charge of munitions studies, and Robert P. Russell, who was surveying the oil bombing, had already returned. We arrived in Washington on June 8 and on June 9 met with the Joint Target Group, which was planning the air assault on the Japanese home islands. What lessons had we derived from the Survey so far? And, particularly, what had we learned from Albert Speer? On June 11, we were interrogated at length by some fifty officers representing all the services, and on June 12, 14, and 15 we held further meetings with the Joint Target Group.

I am not sure that the information we supplied was of great assistance, since the Japanese economy differed drastically from that of Germany and the crucial targets were of a different order. Nor were the questions well formulated. After one long session dominated by General Curtis LeMay, who did most of the talking, I came away dismayed at the shallowness of the views expressed. Just as I was leaving the room, General Lauris Norstad put his hand on my shoulder and said quietly, "George, never forget that individually many of those men are highly intelligent, but when they meet collectively—did you ever hear such goddamn nonsense?"

I shall not undertake to recount other experiences during my stay in Bad Nauheim, since John Kenneth Galbraith has already told those stories with panache in his memoirs, *A Life in Our Time*. We did, as he recounts, deny Nicholas Kaldor a chance to influence the British elections, and we did go to Berlin and get marginally involved in the Potsdam Conference.

Nor shall I describe the appearance of the Red Army in Berlin, since so many others have already written vividly of that period. Apart from the extravagant traffic in Mickey Mouse watches and the extraordinary market demand for any item of underclothing the OSS secretaries were willing to sell, the army impressed me primarily by the primitive quality of its transport. Horse-drawn vehicles were everywhere and, having watched American GIs headed for the front crouched down in jeeps with their feet dangling over the hood ("the only soldiers in history ever to go into battle with their feet higher than their heads," to quote Galbraith), I was astonished that the Red Army had beaten the Germans so badly.

At Bad Nauheim on August 6, we first heard news of the bomb on Hiroshima. I was perhaps the only one not surprised. At lunch in London in December 1944, a British scientist had assured me, "the atomic bomb is on its way," and, when I had returned to Washington the following June, my co-director, J. Fred Searls, who worked closely with Jimmy Byrnes, had told me in some detail of the bomb and of the need to use it on Japan. Our military had calculated that to win the war against the Japanese without using the bomb would, he said, entail an estimated three hundred thousand American casualties. That, at least, was the projection at the time, and whether or not it was correct, it was the basis on which the Hiroshima decision was made. In spite of all the "visions and revisions" since then, I have never doubted that, had I been President Truman, I would have decided as he did.

Second-guessing, of course, is easy, and had we then known what we later learned of the approaching collapse of the Japanese economy some less brutal nuclear demonstration might have been called for. But Truman acted on the information then available and with one bomb changed the world.

With the war now drawing to a close, it was time for the Survey to move its headquarters to Washington, sort out the findings, and put reports in shape—not an easy task, since there were wide differences of view as to the interpretation of the data. Nevertheless, we went at it with vigor—sometimes in my Washington home—and finally arrived at a compromise. The report of Ken Galbraith's group (the Overall Studies Division) would be published separately, while the Survey would publish an overall assessment of its own. In the end, our findings settled nothing; the central arguments are likely to continue for years. How large a factor was our strategic air offensive in shaping the outcome of the war? Could our resources of men and material have been better employed in other ways?

On this score, Speer had provided some curious but fascinating insights. At the time of the massive Hamburg raids in 1943, when the British bombers had first produced a fire storm, the news had made an enormous impact on Hitler and his colleagues. Had the Allies continued those attacks, knocking Hamburg completely out of the war, German morale, he felt, would have suffered a critical blow. But because bomber losses had been heavy and, once forewarned, the Germans had concentrated antiaircraft fire to protect the city, the Allies had moved on to other targets. Again, Speer pointed out that some of our bombing had made little critical difference; by wiping out many small businesses, we had often freed labor for more productive use; by bombing air-frame production at a time when aircraft engines were in short supply, we had gotten their aircraft production back into phase. The most startling statistic he put forward was that, by June 1944, German war production had expanded to roughly three times what it had been at the outset of the war. However, when our Eighth Air Force started bombing oil production in June, we dealt a critical blow, for, even though the Germans faced no immediate shortage, the prospect of continued reduction in oil supplies resulted in curtailing training to the point where German pilots were pushed into combat with totally inadequate training.

Later, the saturation bombing in the Ruhr that began in September 1944 had brought German industry largely to a halt, not so much because we had smashed up machinery—the Germans always had a large surplus of general-purpose machine tools—but because the bombing destroyed internal transport in plant complexes.

Finally, some of us felt that the greatest contribution of our strategic bombing was to force the German Air Force into the air, where our fighters could destroy it. Only by the attrition of the GAF did the Allies gain clear command of the air over the Normandy battlefield—which was essential to victory

Speer Revisited

In the months after his arrest, Galbraith and I saw Speer again at Dustbin, which was the British detention camp at Kransberg castle, near Bad Nauheim. After studying our findings, we found there were still unresolved questions that only he could answer. Speer received us in the garden with the British guards keeping a discreet distance. Though putting a sardonic face on his predicament, he was obviously worried since he had heard rumors of possible war-crimes trials. Half-amused, he said, "Will you be my lawyer, Mr. Ball?" When I told him that was impossible, he replied, "Well, you're making a mistake; many young lawyers have made their reputations by representing notorious personalities, and you'll never get a better chance."

During the 1960s, while Under Secretary of State, I paid occasional visits to Bonn. On two occasions, Speer's daughter, Hilde, came from Berlin to see me. Would I try to get Speer's sentence reduced? To maintain Spandau prison required the labor of 125 to 150 people, and it seemed absurd to keep Speer locked up when Nazis guilty of greater crimes had been freed. But though the American, British, and French governments were agreeable to his early release, the Soviets continued intractable.

In Flensburg, Speer had seemed a resourceful man, not very different from other clever, resourceful men I knew; with charm and apparently spontaneous candor, he evoked in us a sympathy of which we were all secretly ashamed. What had he then known of the Holocaust? But what had my colleagues and I then known about it?

Of course, I had heard dark stories of the treatment of Slavs, Jews, Gypsies, and others who did not meet the Wagnerian standards of the master race. But I believe—though I am uncertain at this point—that I had tended to think those rumors exaggerated. The full horrors of Auschwitz and Buchenwald made a deep impression only after the documented revelations of Nuremburg. It was only then that I became fully and sickenly aware of the atrocious persecution of Jews and Slavs, who were the victims of Hitler's "Final Solution."

That must seem curious today, and even self-serving. Yet I believe it is true, nor do I think I was less well informed than most other Americans, including those, like myself, who had served in the government.[2] Perhaps we were so preoccupied with the squalid menace of the war we did not focus on this unspeakable ghastliness. It may also be that the idea of mass extermination was so far outside the traditional comprehension of most Americans that we instinctively refused to believe in its existence.

At Nuremberg, in contrast to the other top Nazis, Speer forthrightly accepted responsibility for Hitler's outrages and got his comeuppance in a twenty-year sentence. Meanwhile, I had come to think of him, if at all, only as the central figure in a brief encounter that had occurred long ago. Thus, when, in 1970, a representative of the British Broadcasting Corporation called to ask if I would interview Speer in Munich for a television program, I reacted with mixed feelings. After all, had he not been part of the most inhuman gang since Tamerlane's? Still, I could not resist the chance to see what changes two decades of captivity would have wrought in him and to plumb yet further the Speer enigma.

In Munich, there were to be two inquisitors besides myself: Professor Hugh Trevor-Roper, a distinguished British historian, and the very astute and able Michael Charlton of the BBC. Speer had, we were told, learned English, as well as French, during his incarceration, so we would not have to bother with interpreters. Speer greeted us suavely, appearing in remarkably good shape for a man who had spent two decades in prison. He seemed more relaxed than I, who found the interrogation awkward and difficult. I saw Speer with split vision: on the one hand, he was a man of obvious charm, to which it was hard not to respond; on the other hand, he had been part of Hitler's noxious entourage.

Although I was anxious to avoid repeating the obvious, there seemed few questions that had not been answered in Speer's memoirs and in the spate of books and articles about him. All Trevor-Roper and I could do was to fill in details, while picking away naggingly at the central mystery: how could such an intelligent man willingly serve in a vile government under a demented leader?

Speer tried to answer that question for me—and I cannot recall whether it was on, or off, camera—with a figure of speech borrowed from Malraux, striking, yet still far from satisfying.[3] "If," he said, "one spends long enough in the dim light of an aquarium, everything acquires a kind of normality. But if one ever moves outside into the pure light of day and looks into the aquarium, he finds it incredible he could ever have put up with it."

To us, Speer's most baffling reaction was the brooding fascination that, as he frankly admitted, Hitler still held for him even after almost four decades. Though Nuremberg had shown beyond question that Hitler had committed acts of unparalleled depravity, Speer could still not totally free himself of the spell.

Could it be merely the residual awe of a young man—only twenty-eight when he first met Hitler and only forty when Hitler died—a young man dazzled by his unexpected access to the very embodiment of power? Speer had seen Hitler regularly late at night at "artistic" tea parties after the Führer had first conferred with his generals. As the war continued, those tea parties were held later and later—at two or three or four o'clock in the morning. On such occasions, Hitler relaxed and, even though the war was going badly, continued to discuss his building plans with Speer. For Hitler, architecture was, Speer said, "not an avocation but an obsession." Since Speer was the professional and Hitler the architect *manqué,* the young man held an intangible advantage that partially offset the disparity in their positions. Hitler promised Speer the chance to build the world's largest buildings—an opportunity for which Speer succumbed in the banal Faustian parallel. But, if he had sold his soul to the devil and had paid for it by revulsion and long imprisonment, he still could not deny his residual bemusement.

That evening I had dinner with Speer and his wife in the restaurant of the leading Munich hotel. I found Frau Speer a formidable, and no doubt an admirable, woman; through the long years of Speer's imprisonment, she had somehow brought up their family of six children with conspicuous success. Now one son was a successful architect; his daughter had married well; and so on. We talked mainly about how the family had maintained itself and how they reacted to the shame associated with his name.

During dinner, a German friend entered the room and started in my direction. Halfway across the floor, he recognized Speer and abruptly veered off, waving at me and taking a seat at a side table. After dinner,

I stopped at my friend's table to apologize for causing him embarrassment. He had, he said, understood my predicament and the incident had not upset him. My friend was Helmut Schmidt, the current Chancellor of West Germany.

The next morning, the BBC flew Speer and me to Hamburg; from there we drove to Flensburg, past the Naval Training School where the *Patria* had been anchored, and on to Glücksburg and the Duke of Holstein's castle. On the plane, Speer spoke of his experiences after prison. When he first left Spandau for his home at Heidelberg, he had felt like Rip Van Winkle debouched into a drastically altered world. The traffic had upset him, while the mere exposure to the open air had made him physically ill. Now he had developed an adequate pattern of living. He liked the new world he had found. He spoke with enthusiasm of his new car with its rotary engine; his memoirs were enjoying unexpected success; and he was preparing his diaries for publication. He was also working on a theoretical discussion of how an industrial society adapts to war. Whereas Admiral Doenitz, released after serving only ten years, had spoken of having to "feel my way back into the world," Speer had made that difficult passage with relative ease.

I asked about his work as Hitler's architect. He had been commissioned to design the new Berlin to Hitler's gargantuan specifications. The three-mile-long Prachtstrasse (Street of Splendor) was to run on a north-south axis through the heart of the city, which was to be renamed Germania. To the south would be a railroad station three times as large as Grand Central Station in New York City (into which trains would presumably run on time). The avenue itself—almost twice as wide as the Champs Elysées—would pass in front of the Führer Palast, seventy times as large as Bismarck's chancellory. There would be a Reichstag four times the size of the old Reichstag, a general staff headquarters, embassies, and so on. The northern end would be dominated by a secular cathedral modeled vaguely on the Pantheon in Rome but with a copper dome large enough to encompass the dome of St. Peter's seven times over, surmounted by an imperial German eagle nearly fifty feet tall. Hitler's megalomania found its ultimate expression in architecture. A twentieth-century pharaoh, he liked to speculate on how the ruins of his buildings would look in a thousand years.

Did Speer regret never having built Hitler's monstrosities? "God, no," he replied with a shudder. "Weren't they frightful?"

Déjà vu overwhelmed me in Schloss Glücksburg as we sat in the same gilt chairs before the same table where we had conducted our interviews twenty-six years before. Though I had no fresh ideas, some pretense of ritual interrogation was expected for the television public. My questions were, I am afraid, trite, feeble, and contrived. The BBC programmers had, I believe, planned to turn the six or seven hours of filming into an hour-and-a-half show, but the film is still in the BBC archives. I hope it stays there. In spite of the BBC's investment of skill and money, it provided no new illumination of the central enigma.

The Conundrum of Albert Speer

How, then, do I appraise Speer? I have never found a satisfactory answer to that question. The Nuremberg judges decided he deserved a long sentence, and he accepted it as fair. Rather than clarifying my own thoughts, our interrogation—and my renewed acquaintance with Speer— left me even more confused. Looking back, I realize that at the time of our first meeting, I had been insufficiently aware of the full Nazi story to put Speer in proper perspective. But since that time, the revolting disclosures of Nuremberg had left no doubt of Hitler's obscenities. I knew I should feel repelled by Speer because his willing association with the filthy Nazi thugs marked him as a man who had touched evil; yet, try as I might, I could not sustain that mood. Speer was not at all in the mold of the brutal Nazi; instead—and this is what made my relatively tolerant attitude toward him so inexcusable—he seemed, to use Noel Coward's derisive phrase, "like us." Thus, I could find no answer to the obsessive question of how it had all happened.

Or did Noel Coward's phrase suggest an answer that was inevitably unsettling? Were America to experience similar moral degeneration and a regime come to power that punished its dissenters not merely by death but also by torture, might not some of my friends and acquaintances— might not even I myself—yield to temptations such as those that had corrupted Speer?

I have no doubt that at least some of my most righteous acquaintances would go along, advancing up the hierarchical ladder. Like Speer, they would rationalize their actions. If things were bad, that would only be temporary; once the nation achieved its objectives, repression would be relaxed and a benign society could then emerge. Others would stand sadly but prudently by, suppressing their outrage while doing their best to stay out of trouble. Still others would try to flee the country with whatever they could take with them.

There would, one hopes, be a brave few—though I could not identify them with certainty—who would risk the terrors and rigors of a resistance struggle. But I suspect it would be only a thin red line if they knew that, once caught, they might be hung on meat hooks and subjected to all the tortures a demonic imagination could devise.

My question is, of course, contrived. Like any organism with deep and healthy roots, our country's instincts and traditions should enable us to produce the antibodies needed to resist such raging depravity. But we dare not take that for granted. Had Watergate followed a different course—and it could have, but for luck and an indefatigable press—had the scrofulous gang around Nixon been allowed to grow more insolent with each success, our basic institutions could have been dangerously undermined. Nor should we forget the sixties, when hysteria threatened to disrupt our educational institutions and we faced the danger of losing the elite of a generation through drugs and "dropping out."

Because it most acutely touched my own age group, I look back with special horror on the suspicion, meanness, and betrayal of the McCarthy period. America seemed transformed by virulent fear and demagoguery—the same components Hitler used so effectively. Although the McCarthy years did not, thank God, permanently damage the basic framework of our institutions and the great bulk of our people were not corrupted, it was still a portent. Had we then been in the midst of a searing depression or been as angry and divided as during the Vietnam War, I can think of several friends who might well have identified the new "reality" with the wave of the future and thrown rocks as the tumbrels rolled by.

The gravamen of the indictment of Speer at Nuremberg was that he had employed slave labor, a crime which he admitted. But what most preoccupies anyone who speculates about culpability is his association with the contemptible thugs who murdered more than ten million Slavs and six million Jews.[4] No one can establish clearly just how much Speer knew as against what he might have known—and I doubt that even he was totally clear about it.

Yet, is it not the very fact that he seemed "like us"—or at least like what we think we are—that leads us to the judgment that his conduct was inexcusable? In elaborating this point, Professor Trevor-Roper has suggested that, "in Hitler's court," Speer was morally and intellectually alone, for

he had the capacity to understand the forces of politics, and the courage to resist the master whom all others have declared irresistible. As an administrator, he was undoubtedly a genius. He regarded the rest of the court with dignified contempt. His ambitions were peaceful and constructive: he wished to rebuild Berlin and Nuremberg, and had planned "at the cost of no more than two months' war-expenditure" (as he sadly protested in the dock at Nuremberg) to make them the greatest cities in the world. Nevertheless, in a political sense, *Speer is the real criminal of Nazi Germany;* for he, more than any other, represented that fatal philosophy which has made havoc of Germany and nearly shipwrecked the world. For ten years he sat at the very center of political power; his keen intelligence diagnosed the nature and observed the mutations of Nazi government and policy; he saw and despised the personalities around him; he heard their outrageous orders and understood their fantastic ambitions; but he did nothing. Supposing politics to be irrelevant, he turned aside and built roads and bridges and factories, while the logical consequences of government by madmen emerged.

Ultimately, when their emergence involved the ruin of all his work, Speer accepted the consequences and acted. Then it was too late; Germany had been destroyed. [Italics added.][5]

Should we assume, as Trevor-Roper does, that because Speer was the most intelligent and sensitive of the Nazis, he should be judged by a more rigorous code than the others? Or does that question too cavalierly ignore the full range of man's adaptability and the illusion of normality in the dim light of an aquarium?

Following our Munich television interview, Speer sent me a copy of his memoirs. The inscription on the flyleaf thanked me "for today's meeting after twenty-six years"—then he added, "And the questions remained the same!" For me, they always will.

PART III

Monnet, Europe, and Law Practice

6. Jean Monnet

When I returned to Washington in the summer of 1945, I felt, as did many Americans, that the war had put a semicolon, if not a period, to all that had gone before. Ten years earlier I had left the highly charged atmosphere of the yeasty New Deal in search of professional experience. This time I felt no such need to escape from Washington. Thanks to long days and nights in a Chicago law firm of high quality, I was confident of my own professional abilities and, for reasons quite different from those of the young Tom Wolfe, I could not go home again. The New Deal, followed by the war, had shifted the nation's center of gravity to Washington, and I liked being—in the vernacular—where the action was.

But until I had established a private-sector port of return, I wished to avoid further government jobs. Too many bureaucrats, in my observation, had been trapped in frustrating tasks or compelled to carry out distasteful policies because they had no place to which they could retreat. So I decided to join with friends in founding a new law firm to come into being on January 1, 1946. Meanwhile, since the work of the Bombing Survey would terminate three or four months before that date, I took an interim assignment with Jean Monnet as General Counsel of the French Supply Council, which he was then reorganizing.

Early Background

Jean Monnet's name was not then familiar to many Americans, but among those involved in Allied war supply problems, he was a figure about whom legends had already accumulated. Born in 1888 in the little town of Cognac in the Department of Charente in southwestern France, he grew up as the fair-haired child of a middle-class family established in the brandy business. The brand name "Monnet" was known the world over, and the predilection of upper-class Englishmen for brandy-and-soda helped shape Jean Monnet's career. His formal schooling ended at sixteen. He spent two years of apprenticeship in a London merchant bank, after which he traveled as a brandy salesman, chiefly in England but also in Canada and the United States.

His knowledge of English and of British methods served him well when a perceptive French Prime Minister heard him diagnose supply deficiencies during the dark days of World War I and appointed him, at the age of twenty-six, French representative on the Inter-Allied Supply Committee in London. What Monnet brought to that task were two simple but essential ideas. One was the analytic device of the consolidated balance sheet, or *bilan;* the second was a concept of organization: maximum utilization of resources could be obtained by fusing or "pooling" them. Simple as those ideas now sound, they were then regarded with suspicion by bureaucrats and politicians on both sides of the Channel conditioned to thinking only along narrow national lines. With his mind uncluttered by slogans and precedent, Monnet instinctively understood that the indispensable first discipline in operating any international supply system was to relate overall need to overall production and potential capacity. The difference defined the production target. If the target was too high, then requirement figures had to be reexamined and pared down. But more often than not, the exercise resulted in expanding production targets by forcing responsible officials to face realistically the price of victory. Though the technique so described sounds simple and obvious, in relations between the Allies it was a startlingly new approach. Marshal Ferdinand Foch once remarked that fighting a war of alliance made him realize how easy had been Napoleon's job. Alliances have failed again and again because no partner ever knew what the others would contribute or what each ally required to maintain its part of the effort.

Once hostilities finally ended and the cynics at Versailles had produced the League of Nations (which the United States promptly disowned), Monnet became its Deputy Secretary-General. In that capacity, he spent two years working on solutions to the Saar problem between France and Germany, the Silesian problem between Poland and Germany, the Danzig question, and the currency and monetary headaches from which a devastated Europe was suffering.

In 1925, after having restored the family business to a sound basis, he became the French partner of the New York investment banking firm of Blair & Company during the pyrotechnic period preceding the depression of the thirties. Here his belief in consolidated balance sheets was reinforced by grim experience, for while he was in Europe, his partners combined his firm with another to form Bancamerica-Blair Corporation. Only when the merger was completed did the X-ray machine of the consolidated balance sheet disclose that tangled intercorporate relationships concealed liabilities larger than life-size. Monnet once told me he had made and lost $5 million, but what he had learned was well worth it.

Following the stock market debacle he worked in Sweden as liquidator of Krueger & Toll; in Shanghai, as adviser to a League of Nations mission reorganizing Chinese finances; and again in New York, as head of a firm specializing in corporate reorganizations. But, a year before the outbreak of the Second World War, Monnet's career as private citizen ended; thereafter, he was to be continuously in some form of public activity. His Wall Street experience had, however, given him one asset that was to serve him well: the respect and affection of several American bankers and lawyers, including such future movers and shakers as Robert Lovett, John J. McCloy, John Foster Dulles, and Donald Swatland.

Monnet in World War II

In 1938, alarmed at the condition of the French Air Force, he persuaded Prime Minister Edouard Daladier to send him to the United States to buy airplanes for the French government. Later, after the war broke out, he became chairman of the Anglo-French Coordinating Committee in London. Using that position with maximum effect, Monnet, in the words of the official British Economic War History, ". . . confronted the governments with devastating figures comparing Allied aircraft production with German, as estimated by the two Air Staffs and the Ministry of Economic Warfare. In similar 'balance sheets' compiled later on, estimates of requirements on the basis of accepted strategic plans took the place of the speculative figures of enemy production."[1]

During the chaotic days just preceding the French collapse in 1940—in an action that might have changed the course of history—Monnet devised the idea that Britain should offer the French people joint Anglo-French citizenship, with a single cabinet and parliament. The Reynaud government in Bordeaux faced a critical decision: demoralized and defeated, should it capitulate to the Germans or move to North Africa, together with the still intact French navy and as much of the army as could be evacuated? The forty-nine-year-old Under Secretary of War, Charles de Gaulle, in the midst of defeat and exhaustion, supported Monnet's bold proposal for union as a tactical move that might persuade a divided French cabinet to resist. It was one of the few occasions when de Gaulle and Monnet saw eye-to-eye.

Once a convinced British cabinet had persuaded a reluctant Churchill to favor Monnet's scheme, de Gaulle, in London, flashed the word to Bordeaux. But by June 16, 1940, it was a few hours too late. The

Reynaud government had already made the fatal decision to resign, paving the way for General Pétain's succession and—less than forty-eight hours later—a humiliating armistice. It was a shameful moment of weariness and cynicism and disenchantment, of hysteria and the death of idealism. Peering through the distorted lenses of their own despair, the tired, weak leaders of the Third Republic saw nothing but a "plot" by Britannia Militant—or Albion Perfidious—to gobble up the French empire in its hour of ultimate weakness.

With his beloved Marianne trying on her chains, Monnet then volunteered his services to the British government; Churchill made him deputy chairman of the British Supply Council in Washington. Later, following the North African invasion, Monnet played a major part in the *rapprochement* between General de Gaulle, with his London Committee (whose legitimacy as leader of France had not yet been established), and the French general, Henri Giraud, who had been appointed commander-in-chief of the French forces in North Africa by the Imperial Council, which consisted of the Vichy proconsuls still in power. Monnet's deep concern was to avoid a power fight that might tear France apart once victory was achieved.

After V-E Day, Monnet returned to Washington as president of the French Supply Council. It was a job made urgent by the foolish and irresponsible decision of Leo Crowley to halt Lend-Lease on August 21, 1945. Now the French provisional government had to improvise its own machinery to acquire the supplies desperately needed for France's ravished economy.

The Monnet Discipline

To operate that improvised machinery, Monnet needed lawyers. In agreeing to serve as his general counsel, I limited my tenure to the three months until our new firm would open for business. Much to my delight, the assignment proved to be more substantive and less technical than my title implied. Though I hired legal technicians to help establish and operate a procurement apparatus, Monnet wanted my services for quite a different purpose: to help him reduce his ideas to coherent exposition and, in the process, help him think. Jean Monnet did not think like other people. He circled a problem like an airplane approaching an undersized field in a cup of the mountains, volplaning down in ever tightening spirals until he finally reached the runway he was seeking. Yet that metaphor is only partially accurate, for while zeroing in on a problem, he would frequently dart off to explore a new target made visible by a sudden opening in the fog.

Our long communings were never routine. Though Monnet spoke to me in colloquial English, he would often finish an English sentence in

French, quite unaware of what language he was speaking and since I am a linguistic idiot, I would sometimes have to remind him when he made an unconscious shift. He would propound a nebulous idea; I would rephrase what I thought he was trying to say, relating the points he was making to other thoughts he had expressed. Sometimes I would offer an allusion or figure of speech to supply the vivid aphoristic summation he habitually sought.

At the end of each such session, he would ask me for a draft paper by some quite unrealistic deadline, such as later the same afternoon. He was oblivious to the need for allocating time to other requirements, such as sleeping or even eating. If we talked late into the evening, he would still expect a paper to be ready first thing in the morning—and he usually had it.

How he might react to what I had written I could never predict. Sometimes he would exclaim over an individual phrase or paragraph: "Good," or, "That's it!" But more likely than not, he would say with a sad smile: "We haven't got it," or, "That's not it yet." Then we would talk further, often veering off at a sharp angle from what I had written. At the end, I would try again with the same inconclusive results. We put one proposal through seventeen drafts, finally settling on a version much closer to my initial effort than any that had followed. Usually, however, the number varied between six and ten, depending on the purpose of the exercise—whether a formal note to the French or American government, a magazine article, a speech for Monnet, the outline of a project, or a suggested statement for someone else to make.

While Monnet profited by what I called our "collective spiral cogitation," I learned much from helping a wise man shape ideas like a sculptor with a knife. My role was essential for Monnet himself was no writer. I never knew him to draft a document; he evolved letters, papers, plans, proposals, memoranda of all kinds by bouncing ideas against another individual—a combined amanuensis and collaborator. James Reston, of the *New York Times,* once despairingly asked during a strike of his newspaper, "How do I know what I think until I read what I write?" Monnet faced the same problem; he needed to test and sharpen ideas by casting them in the rigorous mold of a simple, persuasive, yet precise, formulation. In addition, he required perfection in thought and statement. Even the simplest letter must convey the exact meaning and nuance intended, which could be achieved only by repeated redrafting and polishing. Once he had achieved a formulation that satisfied him, Monnet might use it again and again. "If an idea has been precisely phrased," he contended, "it cannot be improved by extemporaneous restatement."

That he seemed always able to find men willing to submit to his stimulating but exasperating methods of work testified to his extraordinary charisma—not in the current, vulgar, television sense but rather as Max

Weber used the word to refer to "a certain quality of an individual personality" that sets him apart from ordinary men. The essence of his charisma was that Jean sought nothing for himself. If he could get others to launch—and take credit for—his ideas, so much the better. Thus, anything but an intellectual, Monnet could attract and even captivate intellectuals, drawing on their technical talents without being intimidated by them as Lyndon Johnson later allowed himself to be. He made no attempt to master technical intricacies; that could be left to the specialists on whom he depended. He concentrated on fundamental convictions evolved from his rich experience.

With a rare instinct for the sources of power, he invariably identified those individuals who could advance his special projects, employing his friends as a kind of resource bank, and calling on men of particular talents at the precise times when their skills could be most useful.

In working with Monnet and his colleagues, I was struck by how often we proceeded from our disparate backgrounds to reach agreement on fundamental issues. With almost no formal education, Monnet had his own special method of thought. Most of my other French colleagues, trained in the Cartesian discipline, began with first principles, reasoning, like Aquinas or Hegel, from matter to spirit to matter, while my American friends and I tended to reason like Hobbes and Hume, from effect to cause to effect. Still, though hacking our way through the trees by different paths, we usually came out at the same clearing in the forest, and on one point we were unanimous—that the logic of European unity was inescapable.

Monnet's Personality

From time to time I accused Monnet of behaving like a French peasant—a charge that delighted him. Along with his earthy common sense, he was subject to petty foibles that amused those of us who worked with him. He would never sleep in a city if there were any possible alternative. When in New York City, we might work until two or three o'clock in the morning, but he would still insist on being driven to a friend's house on Long Island for the balance of the night. His personal battle with the weather—and particularly with what he described as the "weight of the atmosphere"—went on interminably. "The air is heavy today," he would say sadly, as though it imposed an oppressive burden. When the air was "good," which presumably meant less humid, we all worked exceptionally hard.

Though he felt at home in America and was inspired by its vitality and spaciousness, he was most at ease in his thatched-roof house in Houjarray, forty-four kilometers from Paris. I would, from time to time, stay there with him and his gifted and enchanting Italian wife, Sylvia. Rising from the breakfast table, Jean would hand me a stick, saying, "Let's walk." As we began to ascend a small hill near the house, he would say, "Start talking," and I would try to regurgitate whatever ideas I had generated overnight. Suddenly, he would grab my arm and point across the soft French landscape to a small church or a peasant cottage. "Did you ever see anything more beautiful?" Standing in respectful contemplation, I would dredge up the appropriate banality; then he would abruptly push me forward along the path and say, "Start talking again."

I do not mean to imply that Jean Monnet was rude or indifferent to personal feelings; he merely put ideas ahead of trite civilities. He was, in fact, genuinely concerned by personal misfortunes and interested in everything his friends were doing. He hated large social affairs, but after Ruth had repeatedly asked him to dinner, Jean finally accepted, conditionally, "I'll come if you won't have anyone but the family." During the entire evening he paid little attention to either Ruth or me, conducting a protracted dialogue with our eight-year-old son, Douglas, whose remarkable knowledge of history he found fascinating.

Helping France Modernize

During our work together in the fall of 1945, Monnet was preoccupied with the problem of how France could modernize and invigorate its devastated and moribund economy. When only partially recovered from the First World War, it was beset by a second, and during the interwar years of the Third Republic, its economy remained ransomed to the past—in thrall to the spirit of Colbert and to habits of thought and industrial practices that disabled it from keeping pace with a changing world. *Immobilisme* contributed to the corruption of its institutions, as confidence and vigor gave way to apathy and defensiveness. Thus enfeebled, France lost the war.

Granted a new chance, France had to act quickly to recover its latent vitality, first by putting its own house in order and then by merging its efforts with those of its neighbors. Anything but a *dirigiste,* Monnet still saw the need to create an economic plan—not a Procrustean bed designed by technocrats, but a mechanism through which, with minimum bureaucratic guidance, representatives of industry, agriculture, and labor could work together to achieve mutually agreed upon targets.

After Monnet had left for Paris in November 1945 to establish and administer the Plan for Modernization and Investment, I remained in Washington, intending to leave the French Supply Council at the end of the year to join my partners in our new law firm. Monnet amd I continued our communication, however, since Monnet was addicted to the transatlantic telephone (in those days, an exercise in masochism because voice transmission was solely by radio). To place a call normally required waiting anywhere from one to ten hours, while few calls were completed without being interrupted by "atmospherics." Frequently, just as Monnet was coming to the hard substance of his message, shouting at the top of his voice, the line would go dead or the sound would be drowned by a crescendo of roaring and crackling. I would be left in disturbing uncertainty, since Monnet might be trying to tell me, as he frequently did, to catch the night plane for Paris.

Léon Blum's Washington Visit

During one of those calls, Monnet made a tempting request. Léon Blum had been delegated to lead a mission to Washington to discuss Franco-American relations. Would I act as Blum's adviser, even though it would mean postponing my joining our new law firm for several months?

Time and events had softened Léon Blum's public image as an irresponsible intellectual, the first Socialist—and, incidentally, the first Jewish—Premier of France. Many people, both in America and Europe, had been upset by his Popular Front government in 1936 and 1937, not merely because of its tolerance of the Communists but also because it failed to expand French military strength to meet the mounting menace of Nazism. Once World War II began, however, Blum had quickly shed his pacifism, supporting French defense efforts, disavowing Vichy, and urging the Socialist party to oppose collaboration. A large man with a massive, well-shaped head and a sensitive face to which large, sad eyes and a drooping mustache gave a quality of *tristesse,* he exuded enormous charm and sympathy. Taken into custody as "dangerous to the security of the French state" on September 15, 1940, he had first been locked up in France, then carted off to Buchenwald, where he was joined by his third wife (who voluntarily made her way to the camp). There they remained together with other important hostages until April 3, 1945, when Blum and his wife were taken by SS guards into the Tyrol. One of his fellow captives—a German general—managed to smuggle out word of their plight to the commandant of the German Army of Italy. As a result, in a scene reminiscent of *La Grande Illusion,* the jittery SS guards were suddenly disarmed by a company of the Wehrmacht commanded by an officer of the old school, who, resplendent in the most correct of uniforms, assured his prisoners that they were now protected by the military honor of the German Army.

On his Washington mission in March 1946, Blum was accompanied by his son, Robert, a quiet self-effacing man who, trained in engineering, had become a top officer of the Hispano-Suiza Company. I was struck by the touchingly close relationship between father and son. Blum lent a sense of solemn dignity to our enterprise, but he left the negotiating largely to Monnet, who was able to arrange with the United States government a $1.37 billion loan for French reconstruction.

The Marshall Plan

When, on July 1, I finally joined my new law firm, Monnet retained us on behalf of the French government so he and I could continue to work together. It was a nervous time, with the economies of the European countries declining alarmingly.

The Marshall Plan came just in time with its promise of help if the nations of Europe could agree on "the requirements of the situation and the part those countries themselves will take in order to give proper effect to whatever action might be undertaken by this government."[2] In response, the British and French first met in a Big Three Conference with the Soviets; then the USSR testily withdrew when faced with the need to cooperate with other European states in determining requirements and allocating American aid.

Blessedly left on their own, the British and French issued a joint communiqué on July 3, inviting twenty-two European nations to send representatives to consider a common recovery plan and sixteen nations accepted.[3] The conference established an interim Committee of European Economic Cooperation (CEEC) to analyze the economic resources of the component nations, develop the principles for a European recovery program, and agree in a preliminary way on what each nation should be expected to accomplish and what aid it might need. The chairman of the Committee was Sir Oliver Franks (now Lord Franks); Jean Monnet was designated vice-chairman. The staff was headed by Monnet's deputy, Robert Marjolin, who was to become one of my closest friends.

On August 10, 1947, Monnet summoned me by telephone, and two days later I was at work in an office under the stairs at 18, rue de Martignac, the headquarters of the French Planning Commission. It was a tiny room (probably no larger than nine by ten feet), but it became my intermittent hideout for several years. Monnet wanted my insights as an American, but since he did not wish the other European representatives to know he was consulting anyone from my side of the ocean, I worked with him and his immediate staff only.

Soon the Committee produced an early draft of its final report. My share in its intellectual content was *de minimis*—dealing largely with drafting changes of tone and style to help make the document acceptable in Washington. But I worried about substance as well, for I foresaw that certain proposals of the Committee might collide with American preconceptions of what the European nations were expected to present. Not only did the cost of the provisional shopping list—$28 billion—seem well above American estimates, but there was, in my view, too great an emphasis on a stabilization fund of $3 billion, which, I believed, would find little sympathy in Washington. Nor did I think that the draft report conveyed sufficient conviction that at the end of the four-year period of American aid, the participating governments would have brought their balance of payments into equilibrium. Increasing uneasiness in Washington had led the United States to propose a three- or four-week postponement of the final draft of the report, but the Europeans seemed bent on concluding their task as early as possible.

I told Monnet of my apprehensions and, with his blessing, flew on September 3 to the United States, taking with me a pirated copy of the Committee draft, which I showed to my old friends who were now in the State Department, Charles Kindleberger and Paul Nitze. They agreed that it would cause problems in its current form and that the State Department would have to take a stronger hand to avert a serious misunderstanding.

I do not know to what extent, if at all, my visit to Washington stimulated American intervention, but the negative reaction of my friends was presumably one of the reasons for an American-European meeting that took place on August 30. At the same time, my telephone comments regarding Washington's reactions strengthened Monnet's resolve to revise the report in a manner more compatible with American opinion. Since I had done all that an outsider could do in Washington, I flew back to Paris on September 8 to help—at least marginally—in drafting the final report.

Washington's views were presented by the Under Secretary of State for Economic Affairs, Will Clayton, who was brilliantly equipped to deal with the Europeans on these issues. A handsome, courtly, soft-spoken southerner with a cotton broker's passion for free trade, he regarded the Marshall Plan as an opportunity to introduce the concept of a common market to Western Europe. As he later wrote in 1963, "I discussed this matter frequently with Jean Monnet who convinced me that Western Europe was too weak in 1947 to accept conditions of regional free trade. I recognized then that Monnet was correct in this viewpoint. Europe had to get a good deal more flesh on its bones before setting up a common market."[4] But Clayton held to his position that a major Marshall Plan objective was to get the Western European countries working together. When representatives of three countries refused to agree to a permanent organization to succeed the CEEC, Clayton replied, with unconcealed asperity, that "perhaps we are all pursuing a will o' the wisp and might as well forget about it." The message was heard and heeded; the three dissenting representatives promptly went home to their capitals and, on returning, dropped their opposition.

I remained in Paris while a Congressional delegation headed by Congressman Christian Herter talked with the French government about conditions in France and the need for foreign aid. Then, on September 28, I flew to London, where Herter was also visiting. Just after I arrived, Monnet telephoned me in distress. A fortnight before, when he and I had been idly chatting about the special qualities of the French peasant, I had called attention to a press speculation that the gold stashed away by French peasants under their mattresses might be worth at least $2 billion. Monnet had replied with a smile of affectionate admiration for the peasants, "That could be true." Apparently he had remembered the conversation, for in emphasizing the inner strength and innate frugality of the French people he had off-handedly mentioned the rumor to Herter.

Though it was only a trifling parenthesis in a long, informal conversation, Herter promptly disclosed Monnet's comment to the press. That evoked cries of anguish both in French governmental circles and the American administration, since stories of rich peasants might give xenophobic Congressmen and Senators an excuse for voting against Marshall Plan aid. At Monnet's urgent request, I met with Herter and persuaded him to make a clarifying—or, more accurately, an obfuscating—statement that somewhat lowered the noise level, but later in November he testified to a Congressional committee about the alleged secret hoard of gold and suggested a Congressional investigation. How diligent legislators could possibly conduct such an inquiry he did not say, since it would presumably involve poking around under several million beds. In any event, the matter again caused trouble when Averell Harriman, leading the fight for the Marshall Plan, testified before the Senate Foreign Relations Committee.

A Permanent Organization for European Cooperation

Meanwhile, Monnet asked me to follow the Marshall Plan legislation and to keep him advised of evolving American ideas of the permanent European organization envisaged in the CEEC report. On this point, the Europeans were understandably confused. In response to American pressure, the drafters of the sixteen-nation report had included a provision for the creation of a permanent organization, and the British and French had agreed to call a second meeting of the CEEC early in 1948 in which that question could be discussed. Toward the middle of January, however, Under Secretary of State Robert Lovett expressed unexpected reservations, primarily on the ground that a meeting at such an early date might annoy Congress. Lovett's reaction was not well received even among other American officials; early in February, the United States Department of State withdrew its objections to reconvening the CEEC, leaving the matter solely up to the Europeans.

Since the French and British still feared some ambiguity in Washington's attitude, Robert Marjolin, who had been given responsibility for the proposed permanent organization, asked me, on February 24, to sound out American sentiments on the substance and timing of European action. Concurrently, the British government sent Adam Denzil Marris to Washington for the same purpose. Marris, a shrewd and perceptive merchant banker, had served in the Ministry of Economic Warfare in London in the early days of the war—then in the British embassy in Washington, where he had learned the political folkways of the United States. During the meetings of the CEEC, he had been deputy leader of the United Kingdom delegation to the initial CEEC meeting and, together with Monnet and Isaiah Berlin, had carried the laboring oar in drafting the final report.

Marris and I consulted separately with the key officials of the United States government, comparing notes at the end of each day. From long conversations with, among others, Henry Labouisse, Dean Acheson, Charles Kindleberger, and Robert Lovett, I concluded that the American government would welcome progress on the proposed permanent organization as early as April. Since Marris reached the same conclusion, we concerted our findings; on February 28, I sent a long message to Monnet and Marjolin in substantially the same words as the telegram Marris sent to his own government.

Meanwhile, Marjolin asked me to come to France to confer on the drafting of plans for the new permanent organization, which would be known as the Organization for European Economic Cooperation (the OEEC) and would replace the temporary Committee for European Economic Cooperation (the CEEC). I arrived in Paris shortly before the second meeting of the ministers of the CEEC countries scheduled for March 15, 1948. The French government hoped that the new permanent organization would become "the expression of the lasting community of the spirit of Europe" and—heavily influenced by Monnet— proposed a formal organization with an executive board that could make decisions and take action between meetings of the larger conference. It also suggested that there be a permanent international secretariat, headed by a secretary-general, to supply the coordinating function.

British Objections

Foreshadowing the arguments that would later arise about the European Economic Community, the British insisted on a loose body limited to periodic consultations, rejecting the idea of an executive board and an international secretariat, and strongly opposing a French proposal to give the new agency and its executive head authority to allocate American aid and stimulate European self-help. There must not be, so the British argued, even the merest hint that the members were relinquishing any aspect of national sovereignty. Nor should the organization, as such, deal with the United States; each European nation should negotiate bilaterally with America for its own share of assistance.

The British still put excessive store in their "special relationship" with the United States and failed, in Disraeli's words, to understand "the relative mediocrity of their circumstances." Fully as important was the fact that Britain, with America's help, had won the war, while the other members of the group were, as one of my Dutch friends put it, "a club of defeated nations." The British thus thought of their country as on a different level from the nations of the continent; being a co-victor, it should deal with the United States as an equal.

Since the smaller European countries feared that Britain and France would dominate the new organization, the eloquent Belgian Paul Henri Spaak was made chairman. In addition, the conferees insisted that all decisions be made by unanimous vote—a provision that the British would have demanded in any event. Monnet's interest in the OEEC ended at this point, for he saw the *liberum veto* as the negation of incisive action. Thus, he did not applaud the elevation of his principal deputy, Robert Marjolin, to secretary-general of the new organization. "I understand," he told me, "why Marjolin wants to play a role in a major affair; it's a big job for a young man. He'll do it as well as possible. But the OEEC's nothing; it's only a watered-down British approach to Europe—talk, consultation, action only by unanimity. That's no way to make Europe."

Monnet and Marjolin addressed problems from different angles of attack. Monnet invariably set goals that might be approached but never attained. Marjolin, whose task was to translate broad concepts into functioning institutions, was necessarily aware of the limits of the feasible and the need for compromise. I refrained from taking sides in the argument, since I was devoted to both men. But their disparate attitudes illuminated the basic question. Was Monnet really right in believing that a change in institutions would cause men and women to conform their thoughts and actions to a new set of principles? Could allegiance to a united Europe some day play the same activating role that national sovereignty had played in the past? Or did it really matter whether he was right or not? Would not the insistent pressure for the unattainable goal at least lead toward greater solidarity and common policies and actions that could never be achieved by more modest objectives?

Marjolin did not believe that the concept of nationality could be displaced within a single generation, or even several generations, merely by creating new institutions. Patriotism had been the coalescing force animating Germany's neighbors to resist her ravaging armies in two world wars, and Britain, in Marjolin's view, was not ready for Europe. He did not think—as Monnet did—that deeply entrenched habits of thought and action could be quickly modified in the pressure chambers of new institutions.

I came out roughly in the middle. I could not believe that there would ultimately emerge anything like a United States of Europe, if by that term one envisaged even a faint shadow of the federal system evolved by thirteen rural colonies on the eastern margin of the American continent. The peoples of the great nations of Europe were burdened by too much history, too much cultural and linguistic diversity, too intense an ethnocentricity, and too many centuries of deliberately cultivating and fiercely defending their national institutions to make the drastic adjustments that federation, or even confederation, required. Still, it was useful to hold out such a grand objective when accompanied by proposals for limited but concrete actions. Even if Europe should not achieve federal or confederal status, it could improve its capacities for common action by a process generally directed toward that goal. What was essential was to keep the process going, not to lose momentum; that was Monnet's constant preoccupation—and his great achievement.

As an American, I saw Europe's developing capacity for common action as essential to a stable world. With the Cold War at its height, the world had split into two camps, each dominated by a colossus. Measured by relevant statistics, the potential of a united Western Europe approached that of the United States, but, so long as the peoples of Europe remained emotionally and politically locked up within tight national borders, they would be unable to participate effectively in affairs outside their narrow parishes.

During 1949, I continued to work with Monnet on projects designed to assure that the French Plan of Reconstruction received enough interim funds from America to move effectively toward rehabilitating the French economy. Since I spent about three and a half months in Paris during that year—largely in connection with the establishment of a Paris office for my law firm—Monnet and I had plenty of chances for long speculative conversations.

The Saar Problem

We spent hours talking about the Saar—and its implications for Europe. During his League of Nations days, Monnet had played a role (albeit, a reluctant one) in working out a settlement that left the political responsibility for the Saar with the League of Nations but gave France full ownership of the coal that was its principal wealth. He had quite accurately noted at that time that "the Saar cannot remain independent. If the population insists, it will sooner or later return to Germany."[5] Though he proposed a referendum, the French objected; they were clearly bent on a takeover of the Saar's economic resources.

Now he saw history repeating itself. Though statesmen talked piously about European unity, they were neither ready nor willing to give that idea reality. French foreign policy was, Monnet felt, slipping limply into outworn molds. Saar coal was being progressively incorporated into the French economy, and negotiations were under way to give the Saar political autonomy—while the Ruhr remained under an International Ruhr Authority.[6] Such arrangements were inevitably a source of festering discontent among the Germans.

The Mood in Europe

It is difficult, after three decades, to recall vividly the suspicions and anxieties that prevailed in Europe—and particularly in France—just four years after V-E Day. Men and women were painfully adjusting to a new and strange world, while still trying to purge their country of the bitterness, shame, and mutual distrust that were the residue of protracted occupation. That France was no longer a major world power as it had been for centuries was a sharp nettle for its leaders to grasp (though less painful than for the British, who only fully grasped it twenty years later). Though the United States nurtured and protected the convalescent West with her money and power, the rising menace of the Soviet Union disturbed the French by nightmare visions that their country might be lost in the shuffle of a bipolar Cold War. Because Frenchmen were fiercely determined that a strong Germany would never rise again, some of them sympathized with the bizarre view advanced by Secretary of the Treasury Henry Morgenthau during the war that Germany should be reduced to a pastoral state.

Still, the future depended on America, and American leaders were now having quite different thoughts. With the intensification of the Cold War, Washington increasingly wished to interpose a strong West Germany between Soviet tanks and the rest of Western Europe. To resist Moscow's pressure, West Germany must be permitted to rebuild its economic strength and develop a political identity. Thus, while France vainly protested, America agreed to the raising of West German production levels. On April 8, 1949, the Accords of Washington recognized the existence of a West German state with elections to follow in April. German rearmament could not be long postponed.

Throughout France, fear and distrust were inevitably revived. In Paris during 1949, even an itinerant American could sense a resurgence of introspection, a slackening of vitality, and the insidious exhumation of old, dark rivalries, fears, and complexes. No one was more worried than Jean Monnet by this accelerating trend. It was axiomatic to him—as to all "good Europeans"—that lasting peace could be achieved only by bringing France and Germany together and exorcising the demons of the past. Such an initiative was urgently needed, and Monnet rose to the occasion.

7. The Parturition of Europe

Unlike Dean Acheson, I was not "present at the creation." During the first half of 1950, an increasingly busy law practice kept me in the United States, and while Monnet and I talked constantly on the telephone, we could speak only in cryptic terms about matters not in the public domain. Thus I first learned from the press that on May 9 the French government had put forward a plan for pooling European coal and steel production. I was sure, of course, that it was Monnet's doing, and I was disappointed that he had not sent for me at the outset. But I knew that, sooner or later, I was certain to be summoned. So I felt relieved rather than surprised when Monnet telephoned on June 18 with his familiar request: "Be here tomorrow." Because my plane was delayed, I did not arrive until evening at rue de Martignac, where I found Monnet, Pierre Uri, whom I then knew only slightly, Etienne Hirsch, who had already become a good friend, and Professor Paul Reuter, of whom I had never heard and who disappeared from the Monnet camp soon afterwards.

The Inception of the Schuman Plan

I found it by no means easy to catch up with all that had occurred in the five intense weeks since the basic concept of Monnet's coal and steel plan had been first disclosed to Foreign Minister Robert Schuman early in May. The action had been kept within a tiny circle, and neither Monnet nor his hard-pressed colleagues could now spare the time to explain the full course of events—not even to a comrade who had fought on the same barricades in the past.

With no comment other than: "Big things are happening. Read this," Monnet handed me a sheaf of papers. For the next hour or so, I quietly tried to assess the exact state of the play, to ingest from memoranda designed for different readers a mass of information, and to trace the evolution of the central ideas. While I was busy with my reading material, an involved discussion swirled around me in French, which under the best of conditions, I could understand only with intense concentration.

Among the papers in the dossier were successive drafts of Schuman's May 9 proposal, which I had seen summarized in the American press.[1] Most revealing was a memorandum of May 3 marked "secret" prepared as a brief for Schuman to use with his cabinet colleagues. Entitled "Notes de Réflexion," it began with a catalogue of French anxieties. "Whichever way one turns, one encounters in today's world only blind alleys—the growing acceptance of an inevitable war, the unresolved problem of Germany, the slow recovery of France, the need to organize Europe and to find a place for France in Europe and in the world." To escape from such a dead end required concrete and resolute action directed at a limited but decisive sector in order to bring about a fundamental change in that sector and, by degrees, modify the terms of the total problem. The coal and steel proposal had been formulated in that spirit.

"With the crystallization of thought on the Cold War," the Notes continued, "all actions and decisions will be viewed in relation to their effect on that War." The rigidity of thought resulting from this narrow objective would block the search for solutions to fundamental problems and would inevitably bring about conflict. To alter that dangerous course required a change in the spirit of men, which could be accomplished not by words but only by "a profound, real, immediate and dramatic action that changes things and gives reality to hopes in which people are now ceasing to believe."

The problem of Germany—so the argument proceeded—was rapidly becoming a cancer; it could be dangerous to the peace and to France if German energies were not directed toward hope and the collaboration with free peoples. Without doubt the Americans would insist that Germany be given its place in the Western orbit not only because they wanted to accomplish something and had no other solution, but also because they doubted French solidity and dynamism. But the German problem could not be settled within the framework of existing conditions. France must seek to change those conditions through a dynamic action that would give direction to the spirit of the German people rather than merely search for a static settlement based on current conditions.

If the question of Germany's industrial production and its capacity to compete were not rapidly resolved, France's recovery would be halted. Germany was already asking to raise its steel production from eleven to fourteen million tons and, though the French would object, America would insist; at the same time, French production would flatten out, or even fall. If nothing were done to change the direction of events, German production would expand, Germany would dump exports, French industry would demand protection, prewar cartels would be recreated, and Germany would move toward the East as a prelude to political agreements, while France would fall once again into the rut of a limited and protected production.

Prompt action was essential, since under American pressure, the decisions that would set these forces in motion would be initiated, if not made final, at the forthcoming conference in London. Yet the United

States did not want matters to develop in that manner; it would welcome another solution, provided it were dynamic, constructive, and—above all—put forward by France.

Pooling coal and steel would render moot the issue of German industrial domination, since it would create the conditions for common expansion with competition but without domination. It would put French industry on an equal footing with German industry, enabling it to participate in European expansion without fear of dumping by the German steel industry and without feeling compelled to join cartels.

All the steps taken so far toward bringing unity—the OEEC, the Brussels Pact, the Council of Europe—had done little to organize Europe. England would agree to nothing that might loosen its ties with the Dominions or commit it to Europe to a degree greater than the commitments America itself made. Germany could not, without change in the existing state of affairs, be brought into the organization of Europe. Thus the course on which we were now engaged would lead to an *impasse,* while we would lose forever this critical moment in which Europe might be organized.

To create a dynamic Europe would not preclude building an association of "free" people in which the United States participated; on the contrary, because such an association would encourage liberty and diversity, a Europe that had adapted to the new conditions would develop its own creative potential and become a force for stability.

Up to now, Europe had never existed; no aggregation of sovereignties meeting together in councils created an entity. A real Europe must be created—a Europe that appeared as such to European and American opinion and had confidence in its own future. "At the present moment," so the paper continued, such a "Europe can be brought to birth only by France. Only France can speak and act," and if France fails to speak and act quickly, the Western nations will cluster around the United States for a more forceful pursuit of the Cold War.[2] England will draw closer and closer to the United States, Germany will develop rapidly, and France will be unable to keep it from arming. France will once again be vulnerable to the Malthusianism of yesteryear, which will, in the long run, bring about its obliteration.

The increase of German production and the escalation of the Cold War would lead the French to fall back again into their psychology of fear at the very moment when audacity could revive the French spirit by the progressive actions for which France was ready. France was marked by destiny. If it were to take the initiative to eliminate fear, bring about a rebirth of hope, and make possible the creation of a force for peace, then it could liberate Europe. "In a liberated Europe the spirit of men born on the soil of France, living in liberty and in constantly improving material and social conditions, can make its essential contribution."

The Haunting Problem of German Rearmaments

That was the essence of "Notes de Réflexion"—the quintessential argument of Monnet and his colleagues. It was a French argument to persuade Frenchmen—not for foreign eyes. Though by no means anti-American, it took full account of the gnawing French preoccupation of the time: France as a nation had lost the power of independent action. As expressed in 1978 by Françoise Giroud, the former French Secretary of State for Culture, France felt itself "chained to a blind giant."[3] In Monnet's view, the giant was not blind, merely busy. America had good judgment, but while it concentrated on the Cold War, Europe's vital interests would be overlooked. Meanwhile, as Britain aligned herself with the United States, Germany would rearm and become economically dominant, leaving France—victimized by fear and impotence—to turn helplessly in on herself. There was a solid basis for such anxieties. Had Monnet not persuaded the weak Third Republic government to put forward the Schuman Plan, which, in turn, made possible (perhaps even inevitable) the later initiative of the European Economic Community, affairs might well have evolved toward the dour situation foreseen in "Notes de Réflexion."

To avoid that drift, France and Germany needed to come to terms on a basis of equality, which was possible, as Monnet saw it, only through a substantial merging of interests. That the merging might be initiated in the limited sphere of coal and steel reflected Monnet's tactical genius. Instead of talking, as politicians constantly talked, about creating unity on a broad front—which meant, in practice, the proliferation of impotent symbols, such as the Council of Europe—Monnet saw the chance for a major breakthrough in a narrow sector. In a figurative sense, he adapted to politics a tank warfare tactic General de Gaulle had futilely advocated in the late thirties: concentrate all available power on a limited point, then spread out behind the lines.

In proposing to act in the narrow sector of coal and steel, Monnet hoped that nations might be willing to entrust sovereign powers to institutions that could form the nucleus of a future European government. Of course, we all knew it was irrational to carve a single economic sector out of the jurisdiction of nation-states and subject it to the control of supranational institutions, but its very irrationality should compel progress. Once coal and steel were pooled, it would become imperative to pool other production as well.

Anticartel Measures

A common market that was simply a customs union was not enough; free movement would also require measures to prevent monopolistic arrangements among producers. But many of Monnet's European colleagues were shocked when he insisted on strong provisions against cartels. Because, of his years in the United States, Monnet was generally familiar with American antitrust legislation, and he quite naturally consulted his old friend John J. McCloy, the American High Commissioner in Germany, who was charged with, among other things, deconcentrating the coal and steel industry of the Ruhr. At the same time, he had to avoid any suggestion that the anticartel provisions of the Schuman Plan Treaty were imposed by the Americans.

Since Robert Bowie, a shrewd and able Harvard law professor, was assisting McCloy in negotiating deconcentration arrangements with the Germans, Monnet consulted him on this particular aspect of the Schuman Plan Treaty. I encountered Bob Bowie on several occasions when he arrived in Paris with drafts and re-drafts of proposed anticartel articles. These were, in turn, rewritten in a European idiom by Maurice Lagrange of the Conseil d'Etat, who, as a skilled draftsman, had major responsibility for giving formal legal expression to the ideas of Monnet and his colleagues.

As a result, two articles of the final treaty (Articles 65 and 66) embodied the most advanced American antitrust thinking, enunciated in language that Europeans could understand. But understanding did not mean ready acceptance; old habits die prolonged deaths, and those provisions provoked a major struggle that lasted more than four months. The problem confronting McCloy and Bowie was delicate. Ruhr coal was still marketed through a common sales agency, which would, as the French saw it, give the Germans too much bargaining power within the Common Market, while failure to break up the great steel concerns would, they feared, further reinforce German dominance of the pool.

From earliest postwar days, the Germans, by conditioned reflex, had resisted deconcentration and decartelization. When the outbreak of the Korean War led America increasingly to look toward West Germany as the main forward element of Western defense, Washington's zeal for deconcentration progressively diminished. Without the Schuman Plan proposal, America's efforts to decartelize Ruhr industry would probably have come to very little.

As a matter of tactics, Monnet found it useful to let his old friend McCloy take the lead in negotiating not only with the German political authorities and the Ruhr industrialists but also with the French and British as occupying powers. Fortunately, Monnet's efforts found sympathy even within the German delegation. Though Adenauer's first thought had been to appoint a German industrialist to represent his country at the Schuman Plan negotiations, Monnet persuaded him that, since the treaty was not a technical matter, he needed a man who could fully appreciate the political significance of the undertaking. Adenauer then selected Professor Walter Hallstein, a distinguished law professor who had taught at Georgetown University in Washington. He understood the American federal system, and particularly, American antitrust laws. With the skillful persuasion of McCloy and Bowie, America's deconcentration proposals and the Schuman Plan Treaty were crafted to reinforce one another. In the end, Adenauer could present the deconcentration measures as his government's proposals, "on the assumption that the Schuman Plan would be in effect."

18, Rue de Martignac

Throughout the year that the treaty was being negotiated, 18, rue de Martignac was the scene of frantic activity. Its graveled courtyard was filled with official Citroens still painted the olive drab that had marked their wartime usage, while helmeted messengers recklessly wheeled their motorcycles in and out. Clearly something important was in progress— a "big affair" as Monnet called it. Few escaped a sense of excitement. "I've been to many international conferences," a seasoned European diplomat told me, "but this is the first time I've ever seen the delegates working to achieve something they all believed in rather than merely trying to defend narrow national concerns."

Happy to be even on the fringes of an event that I felt might eventually transform Europe, I again ensconced myself under the stairs, visiting Monnet only when he called. The house was cut up into tiny rooms crudely furnished. Behind Monnet's modest office was a small dining room, where he and I often ate food cooked by a motherly housekeeper. There were back stairs behind the dining room, which gave me a means of egress in case Europeans arrived. My situation was unique in that I was a private American actively working on the Schuman Plan for a participating government; in addition, other Americans were officially involved in trying to influence various aspects of the treaty. Chief among them was David Bruce, then the United States ambassador to Paris. A resourceful and loyal supporter of Monnet's efforts since his days as chief of the ECA Mission to France, Bruce was a major source of strength. Quite likely his most effective contribution was to give scope and encouragement to his young financial attaché, William M. Tomlinson. Tommy became a central figure in Monnet's scheme of things. Slight of build and only thirty-two years old in 1950, he had grown up in Idaho and retained a Westerner's fierce disdain for protocol and bureaucratic obscurantism. Instinctively grasping the full implications of Monnet's objectives, he was impatient with more plodding intellects who so often missed the point. As financial attaché, he reported to the Treasury Department, where pedestrian technicians had little understanding or sympathy for the political concept of a unified Europe, but Tommy's irresistible force of intellect and energy defeated their obstructionist fumbling. Not only did he dispose of Treasury resistance, he, in time, became a dominant influence on the State Department. A master of maneuver, he reported so copiously as to swamp, and thus paralyze, the less diligent Washington bureaucracy, and, when he received instructions that he found unacceptable, he reacted with such fury and cogency that Washington tended to leave him alone.

I had known Bruce earlier; now Tommy and I became such close co-conspirators that during periods of crisis I would sometimes move my operations to a small office in the embassy chancery adjacent to his. The arrangement was particularly valuable to me, since I needed to dictate in English and embassy secretaries were much better equipped for that purpose than anyone on Monnet's staff. It was an odd arrangement but it worked. Tommy and I conspired with Monnet in full mutual confidence, sensitive to the problems he was encountering. Monnet, in turn, recognized Tommy's problems in dealing with Washington. Such a complete sharing of information and insights could arise only among individuals totally dedicated to a central idea; we all believed fervently in Monnet's goal of a united Europe, which, we thought, was quite as important to Americans as to Europeans.

Very often I found myself working with Tommy late into the night, after which he would disappear to visit the nightspots, since he relaxed as vigorously as he worked. Though he had suffered a cardiac weakness ever since his youth, it did not deter him from committing himself completely to whatever he was doing. In the end, the intensity of his work with Monnet cost him his life. A true hero of the European effort, he suffered a stroke in 1954, at the age of thirty-six, and died a year later.

One minor incident during my work with Tommy illustrates the fatuity of government red tape. At six o'clock one morning, a young marine guard, after searching my briefcase, firmly announced that some documents marked "Secret" could not be taken from the building. It took me ten minutes to explain that the papers belonged to the French government rather than the American government. *"Sekray,"* I said—giving the word an exaggerated French pronunciation—"not *secret.*" He finally, though grudgingly, yielded.

Impact of the Korean War

I shall never forget Monnet's reaction to news of the Korean War. The preparatory conference on the Coal and Steel Community had begun on June 20, 1950, and on Sunday, June 25, 1950, I had gone to Houjarray for a day of work. During the afternoon, after three or four Europeans from other delegations had assembled, someone arrived with word that the North Korean Army had invaded South Korea. Monnet saw the implications in this announcement almost faster than Washington. The Americans, he declared, would never permit the Communists to succeed with such naked aggression, since that would begin the erosion of lines drawn with such difficulty during the postwar years. Yet for America to intervene in Korea would not only jeopardize the Schuman Plan, it might well create panic in Europe and increase American insistence on a larger German role in the defense of the West.

The last point, of course, was of special importance. Morgenthau's idiotic plan to turn the German landscape into a pastoral painting by Millet had been long forgotten. The defeated peoples must be brought back, cautiously at first, into the family of Western civilization, encouraged in their first experiments with democracy, and integrated into a larger Europe. The Berlin Blockade in the autumn and winter of 1948–1949 had pushed the issue to the fore, requiring re-examination of earlier conclusions about German disarmament and speeding up the timetable for ending the occupation and reestablishing German control of their own affairs. But it was not easy for Europeans to adjust their thinking to an arrangement that would mean a reversal of wartime alliances. France and the Benelux countries still bore the visible wounds of Nazi brutality; Coventry remained a scarred city; only five years had passed since the macabre funeral pyre outside the bunker in Berlin.

Saved from the searing scars of invasion and occupation, we Americans found it easy to take a flexible line, but the differences of power and interest, perspective and psychology between America and Europe were becoming increasingly awkward. Monnet, more than anyone else, knew that the prospect of German rearmament could lead Frenchmen to hesitate before entering the Coal and Steel Community with the Germans. But, as usual, he sought to turn every potential setback into an opportunity. Once the United States proposed at a conference in the Waldorf Astoria Towers on September 12, 1950, to bring Germany into NATO, Monnet altered his own timetable.

I think it almost certain that, had the Korean War not accelerated the push for German rearmament, Monnet would soon have pressed the leaders of France, West Germany, and the other members of the Six to create a political community. But events forced the issue. American insistence on rebuilding a German national army could provoke bitter and frightened responses that would drastically set back the cause of unification, particularly if French resistance to such a move separated France from its allies. To avoid such a development, Monnet, although ill at the time, quickly put forward a scheme to organize Europe's defense roughly along the lines of the Schuman Plan. The proposal was first made to Prime Minister René Pleven, who years before had been Monnet's assistant in Polish loan negotiations. Monnet also sent a copy to Foreign Minister Robert Schuman, who was negotiating in New York.

Proposal for a European Army

A few days later, in a second memorandum to Pleven, Monnet proposed that, before meeting again with its allies on October 28, the French government should publicly reject German rearmament on a national basis, suggesting instead the formation of a European army within a European Defense Community, in which the Germans would participate. On Tuesday, October 24, 1950, Pleven presented to the French Assembly what became known as the Pleven Plan, and it was promptly approved.

As drafted, the proposal outlined plans for a European army under a single European executive, with all elements in that army wearing a common European uniform, receiving identical pay, training under a common system, and serving under an integrated command—in the beginning, at the army corps level. Germany would be asked to raise twelve divisions, a tactical air force, and light naval forces. A political commissariat would, in effect, be Europe's defense ministry, with authority to form, recruit, and train the European army, determine common rates of pay and rules of recruitment, and play a major part (in cooperation with the national parliaments) in determining military budgets. These proposals were formally embodied in a treaty signed by France, Germany, Italy, Belgium, and the Netherlands on May 27, 1952. An additional protocol of agreement in April 1954 committed Britain to keeping four divisions and a fighter air force on the continent indefinitely.

Though initially skeptical, Secretary of State Acheson now gave the European army plan strong diplomatic support, but anti-European elements mouthed a ferocious propaganda attack, with General de Gaulle, joined by the Communists, leading the opposition to what he called a "stateless melting pot." Opponents on the Left and Right then tried, with success, to distort the vote into a referendum on German militarism. The result was a four-year fight, which the brilliant French journalist-philosopher Raymond Aron later described as "the greatest ideological and political debate France had known since the Dreyfus Affair."[4]

Meanwhile, the parliaments of four of the six signatory nations ratified the European Defense Community (EDC) Treaty; but the Fourth Republic proved too weak. Prime Minister Mendès-France, preoccupied with extricating his country from Indochina, had other fish to fry; by deliberate inaction, he let the French Assembly kill the treaty.

Years later, it became fashionable in some American circles to regard the European Defense Community as a jerry-built contraption that never had a chance for success. Some even referred to it as an American idea that failed because of excessive American zeal. To anyone who watched the situation from a close vantage point, such comments reflect an abysmal ignorance of the facts, an insensitivity to the tides and currents of the time, and the fashionable but fatuous tendency of some American intellectuals to blame our own country for all blunders or defeats.

Pressure from our government was not the reason for the plan's failure; on the contrary, it was American support that enabled the proponents to come close to success. The primary reason for failure was the unwillingness of any of a succession of flabby French governments to risk putting the plan to a parliamentary test. Meanwhile, Gaullist opposition grew more virulent, national frustration over the Indochinese War took an increasingly disastrous turn (Dien Bien Phu fell in 1954), and Britain's refusal to merge its troops into the "continental army" helped undermine the plan's limited appeal to the French people.

I still lament the failure of ratification. Had an integrated European army come into being, the battalions of retrograde nationalism would have been held in check; fears of a rearmed Germany would have subsided; the momentum toward unity would have continued; Franco-German *rapprochement* would have advanced within a congenial framework; and General de Gaulle might have found it impossible to pull apart the NATO collective security arrangements as he did twelve years later. Ironically enough, only two months after the failure of the EDC, the German Federal Republic became a member of NATO. French fear of German rearmament had created a German national army which the EDC would have prevented; that, to many Frenchmen, meant a beginning of the revival of German nationalism.

In August 1952, with the ratification of the Coal and Steel Community by six national parliaments, Monnet became the first President of the Community's High Authority. Without waiting for the EDC, the Council of Ministers of the Coal and Steel Community had asked the Community's Common Assembly to coopt eight additional members to draft a treaty for a European political—as distinct from defense—community. Within six months, by March 10, 1953, that draft was ready. Unhappily, with the fierce opposition from both the extreme Left and Right focused on the EDC debate, attention to the treaty was postponed; in the end, events overtook it. Nonetheless, had Great Britain joined to balance the weight of Germany, both the EDC and the European Political Community might have come into being.

The failure of the European army (the EDC) was a severe blow to Monnet, and a less resilient man would have regarded it as fatal to his hopes for uniting Europe. But, as usual, Jean accepted it as merely a tactical setback. Still, he could look with little kindness on those who had joined in the destruction of his initiative, and particularly Mendès-France, who, as Prime Minister, had by inaction permitted the French Assembly to deny ratification. Nor could Monnet be enthusiastic when, two months later, Mendès-France collaborated with Anthony Eden in expanding the

Brussels Treaty into the Western European Union (WEU). Many Frenchmen who felt guilty about the EDC's failure hailed this new move as a welcome substitute; in fact, however, it was only a pallid ghost. Though it provided for a consultative assembly, it was little more than a military arrangement.

Pierre Mendès-France

Mendès-France was a man of subtlety and complexity, with a background of scholarship and a deep concern for France's problems. I liked him and admired the skill and incisiveness with which he had extracted his country from its "dirty war" in Indochina. Ten years later, when my own country was fighting its own "dirty war" on the same terrain, I found myself saying, "Mendès-France, better thou shouldst be living at this hour. America has need of you."

To enlist American support for his initiative, Mendès-France planned a trip to America, and since my firm was an adviser to the French government, he asked me to come to Paris to help prepare him for his trip. I worked with him for a week in Paris, then returned to the United States. Meeting him in Montreal, I reviewed and revised his draft speeches and prepared him for press interviews and television appearances.

I was troubled by the assignment and discussed it first with Monnet. He was not pleased by the thought that I might help Mendès-France persuade Americans that the WEU was a legitimate step toward unifying Europe or in any sense a substitute for the European army. Still, he was, as always, realistic. "You're representing the French government," he said, "and you must do what the Prime Minister asks or resign your retainer. I understand, so don't worry about it. You have to do what you have to do." I also consulted my wise friend David Bruce, who was by then America's special representative to the European Coal and Steel Community. He was equally insistent that I avoid passing off the WEU improvisation as a substitute for the EDC.

I enjoyed working with Mendès-France, though, as an intellectual, he regarded the world in a quite different manner from Monnet. During the war, he had been a heroic figure in the Resistance, and I listened with interest to his plans for saving the Fourth Republic from an insidious decline. As Prime Minister, he had started a campaign against alcoholism, calling it an enemy of French efficiency and trying to persuade Frenchmen to drink milk rather than wine. That once led to what might have been an embarrassing situation. One afternoon, when he and I were in a railroad compartment traveling from Washington to New York, a newspaper photographer walked in just as I was pouring a drink from a bottle of Scotch. I shoved it under the table only just in time.

While the Treaty of Paris that created the Coal and Steel Community was still being negotiated, Walter Lippmann insisted that I write a book about it. He even enlisted Cass Canfield, then head of Harper's, to offer me a contract for such a book. The work occupied a great deal of my time over many months. Lippmann read and edited the first few chapters and promised to write an introduction. Though I completed most of the manuscript, the book was never published. Monnet, who had initially approved the book in principle, decided—after reading some of my text—that it was too soon to reveal so much about what had been thought and done.

In November 1954, Monnet announced that he would not stand for another term as President of the Coal and Steel Community and upon returning to private life, founded the Action Committee for the United States of Europe. Meanwhile, I was retained as an adviser by all three of the communities that came into being: the Coal and Steel Community, Euratom, and, later, the European Economic Community. That did not end my work with Monnet, which continued on a nonprofessional basis. I consulted with him informally in Europe and performed my familiar role as amanuensis and intellectual punching bag whenever he came to the United States.

Monnet's Final Years

On Thanksgiving Day in 1977, I dined with Jean and Sylvia Monnet in their home in Houjarray. As a gesture to an old friend and to America, Sylvia had not only procured a turkey, but, by the exercise of considerable effort and imagination, had also found cranberries and made chestnut dressing. It was a quiet, deeply satisfying, but *triste* occasion. Jean and I both knew we would probably never meet again; there was still a sparkle in his eye, but he was very feeble. "I'm not ill, George," he said, "just old." He was very old—eighty-nine at the time—though his mind was clear, and his indomitable optimism scarcely diminished. "It'll go on," he said. "What we've started will continue. It has momentum."

We talked about our work together over the years, and he asked his usual searching questions about my life. Was I happy? How was I spending my time? Then he observed, as he had on so many occasions: "George, you should stop diffusing your energies." That comment had formed the *leitmotif* of many of our conversations during the years that I worked closely with Monnet. Yet, even more persuasive than his words was the testimony of his own career. Men of genius can sometimes validate clichés that have lost their vitality, and Monnet's life confirms the old saying that a deeply committed man can move mountains. Yet to do so he must, like Monnet, possess indefatigable energy, an uncommon measure of both resilience and resourcefulness, and the willingness to forgo all personal gain and glory in the single-minded pursuit of a transcendent purpose.

Monnet and de Gaulle Compared

In later years, I sometimes tried to compare Monnet with that other great Frenchman whom I met on several occasions, General Charles de Gaulle. I have no doubt that, of the two, Jean Monnet was the greater, though that was a matter on which Walter Lippmann and I could never agree. Lippmann was an ardent Gaullist, seeing in the General a man who imperiously disdained the petty affairs that preoccupied other political leaders. In a television interview in 1965, he had described de Gaulle as "a man who can't see very clearly what's right in front of him, who sees pretty well what's across the room, or halfway down the street, but who sees absolutely perfectly what's in the distance. He has the farthest vision, he can see farther than any man in our time."[5] Later, discussing the interview with Walter I called attention to that passage. De Gaulle, I conceded, could see farther than any man in our time. "There is no doubt," I said, "that he can look out over the centuries. But de Gaulle's great weakness is that he habitually faces backwards, seeing the centuries that are past, not the future that is to come. Overlying all his accomplishments has been a sense of nostalgia, a groping back toward a past that can't be recovered or even imitated. De Gaulle's obsession is to establish France on a par with the global powers in spite of implacable facts of population and resources, and, like King Canute, he tries to sweep back the tides of history, to deny the realities of the twentieth century. His great tragedy is that he wasn't born in the time of Louis XIV, when France was indeed the most populous and richest nation in Europe."

I saw de Gaulle as a twentieth-century Don Quixote, seeking to preserve old forms and restore old patterns, always trying to push a modest-sized nation into the front rank alongside superpowers organized on a continent-wide basis—in total disregard of this century's requirements of scope and scale. As Raymond Aron wrote in 1962 in *Peace and War*, the obsolescence of any one of the West European states, acting alone, "assumes, in our period, the appearance of an irrevocable destiny. The approximate proportonality between force and resources, between resources and the number of men and the amount of raw materials, between mobilizable force and power, does not permit any hope that the leader's genius or the people's virtue might reverse the verdict of number."[6] That was a point de Gaulle never understood, or if he understood, never conceded. His whole life was dedicated to prove that a "leader's genius," when combined with "the people's virtue," could somehow "reverse the verdict of number"—that he could somehow make France a superpower in spite of itself.

Monnet never indulged in such whimsical fantasy; he was a twentieth-century man, in contrast to de Gaulle, the brilliant anachronism who disrupted Europe by undertaking a *tour de force* beyond the reach of his extraordinary abilities. As a result, I wrote in 1968, "like King Lear, the General must in the end be reduced to complaining to the heavens—rebelling self-destructively at the deaf neutrality of impersonal forces. As Carlyle said of Napoleon, he 'has words in him which are like Austerlitz battles.' "[7]

De Gaulle was a man who, on two occasions, fulfilled a historical requirement but was at other times a nuisance. He twice bound up the wounds of a nation at war with itself: once in 1946 and again in the late 1950s, when he resolved the corrosive problem of Algeria that was beyond the competence of the Fourth Republic. He found a country with its eyes cast down and restored its self-respect and confidence, and one cannot diminish that achievement.

Yet, even in 1968, I observed that "while he has served France brilliantly during a time of troubles, he has been one of the destructive elements in the larger chemistry of the West. This is not only a personal misfortune, for I am convinced that history will give him bad marks for what he has done to Europe, but it is a tragedy for the European people. It is a tragedy not only because of the breakage caused, but—what is even more poignant—because of the opportunity missed; of all the postwar leaders he has been the only one with the necessary authority to head a Europe that desperately wanted his leadership."[8]

What did the General leave behind him? Not French supremacy in Europe, for today France is progressively slipping behind Germany both economically and politically. He left little in concrete form. The Constitution of 1958 has, so far, given stability to France, yet de Gaulle tarnished that achievement in 1962 by amendments providing for the direct election of a President and the popular referendum—a dubious engine that could someday invite dictatorial abuse in a political sysem lacking America's checks and balances. In addition, he instituted a practice of periodic consultation between the leaders in Paris and Bonn that depends largely on the motivation of individuals, has no institutional underpinning, and is far weaker than it need be because it is bilateral and not embodied in any European system. In essence, de Gaulle was a superb actor, but, unlike architects, actors leave only legends and transient playbills—nothing permanent that affects the lives or sensibilities of future generations. De Gaulle was the Henry Irving of his day.

Since Jean Monnet, in contrast, was a superlative architect, his place in history will not prove evanescent. As a heritage, he has left institutions that, though falling short of their original high purpose, still play a major role in European life. He was preeminently a modern man, who perceived a major dilemma of our complex time—the discord between our technology, on the one hand, with its rapid pace of advance and its requirements of scale and scope, and, on the other, our institutional arrangements, so slow to change and so often parochial in character. Yet I do not mean that Monnet was unaware or disdainful of the past. Though admittedly no scholar, his insight told him that history was not static, not the constant replaying of old themes, but a flow of events that, if man is to survive, must be so channeled as to meet the needs of an evolving age. He was, therefore, never tempted into de Gaulle's error—induced by an atavistic longing for a world that never was—of seeking to recapture the past. As I wrote some years ago in an introduction to the American edition of Monnet's memoirs,

It is because Jean Monnet so clearly perceives the nature of the great tidal forces now at work that he is sturdily immune to disappointments. I was with him on more than one occasion when the progress of a new design seemed irrevocably halted by the abrupt intrusion of obsolete—yet fiercely held—ideas that echoed a distant and earlier age. Invariably—and sometimes almost alone—Jean Monnet remained undismayed. "What has happened, has happened," he would say with a Gallic shrug, "but it does not affect anything fundamental. The important point is for us not to be deflected, not to lose momentum. We must find a way to go forward."

It is because of his apparent imperturbability that Monnet is known—to the admiration of his friends and the exasperation of his opponents—as an incorrigible optimist. Yet his optimism does not stem from any Panglossian idea that all is for the best in the best of all possible worlds, but rather from a belief in the logic of events and the essential rationality of man—a dauntless faith in the ineluctable direction of deeply moving forces. Optimism to Jean Monnet is the only serviceable hypothesis for a practical man or woman with a passionate desire to get things done.

Since the beginning of time many men have tried to alter the structure of world power. When their ambitions have been selfish and hegemonic, they have usually failed. When they have sought to realize their dreams by force, whatever success they have achieved has been transient and illusory. But there have also been those rare men whose visions were ample and generous, whose goal was no less than the good of mankind, and who have relied not on force but on persuasion—the energy latent in an indomitable idea—to accomplish their objectives. Sometimes those men have wrought miracles.[9]

Requiem for an Inspired Friend

In March 1979, I flew to France for Jean Monnet's funeral service in a country church near Montfort l'Amaury not far from Houjarray. It was a bright, spring day, with that special quality of soft light (a "spécialité de la France") suffusing the lush countryside and inevitably recalling our many walks together across the surrounding hills. The church was filled with an oddly assorted congregation—not merely the simple Frenchmen who were Jean's neighbors but also the luminaries of Europe: Chancellor Helmut Schmidt, President Giscard d'Estaing, and foreign ministers or heads of state from other European nations. Conspicuously absent was anyone of comparable high standing from Britain.

Suddenly loudspeakers around the church began to blast forth with an American chorus singing the "Battle Hymn of the Republic" through all five verses. John J. McCloy and a few other of Monnet's close American friends smiled quietly on hearing that fighting song of the American Civil War—a song, as some of us knew, Jean had loved. It was the kind of small joke he would certainly have enjoyed, and he would have been amused at the blank looks of mystification on the faces of the European dignitaries.

The service was a traditional French Catholic service, ceremonious and elaborate. But easily identified on the program was one musical composition of French origin, another of German, another of Italian, and another of English. The spirit of Monnet's Europe was about him even at his death.

After the sermon, Jack McCloy and I stopped a moment to speak to Sylvia Monnet. As she and I embraced, she said to me, "George, did you hear it, the 'Battle Hymn of the Republic'? Wasn't that wonderful?" "Yes," I replied. "It was all wonderful—all those years were wonderful."

8. A Washington Lawyer

Both Ruth and I liked Washington. We could visit friends without the need for time-consuming journeys, and people with varied backgrounds were continually drifting through from the far corners of the world to keep us intellectually alive. At the time, Washington had few cultural amenities. Not until two decades later would the Kennedy Center, under that brilliant impresario Roger L. Stevens, provide a cultural dimension to a society shaped by politics. Unlike present-day Washington, the gastronomic possibilities were then limited to two or three mediocre restaurants and some embassies better known for their chefs than their diplomatic significance. Yet we knew enough people in government, the press, and the diplomatic corps to enjoy a constantly replenished smorgasbord of ideas.

The Lippmanns

Soon after I returned from Europe in 1945, we bought a house on Woodley Road, directly across from the Washington Cathedral, and a week later discovered that Walter and Helen Lippmann lived on the same block. Though we had met the Lippmanns casually on a number of occasions, the new propinquity ripened and enriched our friendship, and during the next twenty-two years, Walter and I met at least once almost every fortnight. Either the four of us dined together at the Lippmanns' or, less often, at our house, or Walter and I would have lunch or exchange late afternoon visits. It was more than a mere neighborly friendship; I sought out Walter to clarify my own muddled thinking, while he used me as a kind of practice dartboard against which he could throw ideas for his columns. Often I would agree with his views, sometimes adding a qualification or an illustrative footnote; on other occasions, I would reject his underlying theses and precipitate an argument. But, however useful he may have found the exercise, I was the greater beneficiary.

For a man with so much to say, Walter was invariably a good listener, tolerant of disagreement, and eager for fresh insights—though impatient of what he deemed patent nonsense. Occasionally I would bring someone to lunch whom I thought Walter might like to meet, but it was not always a complete success. On one occasion, speaking of a man with an inventive but undisciplined mind, he said to me, "Please don't bring 'X' to lunch anymore. He has a flair for eccentric ideas that sound brilliantly plausible, but I can't afford to spend the next week discovering the missing element or the hidden flaw."

Guests at the Lippmanns' dinners were a mixed lot but usually stimulating, and talk over the brandy often introduced me to fresh ideas and diverse points of view. When the four of us dined alone, the conversation would sometimes drift off into gossip, personalities, and satirical comments; Walter had a quiet but acerbic sense of humor, with an underlying taste for gentle malice—while Helen's malice was not always so gentle. At the end of such an evening, Walter might say gleefully, "Well, we've certainly been outrageous tonight, haven't we?"

I remember particularly those occasions when I would goad him into talking about earlier times, particularly his Harvard years with George Santayana, William James, and his classmates of the celebrated class of 1910. At other times, I would ask him to reminisce about his Greenwich Village experiences with Mabel Dodge and the young bohemians of the early 1920s. He spoke with particular affection of John Reed, who was later to write *Ten Days That Shook the World* and be buried within the walls of the Kremlin. Had Reed lived, Walter insisted, he would have outgrown his Communist enthusiasms; he was "far too intelligent not to gain wisdom as events unfolded." His appraisal of T. S. Eliot was less charitable. "Tom was simply too highbrow for me," he said. "Half the time I didn't know what he was talking about and I'm sure he didn't either." I remember one glorious evening when Max Eastman dined with the four of us. At my prodding, he and Walter provided a night of sustained nostalgia.

Establishing a Law Practice

Our law firm had taken form through a succession of accidents. During my interludes in America, while a member of the Bombing Survey, I had talked with Fowler Hamilton about establishing a practice in Washington. Hamilton had long planned to form a new law firm with a friend named Hugh Cox, whom he had come to know when both were Rhodes Scholars at Oxford and with whom he had later worked in the Department of Justice. Though at the time I knew Cox largely by reputation, he agreed that I should become the third member—a result, I knew, of Hamilton's gifted and generous advocacy. Growing up in Nebraska, Cox had made an exceptional record at Oxford. As Assistant Solicitor General in the Department of Justice, he was widely known as a lawyer's lawyer, and his fame had begun to spread throughout professional and business circles. At the time of his death in 1968, a library room in Christ Church College, Oxford, was furnished in his honor and a memorial volume issued with glowing tributes from luminaries of the bar.

In the fall of 1945, our plans for a modest Washington office were drastically revised when four partners of the firm of Root, Clark, Buckner and Ballantine in New York—George Cleary, Leo Gottlieb, Henry Friendly, and Melvin Steen—decided to break away and establish a firm of their own. A third party, friendly both to Cox and the New York group, proposed a merging of efforts, but since I had only casually met one member of the New York group, Leo Gottlieb, I was not a part of the discussions. I was, in fact, about to accept an offer to become a Washington partner of the Root, Clark firm when the secessionists asked me to join them. My new partners were all men of extraordinary ability, and the new firm (which is today known as Cleary, Gottlieb, Steen and Hamilton) grew rapidly from our original seven to where it now consists of more than two hundred lawyers with offices not only in New York and Washington but also in Paris, Brussels, London, and Hong Kong.

My work with Léon Blum delayed my entry into the firm for six months, so that I did not join until July 1, 1946. Shortly thereafter, my practice was interrupted while surgeons removed my right kidney and successfully halted the cancer that had attacked it. I have rarely thought about it since.

We soon found ourselves gratifyingly busy. My partners were more gifted than I in attracting clients, but I represented various agencies of the French government and, in time, began to counsel other foreign interests, both public and private. On my initiative, our firm opened an office in Paris in 1949; both it and the Brussels office which I later proposed have now grown to impressive dimensions.

In 1951, while Europe was still pulling itself together after the war, I was asked to advise the leaders of the French Patronat—an industrial federation that includes the whole of French industry. They needed someone to help prepare the European Patronat for a meeting in New York with the United States National Association of Manufacturers. I was surprised that they selected me as their adviser since they opposed most of the objectives for which I was working (the Schuman Plan and other measures for uniting Europe), but I was happy to have them as a client. My wife and I joined the Patronat delegates in Paris, then crossed with most of them on the *Liberté,* where I gave a daily lecture, preparing my pupils for their encounter with the American natives. I enjoyed the experience for I could and did brainwash my captive audience with my own idiosyncratic interpretation of everything from the American approach to income taxes and antitrust measures to the prevailing American opinion of France and particularly its colonial policies. Many of the businessmen had not been to America since before the war; for others, it was a first visit. The inclusion of German industrialists in the Patronat delegation created awkward moments, since it was only six years after the war, but the presence of an American proved a leavening ingredient.

Thereafter, for several years, I met regularly with French business leaders in Paris for meetings of the "Comité Ball," during which I tried to keep them informed of current American thought, policy, and action. In addition, I wrote long papers covering economic and political subjects that I thought might be of interest. Not only did they have an avid interest in news of America, they were also concerned that the problems and achievements of French industry were not understood in the United States. So, at their urging, I established a regular monthly newsletter called *France Actuelle,* designed to inform Americans of French activities primarily in technology and industry. *France Actuelle* continued publication until 1972, building an established readership and providing a model for other foreign industrial and governmental publications.

I look back wistfully on those postwar years. Part of almost every month was spent in Europe, while my partners and I—particularly Fowler Hamilton—sought every opportunity to enlarge the scope and reputation of our firm. Law practice was for me both a source of income and a base of operations from which I could engage in a *mélange* of activities on the edge of politics and diplomacy. I valued the discipline acquired from work in a firm of rigorous professional standards and I found the law full of intellectual challenges, but, unlike some lawyers, I did not find it all-absorbing. Too many other things interested me as much or even more. So I was not surprised to overhear one of my younger colleagues explaining what he regarded as a critical flaw in my character. "Ball is," he said, "an unmatched *frontalier* but a man without a country."

Liberalizing Trade

Reflecting the lessons I had learned from my Lend-Lease experience and my later work with Monnet, I felt it essential that we rid the world economy of its encrusted barnacles of trade and monetary restrictions. Though Bretton Woods had provided an essential step toward monetary sanity, the movement of goods and services was still badly hobbled. As a great trading nation, we had heavy past sins to expiate. Our mindless protectionism of the late twenties and early thirties had helped to precipitate the world's economic collapse and to create the conditions that fostered the rise of Hitler—at the same time that our isolationism (the other face of protectionism) had induced us to stand numbly by while the world slid toward catastrophic war.

As an ardent advocate of liberal trade, I tried to fit my professional activities to my convictions. Beginning in April 1950, I represented the Venezuelan Central Bank and Chamber of Commerce in a counteroffensive against efforts of domestic oil operators to limit oil imports, and, in 1955, I helped the Cuban sugar industry secure adequate quotas for its product in the highly restricted United States market. I have never liked lobbying and am bored and uncomfortable when I have to importune Senators and Congressmen, even for causes in which I firmly believe. But in acting for the Venezuelans and Cubans I spent little time wandering about the Senate and House office buildings. Instead, we concentrated on showing American industrial and commercial companies how much they depended on their exports to Venezuela and Cuba. In developing the means of identifying the interested American companies—a complex task—we were perhaps the first to use computer technology in a major lobbying effort.

During the years that I assisted these two foreign interests, we managed to frustrate the protectionist lobbies, but our representation in each case was terminated through unexpected events. On June 24, 1953, the President's brother, Dr. Milton Eisenhower, paid a goodwill visit to Caracas; while there, he assured the Venezuelan dictator, Perez Jimenez, that President Eisenhower fully supported the free entry of Venezuelan oil into the United States. That was sufficient assurance for the dictator, who observed that if his own brother were to make such a firm statement, that would settle the matter. So he accepted Milton Eisenhower's word at face value and fired his Washington lawyers. A few weeks later, he was taught a lesson in American democracy: under Congressional pressure, the President imposed tight quotas on oil imports.

The termination of our Cuban representation involved a more dramatic event—the takeover of the Cuban government by Fidel Castro.

My enthusiasm for liberal trading policies led me early in 1953 to help create an organization to resist protectionist sentiment. The prime movers were businessmen of conviction and proven achievement, including John S. Coleman, president of Burroughs Corporation and the Detroit Board of Commerce; Harry Bullis, chairman of General Mills; John J. McCloy, chairman of the Chase Manhattan Bank; and Joseph Spang, Jr., president of the Gillette Company. After a series of meetings in New York and Washington, we established the Committee for a National Trade Policy. I served as a member of the Executive Committee and Board of Directors and as secretary of the Committee.

The Bilderberg Group

Creating the Committee was not of major importance; like most high-minded committees, it ran out of steam in a few years and, for all I know, has long since expired. But I mention it because it led me to involvement in a wholly different enterprise—the Bilderberg Group. That enterprise started as a gleam in the eye of Dr. Joseph H. Retinger, a character who could have stepped out of one of Somerset Maugham's more flamboyant works. A political adventurer in the pattern of a Casanova, Cellini, or Tom Paine, he simply did not think or act the way others did; he was brave and adventurous to the point of being impetuous, romantic, and sometimes just plain foolhardy.

As a student in France at the age of twenty, the Polish-born Retinger made friends among leading Paris literati, including André Gide. Shortly before the First World War, he established a Polish bureau in London, where he became a close friend of another Pole, Joseph Conrad. Moving brashly in high circles in Paris after the war, he made powerful enemies and was expelled. From Spain, he made his way to Mexico, where he ingratiated himself with the political opposition and some years later acted as Plutarco Calles's adviser in expropriating the Mexican oil properties of American companies. With the beginning of the Second World War, he allied himself with General Wladyslaw Sikorski, who was Prime Minister of the Polish government in exile, and worked with Sikorski to negotiate an agreement with the Soviet Union that he hoped might free thousands of Poles from Russian domination. That again made him enemies—this time, among Poles who thought any compromise with the Soviets was treason.

After Sikorski's death in July 1943, Retinger arranged to be parachuted into Poland in order to make contact with the Polish underground, brief them on what was happening in London, and reassure them of Allied support. Though Retinger was fifty-seven, in poor health, and with no training in underground activities, he made the drop and worked in Poland with the underground from April 3 to July 26, 1944. In June he suffered an attack of polyneuritis that deprived him of the use of both feet and hands. For weeks, the underground hid him in a private clinic; then, in spite of his paralysis, he was secretly taken out of Poland by a light British plane sent from Bari, Italy, to collect him.

No longer useful to Poland, he turned his efforts to improving relations between Europe and the United States, approaching former Belgian Prime Minister Paul van Zeeland, Paul Rykens, chairman of the board of Unilever, and Prince Bernhard of the Netherlands. To check the deterioration of transatlantic relations, they should, he urged, take the lead in organizing unofficial private meetings between leaders on the two sides of the Atlantic. The Prince organized a small committee on the European side; then in 1953, proposed a corresponding American committee to General Walter Bedell Smith, a fishing companion who had been Eisenhower's chief of staff. Smith, in turn, referred the matter to C. D. Jackson, a vice-president of Time-Life who was then a White House special assistant. Knowing of our Committee for a National Trade Policy, Jackson passed the responsibility for organizing an American committee to John Coleman, who asked me to work with him since it involved problems outside his experience.

Early in 1954, Coleman and I attended a meeting in Paris at the modest apartment of Joseph Retinger's assistant, John Pomian. On entering the room, we found not only Prince Bernhard but also Guy Mollet, former Socialist Prime Minister of the Fourth Republic, and Antoine Pinay, a conservative ex–Prime-Minister—two men who, I thought, would rarely be seen together at a private conference.

As a result of this and later meetings, plans were made for our first session to be held at the Hotel Bilderberg at Oosterbeek, Holland. It was an old-fashioned summer hotel in a wooded park, and, concerned for the security of so many famous guests, the government had established a plainclothes guard behind every tree. Amused by such highly visible precautions, I told the Prince on the second day that I was going stir crazy; we then speculated on the chances of my getting out of the hotel and to the main road without getting shot.

Thereafter, for twenty-seven years, our group met at least once a year at a quiet retreat (usually a tourist hotel off season) for two and a half days of serious discussion. In addition, there were smaller meetings of the Steering Committee, held until recently at Soestdijk Palace, Prince Bernhard's country home. Except during my years in the government, I was a member of the Steering Committee from the formation of the group until 1979. Then the Bilderberg founders turned it over to a younger group, although I remain an adviser. I have attended every Bilderberg meeting with one exception.

The Bilderberg meetings primarily concentrate on a single objective: to try to clear up abrasive problems and attitudes that could poison effective relations between America and Europe. The meetings are attended by the members of a permanent steering committee of Europeans and Americans and by other men and women of achievement and competence specially invited on each occasion. Attendance is limited to roughly eighty persons. Candor is assured by ground rules that forbid anyone to discuss the meetings except in the most general way or, in outside conversation, to attribute expressed views to any individual. At each meeting, there is a political and an economic problem to which the discussion is addressed. All views are taken as individual expressions; no one speaks for his government, his political party, or any other organization.

The real distinction of Bilderberg is not, however, its ground rules but the extraordinary quality of those who attend the meetings. There is hardly a major political figure from Europe or the United States who has not been invited at least once. Of the present or recent heads of government, Helmut Schmidt, the German Chancellor, has attended several times, and among others who have come one or more times have been Valéry Giscard d'Estaing, Harold Wilson, James Callaghan, Edward Heath, Margaret Thatcher, René Pleven, Guy Mollet, Pierre Mendès-France, as well as Prince Philip, Denis Healey, Dean Rusk, Dean Acheson, Henry Kissinger, and Cyrus Vance.

While the meetings bring together men of strong and differing personal views, they also disclose the national characteristics of the nations represented. At first, those on the American side seemed hesitant to say anything critical of their own government or to depart from a general American policy line. Reflecting a different tradition and political system, the British were bound by no such inhibitions, and a highlight of the early meetings was a continuing pyrotechnical debate between Hugh Gaitskell and Robert (now Lord) Boothby that reflected the intense ideological polarization separating the Labour and Conservative parties.

Bilderberg's most valuable achievement has been to provide for the development of easy relations between individuals of disparate backgrounds, eating, drinking, walking—and constantly talking—together in isolated settings. When I joined the State Department in 1961, I was already well acquainted with most Western leaders. Some I knew particularly well, since we had been together at Bilderberg on more than one occasion. I was sensitive to their attitudes and prejudices, while they understood America much better because of exposure to articulate Americans.

The McCarthy Era and Henry Wallace

Though over the years I usually found Washington attractive, I found it quite unpleasant throughout that sordid period when Joseph McCarthy was throwing his venomous tantrums and when Americans, caught up in a pervasive hysteria, viewed their friends and neighbors with morbid suspicion. During my tours in the government both in the early New Deal days and during the war, I had known many of the familiar names in the McCarthy lexicon of abuse—Alger Hiss, Harry White, Lauchlin Currie, and Frank Coe—but my skepticism and aversion to joining collective enterprises had saved me from any personal connection with ambiguous front organizations. Still, that did not prevent others, less lucky but equally blameless, from being caught up in the national paroxysm of fear and hatred.

Working with me in my law firm during much of this time were two remarkable young lawyers: Leon Lipson and Adam Yarmolinsky. From 1950 to 1954 they threw themselves wholeheartedly into the struggle to protect unjustly accused men and women from suffering the traditional fate of innocent bystanders in a town overrun by bandits. Though both Lipson and Yarmolinsky had experienced the intellectual ferment of the immediate postwar years, they had impeccable anti-Communist records and formed a remarkably effective team. Lipson, now a professor at the Yale Law School and a respected expert on Soviet law, displayed extraordinary erudition, diligence, integrity, and generosity as well as a detached view of life. Yarmolinsky, flamboyant, bright, enthusiastic, and equally energetic, found it harder to separate the desirable from the unfeasible or to recognize the trade-offs effectiveness often requires.

Once satisfied that an accused had not engaged in any activities damaging to America, they successfully set out to establish his loyalty and security. They took many cases, doing their preparatory work largely on nights and weekends. Since precise charges were never disclosed, an accused and his counsel carried an excessive burden of defense; it was necessary to search for clues over the entire life span of the accused and to account for all of his activities during his mature, and sometimes his immature, years.

As head of our Washington office, my principal contribution was to keep the way clear for Yarmolinsky and Lipson to run their own legal-aid bureau, though in at least one situation I did play a central role. On October 6, 1951, Joseph Alsop, the newspaper columnist, called to tell me that Henry Wallace had been summoned to testify before the McCarran Subcommittee of the Senate Judiciary Committee (the Subcommittee to Investigate the Administration of the Internal Security Act and Other Internal Security Laws). The Committee's inquiry was directed primarily at a trip Wallace had taken, at President Roosevelt's request, to Mongolia and Siberia in 1944, where he had been accompanied by such expert advisers as Owen Lattimore and John Carter Vincent, both of whom were in 1951 being accused—quite unjustly—of Communist sympathies. Alsop had met the group in Kunming and had gone along for part of the trip.

Though Alsop had no sympathy for Wallace, he was outraged that

McCarran was rewriting history so grotesquely. He therefore insisted on testifying himself, though he recognized that it would expose him to considerable risk since his acerbic pen had made him many enemies. He was deeply concerned for Wallace, who, unless represented by an experienced lawyer, would, Alsop said, "be slaughtered." Neither my partners nor I were anxious to get mixed up in Wallace's affairs, since we thought him a naïve and muddled man, and normally, I would have refused to represent an individual touched by so much folly. But when Alsop claimed to have tried and been turned down by "every competent lawyer in town," his defense became irresistibly attractive to me; no matter how foolish Wallace may have been, he was entitled to counsel.

Wallace's trip to Mongolia and Siberia had been a curious enterprise. On the advice of Lauchlin Currie (who was later attacked for Communist sympathies), he had taken Owen Lattimore. He had also wanted to take Colonel Philip Faymenville, who had handled Lend-Lease matters in the Soviet Union, but General Marshall vetoed the proposal with the edict that "Faymenville was a representative of the Russians, not of the United States"; the FBI, he said, had a large file on Faymenville.[1] But Wallace did take along a memorandum from Alger Hiss, which he described as "excellent."[2]

Roosevelt's concept of the trip was that Vice-President Wallace, "as an agricultural expert, should observe the ways of life in Siberia, Outer Mongolia and China, and reach some conclusions about how to minimize sources of conflict between China and the Soviet Union." He was also to urge "Chiang Kai-shek to arrange a *modus operandi* with the Chinese Communists" that would assure a more vigorous pursuit of "the war against Japan, and to take steps to control inflation in China."[3]

In spite of my initial hesitation about representing Wallace, I liked the man. I found him modest, compassionate, and gentle, but the obstinacy of his idealism so impelled him to reject all troubling realities that he seemed quite incapable of comprehending his own predicament. He had drafted a statement he proposed to make to the Committee that consisted largely of a frontal attack, calling the Committee members "faceless men" and impugning their motives. His description of his trip to Mongolia and Siberia and his proposed comments on the Russians would, in the climate of the time, have been a disaster.

Even after seven years, Wallace seemed only partly aware of what had happened to him. President Roosevelt had carefully timed Wallace's trip—from early May to the second week in July—to bring him back to the United States only nine days before the Democratic Convention. There he found, presumably to his astonishment, that Roosevelt was dropping him as his Vice-Presidential candidate in favor of Harry Truman. When the President had first proposed the trip, Wallace had, so he told me, replied that he would go only if it served a serious purpose, to which, as he recounted it, the President had replied, "Oh, it will be very useful. I think you ought to see a lot of Siberia." When Wallace told me this in his solemn, trusting fashion, I found it easy to imagine Roosevelt's glee after Wallace had left the room. Did he, as I can imagine it, report to his close confidants: "I've just sent Henry to Siberia and told him to stay there a long time and—the poor dope—he doesn't know what's happening to him?"

In preparing for the Committee hearing, Wallace and I had a long and, I regret, often acrimonious struggle, during which I threatened several times to quit. Finally, I persuaded him to accept my draft statement: a straightforward account of his trip and a factual refutation of the charges made against him. I subjected him to long hours of interrogation—"horseshedding," as lawyers call it—to keep him from blundering onto dangerous terrain.

Alsop led off before the Committee with his own statement, countering aggressive questions with courage and bravura. The room was filled with fanatical McCarthyites, principally old women exuding venom and muttering virulent curses. They were, I thought, spiritual descendants of Madame La Farge and those other scabrous crones who watched the tumbrels roll by. Wallace then followed, stumbling through his testimony without too much breakage, and I was relieved that the long hours of coaching had paid off.

The "Chunnel" Project

My law practice was made not merely tolerable but stimulating by unusual and sometimes bizarre projects that occasionally came my way. Many—in fact, most—were not worth pursuing (at least not worth it to me), and I sent the potential clients elsewhere, but one matter that stirred my imagination was the project for a tunnel under the English Channel—the "Chunnel," as it came to be called—which had been periodically proposed ever since 1802.

What had revived that ancient project once again was the *mal de mer* of two French sisters in 1956. The girls, members of a branch of the wealthy Schlumberger family, then living in New York, were on a holiday in France with their young husbands, Frank Davidson, an American lawyer, and Arnaud de Vitry, a Frenchman with an engineering background who had attended the Harvard Business School. Lamenting their uneasy crossing, one of the wives ruefully remarked that the two husbands should build a Channel tunnel. Reacting to this obvious logic, they founded a company called Technical Studies, which retained me as an adviser. I left for Europe on June 9, 1956, to assist in the jockeying for position then under way.

As a result of much maneuvering, a combined company was finally formed, to be owned by a French group comprising the French Railways and the French Rothschild interests, the British Channel Tunnel Company, and Technical Studies. It established a study group with a steering committee consisting of three representatives each for the three large holders and one representative for Technical Studies. I normally played that role. The Steering Committee was confronted with complex technical and financial problems. Because of ventilation requirements, an automobile tunnel was ruled out as uneconomic. More feasible was a railroad tunnel with facilities for rapidly loading automobiles on flatbed carriages. Should the tunnel be built by boring or by use of submerged tubes? Would not a bridge be more feasible, or, perhaps, a hybrid—half-bridge, half-tunnel? Several great engineering firms made tentative proposals, each trying to demonstrate the advantages of its own method.

Though I thought the logic of the tunnel compelling—particularly after the United Kingdom joined the Common Market—British opposition proved formidable. In a modern world of nuclear bombing, guided missiles, and supersonic planes, nothing seemed sillier than the announcement of Field Marshal Lord Montgomery on Trafalgar Day, 1957, that he opposed the tunnel because "strategically, it would weaken us." "Why give up one of our greatest assets, our island home," he asked rhetorically, "and make things easier for our enemies?" A newspaper cartoon in London promptly showed Napoleon's legions fiercely emerging from the British end of the tunnel accoutered with menacing muskets and the banners of Austerlitz.

When I entered the government in 1961, I lost track of the day-to-day maneuvering on the tunnel. Although many people now believe that the tunnel has become obsolete, I am confident that it will, sooner or later, be built, simply because the logic *is* so compelling. With Britain a member of the European Economic Community, it cannot afford to hold aloof from the Continent. But the tunnel will be built only when enough Englishmen grow tired of waiting for a quieter sea for the Hovercraft, or for the fog to clear so the planes can fly, or for French air controllers to cease sadistically venting their grievances by grounding the airlines. Then—but only then—will governments recognize the stupidity of resisting a land link. I hope to be on the first train to emerge at Sangatte.

PART IV

Adlai Stevenson and Politics

9. Stevenson

I saw little of Adlai Stevenson between December 1944, when we parted in Europe, and the early 1950s, but I heard that he had finally decided to run for Governor of Illinois. Though I sent Adlai a campaign contribution, I did not take his chances seriously. He was, as I saw it, quite unsuited to rough and tumble Illinois politics—but he could only find that out by trying. Thus I thought of his campaign as a therapeutic exercise to purge him of political fantasies.

Stevenson's talents were, I then thought, more social than political, and I did not then recognize how effectively his social charm could be converted into political charisma. In a small group he emanated warmth and bubbling humor. He paid attention to human beings and would listen patiently and sympathetically to their ills and complaints. Though patrician in his view of society, he treated everyone—whether a taxi driver, bus boy, or head of state—with bantering courtesy, and he was a master of the small endearing gesture. Once, when Ruth was standing next to him during a campaign, someone handed him an ice cream cone. Immediately he sought out a small boy in the crowd, saying, "Look at my contours, you need this worse than I."

Even when depressed or upset about some incident, Adlai would express his discontent with a throwaway line or a comic aside that disparaged either himself or some friend or acquaintance who had annoyed or disappointed him. When tired or disconsolate he could on occasion be snide about even good friends but he did not mean it; he was not vindictive, and his moods changed quickly.

For me, his greatest charm was his tolerant view of the world as essentially a comic theater, and he displayed a cynical irreverence. Once, when we were practicing law together, he went to New York to meet with a group of investment bankers. "Though it was a bitterly cold day," he reported later, "greed ran down their faces like sweat." Despite his engaging cynicism, he could speak in eloquent—often slightly purple— terms of the world predicament, the dangers of a nuclear disaster, and particularly the plight of poor people in the poor nations (though I sometimes thought his elegantly expressed sympathy rather an abstraction). He certainly liked the amenities of life—good food, pleasant surroundings, and, most of all, literate conversation. The last was particularly important to him, since, so far as I could see, he read few books and shaped his opinions largely from the comments and suggestions of men and women he respected. At a time when letter writing had become almost a lost art, Adlai constantly used it as a form of conversation.

He was at his best as host in his Libertyville home, which he loved. A comfortable but not elaborate house, it occupied a few acres northwest of Chicago—or, more accurately, southwest of Libertyville, the haven of Chicago's rich. He had the normal equipment of any good farmer of the area: a tennis court, a swimming pool, a horse or two, and a few sheep. His land was totally flat—as was true of the whole region, where a ten-foot elevation was regarded as a hill. Before he became Governor, he and his wife, Ellen, lived a highly social life; she was vivacious and pretty in a pixyish way and at parties was more the center of attention than he. But once Stevenson was Governor and the spotlight shifted to him, she proved quite unwilling to play a supporting role. She refused to leave her circle of like-minded friends for what she apparently regarded as the parochial society of Springfield, Illinois, and became not only embittered but, ultimately, psychotic. Upon Adlai's election, she lapsed into a kind of deliberately obtrusive slatternliness, to the point that, when she and Adlai came to Washington for Eisenhower's inauguration, Ruth and I were shocked by the remarkable change in her appearance and demeanor. She was overweight, dismayingly unkempt, and seemed to flaunt her ineffable boredom and discontent.

I had approached election night in 1948 with distaste and apprehension. The omens were not good for Democrats. Dewey was, I thought, both arrogant and petty, but, though I did not like him, he seemed destined to win: I did not doubt the experts who—even more wrong than usual—predicted that a Dewey landslide would sweep away Democratic candidates all across the nation. On election night, I dined with business acquaintances in New York, sitting up till midnight to listen to the returns. Truman was running better than we expected, but I did not think his chances serious and I went to bed believing that Dewey would be President. The one bright surprise of the evening was a radio report that Stevenson had won in Illinois.

Adlai Plays Hamlet

During the next three years, I saw Adlai only once or twice, although we exchanged an occasional message. On December 11, 1951, I wrote him to apologize for having missed him during his last two visits because I was continuing to "lead the life of an overseas commuter."

Thus, I was not prepared for a visit early in January 1952 from Mrs. Violet Gunther, the political secretary of the Americans for Democratic Action. Did I think that Stevenson would be available to run for President? I told her I had never discussed the question with him, but he was clearly well qualified. There followed a visit with James Loeb, Jr., an assistant to the White House Special Counsel, and a later talk with David Lloyd, also an assistant to the Special Counsel. I had worked with Lloyd during the war and he had traveled with Stevenson during a postwar trip to Italy for the Foreign Economic Administration to survey emergency economic and reconstruction needs.

Lloyd and Loeb were, they said, approaching me with the knowledge of Charles Murphy, then Special Counsel to the President, but without specific Presidential authorization. I do not recall how often we met after that, but I was soon told that President Truman wanted to talk with Stevenson—would I arrange a visit to Washington?

I found Adlai stonily resistant. He had just announced his candidacy for a second term as Governor of Illinois. What did I think he was—"the garden variety of opportunistic pol who charged off looking for a better pasture whenever he heard a distant bell"? During his first four years, he had, he said, started many projects and he intended to finish them; to walk out now would be "bad faith" to his supporters. There was much more of the same—scornful rejection poured out in exasperated phrases. But I had no intention of letting him off easily, and we talked on and on. Several further conversations followed before he grumpily conceded that he could not ignore a "command from Buckingham Palace" and, besides, he did have some official business in Washington. After the Centralia Mine disaster in 1947, he had taken a lead in seeking improved mine safety legislation and now he needed to discuss the question with Secretary of the Interior Oscar Chapman and John L. Lewis, the formidable head of the United Mine Workers. Truman had made clear, I told him, that he would be offended if a Democratic governor came to Washington without calling on him.

On Tuesday morning, January 22, Stevenson was to fly to Washington without announcing his destination and meet with John L. Lewis. He would then come to my home, and, after dinner, I would take him to Blair House, where President Truman was living during the renovation of the White House. Stevenson was late for dinner, and, just before he arrived, Carleton Kent, of the Chicago *Sun-Times*'s Washington bureau, called me. He knew Adlai would be dining with me that night and wanted him to return the call. When Adlai finally arrived, breathless and complaining, he was upset at the message from Kent. "Why can't I do anything without some damn fool leaking it?" "You're lucky," I replied, "that the whole world doesn't know where you are, since your face is on the cover of *Time* that hit the stands yesterday."

During dinner, Adlai rehearsed the coming interview. How could he explain to President Truman, without showing disrespect for the office of the Presidency, that he wished to remain Governor of Illinois? How could he make it clear to Truman that he was not going to run? To seek the Presidency now would be to break faith with the people of Illinois. He had been elected Governor by Republicans as well as Democrats and he would not turn his back on his friends—referring principally to his Lake Forest neighbors—who had worked hard for him.

Already Adlai was beginning to think of himself in the third person. Stevenson the politician was bound by certain standards—*noblesse oblige*—that ruled out the practices of the ordinary "pol." Though pols fascinated him (he often expressed amused admiration and affection for the most cynical), he looked on them with aristocratic condescension.

I tried to get him to promise that if Truman asked him to run, he would not flatly reject the idea. The United States was in a critical period. Taft might well be the Republican nominee, and we desperately needed a President with a broad view of the world who could carry on the grand enterprises begun in the postwar years. I continued on this theme as I drove him to Blair House but with a sinking feeling that I was losing the struggle. When we reached the police barricades on Pennsylvania Avenue, the Secret Service guard blocked the way. Who was this small, dumpy man who arrived in my old Chevrolet? Only after telephoning back and forth did they grudgingly open the barricade.

I told Ruth when I reached home that the interview then in progress would prove disastrous. Truman—brusque and decisive—would never understand Stevenson's subtle rendition of Prince Hamlet. My prediction seemed confirmed when Adlai called me the next morning to say he had "made a hash" of the meeting but, in any event "had put a stop to all the nonsense." He had, he said, told the President "very bluntly" that he did not wish to run. He knew Truman could not understand his reluctance and would think he was afraid to take on a hard fight. At one point, Truman had made a comment that I found particularly endearing: "Adlai, if a knucklehead like me can be President and not do too badly, think what a really educated smart guy like you could do in the job." Stevenson continued in a mood of lamentation. He repeated that he had "made a hash" of the talk and that the President probably thought him an idiot. Truman, he felt sure, had written him off as hopeless; the only advantage was that the interview had definitely put an end to the question of his Presidential candidacy.

But, as morning wore on, I found the issue far from closed. The newspapers had got wind of the fact that Stevenson had seen the President and, with the coincidental appearance of the *Time* cover story, he was clearly the man of the hour. Later that day, I lunched with Stevenson, David Lloyd, and Jim Loeb. To my surprise, Adlai seemed much less negative about his meeting with Truman than he had reported to me. He seemed genuinely interested in the possibility of running, asking a number of questions about his prospects for the Presidency and the electoral mechanics—the dates of the primaries and the amount of money that would have to be raised.

After Stevenson had left for Springfield, I remained in a quandary. Did he want to be drafted? Could an honest draft ever occur? Was he afraid of losing? After all, he had remarked to me on the way to Blair House, "I'll be damned if I want to be a caretaker for the party. If Eisenhower runs, nobody can beat him. And anyway, wouldn't Eisenhower make a pretty good President? There's a hell of a lot of truth in the need for a change."

He was not arguing with me so much as with himself. My contribution to his inner debate was to point out our country's unhappy past experience with generals as Presidents. Stevenson's background, on the other hand, was unparalleled; his Middle-Western origin gave him a feeling for the country uncontaminated by the winds blowing from either Europe or Asia. His international experience made him sensitive to those winds and to the great forces then churning in the world. His experience as a practicing lawyer had given him a feel for the private sector, and during his tours in Washington he had gained an inside view of the bureaucracy. He had run successfully for elected office and demonstrated his administrative capacities as the Governor of one of our most important states. What better qualifications could anyone have? However he felt about it, I told him, I was going to make him better known. Rather to my surprise, he did not veto the idea but merely responded, "Well, don't make it appear I'm building myself up."

That was the *laissez-passer* I needed to set up a "Stevenson information center" in my Washington office, known by the code name Project Wintergreen, after the leading character in "Of Thee I Sing." I raised several thousand dollars and hired a young journalist, Libby Donahue, and a public relations man, Allen Harris, to collect Stevenson material and help feed it to the press. At a suggestion from Arthur Schlesinger, I took my old friend Bernard De Voto with me to Springfield, where we spent several days in the Governor's mansion. De Voto's next "Easy Chair" column in *Harper's* was an eloquent piece entitled, "Stevenson and the Independent Voter." Allen Harris assembled an article for *Look Maga-*

zine and spent some time in Springfield. Together, Harris and Donahue prepared a detailed brochure about Stevenson for national distribution. I wrote Stevenson to tell him about this and many other things on February 20, asking him if he wanted me to desist.

The next day, Stevenson wrote that he had heard "some alarming reports about the activities of Mr. Harris with various magazines in the East" and that there was confusion among publishers "as to whether or not he is my spokesman, and I hope you can restrain him." Still, since he did not explicitly forbid my efforts, we went ahead full steam, though I wrote Stevenson that "to be on the safe side, I have put Harris in a corner and covered him with a rug." I enclosed the brochure we were sending to editors of major friendly papers throughout the country, adding that "if this whole idea appalls you, please let me know and I shall behave accordingly." Again Stevenson interposed no veto, merely replying on February 27 that "I have your letter and have marked it well. I am sorely troubled. My heart is here and my head is not far behind. We will see."

Meanwhile, I concentrated on trying to keep Stevenson from foreclosing the future, telephoning whenever I heard a rumor that he was about to issue a categorical renunciation. We haggled over the issue interminably but with no new ideas or fresh phrasing on either side. Whenever his resistance seemed to be hardening, I would get him to promise to make no negative public statement until I could fly out to Springfield, which I usually did the following day.

I was also keeping in touch with Charles Murphy and David Lloyd, who reported to me that Truman was becoming increasingly impatient. In my letter of February 20, I had advised Stevenson to arrange a secret conversation with the President about mid-March, contending that he owed Truman another talk. That meeting, which took place on March 4, proved even more negative than the previous one. Still, Stevenson cooperated with my publicity build-up, sending me, on March 10, a large file of family photographs. On March 14, Jim Loeb told me that the President wanted Stevenson to have an in-depth talk with Charles Murphy. I tracked Adlai down in Cambridge, Massachusetts. He was planning to fly directly to Florida with his youngest son, John Fell, but, after noisily complaining, agreed to travel by way of Washington. To avoid publicity, he even bought an airline ticket under an assumed name. He and his son spent the night at my house. Jim Loeb joined us for dinner, after which my youngest son took John Fell to the movies while Charles Murphy came by for a late talk.

It was a dismal evening. Stevenson was more obdurate than ever, insisting that he did not want to run and even going out of his way to attack Truman's liberal policies, as though wishing not only to distance himself from the President but also to compel Truman to write him off on ideological grounds. He did not, he asserted, like the idea of public housing. Nor did he favor repealing the Taft-Hartley Labor Law; he wished merely to amend it. Were he President, he would hold firm on stabilization issues; as a result, the country would be tied up with strikes. He regarded education as a state, not a federal, problem; only if the states failed to act adequately should the federal government lend help. He was opposed to "socialized medicine" and the Brannan Plan for agriculture. He thought the states should be responsible for their own civil rights policies and that the federal government ought not to "put the South completely over a barrel." The national debt was appalling; he was an apostle of economy. Reflecting on what he later called the "mess in Washington," he stated vehemently that wrongdoers should not only be fired from the government but also prosecuted. Only on the issue of foreign policy did he seem to approve of what Truman was doing. Yet he did not think he himself could do better; he would, he said, be a "bad candidate and a poor President."

I sat through the long, grim evening with increasing hopelessness, while Charles Murphy, a dedicated Fair Dealer deeply devoted to Truman, cringed at Adlai's blasphemies. Why was Adlai so determined to throw away his chances? Exasperated by his aggressive negativism, I drank too much Scotch to compensate for my chagrin and commemorated a distasteful evening by a repellent hangover.

On the plane to Florida, Adlai wrote Ruth a touching note. As the plane approached Jacksonville, "the miseries," he wrote, were "melting away." Yet the noose still felt uncomfortably tight, and he wished he could see "where the paths of self-interest and family interest converged with paths of duty." Then he added as a postscript: "George's interest and confidence in me is one of the most compelling reasons why I have not taken myself out of this situation conclusively and long before this!"

Three days later, Stevenson wrote Charles Murphy from Florida, listing all the reasons why he did not wish to be a candidate, including his misgivings about "his strength, wisdom, and humility to point the way to coexistence with a ruthless, inscrutable, and equal power in the world." Then he, for the first time, openly revealed his tactical thinking: "Another four years as Governor of my beloved Illinois, and many of these obstacles will have vanished. As a more seasoned politician, with my work in Illinois behind me, creditably, pray God, I might well be ready and even eager to seek the Presidency, if I then had anything desirable to offer."

"I had," he wrote Murphy, been "under the distinct impression from my last visit with the President that, given my Illinois situation, he was quite reconciled to run again himself. If I misunderstood him, or that is no longer the case and the question is whether I would accept the nomination at Chicago and then do my level best to win the election, I should like to know it." If the President has decided not to run, he wrote, "and my decision *is* affirmative, I suppose in sincerity and good conscience I should say publicly and *before* he announces his decision not to run (if such *is* his decision) that all I want is to carry on my work in Illinois; that I have no other ambition, desire or purpose; that I will not seek the nomination; that if my party should nominate me anyway I would accept proudly and prayerfully, of course."[1] The sentence continued, "as should any American in good health with convictions about this tormented world."[2] He was "confident that the people of Illinois would release [him] for a larger assignment that [he] did not seek." Finally, he wrote about his possible nomination: "Now if you have waded this deep and the President should feel that this offers a plausible solution, I should of course like to know so that I can reach a final decision and inform him at whatever time he prescribes."[3]

Murphy, as I later learned, wrote to Adlai: President Truman was "much impressed by what you had to say—impressed in the sense that it confirmed and strengthened the high regard he already had for you. . . . He said that he would like to think the matter over for a few days, and would then talk to me about it again."[4] Murphy then made clear that, in spite of Stevenson's strong rejection of Truman's liberal policies, the President was personally still eager for Stevenson to run.

Launching a Candidate

On Saturday, March 29, 1952, Stevenson came to Washington to appear on "Meet the Press." At the Jefferson-Jackson Day dinner the night before, Truman was expected to announce his own decision about a second term. When Truman flatly announced that he would not run again, the photographers and reporters promptly converged on Stevenson. I went from the dinner to the Metropolitan Club to talk with Adlai about his "Meet the Press" appearance, since I feared he might use the occasion to take himself categorically out of the race. During the television program—to my great relief—he adroitly avoided being forced into a "General Sherman" statement. Moreover, he did not take the same strong line against liberal legislation he had taken during the meeting with Murphy.

That night, Stevenson and I dined with Walter Lippmann, who told Adlai, "I hope you don't run, because you can't possibly beat such a national hero as Eisenhower." To my surprise, Stevenson reacted sharply and indignantly: "What do you mean? Why are you sure I can't beat Eisenhower?" The next morning, Lippmann called me, somewhat upset. "Why did Adlai flare up when we discussed his running? I tried to discourage him because I like both Ike and him, but I think the country needs a change of parties. I'd be put to a painful choice if they both ran." (Later, when Adlai was in the early stages of the campaign, Helen Lippmann sent me a check for $1000. It was the only time, she explained, that the Lippmanns had ever broken their practice of remaining above the battle.)

Several days later, I asked Arthur Schlesinger and Bernard De Voto to prepare a draft statement to launch Stevenson's Presidential candidacy. The pace of events rapidly quickened. A committee of students and faculty members at Yale got in touch with me and then sent Stevenson a telegram asking him to run. My own mail was crowded with letters advising me that I must make Stevenson take a more affirmative position—as though I could possibly control him.

Why was Stevenson so reluctant? Largely, I think, because he thought he could not beat Eisenhower. If it had been clear that Taft would be nominated, he would have taken a different line. He could beat Taft and would feel a duty to do so, since Taft symbolized the Middle-Western isolationism against which he had long fought. But Eisenhower was an internationalist and, in Stevenson's view, a decent man who might improve the moral tone of the White House. He was affronted by the indifferent morality and untidiness of the Truman Administration and was frantic to distance himself from Truman and the messiness, which, as he repeatedly told me, proved that the Democrats had been too long in power. "Twenty years," he said, "is enough for either party." He felt deeply sentimental about Illinois, and he abhorred a partisan struggle that might set him at cross purposes with his Lake Forest friends, who had voted for him as a state governor but would vote Republican in a national election. In addition, he lived under the persistent threat of personal attack, since Ellen, now divorced, was capable of unlimited malice. Finally, he was repelled by the stultifying routine of campaigning. Though he loved making carefully crafted speeches, he hated the constant repetition of banalities, the vacuous irrelevance of campaign issues, and the handshaking, posturing, and babykissing that the public had learned to expect of a candidate. Finally, the vast expenditures involved in campaigning offended the parsimonious instincts of a Calvinist Scot; he loathed the whole process of political fund raising.

On April 16, he issued a statement that, he maintained, would definitively make clear his position. It contained a critical sentence: "In view of my prior commitment to run for Governor and my desire and the desire of many who have given me their help and confidence in our unfinished work in Illinois, I could not accept the nomination for any other office this summer." I found Jesuitical comfort in the fact that he had used the word "could" instead of "would." He well knew the difference between "cannot," which was a simple statement of how he then saw his position, and "will not," which would have denoted a firm decision not to accept in any circumstances. He liked to play with linguistic nuances, and it later appeared that this precise choice of words was not unintentional. The original draft statement prepared by Carl McGowan had read: "I cannot and will not accept the nomination." Stevenson had changed that to "I cannot, in good conscience, accept"; he later deleted the phrase "in good conscience."

I had deep affection for Stevenson, and I admired his contempt for the opportunism that marks most politicians. Yet I did not like the fact that he constantly overdramatized his own predicament—portraying himself as a hero beset by temptations, while at the same time indulging in a self-disparagement that was tinged with artifice. I recall once returning a draft letter he had shown me with the comment: "Why go out of your way to diminish yourself with that self-deprecatory horseshit when you know you don't believe it?" To which he answered with a rueful smile, "Oh, leave it in. I think it's disarming, don't you?"

That Stevenson was sincerely torn between a tempting chance to become President and the desire to avoid any appearance of personal ambition I have no doubt. But his constant harping on the Presidency as an "ordeal" seemed to me overdone. Thus, when he flawed his otherwise brilliant acceptance speech with the words "I have asked the merciful Father—the Father of us all—to let this cup pass from me," I was horrified; it seemed both self-pitying and presumptuous (though I could not help but recall that it was the same figure of speech my old friend Léon Blum had used when the Popular Front's victory in 1936 made him Prime Minister). Blum, however, had had more reason to allude to the cup; in Stevenson's case it was one of his rare gaucheries. The responsibilities of the Presidency were indubitably a heavy burden, but during the life of our nation, the job had been filled by many unexceptional men, and Stevenson was certainly far better prepared and equipped than most of them had been. As for the self-sacrifice involved, that seemed a bromidic emphasis for a man who had spent all of his life preparing for public service.

Meanwhile, events were moving ineluctably toward a draft that—I am convinced—he saw as the solution to his predicament. It would absolve him from the charge that he was Truman's hand-picked candidate or had sought the nomination; even more important, it would end his private torment at the thought of entering a contest he might lose because the timing was askew. The Democrats had worn out their welcome in the White House; they had lost energy and imagination—witness the tawdriness and petty scandals of the Truman Administration. Since, in the pervasive mood of public disenchantment, no Democrat could beat a national hero like Eisenhower, why not let some eager aspirant—Alben W. Barkley or Estes Kefauver—try and fail? Four years in the wilderness might rejuvenate the party; a military President would almost certainly disappoint the exorbitant expectations he was arousing, while time would diminish the luster of Ike's wartime achievements. After a Republican first term, Adlai believed the country might be in a proper mood for a Democratic Second Coming; if, meanwhile, he had done a good job in Illinois—as he was sure he would—he might well be what the hour required. But I told him: "Does anyone remember General Boulanger except as a vain and silly ass who waited too long? Of course, it's too bad opportunity has come prematurely, but *tant pis.* History has bad manners; it won't arrange itself to suit your personal convenience."

He was, I felt sure, deluding himself to think he could wait four years. Barring accident, Eisenhower would almost certainly run for a second term, and history had shown that, except during periods of major catastrophe, an incumbent President is only rarely upset. Since Eisenhower was as yet untested in national politics, it was by no means certain that he would sweep the country; besides, Taft might be nominated. All this I argued with conviction; few people, I said, had been offered the opportunity that now lay open to Stevenson and if he did not walk through the door resolutely, it would close in his face—if not with a bang, at least with a click as the bolt slid into place.

The Nomination

In the beginning, I had believed an uncontrived draft impossible—ruled out by our American political experience. But toward the middle of March I became convinced that, unless Adlai made a definitive "General Sherman" statement, the mounting tide of opinion within the party would lead to his nomination in July. Still, I had moments of trepidation during conversations with professionals in the party who no longer hid their mounting impatience. Adlai's ambiguous conduct was lending substance to the charge that he could not make up his mind, and America needed to be led by a man of decision. "To govern," as Mendès-France was fond of saying, "is to choose."

Meanwhile, Stevenson was being vigorously promoted by a mixed bag of enthusiasts—largely academics and young lawyers, but with a tempering of Southern conservatives—while the pols, such as Mayor Daley of Chicago, Mayor Dave Lawrence of Pittsburgh, and Jack Arvey, were under increasing pressure to declare support for a candidate who, they could be sure, would not back out at the last moment. Stevenson seemed to be enjoying their discomfort. I think he knew that, other than issuing a statement of categorical withdrawal, he could do little to stop the buildup of sentiment, since he offered the Democratic party its only hope against Eisenhower. The small impetus added by Stevenson's friends, including my own efforts, did not, I think, play a critical role in the outcome. Much more important was the fact that, while Stevenson incessantly denied his candidacy, he continued to make—in a wider national setting—speeches that distinguished him from what he referred to as "the current year's crop of political cattle—far from blue-ribbon quality." He continued to demur, however, reveling in the drama of inner struggle: visibly gratified as more and more people urged him to run, called him the indispensable man, and insisted that duty required him to assume the burdens of the Presidency. The more he resisted, the more emotional were the exhortations.

Adlai was more pleased by the praise of the literate than by massive outbursts from those deaf to the eloquence of his thought and expression. He liked particularly to be fussed over by his many female admirers, which sometimes proved a serious handicap. Candidates are invariably surrounded by hangers-on who, if not sycophants, still feel obliged to maintain their tiger's morale, and Adlai was exceptionally vulnerable to uncritical praise and encouragement. He suffered from not having a wife (the institutionalized candid friend). No one was waiting to tell him, after an inept action or uninspired speech; "Well, you were really not up to standard this evening." Instead, he basked in constant encomiums from a bevy of acolytes who loved him dearly and treated him as the long-awaited Messiah; increasingly, he tended to make statements that pleased his admirers but did not advance his more mundane objectives.

During the convention, I took no part in the rounding up of delegates—a task for which I had neither talent nor inclination. Seated among the press corps, I listened to Stevenson's memorable welcoming speech. As the applause grew louder, Joe Alsop climbed onto the chair next to me, waving and shouting, "My God, I would never have believed it, a Brahman intellectual—and they're eating out of his hand." The next day I struggled with the draft of an acceptance speech that I handed to Stevenson's assistant, William Blair, at Blair's family's residence, where Stevenson had gone to ground. (None of my draft was used.) Though the house was staked out by waiting newspaper reporters and heavily guarded by the police, the atmosphere inside seemed strangely hushed—with the same sense of reverence but none of the easy camaraderie of a wake.

The Campaign Begins

Once the convention was concluded, Ruth and I returned to Washington, where I wrote Stevenson a letter offering my services. Before receiving it, he telephoned to ask that I lend a hand to his old friends "Dutch" Smith and Jane Dick in Chicago, who were endeavoring to put together a committee of volunteers outside the regular campaign structure. Dutch Smith had been chairman of the Stevenson for Governor Committee, in which Jane Dick had played a leading role, and they understandably viewed their new enterprise in the same terms as the state committee—merely expanded to a national scale. Such a transformation could not be done literally, however, since a large number of the leaders of the state committee were Republicans who, though supporting Adlai when the issues were local, still believed God wanted a Republican as President.

After several long discussions, the three of us agreed to establish the "Volunteers for Stevenson." (Eisenhower's people had already preempted the "Citizen" name.) Dutch Smith was to be Chairman of the Volunteers and Jane Dick, Co-chairman, while I would have the title of Executive Director. We had one meeting with Stevenson at Springfield and then went to work. Since political organizing was largely a task for the regular Stevenson Campaign Committee and the Democratic National Committee working with local Democratic party leaders throughout the country, I started looking for a finance chairman. Fund raising was, as I saw it, the prime function of the Volunteers. But since the rich and well-placed were, almost by definition, committed to Eisenhower, I had difficulty finding a finance chairman. Eventually someone mentioned Roger L. Stevens, who had recently bought and sold the Empire State Building. He was, I was told, both shrewd and independent. I might possibly persuade him to take the job.

I called Stevens and arranged to meet him in New York City. He was candid and tough-minded, a self-made millionaire but one who did not worship money and disdained the conventional wisdom. The fact that he loved the theater and was a leading theatrical producer added to his charm, yet he was a man with no false pretensions and I liked him immediately. Though inexperienced in politics, he would, I felt sure, add strength to our effort. It proved a brilliant choice; Stevens was resourceful, energetic, and an engaging companion. He was on the way to carving out a commanding place for himself in the New York theater world, and he would years later lead the Kennedy Center in Washington toward cultural eminence.

The New Factor of Television

Wilson Wyatt, an able and personable Louisville lawyer who had in his mid-thirties been mayor of Louisville, became Stevenson's personal campaign manager. He and I agreed that the Volunteers should concentrate on raising funds for Stevenson's television appearances—a task of transcendent importance, since the 1952 campaign was the first in which television was extensively used. During the 1948 campaign, Dewey and Truman campaigned in a manner little changed from the days of Roosevelt, with whistle stops, set speeches to large city audiences, and the customary handshaking and babykissing—supplemented to a limited degree by radio. At the time of the Truman-Dewey campaign, there had been only 345,000 television sets in the United States; by 1952, the number had risen almost fifty times—to 17 million. (It was to increase almost twice again by 1956.) Clearly, in Marshall McLuhan's phrase, the medium had become the message.

We were fortunate that our campaign staff was not taken over by television experts and that the public was not yet accustomed to the contemptuous treatment they later came to accept from political candidates. We took it for granted that Americans had an attention span sufficiently long to absorb rational arguments. The strength of our position, as we saw it, derived from the fact that Stevenson's positions were not only sounder than Eisenhower's but also far more eloquently expressed.

Adlai sincerely believed that a campaign should be used for public education; so we planned a coherent series of speeches, each concerned with a single relevant issue. Television, of course, imposed some constraint on Adlai's oratory, since each speech had to be packed into twenty-seven minutes. But the saturation spot-campaigns that were to reduce Presidential contests to the level of mouthwash merchandising had not yet been devised.

Anatomy of Speech Writing

In retrospect, I am sure we overestimated the impact of Stevenson's speeches. They provided a pleasurable experience, deeply moving to anyone responsive to the cadence and melody of fine writing, but they were not always effective advocacy. Adlai honed and polished words, sentences, and paragraphs, but he paid little attention to structure. He hated to concentrate on a single theme; instead, he would frequently clutter his speeches with unrelated subjects, thus diffusing the overall effect. I struggled with him often over this practice. He was, I assured him, a "gifted poet" but a "lousy architect." While his speeches left a pleasant glow and a sense of momentary uplift, they did not persuade his audience that he knew how to deal with particular problems. By contrast, Eisenhower's far more banal speeches, though leaden and delivered without sensitivity to the nuances of language, almost always set forth a "five-point" or a "seven-point" program, or some similar enunciation of proposed actions. It did not matter if those programs were empty of meaning, they gave the impression that Ike knew exactly how he would resolve all the nation's troubles.

Adlai rejected the practice with a shudder; to list specific projected actions was, in his view, not only casuistical but also an intrusion on the beautiful music of words that he found most gratifying. Television was not a medium well suited to Adlai's style; again, through no fault of his own, he was a victim of unlucky timing. Had he been running four years earlier, when only radio was available, he would have done much better. But he was physically unimpressive—short and with what he called a "receding hairline"—and had no "normal" speaking pace. He would start a speech too slowly, then realize that he might run over his time and abruptly speed up, or he would start speaking too quickly and abruptly slow down. Though we carefully computed the length of each written speech, he failed more often than not to finish on time, thus flawing the effect of his carefully crafted perorations. After a while, the problem of finishing within the required twenty-seven minutes became a phobia that added a sense of the precarious to every appearance.

Nor did television adequately project his personality. Reading his speeches from manuscript, he often failed to look at the camera, inclining his head so that the lights beat glaringly on his shining forehead, which grew more obtrusive as the hairline receded. In addition, he had a habit that suggested a tic: punctuating his comments by flashing on and off a quick smile, which conveyed the unfortunate impression of artificiality and even insincerity. Nevertheless, as we listened to the speeches we felt enormously proud. Our candidate had "class"; he was not a plodding five-star general uttering pedestrian language written by some journalistic hack with all the grace of a gun carriage being hauled across cobblestones; he was a man of culture and intellect seeking not only to educate the country but also to elevate its taste.

In making sure we could pay for the necessary television and radio time, Roger Stevens displayed audacity above and beyond the call of duty. Although the networks would extend credit to a permanent organization such as the Democratic National Committee, they required payment before air time for programs sponsored by organizations such as the Volunteers, which had only a firefly's life span. On at least one occasion—and perhaps even two or three—Roger Stevens either arranged last-minute bank credit or advanced funds of his own literally minutes in advance of a broadcast. It lent our proceedings an extra air of excitement, since we did not know till the last minute whether or not our candidate would be on the air.

Life in Springfield

Once Stevens had taken over the financial problems of the Volunteers, I began spending most of my time in Springfield, working directly with Wilson Wyatt, Stevenson's campaign manager. I not only helped resolve the inevitable conflicts between the Volunteers and the campaign's professional management, but, on Wyatt's request, assisted with the direction of the campaign.

With one or two exceptions, none of us, including Stevenson, knew much about running a modern Presidential campaign. Adlai's insistence that campaign headquarters be located in Springfield imposed intolerable burdens on Wyatt and his colleagues. No doubt a campaign headquarters in Springfield helped reinforce a number of points Stevenson constantly sought to make: he was independent of Truman; he was a child of the Middle West; he was not neglecting his duties as Governor while pursuing the Presidency; and he was demonstrating his abhorrence of slickness and the flamboyant display of wealth characteristic of Republican efforts. Yet no one other than Adlai could have thought it feasible to establish the campaign headquarters in a tiny, run-down frame cottage. The arrangement made the constantly shifting contingent of press and television correspondents, campaign helpers, and political "groupies" restive and cantankerous. Though Springfield was geographically near the center of the country, that was all one could say for it. Direct air service was minimal; no modern hotels existed in the area; and urban amenities were meager. When a distinguished correspondent such as James Reston stayed there for several weeks, he felt as though he had been banished to Ouagadougou—and resented it.

Stevenson cheerfully left such problems to Wyatt, a man of exceptional qualities. Wyatt was invariably good-natured, friendly, and optimistic, while at the same time thoughtful and realistic. Though he dealt with his unmanageable candidate as best he could, he had little staff but volunteers and no place to put anyone. During the whole campaign, we raised and spent only half as much money as our Republican opposition. Yet even though we lacked money, the word that best describes the campaign is "ebullience." We were proud when our candidate attracted men and women of wit and brilliance; Stevenson set the tone, and his speeches contained an unparalleled level of humorous comment. His was the poignant defense of civilized man against the bathos and banality of political campaigning—America's theater of the absurd.

Political Volunteers

Though I was nominally Executive Director of the Volunteers, it was not a role suited to my temperament or inclinations. I have a distaste for high-minded but amateur zealotry. If the heads of our local Volunteer groups were frequently men and women of assertive good will, they were, more often than not, at odds with the local politicians—whom they regarded as a lesser breed. Moreover, the local Volunteer groups were too frequently captured by pushy and overbearing individuals primarily interested in the trappings of power—people who claimed, on the basis of wealth, social position, or connections, a high place in the pecking order. Of course, the sincerely dedicated—and they were legion—effectively promoted the candidate's cause.

I had no flair for politics as an art form; my interest was solely in the content of the candidate's message. Nor could I conceal my revulsion at the groveling deference candidates are expected to show toward power groups. They descend in hordes, seeking by threat or by promise of campaign money or votes to buy the candidate's support of their particular objectives—a sweeping endorsement of the Greek or Israeli government's policies or aid to parochial schools or the rights of Hispanics, Chicanos, or Choctaw Indians or the freedom of any moron to buy a gun. In Springfield, I could avoid most of this. I felt admiration and affection for Wilson Wyatt, and we found it remarkably easy to work together.

I shall refrain from retelling the history of the 1952 campaign but not, in Max Beerbohm's words, because giving an accurate account "would need a pen far less brilliant than mine." My more modest reason is that the campaign story has been told in detail in John Bartlow Martin's comprehensive biography of Stevenson. Nevertheless, two incidents stand out in my mind—for quite disparate reasons.

The Nixon Attacks

Stevenson had started his campaign on August 27. By attacking super patriots and McCarthyites in a deliberately tough speech to the American Legion Convention, he established at the outset his independence and candor. The response clarified Republican tactics. Eisenhower would take the high road with only occasional detours down the slope; Nixon, running for Vice-President, would, by infallible instinct, operate at the level where the language of abuse would have the maximum resonance. Stevenson, announced Nixon—with his penchant for the elegant phrase—was a "weakling, a waster, and a small-caliber Truman" who had been elected Governor by a political organization with "mobsters, gangsters, and remnants of the Capone gang." He was, he said, "Adlai the Appeaser . . . , who got a Ph.D. from Dean Acheson's College of Cowardly Communist Containment." So, he concluded, ". . . the word of Truman and Acheson, as well as that of Acheson's former assistant, Adlai Stevenson, gives the American people no hope for safety at home from the sinister threat of Communism." At Texarkana, on October 27, Nixon was reported as telling a crowd that President Truman and Adlai Stevenson were "traitors to the high principles of the Democratic party . . . [who] tolerated and defended Communists in the government." As he had advised others to do, he "put on a fighting, rocking, socking campaign."[5] Although Stevenson, like Queen Victoria, was "not amused," he scornfully refused to take on Nixon. He was campaigning against Eisenhower and would not demean himself by arguing with Eisenhower's hired gun.

Nixon was propelled to the center of the stage only three weeks after the campaign began when, on September 18, the press broke the story of his $18,000 fund. Had Nixon explained the fund forthrightly both to the country and to Eisenhower it would probably have proved only a passing incident, for most people saw nothing inherently wrong with such a fund if it could be shown that it was not used to buy influence. But, since Nixon could never resist a chance for demagoguery, he adopted a sanctimonious pose of self-pity, seeking to associate himself with other beleaguered Americans burdened by debt and family anxieties who sought comfort in their inner nobility of purpose. The resulting Checkers speech ran the whole gamut of emotional claptrap from the little family dog to "Pat's respectable Republican cloth coat," while Nixon presciently anticipated today's Geritol commercials with the endearing phrase: "I always tell her that she'd look good in anything."

His formula never varied; every speech was a chapter in a child's version of *Pilgrim's Progress,* in which Christian, the hero, nobly resisted temptations to which less worthy men would quickly have succumbed. "There's some that will say, 'Well, maybe you were able, Senator, to fake this thing. How can we believe what you say—after all, is there a possibility that maybe you got some sums in cash? Is there a possibility that you may have feathered your own nest?' " He was, he implied, the noble victim slandered by Democrats. Though he found it an excruciating ordeal to "bare [his] life" on a nationwide hookup, he faced it because his country was in danger and the only man who could save it was Dwight Eisenhower.

I listened to this emetic sciamachy with perverse pleasure; Nixon was confirming for all to see what I had long thought of him. How could any American voter be taken in by such an archetypical confidence man? Even after an unprecedented outpouring of approving telegrams and press comment, I awaited the second wave, assuring Walter Lippmann that "Americans are cannier than you think; in due course, they'll feel the symptoms of *post-coitum tristesse.*" But Lippmann was skeptical. Though he described the reaction to the speech as "simply mob law," we were, he feared, entering a new era in which a candidate could, by exploiting television, make the people feel he was one of them. That would be the end of any serious debate over issues.

The whole incident disturbed me. That I had so lamentably underestimated America's tolerance—indeed, America's avidity—for hypocritical banalities challenged the central assumption of our campaign. Why try to "talk sense to the American people"—as Stevenson put it—if they could be so deceived by cheap claptrap? It would take them twenty-two more years to discover Nixon's vast capacity for fraud.

When Stars Collide

I mention the second incident purely for comic relief. Presidential campaigns throw together men and women of diverse talents, and most of Hollywood clustered about the glamorous Ike. Yet Stevenson also attracted a few devoted stage and screen luminaries—principally Lauren Bacall, Humphrey Bogart, and Mercedes McCambridge. On one occasion, at the request of the playwright Robert E. Sherwood, I arranged for composer Richard Rodgers to meet our candidate, while Rodgers in turn persuaded Tallulah Bankhead and Ethel Barrymore to appear together in a campaign photograph that I supervised. I listened in fascination as Ethel Barrymore tearfully complained to Tallulah, "You deliberately seated us this way so they'll photograph my bad side." To which Tallulah replied in her famous throaty voice, "Dahling, how could you ever suspect me of such a cruel thing? Even if I had thought of it, I would never have done that to you—but, of course, the thought never occurred to me since I don't have a bad side."

The Campaign Concludes

Toward the middle of the campaign, Stevenson began to dislike Eisenhower. He was disgusted when Ike not only failed to repudiate McCarthy but endorsed his candidacy for the Senate. He was even more disgusted when Ike failed to denounce McCarthy's attack on General Marshall (who had done more than anyone else to advance Ike's career) and, even after that insult, had appeared on the same platform with McCarthy. Finally, he resented the tactical benefit Eisenhower derived by announcing that, if elected, he would go to Korea, since Stevenson had himself pondered such a proposal at an earlier point but discarded it as demagogic.

In recounting history, one should try to recreate the mood and emotions of the time. Adlai was right in avoiding strong identification with the Truman Administration. The Democrats had been in power a long time, and the Truman Administration showed signs of weariness; its most talented members had departed, leaving mediocre men in high places to quarrel publicly. The party had been entrusted with power in a period of searing depression and had carried the country through a global war; now the policies and attitudes forged by such cataclysms had lost relevance.

As Stevenson put it to his friends, the party had run out of poor people and run into the Korean War, and the public automatically assumed that a war could best be dealt with by a general. Thus Adlai's candidacy was—as he well knew—out of phase with the times. What the country needed was a soothing father figure who would let people relax; it did not want a man who talked in uplifting phrases of the dangers and challenges of a complex and hazardous age. In view of the public mood, it is surprising that Adlai got as many votes as he did. Though he lost, the 1952 campaign—no matter how ill organized and meagerly financed—was something of which we could all be proud. Stevenson himself felt, as he told me many years later, that it was the high point of his life; everything afterwards was an anticlimax. He had put into that campaign the accumulated thought and experience of many years, and phrases from his 1952 speeches still generate an echo.

Reluctant as he may have been to enter the race, once Adlai made a total commitment to the campaign he convinced himself he could win. That was evident in many of our private conversations during those intense days and nights. For example, when someone insisted that he pay the politician's ritual homage by calling on Cardinal Spellman, he responded petulantly, "For God's sake, don't you characters believe we're going to win big enough so that kind of noxious business isn't neces-sary?" In his definitive biography of Adlai Stevenson, John Bartlow Martin reports that the belief in victory was shared by almost all members of the campaign entourage. But Wilson Wyatt and I were at least two exceptions, as we revealed to one another during a long walk on the afternoon of Election Day, November 1952, when nothing more could be done. Wyatt abruptly asked, "All right, tell me what you think?" I hesitated because I did not want to upset my friend and colleague, who, I assumed, shared the common faith in victory. Then I replied, "Well, we haven't won, but we gave it a hell of a try." Much to my surprise, Wyatt answered quietly, "You're right. It hasn't worked. We haven't had time to turn it around."

I spent the day numb and dreading the evening. A few of us had dinner with Adlai at the executive mansion. Later, Wilson Wyatt and I went to an election-night headquarters in the Leland Hotel, where facil-ities were installed to keep in touch with each state and monitor the returns. Since Springfield was an hour earlier than the East, we put a call through to Connecticut and, the two of us on the line, heard the Connecticut political boss John Bailey report lugubriously: "They're murdering us; it's a total disaster." The dreary evening became even grimmer as we drifted back and forth between the hotel and mansion while the returns were translating nightmares into reality. Finally, well after midnight, several of us went with Adlai to the hotel headquarters to hear his generous and graceful concession speech.

Ten years later, listening to another candidate who had just lost an election for Governor of California, I thought of the stark difference in style and quality of the two men. Stevenson told an Abraham Lincoln anecdote of a little boy who had stubbed his toe in the dark: "He said he was too old to cry but it hurt too much to laugh." The other candidate's comment—so different in spirit—was quite as much in character: "Now you won't have Dick Nixon to kick around anymore."

After the concession speech, we wandered back to the mansion, where a mixed group had gathered. It included a number of Adlai's Lake Forest friends, most of whom had, as they smugly announced, voted for Eisenhower, including one gloating female whose pneumatic bosom was asserted by a diamond Eisenhower pin. When another guest said, "Governor, you didn't win, but you educated the country with your great campaign," Stevenson replied pointedly, "But a lot of people flunked the course."

As I wrote later,

Adlai was remarkably composed and serene, the only blithe member of a doleful group. He had no taste, he said, for political wakes—"especially when I'm the corpse." He consoled us as though we, not he, were the losers, at one point disappearing into the kitchen for a jeroboam of victory champagne someone had sent him. Always the Scotsman, he insisted on not wasting it. Always the considerate host, he insisted on pouring it himself.

Finally, he announced that since he had lost the election the least he could do was to make the toast. And so, with Adlai, we all raised our glasses while he offered a tribute to "Wilson Wyatt, the best campaign manager any unsuccessful politician ever had."

He described himself wrongly, of course, as we all knew. He was no "unsuccessful politician," but a brave leader who had given a whole generation of Americans a cause for which many could, for the first time, feel deeply proud— a man of prophetic quality who, in Arthur Schlesinger's phrase, "set the tone for a new era in Democratic politics."

Only one person present that evening would have dared to call Adlai Stevenson "unsuccessful"—and we loved him for it. For we had each of us, at different times and in different ways, discovered that sense of decency and proportion, humility and infallible good manners which led him so often to understatement—particularly when he spoke of himself. And we would not have had him otherwise.[6]

10. *The 1956 Campaign and After*

For those who fought at the hot gates, the 1952 campaign marked a high point of excitement and exhilaration. Then, abruptly, everything came to a halt. For a day or two, Ruth and I lingered in Springfield; finally—as though to defer getting up on a cold morning— we set off on a leisurely and circuitous drive back to Washington. Adlai saw us off and, as usual, relieved the poignancy of the moment with his wry comment, "What a relief it is to have the damn campaign finished! Next Sunday I won't have to go to church. I can turn over and go to sleep."

Other than a war or protracted intoxication, there is nothing that more completely diverts one from reality than a political campaign; now

I had to pick up the ragged ends of a law practice in disarray. One friend who seemed to be suffering a similar symptom was Senator J. William Fulbright. He had been a buoyant visitor at our Springfield headquarters; now I found him annoyed and disconsolate. Catching the liberal Senators off-guard, the young Texas Senator Lyndon B. Johnson had put himself forward as Democratic leader in the Senate, and it was now too late to block his selection. That meant, Fulbright said, that conservative Democrats would control the Senate, and Johnson would go along with almost anything President Eisenhower proposed. Stevenson, he insisted, must lead the party, yet we both knew that a man out of office could not easily keep himself in the public eye. During one of our frequent lunches or dinners Walter Lippmann expressed the same view. The party, Lippmann said, would be run by Senators and Congressmen; Stevenson would be pushed increasingly into the cold.

Despite this conventional wisdom, Adlai managed during the next four years to maintain himself as far more than the titular head of the party. His *tour de force* attested to the spell he cast over the articulate liberals, and particularly the young who had first tasted politics in the golden days of 1952. His voice was heard and often heeded, and he had an astute sense of timing. In New York early in February 1953, he made a powerful speech to Eastern Democrats, laying out the broad directions of Democratic opposition. Then, after conferring with party leaders and making further political speeches, he left for a trip around the world, returning only in the latter part of August.

Early Planning for the 1956 Campaign

Stevenson knew that if he were to run again in 1956 he not only had to maintain high visibility but gain greater understanding of the issues of the day. Several of us (including John Kenneth Galbraith, Arthur Schlesinger, and Chester Bowles) fretted over that problem, but it was Thomas Finletter who initiated a continuing seminar. From October 1953 to November 1956, the so-called Finletter group met irregularly, usually at Finletter's apartment in New York (though one meeting was held in Chicago with Stevenson and another at Cambridge). Papers were produced on almost every relevant issue facing the United States government. The authors had in most cases served in prior Democratic administrations and, though many were academicians, most of the papers took account of political realities.

Adlai spoke highly of our efforts, but he attended few meetings and when he did attend gave little evidence of having read the position papers. That reinforced my long-held suspicion that he had little taste for the arduous laboratory work of dissecting tough issues, cutting through the gristle to the bone, and paring away the obfuscating tissue. He preferred to talk generally about problems and was bored by their technical complexities. Yet, if we did not educate our potential candidate, we did build up a valuable dossier of position papers that provided Stevenson and his writers with ready-made speech materials during the 1956 campaign. That was justification enough for the time and effort we committed.

Of all Stevenson's achievements during that period, I was most proud of his brilliant, forthright attack on McCarthyism in a speech he delivered in March 1954 at Miami Beach. By denouncing the craven action of the Eisenhower Administration in exploiting McCarthy for its own political purposes, he forced Eisenhower to make at least a *pro forma* reply. Since Ike assigned that task to Nixon, the answer was characteristically cheap and snide.

Whenever Adlai and I met during those years in the wilderness, we talked about his prospects for 1956. Almost by rote he disparaged the idea of a second campaign, yet I grew increasingly convinced that, at the appropriate time, he would make the hard decision. In April 1955, I worked with him on a national radio speech about Quemoy and Matsu—those small, irrelevant offshore islands that were to play such a quaint but important role in the Kennedy-Nixon campaign in 1960. Stevenson sharply cautioned Eisenhower against intervening to save the islands from an attack by the mainland Chinese, though fully supporting the defense of Taiwan.

Stevenson set off for Africa in April 1955, and in mid-June Stephen Mitchell and several others established a steering committee to work for Stevenson's nomination in 1956. During the summer, the committee members began actively rounding up delegates and talking about primaries. Meanwhile, a canny Philadelphia politician, Jim Finnegan, and a political lawyer from Chicago, Hy Raskin, became Stevenson's professional managers. On August 5, I attended a strategy meeting with Stevenson at Libertyville. In the latter months of 1955, we spent a great deal of time developing the themes for a campaign, using the background work and ongoing organization of the Finletter group.

Eisenhower's Heart Attack

On September 24, 1955, I was attending a Bilderberg meeting in Garmisch-Partenkirchen, Germany, when we received word of President Eisenhower's heart attack. Gabriel Hauge, then a White House assistant who lived next door to me in Washington, left immediately. No one knew the extent of Eisenhower's illness, but his heart attack a year before the 1956 election drastically enhanced the odds for a Democratic victory. If Eisenhower should die or be precluded from running by illness, I felt confident that Stevenson could beat Nixon. If, on the other hand, Eisenhower did run, the fact of his heart attack might raise questions about his fitness to be President. By an odd coincidence, Lyndon Johnson was just at that time also recovering from a heart attack, but I did not realize how little such events would affect the Presidential future of either man.

In any event, Ike's illness made most of us in the Stevenson circle more eager than ever to start preparing the campaign. Of course, we foresaw difficulties. Stevenson's divorce would be a problem in heavily Catholic districts. He had alienated Harry Truman by indicating in subtle, and not-so-subtle, ways that he disapproved of the wheeling and dealing that had marred the latter days of Truman's Presidency. Convinced that Ike's ill health would assure a Democratic victory, Truman now seemed to favor Averell Harriman, although he must have recognized Harriman's limitations as a candidate. Adlai was irked by what he regarded as Harriman's lack of grace and subtlety in pushing himself forward, while Harriman showed visible disdain for Stevenson's Cincinnatus pose.

The Minnesota Primary

Meanwhile, Estes Kefauver began to becloud the landscape. Anticipating Jimmy Carter years later, he entered all available primaries and we began to fear that, if he won too many without opposition, he might build up a momentum the convention could not resist. This second time around, the pols insisted, Adlai could not remain passive without risking the critical support of party leaders who were showing increasing evidence of impatience. Though he found the prospect repulsive, Adlai reluctantly decided in November to enter the Minnesota primary. On October 21, he had received a letter of support from the young Massachusetts Senator, John F. Kennedy.

During the months after Ike's heart attack, the Democrats had grown increasingly optimistic, but in December speculation shifted. The White House was using every available conjuring device to create the impression of a resolute Captain Ike vigorously steering the ship of state. They issued a spate of press releases designed to obscure the fact that he did not leave Fitzsimmons Army Hospital until November 11 and spent the next several weeks moving between Gettysburg, Camp David, and Key West. Finally, on February 29, 1956, Eisenhower himself made clear that he would try to retain the Presidency for another four years.

Americans are sentimental and Ike had public sympathy on his side. The people wanted him in good health again, radiating a confidence many trusted because it made them feel good. Even when, in June, he was taken seriously ill for the second time in less than a year and required surgery for ileitis, the question of his fitness to serve was scarcely mentioned.

Stevenson felt pressed by Eisenhower's illness to demonstrate his own vigor, overcrowding his schedule and adding Florida as a primary contest. It was not a sound decision. Stevenson was temperamentally unfitted for primary campaigns and the mindless posturing and glossolalia they involved. He liked public life primarily because it gave him the chance to make speeches of high quality. Presidential campaigns required only a limited number of major appearances before audiences responsive to views on major issues, but in primaries a candidate often had to make fifteen or twenty appearances a day in the hope of informing and educating haphazardly assembled groups of the curious whose cosmic awareness was all too often limited to the jaundiced jottings of a small-town editor or the windy bombast of some illiterate radio commentator posing as the world's greatest all-purpose expert. Under such pressures, a sensitive candidate could retain his sanity only by throwing his mind out of gear and endlessly reciting a fixed speech varied only to salute whatever local political honcho might be in the audience. Stevenson found this excruciating torture. Still, he could have endured it with only passing spiritual damage had it not affronted his sense of the appropriate. "What do they think I am?" he would complain. "A candidate for deputy sheriff? No one worthy of being President should act like a panhandler, standing in front of factory gates or soliciting votes in supermarkets from housewives come to buy toilet paper. I'm no five-dollar whore."

He also hated the thought of running against Kefauver, since it suggested that Kefauver and he were in some way comparable. How could one rationally argue issues with a man whose principal distinction was a coonskin cap? It was humiliating to have to prove that he was superior to a second-rate politician; that should have been evident to all. Meanwhile, he was confused by a surfeit of conflicting advice. Many liberal intellectuals who had vowed undying support in 1952 now complained that Stevenson was acting like an ordinary candidate. They wanted him to stay above the battle. I thought then—and still do—that many would have been happier were he to have lost the primaries; they could then have boasted of having supported a man of rare quality whom the public was too crude to appreciate. Now, they bewailed, the professional "pols" were destroying his exceptionalism.

Those rarified views were not shared by the pols themselves or even by the liberal Senators who attacked Stevenson for not making those traditional genuflections to clamant special interests that were accepted ritual for a Democratic candidate. He balked at the mystic lodge-brother phrases that identified the true believer—the simplistic tag words that transformed the political dialogue into a rote recitation of vapid jargon. Competing as he was against a mine-run candidate like Kefauver or a rigid believer like Harriman for the support of liberal elements, particularly in such self-consciously liberal states as California or Minnesota, he came increasingly to resent the pressures to which he was subjected. His reactions, I once told him, resembled a gyroscope: when pressure was applied to push him off his natural equilibrium, he instinctively generated "precession"—a counteracting motion that discouraged the pressure groups. My figure of speech appealed to him, and he insisted on looking up the word "precession" in a dictionary.

Those of us who knew Adlai encouraged his aversion to doctrinaire poses. He was far more interested in practical measures than in self-indulgent bleeding on the barricades. Civil rights were a case in point. Rather than waving the bloody shirt, as his Northern liberal friends were urging, he saw his proper role as a conciliator, pressing the Southern whites toward progress without driving them into obscurantist resistance. America's policy toward the Arab-Israeli struggle should, he thought, be formulated in Washington rather than dictated from Jerusalem, and he disliked the arrogant manner in which pro-Israeli leaders dangled the prospect of large campaign contributions in exchange for uncritical support of whatever self-serving policy a transient Israeli government might than be advocating. Though sympathetic with the broad purposes of labor, he was averse to putting tight limits on an individual's right to make his own decisions and would have liked to endorse freedom-to-work laws enthusiastically. Nor was he willing to submit to the excessive demands of the farm lobby or any other special-interest group.

Stevenson was, in other words, a moderate in the true meaning of the term. Many of his liberal supporters in 1952 had mistakenly assumed that anyone who spoke so literately and in such high-minded terms would necessarily meet all the esoteric tests of the true lodge brother. When they concluded that he did not, they abandoned him in droves, preferring to see the Democratic party go down to defeat rather than elect a candidate who did not accept every word in their lexicon of shibboleths. It was a phenomenon we would see later, and in spades, in 1968, when American liberals turned viciously against their former hero, Hubert Humphrey, fatuously arguing the nobility of not voting. How they could so recklessly contribute to the election of Richard Nixon, I could not then—nor do I now—understand!

In Minnesota, Adlai's local supporters, Hubert Humphrey, Orville Freeman, and Congressman John A. Blatnik, encouraged him to take the outcome of that state's primary for granted. But as primary day approached, Humphrey began to lose confidence, haunted by the fear that the Republicans might cross over and vote for Kefauver so as to ease the road for Eisenhower. Those forebodings were well founded. When the campaign began, Stevenson had been reported as running far ahead; when the voting took place on March 20, Kefauver received 56 percent of the vote.

I was not involved in the Minnesota primary. I had suggested in

December that, if Adlai wished it, I would come to Chicago in the spring and work on the campaign full-time; however, he was cool to the idea. I was surprised at his reaction, but he told me later that Barbara Ward had expressed a strong distaste for something I had said. Besides, Stevenson implied, I might not fit in well with others on his staff—particularly, I suspect, Willard Wirtz, who had taken over Carl McGowan's task as the principal editor of his speeches, and whom I sometimes found prickly and overly rigid.

If Stevenson did not want me at his headquarters, there were many other tasks that needed to be done. At the end of March, he asked me to keep an eye on the preparations for his Florida primary. He knew that my family maintained a winter home in Florida and that I had spent at least a fortnight there almost every year since the age of eleven. Thus he and I both assumed that I had a working knowledge of the state.

The Florida Primary

To be sure, I had traveled to most of the key centers on both the east and west coasts. But, as I embarked on my new assignment, I discovered that there is more to Florida than meets the winter visitor's eye. Politically it was—and is—not one but several states. As in the case of California, where two-thirds of the population live in the south, the Florida population is also heavily concentrated in Dade County—or, in other words, metropolitan Miami. Since Dade County was at the time composed almost entirely of immigrants from the north, principally New York, the issues that most preoccupied the people were roughly the same as those they had faced in Manhattan, the Bronx, and Brooklyn. In Florida's northwest Panhandle, the prevailing views on civil rights were by contrast roughly those of southern Georgia, just across the border. It was in this more primitive area that Kefauver planned to make his principal gains.

Up to then, my political experience in politics had been almost solely with urban voters; in Florida, I had a closer look at what—to borrow tedious jargon from the economists—one might call "micropolitics." What I saw was not reassuring from Stevenson's point of view. In spite of his moderate approach to civil rights, Floridians in the Panhandle tended to think of him as a liberal who used big words and was ignorant of their day-to-day concerns. The Gulf Coast residents around the Tampa–St. Petersburg area, where wheelchairs far outnumber mopeds, felt much closer to Kefauver; he was, as they saw it, a simple, good man, who would better understand their needs, an "old shoe" type who seemed genuinely concerned for their health and well-being.

Dade County was another matter. There, many residents craved the respectability they associated with Eisenhower and the Republicans and

were lukewarm about Stevenson because he did not meet the litmus test
with regard to Israel. They would continue to support Eisenhower blindly
even in November 1956, after he had ordered the Israeli armies back
across the Sinai with the only tough *démarche* to an Israeli government
ever given by an American President.

In the preprimary weeks, I traveled widely over the state to consult
with local leaders. My mentor and companion was a charming Gaines-
ville lawyer with the euphonious name of Benjamin Montgomery (Ben-
mont) Tenche. When Stevenson came to Florida on April 12, for six
days of intensive campaigning, I accompanied him around the state,
where, in ten or twelve speeches a day, he did his best to concentrate on
local issues. He "bitterly denounced," as he wrote later, "the Japanese
beetle and fearlessly attacked the Mediterranean fruit-fly," then the
principal preoccupation of Florida citrus growers. But he was not happy
with the regime he was expected to follow. Though citrus diseases were
a serious matter, did they, he asked, really deserve "so much attention
from candidates for the highest temporal office on earth? Isn't it time
we grew up?" I was disturbed by his depressed state of mind. The degradation involved in primary campaigning was corroding his soul. He
was tired, plaintively querulous, and increasingly pessimistic.

He felt no qualms about running against Dwight Eisenhower, but to
be measured against Estes Kefauver was an insult. Some might write that
off as snobbism. Yet I remembered the reaction of Walter and Helen
Lippmann after they had spent an evening with the Kefauvers and their
friends; never had I seen them so angry and disgusted, repelled by the
squalor of a conversation laden with puerile obscenities and sniggering
innuendoes. Nonetheless, after his defeat in Minnesota and the general
falling away of support around the country, Stevenson had to pay
increasing attention to Kefauver at whatever cost to his self-esteem. And
there was no doubt that on some liberal issues Kefauver had shown conviction and courage.

Politicians, professors, and columnists constantly dredge up certain
favored historical precedents. The United States, they repeatedly aver,
should take major initiatives "like the Marshall Plan." In political campaigns, they nostalgically recall the Lincoln-Douglas debates. The fact
that those debates did not have the effect ascribed to them does not
diminish the mythology, and in the age of television, when candidates
are measured more by personality than substance, the idea of letting
them slug it out in living color has wide appeal. We initially opposed this
suggestion in the Florida campaign but, after the loss in Minnesota, we
agreed under mounting pressures to a joint Stevenson-Kefauver television appearance. How, we thought, could anyone fail to be impressed
by the contrast between an awkward prosaic Kefauver and our own eloquent tiger? Stevenson was a past master of the apt and eloquent phrase,

and his deep commitment to the public interest could not help but be evident. Thus we finally agreed that, eight days before the Florida primary, on May 21, the two men should meet at a television studio in Miami. Though I was less confident of the outcome than some of the Stevenson entourage, I hoped that we might, indeed, gain a decisive advantage. The debate—or, as we called it, the "discussion"—was to take place on Monday, with Stevenson flying from California a few days in advance to prepare for it.

Bill Blair, Stevenson's personal assistant, telephoned me that the Governor was exhausted and gloomy. Couldn't I arrange a day of total relaxation on a boat, where he could be away from all telephones? I scurried around seeking a suitable vessel, and a campaign worker agreed to borrow one from a friend. I specifically stipulated that the object was to isolate Stevenson so we could brief him for the debate; we would, therefore, want no outsiders aboard. Stevenson grumbled, as usual, when I reported our plans for the outing, but Bill Blair and I reassured him that he would get a good rest and be able to concentrate quietly on the debate.

Nothing could have been further from the truth. In spite of my stern stipulations, the owner of the boat produced not only his wife but also three or four other couples, intending to turn the trip into a floating cocktail party. I heatedly remonstrated, but we did not want an awkward incident that the press might exploit, so Blair and I persuaded Stevenson to go aboard, on the promise that we would segregate him for our briefing. Stevenson was, however, too annoyed to relax. Though Blair and I kept him in the stern of the boat, the sound of revelry from the bow grew louder and louder, and guests drifted back now and then to meet the great man.

Stevenson, in his normal frame of mind, might have enjoyed the absurdity of the situation, but he was tired and bitterly complaining that he had not had time to prepare for the evening's ordeal. That, however, was not really the problem; although intellectually prepared he was both physically and spiritually exhausted. Harry Ashmore, former editor of the *Arkansas Gazette,* and Jim Finnegan, Stevenson's campaign manager, had spent two whole days going over a list of prospective questions with him, and, in any event, the campaign had settled down to a half-dozen stylized questions the press asked by rote.

Stevenson wanted a written text that would assure the eloquence of phrase in which he took such pride. I unwisely discouraged him. The public, I argued, wanted to hear him ad libbing, without benefit of script, displaying full mastery of the issues. I had not foreseen that, in his depressed and demoralized state, he could not give a brilliant performance or persuade many voters.

The boat owner's wife furnished the only comic relief of the afternoon. After insisting that an impatient Stevenson make a tour of her house a few hundred yards from the dock, she exhibited not merely the central area but the "deduction wing," where the family obviously lived. "Why the 'deduction' wing?" Stevenson asked. The lady replied quite innocently, "Oh, Jim keeps a few books and papers around there so he can take it all off his income tax." It was the kind of observation that would normally have delighted Adlai, but that afternoon nothing could make him laugh.

The much heralded television "discussion" proved not so much a disaster as a bore. Fuzzy questions from a panel of local reporters evoked fuzzy banalities about foreign policy, then each candidate avowed his ardor for civil rights. Stevenson was thrown off balance at the outset, when, after he had extemporized some opening remarks, Kefauver read from a written statement. He was equally annoyed at the end, when Kefauver produced another text. Since that was what Stevenson would have done had Blair and I not discouraged him, he was furious. "You left me naked! My God," he complained, "what a humiliation when I can't even show up a fourth-rate hack like Kefauver! I should have had a beautifully written final statement and electrified the country with some blinding oratory!"

Eight days later, Stevenson won the primary by a mere twelve thousand votes, with the Panhandle's wool-hat segregationists providing the winning margin. Feeble though it was, the victory at least saved him from a defeat that—following Minnesota—would have seriously prejudiced his candidacy. A California victory in early June virtually sewed up the convention.

Had Stevenson spent the first six months of 1956 on a world trip, he would have been physically and morally prepared for a hard campaign, since travel stimulated him. But then the nomination might have gone to Kefauver by default. As it was, the primaries destroyed his *élan* and resilience. No longer was he a confident, ebullient candidate; the querulous note was heard far too often as he looked toward the impending campaign as an ordeal rather than an opportunity.

The Convention

At the convention, Senator John F. Kennedy nominated Stevenson, who won on the first ballot; we then found ourselves arguing as to who should run for Vice-President: Kefauver, Humphrey, or Kennedy? An untried alternative was to disregard the tradition that the Presidential candidate select his own running mate, and throw the Vice-Presidential nomination open to the convention. Not only would that save Stevenson the necessity of a bruising choice, it might demonstrate a commitment to open democracy, which was, we felt, one of our candidate's leading assets. Eisenhower had just "dictated" the nomination of Richard M. Nixon; we hoped to dramatize the contrast. But we had not reckoned on the pols; Sam Rayburn, Paul Butler, the new Democratic national chairman, and Lyndon Johnson all opposed the idea.

No decision had been made by Thursday morning, the day before the assembled Democrats habitually nominated their Vice-Presidential candidate. Several of us drifted over to Stevenson's law office, where he was working on his acceptance speech, and once again debated the arguments for and against an open convention. Wyatt and I spoke for it vigorously, strongly assisted by Jim Finnegan. Stevenson finally decided that, while risky, it was still the best course for him to follow—besides, the idea appealed to him intellectually. Late that night, we all went to the Stockyards Inn, next door to the convention hall. There, Stevenson had another battle with the pols, most of whom opposed an open convention. One reason for their opposition, implied if not always stated, was their ingrained conservatism; like Jean Monnet's grandfather, the professionals automatically regarded any new idea as presumptively bad. An open convention was, they thought, a reckless heresy, since the art of politics depended on rigidly controlling the electoral environment.

An open Vice-Presidential contest might choose Kefauver, whom most of the party notables widely despised. They also feared that Stevenson's refusal to pick his own Vice-Presidential running mate would be attacked as further proof of his indecisiveness. Less complicated than Adlai, the pros tended to see everything in terms of a straightforward choice; indecisiveness, like innovation, was sin. In the end, Stevenson held firm with a strong assist from Jim Finnegan.

Unlike several of the pols, Adlai had thought that in an open convention Kennedy would probably win. Kennedy, he thought, had quality; he would have been far more comfortable running with him than with Kefauver, even though he sometimes lamented that "Jack [had] too much of his father in him." Adlai had shown his friendship by asking Kennedy to nominate him, and he was clearly disappointed when Kefauver won the Vice-Presidential race in the open convention. That race provided the one element of drama in an otherwise dreary convention. I thought Kennedy had gained the day when he was only eighteen and a half votes short of the number needed, but when Missouri shifted to Kefauver, it started an inexorable swing. In his shirt sleeves, with his collar unbuttoned and looking boyishly handsome though breathless, Kennedy made a gallant, impromptu speech for the ticket, ending with the traditional motion that Kefauver's nomination be made unanimous. Overnight he was a television hero—a charismatic leader.

Kennedy, so subsequent history suggests, was probably lucky not to win, for he emerged a national hero untarnished by running against an unbeatable general and by Stevenson's lackluster campaign. That, however, was not the mood of the moment; instead, the Kennedy family was angry and bitter. Jack got over it quickly, but Bobby—always the better hater—continued to blame David Lawrence, the politically potent Mayor of Pittsburgh, who was one of Stevenson's staunchest supporters. Lawrence, Bobby claimed, had double-crossed the Kennedys by switching Pennsylvania to the Kefauver side, and there were even insinuations that Stevenson (or at least Jim Finnegan) had played some role in it.

Once the ticket was completed, the only remaining convention business of consequence was Stevenson's acceptance speech. I had seen Stevenson's version of the speech early in the afternoon; Tom Finletter, Carl McGowan, and I had worked over it with growing disappointment. But when Willard Wirtz, then Stevenson's chief assistant, took our version to the Governor, he did not put up a fight for the changes we had recommended, and Stevenson brushed aside our suggestions, which, as I recall, were mostly deletions. It was a bad decision, for after the drama of the afternoon, his acceptance speech seemed a pale reflection of his earlier oratory—largely a compendium of phrases fresh when first uttered but drained of meaning by repetition—the speech of a man who, for the time being at least, had lost his spark. Those of us devoted to his cause felt enormously let down.

The Campaign as Television Farce

Stevenson's first need after the convention was for an effective campaign organization. During the primary period, Jim Finnegan, though campaign manager, had operated with only a small staff. Effective on his home terrain of Philadelphia, he was not used to working with the amateurs who formed the Stevenson entourage; at the same time, he stood in excessive awe of Stevenson himself. During the 1952 campaign, I had worked easily with Wilson Wyatt, Carl McGowan, Bill Blair, and Adlai's personal circle, but my relations were not so easy with Willard Wirtz, who had taken over McGowan's role, nor with some of the younger speech writers, such as Robert Tufts, a young professor from Oberlin College.

Whether for that reason or others that I do not know, Stevenson did not ask me to travel with him but, rather, to take on the task of director of public relations. There was no logic in the assignment other than the fact that Adlai trusted my judgment in dealing with the press and other media. I had no background or experience for the job. I had never been a journalist or advertising executive, and it was not an assignment I wanted in any way. Nevertheless, I set myself up in the campaign headquarters in Washington and worked out an uneasy relationship with our advertising agency—Norman, Craig and Kummel—and particularly with Gene Kummel, who was tolerant of my professional ignorance. I had neither taste nor talent for my most important task, which was to fight with the television networks. I would have been completely useless but for the assistance of our time-buyer, Reggie Shuebel—a remarkable woman of great experience, enormous drive, and unquenchable good humor. Most television entertainment bored me, and I regularly watched only the news broadcasts. I was, therefore, astonished to discover how many changes had taken place in the viewing habits of Americans in the four years since the first Stevenson campaign. That campaign, as I have mentioned, was the first one in which television was widely employed; and it was also the last and only time any candidate used it for a systematic airing of his views. In 1952, we had thought of television primarily as a means for letting a larger nationwide audience listen to our candidate's speeches. But by 1956, 73 percent of American households had television sets, and attention spans had so dramatically shortened that, according to my television advisers, only a tiny fraction of the American public would willingly sit through a half-hour speech. Moreover, we could no longer afford such a luxury, for the cost of a network half-hour on prime time had risen exorbitantly. Whether we liked it or not, we would have to resort to the use of the spots; and even a network spot no longer than a hiccup stretched our meager resources.

Stevenson would, I knew, be repelled by the idea of using thirty-second, or even one-minute, spots with only a scattered handful of nationally televised half-hour speeches. He still sincerely believed that a campaign should be used to educate people, not narcotize them by an endless succession of asinine political commercials. Spots could not convey ideas, only create fleeting artificial impressions—thus putting a premium on manner and personality. "Sooner or later," I predicted in an informal speech in New York, "Presidential campaigns would have professional actors as candidates who could speak the lines." I did not know how presciently I spoke.

In view of some comments four years earlier, I found our need to resort to spots particularly humiliating. During the early days of the 1952 campaign, someone had obtained a bootlegged outline of a proposal prepared for Eisenhower by a New York advertising agency for a blitz campaign of television spots that would be used for saturation effect during the immediate pre-election period. At a meeting of Stevenson followers in Springfield on October 1, 1952, I had made a satirical speech, attacking Eisenhower as a synthetic candidate and using the projected spot campaign as the principal subject of ridicule. Eisenhower, I had pointed out, was being merchandised like soap, or soup, or some other kitchen or bathroom commodity, and I referred to his electoral efforts as "the cornflakes campaign." My argument was straightforward.

In the sale of soap and toothpastes, the saturation of the mind by contrived gimmicks and ear-dinning repetition has become an accepted though painful part of everyday American life. But in the sale of political candidates and ideologies it has its obvious—and proven—dangers. We need not, however, go into that. I think we should hope that Americans, no matter how they determine their choice of cigarettes or chewing gum, are wise enough to realize that they must apply different standards in choosing a political philosophy to live by or men to lead them.

The tyrant, Commodus, in his vanity, ordered the heads chopped off every statue of Hercules in Rome and a reproduction of his own head substituted. Even the most ignorant Romans were not fooled, of course. Hercules ultimately got his head back; Commodus lost his. I do not mean to liken the General to Commodus; but I do suggest that even Batten, Barton, Durstine and Osborne will not be able to make him look like Hercules.

My speech received a good deal of press notice, with the veteran conservative political writer Frank Kent devoting several columns to "Mr. Ball's Bellowing." But it did not deter Eisenhower's spot campaign, which proved effective (so the experts decreed, though they could offer no proof). Ike had spent long hours before the cameras giving pat answers to banal questions from actors selected to represent diverse special interests. The spots had been selectively shown to take account of regional differences, and different answers were beamed to different localities.

Though my "cornflakes" speech reflected my repugnance at the Eisenhower spot campaign, I had not yet grasped the full implications of this new threat to the democratic process. I did not then comprehend the extent to which Presidential candidates would thereafter be presented as commodities, market-tested and packaged to satisfy individual markets. That meant the attrition of serious dialogue. The message to be conveyed was now stylized; two days after voting for a particular candidate, the voter's hemorrhoids would be miraculously cured. By 1956, that mythology had become dogma; most of our limited funds must, the pols assured me, be spent on saturating the networks.

Of course, the concept of canned commercials disgusted Adlai. Only the pressure of the pols persuaded him to film a few spots to be used toward the end of the campaign. It was an art form for which he had neither liking nor facility. Stevenson was a poor actor and refused to learn set answers, so he needed a great many expensive retakes to fit his words to the Procrustean time limit. Even then, the spots were stiff and unconvincing. Edward R. Murrow, who strongly supported Adlai, volunteered to teach him to perform more effectively. He arranged for a studio, and, after a hassle, I persuaded Stevenson to cooperate. Murrow spent a long afternoon of patient coaching, but it did no good. In spite of his friendship with and admiration for Murrow, Stevenson hated the whole exercise and did not conceal his distaste; he even chided me about the expense of the studio.

I will not repeat the sad chronicle of the 1956 campaign. For me, as for many who loved Adlai, it was a prolonged, dismal anticlimax. Management of the campaign was now—up to a point—in the hands of professionals, which deprived it of the charm of improvisation. Worst of all, our candidate had exhausted himself in three stultifying primaries. On many substantive issues—fiscal policy, farm policy, social legislation, and much else—Adlai was more specific and competent in 1956 than he had been four years earlier. The position papers released during the campaign were models of analysis and lucidity; the Finletter exercise had paid off. But Adlai's speeches lacked the same eloquence and drama that he had once demonstrated, and the country did not listen.

As has now become customary in political campaigns, the newspapers concentrated on beating to death two or three "issues" until the whole campaign became little more than a monotonous variation on a few largely irrelevant themes. In a well-orchestrated campaign, the candidate hammers on the points he can handle most advantageously, but our 1956 campaign was anything but well orchestrated.

The Accidental Issues

Oddly enough, Stevenson's proposal for an end to nuclear bomb testing attracted little comment when Adlai first made it and would have been forgotten had he not returned to it on September 5, during the campaign. Here he violated the rules of prudence; he failed to articulate his nuclear proposal in a clear and definitive way and he coupled it in the same speech with the equally explosive proposal that America abandon the draft and develop a volunteer army.

The launching of any new idea in a political campaign calls for certain minimum precautions. It should, first of all, be vetted by experts familiar with its pitfalls, political as well as technical, thus revealing whether or not the idea is sound and politically sustainable. Adlai should have presented the proposal in a carefully drafted text containing the arguments and information necessary to anticipate and counter the attacks of the opposition. In addition, before the unveiling, we should have lined up recognized experts primed to express prompt and enthusiastic public approval.

Now all such precautions were ignored. Stevenson had never studied the bomb-testing issue deeply; instead, he relied principally on conversation and correspondence with friends who were themselves only modestly acquainted with the technical questions involved. Other than Thomas E. Murray, chairman of the Atomic Energy Commission, no one thoroughly familiar with the esoteric problems of verification had ever seen the proposal; it was not an area in which Stevenson had any personal experience and he never made it quite clear what he was proposing. In his original speech to the American Society of Newspaper Editors, he had, in the final draft, dropped out any reference to a prior agreement with the Soviet Union for a cessation of bomb testing, proposing instead that the United States act on its own and resume tests only if the Soviets continued to test. "I would call upon other nations," he said, "the Soviet Union, to follow our lead, and if they don't and persist in further tests we will know about it and can reconsider our policy."[1] Then in his speech to the American Legion in Los Angeles on September 5, after the campaign had started, he spoke about his "proposal asking to halt further testing of large nuclear devices, conditioned upon adherence by the other atomic powers to a similar policy." Later, on September 29, he referred to it as "a moratorium on the testing of more super H-bombs. If the Russians don't go along—well, at least the world will know we tried. And we will know if they don't because we can detect H-bomb explosions without inspections."[2]

Those who argue—as some of Adlai's supporters did after the campaign—that, like the proposal of a volunteer army, Stevenson's proposal for a test-ban moratorium is vindicated by its ultimate adoption by a later administration, are on unsound ground. The partial test-ban agreement concluded by President Kennedy on July 25, 1963, was a formal treaty binding all the parties (the United States, the USSR, and Great Britain) to abjure only from those tests that could be detected by national means—or, in other words, without on-the-spot inspection. Adlai's proposal was that the United States stop bomb tests unilaterally, then reconsider if the Soviets failed to follow suit. Nor did Adlai adequately deal with the verification issue. In the beginning, he talked about the cessation of all H-bomb tests, stating categorically that all such tests could be detected by national means. Later, in a nationwide television speech in Chicago over the weekend of October 25, he referred to his earlier proposal as one to "halt further tests of large-sized nuclear weapons—what we usually call the H-bombs"; we could, he argued, "detect any large explosions anywhere" and could continue to develop and test "smaller nuclear weapons."[3]

Stationed as I was in the East, I could only telephone my dismay at these goings-on. But I watched with sinking heart as Stevenson, having impetuously proposed a unilateral cessation of testing, searched frantically for a defensible fall-back line by putting the emphasis not on disarmament but on the dangers to American health from bomb tests that resulted in nuclear fallout which contained Strontium 90. Though I thought the new argument overstated and insupportable, I did what I could to reinforce it, enlisting Dr. Benjamin Spock, the famous baby specialist, to announce that increasing Strontium 90 in the atmosphere could prove fatal for infants. I also collected statements and testimonials from liberal physicists and chemists all over the country.

Meanwhile, Stevenson was being induced by the speech writers on his plane to embellish his disintegrating case with increasingly insupportable assertions. In a Chicago speech, he said, "With every explosion of a super bomb, large quantities of radioactive materials are pumped into the air currents of the world at all altitudes—later to fall to earth as dust or in rain. This radioactive 'fallout' carries something called Strontium 90, which is the most dreadful poison in the world. Only a tablespoon shared with all the members of the human race would produce a dangerous level of radioactivity in the bones of every individual. In sufficient concentration it can cause bone cancer and dangerously affect reproductive processes. . . . I do not wish to be an alarmist and I am not asserting that the present levels of radioactivity are dangerous. Scientists do not know exactly how dangerous the threat is."[4]

Hyperbole was piled on hyperbole as a beleaguered Stevenson found himself under increasing attack—to the point where he finally charged the Administration with concealing the fact that Strontium 90 was already contaminating the country's milk supply. The campaign reached the ultimate level of silliness when Kefauver declared that hydrogen bombs could "right now blow the earth off its axis by 16 degrees, which would affect the seasons."

As Stevenson was pushed more and more onto weaker ground, I grew increasingly frustrated. Finally, I demanded and obtained a promise from those on the plane that Stevenson would say nothing more on the subject until I could put together a reasoned position paper. I gathered about me in New York the most authoritative experts I could mobilize, cross-examining a stream of them in constant session over two days and nights and growing increasingly appalled by the drastic and complicated qualifications needed to defend Stevenson's position. In the end, I produced a careful—and coherent—paper that set forth the maximum position that could be rationally defended.

Then, in the early morning hours of October 27, I flew to the West Coast to meet Stevenson's plane and give him the position paper. After returning to New York, I awaited its issuance, but nothing appeared until October 29, two days later. I found—to my anger and dismay— that the staff on the plane had rewritten it, putting back the clearly insupportable overstatements. All my lost sleep and frantic effort had achieved nothing, while Adlai's increasingly extravagant pronouncements alienated an even larger number of his better informed supporters.

Nor was Stevenson's proposal on September 5—that we end the draft and substitute a volunteer army—handled any more adroitly. A respectable argument could have been made for it, and it then had some built-in bipartisan backing, though, since adoption by the Nixon Administration in 1972, it has proved disastrous. We had discussed it in a desultory way, and I had even speculated to Stevenson that Eisenhower might seek to match his politically effective declaration "I will go to Korea" with a surprise declaration that he was ending the draft and creating a volunteer army. Stevenson was badly positioned to put forward the volunteer army proposal. Though the country might have welcomed the proposal had Eisenhower offered it, who would accept Stevenson's civilian opinion on a military issue against that of our most famous general? Stevenson's mistake of strategy was fundamental. Instead of continuing to talk about domestic issues on which the Eisenhower Administration was vulnerable and the President an amateur, he tried to tackle the President on the issues of war and peace where a military leader had an overwhelming advantage. Again, he was heavily influenced by his own personal following. Adulatory friends were urging him to take the high road and educate people on cosmic questions, while scolding him for attacking on domestic issues.[5] Moreover, he loved the great generalities of foreign policy, delighting, as James Reston once wrote of another statesman, in "flinging continents about."

Ike was known for his good luck, and, in the end, history played into his hands. On October 29, Israel invaded the Sinai, and two days later England and France attacked at Suez. Major world crises necessarily work to the advantage of an incumbent President—particularly a military man thought capable of protecting American interests. The Suez crisis gave Ike the chance to show he was in charge. He made (without having to buy network time) a major nationwide address, reporting to the people as "your President," and not as a political candidate. In my capacity as Stevenson's director of public relations, I argued frantically with the networks to secure equal time. All three networks referred the matter to the Federal Communications Commission, which finally granted the time. Just then the Russians moved into Budapest to crush the Hungarian revolt. Eisenhower could not have arranged a better atmosphere for the election, and the vote showed it.

On election eve, I flew back from Boston to Chicago with Adlai. In the Blackstone Hotel we heard the bitter news. The Suez affair and the Hungarian revolt served at least one purpose: they provided Stevenson an excuse for losing—though I never doubted we would have lost anyway.

Post-Campaign Anticlimax

The readjustment after an unsuccessful campaign is difficult not only for the candidate, but painful as well for those who have worked closely with him. Since this was the second time around for me, I was becoming an expert at recuperating from unsuccessful political ventures. Once again, I had to reestablish my law practice, which I had all but abandoned for almost seven months. Adlai took a long vacation in the spring of 1957 and thereafter went off to England, where in May he received an honorary degree from Oxford and a tumultuous ovation from the undergraduates. From there he paid a short visit to Africa on behalf of various legal clients.

He returned more preoccupied than ever with the central importance of raising living standards in the Third World. It had, in fact, become an almost obsessive theme: "great wealth and great poverty cannot exist safely side-by-side indefinitely." Yet, though proclaiming the projected ending of the age of colonialism, he was opposed to radical solutions. When the young Senator John F. Kennedy made a widely noted speech attacking French policy in Algeria, Adlai described it to me as "a great mistake." Precipitate independence, he argued, would create only chaos and bloodshed.

In October 1957, Adlai called me to say that Secretary Dulles had asked him to spend six weeks in the State Department helping to prepare the NATO Summit Conference scheduled for December in Paris. Could I help him? He arrived in Washington on October 30, spent the evening talking with Dulles, and called me the following morning. He was ambivalent as to whether to accept Dulles's invitation. Dulles had proposed that Adlai be appointed a special assistant to the President, with an office in the State Department. He would devote most of his time for the rest of the year to developing a United States position paper on points that had been covered in a recent communiqué between Eisenhower and Macmillan. Then he would participate in presenting the position to the North Atlantic Council in December. Dulles envisaged a wide-ranging assignment; Stevenson would be expected to coordinate the American position with the principal allies and to drum up support from Congress and the American public.

Should Adlai undertake the assignment, or shouldn't he? Over the weekend, he and I went back and forth on the issue; Stevenson also talked to Tom Finletter and Lloyd Garrison. If he took it on, he would want me to work directly with him. Could I spare the time? Yes, I said, but meanwhile he ought to stop agonizing. He should either accept Dulles's invitation or flatly refuse it. But I knew Stevenson would never let it go at that; his instinct was for the dusty answer. So he told Dulles that the problems involved in drawing up the position paper were too complex for him to prepare it in time for the NATO meeting. Anyway, the formulation of policy was the responsibility of the President and Dulles and not of an opposition leader. Still, he would be willing to review and discuss the American position before it was put in final form and to do such missionary work as might be useful, even going to Europe as a "special envoy of the President."

In evitably, the matter leaked to the press, compelling Stevenson to issue a statement, since nothing had yet been publicly said by the White House. Though I was interested in, and was currently familiar with,

European political attitudes, I was exasperated with Stevenson's refusal to make up his mind. I was quite prepared to drop my law practice for a few months to help out, but I insisted that my role be approved by Dulles, particularly as I would need appropriate clearance even to see the relevant documents.

Stevenson talked to Dulles about me but met with resistance. Why wouldn't Stevenson be content with the assistants assigned to him from the State and Defense Departments? George Ball, Dulles said, was not cleared, and that process would take too long, The result was a messy compromise. I would assist Stevenson—but secretly. Since I could not go to the State Department to work with him there, every evening Stevenson would carry out the classified papers so he and I could review and revise them during the evening at the Georgetown house where he was staying. Then a messenger would call for the papers and take them back to the State Department.

More worrisome to me than these clumsy arrangements, however, was Stevenson's attitude toward the problems under consideration. He had long since lost interest in NATO; it was, he insisted, a purely military collective security system among the Western powers, and more and more he thought of foreign policy almost exclusively in terms of Third World relationships. Stevenson refused to regard as important the main problem to be faced in the NATO conference: the relation of France to the nuclear issue.

Nor was I happy with his endless conversations with a wide circle of his followers who had had some experience with foreign policy but were, for the most part, unfamiliar with the issues outlined in the Eisenhower-Macmillan communiqué and had out-of-date information in many other areas as well. Even Dean Rusk, whom I met for the first time in this context, wanted to discuss Third World problems that were, I thought, relevant to his work on the Rockefeller Foundation but quite irrelevant to the NATO meeting. Under the circumstances, I urged Adlai to tell Dulles frankly that we lacked sufficient time to develop "definitive ideas" and warn him against going forward with the NATO meeting without adequate consultation with the Congress.

Tom Finletter had prepared a useful paper on the NATO problems, including such matters as placing missiles in Europe. Finletter came to Washington, and he and I drafted a report that Stevenson could give to Dulles, reflecting his reaction to staff papers on NATO prepared by the State Department. But Stevenson had little sympathy for our ideas. His main concern was to include in the paper a strong plea that the United States should lead the "capitalist countries in speeding the development of the under-developed nations." Furthermore, the State Department papers did not, in Stevenson's view, include enough emphasis on disarmament. Dulles replied in a guarded fashion, pointing out that such questions as Third World development would not come up at the December meeting. Meanwhile, Stevenson privately told several of his friends in the press that the Paris meeting "must transcend the current obsession of Washington and London with missiles, rockets, and weapon systems."

It was a disappointing episode. Adlai's interest was in grand concepts and uplifting sentiments, and he was impatient with the practical issues then seriously troubling the Western Alliance. Moreover, he was uncomfortable to be working with Dulles and seemed quite properly concerned by the possible effect of collaboration on his public stance as leader of the Democratic opposition. The more he reflected on the assignment, the more awkward he felt. That is why he did not want to go to Paris: he did not relish being in the shadow of Eisenhower, or even of Dulles—a position I could well understand.

Nor did he try to conceal his boredom with the issues of nuclear defense, all of which he made crystal clear when, on December 6, in writing a critique of the draft of President Eisenhower's statement to NATO, he insisted, against my strong objection, on including the following statement: "I wish the President in his speech could loudly declare that he thinks NATO has a larger purpose than defense; that its purpose is peace and progress; that, as free nations have gathered together to protect themselves, they should also mobilize their resources and skills to help the less fortunate in the human family to advance; that, in this shrinking world, as in our communities, the rich must help the poor; and that this is a higher, better goal for NATO than the accumulation of nuclear weapons, however necessary."[6]

I will have more to say of Adlai in later chapters, but this seems a good point for a summing up. After all, his two campaigns for the Presidency—and particularly the first—were the golden years. All that occurred later was anticlimax.

The debt of gratitude I owe Adlai clearly emerges from the events I have recounted. He was for over three decades a sound counsellor; it was he more than anyone else who was responsible for my six years in the State Department—the most rewarding years of my life. I loved and admired Adlai, and if, in the course of this book, I may point out some of his imperfections, or, at least, eccentricities, it is because I do not like retouched photographs. No one ever had a better friend than Adlai Stevenson—he was unfailingly kind, thoughtful, and steadfast—or a better companion, for he was both wise and witty, with a deep reservoir of anecdote and experience on which he drew to everyone's delight. Nor has America often had so dedicated a leader, able to stir the imagination of thousands and restore thought and civility to the national discourse.

On July 14, 1965, I was returning on a commercial flight from a meeting of NATO in Paris. Halfway across the ocean, the captain brought me a message from the White House: "Governor Stevenson has just died in London and the President wants you to fly there with the Vice-President and bring back his body. A plane will be waiting when you reach Washington." In London the next morning, I saw several of Adlai's old friends and was made aware that the affection he enjoyed was not defined by national borders. Later I attended a memorial service in the Washington Cathedral, where Carl McGowan paid a moving eulogy. When I left the church, President Johnson was just getting into his limousine. He called to me and, with a comforting hand on my shoulder, said, "George, I never trust a man who can't cry for a friend." I had hoped that no one had noticed my tears, but the following week I found them recorded in a *Life Magazine* picture.

It has now been a quarter of a century since the failure of Adlai's second campaign, and during that time many have asked, "Would Stevenson have made a good president?" No one can answer such a question categorically. Every vote is an act of faith, for no one can ever foretell exactly how well any individual will perform under the strains and agonies of the Oval Office. So I can reply only for myself, "Yes, he could have been a great President."

The charge most often made against him is that he lacked decisiveness. As the previous pages have shown, that accusation cannot be totally ignored. But the instances of indecision I observed almost all involved questions of his own advancement or the promotion of his own interest; his hesitancy, in my view, resulted largely from his sense of style and abhorrence at pushing himself forward. On issues of principle, he stood firm—even when the costs were predictable and high. There is no evidence that he was indecisive as Governor of Illinois. On the contrary, he made a distinguished record, launching new initiatives, tidying up the state's finances, and dealing adroitly with the legislature. He was liked and respected, even revered, and his leadership was followed. As President, he would have given dignity to America, improved the moral and intellectual tone, and, in my view, led the country steadily and well.

Unhappily—for him and for America—he never had the chance to prove it.

II. *The French Crisis and Stevenson Again (1958–1961)*

For many years, I shuttled to Paris almost every month until by 1960 I had made over one hundred round-trip crossings. I watched with fascination as France engaged in its reluctant and painful retreat

from empire: from Indochina, then Tunisia and Morocco; until finally—
to the amazement of many of my French friends—even Algeria was
threatened. I discussed the problem incessantly with a wide spectrum of
Frenchmen—ranging from the philosopher and journalist Raymond
Aron to acquaintances in French government and industry. As might
be expected, my clients, the French Patronat, adopted the most obdurate position.

Why, they asked, was my country so intent on dislodging France from
its colonial holdings—why, as they saw it, did Washington show such a
lack of appreciation for all that France had done and was doing for the
indigènes in her overseas territories? Could we not understand why Paris
must take drastic action to check the nationalist frenzy that, they contended, would condemn the natives overseas (who were legally citizens
of France) to a premature and disastrous independence?

To convert me to their point of view, they exposed me to the leaders—both military and civilian—who were trying to fight off the Viet
Minh in Indochina. From them I learned about France's frustrations in
fighting *"la guerre sale."* Not only was the terrain of Indochina clearly
unfit for the type of warfare France's seasoned overseas troops had been
trained to fight, but the irrational willingness of the Viet Minh to take
staggering losses made them an unconquerable adversary. I was to think
of this often nine years later, when America compulsively repeated all
of France's mistakes on the same hostile terrain and against essentially
the same enemy. The French disclosed the same propensity for self-
deception, seduced by the same self-serving arguments that were later
to lead my countrymen astray; they even comforted themselves with the
same statistics of kill ratios and body counts that Americans were to recite
with such macabre assurance during the middle 1960s. Just as the
American civilian and military leaders were later to concoct new sure-
fire ways to win the war, so the French periodically announced new tactical schemes—the Navarre Plan, the Salan Plan, the Leclerc Plan, and
the de Lattre de Tassigny Plan—that would magically assure victory in a
short period.

Visit to the Maghreb

But none of those schemes worked, and by 1954, grieved as they
were by the loss of Indochina, the French were facing mounting threats
to areas that concerned them even more—their possessions in the Maghreb: Tunisia, Morocco, and Algeria. I made no secret of my belief that
they would ultimately have to give up those territories. They, in turn,
tried hard to educate me in the mystique of "assimilation" and "identity"
and the idealistic concepts of Marshal Louis Lyautey. I could only
understand French policy in North Africa, they contended, by viewing
operations on the spot. So when Ruth and I were in Paris in January

1953, the Patronat proposed that we make a tour of North Africa at their expense. I accepted the invitation but only with the stipulation that I be permitted to talk to all sides—the Nationalist groups as well as French officials and leaders of the French communities. Ruth and I spent two weeks in Tunisia, Algeria, and Morocco—our schedules tightly filled with interviews and sightseeing. The Patronat kept their word that I could listen to both sides of the case, arranging meetings for me with representatives of the Neo-Destour in Tunisia, the FLN in Algeria, and the Istiqlal in Morocco.

On my return, my clients no doubt expected me to provide a report they could use to help persuade Americans that their cause was righteous. But the trip only confirmed my conviction that the French were pushing against the tide of history. Though they might be able to postpone coming to grips with their predicament for a limited period, sooner or later their time would run out in the Maghreb. Since I saw no point in rewarding their hospitality by a disquieting report that would stir resentments but make no converts, I followed the unheroic course of thanking them for the trip but writing nothing.

Algeria in Flames

In confirmation of even my most pessimistic predictions, the French were able to buy very little time. Faced with mounting insurrections throughout North Africa and wishing to avoid simultaneous rebellion in all three territories, the leaders of the Fourth Republic allowed both Tunisia and Morocco to become sovereign states in 1956 so they could concentrate on maintaining their position in Algeria. But it was only throwing babies to the wolves; less than two years after our visit, long-simmering rebellion broke out and, by 1958, France had deployed more than 500,000 soldiers in Algeria—as large as our later deployment in Vietnam and the greatest overseas expeditionary force in French history. It was a rearguard action, fought with emotion and cruelty on both sides. Unlike Morocco, Algeria was not a recent French acquisition. The French had controlled the area since 1830 and, unlike British India, where there were fewer than 50,000 British civil servants and commercial representatives out of a total population of almost 400 million, at least 1,200,000 people in Algeria thought of themselves as French—although many, and perhaps most, were of Spanish or Mediterranean origin. French *colons* and their families, many of whom had lived in Algeria for five or six generations, dominated its economic life. But since the natives (the *indigènes*) outnumbered them eight to one, the *colons* feared—not without reason—that in an independent Algeria, they would, as they expressed it macabrely, be forced, to choose between "the ship and the coffin."

Nationalist sentiment had been stimulated during World War II, particularly by America's doctrinal advocacy of self-determination, and, once that war ended, a number of bloody incidents occurred. Though France grudgingly conceded the Muslims a small amount of political power, little came of it, and in 1954 the revolt began to spread over the country. By 1956, the FLN had gained the support of virtually all of the Algerian nationalists. They had occupied a great part of the countryside and were conducting terrorist attacks in the cities. The French had responded by committing massive forces and building electrified fences along Algeria's borders with Morocco and Tunisia. They even crossed over onto Tunisian territory to destroy sanctuaries just as we were later to invade Cambodia.

When Mendès-France extricated France from Indochina and Paris granted independence to Tunisia and Morocco, the *colons* as well as elements of the French army developed a neurotic fear that a weak Fourth Republic government might betray them by negotiating a craven settlement. In November 1957, Felix Gaillard, who had been Jean Monnet's *chef de cabinet* during my French Supply Council days in Washington, became Prime Minister and remained in that post until April of the following year. I visited him several times during that stormy period. The French attack on the Tunisian village of Sakiet, which served as a sanctuary for Algerian rebels, had incited the Tunisian government to retaliate by blockading 15,000 French soldiers at Bizerte. A British and American offer of good offices to help settle the dispute only revived latent suspicion that the United States sought to internationalize the Algerian conflict as a prelude to Algerian independence.

In April 1958, a sudden freshet of anti-Americanism washed away the Gaillard government and, following a protracted crisis, a right-wing army revolt broke out in Algeria. For the moment, France seemed threatened by attack from its own forces in Algeria, much as Spain had been attacked by General Franco's African legions twenty-two years earlier. Since I was in and out of Paris constantly during the period, I shared the general excitement, momentarily expecting a military coup and watching with my friends for an airdrop in the Place de la Concorde. In those anxious hours, the depression that had haunted me eighteen years before returned in full measure. What might befall France under a new and brutal Fascism?

The General on the White Horse

Thus, I was vastly relieved when, on May 16, de Gaulle broke his long silence from Colombey to announce that he was ready to "assume the power of the Republic." After a period of intense and confused maneuvering, that event finally took place on May 27, 1958.

Returning to the United States late in June, I analyzed the prevailing French malaise in a speech before the New York State Bar Association Convention at Saranac on June 28, pointing out that since 1946, France had been constantly at war overseas—first in Indochina, then Morocco and Tunisia, and now Algeria. These King Canute struggles to turn back giant waves of nationalism beating against weakened colonial structures had left a deep mark on the French armed forces. Their disenchantment had begun in 1940, when, though miserably led and finally overcome by the Nazi blitzkrieg, many army units had fought bravely and well. Nonetheless, the army had emerged not only discredited but overshadowed in public esteem by the largely nonprofessional Resistance forces. Thus, in postwar France, the proud officer from St. Cyr learned from a succession of small humiliations that he had lost his status. No longer did the French bourgeois mother concentrate her formidable energies on marrying off her daughter to the bedazzling young lieutenant; army pay had not kept pace with increases in the pay even of civil servants.

This loss of social status as well as the inflated cost of living had, I pointed out, led army officers to connive for posts in North Africa and in other French possessions. In those posts, they had lived in style as the dominant force in the local society. Unappreciated at home, they had found a psychically satisfying life in farflung outposts of the empire. It was a contradiction that bred resentment and suspicion of the politicians who treated them shabbily. After Dien Bien Phu, when sixteen thousand of the army's best troops were trapped in a jungle fortress, the politicians had loudly blamed military incompetence. When a panicky Fourth Republic government gave independence to Morocco and Tunisia, which was more than the Muslim Nationalists were asking at the time, the army felt a deepened sense of betrayal.

Suez confirmed the diagnosis. Though the highly trained paratroopers of General Massu dropped at Port Said with splendid precision, the government yet again snatched defeat from the jaws of victory. The French deputies—"the monkeys in the Palais Bourbon" who comprised the "system"—could no longer be left in charge. Particularly among the more idealistic officers the feeling grew that France needed a reform not merely of her politics but of her national life. Though French tradition taught that the army was "La Grande Muette" (the Great Mute), history had provided plenty of exceptions. Indeed, French history inspired some of my friends in Paris to repeat the adage: "Never trust a man who must put on a disguise in order to establish his authority—be he a priest, a judge, or an army officer."

I hated to acknowledge that Algeria's problems had become too divisive to be resolved by a badly divided French government. In spite of its persistent untidiness, I had always been fond of the Fourth Republic; its very weakness had been its most appealing virtue, for it was incapable of resisting accommodation with the larger Europe I thought essential. What would happen with a strong man now striding on stage? In July, a month after de Gaulle's investiture, I stood on the Champs Elysées as he rode by, standing tall and imperious in an open Citroen, waving his hand with that limp gesture that always seemed out of character. The silent attention of curiously impassive crowds was disturbed by only scattered wrathful chanting of "Algérie Française."

The General had proved an indispensable *deus ex machina:* only he had the strength and audacity to resolve the agonizing Algerian crisis. Yet my relief that France had been saved from a right-wing military coup was dampened by the fear of resurgent French nationalism. I strongly favored a modern structure for Western Europe, and, though the General had spoken of Europe in ambiguous terms, I saw little chance of reconciling his commitment to ersatz *grandeur* with a unified Europe that could play the role of equal partner with America.

For the time being, the European idea would no doubt coast along on its own momentum, since de Gaulle would have to concentrate on Algeria. But, once the Algerian crisis was settled—by, I felt certain, the ultimate conferring of independence—he would be free to focus on Europe and would almost certainly inject a corrosive element into the European chemistry. I discussed this with Jean Monnet but found him unprepared to speculate. Though he had grave reservations about the General, based on long experience in dealing with him in Algeria and later in Paris, he was unwilling to abandon hope that he and de Gaulle might someday achieve a *modus vivendi* that would let Europe go forward.

Adlai Resurgent?

Meanwhile, though France was very much on my mind, I maintained a latent interest in American politics. I saw Adlai intermittently, and we invariably found ourselves speaking of his future. In July 1959, I spent a week with him on the *Flying Clipper,* a 205-foot sailing yacht owned by a Swedish publisher and shipping magnate that had been chartered for a Mediterranean cruise by one of Adlai's old friends, William Benton. Although there were other guests aboard (the yacht could sleep sixteen and had a crew of thirty-five), Adlai and I managed to steal time together, sitting on the forward deck in the sun. He was having a hard time focusing on politics; it was a summer of pure leisure and he delighted in the pleasures of the rich. Wherever he was, Adlai tended to hold court, surrounded by idolatrous and indulgent friends who looked after his every need. Although I hated to inject reality, if we were to avoid one more orgy of indecision, it was time for him to make up his mind what he wanted to do.

I left the yacht mid-cruise to return home, later meeting Adlai at Eze-sur-Mer on the Riviera, where he was again staying with Bill Benton—this time in a villa with seven terraces to the sea. I reviewed a long list of questions that I felt he should be prepared to answer on his return to the United States. We talked at length about his chances for the nomination, confirming my impression that he wanted very much to be drafted. I followed this up on August 8 with a letter addressed to him at Mary Lasker's villa on the French Riviera, describing the general state of the political weather as I saw it. Humphrey, I said, had not yet "gotten his campaign off the ground"; Kennedy was "whirling like a dervish in dead center"; nobody knew who Symington was; "Pat Brown conceded that Stevenson could carry California; and a recent Gallup Poll had persuaded the politicians that a Stevenson-Kennedy ticket would be the strongest one possible." Thus, I concluded, "all this adds up to the fact that events are beginning to respond to an inexorable political logic"; yet, "if the convention insists on nominating you, I am sure it will be because you do nothing about it."

But Kennedy had quite different ideas. He hoped for Adlai's support at the convention and, indeed, was eager that Adlai make the nominating speech for him. On the day after the Oregon primary, which Kennedy won against Humphrey, the future President had breakfast at Stevenson's home in Libertyville. Though several others were initially present, the two men retired for a private meeting. Kennedy then made a strong plea to Stevenson to make the nominating speech but met with resistance. Later that day or the next, Stevenson telephoned me in a fury. "Kennedy behaved just like his old man. He said to me, 'Look, I have the votes for the nomination and if you don't give me your support, I'll have to shit all over you. I don't want to do that but I can, and I will if I have to.'" I had rarely heard Stevenson so angry. It was clear to me that from then on there was no chance of Stevenson throwing his support to Kennedy, who obviously did not understand Stevenson's aversion to crude language. Stevenson said to me, "I should have told the son-of-a-bitch off but, frankly, I was shocked and confused by that Irish gutter talk. That's pretty cheap stuff."[1] Stevenson wrote to Arthur Schlesinger commenting on the meeting and stating, "I can add that he seemed *very* self-confident and assured and much tougher and bloodier than I remembered him in the past."

During the early part of the year, John Sharon, whom I had brought into our law firm after the 1956 convention, and Tom Finney, an administrative assistant to Senator "Mike" Monroney, had begun a quiet drive for Stevenson's nomination. Working out of my law office and Senator Monroney's office on the Hill, they had made up detailed lists of delegates and had begun canvassing them by telephone. They were thorough and professional, and if they erred in judging the situation, it was

from wishful thinking. Though I wanted to believe all they were reporting, I found it hard.

Again, I shall avoid recounting the events of the convention in Los
Angeles. For me, as for other Stevensonians, it had high points—Eugene
McCarthy's inspired nominating speech and the protracted demonstration when Stevenson came to the convention floor. Yet it put a definitive
end to our speculations; we now knew, every one of us, that Stevenson
would never be President, though he could still serve the country in a
lesser capacity. I think it likely that in many ways he would almost have
preferred to be Secretary of State—provided there was a President who
shared his general views. That would have freed him from attention to
grimy domestic affairs, enabling him to concentrate on foreign policy,
which was, and had always been, his consuming interest.

"The Stevenson Report"

Yet I was convinced that, since Stevenson had refused to nominate
Kennedy or to support him for the nomination, Kennedy would not
want him in that post. More likely, he would offer him the job of ambassador to the United Nations. Thus, on July 26, I wrote Adlai a long letter
prophesying that if Kennedy won, Stevenson would have to accept or
reject the United Nations job. Since, if he refused, it might be interpreted as sour grapes, I suggested that, if he did not want it, he should
clarify his position with Kennedy promptly. Though any firm commitments prior to the election would be inappropriate, possibly even illegal,
Stevenson should let Kennedy know that he was interested "solely" in
the "post of major responsibility"—that is, Secretary of State. Because
the Republican ticket would probably consist of Nixon and Lodge, both
of whom could claim some foreign policy experience, Kennedy would
need to associate himself with Stevenson as a foreign policy expert during the campaign; for that reason Stevenson's bargaining position was
probably at its highest point.

You should, I wrote Stevenson, "not only indicate to Kennedy that
you are willing to campaign in certain selected areas, but also mention
the possibility of your setting up an *ad hoc* group to formulate a specific
foreign policy program for execution during the first months of next
year." With matters deteriorating during the latter days of Eisenhower,
the new administration, I wrote, would have to move fast and decisively
to "regain the diplomatic initiative and transform America's reputation
around the world." The new Kennedy Administration should behave as
the Roosevelt Administration had behaved during the crisis in 1933,
promptly putting forth this time not a domestic, but a well-prepared
foreign policy program, and Stevenson should have ready a blueprint
consisting of both specific actions to be undertaken in the first six months

and fresh formulations of long-term objectives and policy.

When Stevenson saw Kennedy at Hyannis Port, he broached the proposal for the task force. Kennedy immediately approved but said nothing about who would be Secretary of State. Stevenson telephoned me the next day to report his meeting with Kennedy, saying, "Now that you've got me into this task force business, it's up to you to do the work. I'm counting on you to come up with a full report. Let me know from time to time how you're proceeding and we can talk it over as the work goes forward."

I immediately set about mobilizing knowledgeable friends and during the course of the summer produced a report that Theodore White later called "Stevenson's most important contribution to the Kennedy campaign." Knowing Adlai as I did, I had been sure from the beginning that I would have to take the laboring oar of drafting the report—at least until we had produced a next-to-final draft that he could polish. In the course of preparing the draft, I met with Stevenson only once—amid magnificent French impressionists in Mary Lasker's beautiful house on Sutton Place. A few days after that meeting of October 5, I sent Stevenson a preliminary outline of the report describing the work I was doing and the people I was involving. Stevenson replied, "I marvel at the rapidity with which you have seized hold of this assignment."[2]

Immediately after President Kennedy's election, I looked for the best ways and means to deliver the report to him at Palm Beach, where he was temporarily resting. I knew Kennedy only slightly and, though we were on a first-name basis, that reflected merely the camaraderie associated with political campaigning. Since anyone who appeared at Palm Beach was immediately beleaguered by the press, and I did not want to upstage Adlai by advertising my own role in the report, I found it awkward to arrange the delivery. Thus, even though I had written most of the report, I turned to John Sharon, a colleague in my law office who had known Kennedy longer and better, and dispatched him to Palm Beach with the document. It was the first time Sharon had ever seen it.

Following my original proposal to Stevenson I had, in part I of the report, listed questions requiring immediate attention: the gold drain, the postponement of discussions of the NATO deterrent, new initiatives in disarmament, assurances on Berlin, and support of the Organization for Economic Cooperation and Development (OECD). In part II, I proposed long-term policies in the fields of economic development, NATO, nuclear cooperation, and arms control. In order to bring about a greater coherence in economic policy, I outlined a comprehensive foreign economic legislation that would provide new aid proposals and give the President authority over a five-year period to reduce tariffs by 50 percent. I included in the appendices papers relating to China, Sub-Saharan Africa, and the organization of the State Department, and I recommended the formation of further task forces to deal with Latin America and Africa.

When Sharon handed Kennedy the document, he called his attention specifically to the immediate recommendations. Kennedy showed particular interest in the OECD and the problems with Cuba. "When he finished Part I," Arthur Schlesinger reports, "Kennedy closed the volume and said: 'Very good. Terrific. This is excellent. Just what I needed.' "[3] Though Sharon handled himself dexterously in fielding Kennedy's questions that were quite out of his field, he did not disclose that he had played no part in preparing the document. That led to confusion. Kennedy assumed that the report was largely Sharon's work and, during the next few days, telephoned John to commission him to undertake additional task forces on other subjects. It took some time to get our responsibilities sorted out. Although there was mistrust of the exercise on the part of Kennedy's Senate staff, who were jealous of anyone intruding from the Stevenson camp, Kennedy insisted on our going forward independently. The assignments he gave me were, among others, to organize and chair forces on the balance of payments, foreign economic policy, and the OECD.

I worked night and day on these task force efforts for the next six weeks, so that they could be ready by the end of December. Meanwhile, the President was going forward with his appointments. He had already designated Dean Rusk as his Secretary of State and Chester Bowles as Under Secretary of State, and there were rumors in the newspapers that he had decided to appoint a liberal Republican businessman, William C. Foster, as Under Secretary of State for Economic Affairs. Foster, whom I knew and liked, had been deputy to Paul Hoffman in administering the Marshall Plan, but he was a Republican and by this time the cabinet had more than the usual share of Republicans in key posts—including C. Douglas Dillon in Treasury and Robert McNamara in Defense. About that time, Chester Bowles asked me to become the Assistant Secretary for Economic Affairs, but I declined. Later I was asked to become the ambassador to the Organization for Economic Cooperation and Development, which I also refused.

I completed the task force reports just after Christmas Day, then joined my family in Florida for the holidays. I was not happy. I felt well equipped to be Under Secretary of State for Economic Affairs, but I had few illusions regarding my chances. Nevertheless, to gain a clear idea as to the views of the new President, I occupied myself in Florida by reading—and outlining—Kennedy's book *The Strategy of Peace*, a collection of his speeches and writings.

I returned to Washington early in January, reconciled to remaining in private life. Thus I was not surprised when, on a flight from New York to Washington, I read in the *New York Times* a long story about the imminent appointment of William C. Foster as Under Secretary of State for Economic Affairs.

Without telling me, John Sharon at this point sprang to action. He telephoned Stevenson, advising him of the rumored appointment and urging him to try to persuade the new President to change his mind. Instead of calling Kennedy directly, Stevenson telephoned Senator William Fulbright, who was then vacationing in Florida. The following day, Fulbright drove to Palm Beach to tell President Kennedy that he was giving Republicans too many top posts in the three principal departments—State, Defense, and Treasury—which would create the impression that the Democratic party lacked men of stature. The President, Fulbright said, should appoint me rather than Foster, since I was eminently qualified for the post. That admonition was reinforced a day or two later when, at breakfast with the President, John Kenneth Galbraith vigorously urged my appointment. As a result, the President changed his mind about Foster and appointed me.

Although I had had considerable experience in the bureaucracy, I had never held an assignment that attracted public attention, and I was not fully prepared for such a drastic change in the pattern of my life. For the next six years, I was to get very little sleep.

PART V

The Kennedy Years

12. Early Kennedy Years

On January 10, 1961, Dean Rusk telephoned to say that the President had decided to appoint me Under Secretary of State for Economic Affairs and that the announcement would be made the following day. At the State Department, I found Rusk in a small office on the first floor normally reserved for visitors, deeply engaged in a frantic but largely futile exercise. He was trying to answer several pages of questions sent to him by the President's assistant and speech writer, Ted Sorensen. It was an impossible assignment since the questions covered every foreign policy issue Sorensen could think of—ranging from the Far East to Latin America and points north, east, south, and west. A staff might have spent several weeks preparing the answers, but because the new administration had not yet taken over and Rusk had not been confirmed, he had to develop the answers without any direct discussion with the State Department. Rusk assigned me several questions, and I mobilized some of my task force collaborators.

Within the next few days, I made the requisite calls on Speaker of the House Sam Rayburn, as well as on my old friend Senator Fulbright, chairman of the Foreign Relations Committee. I appeared before the Committee and on January 30 was confirmed.

The Kennedy Environment

The environment in which I found myself was both familiar and strange. I felt well prepared to deal with those areas under my jurisdiction—principally trade, foreign assistance and monetary policy—as a result of my work in the Lend-Lease and Foreign Economic Administrations during the war, my representation of foreign clients fighting trade restrictions, my participation in the Committee for a National Trade Policy, my work with Monnet, and my role as chairman of a number of Kennedy task forces. I was already on familiar terms with a number of the personalities—both American and foreign—with whom I would be collaborating or negotiating as a result of my prior incarnations. With the conditioned reflex of a blooded bureaucrat, I appraised my own position in the scheme of things, trying to predict who would hold the levers of power and to negotiate an effective division of labor. Though I disliked bureaucratic infighting, I was not unmindful of what Robert Ardrey, the ethologist, later called in a different context the "territorial imperative."

In the years that have since passed, the Kennedy Administration has acquired a nimbus of romance, enhanced by the poignancy of the young President's murder and wistful speculation as to what he might have accomplished. But even at the beginning of his term, there was more than the usual hope and excitement. The President and his lady were both young, handsome, and literate. They displayed those ineffable qualities that an adulatory press referred to as "flair," or "style." Still, though Ruth and I could not help feeling the savor of springtime in the air, it was not the same uncritical excitement we had felt at the beginning of the New Deal. Perhaps we had merely lost the extravagance of youth; we were older and more cynically aware that "plus ça change, plus c'est la même chose." Perhaps we had been in Washington too long, but it seemed to us that there was an inescapable sense of *déjà vu*. Whatever the reason, I could not avoid feeling somewhat detached from the "new team's" exuberance and its confidence in the bright new plans and brilliant insights shortly to be disclosed. As usual, I was on the periphery: I was a Stevenson protégé; I had not been for Kennedy before San Francisco; I had not taught or studied on the Charles River.

Although I still thought of myself as a bright young man, I had to recognize that I had now lived more than a half-century and, in serving John F. Kennedy, was for the first time working for a man younger than I was. Dean Rusk was my senior by ten months, but other luminous members of the new foreign policy repertory company—McGeorge Bundy (forty-one), Ted Sorensen (thirty-three), Bob McNamara (forty-five), and even my old friend, Arthur Schlesinger (forty-four)—were of a generation that had known the depression and early New Deal only in childhood or from the history books they had read or—in the case of Schlesinger—had written. I had unwittingly joined a new youth movement.

The year was unmistakably 1961, not 1933 or 1942. The problems confronting the country were different from those we had faced during my earlier tours in government. In 1933, the country had been in the depths of a searing depression. Urgent and visible action was required not merely to ameliorate widespread hardship but to rescue the disastrously shattered public morale. Events had provided a vivid backdrop for the famous Hundred Days. Again, there had been a pervasive sense of urgency when I had returned to Washington immediately after Pearl Harbor. America's energies were then even more narrowly focused; we had a war to win, and, though there were a thousand ideas of how to win it, our central purpose was never in doubt or dispute.

I found the mood and situation at the beginning of 1961 quite different. America had just enjoyed eight years of relaxed leadership under Dwight Eisenhower. The Korean War had been over for six years; the economy, while suffering a slight slowdown, was by no means in a crisis. Even though Montgomery and Little Rock were place names with epic connotations, those at the top reaches of the Administration showed only a shadowy appreciation of the civil rights movement and the turbulence it would create. The new President spoke of that "goddamn civil rights mess," considering it more an embarrassing problem than a serious cause that had gained many proponents. Of course, we could dimly foresee looming dangers and obstacles, but the world seemed just then to be moving toward one of its rare periods of tranquillity. The Stalin legend had been discredited at the Twentieth Party Congress; a leader whom many regarded as a rough but rational peasant, Nikita Khrushchev, was now in power, and there were intimations of a first thaw in the Cold War.

JFK's Foreign Policy Views

There was not a great deal to know about the new President's views on foreign policy. I hoped he was thoroughly purged of the obscurantist attitudes of old Joseph P. Kennedy, his father. Prior to America's entry into the war, the senior Kennedy had been a rabid isolationist, who, as ambassador to London, had inexcusably undercut President Roosevelt in 1940 by testifying before the Senate Foreign Relations Committee against the Lend-Lease legislation for which his President was valiantly fighting. Nor had he ceased his isolationist frog-croaking even after John Kennedy had entered Congress. Having opposed America's intervention to stop Hitler and the Nazis, he was also a capitulationist when the Soviets threatened to sweep the earth. Believing that the United States could survive as an enclave of freedom, he argued that we "should get out of Korea and stop trying to hold the line at the Elbe or at the Rhine." If the Soviets decided to march, Joseph Kennedy argued, they could easily reach the Atlantic, and it was not for us to try to stop them; indeed, he thought it likely that Europe would, at least for a period of time, be wholly taken over by the Communists. He was against our trying to stay in Berlin, criticized the British loan, and opposed aid to Greece and Turkey, American participation in Korea, and the Marshall Plan.

I had long despised the elder Kennedy, who represented everything

I disliked and mistrusted. He had been a buccaneer on Wall Street, an opportunist in politics, and a debilitating influence when our civilization was fighting for its life; now we were once more engaged against an enemy with the same hard face of tyranny. Before I could wholeheartedly support the new President, I had to satisfy myself that he was free of his father's views and influence. Just after the election I had carefully analyzed his writings and speeches—and had found reassurance that the father's noxious views had not infected the son.

Yet, to my mind, John Kennedy's comments and actions during his years in Congress still reflected a muddy concept of America's role in world politics. He had backed the Truman Doctrine and had supported the Marshall Plan, but he had joined the cacophonous caterwauling of the China lobby that Truman had "lost" China by trying to force Chiang into a coalition with the Communists. Though partially redeeming himself by supporting the deployment of American divisions to Europe, he had qualified that support by insisting on a totally unworkable ratio system. Finally, and this was now of particular interest to me as Under Secretary of State for Economic Affairs, John Kennedy, in February 1949, had voted to recommit the Trade Agreements Extension Act.

Kennedy's most spectacular adventure in foreign policy during his Senate term had been his attack on French policy in Indochina in 1953. No doubt encouraged by the attention these pronouncements had achieved, he had again criticized French colonial policy four years later, in July 1957, this time directing his guns at France's activities in Algeria. One victim of the verbal fallout was our then ambassador to Paris, C. Douglas Dillon, who had expressed firm faith in the French government's handling of the entire matter. (Now Dillon was to be Kennedy's Secretary of the Treasury.) "French insistence upon pacification of the area, in reality reconquest," Kennedy declared in the Senate in July 1957, is "a policy which only makes both settlement and a cease-fire less likely."[1] Algeria, he concluded, was no longer merely a French problem; it was time for the United States "to face the harsh realities of the situation and fulfill its responsibilities as leader of the free world—in the UN, in NATO, in the administration of our aid programs and in the exercise of our diplomacy [to shape] a course toward political independence for Algeria."[2]

Though I had long been trying to convince my French friends that "Algérie Française" was not a policy they could sustain, I was wary of the young Senator's proposal to inject America into a problem only France could settle.

Dean Acheson publicly called Kennedy's Algerian address an insensitive speech that would do more harm than good in resolving the Algerian problem, and I later recalled that speech when Kennedy and successive American Presidents resentfully rejected suggestions that

Vietnam was not exclusively an American affair or that we should fold our tents and go home.

The next year, 1958, Kennedy warned the Senate of a forthcoming Soviet missile gap that would become most dangerous during the early 1960s, when "the deterrent ratio might well shift to the Soviets so heavily, during the years of the gap, as to open to them a new shortcut to world domination."[3] Couched in bureaucratic jargon, that statement was not merely fuzzy in meaning, it was later shown to have been largely an aberration. That it was to become one of the critical themes of Kennedy's campaign against Nixon was not surprising; campaigns are rarely fought over relevant issues, and the controversy over the fictitious missile gap was at least more important than the fatuous hassle over the defense of Quemoy and Matsu—small islands most Americans could not find on the map.

Few Presidents, if any, take office fully armed, like Minerva, with a coherent view of American foreign policy. Wilson was a moderate American reformer with a strong sense of his own superior morality; his romantic foreign policy was shattered on the gneiss of *Realpolitik*. Franklin Roosevelt was enamored of naval power and steeped in the doctrines of Admiral Mahan, but he was also a pragmatist whose vague strategic concepts crystallized during the course of his long and eventful tenure. Eisenhower had an inchoate sense of where America should go but could not articulate it; Nixon's mistakes were concealed under a Béarnaise of Kissingerian abstractions. Ford came to office modest about his mastery of foreign policy and, as Churchill once said of Clement Attlee, "he had much to be modest about."

Prior to inauguration, most American Presidents have had little exposure to foreign policy and approach the subject ill-informed, eager, and pragmatic. Europeans carry more baggage of history and theory. Yet, though Kennedy was certainly not steeped in strategic thought, he came equipped with a bright and alert mind and gathered about him exceptionally able people.

The Kennedy Style

Kennedy was the pragmatist *par excellence;* although he sometimes alluded to conceptual ideas in his speeches, his main concern was action and day-to-day results. When one tried to point out the long-range implications of a current problem or how it meshed or collided with other major national interests, Kennedy would often say, politely but impatiently, "Let's not worry about five years from now, what do we do tomorrow?" I was frequently disappointed by his reluctance to face the longer-range implications of either acting or not acting. In my view, the emphasis of Professor Richard Neustadt that a President should seek, so far as possible, to "preserve his options" provided too facile a rationalization for postponing unpleasant decisions on major issues where results would not be immediately apparent. Though I found Kennedy intellectually alert and quick to understand a given problem, he was not, in my opinion, profound in either his analyses or his judgment.

On only one occasion did I ever hear anyone try to force him to a long-range decision he clearly wanted to postpone. He had asked Dean Acheson to attend a meeting during which we discussed every facet of a burdensome problem. At the end of the long evening, President Kennedy announced that he would have the question studied further. Acheson flared up, "There's no point in studying the matter further, Mr. President; you know all you'll ever know about it. The only thing to do with the issue is to decide it." Though obviously taken aback, the President responded politely, but Acheson did not immediately cool down and the meeting ended uneasily.

Kennedy was without doubt an effective advocate, but if it is now part of the mythology that he was a gifted speaker, that is only by contrast to those whom we have since endured. He spoke with a peculiar Bostonian cadence, letting his voice fall just when it should have risen to gain maximum effect. An attractive figure on the platform, easy in manner, armed with eloquently phrased speeches interlarded with quotations and poetry, he projected charm but little passion. Though audiences liked him and found him disarming, they were rarely roused as Roosevelt, for example, had roused them. He was young and boyishly good looking; he and his stylish wife brought a glamour and gaiety to the White House unknown perhaps since the days of Dolly Madison. Nevertheless, he could not impose his own personality on the events of the day, as I had seen Roosevelt do three decades earlier.

Dean Rusk, My Self-Contained Leader

My immediate chief was Dean Rusk, for whom I developed both respect and affection. Though he gave many the impression of coolness, he quickly became a warm friend. I could talk freely to him on any subject. Thoughtful and reserved, he possessed a quiet humor, enormous moral resources, and had a deep commitment to strongly held ideas and principles. His ample reservoir of fortitude sustained him during critical periods, and he displayed an almost excessive dedication to work. Indeed, his unrelenting efforts over his eight-year tenure as Secretary of State permanently impaired his health.

His desire, as he expressed it on many occasions, was to leave the next Secretary of State with problems no worse than he had found them when he took office. It was not a sentiment I shared; I would have chased far more rabbits than he, but that reflects a difference in temperament and philosophy. During my first months in the Department, when my jurisdiction was limited to economic affairs, Rusk's apparent indifference to my activities bothered me; I was making important decisions and felt the need for a continuing dialogue with the Secretary. I expressed that concern to Lucius Battle, the wise and perceptive head of the Department's secretariat who had known Rusk well for many years, and much to my surprise he burst out laughing. "Only the other day," he said, "Dean told me, 'I wish I knew what Ball's doing; he goes his own way and never talks to me.' " That colloquy cleared the air; thereafter, the Secretary and I established regular and thoroughly satisfactory communications.

Rusk shared my general views about European unity, although he did not feel as strongly about it as I and was skeptical of the reactions of European governments that all too often tended to regard the world's major conflicts as a spectator sport. For example, when the Dutch government pressed us hard to defend their interests in New Guinea (West Irian), then under threat from President Sukarno of Indonesia, Rusk's response was unequivocal and, I thought, unanswerable: "If the burghers of Amsterdam are not prepared to send their sons to save the area," he said, "why should we ask American boys to fight and die for it?"

Rusk's discipline and patience admirably equipped him to deal with the Soviet Union. When, during the summer of 1961, he conducted a marathon negotiation with Gromyko over Berlin and Germany, he was as competent as his adversary at reiterating the same positions again and again, varying the exact formulation just enough to keep the dialogue going without giving away a single nuance.

Unlike several of my more flamboyant colleagues, Dean never let personal vanity color his views. His loyalty to his country, and indeed to the President, contributed to a reserve that limited and often distorted the impression he made on those about him. With his quiet humor, he could easily have adopted a public personality that would have provided the press with far better and more sympathetic copy. It would have increased his popularity and even in some instances his effectiveness. But instead, he kept the press at arm's length, rarely telling them anything they did not know already or could not easily obtain from others.

Consistent with his view of the relations between a Secretary of State and his President, he expressed his opposition to the projected Bay of Pigs expedition only privately to Kennedy. When that expedition proved a fiasco, he never disclosed that he had cautioned against it. Later, de Gaulle expressed his admiration for Rusk as a man who would never embarrass his chief; Rusk would never put the President in the position of publicly rejecting his advice if the President decided to go forward with a project Rusk opposed. He followed the tradition of Secretary of State George Marshall whom he greatly admired.

Chester Bowles, the Idealist

In contrast to Dean Rusk, Chester Bowles, the Under Secretary of State during the initial months, was far too open and voluble. When the Bay of Pigs failed, he made the mistake of letting it be known in public that he had advised against the venture. I had become acquainted with Bowles during the 1956 Stevenson campaign. I found him sympathetic with what I was trying to achieve, but his interest in economic policy was largely concentrated on assisting the Third World—particularly the nations of Asia and, to a lesser extent, Africa. Bowles was a warm and generous spirit who inspired affection. Too noble for life in the bureaucratic jungle, he still held courageously to his principles. Given their disparity in temperament, Dean Rusk and he could not possibly work together effectively. Rusk was impatient of windy abstractions, while Bowles, who had begun his career in the advertising business, was enamored of sweeping statements and broad concepts that often seemed little more than catch phrases.

Bowles favored those romantic clichés to which Adlai Stevenson was also addicted, but he lacked Stevenson's grace of expression, underlying earthiness, and cynicism. He genuinely believed that the basic world conflict was "a struggle for men's minds," that the world's central drama was "the revolution of rising expectations," that "Point Four may go down in history as the most important idea of our generation,"[4] and that the Soviets now realized that military aggression and the threat of aggression had become a "dead end." It was not that he frivolously discounted the Soviet military threat, but he disliked coming to grips with Soviet bloody-mindedness on a day-to-day basis, preferring to concentrate on schemes to elevate what we then called the underdeveloped countries.[5] He saw enormous possibilities in grandly conceived public work projects that would benefit large areas of Southeast Asia; indeed, he talked about one project so often that iconoclasts of the press began referring to his weekly background briefings as "Up and Down the Mekong River with Gun and Camera."

I was fond of Chester Bowles. Who would not be? Yet, though we maintained the warmest relations, we had few useful exchanges of views. We were always promising one another to have a long talk in which we could deeply review current policies, but when we did meet our conversation produced little. As I saw it, Chester Bowles's views were—superficially, at least—much closer to Stevenson's than to mine. I did not question the need to provide foreign assistance to the poor countries of the Southern Hemisphere, but I saw little chance for rapid improvement in the standard of living in countries where the demographic curve kept rising precipitately.

Even though his tenure in the Department was brief, Chester Bowles achieved many useful things. He helped ambassadors carry out a consistent policy by arranging for a circular letter from President Kennedy that authorized them to "oversee and coordinate all the activities of the United States government" in the countries to which they are accredited—with the exception, of course, of military forces in the field under United States or area military command. Securing that letter was no mean achievement; it was opposed by the Defense Department, the CIA, the Departments of Agriculture and Interior, the Peace Corps, and even by some older foreign service officers who wished to confine the responsibilities of the foreign service to traditional diplomatic relations.

Most of all, Bowles enriched the foreign policy establishment by recruiting extremely able men, such as Edwin Reischauer, who became a brilliant ambassador to Tokyo, Edward R. Murrow, who headed the United States Information Agency (which included the Voice of America), Thomas Hughes, the astute and informed head of the Department's Bureau of Intelligence and Research, and Abram Chayes, the Department's legal adviser. But Bowles was far too gentle and imprecise to be effective in the day-to-day work of the Kennedy Administration. He tried to see every question in the long view, whereas the Kennedy *modus operandi* required quick answers and prompt action.

Broadened Responsibilities

From January to November, 1961, my limited role as Under Secretary of State for Economic Affairs excluded me from the initial discussions regarding our broad military and political strategies. But it did save me from involvement in—or even any advance knowledge of—the Bay of Pigs adventure in April of that year. I like to think I would have opposed that project, as I later opposed the Vietnam War, but I cannot be sure; I was then new at the job; I did not know either the President or the Secretary of State very well, and I do not know how loudly I would have expressed opposition.

One day during the latter part of the summer of 1961, Rusk drew me aside to say, "I want you to take over more and more political matters and get yourself injected into them. Chet isn't up to it." From August 4 to August 10, both the Secretary and Bowles were out of the country, and I had my first experience as Acting Secretary.

As the months wore on, I became more and more involved in noneconomic matters. During October and November, Dean Rusk showed me the daily reports of his discussions with Gromyko on Berlin, and I was given a full account of President Kennedy's meeting with Khrushchev in Vienna. As Rusk and I became better acquainted, a new working pattern evolved. In early September, he assigned Bowles responsibility for administration and personnel, policy planning, and long-term operations; I was to spend more time backstopping him in crisis situations. On November 25, I was in Geneva at a ministerial meeting of GATT (the organization supporting the General Agreement on Tariffs and Trade that administered a set of rules and provided a forum to facilitate the liberalization of commercial policy). Late in the evening, Rusk telephoned to tell me that I was being appointed the Under Secretary of State and that Bowles would take an assignment in the White House. He also said that the President was appointing Averell Harriman Assistant Secretary of State for Far Eastern Affairs. Harriman, who was then involved in negotiating the Laotian settlement and staying in the same hotel, called me a few minutes later to ask for details. The Secretary had, he said, asked him to take a new job and he had accepted. He had not heard clearly whether he was to be Assistant Secretary for European affairs or for Far Eastern affairs, but, with characteristic good spirit, had accepted anyway.

McGeorge Bundy

Almost more important than my relations within the State Department itself were my continued dealings with the White House, and particularly with the national security adviser, McGeorge Bundy. Bundy, who had been Dean of Arts and Sciences at Harvard, had, as a Republican, worked in Thomas Dewey's Presidential campaign in 1948 and then backed Eisenhower in 1952 and 1956. But, after the Republicans had nominated Nixon in 1960, he crossed the aisle to organize a scientific and professional committee to support Kennedy.

Though I did not know it at the time, Kennedy had originally wanted Bundy as Secretary of State but felt that a forty-six-year-old President could not have a Secretary two years younger. When Kennedy had then suggested that Bundy be made Under Secretary of State, Rusk had demurred. (Had Bundy taken that job, my own role in the government would have been quite different.) Kennedy had then appointed him Special Assistant to the President for National Security Affairs and encouraged him to build what amounted to a foreign office in microcosm, which, he hoped, might move more quickly and incisively than the State Department, for the President thought the Department muscle-bound by habit and tradition. Not only was the Department regarded as overstaffed and bureaucratic, but the persecution of the McCarthy period had conditioned career foreign service officers to hedge their bets and make compromise recommendations rather than urge clear-cut decisions.

Because of Bundy's estimable qualities—his devotion to ideas, his loyalty to the President, his sense of fair play, and his recognition of the primacy of the Secretary of State as the President's foreign policy adviser—he played a strong hand in formulating our foreign policy with only a minimum of friction with the State Department. Every President should be entitled to organize the top reaches of his government to accommodate his own habits and predilections, and with Bundy in the White House, the machinery worked smoothly. Yet subsequent events have shown the dangers of such an arrangement when the man holding that position is self-centered and conspiratorial. During the years from 1969 to 1973, Henry Kissinger used the office to undermine the Secretary of State, William Rogers, and in the Carter Administration, Zbigniew Brzezinski drove Cyrus Vance to resignation. Setting themselves up as spokesmen for American foreign policy in competition with the Secretary, each in turn preempted major areas of policy and connived to exclude the State Department from effective participation.

During the shakedown months of the new administration, Bundy's operations and mine were not without friction, but we soon developed an effective pattern of collaboration. For a time, I was confused about Mac Bundy's role—and by his extraordinary facility to grasp an idea, summarize or analyze it, and produce an orderly response as fast as a computer. Lacking the gift for such quick assimilation and fluency, I initially felt at a disadvantage when the President would address a question to me and Bundy would respond with a well ordered answer before I could even begin to talk; on one occasion, I recall, I demanded equal time. But the problem solved itself as we came to know one another better; he was extremely helpful to me, and the fact that we both regarded the world as confusing but comic overcame a slightly prickly beginning.

Unlike his successors, Bundy was too sure of himself to crave popular acclaim. Thus, he left the public interpretation of policy to the Secretary, made almost no speeches during his tenure in the White House, avoided appearing on television, and never aspired to be an ambassador-at-large, traveling around the world lecturing the natives, befuddling our ambassadors, and complicating already complex problems. If a foreign ambassador was to be called in, it was the Secretary who did it—or Bundy with the Secretary's knowledge and approval. I was to think of this nostalgically during Kissinger's and later Brzezinski's tenure, when the national security adviser even had his own press officer.

Robert McNamara

The personalities who played key roles in my own spheres of interest varied depending on the nature of the particular problem. I would sort out economic or financial problems with the Secretary of the Treasury, Douglas Dillon—though the Secretary of Commerce and the Secretary of Labor were also sometimes involved. But, in any group where Robert McNamara was present, he soon emerged as a dominant voice. I was impressed by his extraordinary self-confidence—based not on bluster but on a detailed knowledge of objective facts. He gave the impression of knowing every detail of the Defense Department's vast operations and had concise and impressive views on any subject that arose, reinforcing his opinions with huge verbal footnotes of statistics. Since I am quite incapable of thinking in quantitative terms, I found McNamara's performances formidable and scintillating.[6] He quoted precise figures, not mere orders of magnitude. During the Vietnam War, if asked to appraise the chances of success for different operational projects, he would answer with apparent precision: one operation would have a 65 percent chance, another a 30 percent chance. Once I tried to tease him, suggesting that perhaps the chances were 64 percent and 29 percent, but the joke was not well taken.

It would be quite unfair to imply, as some have done, that McNamara was so accustomed to thinking in terms of numbers that he was unaware of broader considerations. His mastery of that capricious behemoth, the defense establishment, was not achieved merely by a virtuosity with statistics; it required force of character. McNamara, moreover, is a man of humanity and imagination, capable of strong commitments to causes, no matter how unpopular, and relentlessly determined to apply enlightened concepts against obscurantist opposition.

Rusk, Bowles, Bundy, McNamara, these were the colleagues who played the most important part in my activities. They were an extraordinarily gifted group; had the phrase not acquired a special connotation, I might say "the best and the brightest." Though I found myself later in fundamental disagreement with every one of them over Vietnam, personalities did not intrude in the argument, and we retained our respect for one another. In comparison with other administrations, there was almost no feuding and fighting: we knew why we were there, we were all busy, and we had no time to waste in petty maneuvers.

13. The Context of the Time and the Kennedy Program

The requirements of foreign policy, as I envisaged them in 1961, were steadily changing, yet, consistent with Alphonse Karr's aphorism, they still remained essentially the same. World peace still depended primarily on a precarious power balance, and while trendy thinkers decreed that the balance was no longer bipolar but multipolar, the competition of the Soviet Union and the United States still dominated world politics. Meanwhile, what for centuries had been the major Western powers were completing their withdrawal from world political and military involvement largely as a result of two parallel developments.

Dissolution of Colonial Systems

The first was the dissolution of the great colonial systems that had concentrated control of a large part of the globe in a handful of metropoles. Prior to the Second World War, no more than eight major capitals ruled not only Europe but over a billion men, women, and children on five continents. Deals and maneuvers among the members of this tight little club settled the fate of peoples in areas little touched by the Industrial Revolution. Although by the beginning of the Kennedy Administration, the great empires were far down the road to dissolution, huge populations were still making the perilous passage from colonial dependency to some form of juridical independence. As new and inexperienced players scrambled for seats at the diplomatic board, the old rules of play badly needed rewriting.

I recall a quip about the Australian political leader, Robert Menzies, who became Prime Minister when the British Commonwealth was still a small group of white nations and only just beginning to include new nations of every color. "Bob," someone remarked, "was always keen on the Commonwealth until he found he had not joined Boodles but the Royal Automobile Club."

Already it was clear that much of our foreign policy, and indeed much of my own time, would be focused on problems involving the bits and pieces of disintegrating empires. So long as the metropolitan powers retained control, the ethnic, religious, and tribal quarrels that threatened civil war and insurrection could be effectively contained—albeit sometimes with bloodshed—but with the British empire in liquidation, bloody communal riots killed hundreds of thousands in India and Pakistan, while the Greek and Turkish communities slaughtered one another in Cyprus. With France withdrawing from Indochina, the Vietnamese began a civil war, while Belgium's headlong flight from the Congo unleashed tribal fighting that threatened a great power clash in the heart of Africa.

The once great powers could no longer continue the ancient game of bluff and finesse; there were now too many wild cards in the deck, while the board was far larger. Though the United Nations had been established to make new rules, it could not effectively keep peace between the superpowers; its principal role was to serve as midwife for the birth of new nations and to provide a forum where leaders of those nations could make their voices heard, if not heeded. In the schoolroom of the United Nations young leaders, thrown up by revolutionary convulsions, hung together like new boys, forming little cliques—or, as they were called, regional blocs. Since their governments were far too weak to tip the balance in the continuous Indian wrestling between Washington and Moscow, they chose to separate themselves from that contest by announcing their neutrality, which they referred to as nonalignment. As early as 1955, a number of Third World leaders met at Bandung under the leadership of Nehru, Sukarno, and Tito in an effort to convert non-alignment into a political force.

The Climactic Effect of the Suez Crisis

If the disintegration of empire created new states to complicate the peace, it also removed the old metropoles from world power roles. That second change, long in process, was abruptly confirmed by the Suez crisis in 1956. That crisis resulted when the neurotic reaction of British Prime Minister Eden and the French Prime Minister Guy Mollet to Nasser's nationalization of the Suez Canal led them to conspire with Israel behind President Eisenhower's back. Their misconceived and badly bungled military actions against Egypt forced Eisenhower to oppose America's traditional allies in the UN Security Council with cataclysmic results. By exposing the relative impuissance of two nations with rich histories, it expanded America's own burdens. Neither France nor Britain would any longer share responsibilities outside Europe, contracting their field of vision to the narrower sphere of regional powers.

A few weeks after the Suez debacle, I had called on Mollet. An emotional man, upset and embittered by the Suez fiasco, he felt a sudden compulsion to unburden himself to an American friend, so for more than an hour he poured out his version of the Suez story. The point he primarily emphasized was that the Americans incorrectly claimed to have been taken by surprise; Eden had warned Under Secretary of State Robert Murphy that the French and British might feel compelled to act. Even so, he insisted, the French would have gone ahead even against American disapproval had not Eden succumbed to a protracted sobbing spell when faced with displeasure. Later I asked Bob Murphy about the story and he gave me a detailed account of American efforts to prevent the rash and foolish action.

The Suez debacle not only ended British and French pretensions to great-power status, it drove Nasser toward the Soviet Union and titillated Israel's expansionist ambitions. But Eisenhower and Dulles were evenhanded. If our European allies had to withdraw, so had the Israelis. By threatening to cut off America's public and private subsidies to Israel, they forced Ben Gurion—kicking and screaming—to pull the Israeli army back from the Sinai. It was the last time America applied the same rules to Israel that it applied to other allies or other friendly countries. Thereafter, when Israel embarked on adventures in total disregard of American views or interests, it risked little more than a gentle *pro forma* rebuke from Washington.

Meanwhile, Secretary of State Dulles continued to wage the Cold War as a religious conflict, ranting against "godless Communism." A literal-minded lawyer, he approached the problem of Soviet expansionism as though he were resisting a corporate takeover. Treating the complex relations between nations as business arrangements between corporations operating under national laws, he negotiated security treaties that committed us to defend forty-two nations. Lacking a sense of the absurd, Dulles had no sense of perspective. As my friend Walter Lippmann wrote, he was "not a prudent and calculated diplomat, but a gambler . . . with promissory notes engaging the blood, the treasure and the honor of the country." Nor was there a consistent strategy; while Dulles expanded America's commitments, Eisenhower reduced our military budget in the name of fiscal responsibility. Entrapped by that contradiction, Dulles fell back on his fanciful doctrine of massive retaliation (or, as it was topically called, "more bang for a buck"), which, he inanely claimed, somehow gave the United States the "initiative"—whatever that might mean.

The new Kennedy Administration thus came to power in a time of confusion. America had survived the shock of the Sputnik in 1957, though not without angry accusations that America had lost the technological lead and might no longer possess "an adequate margin of deterrence" over the USSR—all of which foreshadowed a similar brouhaha in the latter 1970s. For a brief moment, some Americans regarded the Russians as ten feet tall and even took seriously Khrushchev's boast that the USSR, with its fast economic growth, would "bury" us—until saner heads provided a more realistic perspective.

In the months that followed, there was much talk of the relaxation of East-West tensions, but there were also a number of disquieting incidents. Vice-President Nixon encountered angry demonstrations on a trip to South America; Castro took over in Cuba, slowly strengthening his dependence on Moscow and thus confronting America with a patent violation of a revered item of our national credo: the Monroe Doctrine. That doctrine forbade European powers from intrusion into the Western Hemisphere, which we regarded—though we avoided stating it in those terms—as our exclusive sphere of interest and influence.

Khrushchev brought the United Nations briefly into the limelight by waving his shoe and pounding it on the desk, while the breakdown of the Summit Conference in Paris in May 1960 over the U-2 incident, when Francis Gary Powers was shot down, set the West's teeth on edge. Meanwhile, a small-scale war in Laos was occasionally noted in the back pages of the newspapers.

It was clear long prior to President Kennedy's inauguration that Khrushchev was far different from Stalin and that Soviet methods and manners had undergone substantial change. The Soviet regime, as I then saw it, was no longer primarily driven by an evangelical compulsion to extend the reach of Communism—if it had ever been; its major engine of expansion was merely old-fashioned, imperialist compulsion. So long as we maintained our moral and military defenses, Moscow was unlikely to risk a frontal challenge; yet I had no doubt that the Soviets would lurk patiently in the bushes to pounce on any emerging target of opportunity they could exploit at acceptable costs and risks. "The long twilight struggle" of which the new President spoke in his inaugural address required that the United States at all times have enough force available to assure that, if the Soviet Union challenged significant strategic interests of ours and our allies, the risks and costs would be unacceptable.

That meant we had to be prepared to fight limited wars—or at least assist Third World nations to fight them—a view that directly collided with Dulles's fraudulent theory of "massive retaliation." To the extent that that theory was ever rationally articulated (Dulles wrapped it in opaque rhetoric), it meant that whenever America faced even a marginal challenge in any part of the world, we would threaten to use our nuclear arsenal. As Vice-President Nixon put it, "rather than let the Communists nibble us to death all over the world in little wars, we will rely in the future on massive mobile retaliatory power."[1]

What dangerous nonsense! I had long followed the scholastic speculations of the nuclear theologians. At Denis Healey's instigation, I had attended a famous conference at Brighton that led to the creation, in 1958, of the International Institute for Strategic Studies in London. It was there I first met a young, articulate practitioner of the new metaphysics named Henry Kissinger. But I could never bring myself to believe that, so long as we maintained a reasonable nuclear striking force of our own, nuclear war between the superpowers was more than an intellectual abstraction. Barring the domination of a lunatic such as Hitler—the prototypical "irresponsible" leader—no great nation was going to commit suicide. Even Hitler had been unwilling to use poison gas.

The real concern was that the Soviets would test us in areas where our interests were too marginal to justify a suicidal response. We desperately needed to build up our conventional forces—particularly our capability for quick flexible response—which the Eisenhower Administration had permitted to fall into disarray. Though the antipathies between the new, poor, weak nations largely in the Southern Hemisphere and the old, powerful nations of the North would inevitably increase, I did not foresee an ultimate class struggle on a global scale, which was then a trendy prophecy. The vast populations of the poor nations of the Southern Hemisphere did not possess modern military power nor were they likely to obtain it for many decades.

To be sure, the Soviet Union had announced that it would encourage "wars of national liberation" to establish its increasing hegemony over Third World areas. But such wars, by their nature, would tend to remain limited—threatening to evolve into Armageddon struggles only if the territory in question were of major strategic significance, whether because of geography or the possession of a vital resource (and oil was probably the only commodity worth a big war).

Fear of China

Nor did I share the view then popular in some quarters that China—more than the Soviet Union—was the nation we should fear in the future. In spite of its overswollen population, China seemed unlikely to become a major danger to the West. By 1961 it was only just beginning to experience the Industrial Revolution. Its economy was decades behind that of either the Soviet Union or the Western democracies, and, as I saw it, its huge population was more a source of weakness than of power. There were simply too many mouths to feed, too many illiterate peasants to train, and too thin a layer of education and sophistication for China to be able to mobilize its teeming hordes with any effectiveness. Yet during the middle sixties, while we were preoccupied with the Vietnam War, the fear of a militarily powerful China on the march was to become an obsession within some Administration circles. In 1965, after the famous Lin Piao speech about "Peoples' Wars of National Liberation," Secretary McNamara in particular became concerned with that possibility.

Kennedy Initiatives

All this was background for the shakedown cruise of the new administration. Though each new administration regularly strives to put its own *imprimatur* on events and to claim patent rights to a fundamentally different foreign policy, the broad lines of our international strategy had changed only marginally since World War II. Time had shown that most noisily announced innovations might be novel in style or method but rarely in substance, and, though pipe-smoking experts in ivy-covered halls periodically proclaimed the end of old eras and the beginning of new ones, that proved more an academic fad than anything consequential. We had, they wrote, reached an end to the age of alliances and had shifted from a bipolar to a multipolar or polycentric world (depending on whether the author preferred Greek-based on Latin-based neologisms). We were, some proclaimed, entering the post-industrial or technetronic age—whatever that might mean.

In claiming to offer a new foreign policy, the Kennedy Administration was thus following a normal practice. Its policies reflected no seminal change, nor did they represent a coherent body of doctrine or even a well-articulated strategic plan; at the most, they consisted of aspirations, slogans, and changes of emphasis—certainly an improvement over the two-dimensional thinking of Dulles's Manichaean crusade.

The first broad formulation was put forward in the elevated language of the President's inaugural address. It was eloquent and aphoristic, and, as Ruth and I stood in twenty-degree (Fahrenheit) weather on the steps of the Capitol, we were warmed by the pervasive excitement and expectations. Several of my friends had, I knew, contributed language for the speech, and I had already heard some of the key phrases. But, while admiring its elegant rhetoric, I could not help thinking: "What enormous open-ended commitments the President is making!" Over the years, Walter Lippmann had repeatedly complained to me that the Truman Doctrine had promised far more than America could, or should ever try to, undertake; now Kennedy's inaugural address was, if anything, going even farther. We would, the President said, "Pay any price, bear any burden, meet any hardship, support any friend, oppose any foe to assure the survival and success of liberty." We were not prepared "to witness or permit the slow undoing of those human rights to which this nation has always been committed, and to which we are committed today at home and around the world." What we would seek, so the new President said, was "not a new balance of power, but a new world of law," thus giving the address a strong Wilsonian flavor. Finally, the music swelled to a crescendo: "Now the trumpet summons us again—not as a call to bear arms, though arms we need—nor as a call to battle, though embattled we are—but a call to bear the burden of a long twilight struggle, year in and year out, 'rejoicing in hope, patient in tribulation'—a struggle against the common enemies of man: tyranny, poverty, disease, and war itself."[2]

Those were brave words, spoken in that special cadence with a dying fall that was a trademark of all the Kennedys. But what did it all mean in specific terms? Implicit in the President's noble words was the repudiation of two practices of the past: we would no longer use our foreign aid primarily as an anti-Communist weapon nor would we demand, as Dulles had done, that the recipient countries must regard our aid as a vaccination against "immoral" neutralism. To the "unhappy people in the huts and villages of half the globe, struggling to break the bonds of mass misery," the young President pledged that we would "help them help themselves" for whatever period was required, "not because the Communists may be doing it, not because we seek their votes, but because it is right." And, again of the new states, he said, "We shall not always expect to find them supporting our view. But we shall always hope to find them strongly supporting their own freedom . . ." These were two excellent principles our new administration asserted and tried to follow—though we often had to yield before the imperatives of *Realpolitik*.

The New Political Approach to Third World Countries

In dealing with the new nations just broken away from their Western metropoles, the Administration sought to change the traditional emphasis on political stability. Postwar diplomacy had largely rested on the assumption that the United States in the latter twentieth century was a *status quo* power, while the Soviet Union was essentially a revolutionary power, and that the United States would benefit by encouraging stability; the Soviet Union, by exploiting turbulence. In critical areas, America was accustomed to favor regimes that offered at least transient stability, even when their practices often offended our ideas of freedom and human dignity. If stability could be assured for a reasonable period through colonial structures, such as Portugal's, there was no reason for America to rock the boat.

The Kennedy doctrine frontally challenged this approach. America should not think of itself as a *status quo* country; its own traditions were revolutionary. Old structures were crumbling; American policy must accommodate to the new spirit of change and even revolution. If America failed to encourage the young revolutionaries in the new countries, they would inevitably turn toward the Soviet Union.

America should, therefore, stop trying to sustain traditional societies and ally itself with the side of revolution. The Kennedy Administration was the first testing ground for these new theories. It applied them in devising the Alliance for Progress—an effort to help the Latin American countries break out of the old feudal molds. I am afraid it left little permanent residue.

Though the new President did not make human rights an obsessive doctrinal theme as would President Carter sixteen years later, he still spoke bravely of protecting them. We would position ourselves on the side of change, showing empathy with the young leaders in the new countries even at the risk of transient instability; but, since the Soviets regularly exploited instability, rhetoric did not answer the hard questions. How much instability could we accept without risking a shift in the power balance?

For America to put itself on the side of change meant, with regard to most countries, the encouragement of young revolutionaries. Because many of those revolutionaries had been exposed to Western education either at the London School of Economics, the Sorbonne, or some American university, they were bent on pushing their countries into the industrial age. But how to do it? Much of their Western instruction had stressed the evils of capitalistic societies; many of their most sympathetic instructors and professors had shown Marxist or Fabian leanings. Western capitalism, they had been taught, required an entrepreneurial class that, in most new countries, existed only in corrupt or primitive form.

Market economics assumed the availability of private capital, but, if capital existed at all in the new states, it was usually in the hands of a small feudal oligarchy, interested only in perpetuating its own privileges and quite indifferent to the state of the masses.

All true, of course, but their professorial mentors had not bothered to point out that socialist governments were miserably inefficient. Those Third World countries most successful in entering the industrial age—such as Korea, Taiwan, Singapore, and Brazil—relied heavily on private enterprise, while states making relatively little economic progress, such as India or Indonesia, depended on public sector solutions. The choice involved the central issue of power. Young leaders in a hurry normally preferred to preempt the power of decision; they opted for centrally planned and directed societies, where they could serve as philosopher-kings resplendent with their medals of authority—Western graduate degrees in economics or political science.

The State of the Union

In spite of the exhilarating tone of Kennedy's inaugural speech, the domestic sky was already speckled with small clouds. The storms to come would involve more than the play and counterplay of political, military, and social forces; latent social and economic troubles would also test our unity and national purpose.[3] During a period in which Soviet economic growth had fallen well below prior predictions, the United States had enjoyed eight years of prosperity at stable prices. But that concealed disturbing trends. Our international balance of accounts was beginning to show persistent deficits. By the beginning of the Kennedy Administration, economic growth had ceased to increase at a rate sufficient to match the increases in our labor force and in productivity. During the eight Eisenhower years, from 1953 to 1960, America needed to increase its Gross National Product by 4.5 percent a year to create the necessary new jobs required by a burgeoning population, but, instead, GNP growth had averaged only 2.4 percent. By the time of Kennedy's inauguration, unemployment had risen to 6 percent, though it was not widely visible since the bulk of the unemployed were black or unskilled workers in the inner cities. It was both the best and worst of times.

14. Assisting and Resisting the Third World

During my first eight months in the State Department, while I served as Under Secretary for Economic Affairs I was faced with actions and decisions in all three principal areas of my responsibility: foreign

aid, trade, and finance. I had favored foreign aid from the beginning
and I thought the level of our effort inadequate. It was the theological
aspect of foreign aid that depressed me. In 1961, development economics was at the height of its vogue. Inventing an overblown nomenclature,
the professors swarming into Washington talked tendentiously of "self-
sustaining growth," "social development," the "search for nationhood,"
"self-help," and "nation-building." President Truman's Point Four Program had been concerned merely with technical assistance, but the
experts now clamored for us to increase the flow of capital to the poor
countries. Young men in the governments of those countries (mostly
former students of the American experts) would, with the guidance of
those experts, devise development plans for spending that capital.
Instructed by the American experts, they would build a whole multitude
of new Jerusalems. They would construct new political systems, modernize their economic life, re-draw trade lines, re-train labor, develop programs of land reform, expand education, design public health services,
and, with American hardware and technical help, acquire an appropriate military capability.

The prospect of leading the Third World into the twentieth century
offered almost unlimited scope for experimentation not only to economists but also to sociologists, psychologists, city planners, agronomists,
political scientists, and experts in chicken diseases. It was the golden age
for development theorists. Some university faculties were almost de-
nuded as professors left their tranquil campuses to instruct the natives in
the dank far reaches of the world. A story current at the time told of the
professor who boasted that he occupied "The Pan American Chair of
Development Economics." By that he meant a first-class seat on Pan
American Airways to any destination in the world.

But the most presumptuous undertaking of all was "nation-building,"
which suggested that American professors could make bricks without
the straw of experience and with indifferent and infinitely various kinds
of clay. *Hubris* was endemic in Washington.

The Agency for International Development (AID)

As I had recommended in my foreign aid task force report, President Kennedy directed that we reorganize and consolidate our foreign
aid programs. In his first foreign aid message, in late March, he called
for a unified administration that would absorb the Foreign Operations
Administration, the Development Loan Fund, Food for Peace, the Peace
Corps, and even certain functions of the Export-Import Bank. New task
forces were established within the Administration to develop the plans
for a new agency. At the same time, Robert Komer on the White House
staff was charged with making a parallel reappraisal of the military

assistance effort.

According to the development economists, foreign aid should not be directly used as an instrument of American foreign policy but have a life and *raison d'être* of its own. Thus, they insisted, the new Agency for International Development (AID) should be quite independent of unenlightened bureaucrats of the State Department who were not zealous converts to the new theology. In the little boxes that comprised the organization charts, the agency would be shown as reporting directly to the President; though the organic legislation included some propitiatory words about receiving "foreign policy guidance" from the Secretary of State, it could largely go its own way. That meant, in theory, that it would be guided by the standards of development economics rather than any specific political or economic interests of the United States. I doubted such a principle of operation could long survive the captious scrutiny of Congress and that surmise ultimately proved correct.

I was delighted when the President chose Fowler Hamilton to head the new combined agency. He and I had worked together long and closely; we had started our new law firm and seen it prosper, and the thought of my old friend playing a key role in the Administration enormously pleased me. But it proved by no means an easy assignment. The disputes among the foreign aid theologians as to how to organize and administer a foreign aid program seemed to him—as they did to me— bureaucratic, academic, tedious, and frivolous. At the same time, some of the businessmen brought into the Administration on the urging of Vice-President Johnson did not easily adapt to the Kennedy Administration ethos. Fowler Hamilton had to spend much of his time on Capitol Hill, where foreign aid programs had only a limited constituency. During the years since the initial suggestion by President Truman of his Point Four Program, foreign aid had been in an almost constant state of reorganization—to the point where the recruitment of competent personnel was difficult, and efficient administration impossible. Stories of ineptitude and wasteful expenditure had become part of the folklore, and Congressmen could recite them by rote.

The Harvard and MIT development economists then at the height of their influence not only pressed for the United States to provide maximum development dollars to the Third World but insisted that we try to squeeze further dollars from our Western allies—particularly, the Germans. My notes of the period are full of telephone calls, particularly from Walt Rostow, urging me to demand this or that additional amount from the Federal Republic for the Indian or Indonesian Consortium or some other pet aid project. On my first official trip to Europe in the middle of March, the White House had charged me to press Ludwig Erhard, then Minister of Economics of the Federal Republic government, to increase the German aid effort. I thought it a mistake to treat our Western allies as a bank to provide capital resources for our grandiose Third World programs. But President Kennedy was not impressed by my cautionary advice.

The Volta Dam

The African Bureau of the State Department took readily to the Administration's new Third World policies, interpreting them to suit the vagaries of African politics. Headed by Assistant Secretary G. Mennen Williams, it enthusiastically supported the new young African leaders whose "one-party" democracy seemed to me a contradiction in terms. The Administration greatly expanded the number of American embassies throughout Africa, encouraged in this course by the new self-consciousness of American blacks. Though few of them had ever been to Africa or even thought much about it, sociologists and social workers were busily urging black Americans to seek "identity" by attention to their African roots. I thought it a questionable thesis. Black Americans were, after all, Americans, and their problem was to cope effectively in American society. The new emphasis on ethnic identification seemed to me not only politically distracting but a cruel joke on the ethnic peoples.

The largest and most controversial project during the first year of the Administration was the Volta Dam in Ghana. The commitment of substantial sums (in the neighborhood of $133 million) was critically complicated by the fact that Kwame Nkrumah—the first of the young, black nationalist leaders to gain freedom for his African country—showed increasing sympathy for the Soviet Union.

The Volta Dam would provide power not merely for Ghana but also for Togo and Dahomey; in addition, it would supply energy for an aluminum reduction plant and smelter to be built by the Kaiser Aluminum Company. What particularly recommended the project to the President were the personalities involved. Its primary promoter was Sir Robert Jackson, chairman of the Development Commission for Ghana, a man of drive and imagination whom I had known casually when he had worked with the United Nations in the 1950s. Jackson's name and reputation would, however, have meant little to the President had he not been married to the persuasive Barbara Ward Jackson, who had exercised such a strong influence on Stevenson. Lady Jackson lighted up Kennedy's imagination by recounting the benefits to African unity from a project that cut across country lines. By financing the dam in a country leaning toward Moscow, we would prove that America was prepared to help Africans for their own sake and not merely to further our own political interests. It might even keep Nkrumah neutral.

Intrigued by these arguments, Kennedy received Nkrumah at the White House early in March 1961, when the African leader came to the United Nations, although Eisenhower had earlier refused to extend such an invitation. Nkrumah made such a good impression on Kennedy that the President wrote him in July that we were prepared to go ahead with the Volta project. Then, when Nkrumah made a tour of Iron Curtain capitals, Kennedy's enthusiasm began to cool down. Should we commit such a large share of the aid funds earmarked for Africa to a country turning rapidly toward the other side?

I suggested to the President that we send a fair-minded American industrialist to survey the project. Should we decide to go ahead, he would be in better shape with Congress if the industrialist made a favorable report. I suggested Clarence Randall, the conservative head of the Inland Steel Company, whom I knew and liked. Though Randall was, within a few months, to be the steel industry spokesman when President Kennedy sought to block a steel price increase and though he had, in the 1950s, opposed me in a national radio debate on the Coal and Steel Community (which he then called a "cartel"), he would, I felt confident, provide an honest opinion. I thought he might also help persuade Nkrumah that he must stay nonaligned if he were to receive American bounty.

The British were pressing us to push forward with the dam. Sensitive to Kennedy's soft side, Prime Minister Macmillan wrote that our withdrawal from the project could have the same tragic consequences as Dulles's decision to pull out of the Aswan Dam; it would enormously strengthen the Soviet hand. The United States had been negotiating the dam project with Ghana for three and a half years, and the Ghanaians had already invested a considerable share of their meager resources. Thus the affirmative argument took shape: Dulles had made a frightful mess of Suez—one of the most tragic and far-reaching diplomatic blunders of the century—and we should not repeat the same mistake simply because the American right wing was breathing hotly on our necks. The dam would take ten years to build, and, in the meantime, Nkrumah might well disappear as Ghana's leader—which in fact he did.

Clarence Randall left for Ghana on October 19 and returned on October 31. I took him to see the President on November 3. The burden of his report was that we not make an immediate commitment but postpone the decision for a year. But that was not a practical solution, since, as I explained to Randall, the Africans would see it as a flat rejection. Sophisticated and reasonable, he readily accepted a vow of silence, recognizing that public knowledge of his report would tie the President's hands. I discussed the problem with the President at Hyannis Port on November 24 and reviewed the situation at a National Security Council meeting on November 28.

Meanwhile, Queen Elizabeth was scheduled to visit Ghana from November 9 to November 20. If the United States torpedoed the Volta project just before her arrival, it might incite dangerous demonstrations. Thus I promised the British that we would not announce the decision until the Queen's visit was completed. Administration opinion was far from unanimous, and, for the first time to my knowledge, Attorney General Robert Kennedy differed from his brother. We should not, he argued, make a large aid commitment to Nkrumah, who was more and more moving toward the Soviet side.

After repeated discussions, the President finally said to me, "All right, George, you make the decision." I replied that he knew all the arguments for and against the project. It seemed to me that we might secure a long-term gain from going forward, but that did not mean we had to go the whole way immediately. We could move forward on a limited, conditional basis, while we kept a sharp eye on the evolution of Ghanaian politics. Our total disbursements during the first three years need not amount to more than $28 million, and we could turn off the tap at any time if Nkrumah behaved too badly.

Meanwhile, before a final decision was announced, we asked Clarence Randall to return to Ghana and impress Nkrumah with the seriousness of the conditions attached to our financial assistance. If Nkrumah got out of line, our flow of funds would promptly dry up. Randall left for Ghana on Friday, December 15. President Kennedy announced his decision to go ahead with the dam on Saturday, December 16, after we had touched the appropriate Congressional bases. Thereafter, Nkrumah developed a raging megalomania, calling himself Osagyefo, or "redeemer," and imposing a repressive dictatorship. He turned increasingly against the West until, in 1963, the President instructed AID to stop extending any further credit for the dam project. We had then spent a total of $40 million on it.

Resisting the Third World

Dealing with foreign aid was, in many ways, far easier than maintaining a rational trade policy. During the Marshall Plan days, the slogan "trade not aid" had a glib appeal, but vested interests still got in the way. In our trade with the Third World, the slogan was even harder to apply; our affirmations of solicitude gave an impression of cant and hypocrisy.

According to classical doctrine, each country should concentrate on that type of production in which it has some comparative advantage. Apart from proximity to raw materials, the comparative advantage of most Third World countries was limited to a large supply of low-cost labor; logic called for those nations to assume the lion's share of labor-intensive production. But logic was no match for the realities of domestic politics. Labor-intensive industries, by definition, employ large numbers of voters and in democratic nations have exceptional political clout. Whenever Third World countries ship substantial amounts of labor-intensive products to America, our domestic producers and their trade unions complain that cheap foreign labor is taking jobs from our workers.

For some Americans foreign aid has served as an excuse for denying

Third World nations free access to our markets. It is politically easier to obtain foreign-aid appropriations than to keep open our markets for Third World products, even though that has meant depriving poor countries of the chance to earn their living in the world economy.

Textiles—A Major Headache

Textiles (a prototypical labor-intensive product) posed a specially critical problem for President Kennedy. He had been a Senator from New England, where textile manufacturing flourished early, and, in addition, had sought support in the southeastern states to which the textile industry had largely migrated. During his Presidential campaign, he had committed himself to taking care of textile import problems, and the industry promptly demanded that he redeem his promise. The President turned the problem over to me. It caused me more personal anguish than any other task I undertook during my total of twelve years in different branches of the government.

What, after all, was the American textile industry complaining about? It was that entrepreneurs in Hong Kong, Japan, Korea, Taiwan, and other developing countries were using low-cost labor to manufacture textiles for export to America. But why had our American industry failed to establish sources of production in the low-cost labor areas of the Third World? The Japanese textile industry had done so, as had other American labor-intensive industries, such as electronics. Had they been willing to utilize the huge pools of Third World labor, the American textile industry could have provided low-priced textiles to American consumers. Rather than concentrating 1.3 percent of our labor force on the production of textiles, our country might have shifted more rapidly to the capital-intensive and knowledge-intensive industries and services that befitted a nation with an advanced economy.

Textile company management personnel did not think in those terms. Because textile production requires only limited capital and is, therefore, easy of entry, almost every American community acquired its own textile mills at an early date. Certainly, that was the structure of the industry until shortly before the Second World War. With family-owned mills scattered over most of America's fifty states, the industry was politically powerful—since company owners living in a Congressional District have far more political influence with their Congressmen or Senators than do large corporate absentee owners, no matter how economically powerful. In addition, because of the vast number of employees and the protectionist policies of the textile unions, the industry could apply almost as much pressure as organized agriculture.

In spite of increased productivity resulting from concentration and modernization during the period following the Second World War, industry leaders still claimed that imports from Hong Kong, Japan, and other Asian countries were driving them into bankruptcy, while labor leaders chanted contrapuntally that imports were taking jobs from American workers. I did not find the case persuasive, but the President felt too deeply committed to stand against the mounting pressure. He assigned the task of the following up on his commitment to his Deputy Special Counsel, Myer Feldman, who had come to the White House from Kennedy's Senate staff. Feldman reflected the views of the industry's lobbyists and constantly pressed me to take steps against my liberal trade convictions. No doubt he was merely doing what he was assigned to do, but I wished he would not pursue the task so assiduously. Whenever I told him about actions we were considering or sent him papers we had drafted, the industry immediately knew about it.

To institutionalize the internal pressures, the President appointed a Cabinet Committee on Textiles under the chairmanship of Secretary of Commerce Luther Hodges, a former Governor of North Carolina—the nation's second largest textile-producing state—who had at one time been general manager of all the Marshall Field textile mills. He responded by conditioned reflex to the textile industry's cries of distress. Nor were the other members of the Textile Committee, Willard Wirtz, the Under Secretary of Labor, and Henry Fowler, the Under Secretary of the Treasury, always as firm as I would have liked in resisting the demands either of the industry or its unions. Outside of colleagues in the State Department, I received my strongest support from McGeorge Bundy's staff, particularly from Carl Kaysen. But jurisdiction over the problem belonged to Feldman rather than Kaysen, and the Bundy staff could do little to persuade the President to call off the pressure.

I was thus largely alone in trying to hold back the sentiment mounting on the Hill, in the White House, and elsewhere in the Administration to go along with the industry's request for mandatory quotas on practically every textile and apparel item. I was determined at all costs to block quotas. They would make a mockery of our concern for the Third World and our commitment to liberal trade; moreover, they would put us crosswise with the textile-importing countries of Europe, on which the full weight of Asian exports would then be deflected.

In due course, the textile leaders fell back on the shopworn contention that their products were essential for national security—by which they meant, I assumed, that naked American soldiers would be easier to shoot than fully clothed enemies. I had heard it all before and was understandably annoyed when, with no notice to me, the Director of Defense Mobilization made a "finding" that the textile industry was essential to national security. The problem was, of course, posed in absurdly unreal terms. No one expected the industry to disappear; all that had happened was that some textile imports had gained as much as

10 percent of the American market. Though I did not regard that statistic as shocking, I well remember a session with one of the industry leaders, Mr. Robert T. B. Stevens, who almost tearfully insisted that the industry would collapse unless we promptly closed our borders to "cheap labor" products.

I had not joined the government to reinstate a regime of quantitative restrictions that America had spent so much diplomatic effort to dismantle. But pressures continued to mount. Early in February 1961, soon after the President's inauguration, the Special Subcommittee to Study the Textile Industry of the Senate Committee on Interstate and Foreign Commerce, under the chairmanship of Senator John O. Pastore of Connecticut, issued a report recommending mandatory sanctions. At the same time, a formidable number of Senators and Congressmen joined in a letter to the President attacking me and demanding action.

The Counter-Proposal—An International Agreement

To be sure, a few Congressional voices were raised on behalf of the American consumer and against quotas. Senator Gore of Tennessee pointed out that the American textile industry commanded more than 90 percent of the domestic market and also maintained a thriving export trade. He knew of no other industry in such a favored position. But my colleagues on the Textile Committee were not impressed, and they overruled me by voting for mandatory quotas. Totally isolated, I could block such a move only by a counter-proposal. With no idea how I would go about it, I confidently asserted that I would negotiate an international agreement that would limit textile imports, while permitting some gradual increase at a systematic, hence nondisruptive, pace. To help me develop a feasible approach, I co-opted Warren Christopher, an able young Los Angeles lawyer, who was later to be Deputy Secretary of State in the Carter Administration. I also borrowed a textile expert named Stanley Nehmer from the World Bank.

Meanwhile, through Myer Feldman, the industry was frantically demanding that I meet with their representatives and outline the Administration's intentions. That raised a major question of tactics since the textile lobby defined the textile industry to include producers of every product that could be directly or even remotely called a textile. But jute bags, wool tops, burlap, carpets, and the like had little in common; individual sectors of textile production faced disparate problems, and I insisted on meeting with the various sectors individually—first with cotton textile producers, another time with the silk textile industry, a third time with wool, then jute, and so forth. Though that evoked an angry response, I held fast and soon found myself enjoying the confrontation, acrimonious and unpleasant as were my meetings with the industry. For my private and secret gratification, I appeared before each textile group dressed in a British-made suit, a British-made shirt, shoes made for me in Hong Kong, and a French necktie. I made no promises other than assuring the cotton textile producers that we would take their problem up in an international meeting in July. As I was leaving one meeting, I heard an industry representative say, "That's the slyest bastard I've seen in years. We certainly have to watch him." I found such praise heart-warming.

Meanwhile, the industry insisted that its minions participate in the forthcoming negotiations. I refused. I was representing the totality of United States interests, not a single industry, and there was no more reason for industry representatives to participate than for representatives of domestic consumer groups. Unfortunately, my position was weakened when the French included a textile industrialist in their delegation and the Germans proposed to bring over three textile people as observers. At the end, we compromised by arranging for the American cotton textile industry to send a delegation to Geneva. Its members would not participate in the meetings or even attend as observers, but we would keep them currently briefed and discuss developments with them. Meanwhile, nearly half the members of Congress signed letters in favor of mandatory quotas; if I failed at Geneva, they had the votes to pass the necessary legislation.

I left for the Far East on June 30, to attend a meeting of the Development Assistance Group which I shall shortly describe and to disclose our textile predicament to the Japanese government and to the textile industry in Hong Kong. Meanwhile, it was arranged that Warren Christopher would go on to Geneva early in July to prepare the meeting.

Bitter Tea

From July 3 to July 6, I met with the British authorities in Hong Kong. Since Chinese entrepreneurs owned most of the Hong Kong textile industry, I followed the suggestion of the United States Consul General and invited industry representatives to a tea party at the Peninsula Hotel. Cushioning the blow as much as possible, I broke the sad news that the United States government felt required to negotiate restraints on their exports and that we would be discussing the matter in Geneva beginning on July 17. I also visited Osaka to give the same word to the textile industry there. When I returned to Tokyo the following day, I saw a placard draped over a newsstand in front of my hotel hawking in big, black letters a piece in the *Far Eastern Economic Review*, "Ball's Bitter Cup."

Meanwhile, on July 7, Warren Christopher telephoned from Geneva to say that the proposal I had forwarded to him from Okinawa for a series of bilateral agreements seemed too complex and cumbersome to achieve results by 1962. Christopher, himself, was working on a new *ad hoc* position. Since it was urgent that we have a plan well prepared before the meeting, I agreed to fly directly to Geneva from Tokyo, arriving on Friday, July 14. I still had not found a formula that met our political requirements without mandatory quotas. I was deeply troubled.

Awake until early morning on the night of July 15, I hit on a promising approach. To avoid the rigid constrictions of fixed quotas, we might give importing nations the right to call for restraint only when sudden surges of imports threatened to disrupt the market for specific categories of items. I climbed out of bed, got myself a yellow pad, and by sunrise, I had blocked out the outline of a scheme.

As perfected during the next few hours, my outline provided that if a signatory importing nation found that a certain category of cotton textile import was "threatening to disrupt the market," it could request exporting nations to restrain their exports of that offending category to a specified level, not lower than that prevailing for the twelve-month period ending June 30, 1961. If, within thirty days, the exporting countries would not agree to such restraint, the importing country could take steps to refuse imports above the level specified. To sweeten the medicine for Third World countries, I included a statement of intention that "this procedure will be used sparingly, with full regard for . . . the agreed objective of obtaining and safeguarding maximum freedom of trade, and only to avoid disruption of domestic industry resulting from an abnormal increase in imports."

Of course, the document was tailor-made for abuse. Once we gave an importing nation the unappealable right to decide when its markets were "threatened by disruption," protectionist pressures would be hard to resist. But it was the best I could do—or, more accurately, the least I could get away with, since I had to get the American cotton textile industry off the President's back.

I could persuade the Third World exporting countries to join the agreement only by putting emphasis on its stated purpose "to significantly increase access to markets," arguing that this would permit their exports to grow, though precluding the disruptive growth of individual items. I recognized, of course—and the more sophisticated representatives of Third World countries also recognized—that the proposal was smothered in a Béarnaise sauce of sham and sanctimony. Talk of "increased orderly access" provided me a debater's advantage, but I was quite aware that the Third World textile-exporting countries would sign only under duress, knowing that if they did not agree, the United States would impose mandatory quotas. It was as simple as that.

I met individually with representatives of exporting countries for intensive quiet talks in which I emphasized the growing pressure for quotas in America and my desire to cushion the blow as much as possible. Meanwhile, I had to fight a rearguard action against the trade association and labor union representatives who had established themselves in the same hotel and were blowing down our backs. I was annoyed by their immoderate demands to the point where I could scarcely sit through further long sessions with them without showing my irritation. Fortunately, Willard Wirtz, then Under Secretary of Labor, and Warren Christopher rose valiantly to the occasion, spending a whole wrangling night working out compromises.

When, at the end, I was congratulated by my colleagues, I made it clear that I was not proud of what we had achieved. My forebodings proved well-founded. The Department of Commerce assigned a man who had spent his working life in the textile industry to administer the agreement, and he so applied it as to be almost as restrictive as mandatory quotas. I felt chagrin that I had persuaded the developing countries to go along on the promise of orderly growth.

The UNCTAD

Even after my appointment as Under Secretary, I continued to keep a vigilant eye on our foreign economic policy, to assure that we were fighting effectively to maintain liberal access to the American market for the products of other nations and particularly those of the Third World. Meanwhile, the Third World countries organized themselves for a frontal assault on markets of the great trading nations. The intellectual author of this effort was an economist from Argentina, Dr. Raoul Prebisch. Dr. Prebisch argued that Third World countries could best increase their foreign exchange earnings by expanding their export of manufactures produced with the comparative advantage of cheap labor. The industrialized countries should, in turn, grant preferential access to their markets for such Third World manufactures.

Though logical by the standards of a perfect world, the scheme ignored political reality. The industrial nations would never give preference in their markets for any significant amount of labor-intensive, manufactured or semi-manufactured products of Third World countries; the most we could possibly hope to do was to prevent discrimination against those products by quotas or specially high tariffs. The protectionist lobbies were constantly mouthing the old bromide that the American worker's living standard would be destroyed if he had to compete directly with the "slave labor" or "sweat-shop labor" of poor countries.

Yet, despite their political unreality, the Prebisch proposals supplied the central theme for the first United Nations Trade and Development Conference (UNCTAD), scheduled to be held in Geneva on March 23, 1964. That conference was a mass affair with representatives from 116 nations. I would formally head the American delegation and make the initial American address on March 25. What, then, should I say? Veterans of such international conferences urged me to employ the traditional sympathetic waffle, and my colleagues in the State Department and the White House were horrified when I announced that I intended to make an honest, realistic statement to the conference. America, they argued, must never appear negative and indifferent to the aspirations of Third World nations; if we took an honest stance, other nations would take advantage of our forthrightness with empty promises.

The latter part of that argument was undoubtedly true. Speaking on the day preceding my speech, the French Finance Minister, Valéry Giscard d'Estaing, proposed that world markets be organized so as to guarantee higher prices for the raw materials and agricultural commodities of underdeveloped nations and that tariff reductions be negotiated to give the semi-manufactures of those countries access to the markets of advanced countries from which they purchased machinery and equipment. It was odd to hear such piety from a country that still revered the spirit of Colbert. But Giscard's speech evoked applause, even though most of the delegates knew nothing would come of it.

I was aware that the delegates expected the United States to offer similarly generous-sounding promises. But I held to my commitment to candor. As I had expected, the speech fell like cold rain, but I am sure that the realism I injected at the outset saved the conference from even more absurd and unachievable recommendations than was finally the case. Not only the frankness of my speech but also its brevity differentiated it from the bombast of Che Guevara. For forty-five minutes he spoke with such emotion as to hold the conference in the palm of his hand, then lost it completely during the next hour and a half. Guevara was, as I later commented to my dear, long-winded friend Hubert Humphrey, the "Humphrey of Latin America."

When I returned to Geneva on June 10 to make a wind-up speech, there was again a sense of great expectations, a pervasive hope that the United States would, as so often in the past, produce some major and generous proposals. I had, however, no new initiative to put forward and I was not prepared to utter sanctimonious platitudes and make promises we could not keep. So, to the surprise of everyone, including my own delegation, I threw away my prepared speech and told the conference to get to work. I pointed out that the huge assemblage had been toiling for almost three months but had agreed on nothing. Rather than have me take up their time, they should roll up their sleeves and finish their business.

My speech shocked the delegations but failed to inspire useful action. To prevent the conference from going down in history as a monument of expensive futility, the delegation leaders concocted a Trade and Development Board that would meet twice a year to spur the economic growth of the poor nations. It was a mouse not a mountain and it could not roar above a whisper. But an agreement to create a permanent

UNCTAD secretariat did lift hearts; it provided new international jobs for Third World bureaucrats.

Perhaps the most significant result of the first UNCTAD conference was the emergence of the so-called seventy-seven-nation Latin-Asian-African bloc that would in subsequent years seek to promote that catch phrase of the seventies—the New International Economic Order.

Neither my delegation nor some of my colleagues in the White House were altogether happy that I had spoken so flatly, but I have never regretted it. It was not that I was insensitive to the plight of Third World countries; on the contrary, as I told Dr. Prebisch many years later, I thought his program inherently reasonable and I would have liked to see it given a fair run. Though wary about exceptions to the most-favored-nation doctrine that might open the way to special interests, I saw logic in the concept of the advanced countries opening their markets to Third World manufacturers; the only problem was that they would never do it, and I did not want to be a party to a fraud. To gain transient popularity, great nations should not misinterpret the realities of their own national politics. We had done that too often in the past.

15. The Tradesman's Entrance to Foreign Policy

With the expansion of the OEEC into the OECD, the Development Assistance Group (DAG), which included America, could now be incorporated in the OECD and renamed the Development Assistance Committee (DAC). By the eccentric standards of bureaucratic custom, to evolve from DAG to DAC was a mark of progress. The responsibilities of DAG, which the DAC would now inherit, were to keep track of the technical and development assistance provided the Third World by individual Western countries—a necessary mechanism since the ex-colonial powers often kept secret the aid provided their former dependencies. Not knowing how much, or the nature of, the aid any Third World country might be receiving from other industrialized nations, we could not effectively help with their development planning, nor could we be sure that a recipient country was not using our aid merely to service its debts to Paris.

I briefly indulged in a grandiose vision that, in addition to channeling aid through international organizations such as the World Bank, we might use an improved version of DAC to coordinate national aid. DAC would then not only serve as a clearing house but would also help finance developing countries by organizing syndicates of its members to make common grants or loans. Except for aid consortia for a few particularly troubled countries, the concept proved fantasy. Changing the acronym from DAG to DAC did little to transform the scope of the enterprise; it remained little more than a secretariat scrambling to accumulate and publish such statistics of national foreign aid contributions as it could come by. If Macy's does not tell Gimbels, France will certainly never tell America the details of its aid to the African Francophone countries. Nor has the concept of foreign aid ever been clearly defined. To what extent is so-called "aid" simply a commercial credit? To what extent is it a political bribe? To what extent is it a genuine contribution to economic sustenance or development? Those remain controversial questions.

Japan

The DAG was one of the few transatlantic institutions that included Japan, and I hoped it might provide leverage to help bring the Japanese into the OECD. With Japan's exuberant economic growth, it should begin to play an expanding world role—initially economic then, ultimately, political. Though no one in the early 1960s talked of "trilateralism," that was, in essence, what I had in mind.

The meeting to convert the DAG to the DAC was to be held in Tokyo on July 11 to July 13, 1961. I arrived in Okinawa on July 1 and spent an afternoon and morning talking with General Paul Wyatt Caraway, whose mother, Hattie Caraway, the first female Senator, had co-sponsored the Equal Rights Amendment in 1943. General Caraway was a feisty little man: brusque, precise, and widely regarded as a martinet. But he showed sensitivity to the political problems we faced with the Japanese.

Until then, I had thought of Okinawa merely as a major World War battleground. Now, observing our vast stores of supplies and the proprietary manner in which our military administered the island, I thought it preposterous that fifteen years after the war we should still be treating it as our colony. I understood why our military wished to preserve arrangements that enabled them to do what they pleased without interference from local authorities. Yet the situation was tailor-made to generate trouble between Tokyo and Washington. How could we decry the colonial practices of our European allies yet persist in similar practices in Okinawa?

Encouraged by Carl Kaysen, an old friend from Bombing Survey days who was traveling with me as a representative of Mac Bundy's White House Staff, I sent the President a telegram describing the dangers implicit in our position. Later, pursuant to that telegram, the Kaysen Mission was dispatched to make a full study.

In Tokyo, Ruth and I enjoyed the warm and thoughtful hospitality of Ambassador Edwin Reischauer and his brilliant and charming Japanese wife, Haru. Reischauer, a distinguished Far Eastern scholar, had been one of Chester Bowles's nominees. The son of an American educator who had devoted his life to Japan, he had been born in Tokyo only a few blocks from his wife's birthplace, though they never met until many years later in the United States. His appointment initially drew heavy fire. Should the American ambassador to Japan be married to a Japanese? But the two together had proved precisely the right team in the right place at the right moment. I can think of no two people during that period—still tense from war and defeat—who could have done so much to consolidate American-Japanese relations.

Because I was the first high official of the new Kennedy Administration to visit Japan, Ruth and I were accorded almost embarrassingly elaborate hospitality. The high point was Prime Minister Hayato Ikeda's party for us at Geihinkan, a government guesthouse in the Shirokane section of Tokyo. In effect, there were two dinners: the succulent shellfish fried in batter called tempura and the other components of a traditional Japanese dinner, then a Western-style dinner, where we sat on chairs rather than on the floor. For entertainment, there were both Noh and Kabuki performers. Since it was an exceptionally balmy evening, we wandered happily after dinner across graceful bridges over lily ponds scattered throughout the gardens. It never occurred to us that the Prime Minister would later be attacked in the Japanese Diet for his extravagance in providing such lavish entertainment to a mere Under Secretary of State.

Between sessions of the DAC I met quietly with individual delegations to gain their support for Japanese membership in the OECD. I also reviewed with Japanese ministers the festering trade problems between our two governments. I had already expounded my own approach toward trade liberalization in the task force report on foreign economic policy I had submitted to the newly elected President in December. We should, I urged, use the European Economic Community both as a justification for a major new round of trade negotiations and a precedent for reducing tariffs by percentage cuts across the board rather than the traditional item-by-item haggling.

The Trade Bill

Soon after I joined the State Department, I began to agitate for new legislation to make this possible. A major round of trade discussions—the first phase of the so-called "Dillon Round"—would soon be concluded, with the result that over a period of years, tariffs would be cut by an average of 10 percent; I was now determined to use the momentum for much broader legislation. A new trade bill should, as I saw it, not merely provide trade liberalization for its own sake, it should encourage the buildup of a rational structure for the West's economy. At the same time, I was anxious to avoid the type of trade legislation that might, by promising to reduce the common external tariff of the Common Market, provide the British opponents of accession with an excuse for staying out of Europe.[1] For a while I toyed with the idea of postponing the legislation for a year until Britain had gained access. President Kennedy wisely overruled my concerns and insisted that we go forward without delay.[2]

I had been involved in commercial policy matters for many years and looked forward to leading the Congressional fight for the new legislation, but President Kennedy had other ideas. He had twice complimented me on my appearance before Congressional committees, and I was unaware of any reservations until one day he said to me, "Just a suggestion, George; don't give the committees the impression you're too well prepared. A Senator told me the other day that some of his colleagues thought you had too many answers. They don't like a witness that seems to know more than they do."

It was a useful rebuke. Though I did not mean to appear cocky, I enjoyed fencing with antagonistic Congressmen and Senators. I had the advantage of total immersion in subjects that Congressional committee members had only briefly encountered. Yet, as I discovered later, it was not my obnoxious self-assurance that induced the President to select Luther Hodges, the Secretary of Commerce, to lead the trade bill through Congress, but Wilbur Mills, the powerful chairman of the Ways and Means Committee, who insisted that Hodges, a former Governor of North Carolina, would reassure industrialists. He was, they thought, on their side, while the State Department, according to the perennial mythology, was more concerned with improving our foreign political relations than protecting American industry and agriculture.

As it turned out, the President's choice was wise. In his bumbling but forthright manner, Hodges convinced the committees that he wished only to advance American business interests and that the proposed new legislation was essential, since otherwise our exports could not compete over the external tariff of the Common Market. I had known Hodges ever since the days of the first Stevenson campaign, and we worked out an agreed strategy. He would testify on the first day, leaving me to pick up the pieces. The country was more prepared for the new legislation than most of us had thought. It passed easily by a vote of 298 to 125 in the House, and 78 to 8 in the Senate.

As a concession to Congress—and business—the negotiation of trade legislation was taken away from the State Department. The President's Special Representative for Trade would now have overall charge of the negotiation of all trade agreements. The President asked me to recommend someone for that assignment who would seem sufficiently conservative to reassure Congress and the business community while still firmly believing in liberal trade. I suggested Christian Herter, who, after the death of Secretary Dulles, had served as Secretary of State under

President Eisenhower. He was a courtly New Englander, gentle in manner and with high integrity. Since he was a Republican, his appointment would not be regarded as partisan.

Key to successful negotiation was the selection of an effective assistant to Herter to do the actual bargaining. A formidable assignment, it required persistence, tough-mindedness, and the fortitude to stand up to industry and labor pressure; it also meant spending an unpredictable number of years in the pleasant but constricted atmosphere of Geneva wrangling with other negotiators who were feeling equal but opposite domestic pressures. Our negotiator should be reasonably fluent at least in French and German. He must understand, and sympathize with, the basic tenets of liberal trade policy.

For that assignment W. Michael Blumenthal was uniquely qualified. Fleeing Germany with his family, he had spent his adolescence as a stateless person in Shanghai. Blumenthal had learned the harsh ways of a huge, exotic city, been interned for two years by the Japanese, and had finally found his way to America after the Japanese surrender. Making his way through the University of California at Berkeley—in part by working during summers as a shill in a Las Vegas gambling house (an excellent preparation for his later career as Secretary of the Treasury)— he had acquired a Ph.D. in economics at Princeton, taught briefly, had a brief but successful experience in business, and, with the advent of the Kennedy Administration, joined the State Department's Economic Bureau. There, as his unusual competence became evident, I gave him increasingly more difficult assignments.

During my early months in the State Department I was continually told by my colleagues that one proposal or another must be rejected because it "was not State Department policy," and I had formed the habit of replying, "Well, it is from now on." That had been the case with commodity agreements, where our traditional position of automatic rejection seemed to me far too rigid. I had no illusion that such agreements worked effectively. Member countries would either break the rules and overproduce, or the scheme would be upset by the vagaries of wars, weather, or some other natural or unnatural disaster. Nevertheless, Third World countries were loudly agitating for income stability and for an improvement in the terms of trade (which all of them regarded as persistently adverse), and it was, I thought, time to reexamine the whole question.

So I assigned that task to Blumenthal, watching with interest and admiration as he wrestled with an international coffee agreement, a long-term cotton textile agreement, a cocoa agreement, a tin agreement, and other commodity arrangements. Thus, when the choice came to select a negotiator for the Kennedy Round, I felt no qualms in overriding the sacred principles of seniority and persuading the President to accept Michael Blumenthal, then only thirty-seven years old. The task before him was exacting and formidable: to carry through to success a negotiation involving many nations that was to last five years. He performed brilliantly.

First Signs of Détente

Implicit in the Kennedy Administration's Grand Design was the hope that, as the West grew more cohesive, America could begin "to build bridges" to the Soviet Union. In October 1962, the Cuban Missile Crisis had cleared the air, and the following year, President Kennedy began to probe for areas of common interest between the United States and the Soviet Union. That initiative led Walter Lippmann to begin writing about the possibilities of *détente* long before it had become a household word.[3]

In a commencement address at American University on June 10, 1963, Kennedy tried to put America's position in more rational terms than Dulles's perfervid anti-Communist *jihad*. What the United States sought, he said, was "not a *Pax-Americana* enforced . . . by American weapons of war . . . but peace for all men" and "peace for all time." Though acknowledging that the dreamer's "absolute, infinite concepts of universal peace and good-will" were merely invitations to "discouragements and incredulity," he saw the chance for a practical approach to peace "based not on a sudden revolution in human nature, but on a gradual evolution in human institutions." To be sure, there was a widespread feeling "that it is useless to speak of world peace . . . until the leaders of the Soviet Union adopt a more enlightened attitude," but "I believe," he said, "we can help them to do it," though to assist that process "we must reexamine our own attitude. . . . History teaches us that enmities between nations . . . do not last forever; the tide of time and events will often bring surprising changes in the relations between nations."[4] Finally, he stated emphatically that, though the United States would never start a war, we would be prepared for war if others initiated it.

Following the speech, the President went to Europe to reassure our European allies but avoided the customary Cold War rhetoric. On the night he flew back to Washington, word came that the Russians had expressed a willingness to negotiate a limited test ban treaty. I met the President when his plane arrived at Andrews Field on July 2, 1963, and gave him a hastily dictated memorandum that tried to interpret the Soviet announcement. To the extent that historical guideposts ever mean anything (they rarely mean much), that message marked the beginning of the *détente* Lippmann had foreshadowed. During the next few months, the President's search for areas of common interest produced tangible results: not only a test ban treaty, but a consular treaty, the ending of the India-Pakistan War through Soviet mediation, and, finally, the sale of American wheat to Moscow. That last transaction was to occupy a considerable part of my time for an intense period in 1963.

Soviet Wheat Sale

For several years there had been poor harvests on the Russian steppes, and the New Lands experiment had been disastrous. The Soviet government had found it impossible to achieve efficient agricultural production through collective farms and Communist methods, and the Soviet people were faced with a serious grain shortfall. Moscow had, therefore, bought a substantial amount of wheat from Canada and Australia and, through indirect channels, had indicated a wish to buy some of the several hundred million bushels of surplus wheat we held in storage. I saw no reason why we should not make a profitable deal with the Soviet Union, but some Americans—even some in public life—still felt that if we bought or sold goods across the Iron Curtain we might become the dupes of Soviet commissars. That puzzled me: Freudian psychoanalysts, I pointed out, could have a field day spinning theories to explain the prevailing sense of guilt and fear of contamination from commercial dealings with the East. I thought the reaction out of character; it insulted the skill and integrity of our Yankee traders, contradicted the experience of our own history, and seemed an over-reaction to Marx's contention that politics in capitalist societies were always responsive to greed.

From the colonial period down to the First World War, America had depended heavily on foreign trade. In 1812, our insistence on the protection of neutral trading rights had brought war with England. During our Civil War, there had been substantial cross-border "trading with the enemy." But by midcentury, our domestic market had greatly expanded, while our foreign trade accounted for hardly more than 5 percent of our national income; so long as we ran a surplus in our balance of external accounts we could afford a certain margin for moralism and ideology.

Reflecting the prevailing bigotry, Congress had passed an amendment to the Agricultural Act of 1961, expressing opposition to the sale of subsidized agricultural commodities to unfriendly nations, but, though troublesome, it was only a declaration of "the sense of the Congress" without binding effect. Applied to the proposed wheat sale, it made no sense. We had for many years been selling the Russians nonsurplus agricultural commodities and a dozen other items. They would not benefit by the subsidy since it did not go to the foreign buyer but to the American wheat farmer, regardless of where and whether the wheat was sold. Still it was a handy partisan issue and some Republicans could never resist a chance to heckle the Administration. The President, they indignantly complained, had not adequately consulted Congress; he had merely informed them prior to October 9, when he announced his decision to go forward with the negotiations.

The exploitation of domestic bigotry provided useful leverage to interests seeking commercial advantage. Under pressure from ship owners and maritime unions, the President agreed that if we sold wheat to the Russians at subsidized world prices, it would have to be carried in American bottoms. In addition, since the Soviet's gold reserves were being drawn down faster than their mines could replace them, Moscow was asking for credit which raised a separate problem.

The Soviet proposal involved only 65 million bushels of surplus wheat—a small amount relative to our several hundred million bushels in storage. But we had to consider the initial sale as opening the way for later purchases that would improve our balance of payments. In addition, though the Soviets were clearly not so desperate that they would grant political concessions for wheat, our willingness to sell on normal terms would signify to Moscow that an improved climate of opinion could be mutually beneficial. Substantial preparatory work had gone into the negotiations. Ambassador Llewellyn Thompson, who understood the habits of Moscow, sounded out the Soviet ambassador and, on October 5, was told that the Soviets would be interested in buying wheat on customary commercial terms and at the world market price. Much to my surprise, the ambassador did not object to the use of American ships, though American shipping rates were the highest in the world.

President Kennedy asked me to lead the negotiation with the assistance of Franklin Roosevelt, Jr., the Under Secretary of Commerce. On November 21, 1963, the Soviet purchasing mission arrived, led by First Deputy Foreign Trade Minister Sergei Borisov, a genial, straightforward *fonctionnaire.* It took no more than one meeting to discover that, in their own confusion, the Soviets had confused us. Some political commissar must have decided to use American ships to avoid problems with our longshoremen and port security restrictions. Someone—perhaps a commercial commissar—must have pointed out later that American shipping was prohibitively expensive. (Today the poor political commissar is probably running a power station in Siberia.)

Our talks quickly became a protracted haggle. The Soviets were quite unable to understand how American longshoremen could refuse to load Soviet ships that might be sent to lift the wheat. "I don't understand," Borisov said, "how your unions can be so unpatriotic as to defy the government. In my country, when the government wants something done as a matter of policy, our unions do it, and nobody asks any questions." Though I gave Borisov a lecture on the beauties and glories of our American free labor movement, it made no impression. The Soviet Communist party represented the workers, and the unions could not press claims against the wishes of the party. (It foreshadowed the argument in Poland two decades later.)

I regretted that President Kennedy had so quickly capitulated to the longshoremen's demands—and I think he did also. No private organization should be able to thwart government policy from motives of cupidity cynically disguised in patriotic clothing. Once we decided to sell wheat to Russia we should have offered Moscow the same terms and conditions as any other buyer.

I was fascinated by the puritanical attitude of some members of the Congress. Though on humanitarian grounds they would give wheat to starving Russians, they felt its sale was immoral. Yet we did not establish a moral principle by imposing discriminatory conditions on that sale; we simply appeared cheap and grasping. I had had previous experience with the avidity of the greedy for wrapping themselves in the flag. At the time of the wheat negotiations there was an organized campaign to boycott all cigarettes that included even a tiny amount of Yugoslav tobacco. A little later, when the Soviet Union proposed to bid on some turbines to be used in a United States publicly owned hydroelectric facility, the Soviet producers were excluded from the bidding on the ground that the installation of Soviet equipment might "jeopardize security." A candid American official was quoted as admitting that he advocated rejecting the Soviet request because it would "cast a shadow on American technology."

In the end, we finally reached an agreement to sell the Russians about half as much wheat as originally requested with the concession that the Soviet Union could lift 50 percent of the wheat in foreign flag ships. But, limited as it was, that sale was not happily received in all sectors of the Administration. Vice-President Lyndon B. Johnson declared—as I learned later—that "the wheat deal was the worst political mistake we made in the foreign policy of this Administration."

Since that first wheat sale in 1963, sentiments have shifted 180 degrees. American farmers are now so eager to sell wheat to Russia that President Carter triggered a farm belt revolt when he imposed a wheat embargo in reaction to the Soviet invasion of Afghanistan, only to have President Reagan stultify his own anti-Soviet ideology by withdrawing it shortly after assuming office. Moralism has given way to pragmatism; doctrine, to politics.

The Dollar Gap

Even by the early 1960s, we Americans could no longer afford the luxury of refusing to sell our produce abroad merely to prove our piety; our financial reserves were no longer increasing as they had been in the late 1940s and early 1950s, when I worked with Jean Monnet on the French Plan and with Léon Blum on French financial problems. At that time, my economist friends solemnly shook their heads over an intractable "dollar gap" that reflected the inability of major European nations to earn foreign exchange. Because America had such a wide technological lead, European nations would, they predicted, continue to suffer balance of payments deficits, since the problem was "structural." That was like telling a sick man he had an inoperable cancer; the world would have to accept the dollar gap as a fact of life or death.

By 1963 the perspective had changed drastically. Instead of piling up reserves, America was running deficits in its own balance of payments. Those deficits, first appearing in 1958, had persistently increased. The danger was no longer a "dollar gap" or dollar shortage, but a dollar glut. Our net outflow of gold between 1950 and 1962, aggregating over $8 billion, had reduced our gold reserves to about $16 billion; meanwhile, foreign countries had increased their short-term dollar claims by over $17 billion to the point where they now aggregated $25 billion. As chairman of the task force on the balance of payments appointed by President Kennedy prior to inauguration, I had been given a crash course in international monetary policy by the finest monetary experts in America, including Paul Samuelson, Robert Triffin, Robert Roosa (of the New York Federal Reserve Bank, later to become the Kennedy Administration's Under Secretary of the Treasury for Monetary Affairs), Richard Gardner, Otto Eckstein, Edward Bernstein, Peter Kenen, and Joseph Pechman. Key features of the report, which I drafted with the help of Myer Rashish, have been noted by Dr. Robert Solomon of Brookings.

The report recommended that the Secretary of State arrange for informal consultations with American companies before they made substantial overseas investments. . . . It recommended legislation embodying proposals for systematic machinery to restrain cost-price spirals. It recommended a change in the U.S. agricultural program from price support to income support, to enhance the competitiveness of U.S. farm products in world markets. It proposed that countries accumulating foreign exchange as a direct result of expenditures by other countries in furtherance of the common defense or of development assistance should take a series of measures to increase imports and other payments abroad. But, surprisingly and without explanation, the report rejected the idea that the United States should urge Germany to revalue its currency.

The Ball report also suggested study of the desirability and feasibility of giving a gold-value guaranty to foreign official holders of dollars, but it explicitly refrained from recommending such a step. Finally, in a section entitled "International Monetary Reform," it suggested study within the government of alternative ways of meeting the world's growing reserve needs, and it summarized a series of possible reforms, ranging all the way to a world central bank, along the lines of the proposals of Robert Triffin, who was a member of the Task Force. There is reason to think that the details on international monetary reform were not to the liking of Secretary of the Treasury Dillon; he was quoted in *Fortune* as saying, in reaction to reform proposals such as those of Robert Triffin or E. M. Bernstein, "The United States should continue as banker for the world."[5]

Despite Secretary Dillon's disagreement, I tried to promote the acceptance of the report's recommendations.

Balance of Payments Obsession

President Kennedy's brooding concern with the problem of our depleting gold reserves reflected the influence of his father, Joseph P. Kennedy. As a brilliant speculator and market manipulator, the elder Kennedy was obsessively conservative with regard to public finance; to him our gold resources were a significant measure of our national strength and authority. Those of us struggling to keep the problem in perspective were apprehensive whenever the President was planning to go to Hyannis Port for a weekend, and the President, I thought, sometimes shared that apprehension. He feared that his father would scold him for leading the country toward destruction by permitting balance of payments deficits and the reduction in our gold stocks. So, whenever the President returned from Hyannis Port, we braced ourselves for a sermon on gold and the hellfire awaiting us if we did not promptly correct the balance of payments deficit. Twice when I argued with the President about some aspect of the problem, he said to me ruefully, "All right, George, I follow you, but how can I ever explain that to my father?"

In time, the President's increasing obsession with our worrisome balance of payments threatened to produce serious distortions of policy. Compared with our later experience when, in 1977, for example, the deficit in our overall balance of accounts amounted to $20 billion, the deficits of $2 billion we were then running now seem almost *de minimis*. But at that time, Americans were not yet adjusted to the idea that America should be other than a surplus nation.

To cope with the problem, the President established a Balance of Payments Committee under the chairmanship of Secretary of the Treasury Dillon, which included, among others, Secretary McNamara; the chairman of the President's Council of Economic Advisers, Walter Heller; and the chairman of the Federal Reserve Board, William McChesney Martin. I was the State Department member. Management of the problem on a week-to-week basis was entrusted to Robert Roosa, who, as a financial expert, had been part of my task force. During 1961, Roosa engaged in a series of dexterous operations and negotiations to build some short-term defenses for our gold position; with considerable ingenuity, he devised a series of so-called "Roosa Bonds" and developed an extensive network of currency swaps and bilateral arrangements. Meanwhile, our committee sought, by a series of improvisations, to reduce the effect of our increasing balance of payments deficits. Though it was blasphemy to philosophers of economic development, we tied most foreign aid to purchases in the United States; overseas military expenditures were cut, largely by bringing home the families of our troops in Germany, and there was talk that we might have to reduce the size of our troop deployments. That was fodder for Europe's neutralists, who questioned the firmness of our defense commitments.

Still, more and more, the pressures generated by the President's balance-of-payments preoccupation threatened to drive us toward restrictions and protectionism. The duty-free allowance for goods brought back by returning tourists was drastically reduced, and "Buy America" provisions were tightened to the point where domestic goods had to cost 50 percent more than similar imports before the Defense Department could buy abroad.

I was not happy at our heavy reliance on purely technical manipulation among the central banks, and I enlisted the support of Walter Heller, together with another member of the Council of Economic Advisers, Professor James Tobin, and Carl Kaysen in the White House, to press for a more fundamental approach. Concern about that evanescent concept called "international confidence" had begun to affect even our domestic policies. I resented the sanctimonious, school-masterish scolding of European bankers, since our deficits resulted in part because we were carrying an inordinate share of the Free World's defense. So my colleagues and I argued that we should not leave our gold stock to the mercy of European bankers and speculators but should develop multilateral agreements among governments to insulate the United States from excessive gold losses—while we worked toward a longer-term equilibrium. As I put it in a memorandum I wrote to the President on July 24, 1962,

I am convinced that our Atlantic allies will never behave in a more enlightened manner so long as our international financial problem is considered as something to be resolved according to a special body of arcane rules to satisfy a special priesthood—something to be resolved outside the general body of political problems that exist among the Free World powers. If we are to avoid trouble and humiliation, we must raise the negotiations to a political level. We must solve this problem as we solve others—by cooperation with those leaders of the major Atlantic powers who have *political* responsibility for the maintenance of effective Free World relations and who, unlike central bankers, regard our exertions for Free World strength and security not as reckless and imprudent conduct but as vital to the survival of their own countries.

I pointed out that, since the war, we had given the Western European nations in outright grants roughly $40 billion, which was closer to $50 billion in then current value. Europe needed a secure dollar just as much as we did, and constant fear of a flight from the dollar could not be tolerated. We were attempting to improve our payments figures by means that often involved distortions of policy out of all proportion to the results; thus we had created an impression of weakness and insecurity that was "seriously eroding our authority and bargaining power—and our freedom of action and decision."

The pressure to sustain the "confidence" of private financial circles was, I wrote, "confining us in a constantly shrinking and more uncomfortable box. . . . The result is that every currency speculator in Europe regards himself as a self-appointed financial adviser to the United States government." If we were to break out of the box, we had to "entrust the dollar, and the other convertible currencies, not to the daily whims of private and official 'confidence' but to a structure of long-run reciprocal assurances by governments." That meant that we must tell our European allies: ". . . if we are to continue to carry our heavy share of the free world's burdens, we can do so only under conditions where our exertions in the common cause do not imperil the dollar and, in fact, the whole international payments system."

Under existing arrangements, I pointed out, even cutting down our balance of payments deficits would not eliminate the danger that one or more central banks might suddenly decide to turn dollars into gold. It was a mistake for us to try to maintain "confidence" merely by unilateral efforts; we should seek multilateral agreement at the political level to insulate ourselves from the danger of excessive gold losses. If we persisted in our present effort "of trying to bring about payments equilibrium under forced draft," we would find ourselves pursuing "lines of policy that would undermine years of effort to build a world of expanding trade."

To get out of the present predicament, we should reach a prompt political agreement that would "provide effective interim defenses against the runs on our gold supply" and thus give us the time necessary to deal with the basic payments balance problem in an orderly manner. Ultimately, "we should seek a thoroughgoing revision of the payments system that will make provision for increasing requirements for liquidity over the longer future without undue dependence either on gold or deficits for key currency countries." My comment foreshadowed the increased liquidity later achieved by the creation, in 1969, of SDRs, a kind of international money evidenced by an entry in a member country's bank balance with the International Monetary Fund, to be made available to each country in proportion to its IMF quota.

My memoranda were written when the international markets were filled with rumors that President de Gaulle might be preparing to exert political leverage on the United States by withdrawing gold from our country. My efforts to broaden our approach to the problem in time created some tension between Douglas Dillon and me, which worried the President. But as the drain on our gold supply again began to increase toward the end of 1962, even the Treasury was beginning to recognize that additional multilateral understandings were necessary for a longer-term solution.

16. The Mystique of a Grand Design

The young movers and shakers of the Kennedy Administration thought of themselves primarily as pragmatists, well equipped to resolve America's emergent international problems with flair and imagination. Though they had, if anything, a surfeit of theories regarding the economic development of the Third World, they had fewer settled views on the structure of relations among the Western industrialized democracies.

Evolution of a Concept

Still, they were sympathetic to what was, to me, a familiar idea developed during my years with Jean Monnet: the long-term objective of building what we referred to as a European-American "partnership." To be more than a metaphor, such a partnership required a new European political structure since, fragmented into moderate sized nations, Europe was far less than the sum of its parts. No longer possessing world-wide colonial systems, the once great European powers could no longer play in the global league with the two continent-wide nations—the United States and the USSR. A world power needed vast resources to meet the requirements of scope and scale in a world shaped by fast transport, instant communications, mass production, and increasingly sophisticated technology. Though the peoples of Western Europe commanded aggregate resources approaching our own, that aggregate was, in political and military terms, a meaningless statistic. Lacking a common political structure through which they could mobilize and deploy resources in response to a common will, they could play only a marginal role beyond the boundaries of their own continent.

The creation of first the Coal and Steel Community and then the European Economic Community, had set Europe on the way toward integrating its national economies. Six European countries—France, West Germany, Italy, Belgium, the Netherlands, and Luxembourg—had organized a common market in which goods and services could move freely across national boundaries, and institutions had been established at Brussels to shape common rules and supervise the Community's activities. Blueprints had been drawn to enable the central institutions of the Common Market, particularly the Commission of the Community, to acquire increasing political power that might lead, by gradual evolution, toward something approaching confederation. Americans, I had long believed, had much to gain by encouraging Europeans to develop their own European identity and institutions. Europe as a collectivity could share world responsibility as our "equal partner."

Soon the Kennedy Administration began to incorporate the partnership concept in the body of doctrine they were evolving, which suggested to the columnist Joseph Kraft that that concept was the Kennedy Administration's "Grand Design."[1] America would benefit by having a strong ally. The trade disadvantages of having American goods subjected to the Community's common external tariff should be more than offset by the increased volume of trade resulting from Europe's economic expansion. Even more important, we Americans could afford to pay some economic price for a strong Europe that would sustain its share of world responsibilities. Obviously, we could not expect a united Europe always to agree with us. But if Europe expressed views of its own, so much the better; we certainly had no monopoly of wisdom.

Absence of the British

The missing piece in the European jigsaw map was Great Britain, which had so far refused to join either the Coal and Steel Community or the European Economic Community. Though disappointed, Jean Monnet predicted that London would sooner or later fall in line. "The British know a *fait accompli* when they see one," he would say, "and once the Community is operating successfully, Britain will join." Monnet knew the British about as well as he knew the French and Americans, since he had worked closely with all three during two world wars.

It was easy to understand why Britain failed to accept the new reality. Not only did it carry the heavy baggage of history, but it saw the Community as a club of defeated nations; Great Britain and the United States had fought the war together and had won. Besides, the British felt more at home with Americans, who spoke a quaint variant of their own language. Disliking the Germans and mistrusting the French, they thought of their undefined and frequently disavowed "special relationship" with the United States as a fundamental source of prestige and security and shied away from commitments that might undercut it.

In a memorandum to President Kennedy in May 1961, I pointed out that Britain's aloofness reflected its long habit of balance-of-power politics. Recalling Napoleon and the continental system, Prime Minister Macmillan had told President Eisenhower in 1960 that "should France and Germany go down the road toward a unified Western Europe, Britain, in the long run, had no choice but to lead a peripheral alliance against them." Such anachronistic nonsense showed that Great Britain had not yet adjusted to reality; no longer an empire, it was now merely an island nation on which the sun not only set, but set every evening—provided one could see it for the rain.

Under Macmillan, Britain both kept its distance from the European Community and seriously tried to "lead a peripheral alliance" against the Six. By proposing that the Community become part of a broad but loose Free Trade Association, it sought to transform the Community into a purely commercial arrangement. Thwarted in that maneuver, it then organized the so-called "Outer Seven" countries (the United Kingdom, Switzerland, Sweden, Norway, Denmark, Austria, and Portugal) in what was known as the European Free Trade Association (EFTA). EFTA offered no redeeming benefits in the form of economic integration nor any promise of political unity; it was merely a commercial trading bloc that discriminated against the United States and all nonmember countries. It excluded agricultural trade, did not provide for a common external tariff, and established only rudimentary institutional arrangements.

In time, as all "good Europeans" predicted, EFTA became a headache even for the British, and, as Britain's economy declined while the continent's flourished, her most astute businessmen and intellectuals began to recognize that, sooner or later, the United Kingdom would have to join the Common Market. Particularly among the senior civil servants, there was a growing sense of urgency; time was not working on Britain's side. The statistics were eloquent and unanswerable; the member countries of the Common Market were enjoying a far faster and more dynamic growth than a sluggish Britain—an inescapable reality even Prime Minister Macmillan could no longer ignore. Abandoning the defensive concept of a "peripheral alliance," he told Canadian Premier John Diefenbaker that it was "better that the United Kingdom should join the European Economic Community and become a live partner in a growing trade association than go bankrupt on its own."

I watched with increasing hope as Europe's *fait accompli* began subtly to change British views. An enduring European edifice could never be built merely on a Franco-German *rapprochement;* yet an enduring structure was essential. Germany must be incorporated into a European framework to neutralize aberrant forces generated by the irredentist desire for reunification. So long as the United Kingdom remained outside the Common Market, it was like a giant lodestone exerting uneven degrees of attraction on individual member states of the Six, and even on individual factions within those member states.

Even before the inauguration of President Kennedy, some of my British friends had told me that the Macmillan government was having second thoughts about Britain's isolation from Europe. Once in office, I saw my responsibilities as twofold: I would encourage the British to take the plunge, but, at the same time, I must not let insular British elements destroy the institutional potential of the Rome Treaty and turn the European Community into a mere trading bloc. I had no idea how quickly I would have to face the issue.

Meeting with Edward Heath

Toward the latter part of March 1961, when I was in London for a meeting of the Development Assistance Group, the Joint Permanent Secretary of the Treasury, Sir Frank Lee, an old wartime friend, invited me to meet with Edward Heath, the Lord Privy Seal, and a group of British civil servants. I knew that Heath was regarded as more sympathetic to the Common Market than his predecessor, Reginald Maudling, but I had never met him. I was instantly impressed by his cordiality, frankness, and absence of foreign office cant.

Heath opened the meeting by reviewing developments since July 1960, when Great Britain had decided to jettison the original free trade area proposals. Thoughtful Britons were increasingly worried that the economic division of Europe might create a political split. Chancellor Adenauer had told Prime Minister Macmillan that he felt it politically urgent to resolve the issue of Britain's relations with the continent, and the two had agreed on official-level meetings to develop the basis for a solution.

Provided an overall settlement could be found to take care of the Commonwealth, agriculture, and EFTA problems, the United Kingdom government was, Heath said, now ready to accept a common, or harmonized, tariff. That was a basic change in attitude. Equally important, the United Kingdom was prepared to accept any institutions that were "consequent upon the establishment of a common, or harmonized, tariff." Finally, it was ready for the Six to negotiate with the Commonwealth countries regarding the reduction or elimination of British preferences, although arrangements would have to be made respecting the preferences now enjoyed by overseas territories in the United Kingdom and the Common Market. His government, said Heath, now wished to explore whether there was a basis for negotiation.

At that point, Heath left to attend a House of Commons debate on Laos. Sir Frank Lee then took the chair. The Danes, Norwegians, and Austrians, who maintained the largest trade with the Common Market Six of any of the seven EFTA countries, were, Sir Frank told us, pressing Britain hard to work out some arrangements between the Six and Seven. The Dutch and Italians, on the other hand, were more concerned that an economic division in Europe might lead to a political split. What was America's position?

We had, I replied, consistently supported European integration. Some form of German-French *rapprochement* was imperative; a structure must be built to assure Germany's retention in the West, particularly in view of the "unpredictability" implicit in the fact that the powerful leaders of both Germany and France were both old men. As the Germans grew increasingly self-confident, they might be tempted to move independently in search of reunification.

The United States, I said, was prepared for some temporary sacrifice of commercial interests to facilitate the political promise of the EEC. We regretted that the United Kingdom had not joined the Rome Treaty; the political genius of the British would have greatly accelerated progress. Now—particularly in light of our balance of payments deficits—we could accept the added discrimination resulting from British entry only if it would reinforce the political character of the EEC. We opposed the merger of two preferential systems for Africa—the British Commonwealth and the French system. Preferential arrangements not only encouraged the expansion of uneconomic production and the drawing of distorted trade lines, but if expanded to cover the whole Common Market, would create major problems for outside producers, such as Latin America. Though we could not precisely define our position regarding a hypothetical set of facts, I doubted that Britain was yet ready for a solution that would fully satisfy United States requirements.

Sir Frank Lee then put the question directly: "Does the United States want Britain to join the Common Market? Might America perhaps even welcome some derogation in the agricultural field, since United States trade would benefit if the EEC did not adopt a common agricultural policy?"

My assistant, Robert Schaetzel, then interjected that he thought a common agricultural policy essential to the development of the EEC, since there had to be a balance between industry and agriculture. In answer to my expressed concern that derogations to take care of Commonwealth trade might involve the expansion of preferences, Sir Frank replied that he did not foresee increased preferences outside of Europe, except in the field of tropical products. Other problems with the Commonwealth primarily involved temperate foodstuffs where the United Kingdom could either continue duty-free treatment or agree to some change.

I then emphasized the importance we attached not only to "noncommercial" aspects of the European Economic Community, but also to the Community's institutions established in Brussels. Sir Frank responded encouragingly that his government had made a serious study of the non-trade aspects of the Rome Treaty, and, with the "changed temper" in the United Kingdom, he felt the government was now prepared to go farther in this respect than ever before.

The EEC's institutions should not, I insisted, become mere technocratic bodies; they should continue to develop politically. If Britain joined the EEC, it should be on the understanding that the present institutions did not form a completed edifice but would continue to evolve and that the Rome Treaty was not a "frozen document" but a "process."

Sir Frank replied that he fully understood the significance of what I had been saying. Although the movement toward political federation in

Europe had been checked for the moment, it would later resume its forward march; he, himself, did not shrink intellectually from the idea of full political union. I answered that, if the British joined the EEC in the proper spirit, "the internal logic of the movement would carry them along toward the ultimate goal."

Sir Frank summarized this dialogue for Edward Heath on his return. Heath seemed impressed by the spirit and content of the conversation, acknowledging that the proposed steps would require a major United Kingdom political decision. The British were still not clear whether the French wanted them in Europe. I again emphasized that the United States would regard an unqualified British move into Europe as a major contribution to Western cohesion.

Since we had covered a great deal of previously uncharted ground, I emerged exhilarated but feeling as though I had bailed out of an airplane without knowing the terrain underneath. Both Heath and Lee had gone much farther than I had expected—but then, so had I. The President had given me no mandate to state American policy with such assurance; I had never reviewed the nuances of the subject with him, nor even asked his views on the critical questions Heath and I had covered. Thus, in describing the American position, I was not sure whether I was making American policy or interpreting it.

Nor were my colleagues uniformly happy at the line I had taken. I remember particularly Joseph Greenwald, one of the ablest men in the American embassy in London, upbraiding me for encouraging Britain to move toward Europe. Having long watched British maneuvers to water down the European institutions and to undercut European efforts toward unity, he felt that I had given them too much encouragement. He implied, without saying so explicitly, that he did not believe Britain would ever play more than a foot-dragging role in Europe, resisting any move toward political unity.

Macmillan's Washington Visit

Since my meeting with Heath on March 30 had obviously been arranged in preparation for Prime Minister Macmillan's visit to Washington, which was to begin on April 4, 1961, I quickly sought to prepare President Kennedy for the forthcoming discussions. The Prime Minister, I wrote in a memorandum to the President, probably still hoped to solve the problem by a "traditional British-type compromise that would give the UK the best of both worlds—the full commercial advantages of a loose association with the Common Market without any economic or political involvement in the Continent." However, I pointed out that senior British civil servants had lost faith in that course and would be cheering for the President to disabuse the Prime Minister of such wishful thinking. If we forced Macmillan to recognize that no easy compromise was possible, he and his government would then have to decide whether to stay aloof from the Six or make a full commitment to Europe.

In that connection, I pointed out that, in the course of my London visit, I had also gone to Bonn to see the German Economic Minister, Ludwig Erhard, as well as the Defense Minister, Joseph Strauss. Germany was well along with two major postwar projects: the rebuilding of her economy and the creation of a modern military establishment. Sooner or later an increasingly self-confident post-Adenauer Germany might be tempted toward an independent bilateral negotiation with the Kremlin, looking toward reunification. If Britain remained aloof, such men as Erhard and Strauss, who did not share Adenauer's commitment to a Franco-German *rapprochement,* might exploit the "division of Europe" as an excuse for breaking free from the Six, but if the British should wholeheartedly join the Six, the Community could furnish the glue to bind Germany irrevocably to the West.

In Washington on the morning of April 1, as we sat across the cabinet table from our British visitors, almost the first question Prime Minister Macmillan asked the President was how he and the American government would react if Britain applied to join the European Community. President Kennedy responded briefly, then said, "I'll ask Under Secretary Ball to reply to your question." I then repeated what I had said to Heath in London—that America would welcome it if Britain should apply for full membership in the Community, explicitly recognizing that the Rome Treaty was not merely a static document but a process leading toward political unification. I elaborated upon this theme at some length, noting the dangers of a mere commercial arrangement that would drain the EEC of political content. The Prime Minister seemed on the whole pleased and satisfied.

The following evening, April 6, during a dinner at the British embassy, the Prime Minister twice took me aside for private conversations. Despite his reputation for imperturbability, he seemed excited, speaking with enthusiasm about the new President and the people around him "who all seem to be full of such ideas and drive." I mentioned the enormous help we had received from Sir Frank Lee and that I had had a long and searching talk with Heath and Lee on the Common Market. "But, of course, I know all about that," he replied. "Could you possibly think I would have spoken so freely if I had not known all you said to Lee and Heath?" Then, later in the evening, he approached me again. "Yesterday was one of the greatest days in my life," he said with apparent emotion. "You know, don't you, that we can now do this thing and that we're going to do it. We're going into Europe. We'll need your help, since we'll have trouble with de Gaulle, but we're going to do it."

Disappointing Aftermath

I went home elated, sharing Macmillan's feeling that yesterday had, indeed, been a great day and that Britain was getting ready to take an epic step. But, as I was to discover later, Macmillan's private conversations, particularly with regard to such sensitive political issues as Europe, were often far more forthright and eloquent that his public statements or official actions. When, on May 1, the Prime Minister wrote the President outlining the British position and suggesting points the President might usefully make when he met President de Gaulle, he seemed still stuck in the old grooves, insisting on special arrangements for British agriculture and for the EFTA. To help the President draft a proper reply, I spelled out, in a long memorandum, the basic rationale for our position. The effect of Macmillan's highly qualified approach would be, I pointed out, disastrous to Western cohesion; it would loosen Germany's ties to the West, as well as encourage General de Gaulle to pursue his most nationalistic policies. The Prime Minister's letter demonstrated the inherent contradiction in the British position. Though ostensibly agreeing that Britain should join the Common Market, Macmillan wanted the President to help him evade the political implications of full entry into the European Community.

By being firm and clear, we could strengthen the hand of those in London who wished to face the problems squarely, while discouraging those ministers fighting a rearguard action against anything approaching full British membership. Great Britain unquestionably had special problems, but so had the other Common Market members when they first joined; those problems could be dealt with by transitional arrangements within the framework of the Rome Treaty. Such arrangements might, for example, permit the phasing out of Commonwealth preferences over several years, while special provisions could be adopted for British agriculture. Such technical adjustments should, however, be left for solution after Britain had joined the Community.

All during the summer of 1961, I was oppressed with the thought that timing was askew; events lacked synchronization. Several times in my life I was to watch the divergence of trends that might—with better luck—have come together. The result was frustration—at least at the time. Adlai Stevenson, for example, might have been elected President had he run against anyone but a triumphant general. The country might have been saved the obscenities of a Nixon Presidency had there not been riots in Grant Park—or, in larger terms, the anti–Vietnam-War hysteria.

Had Britain embraced the original Schuman Plan proposal, it could have dominated the evolution not merely of the Coal and Steel Community but also of the European Economic Community. Reinforced by a dynamic and evolving Economic Community, the Fourth Republic might have been able to cope with the Algerian crisis without the need to bring back the First Citizen of Colombey. But Britain, though shedding all but the memories of empire, had not yet recognized the limited capabilities of an island nation trying to go it alone. The timing was wrong, and a great opportunity was missed.

Now the timing was still askew, but in a different way. The British were awakening to the mediocrity of their situation just when the increasingly confident leaders of France and Germany were resenting the British for quite different reasons: de Gaulle because Britain had been on the victors' side while France had not, and Adenauer, in part at least, because the British army had locked him up at the conclusion of the war. With Britain finally in the position where, with encouragement, it was prepared to join Europe, it might not have the chance.

British Reaction

During the summer, opposition to British entry built up from not only right-wing Conservatives but left-wing Socialists as well. The politically canny Macmillan well knew that his decision to join Europe would be regarded as an about-face—the contradiction of statements and actions during his five years as Prime Minister and before. Only by a considerable *tour de force* had he gained the support of his own cabinet. But the British people were ahead of the politicians; a Gallup Poll taken in June showed that 46 percent of those questioned favored Britain joining the Common Market, with only 20 percent against and no less than 34 percent with no opinion.[2] Badly split on the issue, the Labor party was assuming a neutral stance—its leader, Hugh Gaitskell, waffling. The farm organizations were loudly insisting that nothing material be done to alter British agricultural policy, though there was no way Britain's existing agricultural policy could be harmonized with the Community's common agricultural policy, since the two were based on quite different principles. Finally, the Commonwealth and the member nations of EFTA were uttering loud cries of fear and outrage.

All this uproar did not deter two courageous advocates of European unity from speaking eloquently in favor of British entry. In the House of Commons, on May 17, Ted Heath made the case with emphasis on the political implications, while in a speech in Chicago on June 16, Sir Alec Douglas-Home (later Lord Home), the British Foreign Secretary, stated the argument in even grander political terms, contending, among other things, that "a united Europe would finally cement that *rapprochement* between France and Germany which has been one of the great features of the postwar world and acts like a tremendous magnet for that part of Europe which has been artificially cut off from the mainstream of European development by an alien creed. Interdependence for Britain must include European interdependence."

Though the political arguments were more cogent and exciting than the economic, they were also more subtle and delicate. Did Britain wish to face a European coalition hostile to its interests, or a group of European nations working closely with the United States that did not include Britain? To avoid these dangers, Britain must try to become the leader of Europe. But no British government could publicly admit that it hoped, by taking leadership of the Community, to regain leverage lost through the shriveling of empire; that would stir resentment among the continental powers. Nor did Britain wish to turn its back on those tattered vestiges of empire that were the sole remaining residue of the Commonwealth; the British felt sincere obligations, particularly to members of the old Commonwealth—or, in other words, the former white dominions.

Finally, the British were proud of the fact that their island kingdom, with its peculiar set of Anglo-Saxon institutions, differed sharply from the nations of the Continent. They had different customs, thought in different terms, and cherished their eccentricities. Any suggestion that entry into Europe might diminish Britain's political sovereignty would have rendered the idea widely unpalatable.

Macmillan's Tactics

So, no matter how much Macmillan privately asserted that entry into Europe was an act with wide-ranging political consequences, he presented it to the British people as an economic move dictated by commercial imperatives. Britain could not make the structural adjustments necessary to maintain an adequate growth rate without what Macmillan referred to as "the cold douche of competition" in a large mass market. It needed to join Europe to attract capital from overseas and put its financial house in such shape as to avoid recurrent sterling crises.

But arguments couched solely in tradesmen's terms do not lift men's hearts or quicken their pulses. A de Gaulle, Churchill, or Roosevelt might have revelled in the flamboyant gesture, the dramatic announcement that Britain had decided to join the Community without reservation, confident that it could work out the necessary adjustments once it were inside and leading the pack; that was the course of action I urged on my British friends. But it was not Macmillan's style: he preferred to play down the importance of the EEC as though he could casually ease Britain in without excitement or fanfare or much more than a brief squib in the *Financial Times*. "I must remind the House," he said on July 31, "that the EEC is an economic community, not a defense alliance or a foreign policy community, or a cultural community."

In a memorandum to President Kennedy, I wrote on August 5 that the Prime Minister was trying to "slide sidewise into the Common Market." By stressing the need to find accommodation for all of Britain's interests, particularly those of the Commonwealth and EFTA (the European Free Trade Association), he had raised problems that would almost certainly assure a protracted and complex negotiation. The implications of Britain's adherence to the Rome Treaty were, I pointed out, enormous: "If the negotiation preserves and extends the political content of the Rome Treaty, it will mean substantial additional weight on the Western side of the world power balance. At the same time, it will require a major sorting out of political relationships. The economically advanced non-Communist world will be divided into two principal parts, the United States and the European Community. Japan will be the only great industrial power not having [free] access to one of those two great markets, although other smaller countries will be in the same boat. Its effects will be profound not only for world politics but for the world."

I, therefore, recommended that, at his next press conference on August 10, the President should express gratification at Prime Minister Macmillan's announcement and emphasize United States support for the political and economic integration of Western Europe. We should play our cards with full awareness that America's role, though important, was still peripheral. We had encouraged the Macmillan government to begin negotiations; now we must watch from the sidelines, making sure, as best we could, that our own interests were consulted. My task, as I saw it, was to stand like Horatio at the bridge and forestall any British deal that would either seriously dilute the political significance of the Community or discriminate against America.

In holding that line, I inevitably engendered resentment, although, since my British opposite numbers were professionally polite, I did not, at the time, know its intensity. The British publisher, Cecil Harmsworth King, mentions in his diary that in 1966 he and I dined together in Washington with some British embassy personnel, including Sir Michael Stewart and John Killick. "When he had left, Killick of the Embassy chancery and Stewart were saying how much he [Ball] was disliked by successive British governments: they thought perhaps because he told them too many home truths!"[3] In his memoirs, Prime Minister Macmillan also attested to my unpopularity. "President Kennedy was . . . helpful and sympathetic," he noted, but "there was always Mr. George Ball of the State Department who seemed determined to thwart our policy in Europe and the Common Market negotiations."[4]

The European Free Trade Association

If unpopular in certain British government circles, I was a pariah in the capitals of the neutral countries of EFTA. That resulted not only from the position I took with their representatives in bilateral meetings, but also from a public statement in London on April 3, 1962, suggesting that while the European Economic Community could make some useful economic arrangements with the neutral members of EFTA—Sweden, Austria, and Switzerland—it would be wrong to accord free access to the Common Market to any nation that would not accept the Community's political commitments. I had sympathy with the problems Britain faced, particularly with agriculture and its relations with the Commonwealth. But EFTA was another matter. The British had brought that problem on themselves by Macmillan's foolish attempt to organize a "peripheral alliance" directed against French and German efforts to build a unified Western Europe; now they were finding that the shoddy little creature they had spawned was embarrassing their efforts to face reality.

Ireland, Denmark, and Norway could, if they wished, join the European Community, accepting the same political commitments as other members; but Sweden, Switzerland, and Austria claimed that would compromise their neutrality. They wanted it both ways, demanding the commercial benefits of the Community without assuming its burdens. In my view, Sweden and Switzerland defined "neutrality" to suit their own purposes, and I had no sympathy for such casuistry. The United States would also be left on the outside of the common external tariff, but we were not asking for special treatment; if the neutrals opted not to join Europe, then let them help us negotiate a general liberalization of trade.

Since I expressed myself without ambiguity, I bore the brunt of the attack. (One of my Swiss friends predicted that I would be burned in effigy in front of the American embassy in Bern.) There was, I felt, sound reason for me to accept the obloquy for an unpopular position. I had assured the British negotiators—including Ted Heath—that America would run interference for them until we had pushed the neutrals into a forthcoming position; then, at the right time, I would soften our objections so they could make some compromise arrangements that would not damage the Community. It was the kind of tactic the British understood—and, I think, quietly approved.

My impatience with the Swiss and Swedes, who hid behind neutrality for their own benefit, did not extend to Austria, which was not a free agent. Austria's neutrality was required by the 1955 Austrian State Treaty, through which Austria gained its independence from the Soviet Union. Now, at the end of August, the Soviet government insisted that, since the members of the EEC were NATO members, Austria's membership would contravene the treaty. The effect of Austrian participation in the Common Market would amount, so *Pravda* argued on December 1, 1961, to economic and political union with West Germany, which the Treaty forbade.[5] To its great credit, the Austrian government shrugged all this off and applied for "association" with the EEC. The Austrians were, as I saw it, the victims of Swiss stubbornness; had Switzerland adopted a less rigorous definition of neutrality, the Austrians could have had more freedom of maneuver, since Austrian neutrality was tacitly defined in terms of the Swiss position. Though I initially took a firm line with the Austrians, I always intended, in the end, to help them find a solution. After a while, they began to understand that we did not wish to damage their interests, nor would we do so.

The Commonwealth

If the EFTA countries were an impediment to Britain's entry into Europe, that obstacle could be overcome by firmness. Britain faced far more difficulty in satisfying the commercial interests of both the old and new Commonwealth countries. Though the Australian Prime Minister, Robert Menzies, and I had tense initial disagreements, I was finally able to find a solution Australia could live with. I put major effort into that achievement not only because the problem was important, but because I had great admiration for Menzies—one of the most effective political figures of the postwar world. A colorful man of boundless energy and robust good humor, he delighted me by singing Australian country songs as we rode about together.

Another member of the old Commonwealth facing even more acute problems was New Zealand, which, in 1961, had earned 54 percent of its foreign exchange by selling its bacon, butter, and other products to the United Kingdom. In the end, even the continental European nations agreed on the need for special arrangements to solve New Zealand's unique problems.

The OECD

If the EEC, with British membership, could evolve the core institutions for European political unity, we would be well on the way toward our Grand Design. That concept had already caught the imagination of some fanciful commentators who named it the "dumbbell theory"—more, I liked to think, as a graphic representation of what its proponents intended than as a derisive comment on their intelligence. A dumbbell consists of two massive spheres connected by a thin rod. If a unified Europe were to play a partnership role with the United States, some institution was required to provide a common forum for the entities on the two sides of the Atlantic. Though initially any such institution would concentrate on economic matters, I hoped that it might some day be supplanted by a body with increasing political interests.

The institution most easily adapted to serve that purpose was the Organization for European Economic Cooperation (the OEEC), which had evolved from the temporary committee (the CEEC) established at the time of the Marshall Plan. Meanwhile, the Eisenhower Administration had already proposed that it be expanded to include the United States, giving it the new name of the Organization for Economic Cooperation and Development (OECD). I had written a report on this for President Kennedy in December 1960, prior to his inauguration, and we had talked about trying to dismantle the old organization and beginning from scratch.

The OEEC had never achieved the optimistic objectives we had held for it when I had worked with Robert Marjolin during the drafting of its charter. Although Marjolin brilliantly led the organization during the first decade of its existence, British aversion to anything supranational had prevented its development into much more than an instrument for consultation—a body that could collect statistics, make studies, and formulate ground rules for cooperation. Now it had lost most of its vitality, and I was convinced that we could create an effective machine for common transatlantic decision and action only by beginning afresh. A new organization generates excitement, attracts first-rate talent, and, with proper leadership during its early months, can break new ground. But an institution in business for more than a decade succumbs to a creeping sclerosis from bureaucratic practices and tired bureaucrats. Excitement is replaced by routine; there is a drying up of initiative and fresh thinking to the point where a Gresham's law drives out the ablest people.

Unhappily, it was too late to create anything new; in November 1960, the Eisenhower Administration had committed the United States to join an expanded OEEC. The failure to scrap what existed and make a fresh start condemned the expanded organization to a pedestrian role, but, while lamenting the bad timing, I had no option but to support the enabling legislation; it was finally passed on March 16. After some scrambling about, we arranged for the President to appoint an excellent career officer, John Tuthill, as United States representative to the OECD.

Failure of the Grand Design

The Grand Design never became much more than a figure of speech. Britain's efforts to join the Community were, as I shall recount in a later chapter, frustrated after long, wearying negotiations by a willful French leader who resented the United Kingdom's close ties to America and feared that Britain would frustrate French hopes to dominate Europe. By the time the British were finally permitted to enter, a whole decade later, their economy had already fallen so far behind that of France and Germany as to preclude them from taking leadership or even playing a strong constructive hand.

Today the fashionable second-guessers dismiss our efforts to promote a politically unified Europe as mere wishful thinking. We were, they contend, obtuse not to recognize that political patterns have been fixed by history and that habits of nationalism are deeply entrenched. Yet I remain unreconstructed. Britain had emerged from the war with enormous prestige, while France was still trying to pull together her shattered society and Germany was a beaten and humiliated nation. The Marshall Plan saved Europe and initiated a period of vaulting prosperity and increasing self-confidence; wise American leadership brought about monetary stability and the progressive liberalization of trade. By neutralizing French fears, the Schuman Plan and the European Economic Community made it possible for the Germans to rebuild their economy, freeing them from discriminatory restrictions without reviving old fears and jealousies. Finally the Community brought France and Germany into effective working relations through participation in a common enterprise. Had Britain joined the Schuman Plan at the outset, it could have taken the laboring oar in drafting the Rome Treaty that created the EEC, and the peoples of Western Europe might today be combining their energies in a broader framework that could give real meaning to the concept of an Atlantic partnership.

If I look back with regret at events since the early 1960s, it is not because I spent so much time and effort trying to advance the building of Europe, but because the effort failed. Although, God knows, American governments have made plenty of mistakes, our encouragement of a unified Europe was not one of them. Failure came from no fault of ours, but because, when key decisions were made, the European leaders of the moment lacked adequate vision; the puckishness of history prevented events from occurring with the right timing or in the right sequence. We were pursuing a worthy and—at the time—not a wildly unrealistic goal. Had our Grand Design been even partially realized, the world would be a better place today.

17. Troubles in the Congo

As Arthur Schlesinger, Jr., has pointed out, John F. Kennedy was the first American President to show much interest in African affairs. As chairman of the Senate Foreign Relations Committee's African Subcommittee, he had, as early as 1959, called attention to the new explosive forces in Africa with which America and the West must reckon: "Call it nationalism, call it anticolonialism, call it what you will. Africa is going through a revolution. . . . The word is out—and spreading like wildfire in nearly a thousand languages and dialects—that it is no longer necessary to remain forever poor or forever in bondage."[1] During the 1960 campaign, he had strongly attacked the Eisenhower Administration; America had, he said, "lost ground in Africa because we have neglected and ignored the needs and aspirations of the African people."[2]

During the 1950s and 1960s, the new countries were still led largely

SUDAN

CENTRAL
AFRICAN REPUBLIC

FR.
CONGO   Stanleyville •   UGANDA

REPUBLIC OF
THE CONGO   RWANDA
BURUNDI

Léopoldville •   TANGNYIKA

Indian Ocean

ANGOLA   Elisabethville •

FEDERATION OF
RHODESIA
AND NYASALAND

Atlantic Ocean

0   1000   2000
KILOMETERS

0   1000   2000
MILES

THE CONGO -1962

by their emancipators for whom anticolonialism remained the obsessive driving force long after they had won the battle. Their talents lay more in revolutionary agitation than in the sober management of poor fledgling nations. It was as though Sam Adams rather than George Washington had become America's first President. Following the Suez debacle, a swollen freshet of new nations shifted the UN center of gravity from experienced to immature governments and the single-minded zeal of those new leaders distorted United Nations proceedings. By 1960, the largest organized group in the United Nations was the Afro-Asian bloc, and its members reacted by conditioned reflex to almost every issue with anticolonialist rhetoric expressed in an indiscriminate condemnation of the Western powers. Since colonialism, in their experience, involved racial discrimination, they ignored the repressive colonialism manifest in the Soviet Union's Eastern European empire and failed to recognize the USSR as the largest of all "colonialist" powers. Thus many were seduced into serving Moscow's interests.

In this environment, John F. Kennedy found his African theories tested earlier than he would have preferred when his new Administration faced the imminent explosion of the Congo. Lightning could not have struck in any spot more dangerous or difficult for firefighters. The Congo presented all the evils and dangers of premature independence for a sprawling territory strategically important to both the West and the Soviets.

Introduction to the Congo

I had been first introduced to the Congo's problems in the late 1950s, when one of my European law partners brought a minister of the Belgian government to my house in Washington. The minister knew that, as an adviser to the French Patronat, I had shown interest in France's colonial problems in North Africa. He wished to persuade me that the Belgians could succeed where the French were failing. By its enlightened economic policies, Belgium could maintain control of its Congo territories without fear of the turbulence bedeviling the French in the Maghreb. During a long afternoon, he displayed an impressive portfolio of charts, pictures, and plans to demonstrate how Belgium was improving the physical environment and elevating the living standard of the Congolese. He exuded smug confidence that Belgium was in the Congo to stay. The benign attention of the government in Brussels was, he said, fully appreciated by the Congo *indigènes*.

Obviously a man of good will, he amazed me by his insensitivity to the realities of the colonial predicament, cherishing a fallacy endemic among former colonial powers that Third World peoples would be tranquilly grateful for the paternalistic improvement of their physical lot. In return for economic aid they would placidly continue to accept rule by foreigners and the racial discrimination that went with it. (Years later I could not help but recall the minister's attitude when, on a brief visit to Soweto, one of my American companions exclaimed with indignant incredulity, "What are those African blacks complaining about? I've seen far worse slums in Harlem!")

In spite of the minister's self-assurance, I remained unpersuaded. Belgium, I told him, would have no better luck than other countries in trying to buck the tide of history. The domination of colonies by a European metropole could not, I declaimed—perhaps too pompously—long withstand the rising force of Third World nationalism.

The End of the Belgian Congo

Even so, I certainly did not expect the speed with which Belgium's colonial hold would be broken. The abrupt dying fall in Belgium's colonial music was heard right after August 23, 1958, when General de Gaulle, on a visit to Brazzaville in the French Congo (just across the river from Léopoldville), announced that France would grant complete independence to any French dependency that desired it. No doubt the General knew that this startling offer would resound through the Belgian territories to the south, but he took mischievous delight in making problems for his neighbors (as he amply demonstrated nine years later when he shouted "Québec libre" to a cheering crowd in Montreal). His Brazzaville statement inspired immediate demands by Congo nationalist leaders that the Belgian government make a similar offer; attending the Brussels Exhibition in the same year, they found further stimulus for their impatience when they met Belgians who showed sympathy for independence.

The Belgian authorities still felt no sense of urgency until riots broke out in Léopoldville in January 1959, and Brussels was caught completely off guard. Almost overnight, the gears of official policy shifted with a resounding clash as the Belgian King Baudouin on January 13 announced his government's intention "to lead the Congolese population forward to independence" and outlined a plan for increasing self-government that promised independence in four or five years.

As so often happens in a revolutionary period, this limited concession inflated expectations and increased pressures for more rapid and drastic action. King Baudouin's promise of leisurely change heightened the turmoil. Many Belgians in the Congo began to send their families home. In a panic, the Belgian government called a round-table conference in Brussels. Though its representatives had come prepared to offer a shorter transition period, they were met by demands for immediate independence. Faced by tribal rampages in Léopoldville and other parts of the Congo, the government suddenly caved in; on June 30, 1960, the Congo's independence was formally celebrated. It seemed symbolic that, during the ceremony, a spectator stole King Baudouin's sword.

Belgium's colonial policy had failed not because it had overexposed young Congolese to the ideas of the Enlightenment, quite the contrary. There had been no university at all in the Congo until 1954, nor had there been provision for educating ambitious Africans at Belgian universities. Belgium's leaders, unlike their British counterparts, had done little to prepare the *évolués* for independence.

To their surprise and sorrow, the Belgians discovered overnight that rather than restraining the Congolese from demanding too much too soon, Belgium's failure to prepare them for independence engendered chaos that induced a panicked exodus of Europeans followed by repressive rule. Nor had the paucity of education prevented black leaders from emerging. Denied the normal avenues of political action, they had organized revolutionary activities through tribal structures supplemented by associations of "old boy" mission school graduates. Of the leaders who were to play a major role, five in particular deserve special comment.

The New Congo Leaders

Joseph Kasavubu was a member of the large and powerful Bakongo tribe. In 1955, he became president of a cultural-political association developed for political action in defiance of Belgian authorities. With that institutional backing, he was elected a district mayor of Léopoldville.

As politics shifted toward a national setting, *Patrice Lumumba* emerged as his principal opponent. A member of the small Batelela tribe in the Orientale Province, of which Stanleyville was the capital, Lumumba had clawed his way up through the trade-union movement to become the first truly national politician.

Joseph-Désiré Mobutu (now known as Mobutu Sese Seko), at first a subsidiary figure, began his career in 1949 as a clerk in the Belgian Congolese Army. He rose through the ranks of Lumumba's political party. Shrewd, ruthless, and corrupt, he showed little of the popular appeal of his mentor but cunningly exploited his increasing military stature to force his way to the top. American business interests found him acceptable because he favored foreign investment and was anti-Communist.

A protégé of Lumumba's from Stanleyville, *Antoine Gizenga*, frightened Americans most. Lacking the political skills of Lumumba, he gained power through close ties with the Soviet Union.

The personality whom many Westerners found the most interesting and attractive was *Moise Tshombe*. A member of the Lunda tribe in the Congo's southernmost province and son of a wealthy family, he drew support both from his tribal group and from Belgian copper interests. A cynical and ambitious politician with considerable charm and a sense of humor, he was a bold and skillful operator.

The African palaver—a kind of talk marathon—is a unique form of diplomacy and it was only after frenetic talking and maneuvering that a government was finally formed on June 23, 1960, with Lumumba as Prime Minister and Kasavubu as President. By then the country was already in trouble; Congolese troops had deposed their Belgian officers and embarked on sadistic riots—looting Belgian houses and raping-European women—outrages that precipitated a mass exodus of white residents. Now history imitated art; though Lumumba had almost certainly never read Evelyn Waugh's classic satire, *Black Mischief,* he tried to appease his army by precisely the same tactics employed by Waugh's hero, King Seth: he promoted every man to the next higher rank, thus leaving the army without a single private soldier. To protect the lives and property of its remaining 90,000 citizens, the Belgian government sent in paratroopers in July 1960, which aggravated the mounting resentments.

The United Nations in the Congo

Lumumba appealed first to the United Nations and then to the Soviets to end the Belgian "aggression." The UN Security Council—under pressure from the Afro-Asian bloc—adopted a hasty resolution on July 13, 1960, calling on Belgium to withdraw its troops from the Congo and authorizing the Secretary-General "to take all necessary steps in consultation with the Congolese government to provide it with such military assistance as may be necessary." Dag Hammarskjöld, the last strong, independent-minded Secretary-General the United Nations is ever likely to have, responded by approving the creation of a UN force to replace the Belgian troops, thus undercutting the Soviets' excuse for inserting forces of its own. Hammarskjöld then held his ground against a diplomatic counter-offensive.

As the fragility of the new government became increasingly apparent, tribal groups in several parts of its vast territories proclaimed their independence. In the eastern province, Antoine Gizenga announced the formation of a government at Stanleyville that claimed sovereignty over the whole of the country. In the southern territory of Katanga, containing rich copper and diamond mines that provided half the Congo's foreign exchange and tax revenues, Moise Tshombe announced the creation of an independent state. Lumumba responded by asking the Soviet Union to help put down the Katanga rebellion.

Supported by Russian and Czech "technicians" and Soviet military equipment, Lumumba's army tried to push into Katanga but was repulsed by Tshombe's forces, which included Belgian volunteers and hired adventurers. The victory of Tshombe's mercenaries critically weakened Lumumba's prestige and authority.

On August 3, 1960, Hammarskjöld announced that United Nations troops would enter Katanga on August 8, but cancelled the order when Tshombe refused entry. The news that the upstart Tshombe had defied the United Nations created a sensation. The Soviet Union proposed to send troops if the Belgians were not withdrawn and the Congo's territorial integrity safeguarded. The Secretary-General now decided to visit Katanga to talk with Tshombe. Though no one can say with assurance just what passed during their private interview, Hammarskjöld presumably reassured Tshombe that the United Nations would not assist the Congolese government to subdue Katanga. On that understanding, Tshombe agreed to permit the entry of the UN force.[3]

With Lumumba humiliated by his military fiasco, Kasavubu dismissed him as Prime Minister. That led to a protracted tug of war between Kasavubu and the new parliament, resolved only when Colonel Mobutu, then commander of the *Force Publique,* took temporary control of the country. He promptly expelled the diplomatic representatives of the Soviet Union and Czechoslovakia, leaving the Communists to try to regroup in Stanleyville.

The Situation Confronting Kennedy

That then was the tangled Congo mess when President Kennedy was inaugurated. A United Nations force had been sent to the Congo on a limited mission to keep the peace, pending the withdrawal of Belgian forces and the building of an adequate army under the national government's command. Kasavubu was holding Lumumba in prison; Tshombe was persisting in his secessionist drive in the Congo; Gizenga claimed to head a Congo government in Stanleyville. To complicate matters, Kasavubu turned Lumumba over to Tshombe, and, on February 13, 1961— only about three weeks after Kennedy came to power—the Katangese authorities confirmed the killing of Lumumba under highly ambiguous circumstances, thus making him an instant martyr in radical Third World circles.

That was rich fuel for the Soviets' anti-UN campaign, and they moved rapidly to capitalize on it. Though they had encouraged the original commitment of a UN force to the Congo as a means of getting the Belgians out and giving them a free hand, it no longer served their purposes. They launched a campaign to try to destroy the United Nations as an effective institution, demanding that Secretary-General Hammarskjöld be dismissed as "an accomplice and organizer" of the murders, calling for the arrest of Tshombe and Mobutu, and insisting on support for the "legitimate" Katanga government of Acting Prime Minister Antoine Gizenga.

We saw all this as a major headache, but if America were to have an African policy at all, we could not ignore the Congo. It was, as I later described it, "a keystone of central Africa." Superimposed on a map of Europe, the Congo would extend from the Atlantic to the Soviet frontier. From Elizabethville to Leopoldville was as far as from Bucharest to London; as one writer has put it, "between the inhabitants of Katanga and those of the Bas-Congo, there is about as much resemblance as between a Rumanian peasant and a cockney."[4] With two hundred tribes speaking a score of dialects, the Congo was unmanageable by a centralized government.

Even more important than its size and diversity was its strategic position. As I wrote in 1961, "It has a long frontier with each of the three major areas in which we divide the African continent south of the Sahara Desert: West Africa, already independent and divided into a number of states of varying sizes; East Africa, now rapidly evolving from British tutelage into what we hope will be a stable and prosperous independence; and the southern part of the continent, beset with critical problems that are now beginning to emerge in sharp relief on the world scene."[5]

On February 25, 1961, as one of his first acts, President Kennedy warned that America would "defend the Charter of the United Nations by opposing any attempt by any government to intervene unilaterally in the Congo."[6] To keep the UN force in place, the United States then made up the financial shortfall resulting from a refusal of the Communist countries to bear their share of the cost.

Death of Hammarskjöld

On September 13, Hammarskjöld took off for North Rhodesia to meet again with Tshombe and arrange a cease-fire. He was killed on September 18, when his plane crashed before landing at Ndola.

By an odd quirk of circumstance, I seemed always to hear of portentous events at international meetings. I was at a Bilderberg meeting in Garmisch-Partenkirchen in 1955 when President Eisenhower had his first heart attack. At a Fiuggi (Italy) Bilderberg meeting in 1957, I first learned of the Soviet's Sputnik. Finally, on September 18, 1961, at the annual meeting of the International Bank and Monetary Fund in Vienna, a shocked conference hall heard the announcement of Hammarskjöld's accident.

Until Hammarskjöld died, I had been far too occupied with other matters to pay much attention to the Congo, but now I took overall charge of the State Department's direction of our Congo policy. In a sense, it was no policy at all; it had evolved in response to events, and I could discern no clear, central strategy. Even within the Department there was a confusion of voices; each bureau seemed determined to advance its particular bias. That was normal. Indeed, it was as it should be; to achieve perspective and a three-dimensional strategy, a subject had to be viewed from more than one point of vantage. But the system could work effectively only if someone with overall responsibility—either the Secretary or his deputy (then known as the Under Secretary)—was prepared to distill from these disparate attitudes and opinions a policy expressing the nation's larger interests and to assure that that policy was faithfully executed.

Disparate Opinions

With its strong—and understandable—anticolonial bias, the African Bureau tended to reflect the views of the African bloc; it saw secession as the effort of Belgian interests to preserve their entrenched positions, using Tshombe as their instrument. As my own responsibilities were not geographically limited, I tried to fit our policies toward the Congo into a context larger than African politics. I could not wholly agree with Chester Bowles or "Soapy" Williams. Bowles, who had written a book about Africa, felt deeply about its peoples and, like Williams, was moved by an idealism that, in my more cynical view, expected too much of the new African leaders.

Understandably, the African Bureau's views were heavily influenced by the opinions of our ambassador to the Congo, Edmund Gullion. A strong and effective career officer, Gullion had come to share the view of the United Nations representatives in the Congo that the Katanga secession must at all costs be repressed. Thus, we were constantly receiving what I thought of as "Tshombe *delenda est*" messages from our Leopoldville embassy.

The Bureau of International Organization Affairs, headed by Harlan Cleveland, had a different point of reference—the anxiety to assure that the United Nations demonstrate its authority and effectiveness. While not unsympathetic with the African Bureau and definitely anti-Tshombe, Cleveland and his colleagues cautioned restraint, fearing that the UN forces might become bogged down and UN authority undercut by a protracted (and necessarily bloody) attempt to end the Katanga secession, which was outside their mandate. They were necessarily sensitive to the views of Adlai Stevenson, who was then our UN ambassador, and, because the primary role of the Bureau of International Organization Affairs was to serve as the conduit between the Department and our New York mission to the United Nations, they constantly found themselves in the middle. It was not always easy to interpret the views of the mission to the Department and the views of the Department and the White House to the mission. Adlai spent his days and nights in the United Nations environment and could not ignore the vehement anti-Tshombe demands of the Afro-Asian bloc. He also had to maintain harmonious relations with the Secretary-General and Secretariat; the cooperation of both was essential.

Finally, the European Bureau was, by definition, concerned with the reactions of major European governments. The French government, having abstained from voting to commit UN forces to the Congo, now refused to pay its share of the expenses. The British government, under Prime Minister Macmillan, sympathized with Tshombe. It had its own colonial interests to consider; the southern boundary of Katanga bisected both the Lunda tribe and the copper belt, which extended into what was then the Federation of Rhodesia and Nyasaland. Key members of the British government saw an independent Katanga as a buffer against the more radical elements in Léopoldville. Furthermore, some of the more cynical of us suspected, rightly or wrongly, that certain members of the British government might have a financial interest in Tanganyika Concessions, which owned 30.78 percent of Katanga's Union Minière.

Shaping a US Strategy

My first order of business was to develop a clearly articulated United States strategy. It was not on our initiative that the United Nations had sent troops to the Congo; the United States had merely supported a move by the Afro-Asian bloc. The Eisenhower Administration's failure to define and explain a clear American policy—a failure we had not yet rectified—now made President Kennedy vulnerable to conflicting pressures. The Belgians had left the Congo in a frightful mess, and I was never convinced that an inexperienced government in Léopoldville could make its writ effective throughout a huge, sprawling tribal conglomerate one-third as large as the United States. Léopoldville's tenuous authority extended through a primitive system of roads and communications to diverse peoples and areas with little in common. Some argued from these facts that we should try to salvage Katanga as the one area that might— with continuing help from Belgian interests—sustain itself and evolve as an effective small nation-state. In spite of all the hatred of Tshombe as a tool of colonialism, he had—in contrast to the demagogues in Léopoldville—demonstrated some capacity for leadership.

But logic is irrelevant in Africa, where national boundaries are merely lines marking the fortuitous collision of expansionist colonial powers. They bisect tribes and language areas, ignore topographical facts such as rivers or mountain ranges, and are even more irrational than gerrymandered electoral districts in America. That built-in fragility was, in fact, the main argument for keeping the Congo together. If any of the new African nations were to be broken into its logical parts, the resulting chain reaction of fragmentation would turn Africa into an unmanageable sandheap of small, poverty-striken tribal entities. Moreover, were we to offer even the most qualified support to an independent Katanga, we would, in the eyes of the Third World, identify ourselves with the Belgian colonialists; that would give the Soviet Union a golden opportunity to exploit the resulting disaffection of those areas of the Congo that had, in losing Katanga, lost also their major source of revenue.

As a lawyer who regarded the adversary process as the most effective engine to elicit the truth, I put hard questions to my colleagues who espoused divergent lines of policy. What was the United Nations really trying to do? Was it trying to protect its own forces? Was it trying to destroy Tshombe's army, which was largely manned by white officers, mercenaries, and volunteers? Was it primarily seeking to end the Katanga secession? If so, was that consistent with the objectives for which it had originally entered the country? The British, I knew, were contending that such an intervention in Congolese internal quarrels had been explicitly barred by one of the earlier Security Council resolutions adopted in December 1960.[7]

I had no doubt that the UN forces were clearly exceeding the mandate provided by the Security Council—or even perhaps by the Charter itself. But I still had to balance that item against America's *Realpolitik* interest in supporting that makeshift fighting force. We had, I thought, a compelling reason to prevent a secession that would tear the Congo in two. Gizenga, Lumumba's ideological heir, was based in Stanleyville; the Tshombe regime was established in Elisabethville; Kasavubu presided in Léopoldville. If the Soviets obtained a base in the heart of Africa, we would have to drive them out. The United Nations military force seemed the best hope of avoiding such a dangerous confrontation. If it could not bring the great powers together, it might at least keep them apart in a highly strategic area. Moreover, we could not exclude past history from the equation; two American administrations had gone along with UN activities in the Congo, and the costs of reversing our course would be high.

Speech on the Congo

A policy not carefully articulated is, in my view, no policy at all. Whenever I encountered a difficult question as to where American interests lay, I hammered out a formulation as free as possible of diplomatic obfuscation; it was, I suppose, a lesson learned from Jean Monnet—one could best test and order his thoughts by writing them down. So I set forth our Congo position in a speech on December 19, 1961, at

Los Angeles. Later, with the approval of President Kennedy, who liked the speech and suggested a few additions, we had it published as a pamphlet and widely circulated as the definitive statement of our Congo policy.[8] In that speech, I pointed out that the "Congo's main political issue, perhaps the only real 'modern' issue, was Congolese unity," and that, "if the Congolese government should prove unable to deal effectively with the Katanga secession of Mr. Tshombe, militant extremists, such as the Communist-chosen instrument Mr. Gizenga, would bid to take over the central government in the name of Congolese unity. In the resulting civil war, our main objectives in Central Africa would be drowned in blood." I posed the alternative: "Why shouldn't Katanga be independent? For that matter, why shouldn't every other tribe in Central Africa that wishes to declare its independence have the right to do so? . . . to those who approach the problem from the viewpoint of protecting a particular interest, something may perhaps be said for carving enclaves out of the Congo, though I am convinced that even this calculation is mistaken. But if one looks at the problem from the viewpoint of saving all of central Africa from chaos and Communist infiltration, then clearly the acceptance of armed secession by a tribal area, no matter how rich and well-supported, can lead only to disaster." There was, I contended, "simply . . . no legal case, no political case, no economic case, and no moral case for Balkanizing the heart of Africa."

Peace could be restored only through negotiation. With Katangese authorities engaged in a steady buildup of men, munitions, and equipment (including airplanes) obtained through the devious international arms trade, there would, I predicted, be an inevitable clash with the UN forces. That clash finally occurred at Elisabethville. On December 3, Ralph Bunche (who was the Acting Secretary-General following Hammarskjöld's death and before the election of U Thant) had directed the UN force to reestablish law and order and, in the face of threats of an impending Katangese attack, had authorized it to take any action necessary to restore the rights of the United Nations in Elisabethville. Heavy local fighting erupted on December 5, increasing in scale during the following days. Then gradually the UN force gained control of the situation, using US Globemaster aircraft to airlift UN troops.

If we were to counter the threat from the Communist-dominated Stanleyville in the eastern Congo, we had to arrange a deal between controlling factions at the two other points of the triangle: the Leopoldville leaders in the north and Tshombe's Elisabethville faction in the south. Tshombe must be persuaded to halt the secession and bring Katanga into some kind of Congo federation, and the Kasavubu regime must abandon its insistence on a centralized government.

Unfortunately, American opinion did not fully support such a course, and—as we were to learn bitterly in Vietnam—no American foreign policy can succeed without the support of both Congress and the public. Tshombe not only had the strong financial backing of Belgian financial interests but was rapidly becoming a folk hero of the American right. He was, claimed his apologists, a determined anti-Communist trying to save the richest area of the Congo from the encroachments of leftist forces in Léopoldville. Southern Senators, in particular, favored him, because his secessionist ambitions evoked atavistic memories of the old South. They also saw him as being harassed by an Afro-Asian bloc that expressed its residual anticolonialist sentiments in a vindictive effort to destroy the only leader really interested in the country's welfare. Several vocal and influential Protestant ministers also championed his cause. Tshombe was their man; in contrast to Kasavubu and Lumumba, both products of Catholic mission schools, Tshombe had been trained by Methodist missionaries.

Tshombe mounted a noisy public relations campaign financed by Belgian financial interests under the direction of a man named Michel Struelens. The Katangan lobby's principal instrument was the American Committee for Aid to Katanga Freedom Fighters, founded in 1961 under at least the nominal chairmanship of Max Yergan, a black educator. On December 14 of that year, it published a full-page advertisement in the *New York Times* and seventeen other major newspapers under the headline: "Katanga is the Hungary of 1961," demanding the withdrawal of financial aid to the UN mission in Katanga. That appeal brought more than three thousand contributions from commercial and industrial companies. Further support for the campaign came from conservative or isolationist organizations, such as the John Birch Society. In March 1962, the Katanga Freedom Fighters Committee organized a meeting in Madison Square Garden where $80,000 was collected for the pro-Katanga struggle.[9] Richard Nixon complained in a syndicated article in the *New York Herald Tribune* on December 19, 1961, that our Congo policy had failed and that the Kennedy Administration was leading us toward a Communist takeover of the Congo—a remarkable charge from one who had been Vice-President in an Administration responsible for the initial commitment of UN troops to the Congo. Tshombe, said Nixon, was "a dedicated anti-Communist." Senator Thomas J. Dodd of Connecticut went even farther, accusing United Nations troops of "naked aggression" and "atrocities" against Katanga and demanding a Senate investigation—a statement endorsed on December 30 by former President Herbert Hoover.

It was formidable conservative frog-croaking, especially when Senator Richard B. Russell of Georgia recorded his disapproval in a letter to President Kennedy. That lent solidity to the opposition, for Senator Russell was not one of the usual suspects in the front ranks of partisan conservatives. He commanded respect from a young President who only a

George Ball, *c.* 1920.

George Ball as an undergraduate at Northwestern University, 1929.

Ruth Murdoch in 1929. She married George Ball in 1932.

George Ball, a director of the U.S. Strategic Bombing Survey, in front of the Ritz, Paris, 1944. Note the breach of military decorum in an unbuttoned overcoat.

Ruth Murdoch Ball, 1944.

John Colin Ball, the George Balls' first child (*above*),
and Douglas Bleakly Ball, their second, in 1947.

Bernard De Voto. Writer, frontiersman, and historian.

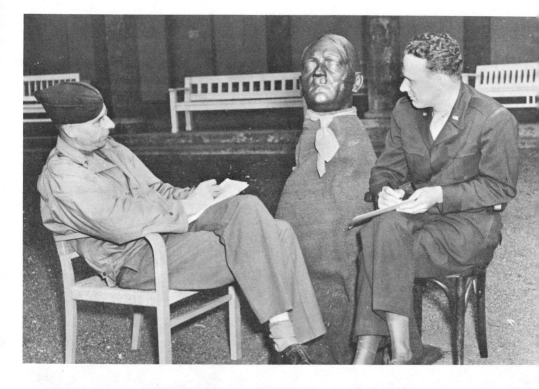

Above: George Ball and his fellow director of the U.S. Strategic Bombing Survey, John Kenneth Galbraith (*left*), viewing the bust of Hitler at Bad Nauheim in May 1945.

Below: With Wilson Wyatt, campaign manager for Adlai Stevenson in 1952.

Adlai Stevenson in 1952 inscribed the photo: "With apologies to a dear friend and political widow, Ruth Ball."

DUBOIS, THE DRAKE

G.W.B.   J.F.K.

☆ OCTOBER 1962 ☆

SUN	MON	TUE	WED	THU	FRI	SAT
	1	2	3	4	5	6
7	8	9	10	11	12	13
14	15	16	17	18	19	20
21	22	23	24	25	26	27
28	29	30	31			

Sterling silver plaque showing the dates of the Cuban Missile Crisis—a gift from President Kennedy.

Cartoon appearing in *Canard Enchaîné* during argument over British entry to the Common Market, 1963.

M.L.F. : ENTRE LONDRES ET PARIS ON SE RENVOIE LE BALL.

"For George Ball—with highest esteem and best personal regards, John Kennedy."

Averell Harriman sworn in as Assistant Secretary of State, 1963.

With Portugal's Premier Antonio de Oliveira Salazar, September 1963.

With Chancellor Ludwig Erhard of West Germany, 1964.

Under Secretary of State Ball at Checkpoint Charlie overlooking East Berlin, November 1964.

With President Lyndon Baines Johnson and former Secretary of State Dean Acheson, 1964.

With Archbishop Makarios III, Cyprus, 1964.

McGeorge Bundy, George Ball, Dean Rusk, and President Johnson, April 1964.

A reception at Buckingham Palace during May 1965 SEATO meetings.

*To my friend and alter ego George Ball
as proof that we look at things alike!
Dean Rusk*

Inscription reads: "To my friend and alter ego George Ball as proof that we look at things alike! Dean Rusk." July 1965.

Aboard Air Force One with Ambassador Llewellyn Thompson, NATO trip, 1965.

To George Ball
may we always be this relaxed
Lyndon B. Johnson

Meeting at the White House with (*left to right*) Robert McNamara, McGeorge Bundy, Hubert Humphrey, and President Lyndon Johnson.

With Dean Rusk and President Johnson, July 21, 1965.

With Ruth Ball and Vice-President Hubert Humphrey, January 1966.

Audience with Mohammad Reza Pahlavi, Shahanshah of Iran, at the time of the coronation, Teheran, October 1967.

Presiding at Family of Man Award dinner honoring Jean Monnet (*at lectern*).
Left to right: George Ball, The Hon. John J. McCloy, and Norman Vincent Peale,
1967.

Robert F. Kennedy and Jean Monnet at Family of Man Award dinner, 1967.

With King Faisal of Saudi Arabia, 1968.

Sworn in by Chief Justice Earl Warren as Permanent Representative to the United Nations, April 1968. Ruth Ball and President Johnson witness.

Cartoon appearing in the *Christian Science Monitor* following resignation from the UN to assist Hubert Humphrey's presidential campaign. September 1968.

To: George W. Ball

With best wishes.

(Lee Kuan Yew) 17-3-70

ON THE OPPOSITE PAGE

Above: with Prime Minister Lee Kuan Yew of Singapore, 1970.

Below: with Albert Speer during interview at Duke of Holstein's castle known as Schloss Glücksberg, March 1971.

Family Portrait. *Left to right, rear:* Douglas Bleakly Ball, John's wife Linda Ottenant Ball, John Colin Ball. *Seated:* Ruth Ball and George Ball. October 1981.

JOHN W. ALEXANDERS

year earlier had been a junior Senator and never a member of the inner club. So Kennedy sent Under Secretary of State for Political Affairs George W. McGhee to explain the situation quietly to him. McGhee, a highly personable Texan, was well-liked by southern Democrats in the Congress, and he could never be dismissed as an anti-Tshombe fanatic. Meanwhile, we concentrated on trying to set up a meeting between Tshombe and Premier Adoula (now head of the Leopoldville government) that might produce not only a cease-fire but also a settlement.

Since so many forces were pushing in different directions, caution was required. In December 1961, U Thant and the commander of the UN forces, intent on pushing into Katanga, rejected any idea of a cease-fire until settlement conversations had actually begun between Tshombe and Adoula. Adlai Stevenson and our UN mission in New York, necessarily sensitive to the Secretary-General's views and the prevailing UN sentiment, urged that the UN forces be permitted to push forward. Our concern in Washington was that a UN effort initiated to prevent great-power intervention had, under pressure from the more radical African countries, been transformed into an anti-Tshombe crusade; we wished to avoid any appearance of supporting such a crusade.

Given this basic divergence, I found myself conducting a running argument with Stevenson, who had little patience with a White House and State Department he thought insufficiently sensitive to Third World sentiments. Moreover, being outside the range of fire from leading members of the Senate and the House, he did not feel the domestic heat as we did.

With the UN forces poised to drive into Elisabethville, we were eager to get Tshombe to come forward with some specific proposals. The President was determined that the United States not press for any UN action that might appear to be aimed at Tshombe's destruction; before the military action got out of hand, we must, therefore, make it clear to U Thant that we would support the United Nations only for limited military objectives and not for a general offensive. Stevenson was equally firm that the UN forces should continue the fight, even after they took Elisabethville, until Tshombe was prepared to talk. Thus I was caught in a searing predicament between the President's instructions, which I had helped to shape and fully supported, and deference to the convictions of an old friend whom I loved and admired and who—more than anyone else—was responsible for my role in the government.

Meanwhile, we were asking the French and other Europeans to help push Tshombe into line, and, perhaps in response to French pressure, President Kennedy, on December 14, 1961, received the following appeal from Tshombe: "For ten days, troops of the United Nations have been putting pressure against Katanga, causing the loss of human lives and material damage. Force alone will never be able to resolve the Congolese problem. I confirm my desire to negotiate with Monsieur Adoula the various aspects of this problem. I ask your intervention as a free man and as a Christian to designate a suitable negotiator to stop at once this useless infusion [sic] of blood."

What reply should the President give to Tshombe's *cri de coeur?* U Thant, Stevenson told me, would insist that the President flatly reject Tshombe's proposal; we would be interfering with a UN operation if we designated a negotiator or mediator. But in Washington we were convinced that Tshombe would never negotiate with a UN mediator. As a compromise, we proposed that U Thant request the President of the United States to undertake mediation through any agent he might appoint. We did not intend to let a possible settlement break down over a silly jurisdictional quarrel as to whether the United States or the United Nations should designate the negotiator.

U Thant proposed to advise Tshombe that he was designating Deputy Secretary-General Ralph J. Bunche and Robert A. K. Gardiner to mediate and that a plane would be sent for Tshombe. No mention was made of a cease-fire. I was convinced that if U Thant spoke for us, Tshombe would never negotiate, since, as Tshombe saw it, the United Nations forces in the Congo were trying to kill him.

That disagreement over tactics led to the most heated argument I ever had with Stevenson, and it was painful for both of us. I felt he was being unrealistic, while he, no doubt, thought I had sold out to the nationalistic types in Washington. The United States should, he argued, not try to preempt what was clearly a United Nations role. If we chose to go ahead, U Thant would simply refer the matter back to the Congolese delegation and then to the Security Council, which would destroy any possibility of negotiation.

We settled the long haggle by simply advising the United Nations that the President was designating Ambassador Edmund A. Gullion as his representative to facilitate a meeting between Adoula and Tshombe and was so notifying Tshombe. Though we omitted an explicit assurance of a cease-fire, we authorized the United States consul in Elisabethville, Lewis Hoffacker, to say, when he delivered the message, that a ceasefire would be in effect. In Kitona in the southwestern Congo, Ambassador Gullion and UN Deputy Secretary-General Bunche looked over their shoulders as Tshombe and Adoula engaged in an African pow-wow that lasted seventeen hours. An agreement was finally reached and signed on December 21, 1961. Tshombe explicitly acknowledged the authority of the central government and undertook to comply with various UN resolutions requiring him to get rid of his mercenaries and stop behaving independently.

On its face the agreement seemed to have settled all the difficult issues, but we remained skeptical. Based on past experience, we doubted that Tshombe would live up to its terms, particularly after he had told the press in Kitona that they had been unsatisfactory and would have to be presented for approval to his Parliament, which might take a week or two.

On December 22, I telephoned McGeorge Bundy in Bermuda (where the President was meeting with Prime Minister Macmillan) to report that the Tshombe cabinet had broken up after a three-hour session the night before and that Katangese representatives had released a communiqué denouncing the agreement as not binding since Tshombe had no advance mandate from the provincial parliament. With the cooperation of Brussels, we were working on an economic program to cut off Tshombe's sources of financing. To my mind, only the prospect of financial stringency would persuade Tshombe to live up to his commitments.

By this time, U Thant, under pressure from Adoula and anxious to dispose of the Katanga problem so he could begin reducing the UN force, was strongly urging a speedy settlement. In July, a new plan was drafted, largely in the State Department, for graduated economic and financial pressures on Katanga. Meanwhile, the situation was, Stevenson and I agreed, rapidly deteriorating. The French were dragging their feet, and, though Belgian Foreign Minister Paul Henri Spaak was doing his best, the Union Minière was actively working to sabotage the effort.

In the United States, the Cuban Missile Crisis and the approach of Congressional elections deterred us from any new Congo initiatives, though a mission by George McGhee strengthened hope that conciliatory measures could succeed. We were increasingly anxious that they succeed soon, for the Adoula government seemed to be falling apart, which would create new openings for Soviet infiltration. A serious question had also arisen as to how long the UN force could be held together; India, after the Chinese attack over the Himalayan mountain barriers, was threatening to withdraw its contingent.

Sanctions were a sticky problem. A new plan drafted by George McGhee in November 1962 proposed a milder formula for the division of revenues and thus proved helpful in winning Spaak's support for economic pressures. Great Britain still held back, as did the Union Minière. On December 27, after Katangese gendarmes opened fire on UN forces, the UN troops began a counter-operation that put them in full control of Elisabethville by December 29. A second contingent occupied Kamina, and a third the rail and mining center of Jadotville. The UN Command on the spot then decided to act on its own and expand the fighting without regard to any instructions from New York, where U Thant had announced on December 29, 1962, that military action by the UN forces had already ended. Denying that the Katanga secession had been ended by force, he repeated on December 31 that the military situation was stabilized, even though fighting was actually continuing.[9]

This, then, was the first stage of our involvement in the Congo, but it was not to be my last embroilment with that beleaguered and unhappy land, where, as I shall describe later, affairs took one bizarre twist after another.

18. The General and His Thunderbolts

Charles de Gaulle's obsessive ambition was to make France top dog in world councils; that was possible, he believed, only if he were top dog in France. His misfortune was to be constantly at war with history, for he had the bad luck to come too late on the scene. France was no longer, as in the eighteenth century, the richest and most populous nation in the Western world; she was not even self-sufficient in defense but dependent on America's military presence and on the American-dominated NATO. That, to de Gaulle, was intolerable, and he tried by the levitation of his own will to raise France to an equal rank in superpower councils.

Proposal for Directorate

He had disclosed that intention on December 27, 1958, when he proposed to President Eisenhower and Prime Minister Harold Macmillan that the three nations constitute a directorate. They should establish tripartite machinery for global strategy outside of NATO, carve the world into areas of assigned responsibility, make joint decisions, and develop common military strategies that would include plans for nuclear warfare even though the French bomb was still eighteen months in the future. In Washington, the proposal created more surprise than it deserved, as it had long been obvious that Paris was out of phase with American thinking. Nonetheless, early in July 1959, Secretary Dulles made a special trip to sort out problems with the General. De Gaulle insisted that, unless France were properly represented in the world's top councils, his country would quickly deteriorate. Dulles replied that a world role for France could come about only concomitant with its development of internal strength, and that formalizing such a role would engender jealousy in Italy and Germany. Though groupings for directing the free world might exist in fact, they would be resented if explicitly acknowledged.

With his directorate scheme rebuffed, de Gaulle shifted tactics. Conceding that there was no need for a permanent strategic understanding (*entente*), he argued that NATO should be extended to cover the Middle

East and at least all of Africa north of the Sahara and that the structure of the alliance should be revised. Apart from France, the United Kingdom, and the United States, Germany was the only other country that "need realistically" be considered, but Germany could not yet speak on an equal basis with the other three powers. In an effort to placate de Gaulle, Dulles invited French participation in tripartite military consultations. The French asked for a study of strategy in the Far East—particularly with respect to Laos. But the American military took the position that, since neither British nor French forces could contribute much to Far East defense, there was no point in joint command relationships.

That marked the end of de Gaulle's initial efforts to raise France to superpower status. Thereafter, he tried in a half-hearted way to gain control of Europe on French terms. About a fortnight after Kennedy had assumed office, the six European Economic Community (EEC) countries—meeting in Paris—set up a commission headed by the French ambassador to Germany, Christian Fouchet, to develop proposals for a political union—a *"union des états"* with no supranational aspects. After several versions and revisions, the scheme foundered in April 1962, when the Dutch and Belgians refused to go forward so long as Britain was not a member of the Common Market.

This is background for four events occurring on different levels during the latter months of 1962 that were finally to interact in a dramatic fashion.

Converging Activities

First, the British–EEC negotiations were proceeding at a snail's pace, with the parties still far apart. Heath, with the brilliant assistance of my old friend from wartime days, Eric Roll (now Lord Roll), was bargaining hard, withholding for tactical reasons offers of compromise on certain key issues, which he could, at the eleventh hour, concede in concluding a final settlement.

Second, de Gaulle was pursuing a new option in his quest for the leadership of Europe—an *entente* with Adenauer, in which France would be the predominant power.

Third, America's nuclear partnership with Britain was facing a crisis, as Britain neared the end of a generation of delivery vehicles.

Fourth, to forestall the resentment that might develop from Germany's continued exclusion from the nuclear club the United States was proposing the creation of a mixed-manned fleet of nuclear vessels to be operated on a collective basis by the United States and other European nations, including Germany. Such a proposal had been foreshadowed in March 1960, when the NATO commander, General Lauris Norstad, suggested that US, British, and French battalions be assigned to a supranational force under NATO command. Later, in November, he suggested a "multilateral atomic authority" within NATO that would give alliance members "an essentially equal voice" in controlling the nuclear components of NATO systems. At the December 1960 NATO ministerial meeting, Secretary of State Christian Herter put forward a two-part proposal. Five United States Polaris submarines would be assigned to NATO and a sea-based, mixed-manned Polaris force, multilaterally owned, financed, and controlled, would be established. One hundred missiles would be committed to the latter force on terms that would prevent their withdrawal from NATO.

When the Kennedy Administration took office, the problem was immediately reviewed and in a speech at Ottawa on May 17, 1961, President Kennedy announced that, "to make clear our own intentions and commitments to the defense of Western Europe, the United States will commit to the NATO command five—and subsequently still more—Polaris atomic missile submarines. . . . Beyond this, we look to the possibility of eventually establishing a NATO seaborne force, which would be truly multilateral in ownership and control, if this should be desired and found feasible by our Allies, once NATO's non-nuclear goals have been achieved."[1] During succeeding months, several members of the alliance expressed interest in studying the creation of a NATO multilateral seaborne missile force, and, in October 1962, we sent a United States team headed by Gerard Smith and Admiral John M. Lee to Europe to present technical information.

Though I was, of course, generally aware of the proposals for a multilateral force, I did not at first take them seriously. But as the French increasingly flaunted their *force de frappe* as a badge of great power status, I began to fear that the Germans might, over time, develop a sense of grievance. At the same time, for the Federal Republic to acquire a nuclear capability of its own would create great tensions with a Soviet Union that still exploited German *revanchism* for its own purposes and would be totally unacceptable to other Western European powers. As I said in a speech on January 11, 1965,

It is not enough to say that there is no desire in Germany to become a nuclear power. Not only is this proposition dubious, but it is largely irrelevant. In approaching the problem of nuclear management, we must concern ourselves not merely with the situation of today, but also with that of tomorrow. . . .

We cannot safely proceed on the assumption that the Germans will be prepared over the years ahead to refrain from efforts to obtain some nuclear capability. We cannot count upon German willingness to resign themselves to a second-class status, nor upon our ability to compel Germany to do so.

When the Western European Union was created, Germany gave a very limited commitment not to manufacture nuclear weapons on her own soil. But Germans are as familiar as the rest of us with *rebus sic stantibus* and in 1964—when that commitment was given—France had not yet made the decision to become an atomic power. . . .[2]

Germany rearmed after World War I in the face of clear commitments that it would not do so because the Allied nations lacked the sustained will to enforce those commitments. That failure of will, I said, arose in large part from the feeling, rightly or wrongly, "that the doctrine of original sin had no place in international arrangements and that discrimination against Germany should not be perpetuated."

There were, I contended, two lessons that the last fifty years should have clearly taught us about Germany. "First, the Germans should not be left alone to develop a feeling of isolation from other people of the Free World; second, they should not be left with a real or imagined sense of grievance or discrimination. Such feelings can be dangerous in any country. They can be particularly dangerous in the case of Germany."

That was the reasoning which led me to support the proposed creation of a collective military force. A land-based force was excluded because it would have to be deployed within the national territory of a member state; a sea-based force could spend its life in international waters. The nuclear weapons system on the mixed-manned ships or submarines would be under the collective control of a group or committee representing the participating nations. The weapons could be fired only by unanimous decision of that group, acting under instructions from their governments.

Such a scheme was obviously more complicated than nuclear management by a single state, and in practical effect a mixed-manned force would have little military value. But that was not the point; I saw it as serving a political objective. I thought we might offer such a force to our allies—not seek to impose it; only if they showed sufficient interest would we invite them to work with us in transforming the concept into a reality.

The Failure of Skybolt

Besides enabling West Germany to share the management of a nuclear weapons system I hoped that the multilateral force might provide the British an excuse for relinquishing their own national deterrent. Britain had a special claim to be a nuclear power since she had closely collaborated in developing the nuclear bomb. But with her postwar troubles, she had not been able to keep pace in the development of delivery systems, and in the early 1960s manned aircraft capable only of dropping bombs over targets were no longer adequate. As a result, after abandoning an initial effort to develop a missile of their own, the British had agreed to join with the United States in developing a new air-to-surface missile called Skybolt. Mounted beneath the wings of B-52 bombers and the British V bombers, it could be launched at ground targets one thousand miles away. At American insistence, the agreement provided that either party could terminate the arrangement after consultation with its partner. Nevertheless—albeit the point was not made explicit—the British regarded the agreement as an American commitment to underwrite Britain's nuclear future.

By the spring of 1962, Secretary McNamara had decided that Skybolt was an excessively expensive project with serious technical flaws, and that the progress achieved with the Polaris and Minuteman missiles made it redundant. But cancellation would have to be carefully worked out with the British. I knew the Pentagon was unhappy with Skybolt, but I spent little time thinking about it. Both the President and Secretary Rusk considered it as primarily a military matter to be handled by McNamara; it had, they assumed, only incidental political overtones.

Since all of us were, at the moment, weary from the Cuban missile ordeal and preoccupied with sweeping up the debris, none of us regarded a forthcoming meeting between Macmillan and Kennedy at Nassau as more than a routine affair—merely the sixth in a series. Skybolt had not originally been on the agenda, and the Defense Ministers had not planned to attend until McNamara telephoned me on December 7 that he had decided to go. That meant, as I told him, that the British Defense Minister Peter Thorneycroft would also insist on attending, which would make Skybolt the principal subject of discussion. Rusk opted to stay home, since he had earlier scheduled our annual diplomatic dinner for that night and did not want to offend the diplomatic corps. I was a last minute recruit.

The Nassau Conference

Secretary McNamara telephoned the British Minister of Defense on December 8 to advise him that the final decision to cancel the Skybolt had not yet been taken, though it obviously outraged his own concepts of cost-effectiveness. Whether or not that call was intended to satisfy the "prior consultation" clause I do not know. The decision to scrap Skybolt had, in fact, already been effectively made, but officially McNamara and Rusk took the position that there had been no final decision.

Since the matter obviously had to be discussed with the British in advance of Nassau, McNamara decided to visit Thorneycroft. Roswell Gilpatric, McNamara's able Deputy, called me on Saturday, December 8, to discuss the position McNamara should take with the press when he arrived in London. According to Gilpatric, he planned to say that Skybolt was being carefully reappraised because of its marginal character in terms of time and cost and because all such programs came up for review at budget time; the purpose of coming to London was to consult the British. But on the evening of December 10 Secretary McNamara sent me a draft press statement he proposed to make on arriving in London which made clear that the Skybolt had failed its flight tests. I immediately telephoned McNamara to urge that he eliminate any reference to the flight tests. He had to make clear he was coming to consult and not to cancel. He would, moreover, violate protocol were he to say anything substantive to the press prior to meeting with the government. To suggest that the Skybolt test had failed—implying that we would cancel the missile—would needlessly embarrass Thorneycroft.

But the advice was not taken and when McNamara arrived at Gatwick Airport, his press statement made clear that all five tests of the Skybolt missile had failed. That aroused British anger. Only six days earlier Dean Acheson had made his famous comment at West Point that Great Britain had lost an empire but not yet found a role, and the more chauvinist leader writers had responded explosively—no doubt because that comment struck too close to home. Now they played variations on the theme, implicitly assuming that Acheson's statement reflected the considered view of the Kennedy Administration.

McNamara's insistence on announcing the failure of Skybolt illustrated both the strength and weakness of his temperament. Once he had made up his mind something should be done, he would damn the torpedoes and full steam ahead, in spite of any incidental breakage caused by inappropriate timing. The doctrine of cost-effectiveness required that Skybolt be dropped, and he was not prepared to keep it temporarily alive merely for political reasons.

McNamara's meeting with Thorneycroft was a foregone disaster. Thorneycroft accused the Administration of wishing to deprive Britain of its national nuclear deterrent; the British press and government insisted that the United States was tactless, heavy-handed, and abrupt. We were, they implied, either grossly insensitive to the pride and security of an ally or wished to push Britain out of the nuclear club. Some charged that Skybolt had not failed but that the United States was threatening cancellation to force the British to fulfill their troop quota in Western Europe.

Maneuvering Prior to Nassau

Shortly after McNamara's talk with Thorneycroft, Prime Minister Macmillan met President de Gaulle at Rambouillet. Just what transpired is not altogether clear. Some of my British government friends feared afterwards that Macmillan had spent too much time alone with de Gaulle, and we all knew the hazards when two heads of government get together without the benefit of chaperones to record their conversation. Perhaps, they surmised, the Prime Minister overestimated his own comprehension of the shadings and nuances of the French language. He apparently gave de Gaulle a full account of the Skybolt project and told him that he planned to "protect the continuity of British nuclear power" by persuading the Americans to provide a satisfactory alternative; if one were not forthcoming, Britain would build its own delivery system. He indicated to de Gaulle that he would ask the Americans for Polaris submarines. Though the submarines might nominally operate within NATO, he would insist that Britain keep control of the weapon in time of crisis.

He did not, of course, know any more than we did about conversations then under way between the French and Germans. As early as the end of September, de Gaulle had given Chancellor Adenauer a draft proposal for a Franco-German *entente*. On November 12, after prolonged debate inside the German cabinet, a memorandum had been sent to Paris that accepted de Gaulle's proposals in principle but insisted that Franco-German military cooperation must be developed within the framework of NATO and in agreement with it. These matters were all discussed when French Foreign Minister Couve de Murville and German Foreign Minister Gerhard Schroeder, met on December 16 and 17, immediately following Macmillan's visit to Rambouillet.

All this was in progress when we met the British at Nassau from December 18 to 21 in what was probably one of the worst prepared summit meetings in modern times. Hasty preparations for the Nassau Conference forced me, for the first time, to take a careful look at the Multilateral Force (MLF), to which I had not, up to then, paid much attention. With the failure of Skybolt, we faced the question whether, and by what means, we should extend the life of Britain's deterrent into a new weapons generation. Without providing some collective control of the new delivery system, such a reassertion of the nuclear special relationship would almost certainly upset the French—a point eloquently urged on me by Assistant Secretary of State for European Affairs William Tyler, a member of our Nassau delegation. Bonn might also react badly since the action emphasized Germany's exclusion from the nuclear club.

The issue of the conference was largely settled even before we arrived. Soon after the plane took off from Washington, the British ambassador, Sir David Ormsby-Gore (now Lord Harlech), a close friend of Kennedy's for many years, talked with the President in his private cabin, where the President had changed into pajamas for an hour or more of rest. As I reconstructed the conversation later, largely from what the President told me, Kennedy had been taken by surprise at Ormsby-Gore's dour appraisal of the situation. The Macmillan government, so the ambassador stated, was in a precarious position. Macmillan had made much of the "special relationship" and his ability to use it for Britain's benefit; if he now went home empty-handed, America might have to deal with a more neutralist and less pro-American Labor government under Hugh Gaitskell.

The Nassau Meeting

When the plane landed, Prime Minister Macmillan was waiting at the Nassau airport to greet the President, and, during the usual airport ceremonies, the local police band struck up an old English song "Early One Morning." Remembering it from my childhood with my English-born father, I suggested to one of my colleagues that the British had carefully chosen the piece for the occasion. The words, as I recall them, were:

> Oh, don't deceive me,
> Don't ever leave me,
> How could you use
> A poor maiden so?

Nassau was a pleasant meeting site. The President lived on the side of a hill adjacent to the Lyford Cay Club, in a handsome house that belonged to Canadian industrialist Ed Taylor, whom I had casually known in my Lend-Lease days; Prime Minister Macmillan occupied another house farther up the hill. The rest of us were housed in the club. But the British had not come to enjoy the golf or to let us enjoy it; their mood seemed not merely subdued but grim. Macmillan met privately with the President that night and told him of the political problems we were causing him by proposing to cancel Skybolt. The British people had come to believe in the special relationship; they had placed all of their nuclear hopes on Skybolt. What was his government to do now?

Next morning the meeting began somberly. I thought Thorneycroft, in particular, suspicious and resentful almost to the point of hostility. Macmillan beat the drum heavily for the special relationship and urged us to provide Polaris as a substitute for Skybolt. He dismissed any thought that it might prejudice the United Kingdom's pending application for membership in the European Community; Britain's disagreements with the Community were, he said, over agriculture, not nuclear policy. When he talked with de Gaulle at Rambouillet, the General had fully understood Britain's nuclear predicament.

But how could we provide Britain with a new nuclear weapon not committed to a multilateral force or even to NATO, without creating problems, not only with France but potentially with Germany? Should we not seek some kind of multilateral solution? Kennedy asked me to speak to the question. I recited the arguments developed by the group working on the Multilateral Force, but Macmillan would have none of it. Britain was going to remain a full-fledged nuclear nation; he had no interest in participating in any multilateral experiments. He was in fine form, eloquent but self-contained, forceful but sad. His government, he said, was in a shaky position; he had to bring back something concrete, which could only be Polaris without strings. Otherwise, our "special relationship" would be irreparably damaged.

At one point, when I stressed the need that any Polaris offer be linked to a nuclear fleet manned by crews of mixed nationalities, Macmillan said to me disdainfully, "You don't expect our chaps to share their grog with Turks, do you?" Remembering a fact I had learned from my historian son, I replied, "Wasn't that exactly what they did on Nelson's flagship?" I was pleased with that glib answer but made no converts, even when I pointed out the dangers of the course Macmillan was advocating. We had turned down France's request for aid in connection with an enriched uranium plant in March 1962 and had rejected General Norstad's scheme for a land-based MRBM force for NATO; now other European nations—particularly France—would regard an unqualified Polaris deal as offensive in emphasizing America's preferential treatment of Britain. At that point, the President came to my support, expressing concern at the growing number of nuclear nations. For each nation to develop its own separate deterrent made it almost impossible for the West to have a coherent strategy.

I understood the President's dilemma. He was fond of Macmillan (their friendship went back many years) and he was always sensitive to the distress cries of a fellow politician. He certainly preferred a Macmillan Conservative government to a Gaitskell Labor government that might reverse the British decision to enter Europe and pursue a neutralist course. Moreover, our nuclear arrangements with Britain were unquestionably reciprocal; Britain had agreed to make Holy Loch available for our Polaris submarines and had let us establish our missile warning station at Fylingdale.

During the entire session, I found Macmillan both shrewd and impressive: shrewd in the way he played on the President's sympathy, and impressive when he suddenly spoke about the need for a United Europe. I described the scene later as follows:

"During the First World War," he told us, "most of my comrades and my closest school friends were killed. I saw my Guards battalion destroyed at Loos in 1915 and on the Somme a year later." He and his older brother, Daniel Macmillan, were "invalided out of the war" with severe wounds in five engagements. He had known the desolation of the battlefield and the futility of war. He was haunted by the slaughter of 1914–1918 and did not believe the world could stand a continuation of the vicious national rivalries of Europe. He said all this to us at Nassau, and was to repeat much of it in the first volume of his memoirs published three years later. Writing of his war experience (*Winds of Change*, p. 98), he said,

"I brooded over these dire events . . . few of the survivors of my own age felt able to shake off the memory of these years. We were haunted by them. We almost began to feel a sense of guilt for not having shared the fate of our friends and comrades. We certainly felt an obligation to make some decent use of the life that had been spared to us."

His major motivation for trying to lead Britain into Europe, the Prime Minister assured us, was political and not economic. He wanted Britain to participate in building something better than the self-destructive system of the past. Yet when the debate began . . . , Macmillan put his case to the country almost entirely in terms of commercial and economic expediency. British industry, he said, needed the "cold douche" of competition in a great market, but this was not an argument to stir men's hearts or inspire their imagination, and the government made little effort to educate public opinion on the larger issues.[3]

At the conclusion of a strained and uneasy day, McGeorge Bundy for the Americans and Philip de Zulueta for the British were commissioned to draft a communiqué. They produced a monument of contrived ambiguity, so obscurely drafted that the two sides could construe it differently. Still, even fuzzy language on the multilateral issue seemed to me better than nothing, and, after I had offered Bundy a few suggestions, I decided to struggle no longer. Macmillan had achieved what he had told de Gaulle he would achieve: he had obtained a clause that permitted the British to withdraw their Polaris forces from NATO "when HMG may decide that supreme national interests are at stake." That assured them, in effect, the continuance of their own national deterrent, making nonsense of most of the other commitments.

Bill Tyler, who was closer to the problem than I, saw more clearly the destructive implications of emerging events. The agreed arrangements would, he told me, outrage de Gaulle, as they would document beyond question Britain's incestuous ties to America. They could well push de Gaulle toward refusing Britain entry to Europe on the ground it was an American "Trojan horse." We must, he insisted, make at least a gesture toward the General, so President Kennedy and Prime Minister Macmillan sent separate draft letters to de Gaulle. Kennedy's letter offered to make Polaris missiles available to France on the same terms as those offered Britain. Macmillan's letter stressed the fact that Britain had preserved its independence under the agreement. With what I suspect was deliberate whimsy, Prime Minister Macmillan told the press in London on December 23 that he had never fully understood what the "special relationship" meant, though he had just proved his mastery at exploiting it.

The Nassau meeting had been a crushing defeat for the Grand Design. We made a strictly British-American deal, and the British did not take seriously its multilateral overlay. Since France had been absent, our offer to the General would inevitably appear as an afterthought—and the General was not one to wear anyone's cast off clothing.

De Gaulle's Thunderbolt

Those apprehensions were well founded. Early in January 1963, I flew to Europe, primarily to talk with Chancellor Adenauer regarding the Multilateral Force. On Thursday, January 10, I met with the French Foreign Minister, Maurice Couve de Murville. Since I had known him for a number of years, I felt we could speak frankly. I was principally concerned with de Gaulle's attitude toward Britain's application to join the European Community. What would the General say about it at his forthcoming press conference the following Monday, January 14?

A French friend, Charles Gombault, editor of *France Soir,* had already telephoned to say that the General was climbing Mount Elysée with a bundle of thunderbolts under his arm. He had provided a quick outline of what the General planned to say at his press conference, including his final rejection of British entry, and I told Couve what I had heard. If the French President did take such a position, I said, it could create serious problems between Paris and Washington. The Foreign Minister seemed quite unperturbed. "You are," he said, "far too experienced to believe what you hear from press circles; you've been around too long for that. I can assure you there are no such ideas in this house."

That night Edward Heath and I had dinner together in a private room at the Hotel Plaza Athénée. Heath was in ebullient good spirits, since he had lunched with Couve de Murville and received what he thought was an unambiguous assurance that the way for British entry was still open. Serious obstacles, of course, remained, but Heath seemed confident the British application was in no serious trouble. Next day I was not so sure. M. Gombault brought to my hotel a reporter who had attended a background briefing at the Elysée Palace early in the week, where a select group of correspondents had been given an advance *précis* of President de Gaulle's press conference. The account he then recited proved a completely accurate statement of what de Gaulle did in fact say the following Monday.

Couve de Murville's unqualified assurance has haunted me ever since, and I have discussed it with Ted Heath, who feels equal mystification. Could de Gaulle have failed to take his own Foreign Minister into his confidence? The late Sir Pierson Dixon, who was at that time Britain's ambassador to Paris, is reported to have believed that at the time Couve de Murville knew nothing of President de Gaulle's decision.[4] I would like to believe that, but even though the General was famous for his secrecy, how could his Foreign Minister have been unaware of a matter on which the press had already been briefed?

On Sunday, I flew to Bonn and the following morning met with Chancellor Adenauer to discuss the MLF and our other bilateral German-American problems. The Chancellor was in a mischievous mood. He greeted me with a sad face, "I couldn't sleep last night. I dreamed all night that this morning Mr. Ball and I were going to have a fierce fight because I would not like anything he proposed. Now, tell me what you have to say, Mr. Secretary."

I held forth on the merits of the multilateral nuclear force and how it would enable the Federal Republic to play a nuclear role without evoking cries of alarm from the rest of Europe or even the Soviet Union. At the conclusion of the morning he said (as he had planned to say all along), "You've set all my doubts to rest, Mr. Ball. I am quite in accord with what you've told me. This afternoon my government will announce its full support for your proposals." We had what the Chancellor described as a "celebratory lunch," and as we talked, I discovered the depth of Adenauer's anti-British feelings. With a scorn verging on bitterness he said, "You don't seriously think Macmillan is ready for Europe, do you? You can't really think that the British can catch that bus?"

Late that afternoon, Monday, January 14, we learned the details of de Gaulle's dramatically stage-managed press conference. The General had concentrated his fire on Britain's entry into the Common Market, on the Nassau agreements, and on Franco-German cooperation. There were, he stated, three objections to British entry: (1) Britain's economic background differed from that of the Six, and it was clear that she lacked the determination to change it; (2) The present six member nations showed more resemblances than differences; (3) Britain's entry would be followed by other EFTA members, and that would change the character of the Community completely.

He then turned to the Nassau agreements. Because the Soviet Union's long-range ballistic missiles now threatened America, the United States had only a secondary interest in European defense. Our handling of the Cuban Missile Crisis had shown that the Americans would use nuclear weapons to defend themselves without any consultation with their European allies, even though those allies would have received the main thrust of any Soviet retaliation. America's nuclear force was still the guarantor of world peace, but it did not respond to all the needs of Europe and France; thus France had developed her own nuclear forces. The Nassau agreements had given Britain Polaris missiles and American know-how to construct the submarines to launch them. France, on the other hand, had neither submarines nor nuclear warheads, and thus could not use the Polaris missiles offered to her. The French deterrent must always be under French control.

The most enthusiastic passages in the General's dissertation concerned Franco-German cooperation. Two great peoples that had for so long fought one another had now achieved a new spirit of sympathy and understanding: as though two cousins had discovered one another, each seeing the other as useful and attractive. For the first time in many generations the French and Germans felt solidarity. And he extolled in rhapsodic terms the potential of a Franco-German *rapprochement.*

If the General had expected this to be well received in Bonn, he was manifestly mistaken. That night at dinner at the American embassy, I found German ministers quite as upset as I. The theatrical elegance with which de Gaulle dismissed the British angered Americans and greatly offended other European governments. The General was asserting a French primacy—unsupported either by military force, industrial achievement, or population—that flatly contradicted the concept of equality among the Six. He was suggesting a degree of agricultural protectionism contrary to the spirit of the Community, and was gratuitously insulting the Brussels Commission. It was vintage de Gaulle.

The Franco-German Treaty

On January 29, just over a fortnight after de Gaulle's press conference, Couve de Murville fulfilled his appointed role as chief executioner, thus effectively ending any immediate British hope for accession to the Rome Treaty. Even before then, Adenauer had journeyed to Paris to sign a Franco-German Treaty. That Treaty provided for meetings at least twice a year between the heads of state of the two governments and at least three times a year between the ministers of foreign affairs. High officials of the two foreign affairs ministries would meet at least once a month; the ministers of national defense at least every three months; and the chiefs of staff at least every other month.

The two governments would consult each other before making decisions on any important external matter in an effort to concert a common position on problems of the European Community, political and economic relations with Communist East, all matters debated in international organizations (such as NATO and the United Nations), and aid to underdeveloped countries. The two governments also agreed to develop common strategic and tactical military doctrines, with their armed forces cooperating and their armaments industries working in close consultation. The Treaty had no time limit and no provision for unilateral renunciation.

Washington Reaction

I can hardly overestimate the shock produced in Washington by this action or the speculation that followed, particularly in the intelligence community. There were wild rumors of a plan to pave the way for France, with Bonn's assistance, to negotiate with Moscow for a whole new European arrangement. We compared and supplemented our intelligence reports with bits and pieces gathered by the British. We looked at all possibilities of a Paris-Bonn deal with Moscow, leading toward a Soviet withdrawal from East Germany to be followed by some form of confederation between the two parts of that severed country. That would, of course, mean the end of NATO and the neutralization of Germany.

In the early days of February, we asked the German government pointed questions as to its interpretation of the treaty in the light of France's rejection of United Kingdom entry into the Common Market, and the anti-American overtones of the General's press conference. Was it true that Germany no longer welcomed the United States' views and presence? Was it not a tragic mistake, just when the Communist world was in disarray following the Cuban Missile Crisis, for the Western nations to reverse the drive toward greater unity? How, finally, could the fuzzy military clauses of the Treaty be reconciled with relations and responsibilities in NATO, particularly in view of de Gaulle's known antipathy to NATO and his desire to play a smaller role? Finally, we emphasized that, once Western Europe and the United States began to make separate demands on, and conflicting approaches to, the Soviet Union, Nikita Khrushchev would play one off against the other. That would mean the disintegration of our common security.

A Comforting Preamble

We soon found that many German government ministers and officials were as alarmed as we by the implications of the new Franco-German relationship. They were angry and embarrassed by Adenauer's trip to Paris to sign a document that threatened German-American relations. While Adenauer was away on a holiday at his home in Cadenabbia on Lake Como, the caucus chairman of the Bundestag, Heinrich von Brentano—already resentful because Adenauer had removed him as Foreign Minister—worked with Foreign Minister Schroeder to draft a preamble to the Treaty that was finally adopted on May 16. That preamble noted specifically that the rights and obligations of the Federal Republic resulting from multilateral treaties to which it was a party would not be modified by the new Treaty. It expressed the "resolute wish" that the Treaty be so implemented as to achieve the principal objectives that had guided the Federal Republic in cooperation with its allies and which determined its policies. It mentioned in particular: the maintenance and strengthening of the North Atlantic alliance and particularly the close association between Europe and the United States, the right of self-determination for the German people and the restoration of German unity, common defense within the framework of the alliance, and the integration of armed forces of the member states, the unification of Europe according to the pattern set up by the existing European Communities, and the lowering of tariffs in negotiation carried out within the framework of GATT. The Federal Republic government also sent Dr. Karl Carstens, the Secretary of State for Foreign Affairs, to Washington to calm the waters, and I had long talks with him during his visit. I liked him and regretted that, in view of the anxieties of the moment, we had to give him a hard time. Carstens, a German lawyer, who is now the President of the Federal Republic, is a sympathetic man with a lucid understanding and unquestioning commitment to Western values.

As the form and content of the preamble emerged, the clouds of conspiracy enveloping the Treaty began to dissipate. What we had thought was the coming together of two governments had been merely the final act in a love affair between two old men—de Gaulle and Adenauer—in which de Gaulle was clearly the dominant partner. Adenauer had long dreamed of a Franco-German *rapprochement,* seeing it essential to European peace. Beyond that he had a profound mistrust of the British. Though this mistrust has been usually attributed to the treatment by the British military when he was Burgomaster of Cologne during the British occupation, I suspect it resulted quite as much from Britain's weakness and its temptation to concessions during the Berlin crisis in 1958 and 1959. In addition, support costs for forces in Germany were a thorny issue not only between Britain and Germany but also the United States and Germany. Finally—and no doubt the conclusive point—de Gaulle had cast a powerful spell on the old man, shrewdly playing on Adenauer's vanity and weaknesses.

The preamble effectively repudiated all that de Gaulle was seeking to accomplish through the Treaty. Submitted first to the German Federal Council (the upper chamber), it was adopted by twenty-nine votes. Realistic as he could be on occasion, de Gaulle realized that his maneuver had failed. On July 2, 1963, at a dinner for French parliamentarians he remarked in reference to the Treaty, "You see, treaties are like young girls and roses; they do not last long. If the Franco-German Treaty is not to be implemented, it will not be the first case in history." On July 23 of the following year, he, in effect, told the Germans that if they continued to cling to their Atlantic concepts and failed to align their foreign policy with his, he would undertake his own explorations with Moscow, which indeed he sought to do.

Thereafter, in conducting France's affairs he paid no attention to the Treaty's commitments. In 1964 he recognized the Communist government of China and in 1966 decided to withdraw from NATO without bothering to consult Bonn, while, on its part, the Federal Republic adhered to the Treaty of Moscow and the suspension of nuclear tests even though France refused to do so.[5]

For Adenauer, the rebuff implied in the passage of the preamble was the beginning of the end. In March and April of 1963, there were rumors of an attempt by an SPD-FDP coalition to replace Adenauer with Ludwig Erhard, who strongly favored British entry. The pressure plainly building up for the retirement of the eighty-seven-year-old Chancellor finally succeeded when he tendered his resignation on October 15 and Erhard took over.

An Obit for the MLF

Though I have sometimes been spoken of as the principal advocate of the Multilateral Force, I never felt fervently about it, seeing it solely as a political instrument and fully recognizing that it was a clumsy if not unworkable military concept. In retrospect, I no doubt overestimated the effect on the German people of permanent exclusion from the management of nuclear weapons. Particularly after the emergence of *Ostpolitik,* in the early 1970s, Bonn became heavily preoccupied with developing operational arangements with the Soviet Union and Eastern Europe that would permit the return of Germans from Poland and alleviate the hardships of divided families on the two sides of the Iron Curtain. Any suggestion that West Germany might become even a modest participant in controlling a nuclear weapon would have created insurmountable problems with Moscow—and the Germans had a clear sense of priorities.

In the end, the MLF failed for want of enthusiastic European support. Even the possibility of a Multilateral Force was ruled out by the final draft of the Nuclear Nonproliferation Treaty. Long before that, however, the idea had passed into the limbo of aborted projects. Although Bob McNamara and I had continued for a time to support it, President Johnson became increasingly cool toward the idea, and it was finally dropped. I had no deep regret at its passing.

Looking back from the vantage point of 1981, I can derive one lesson from the futile episode of the Multilateral Force. In designing policy to meet particular political or military requirements, we are sometimes tempted to conceive solutions in the spirit of that whimsical cartoonist, Rube Goldberg. Certainly that was true of the MLF, which, on its face, was a manifestly absurd contrivance. At the moment of writing, the same point can also be made regarding the MX—the proposal to scar the American desert with a bizarre set of tunnels through which nuclear weapons would constantly be moved. The lesson, as I see it, is this: once a project assumes the attributes of the grotesque it will never succeed. The American people still possess a sufficient residue of common sense to recognize the ridiculous when they see it.

19. *Ayub Khan and Salazar*

Ever since the Italian city-states first established permanent embassies in the sixteenth century, relations between governments have been effectively conducted through what are banally known as "normal diplomatic channels." Although today the jet plane has tended to encourage special diplomatic missions, they should be used sparingly—only when relations with foreign governments have, for one reason or another, become particularly sensitive and complicated. That was the situation in the early fall of 1963, when President Kennedy asked me to hold in-depth conversations with the Prime Minister of Portugal and the President of Pakistan.

Background of Discontent

As a NATO member, Portugal's chief contribution to Europe's defense was the Azores air base. But those arrangements were uneasy, since we were not getting on at all well with Prime Minister Antonio Salazar, Portugal's undisputed ruler. Salazar not only resented our public pressure on his country to offer independence to its two principal African possessions—Angola and Mozambique—he also believed we were actively helping insurgent movements in those areas. Holden Roberto, who headed an African liberation movement known as the National Front for the Liberation of Angola (FNLA), had established a government in exile in Zaire and controlled much of the northeast of Angola with the exception of Cabinda. Our African Bureau, I knew, maintained sympathetic contact with him but I was assured that the only assistance we were providing was limited to educational activities in the rebel camps. The Salazar government strongly suspected that our assistance went much further, and there was concern that, if we could not clarify our position, the Azores bases might no longer be available.

Our relations with Pakistan were equally sour. In 1955, when the British with the encouragement of Secretary Dulles were putting together the bits and pieces of the so-called "northern tier" barrier reef, Pakistan had joined in the creation of the Baghdad Pact (which subsequently became known as CENTO); it later joined SEATO as well. As envisaged by the Pakistanis, their alliance commitments entitled them to preferential treatment from America. Though there was a qualification in the CENTO Treaty limiting America's defense obligations to resisting Communist aggression, Pakistan saw the alliances primarily as a source of support in its struggle with India.

Soon after the Kennedy Administration took office, the Pakistan government detected a change in our policy. Rejecting Dulles's view that any country not explicitly for us was against us in the East-West conflict, the new Administration made its peace with nonalignment; America, according to the new doctrine, would no longer press Third World countries to choose sides. That drastically devalued the claims to preferential treatment for so-called "allies" such as Pakistan, and some Pakistanis felt betrayed. With our most devout economic developers from Harvard and MIT fascinated with India, they saw their huge neighbor receiving far the largest share of our total foreign aid—in spite of the fact that Nehru was the noisiest cheerleader for nonalignment.

The Pakistanis obviously found this galling and said so. Still they might have become reconciled had the Chinese, in September 1962, not attacked India over the Himalayan mountain barriers. Taking account of India's global importance, our outspoken and effective ambassador in New Delhi, my old friend, Ken Galbraith, persuaded Kennedy that we should help India restore and strengthen its armed forces. At the Nassau Conference in December 1962, he obtained approval of a substantial military assistance package that left the Pakistanis bruised and surly. In their eyes, the United States was arming a neutral country against an ally—a sentiment stridently voiced by Pakistan's anti-American newspapers.

Faced with these two edgy situations, I arranged to visit both Salazar and President Ayub Khan.

Visit to Salazar

Salazar had long seemed to me a figure "out of joint with his times" (to borrow a phrase from Portugal's famous epic poet, Luis de Camoens, who used it some years before Shakespeare). In the mid-1920s, after the Portuguese economy had been wrecked, in large part by a brilliant banknote fraud, Dr. Salazar had been drafted from the economics faculty of the University of Coimbra to rescue the country.[1] Beginning as Finance Minister, he had become Prime Minister in 1932 under a new constitution that established Portugal as an authoritarian state. When I went to see him in 1963, he was very much in command and never hesitant to use his full powers. But in manner and appearance he seemed more the professor than the archetypal dictator. Dapper in dress, slightly built, and pale, he was formally courteous in an Old World way. Consistent with his style of frugal simplicity, his office was sparsely furnished and he gave an impression of frailty and shyness quite out of character for a notorious "strong man."

In advance of my trip, I had re-read Portugal's great national epic poem. Composed in the seventeenth century, *The Lusiads* told of Portuguese conquests with a sense of national pride mingled with Christian purpose. In introducing *The Lusiads,* its author, Camoens, proclaimed, "This is the story of heroes who, leaving their native Portugal behind them, opened a way to Ceylon, and farther, across the seas no man had ever sailed before. . . . It is the story, too, of a line of kings who kept ever advancing the boundaries of faith and empire. . . ."[2]

The mystique of "advancing the boundaries of faith and empire" was central to Salazar's convictions. It explained both his conservatism and his profound confidence in the righteousness of his cause. I quoted

Camoens at an early point in our conversation, and Salazar responded with a grateful smile. During our talks, history constantly intruded, so that our whole conversation seemed set against the backdrop of the grand but pathetic saga of Portugal. Salazar was absorbed by a time dimension quite different from ours; it seemed as though he and his whole country were living in more than one century, and the heroes of the past were still shaping Portuguese policy. That impression was so acute that, after our second day of conversation, my reporting telegram to President Kennedy observed, among other things, that we had been wrong to think of Portugal as under the control of a dictator. It was, instead, "ruled by a triumvirate consisting of Vasco da Gama, Prince Henry the Navigator, and Salazar." I also telegraphed Galbraith in New Dehli, advising, "Having just spent two days with Salazar, I now know what it means to give serious political responsibilities to a professor of economics."

Early in our conversation, Salazar put great emphasis on Portugal's relative poverty; it was, he said, the poorest nation in Western Europe, having a per capita income of $460 and an illiteracy rate of 40 percent. But he seemed unaware that the deflationary policies he had imposed on the country for three decades were in any way responsible for that dismal situation. What did disturb him was that a successful African insurgency might debouch more than half a million refugees into a crowded metropole of nine million people at a time when Portugal's agriculture was stagnant and her industries undergoing painful readjustment.

The end of the Lusitanian presence in Africa would, he pointed out, almost inevitably precipitate an acute and prolonged depression in Portugal, complicated by a balance of payments squeeze. In losing a monopolistic colonial market for her exports, Portugal would also be deprived of the artificially cheap raw materials her obsolete industries needed to compete in world markets. Thus the Prime Minister was convinced that, if Portugal were to lose the last 800,000 square miles of her colonial empire, she would forfeit even the shadow of respect as a small but solvent power and would sink to the level of an Iberian Graustark.

That such a fate should befall his tiny country was insupportable to Salazar. His mind was still in the fifteenth and early sixteenth centuries, when Portugal, a tiny nation of 1,500,000 people, had surpassed herself; Lisbon had been the center of excitement, the heart of world exploration, the capital that stirred the imagination of all civilized men. But, after only a brief flowering, a spectacular day in the sun, Portugal had fallen on evil days. When King Sebastian and the cream of the Portuguese nation were annihilated by the Moors in the Battle of the Three Kings near Alcazarquivir, the golden age abruptly ended. Portugal's troubles mounted one on another: it lost its independence to Spain for long periods; it saw its maritime preeminence usurped; and the Dutch captured its Asian possessions. Only the obdurate resistance of the settlers in Angola and Brazil had saved those territories from foreign conquests and its most bitter blow came when its exhausting nineteenth-century struggle against Napoleonic aggression was perversely rewarded by the revolt and independence of Brazil, a possession larger than the United States. That marked the beginning of the end of empire. When I saw Salazar, Portugal had its back to the wall and knew it. Even though the United Kingdom could face the loss of one-quarter of the globe without ceasing to be a major nation, the loss of Angola and Mozambique would be catastrophic for Portugal.

Dr. Salazar was determined that this would not happen. In spite of its limited resources, Portugal, he insisted, was improving and extending education in its African provinces. Racial discrimination, he stated flatly, did not exist as in other parts of the White Redoubt; there were no laws against intermarriage between Portuguese Europeans and blacks and few social bars to people of mixed blood. Why then were we interfering in what, I am convinced, Dr. Salazar still thought of as Portugal's "civilizing mission"? I was sure such a conception seemed as vital to him as to St. Francis Xavier and the leaders of the Reconquista borrowed from Spain.

I set forth in detail America's belief in self-determination, but Dr. Salazar would have none of it. To promise self-determination would, he argued, destroy Portuguese influence in Africa, as well as the Portuguese presence. Experience in other countries had shown, he said, that announced time schedules, no matter how foreshortened, were always accelerated under pressure from the more radical African politicians. The peoples of Angola and Mozambique were not yet ready for independence. Considering all that had happened in the Congo (this was not long after the Katanga episode), the maintenance of relative stability in Portuguese Africa was, he argued, a real contribution to peace.

All this was said in answer to what he regarded as undue American pressure. We had long urged Portugal to offer self-determination on a reasonable time schedule; we had, in addition, supported Afro-Asian initiatives in the United Nations designed toward that end. We had discouraged American private investments in Angola and Mozambique, refused Export-Import Bank loans to those areas, and prohibited the sale of arms for use in the Portuguese overseas territories. Nonetheless, in spite of the awkwardness in our relations, the Portuguese still permitted us to use the Azores base for NATO purposes.

At the end of our second day of talks, Salazar mentioned that he understood that I was going on to see Ayub Khan. Could I stop in Lisbon again on my return trip to Washington? He wanted, he said, an opportunity to collect his thoughts and he hoped to be able to answer some of my questions better on a second visit. After my return from

Pakistan at the conclusion of our second set of meetings, Dr. Salazar made a request that violated established protocol. "I have found our conversations useful and interesting," he said, "but I would like to give you a more reasoned reply. When you get back to Washington would you please write me a letter setting forth in detail the position you have outlined in our conversations? Write it to me personally, and I will send you a personal reply."

Obviously, it was odd for a mere Under Secretary of State to be writing a head of government. But on October 21, 1963, I sent him a fifteen-page, single-spaced letter, and, on February 27 of the following year, he sent me a reply of roughly equal length. Even today the exchange is, I think, of interest, not merely as an odd departure from protocol but also because each letter was a thoughtful, honest effort to express a point of view. Even though those points of view could not be reconciled by our two governments, we still understood one another better.

Letter to Salazar

In my letter to Dr. Salazar I pointed out that Europe, following the Renaissance, had broken out of its small peninsula to extend its influence to the corners of the earth. But the ravages of two world wars had drained Europe of the power necessary to sustain world-wide control and the new technology that made possible the instantaneous communication of "those subtle *provocateurs* of change—ideas" had made a new order inevitable.

Europe had assured the demise of its imperial system by educating its dependent peoples in the doctrines of Western political thought—the dignity of the individual, the notion of the nation-state, the right of societies to self-determination. Now the drive toward self-determination could be frontally opposed only at an exceptionally high price—and a price that, once paid, tended to go higher. Wise nations had not sought to block the tide but to build canals and conduits to direct its flow—seeking to work with the forces of history rather than against them. When the metropolitan powers had built a trained civil service and given their colonies substantial self-government, they had been able to maintain close and mutually profitable relations after independence.

Because we saw value in retention of close ties between the new states and their metropolitan patrons, we were anxious for Portugal to play an effective and continuing role in Angola and Mozambique. The problem would not be resolved by military might. Whenever colonial powers had sought to maintain their hold on dependent areas by force they had sooner or later given up the struggle.

Time, I insisted, was not working in Portugal's favor. It had no longer than a decade to prepare its territories for self-determination and the time factor had to be realistically incorporated in Portuguese government policy. Thus Portugal, in our view, should immediately make clear that its goal was self-determination within a reasonable, although not necessarily explicit, period.

There were, I pointed out, responsible African leaders anxious to work with the West and, though Salazar had expressed doubt on this matter, I had rechecked our information since returning to Washington. We recognized that immediate independence would be a disaster—there had to be a transition period lasting over a period of years if there were to be a continuing Portuguese role. But it was necessary to establish immediately the *right* of self-determination—not its *implementation,* which could come about only after a gradual process of preparation.

Letter from Salazar

Dr. Salazar's reply presented a careful apologia for his firmly held position. His letter began by noting that American leaders regarded the nationalist movement of peoples in Africa toward independence as an inevitable fact that "must deny the pre-existing right and attempt to create a new right." That being the case, Salazar wrote, "the United States naturally considers itself unobligated to defend the former and disposed to recognize the latter."

The drafters of the United Nations Charter found that a number of states had dependent territories in which the geographic situation, social structure, or economic or cultural development, as well as the race and language of the majority of the inhabitants, substantially differed from that of the metropolitan power. Those territories were politically on a more or less inferior plane.

The Portuguese overseas territories, on the contrary, were not dependent territories, but politically integrated. Portugal had been admitted to the United Nations in that constitutional form, but the United Nations resolutions since voted with regard to Portugal had not treated "self-determination" as a choice among various alternatives provided in the Charter; they had demanded the imposition of a single alternative—independence. Yet immediate independence denied the natural evolution of the peoples and the existence of an enlightened political preparation.

Salazar was, he wrote, not questioning the sincerity of the American government's adherence to the principle of self-determination, nor did he regard our position as inspired by self-interest. But we had not been consistent in applying the principle. Our vigorous actions had in some cases resulted in territorial fragmentation, in others we had, by force of arms, imposed political unity on a particular territory. The experience of the new states had shown that, when tribal leaders constituted the political elite existing at the time of independence, one might expect political institutions with a certain stability—arising in effect from tribal discipline; when that condition did not exist, the political structure of a new state was precarious and could survive only with substantial economic and military support from the former metropole. To the extent that political stability depended primarily on the tribal structure, movement was retrograde toward a more primitive organization of the country; when it was based on exterior assistance, the new nation had merely a kind of pseudo independence or disguised sovereignty. Portugal was prepared to provide resources for the normal development of its overseas territories so long as they remained under existing constitutional arrangements. But it could not and would not support the vast subsidies needed to maintain the economy of newly independent African states for the benefit of foreigners and for unlimited periods. If, therefore, we forced independence too quickly, Portugal's responsibilities would have to be assumed by a third country.

Thus, Salazar concluded, the full independence of Portugal's overseas territories would neither guarantee the progress of the peoples nor assure the continuance of a Portuguese "presence, influence and interest" in Africa (the language I had used in my letter). I had suggested, however, that an intermediate preparatory period might be useful and possible. The Portuguese government had considered this possibility and accorded some good faith to the declaration of certain African leaders in favor of a program of evolution toward independence. But, wrote Salazar, such a program was not feasible, not only because of the violence of the African revolutionary movement, but because of the inevitable intervention of "interests foreign to the African continent itself." After all, it was the violent elements who gave the orders and, as Salazar dryly commented, he had not observed that the great powers opposed them.

For these reasons, Salazar did not believe it feasible on the practical plane—to say nothing of the juridical plane—to develop in concert with any other countries a plan of action that would assure a continuing Portuguese presence in the African territories.

Finally, he concluded, we must be wary of Communism. We had put great emphasis on the obvious lack of suitability of the Communist structure to African societies, but that did not mean that Africa would remain hostile to international Communism or that Communism could not operate in Africa as it did in Europe and in America. Having made a false step in its African policy, the Soviets would, he felt, stop forming African political parties with the Communist label. Though they might make use of local elements that would set up Communist governments, they would direct their energies, he suggested, at taking over Africa for the purpose of nationalizing its wealth, halting its economic progress and then bringing about "its ideological and strategic neutralization."

Though he granted that Western policy and even Soviet policy seemed to be aimed toward preventing a general conflict, little by little positions and interests would be lost and in the end the sum total of these losses might be about the same as those that would result from a defeat of the West in a general war.

Today this exchange of letters is of merely historical interest. Angola is under the control of a government friendly to the Soviets, though the guerrilla forces of UNITA under Jonas Savimbi still challenge the government's control of the rural areas in the southern half of the country. Twenty thousand Cuban troops train Angolan forces and help fight the "insurgents," while eight thousand Cuban civilians deal with education and services. More than three hundred thousand Portuguese have returned to the metropole. Salazar is dead.

Visit to Ayub Khan

In contrast to Dr. Salazar, a man of the sixteenth century, President Ayub Khan of Pakistan was straight out of Kipling's nineteenth-century Indian tales. A graduate of the old Indian Army prior to the partitioning of the subcontinent, he was almost a caricature of the spit-and-polish British officer; immaculately turned out in tailored uniform with a carefully cropped moustache, he carried about him the aura of command and the bluntness of a seasoned soldier. A conversation in depth with Ayub Khan did not require the subtlety and *délicatesse* of a similar talk with Salazar. He and I could come straight to the point and stay on it. The gravamen of the Pakistan complaint was simple and straightforward. When we provided military aid to the Indians, we not only turned our backs on an ally but also undercut its security. Could Pakistan, therefore, count on us? My country was, on its side, equally concerned about Pakistan's tilting toward China.

The corrosive relations between America and Pakistan that were rapidly developing reflected, in part, the festering enmity between Pakistan and its neighbor India that had existed ever since the partition in 1947. Kashmir was a continuing bone of contention; the Pakistanis were implacably furious at India's unwillingness to subject the issue to a referendum. During the winter of 1963–64, the United States had done everything possible to bring about a settlement. Meanwhile, conspiratorial elements in Pakistan, largely led by Foreign Minister Zulfikar Ali Bhutto, were cautiously flirting with the Chinese, on the classical principle that the enemy of their enemy, India, was automatically their friend. Bhutto assured his countrymen that China would come to Pakistan's defense in the event of an Indian attack.

In order to calm Indian feelings, I had initially intended to go not only to Pakistan but also to New Delhi. But Chester Bowles, who had only just returned to New Delhi as ambassador, vehemently rejected the idea on the ground that he could not, without loss of face, receive the man who had so recently succeeded him as Under Secretary. Thus, New Delhi was canceled from the itinerary.

Even without a visit to India, arrangements for my trip proved awkward. Initially the Pakistan government—no doubt inspired by Bhutto's anti-American drive—tried to restrict my conversations with the President and reduce the visit generally to a discussion with the Pakistani foreign office, of which Bhutto was head. When we made clear that I would not make the trip on that basis, that edict was reversed, but the road remained filled with booby traps.

On August 30, four days before my visit, Pakistan signed a civil air agreement with Communist China, giving China landing rights in Pakistan and, among other places, in Dacca. In response, we held up a promised $4.3 million loan to Pakistan that would have provided Dacca with a new airport. Then Pakistan further offended Washington by raising its legation in Cuba to embassy status. Finally, just on the eve of my arrival in Pakistan, an influx of Chinese Communist trade delegates descended on Rawalpindi, the garrison town that served as Pakistan's temporary seat of government pending the building of its new capital at Islamabad.

Under the circumstances, my talks with Ayub Khan were destined to be difficult, since the whole Pakistan–United States relationship was now in the balance. I was in no position to agree to President Khan's demand that the United States reduce its military aid to India. As a sanction, we could, if necessary, cut off our foreign aid to Pakistan then running at the rate of nearly $500 million a year, but that would tend to drive the Pakistanis even further toward Peking. The Pakistanis, on their part, were making self-destructive threats, suggesting that they might refuse to accept our foreign aid if we attached any strings. We had already provided Pakistan with something like $2 billion of aid, but I had long ago learned that nations did not necessarily respond to their own enlightened self-interest; I deeply distrusted Bhutto and the faction he commanded.

Since my task was not only to persuade President Ayub Khan that we would defend Pakistan, but also to show the Pakistani army and air force how effectively we could do so, I asked Secretary McNamara to lend me a competent military spokesman. He designated Major General William Quinn—an exceptionally engaging officer, with a gift for lucid exposition. Quinn, in turn, produced an airplane. We arrived in Rawalpindi on September 3. I spent Tuesday morning with the embassy staff, then met with President Ayub Khan late in the afternoon. Our conversation was gratifyingly direct, and we at least gained a full understanding of each other's views.

Kashmir was an issue we could not avoid, but the main focus of Ayub Khan's comments concerned our arming of India. Though I emphasized our good-faith commitment to defend Pakistan, Ayub Khan was by no means fully persuaded, although our conversation quieted some of his anxieties. I pounded away on our disquiet over Pakistan's drift toward China and I warned him not to be seduced by Chinese overtures. That the Chinese were engaged in such a seduction was suggested by the poem of a member of the visiting Chinese trade delegation, published on the day of my arrival.

> You [Pakistanis] are on the western
> coast of the sea and we are on the east.
> The tidal waves on the ocean roar, and,
> intermingled, we can hear the sound of
> our heartbeat.

Though I spent some time with Ayub Khan that first evening, he seemed disinclined to go very far with our conversation until after I had been subjected to a series of expositions by Pakistani military and foreign policy experts. They would, I assumed, give me their highly charged view of Pakistan's attitude toward the issues in question.

Ayub Kahn's intention was, I assumed, to pass the responsibility to Foreign Minister Bhutto and to give the commander of the Pakistani army, General Mohammad Musa, and his colleagues a chance to air their feelings. Ayub Khan was clearly not trying to avoid further confrontation, as he asked me to lunch the following day and said that he would be available whenever I wanted to confer with him.

The following day I met with Bhutto and his staff as well as with the Pakistani military. The military discussions went into considerable tactical detail. The Pakistani high command gave us a detailed look at their vulnerabilities, while General Quinn briefed them on our assessment of the situation and what the United States could do to assure their security.

I had a long tête-à-tête with Ayub Khan on September 5 and left late in the afternoon. I gained the clear impression that he genuinely wanted to repair relations with the United States but, hard pressed by others in the leadership, was not a wholly free agent. For the time being, he was quite ready to put the Kashmir issue in cold storage; the main thrust of his argument was that we should do everything possible to stop the competitive arms buildup between Pakistan and India. He was not seeking fresh offers of military hardware from us so much as the assurance that we would try to cut down military expenditures on both sides. Since the military element in his government's budget was already excessive, he was anxious to limit further defense outlays.

Clearly he was under domestic pressure, fearful of palace struggles led by such insidious connivers as Bhutto and disturbed by the mounting public hysteria stimulated by an intemperate Pakistani press. The news columns were filled with slogans, such as "Better Communist domination than Hindu domination" and "A new devil is better than a thousand-year-old devil." While I was still in Rawalpindi, Ayub Khan felt compelled to crack down with new harsh censorship measures.

I did my best to persuade the Pakistanis that the critical threat to their security was from Communist China, not India, and that India and Pakistan ought to concentrate on their mutual defense against Peking. If Pakistan got too close to Communist China, it would nullify any alliance between the United States and Pakistan.

My visit was anything but relaxed. (After my first interview, my colleagues and I sat up until two in the morning drafting telegrams and planning strategy.) Yet it was not wholly without humor. Knowing Ayub Khan shared his own passion for golf, General Quinn had come equipped for a game. I gave him mock-serious instructions beforehand about the need to let Ayub Khan win; by beating the President he would, I told him, jeopardize our mission. After the game, the General reported shamefacedly that he had definitely planned to lose on the final hole, but, when they had finished the seventeenth green and he was still two strokes ahead, it had abruptly started to rain. I made the appropriate gestures of dismay.

Later, on September 9, I met with President Kennedy to brief him on our trip and asked General Quinn to accompany me. After reporting on all that had happened in Portugal and Pakistan, I said, "Mr. President, I would like you to know that General Quinn was a monument of strength for our mission. His briefings were brilliant, and he made a great impact on the Pakistan military command. At the same time, in all candor, I must say that he violated my orders on one matter and almost destroyed the effectiveness of the mission."

"What did he do?" asked the President. I explained that I had told General Quinn to lose to Ayub Khan but that he had come back with the obviously unconvincing explanation that his plan to lose had been thwarted by a sudden rainfall.

"Is that true, General?" asked the President. General Quinn looked embarrassed and uneasy. "Yes, I'm afraid it is, Mr. President." "General," said the President, "that's a very serious accusation. What's your handicap?" The general named a figure which was, as I recall, 6 or 7. "Well," said the President with a broad grin, "you and I must have a game some day."

I remember another anecdote that involved my final tête-à-tête with President Ayub Khan. Just as I was leaving, I said to him, "Mr. President, I would like to ask you a question quite unrelated to my mission, merely to satisfy my own curiosity. Pakistan is a nation of more than ninety million people; it is Islamic by constitution and non-Arab. There is only one other country in the world with similar characteristics and that's Indonesia. It has a population of perhaps one hundred million people, is Islamic by constitution and non-Arab. I've often wondered why you don't make more common cause with the Indonesians."

"Do you really want to know, Mr. Secretary?" When I nodded in the affirmative he replied, "Well, the answer's very simple. Sukarno's such a shit."

It was a conversation I enjoyed reporting to the President.

20. The Cuban Missile Crisis

On a coffee table in my house in Princeton is a small piece of wood surmounted by a silver plate, on which is inscribed in the top left-hand corner "GWB" and in the top right-hand corner "JFK." Engraved on the plate is a calendar for October 1962 with the days from the sixteenth to the twenty-eighth heavily outlined. The fortnight thus celebrated has a special meaning for all who possess similar plaques; it was the period of what has come to be called the Cuban Missile Crisis, and the plaques were gifts by President Kennedy to members of the so-called ExCom, who worked with him during that intense period. Although those two weeks left a permanent mark on all involved in that crisis, I find the subject difficult to write about. More than any other event of the brief thousand days of John F. Kennedy's leadership, the Cuban Missile Crisis has been minutely described and endlessly dissected.

Background of the Crisis

There were good reasons not to expect the Soviets to put offensive missiles in Cuba. After the fiasco of the Bay of Pigs in April 1961, Chairman Nikita Khrushchev had sent President Kennedy two notes; in the first, he warned that Cuba could count on Soviet support to resist any armed attack from the United States, and, in the second, he stated that "the Soviet Union did not have any bases in Cuba" and did not intend to establish any. We took that latter assurance at face value; the Russians had never put offensive missiles on the territory of other nations, even members of the Warsaw Pact.

But, beginning in late July 1962 our reconnaissance planes reported a substantial increase in ship traffic from Soviet ports to the Cuban port of Mariel. That awakened curiosity in intelligence circles, particularly as the ships seemed to be carrying transportation, electronic, and construction equipment—presumably to improve coastal and air defenses. They might also, we suspected, be carrying SAMs (surface-to-air missiles), which were sophisticated antiaircraft weapons, defensive in character, which the Soviets had already supplied to Iraq and Indonesia. In addition, several thousand Soviet military technicians were reported to have arrived, though they were never seen in uniform.

On August 29, one of our U-2 spy planes obtained photographic proof that two SAMs had been put into position and that six more were tentatively located, but that in itself seemed no cause for concern. The Soviets, I assumed—to the extent I thought about it at all—were simply reacting to post-Bay-of-Pigs Cuban pressure to protect Cuba against another attack. They had been careful to deny any objective beyond that, and I doubted that even Khrushchev would run the risk of being caught in a flat lie to the President of the United States.

John McCone, the head of the CIA, was somewhat more skeptical. Why would the Soviets, he speculated, install expensive SAMs unless they had something valuable of their own to protect, such as offensive missiles to be implanted at a future time? He had, so he later said, worried for some time that, once the Soviets found themselves free to use Cuban territory, they might introduce offensive missiles. They had refrained from installing offensive missiles in their Eastern European satellites from fear that the Poles and Hungarians might fire them at Moscow, but missiles in Cuba with a one-thousand-mile range could not reach the Soviet Union.

But, however much McCone may have worried, he did not, to my knowledge, mention his concerns to the President or to the rest of us; instead, prior to the actual discovery of the missiles, he went off to Europe on a honeymoon. Meanwhile, Soviet Ambassador Anatoly Dobrynin passed on to the President's brother, Attorney General Robert F. Kennedy, a private assurance from Khrushchev that he would not create trouble for the United States during the election campaign. Dobrynin also said, in answer to Robert Kennedy's inquiry, that his government certainly did not intend to arm any third party with the power to begin a thermonuclear war. Even with that assurance, the President—at Robert Kennedy's instigation—had issued a warning that the introduction of offensive ground missiles in Cuba would raise grave issues and on September 7 had asked for Congressional authorization to call up 150,000 reserve troops.

Until then, we had been sending biweekly flights of U-2 spy planes to overfly Cuba, but, once the SAMs were discovered, the schedule was stepped up. On September 21, the CIA received an eyewitness report from an agent in Cuba who reported that, on September 12, he had seen the tailpiece of a large missile on a Cuban highway. Other bits of evidence soon tended to confirm that this could have been an offensive missile. Until then, no U-2 flights had been scheduled over the western end of the island for fear of losing a plane, but that territory was now targeted in a flight plan approved on October 9. Five days later, on Sunday, October 14, U-2 photographs showed what was presumably a missile site in preparation, although no missile was yet in sight.

Discovery of the Missile Sites

For the preceding several days, I had been in Panama and Colombia and did not return to Washington until Sunday night. On Monday, October 15, I had been scheduled to attend a reception for the National Foreign Policy Conference, and later a black-tie dinner for West German Foreign Minister Schroeder. For reasons not now clear to me, I had cancelled the dinner and was at home when Roger Hilsman, Director of the State Department's Intelligence and Research, telephoned to report that a preliminary analysis of U-2 pictures showed that the Soviets were installing offensive missiles in Cuba. That news was a shock, since I had long thought McCone too hard-line and suspicious. Moreover, along with others in the top command, I had been vigorously trying to refute the charges, then being repeated by Senator Keating in a whole series of speeches, that the Soviets had put offensive missiles in Cuba. He was, we thought, overinterpreting the same unverified intelligence report we had received.

I slept little that night and the next morning was called to a secret meeting at the White House at 11:45. At the direction of the President, McGeorge Bundy had assembled a special group, consisting of Secretary Rusk, Secretary McNamara, Attorney General Robert Kennedy, General Maxwell Taylor, General Carter (the acting chief of the CIA while McCone was temporarily out of town), Roswell Gilpatric (the Deputy Secretary of Defense), Edwin Martin (the Assistant Secretary of State for Inter-American Affairs), Theodore Sorensen (the President's Assistant and speech writer), Secretary of the Treasury Dillon, Ambassador Charles Bohlen, and the President's appointments secretary, Kenneth O'Donnell—in addition to Mac Bundy and myself. It was an *ad hoc* collection; such a sensitive matter seemed inappropriate for the National Security Council, which included among its statutory members such extraneous figures as the head of the Office of Emergency Management (concerned primarily with domestic housekeeping).

We agreed at the outset that no one should cancel any appointments under circumstances that might lead the press to suspect a crisis. Thus, Secretary Rusk left to meet the Crown Prince of Libya at the airport, while Adlai Stevenson came down from New York to attend a White House luncheon for the prince. All of us recognized that we faced a critical challenge from Moscow. Khrushchev, having harassed America for more than a year by demanding a Berlin settlement on his own terms, was now, we believed, about to try a new tactic. As soon as his missiles were installed, which would be sometime after the United States election, he would try to force the Western powers out of Berlin in exchange for their removal. Another possibility was that he wished to trade off the Cuban missiles for the American Jupiter missiles based in Turkey and Italy, but since the Jupiters were antiquated and not very useful, that seemed unlikely. Clearly the whole affair must be kept secret until we could develop a carefully reasoned response. It would be far better to announce the emplacement of the missiles at the same time we disclosed the measures we were taking to force their removal. Meantime, we would greatly step up the number of overflights.

We knew, of course, that we were operating under time constraints. We had to force the issue before any missiles were fully installed or we risked their being fired. During the first day, the discussion proceeded with little structure, each of us putting forward his view as to what to do. In the afternoon, we moved the locus of the meeting (minus the President) from the White House to my conference room in the State Department but returned to the White House at 6:30 P.M. for more discussions.

One question in dispute was whether the emplacement of the missiles would in any way change the power balance. At the beginning, McNamara pointed out that the Cuban missiles would give the Russians no advantage not already provided by their intercontinental missiles in the Soviet Union, except for the reduction of the warning time from fifteen minutes to two or three minutes. And at first McGeorge Bundy contended that we should not treat the matter as a major issue. But alteration of the strategic military balance was not the only consideration; United States' acquiescence in the emplacement of the missiles would have a disastrous political effect. The thought of having missiles so close to our shores would deeply upset our own people—not to mention the Latin Americans. It would be a critical blow to the Monroe Doctrine— or, to put it in more modern terms, an unacceptable Soviet encroachment on the United States' sphere of influence.

Even the military analysis seemed, as we thought about it, subject to question. We could not be certain that our intelligence services had not overestimated the number and accuracy of long-range Soviet intercontinental missiles, in which case shorter-range missiles in Cuba might greatly increase Soviet capability. Paul Nitze, then Assistant Secretary of Defense for International Security Affairs, was particularly concerned that, if the new missiles should become operational, the Soviets could destroy a large part of the American strategic bomber force.

Hawks and Doves

As the conversation proceeded, the ExCom began to break into two groups. Nitze, Douglas Dillon, and John McCone, among others, felt that we should promptly launch an airstrike to remove the missile bases by force. McNamara, Gilpatric, Ambassador Llewellyn Thompson (just returned after several years in Moscow), and I opposed any irrevocable action, since it would involve killing probably as many as twenty-five thousand Russians and thus risk a violent Soviet reaction.

The next morning, Wednesday, October 17, while the President was out campaigning, the ExCom continued its intensive meetings in my conference room, now unimaginatively nicknamed the Think Tank. It was in a special compound on the seventh floor directly across a corridor from my office, which, in turn, was separated from the Secretary's office only by the office of the secretariat. Thus it was well segregated from the rest of the Department. During that first week, our meetings went on every day and late into the night; sandwiches and coffee were sent for as needed. Dean Rusk attended only a few of the meetings—and then only briefly. He felt that as the principal foreign policy adviser to the President he should not air his comments in a general meeting with lower-level people but reserve them for the President himself. In the course of the hours and days that passed, two participants carried the greatest authority: McNamara and Robert Kennedy. McNamara has a natural flair for command and whenever he was in the room he tended to dominate the discussion. He has an unusually quick and incisive mind and supreme self-assurance. During these meetings I found him both impressive and slightly exasperating—exasperating perhaps because he was so forceful.

Robert Kennedy surprised me. Until then I had not had much respect for his judgment; he had seemed to me—particularly in comparison with his brother—immature, far too emotional, and inclined to see everything in absolute terms with too little sensitivity to nuance and qualification. But during the Cuban missile affair he was a stabilizing influence. Aware of the gravity of the situation, he was a force for caution and good sense.

Eventually, we reduced the possible responses to six. They cut across the full spectrum, including such actions as confronting the Soviet Union with photographic evidence and demanding the removal of the missiles, sending an emissary to Khrushchev, and dragging the Soviet Union and Cuba into the United Nations Security Council. Soon, however, attention narrowed on the two remaining: embargoing military shipments to Cuba through a naval blockade (which we came to refer to as the "Slow Track"), or mounting a surprise bombing attack on the missile installations (known as the "Fast Track"), which involved, if necessary, following up with an invasion.

From the beginning, I opposed an airstrike, not merely because it would kill several thousand people, but because it was an irreversible step. Moreover, as I first argued on Wednesday, a great power should never act in contravention of its own traditions or it would lose its world authority; to launch a surprise air attack would seriously undercut the effectiveness of our leadership. To my gratification, the Attorney General later restated my argument in much more vivid and compelling terms. A surprise airstrike, he said, would be another Pearl Harbor and he added, with obvious conviction, "My brother is not going to be the Tojo of the 1960s." It was a telling phrase, and I thought at the time that it altered the thinking of several of my colleagues.

I was disturbed by the reaction of my long-time friend Dean Acheson, who attended several of our meetings. Acheson, I knew, thought Bobby Kennedy an upstart. He had not liked Bobby since his association with Joe McCarthy, and he now thought, as he clearly indicated not only by his words but also by the emphatic way he spoke, that Bobby was talking sentimental nonsense. The United States, Acheson argued, had specifically stated in the Monroe Doctrine that it would not tolerate the intrusion of a European power in this hemisphere; the President had explicitly told Congress that America would be forced to act if the Soviet Union installed offensive weapons in Cuba; and, on October 3, a Congressional resolution had authorized the President to prevent "by whatever means may be necessary, including the use of arms, the creation in Cuba of a foreign military base that endangered United States security." Thus, concluded Acheson, there had been adequate warning, and whatever we did could not be regarded as a surprise attack. As eloquently expressed by Acheson, the argument was plausible, but I could not accept what seemed to me its fundamental disregard for our international standing and our relations with other nations. Oddly enough, I found myself sounding more legalistic than he. Because Cuba did not belong to the Warsaw Pact, I conceded that an air attack on Cuba would not necessarily bring the Soviets into a state of war, but a naval blockade would have more "color of legality." Acheson's insistence on an immediate attack was not, I thought sadly, his finest hour.

On Thursday, October 18, we met twice with the President, at 11:00 A.M. and 10:00 P.M. Meanwhile, the Pentagon was positioning formidable numbers of men and planes in case a decision was made either to bomb or invade, and rumors of troop movements were beginning to appear in the newspapers, though with no explicit linkage to Cuban missiles. On the political side, I had instructed the State Department to draw up detailed plans for obtaining the support of our Latin American and

European allies. That morning (Thursday) the Intelligence Board reported that the first Soviet missile could be ready for launching in eighteen hours. We were, therefore, nearing the moment of action. When I later met with Secretary Rusk, he expressed himself firmly against a surprise attack; it would destroy any hope of political support. We would invite universal opprobrium were we to act without first consulting the Organization of American States and the United Nations and making a prior effort to approach the Russians.

That evening, while Rusk was giving a dinner for Soviet Foreign Minister Gromyko on the eighth floor of the State Department, the ExCom continued to argue the central issues in my conference room, one floor below. To sharpen the argument, we divided into two groups: McGeorge Bundy headed the group developing the case for an airstrike and the kind of scenario it would involve; I headed the team favoring a blockade. On my side of the argument were McNamara, Gilpatric, Robert Kennedy, Ambassador Thompson, and, finally, Robert Lovett, who had been enlisted by the President. On the airstrike side were McCone, Dillon, Taylor, Acheson, Nitze, and, finally, Bundy, who had reluctantly swung toward an incisive response.

Advantages of the Blockade

There were risks in either course, but to my mind the blockade had the incomparable advantage of giving the Russians time to back down before we had taken any irrevocable action. Still, we knew that even a blockade might degenerate into armed conflict if we were forced to sink a Russian ship and a Russian submarine retaliated by sinking one of ours. In the course of that evening, Dillon came over to the blockade side, largely persuaded by Bobby Kennedy's argument that we must be true to ourselves as Americans. We supporters of a blockade felt it tactically necessary to point out that such a course would not automatically exhaust our options: we could limit the contraband list in the first instance to offensive weapons and then expand it. We reinforced our position by pointing out that we could still launch an airstrike or even an invasion if the blockade proved ineffective.

At 10:00 P.M., we went again to the White House. We were afraid too many black limousines would attract undue attention, so nine of us piled into my car, sitting two or three deep and instead of going directly to the White House, we went to the Treasury, then by a secret set of passages through the White House bomb shelter into the White House basement.

We stayed with the President until after midnight. During the meeting it became apparent that he was strongly leaning toward a naval blockade. He asked Ted Sorensen to draft a speech, and later that night

I asked George Springsteen to call home the State Department's legal adviser, Abram Chayes, who was at a shipping meeting in Paris. Springsteen, a model of effectiveness, did not waste words or the chance of a leak from an insecure telephone. He told Chayes simply to come home. When Chayes asked what was happening ("Is it Cuba?"), Springsteen replied with masterful succinctness: "Just shut up and get back here."

The following morning, Friday, October 19, the President again went campaigning, but before leaving he heard second thoughts from some of his advisers. The Joint Chiefs of Staff wanted him to reconsider and order an airstrike or invasion, while Dean Acheson still obdurately opposed a blockade. That morning, Pierre Salinger, the President's press secretary, had reported that reporters were beginning to ask questions about troop movements in the direction of Florida, and we were deadly afraid that the press would break the story before we had everything in place. Rusk had raised some eyebrows among the reporters when he cancelled a speech before the Business Council at Hot Springs, which made it even more important that I keep a date to speak that same evening in Washington before the board of directors of the United States Chamber of Commerce.

It was one of the most unpleasant evenings I can recall. Given the restlessness throughout the country, I knew I would be asked questions about missiles in Cuba and though I hated the idea of lying, any equivocation on my part could spark dangerous rumors. I therefore couched my answers in circumlocutions, using diversionary and elaborate obfuscation. Later, the head of one of Chicago's largest banks complained angrily to my brother that, in the light of what had subsequently happened, it was clear that I had not been candid with the board of directors; he was quite outraged about it. Just how I could have been candid and still have preserved an essential American strategy, he seemed neither to know nor care. Fortunately for America, he was not making the decision. Immediately after my speech and the question period, I returned to spend most of the night in the Think Tank, helping to develop alternative scenarios.

During these hours, I formed great admiration for the technical competence of some of my State Department colleagues, and particularly Edwin Martin and U. Alexis Johnson who, working with Paul Nitze, drafted the blockade scenario that took into account such contingencies as a Russian *riposte* in the form of a Berlin Blockade, the possibility that an air strike might be necessary even after our quarantine, and the chance that the Soviets might attack the Jupiter missile sites in Turkey or Italy or move against Iran. Throughout the whole of our sessions and the weeks that followed, Ambassador Llewellyn Thompson showed almost infallible judgment in predicting Khrushchev's probable reactions.

Among other things, he advised us that the Russians were impressed with legality and might give weight to a resolution by the Organization of American States endorsing the blockade. We set the lawyers to work drafting the proper papers and examining whether a blockade would be considered legal in international law if we could not obtain an OAS resolution. All this concern for legality and for the reaction of other countries annoyed Dean Acheson, who, recognizing that he was losing the argument, departed for a weekend at his farm in Maryland. Meanwhile, as the airstrike proponents found themselves increasingly outvoted, we tried to mollify them by reiterating that a blockade was merely the first step; if after a reasonable chance, it did not work and the Russians continued to emplace missiles, then we could again consider an airstrike.

Moving Toward Decision

The following Saturday, October 20, the President broke off campaigning in Chicago on the excuse of a bad cold and a fever and returned to the White House early that afternoon. That day, the Chinese started to attack India over the Himalayan mountain barriers, which led some of us to speculate that the Chinese might be moving in coordination with the Soviets' Cuban adventure. We met in the Think Tank at nine in the morning to review the President's speech as drafted by Ted Sorensen. At 2:30 P.M., we met with the President in the Oval Office. Dean Rusk had prepared a summary in his own handwriting, which he read to us and then handed to the President, recommending the blockade track primarily on the ground that an airstrike would be irreversible. After hearing additional arguments from McNamara for the blockade, the President told us that he wanted to begin with a limited step and that bombing was too blunt an instrument. In his view, the blockade was the way to start, though that did not rule out an airstrike in the future. He was still expecting a Soviet move against Berlin, no matter what happened in Cuba.

The Stevenson Dissent

Adlai Stevenson, who had just arrived from New York, then outlined a dissenting position. He proposed that, simultaneously with the President's speech, which had been set for 7:00 P.M. on Monday, the United States should call for an emergency session of the United Nations Security Council, so that we could get a resolution on the table before the Russians could submit one. The crux of Stevenson's argument was that we should not only utilize the United Nations and the OAS but also pursue other diplomatic moves, such as offering to withdraw from Guantanamo as part of a plan to demilitarize and neutralize Cuba. He also wanted the President to consider offering to remove the Jupiters in Turkey in exchange for the removal of Russian missiles from Cuba.

The President rejected both of these proposals, though he was willing to discuss removing the Jupiters at the right time because they were obsolete and had little military value. But they were there for the protection of NATO, and he did not propose to confirm the suspicions of de Gaulle that the United States would sacrifice its allies' interests.

Though the President was courteous but firm, some of the others present were outraged and shrill. Dillon, Lovett, and McCone violated the calm and objectivity we had tried to maintain in our ExCom meetings when they intemperately upbraided Stevenson. The attack was, I felt, quite unfair, indicating more the state of anxiety and emotional exhaustion pervading the discussion than any reasoned reaction. After all, there was nothing new in any of Stevenson's proposals. We had from the beginning discussed a possible trade involving the removal of our missiles from Turkey and even from Italy as a way out of the impasse, and such a solution had at one time or another been put forward by, among others, Averell Harriman and Harlan Cleveland. The President, in addition to a number of his advisers, including both Bobby Kennedy and Bob McNamara, had expressed the view that some such trade would probably be necessary before the Soviets would accept our demand for the missiles' removal. McNamara had even suggested that we might have to withdraw our missiles both in Italy and Turkey and even conceded that we might ultimately have to abandon Guantanamo. I recognized the cogency of these predictions and on Wednesday, October 24, after the quarantine had been imposed, I notified Raymond Hare, our ambassador in Turkey as well as our NATO ambassador, Thomas Finletter, that we were considering the possibility of a trade and asked their advice as to probable Turkish and NATO reactions to such a move. The reply in each case had been emphatically negative. In the end the President did obliquely promise Khrushchev that the Turkish Jupiters would be withdrawn, though only on condition that such a withdrawal would not appear as a part of the Cuban missile settlement.

Thus, in urging that we offer such a trade, Stevenson was not putting forth an idea not already discussed. The reason for the excessive expressions of outrage was that he proposed it late in the day, after the President and the ExCom had already settled on another course. Not having been present during the week-long argument, Stevenson appeared to the weary members of the ExCom as ignoring all the anguished hours of discussion that had already taken place. To be sure, all but the fiercest hawks thought that we might have to offer the concessions Stevenson suggested, but we would not offer them at the beginning; only after we had tested out Soviet reactions to our quarantine and with luck had put Khrushchev on the defensive.

Stevenson was obviously at a disadvantage. While we in Washington had been arguing day and night under strong pressures for incisive action, he continued to live in the United Nations shadow world, where compromise was the invariable formula for solving all problems. He necessarily considered actions in terms of their defensibility in UN proceedings; he, after all, would have to carry the burden in the Security Council and he wanted our case to be one he could win. He wanted, as he told me, to show that we were willing to pay at least a token price for neutralizing Cuba.

I felt protective of Adlai, embarrassed for him, and exceedingly annoyed with my colleagues. I wondered if I might have saved him from their anger by briefing him more adequately in advance as to the probable mood of the meeting. On balance, I do not think so. He spoke out of strong conviction. He was not a man to tailor his opinions to his audience, and I doubt that the personal attack greatly bothered him. I felt sorry for him and proud at the same time. Though he seriously hurt his position—particularly with Robert Kennedy, who never liked him much anyway—he maintained the respect of most of us (including the President) as a man of forthright opinion.

To cushion the shock for our allies and minimize resentment at the lack of advance consultation, the President proposed to send some of his most respected advisers to inform the European heads of state. In spite of Dean Acheson's discontent with the course chosen, the President still coopted him to call on the most prickly allied leader, President de Gaulle. When Rusk telephoned Acheson on Saturday night to ask him to fly to Paris the next day, he replied, "Of course, I'll do what the President asks." Then he quoted a saying of Judge Oliver Wendell Holmes, one of his idols, "We all belong to the least exclusive club in the world, but it's the club with the highest dues: the United States of America."

The Story Finally Leaks

I constantly marveled during the whole week of tension that we had managed to avoid any serious press leak. I think we all expected the story to break at any moment. My forebodings were confirmed on Saturday night when I received a call from Scotty Reston of the *New York Times*. From what he told me, it seemed clear that he had learned most of the essential facts about the Soviet action and the proposed American response. I was horrified but relieved that the story belonged to a correspondent of such integrity. Would he please, I asked, hold off printing anything? I strongly emphasized how badly America's position might be harmed by premature publication during an extremely grave crisis. We talked for a while, and I exacted a promise that he would next call McGeorge Bundy. The President then telephoned Orvil Dryfoos, the publisher of the *Times,* who agreed to denature the story to the point of harmlessness. Subsequently that decision to withhold the news was seriously debated within the precincts of the *Times* itself, and some contended that the paper should have broken the story without regard to any Presidential request or consequences to the country. I find the argument tendentious and presumptuous; I cannot agree with Harrison Salisbury, among others, who contends that the *Times*'s judgment as to what is good for the country in a highly dangerous situation is better than the President's. What was at issue, after all, was not a story of Presidential chicanery or a cover-up of something that would have been embarrassing to the Administration; it was war or peace.

To throw the press off the Cuban scent, we undertook diversionary tactics. On Sunday, October 21, Averell Harriman, then Assistant Secretary for Far Eastern Affairs, Martin Hillenbrand of the German affairs office, and Phillips Talbot, Assistant Secretary of State for Near Eastern Affairs, arrived conspicuously at the White House in order to inspire press speculation about crises in China, India, or Berlin. Meanwhile, ExCom members continued to use the basement passageway from the Treasury through the White House bomb shelters. We met that morning in the Oval Office at 10:00 o'clock. While we were going over Sorensen's third draft of the speech that the President was to make Monday evening, I broached an idea I had been toying with during the night. Should we not try to spread the responsibility by holding Castro equally responsible with Khrushchev? That might help Khrushchev get off the hook. In practical terms, it would mean extending the blockade to include petroleum shipments and other cargo the Cuban economy needed. But it was, I instantly realized, a bad idea; as McNamara promptly pointed out, the blockade should be kept as narrowly targeted and as simple as possible. We had only one aim: to get the missiles out of Cuba. Adlai Stevenson raised a valuable point by challenging the sentence in the Sorensen draft that called for the Russians to "render the missiles inoperable"; the language should be made more explicit by demanding that the Russians "dismantle and remove" the missiles.

Once the blockade decision had been made, the State Department went into full action. Again the professionals showed their competence. Top secret telegrams were drafted to our ambassadors all around the world; a message was prepared for dispatch from the President to Khrushchev; and special letters were drafted to forty-three heads of government, including de Gaulle, Adenauer, Diefenbaker, Macmillan, Nehru, and Fanfani.

What provided a particularly macabre background for our activities was the weather. Though we might be about to blow up the world, nature had never seemed so luxuriant. The air was light and the sky crystal clear. As Bob McNamara and I walked through the White House Rose

Garden that Sunday, I remarked: "Do you remember the Georgia O'Keefe painting of a rose blooming through an ox skull? That's exactly how I feel this morning."

At 2:30 on Sunday we met together with the full membership of the National Security Council for the first time since the beginning of the crisis. Some cabinet members learned only then of the crisis, and they gave their formal approval to the President's projected course of action. The following day, the Security Council validated the creation of the Executive Committee by formally approving Action Memorandum 196, which had established it. From then on until further notice, the ExCom would meet with the President at ten o'clock each morning in the Cabinet Room.

The Day of the Speech

Monday, October 22, was a day of extreme nervousness. We heard in the morning that Soviet Foreign Minister Gromyko would have an important statement for the press before flying home to Moscow that afternoon; we were afraid that the Russians had discovered what was about to happen and were planning some drastic countermove. There were ominous rumors also to the effect that a Soviet prop jet was headed for Cuba. At five o'clock, the President met with the Congressional leaders only to find that most of them considered his quarantine idea inadequate. None doubted that we must take all necessary steps to get rid of the missiles, but they thought a blockade not strong enough and would have preferred an airstrike or some other aggressive military action.

Following the schedules Alex Johnson had worked out, at six o'clock (one hour before the President was to speak), Rusk told Soviet Ambassador Dobrynin what the President intended to say. He gave Dobrynin a copy of the speech and read portions out loud. Also in accordance with the schedule, I briefed forty-six ambassadors of allied countries at 6:15 in the State Department's International Conference Room. Included were the representatives from North Atlantic Treaty countries, those belonging to the Central Treaty Organization, the Southeast Asian Treaty Organization, and ANZUS. I described the background of our relations with the Soviets over the use of Cuba as a military base and showed them the evidence of the missile emplacements in Cuba, leaving it to Roger Hilsman to supplement my statement by a more technical explanation of the photocover. After outlining the main points of the President's message, I invited the ambassadors to remain and watch the President on television. Just as the speech was about to begin, a note of black humor crept in when a Savings and Loan commercial appeared with the question, How much security does your family have? It sent the ambassadors into nervous laughter. While I was briefing our allied ambassadors, Dean

Rusk was briefing the ambassadors of the nonaligned and neutral countries, and Edwin Martin was briefing the ambassadors of the Organization of American States.

Immediately after the President's speech, I met with the diplomatic press. I raised almost as many questions as I answered. "What will Khrushchev do? Is he going to abide by the quarantine we are about to establish? Is he going to try to run that quarantine or to break it? Is he going to reply somewhere else in the world? We are prepared for whatever Khrushchev may decide."

That night I slept fitfully on a couch in my office, waking from time to time for a message from our Operations Center indicating any Soviet reaction. The next morning, Secretary Rusk, who had gone home for a quick nap, woke me with cheering news: "George, we've won a great victory. You and I are still alive." It reflected the prevailing mood. So far the Russians had not moved against Berlin or bombed the Jupiter bases, and we gained the impression that they had been taken by surprise and were trying to decide what to do. (Perhaps somewhere in the Kremlin another "think tank" was feverishly operating.) Then, in the morning the Tass News Agency transmitted the Soviet government's statement charging President Kennedy with piracy, violations of international law, and provocative acts: the standard Soviet farrago.

That Tuesday, October 23, after Rusk appeared and argued personally, the Organization for American States (OAS) approved the quarantine action by the unexpectedly large vote of nineteen to zero, thereby legitimatizing our blockade, which, under the terms of the President's proclamation, was to be put into effect Wednesday, October 24, at 10:00 A.M. Eastern time. The question we asked ourselves, and one another, was what would happen next. The U-2 photographs showed work still continuing on the missile sites.

As the blockade line was drawn, nineteen ships of the United States Second Fleet took up stations in a great arc extending five hundred miles out to sea. On Monday, twenty-five Soviet ships had been reported strung out across the Atlantic bound for Cuba. They had been spotted by naval reconnaissance planes, and particular note was made of those carrying deck cargo and those with extra large hatches wide enough to accommodate missiles.

Meanwhile, our emissaries had touched base with our principal allies. President de Gaulle distinguished himself not only with our government but also with the American people by his unequivocal response to Dean Acheson—even before he had seen the missile photographs—that he understood why the American President had acted and that France would fully support us. But leading British newspapers failed to meet that standard of trust. They offended Americans (and infuriated our embattled group in Washington) by challenging the authenticity of the missiles and deploring the President's action. Some even snidely suggested that it was an election ploy; and the British nuclear disarmers did not fail to display that sanctimonious rejection of realism that has become their hallmark.

During a long ExCom session Wednesday morning, we continued to worry about how to deal with the first ship interception, which, we expected, would occur sometime during the day. Our forebodings deepened with the report that work on the missile sites was proceeding at an accelerated pace. That afternoon, the President authorized our information service to release aerial photographs to give the lie to scoffers and to establish with our friends that the missiles were irrefutably there. The question of releasing the photographs had been hotly debated, and even the President had been hesitant to disclose the extraordinary definition achieved by our cameras, but events fully vindicated the wisdom of disclosing the pictures to the world. Even the most cynical critic or naïve nuclear disarmer could no longer question the existence and location of the missiles.

We carefully dissected all indications of Soviet reaction no matter how fragmentary, including a curious message Chairman Khrushchev gave to American businessman William Knox, whom he unexpectedly summoned to the Kremlin. In the course of a long harangue, Khrushchev admitted that the Soviet Union had missiles and attack planes in Cuba, but he wanted the President and the American people to know that, if the United States navy tried to stop Soviet ships, his submarines would start sinking American vessels.

Wednesday morning I learned from Adlai Stevenson that U Thant, responding as always to the pressure of nonaligned nations, was calling on the Soviets to suspend all arms shipments to Cuba and on the United States to suspend its blockade for a period of two or three weeks. That was anything but helpful. For us to accept the proposal would so relieve Khrushchev of pressure that we would probably never be able to get the missiles out of Cuba. In addition, the Thant proposal contained no provision for verification.

It was a day of intense anxiety. We believed that if our navy sank a Russian ship, Khrushchev would react vigorously. Thus we were momentarily relieved when, while meeting with the President in the Cabinet Room, we received word that a dozen of the Soviets' twenty-five ships had changed course or stopped. Still, we remained skeptical, speculating that Moscow might have some other purpose in mind: perhaps that they rendezvous with Soviet submarines. Since the essence of our blockade strategy was to avoid precipitate action and to give Khrushchev time to think, the President directed that there be no shooting. Our navy was to keep Soviet ships in view but not to board them without fresh instructions.

Waiting for a Collision

That night (Wednesday) I again stayed in my office, sleeping inter-mittently, waking to read each report as it came into the Operations Center. In addition, I had a problem to sort out with Stevenson; Wash-ington and New York differed as to how the President should answer Thant's proposal, which was to be put to the Security Council that night. I had urged Adlai to try to talk to Thant before the Security Council meeting, since I wanted our objections on record before Thant spoke, but Stevenson thought Thant would resent it. We were concerned in Washington that the Soviets would immediately accept Thant's proposal, leaving us in the lonely position of rejecting the Secretary-General's unacceptable idea. We had expressed our opposition in a letter from the President, which we wished Stevenson to deliver that night, but he thought the letter was too rigid. He wanted its tone softened so that we would not seem to be rejecting Thant's proposal outright or indicating that we were not even prepared to talk. I told Harlan Cleveland, the Assistant Secretary for International Organization Affairs (and thus Ste-venson's conduit to the State Department), that if Stevenson continued to resist our instructions I would have to get the President to overrule him, since Kennedy wanted the letter delivered without delay. I tele-phoned the President to tell him that I would try to persuade Stevenson to talk with U Thant before U Thant spoke in the United Nations, but that Stevenson might insist on hearing those instructions directly from the President. At 11:15 that night, I again called the President to say that I had just talked with Stevenson and had pointed out that the U Thant proposal was unacceptable, among other reasons, because it did not provide for inspection or verification. But Stevenson, I told him, had dismissed the point, arguing that if we accepted Thant's proposal, we could then take up those questions in the conversation.

As the night wore on, we received regular reports that Soviet mer-chantmen were approaching closer and closer to our line of destroyers. All evening I had been trying to think of precautionary steps we might have neglected. With the ships in motion, a clash might come at any moment; events could then get quickly out of hand. Finally, I decided that we should try to get Thant to call upon Khrushchev immediately to stop his ships for twenty-four hours to avoid an irrevocable clash; we would then have time to try to work things out. That would give Khru-shchev a public excuse for doing what he might wish to do anyway.

I knew that Stevenson would resist if I tried on my own initiative to get him to move that night, so toward midnight I called the President, who favored the idea. I promptly telephoned Stevenson to ask that he try to get Thant to act that same night. Adlai was reluctant to call Thant, who had already gone home, but I pressed him and he promised to try.

Later we talked again, and, at 12:20 in the morning, he called to say that he had got Thant out of bed and Thant had agreed to send such a message—but not until morning, because the communications were poor at night.

Earlier that evening, Stevenson had had his now-famous altercation with Soviet Ambassador Valerian Zorin. When he put it directly to Zorin as to whether or not the Soviets were placing medium and intermediate range missiles in Cuba, Zorin had promised him an answer in due course. Stevenson had then dramatically replied, "I am prepared to wait for my answer until hell freezes over, if that's your decision. And I am also prepared to present the evidence in this room." Thereupon he had revealed the photographs with devastating effect. For Adlai, it was the kind of triumph he liked the most and richly deserved.

Next morning, our air surveillance still showed work rapidly going forward on the missile bases, but Naval Intelligence now definitively confirmed that twelve of the twenty-five ships had in fact turned back. Presumably those twelve carried incriminating cargo and could not risk running the blockade. Meanwhile, I repeatedly needled Stevenson to get Thant to send his appeal to Khrushchev to stop all the ships for twenty-four hours. Finally, at 2:26 P.M., Thant did send such a message, asking that Soviet ships keep out of our interception area for a limited time "to permit discussion of the modalities of a possible agreement. . . ." He also sent a letter to President Kennedy referring to his message to Khrushchev and asking that "instructions be issued to United States vessels to do everything possible to avoid direct confrontation with Soviet ships in the next few days in order to minimize the risk of any untoward incident." To that Kennedy replied that if the Soviet ships already on the way to Cuba were to "stay away from the interception area for the limited time required for preliminary discussion," Thant could be assured that United States vessels would abide by his request. On Friday, Khrushchev advised Thant that the Soviets would also abide by his request but insisted that the period of such constraint could not "be of long duration."

My modest initiative had at least helped to bring a brief delay in a possible clash between our navy and a Soviet ship that refused our boarding demand. That danger was further diminished when the President ordered our navy, against strong protests from some of the more hard-line ExCom members, to let a Soviet tanker, the *Bucharest,* pass through without boarding after identifying herself by radio and declaring that she carried only petroleum. The same treatment was also accorded to an East German cruise ship. Though I supported the President's action as strongly as possible, some of my ExCom colleagues vigorously protested that our failure to board every ship would send the wrong signal to Khrushchev. We all knew that at some point soon we would have to stop a ship if our blockade were to be credible, so a Panamanian-owned ship, the *Marucla,* under Soviet charter, was chosen as the least provocative. Our navy boarded it Friday morning and, as we had fully expected, found it to contain no contraband. We received the news while the ExCom was meeting. We would have felt greater relief had our intelligence not continued to report that work on the missile sites was being speeded up.

That led the ExCom's more belligerent members to step up their pressure for an immediate airstrike before the missiles were ready to fire. They had a certain logic on their side; the objective of the blockade was to induce the Soviets to dismantle the missile sites in Cuba before they became operational, and, if we could not achieve that objective merely by a blockade, we might have to take some other action. We could not, as we saw it, let the missiles become operational, since once that occurred relative bargaining positions would be irrevocably altered, and the danger of a nuclear foray greatly increased. Once the missiles were on station, an airstrike might precipitate their firing, since no strike could be sure of taking out all of them. So most of my colleagues seemed convinced that, if the Soviets continued work on the sites, we could not wait much beyond Sunday to make the decision to send in our planes. Moreover, my more hawkish colleagues, such as Nitze and McCone, were skeptical that an airstrike would by itself be enough; they would almost certainly press for an invasion, and plans went forward on that basis.

Message from Khrushchev

We were intently alert for any signs that might indicate a softening of the Soviet position. So far, communications between the President and Khrushchev had elicited only traditional Soviet bellicosity. Then news came from an unexpected quarter. John Scali, a correspondent for the American Broadcasting Company (later our ambassador to the United Nations), was suddenly invited to lunch by a counsellor at the Soviet embassy named Alexander S. Fomin (who was presumed to be a KGB colonel and chief of the Soviet intelligence operations in the United States). Fomin, in a high state of excitement, asked if the State Department would be interested in settling the dispute on the following basis: the Soviets would dismantle and remove the missiles in Cuba, and the United States would pledge not to invade Cuba. If Stevenson were to suggest something along this line in the United Nations, Fomin said, Ambassador Zorin would be interested. After checking with the President, Rusk authorized Scali to indicate America's interest, and Scali passed that word to Fomin at 7:45 that Friday evening.

At about six o'clock, the famous personal message from Khrushchev to Kennedy had begun to come in on the teletype from Moscow. Rusk and I met with the President and some of our colleagues in the Oval Office to try to decipher what Khrushchev was trying to tell us. It was an extraordinary letter—personal, discursive, and emotional—unquestionably a *cri de coeur* by Khrushchev and untouched by any banal foreign-office hand. At the time, I remembered that I had once been told by a Soviet expert that when Khrushchev composed a letter or message, he turned his chair toward the wall and dictated in a loud voice to a stenographer sitting behind him. Reading the letter on that fateful Friday evening, I could picture the squat, morosely unhappy Chairman facing a blank wall and a doubtful future. I felt his anguish in every paragraph.

After a long apologia offering Khrushchev's excuses for putting the missiles in Cuba and explaining why the United States should not be concerned about them, he came to the heart of the matter. The Soviets, he proposed, would withdraw or destroy the missiles now in Cuba and would send no more, on condition that we stop our blockade and not invade Cuba. He then acknowledged the dangerous collision course on which our two nations were headed. "If you have not lost your self-control and sensibly conceive what this might lead to, then, Mr. President," he wrote,

we and you ought not to pull on the ends of the rope in which you have tied the knot of war, because, the more the two of us pull, the tighter that knot will be tied. And a moment may come when that knot will be tied so tight that even he who tied it will not have the strength to untie it, and then it will be necessary to cut that knot, and what that would mean is not for me to explain to you, because you yourself understand perfectly well of what terrible forces our countries dispose. Consequently, if there is no intention to tighten that knot, and thereby to doom the world to the catastrophe of thermonuclear war, then let us not only relax the forces pulling on the ends of the rope, let us take measures to untie that knot. We are ready for this.[1]

Considered against the background of the Scali incident, the Chairman's letter seemed to be the break in the clouds we had been waiting for, and I slept at home for the first time in several nights. Meanwhile, experts from the State Department's Bureau of Intelligence and Research settled down to analyze the Khrushchev letter and the Scali message to determine what, if any, traps they might contain.

For the past ten days I had felt caught up in irresistible forces moving us toward catastrophe—and I began to think of the hawks among us almost as enemies. I could not tell Ruth, or anyone else, the details of what was happening—though I had told her earlier in the week that she ought to try to turn the basement into a small bomb cellar, since I would be taken off to a secret command center if hell broke loose. Wishing not to alarm anyone, she had made meager and almost pathetic preparations. She moved some canned food into the basement, stored water in large jars, laid in a supply of flashlights, and cached away some books for herself to read and a Bible for our black cook, who was devoutly religious.

The Second Message

Though I was encouraged Friday night that a resolution might be at hand, hope rapidly dissipated Saturday morning. Just after the ExCom assembled at ten o'clock, the news ticker reported that a new letter from Khrushchev was being broadcast by Radio Moscow. Totally different in tone and substance from the idiosyncratic and highly personal message of the night before, it had clearly not been written by Khrushchev but by a committee; it bore the unmistakable marks of an official communication—an art form with which we were all too familiar. To our dismay, it changed the terms of the offer by establishing a parallel between the Soviet missiles in Cuba and our Jupiters in Turkey; as the price for Moscow's removing its offensive missiles, we must remove the Jupiters.

Why had the terms been changed? Had Khrushchev been overruled, or had the mention of such a face-saving swap in the Washington press—particularly in a column by Walter Lippmann—led Khrushchev to believe that he could safely raise the ante? To increase our anxiety, John McCone reported that a single Soviet ship had detached itself from the others and was headed for Cuba and that work on the missile sites was proceeding day and night. Even more alarming, we were advised that Soviet SAMs had shot down one of our U-2 reconnaissance planes—the first fatality of the crisis. Earlier in the week, the ExCom had solemnly decided that if one U-2 were shot down, we would send our aircraft to take out a single SAM site and if a second were attacked, we would destroy all the SAM sites. The more blood-thirsty members of the ExCom were insisting that we act Sunday morning.

Here the President showed the judgment that invested his handling of the affair with high statesmanship. Refusing to be panicked into a step that would almost certainly mean escalation, he postponed the decision for at least another day. But it was unmistakably Black Saturday, since in spite of the Khrushchev letter, one might reasonably infer from the evidence that the Soviets really intended war and were simply stalling until they were better prepared. What gave a certain irony to our predicament was that the Jupiters, an early form of liquid-fuel missile, were obsolete; no one could even be sure they were operable. In a purely military sense, we did not even need them; Polaris submarines stationed in or near Turkish waters would be far more effective. Even Robert Kennedy commented at that Saturday morning meeting that the Soviet proposal was "not unreasonable." But the Jupiters were in Turkey as part of our whole NATO commitment, and the United States could not trade off equipment committed by NATO to serve interests of its own without undercutting the confidence of our Western allies.

The Problem of Withdrawing the Jupiters

The problem was political, not military. Because the missiles, lacking military value, were clearly a provocation, there was every reason to withdraw them but it had to be a voluntary act worked out in agreement with our NATO allies. The President had wanted to withdraw the Jupiters from both Turkey and Italy for some time. But the history of our efforts to withdraw them has been garbled and, since that distortion impugns my own record of responsibility, I would like to dispose of a personally annoying bit of historians' gossip that implies that the President had ordered me to remove the missiles from Turkey prior to the missile crisis and that the missiles were still in place at the time of the crisis only because I had failed to carry out his instructions. I am grateful to Professor Burton J. Bernstein of Stanford University for effectively refuting that annoying canard. Rather than burdening the text with a distracting digression, I am including a full clarification in a footnote.[2]

After carefully reviewing all evidence available to him, Professor Bernstein pointed out that "it is too simple to conclude, as have some analysts, that Kennedy ordered removal of these missiles and that the bureaucracy thwarted his instructions. Indeed, according to Bundy's recent recollection, the President did not order withdrawal of the missiles until *after* the Cuban Missile Crisis.[3]

The Trollope Ploy

The situation on Saturday morning seemed darkly foreboding. The blockade, the hawks insisted, had not worked; it had simply allowed the Soviets time to complete the missile emplacement. When the Joint Chiefs of Staff joined our meeting, they proposed that we launch an airstrike Monday, to be followed by an invasion. One or two of my colleagues seemed, I thought, almost pleased that things had worked out as they had predicted; they had always regarded the blockade as an illusory course and feared it might lead us into a trap.

Of all the people in the room, the President was by far the most calm and analytical. If we launched an airstrike, would the Soviets respond by an attack on Turkey—which would lead to the Jupiters being fired off? To avoid such a drastic escalation, he ordered them defused (much to the disgust of those eager for dramatic action). How supremely fortunate that the President was John F. Kennedy rather than one of my hawkish colleagues!

Rusk, Llewellyn Thompson, and I drafted a note rejecting the Turkish deal and demanding that the Soviets immediately halt work on the missiles. When we brought it back to the ExCom, Robert Kennedy objected both to the content and tenor of the draft. Instead, he proposed what McGeorge Bundy was later to call the Trollope Ploy—evoking the image of a Victorian maiden who would construe even the tiniest gesture as a marriage proposal she could then eagerly accept. Why not, Robert Kennedy proposed, ignore the second formal note? Why not reply to Khrushchev's personal letter as though the second note had not existed? I like to think that only fatigue and anxiety led me to overlook the artistry of the proposal. Of course, Bobby Kennedy was right, but my first reaction was skeptical.

Robert Kennedy and Sorensen drafted a response that was promptly dispatched to Khrushchev. Meanwhile, Robert Kennedy delivered a copy to Ambassador Dobrynin, with a severe warning that the United States would react strongly unless Khrushchev immediately advised that the missiles would be withdrawn. In addition, Kennedy suggested to Dobrynin privately that the President had wanted to remove the missiles from Turkey and Italy for a long period, but it could not be part of the deal, since it was not an arrangement that could be made under threat or pressure. He had ordered their removal and it was "our judgment that, within a short time after the crisis was over, those missiles would be gone."[4] Dobrynin, however, told Bobby Kennedy that in his opinion the Kremlin was far too committed to agree to the deal envisaged by the President's letter.

I woke early on Sunday morning with a sense of depression, but it did not last long. A few minutes before nine o'clock, Radio Moscow announced it would broadcast an important statement. We knew that if the Russians gave a negative answer, we were poised to launch an airstrike no later than Tuesday morning. Even then I doubted if that schedule would be kept, in view of the President's manifest desire to avoid any irrevocable act. But fortunately, we never had to find out. What the radio relayed was another long, tortured letter from Khrushchev that told us what we were eager to hear. In response to President Kennedy's promise that there would be no attack or invasion of Cuba, Khrushchev wrote that he had instructed Soviet officers to discontinue construction of the missile sites, dismantle them, and return them to the USSR, and that UN representatives would be permitted to verify the dismantling. Khrushchev also added that he was sending Vasily Kuznetsov, the First Deputy Foreign Minister to work with U Thant in eliminating the present crisis. The ExCom once more went to work, and we drafted a quick acceptance statement. I shall never forget the relief we all felt that morning. Unless something unforeseen happened, the crisis had passed.

Sweeping Up

That did not mean, of course, that we could avoid a long period of sweeping up. The President appointed John J. McCloy to head the negotiations with Kuznetsov and designated Deputy Secretary of Defense Roswell Gilpatric and me to work with him. That, as it turned out, was not necessary. I had so much catching up to do with work deferred during the crisis that I did not have time to go to New York, and McCloy, with some help from Gilpatric, carried on successfully. In time, we were satisfied that the missiles had all been removed. A problem developed over securing removal of the Ilyushin 24s but that, too, was ultimately worked out.

No doubt part of the delay in cleaning up was due to Castro's foot-dragging. The Kremlin was in an awkward spot, and Castro made the most of it. To persuade the Cubans not to obstruct Soviet actions, Khrushchev sent Deputy Premier Anastas Mikoyan to Havana on November 2. Castro, Mikoyan found, was outraged and intransigent. At the end of the month, on November 30, Mikoyan came to Washington for a talk with President Kennedy; that night Ruth and I dined with him informally at the home of Secretary of the Interior Stewart Udall. The only other guests were, as I recall, the President's Economic Adviser, Walter Heller, and his wife and Soviet Ambassador Dobrynin and Mrs. Dobrynin. The Udalls lived modestly in a small house in a wooded area of McLean, Virginia, and when we arrived the place was surrounded by a Secret Service army.

It was a strange, seemingly unreal evening. The liquor flowed plentifully, and Mikoyan demonstrated the resourcefulness that had kept him alive and in power for many years. He was widely famed as the prototypical "survivor." Though Mikoyan had been a close associate of Stalin in the State Defense Committee during the war, Stalin had still exiled Mikoyan's younger sons to Siberia; yet Mikoyan remained as Deputy Premier and continued to hold that post under Khrushchev. A whimsical anecdote then circulating in Moscow related that the Communist government had been overthrown, Khrushchev exiled to America, and the Czar restored to the throne. Many years later, the story went, Khrushchev telephoned the Czar to petition for the right to return so he might die in his native land. The Czar replied "Just a minute, let me consult." Then over the telephone the Czar was heard asking, "Anastas, what do you think?"

Now Mikoyan—in the living room of a typical middle-class American home—regaled us with a straightforward account of Castro's anger and rudeness. Castro had refused to see him for two weeks, letting him wait impatiently in a Cuban resort town; when they finally met, conversation had been angry and difficult. During the evening he spoke of his wife who had died the day after he arrived in Cuba. Though they had been married for many years he had made no effort to return to Moscow for the funeral. At the beginning, as young revolutionaries, he and his wife had, so he told us, "lived together only as brother and sister" because they did not want love-making to deflect their thoughts and energies from their single revolutionary objective. Later they apparently made up for lost time since they had five sons, one of whom, a pilot, had been killed in action in World War II.

It was an odd, and for me somewhat disquieting, evening. Just recovering from the intense strain of the Cuban Missile Crisis, Ruth and I found it difficult to join wholeheartedly in the singing and conviviality that ensued. Mrs. Dobrynin, an aggressive woman and quite sure of herself, insisted on becoming the life of the party, hammering American songs on the piano quite noisily and mechanically and demanding that everyone sing as loudly as she. Then came many toasts extravagantly expressing the eternal friendship of our two countries.

Had anyone been alert enough to notice, I would have appeared especially quiet, if not a little surly. Mikoyan, a wily Armenian, joined the festivities with apparent gusto, though I felt he was secretly laughing at what he considered the sentimental, and even gullible, Americans.

Stewart Udall is an admirable man, outgoing and friendly, for whom I have great affection, and I did not fault him for his manifest decency. Not having endured the agony of the missile crisis as a direct participant, he could not share my sense of constraint in socializing with the representatives of a country with which we had only narrowly averted a war.

Retrospective

How, finally, should one assess the missile crisis? It was almost certainly a watershed in our relations with the Soviet Union. By bringing Moscow face to face with the reality of nuclear catastrophe, it paved the way for *détente*. At the same time, it no doubt helped stimulate the Soviets' subsequent buildup of both strategic and conventional weapons. Never again would the Soviets knowingly permit themselves to be caught at a tactical disadvantage requiring a humiliating retreat.

Whatever the views of the academic second-guessers as to how the affair should have been handled—and they have not been reticent—I thought then, and still do, that under John Kennedy's firm leadership we gave a superior performance. We did not move precipitately but argued out all available courses of action in an intellectual interchange that was the most objective I ever witnessed in government—or, for that matter, in the private sector. Surviving ExCom members look back on it with pride. We were present at a moment of high challenge and, with John Kennedy's steady but cautious guidance, we won the day without a shot being fired.

21. *Day of the Murder*

In the early evening of Wednesday, November 20, 1963, I returned from Paris where I had been attending a ministerial meeting of the OEEC. As soon as I reached the State Department at 9:20 P.M. I called the President. We talked principally about our problems with the European Common Market—primarily with France and the European Community's common agricultural policy. I told him that Chancellor Ludwig Erhard had given me the impression that the Germans understood the difficulties Europe's policies were creating for the American farmers and that he wanted to be helpful. We also discussed the pending wheat negotiations with the Soviet Union and a *New York Times* story of the previous day, which the President feared might be read as implying that he was contemplating a trade offensive against the Soviet Union. Finally, I reported on a talk I had just had with ex-Chancellor Adenauer and on the pending Mundt bill, on which I planned to testify the next day.

Kennedy seemed in a relaxed mood. He said he would return from Texas Saturday evening and would lunch with Cabot Lodge on Sunday. He thought that he and I should have a visit Sunday evening. Either we could meet at the White House or I could come down to Middleburg Sunday afternoon to brief him for his meeting with Erhard on Monday. Among other things he wanted to show me his new house. It was our last conversation.

Almost every American who was of sentient age on Friday, November 22, 1963, remembers where he or she was and what was happening when word came of the President's assassination. The private reactions of millions of Americans were imprinted indelibly on their memories. For me it was a day of anguish and anxiety. Secretary Rusk had left that morning with most other members of the United States cabinet to attend a joint cabinet meeting with the Japanese in Tokyo, so I was Acting Secretary. The morning had followed a routine course. I had held a staff meeting, met with several of my colleagues, and had lunch in my office with McGeorge Bundy, who had to leave early to meet with Secretary McNamara. Then, at approximately 1:40 P.M., a messenger handed me a bit of yellow paper torn off a ticker with a UPI flash; three shots had been fired at the President's motorcade. Almost immediately it was confirmed that the President had been shot in the head.

Within no more than ten minutes Secretary Rusk telephoned from his Tokyo-bound plane, then thirty thousand feet in the air the other side of Hickam Field, Hawaii. He had already heard the news and I could give him little amplification. "We'll be back at Hickam Field in forty-five minutes. Shall we come to Washington or go straight to Dallas?" I told him I did not know but would find out. "I'll call again from Hickam Field," Rusk replied. Within half an hour we knew the President was dead.

What had happened? Was it a plot? The beginning of a Soviet move? The first step in a coup attempt? I telephoned John McCone, the head of the CIA, and suggested that he activate the Watch Committee, which monitored crises and interpreted every fragment of news from all over the world, tapping foreign intelligence services and assembling every source of information available. He had, he said, already done so.

While watching the television screen in my office for news, I discussed with George Springsteen, my top staff assistant, and others on my immediate staff what to do first. When word came that Lee Harvey Oswald had been captured, I immediately ordered his name checked in the Department's files for any information that might cast light on his activities. Within minutes, word came back that he had spent thirty-two months in the Soviet Union as recently as June 1962.

In the minutes that passed, my staff tapped every available resource of the State Department to develop an agenda for action. Obviously there were many things an experienced foreign office automatically did: reassure the diplomatic corps and send messages to our embassies, try to assess the reactions of various countries and head off precipitate speculation. But beyond that, I discovered duties of the State Department I only dimly recalled from early American history studies. The Act of Congress of September 15, 1789, which had created the Department of State, had not only invested the new department with the responsibilities of what had been known as the Department of Foreign Affairs but had also assigned it certain special responsibilities originally conducted by the Secretary of the Continental Congress. These extra duties were the product of a compromise; some members of Congress had been advocating that they be given to a new Home Department. Among the domestic assignments entrusted to the Department were the custody of the Great Seal and responsibility for publishing the laws enacted by Congress. In addition, there were some special tasks to be performed on the occasion of a President's death.

The Secretary of State was required, among other things, to send messages to the governors of our states and territories, informing them of orders for the thirty-day public mourning period and supplying details of the funeral service; he also had to request notification whether they intended to be present at the funeral ceremonies, to issue instructions closing all executive department agencies on the day of the funeral, and to direct the Secretary of Defense that all military commands and vessels under the control of the Secretary of Defense should fly flags at half-mast for a thirty-day period of mourning. He had to notify all foreign embassies that the President had died and inform them that the new President had taken the oath of office.

I gathered two or three of the most skillful writers in the Department, including Harlan Cleveland and Walt Rostow, and together we began drafting the necessary proclamations and messages. Included among them was a Presidential proclamation appointing the day of President Kennedy's funeral as a day of national mourning and prayer.

By the time the Secret Service inquired through channels as to whether the State Department had a dossier on Lee Harvey Oswald, we had already discovered that he had not only been in Moscow but had also applied for Soviet citizenship. What was the connection? I called in Ambassador Llewellyn Thompson and Averell Harriman—both of whom had served in Moscow. "Could this," I asked, "be a Soviet move to be followed up by a missile attack?" The answer was a resounding negative. The leaders of the Soviet Union, they insisted, would never sanction the assassination of other heads of state, as that might invite similar attacks on themselves. Nevertheless, there was the danger that Oswald's pretense to Marxist convictions might set off violent anti-Soviet sentiments that could undo all our efforts to develop working arrangements with Moscow.

Two or three times during the afternoon I talked with McGeorge Bundy in his White House office. Once he said to me poignantly, "It's lonely over here." Meanwhile, we awaited the arrival of the airplane carrying the body of President Kennedy and the new President, Lyndon Johnson. I went to the White House to find old friends in tears, including Arthur Schlesinger, who said, "They've killed him," without being very specific as to just who "they" might be.

Helicopters were leaving from the White House lawn for Andrews Field, and I climbed aboard carrying a memorandum for the new President listing the routine tasks he must immediately perform. The MATS terminal at Andrews Field was surrounded by Secret Service men, marines, and a growing crowd of excited people. I had some coffee in the mess and waited. Soon the big plane came in, and a fork-lift removed the heavy casket. Mrs. Kennedy emerged and departed with the casket for Bethesda Naval Hospital. Finally, the new President came down the ramp. Lyndon Johnson moved directly to a cluster of microphones and made a little speech, which we could only indistinctly hear, except that the words, "I will do my best. That is all I can do," came through loud and clear. Since the President had sent word that McNamara, Mac Bundy, and "someone from the State Department" were to accompany him to the White House, the three of us followed him to the waiting helicopter. I handed the President my memorandum describing the formal tasks that had to be performed and a draft of a proclamation. Bob McNamara asked me, as Acting Secretary of State, to sit opposite the President, but I insisted that he take the seat. Mrs. Johnson moved across to a couch between Mac Bundy and myself.

President Johnson seemed near a state of shock. He moved erratically, and I saw twitches in his face. During the ten-minute ride from Andrews Field to the White House he spoke to the three of us with deep emotion. Mrs. Kennedy, he said, had been incredibly brave. Although her stockings were covered with blood, she refused to change them— since it was her husband's blood—even as she stood by Johnson during the swearing-in. He then turned to us and said, "You're men I trust the most. You must stay with me. I'll need you. President Kennedy gathered about him extraordinary people I could never have reached for. You're the ablest men I've ever seen. It's not just that you're President Kennedy's friends, but you are the best anywhere and you must stay. I want you to stand with me." He then asked each of us to tell him what we had done during the day and what needed to be done immediately. Mac Bundy and Bob McNamara spoke briefly, and I dwelt largely on the effect of the assassination on foreign governments and what we must do to reassure them.

When we landed on the White House lawn, a few yards from the Oval Office, where all of us had landed with President Kennedy on so many previous occasions, everything seemed to have a different, sad, almost macabre appearance. The President headed for the West Wing, where he was meeting with the Congressional leadership. Bob McNamara and I entered through the Cabinet Room and sat together for the next twenty minutes talking of the meaning of everything that had occurred in the last few hours, as well as the significance of the Kennedy Presidency. We agreed how unfortunate it had been that JFK had felt his freedom of action limited because he had been elected by such a narrow margin. With a new election and a new mandate in 1964, we had hoped he could operate with less restraint. It could have been a brilliant, innovative period for America.

Later that night, I went back to Andrews Field. A half-hour after midnight, on November 23, the plane carrying most of the Johnson Administration cabinet taxied up to the MATS terminal. Dean Rusk, as the senior member of the cabinet, disembarked first. He made a statement on behalf of his colleagues, addressing those "who had the honor of serving President Kennedy" and who "value the gallantry and wisdom he brought to the grave, awesome, and lonely office of the Presidency."

I seized Dean Rusk's arm and rushed him off to a limousine so we could talk about what had to be done as well as the meaning of what had occurred that day. No one could yet be sure that Oswald had acted on his own; there was still a chance of a larger plot. Among other things, we spoke of the dangers of a mindless reaction on the part of extremist groups within the United States. Pat Moynihan, whom I had seen in the MATS mess, was particularly concerned that the Dallas police might behave irresponsibly. He knew the police mentality, and he was eager for us to do something to prevent unnecessary reaction.

The next day, we faced many routine chores. Working with Averell Harriman and Alexis Johnson, I drafted a brief speech for the nation, which the President decided not to make, and I talked with the President and Mac Bundy about which foreign visitors the President should personally see from among the large number arriving that evening. We also discussed at length the kind of reception that would be held after the funeral.

That night, Dean Rusk, Averell Harriman, and I went to Dulles Airport. Unique among American airports, planes land far out on the tarmac, and passengers are ferried to the airport terminal by mobile lounges that connect directly with the planes. Then the lounges kneel down to ground level like giant elephants, debouching the passengers through a corridor directly into the terminal. In view of the large number of foreign heads of state and chiefs of government coming in their own private planes, no one of us could handle the task of greeting each man. To the extent possible, Secretary Rusk met the principal heads of state, while I met most of the others. As might be expected, de Gaulle's arrival attracted the greatest attention.

The next day, Rusk and I worried over the possibility that one or more heads of state might be attacked by an assassin. The funeral party was scheduled to walk eight long blocks between the White House and St. Matthew's Cathedral through a densely populated section of the city. De Gaulle, with his great height, would be the most conspicuous target, and, as Dean Rusk noted to me, he had already been the object of four assassination attempts. A bullet striking Mikoyan could create a crisis between the United States and the Soviet Union.

Alone among the top officials of the government, I declined to go to the funeral. I had two motives. One was a personal one: I have a distaste for the pomp and panoply of state funerals; we were treating the dead President as a king, rather than as a warm, human, lively, glittering young American elected by the popular vote of a great nation. I could, however, have set aside my personal predilections, but I felt it imperative that a responsible official remain at the center of communications, ready to deal with an emergency, such as an assassination attempt. As Alexis

Johnson and I sat in my office watching the slow procession on television, we felt an oppressive apprehension. God knew what the future would hold! But no disasters occurred.

That evening 220 guests came to the reception rooms on the top floor of the State Department, where Rusk and I, and our colleagues tried to make them feel welcome, be certain that no one was slighted, and make sure that the new President was briefed a moment in advance before he received each distinguished visitor. Sixteen of the guests were accorded such special treatment. The President seated them for a few moments for private conversation, but he was uncharacteristically laconic; he knew few of his guests and let Dean Rusk do the talking.

I devoted most of the following day, November 26, to helping the President receive foreign visitors—Emperor Haile Selassie in the morning, then Prince Philip and Prime Minister Alec Douglas-Home, and, at noon, Chancellor Erhard. Thursday was Thanksgiving. On Friday, at his insistence, I took Pakistan's Foreign Minister Zulfikar Ali Bhutto to see the President. Relations with Pakistan were still extremely sticky, and Bhutto had persistently undercut us. Thus, though Bhutto had intended the visit as a means of ingratiating himself with the new President, I took the occasion to interject some critical comments. The President—whom I had briefed in advance—picked up and elaborated on my comments, giving Bhutto an uncomfortable time. As he and I walked out of the President's office together, he turned on me furiously: "How dare you treat me like this? Don't you know I spent fifty thousand dollars for an airplane to fly over here and I didn't expect such a discourteous reception?"

The comment did not disturb me, since Bhutto had earned the diplomatic chastising he had just received. Yet, I thought of the incident years later when Bhutto was brutally confined in a small prison for many months and finally hanged. Two men I have known, former Prime Minister Bhutto and Adnan Menderes of Turkey, have been executed by hanging; a third, whom I regarded as a good friend, former Prime Minister Amir Abbas Hoveida of Iran, was killed by a firing squad. *Sic transit.*

None of us could see the future clearly. Most of us had joined the government when John F. Kennedy was inaugurated. We had worked together closely and harmoniously for almost three years. Now suddenly the climate had drastically changed. The bright promise offered by the young President had suddenly darkened. We felt chilled and apprehensive.

Few of us were well-acquainted with our new leader. As Vice-President, he had been an unhappy, brooding, sometimes irascible man; one had dealt with him carefully but given him only secondary attention. Nothing a Vice-President did was important, yet no one wanted to cross Lyndon Johnson for fear of an eruption. How many of us would stay once we had tested the new leader and he had tested us? No one could say. Some had been so closely identified with JFK as to make an adjustment difficult both for them and for Lyndon Johnson. Certainly, a large component of the top command recruited from Harvard and MIT would be likely to find the new atmosphere less congenial. Could they happily function under a Texan who had made his way by slicing through the political sagebrush with a machete and was burdened by the baggage of regional attitudes and prejudices?

I was by no means sure of my own plans. Though I knew the Vice-President officially—and we had been on friendly terms—I had had no personal relations with him. During my Stevenson years, I had looked on him as a political primitive—tough, effective, yet hardly exuding the liberal democratic values to which I felt committed. Now I could do nothing but watch and wait.

PART VI

The Johnson Years

22. Sailing under a New Skipper

President Kennedy was dead. He had been my friend and then my chief and the shape of the future was now obscure. I thought I had understood Kennedy. He resembled other men I knew well who had gone to good schools, were informed, literate with a wry wit, and had a receptive ear for historical or literary allusions. His being President necessarily imposed a slight barrier between us, but he was friendly and outgoing, and we could talk with the easy assurance that friends enjoy together.

Rapport with Lyndon Johnson did not come so easily. He was of a breed I had known only from literature, legend, or at a distance. As a Stevenson Democrat, I had shared the prevailing stereotype of LBJ as a shrewd political manipulator—an "operator" ready to make a deal even by compromising policies in which I strongly believed. I did not think of him as a "liberal," which for many of us was still the shibboleth of acceptability, but as a Texan and a southerner—with the qualities those two words connoted in the stilted vocabulary of our parochial politics.

I assumed I would never understand Johnson as I had John Kennedy, for he was, as I saw it, a man from a different culture. Lacking the tone and manners one expected of a President—with a breezy Texan tendency to oversimplify and overstate, overpraise and overblame—he would not, I thought, be easy to work with. That I would never fully comprehend him was correct, since he was far more complex than Kennedy and, as I came to perceive him, capable of strengths he did not visibly display and weaknesses he could not effectively conceal. I look back on Lyndon Johnson as both imposing and enigmatic, with abilities as impressive as his imperfections.

Prior to the time he took his oath of office on Air Force One in Dallas, I had had only a few encounters with him, including one momentarily abrasive. Hypersensitively fearful that someone might take him for granted—a concern built into the office of Vice-President—he had at one point protested angrily at what he regarded as my inadequate response to some request (I do not remember what). But when I wrote him a detailed explanation, he seemed completely mollified and apologetic; indeed, he gave me the ultimate accolade—I was, he told me, a "can-do man."

Building a relation of mutual confidence required, among other things, that I be ready to devote more time than I could comfortably spare to listening to his anecdotes and reminiscences. Indulging the occupational habit acquired by politicians from years of *bavardage,* he loved to sit back in his chair and tell long, colorful, Texas stories, or talk about past experiences—often with little relevance to the subject at hand. Though I tried to avoid it, he would sometimes catch me after meetings around the cabinet table and lead me into a tiny room just off the Oval Office that he used as a kind of hideaway. Then, after a long conversation—or more accurately, a soliloquy—he might suggest that I go swimming with him in the White House pool. I unfailingly declined, not only because I swim badly but because I was always hard-pressed for time. The fact that I might have a foreign ambassador waiting in my office seemed of little concern to Lyndon Johnson, and I felt foolish saying, "Mr. President, I just can't do it, I've got meetings and problems I must take care of this afternoon"—which seemed to imply that I was busy while the President was not.

The Vision of LBJ

In time, I gained fuller appreciation—to the point of admiration—for his capacities and qualities. For all of his disarming simplicity of manner, he was a remarkably effective man with extraordinary shrewdness, phenomenal driving force, and an implacable will. He could sometimes be harsh and obdurate, relying more on cunning than subtlety, but he was always kind to me, and in time we developed an affectionate rapport.

Yet in the beginning there was an inevitable sense of constraint. Though Lyndon Johnson tried, so far as possible, to create the appearance of continuity with the Kennedy Administration, the atmosphere perceptibly changed. As the months wore on, the imprimatur of LBJ was stamped on almost everything we did—and on our method of doing it. From the first weeks of his Administration, he concentrated intensely on two almost obsessive objectives: the first was to break loose Kennedy's legislative measures then jammed in the Congressional machinery; the second was to bring into being the so-called Great Society, which represented the essence of all he had dreamed about and worked for during his long career. It is easy to be cynical about many of Lyndon Johnson's attitudes and activities; what the public saw was an earthy man with little skill at concealing often crass political motives and methods. But an equally authentic picture was of a man possessed by a vision and the desire to realize it: the vision of his country freed from poverty and discrimination in which everyone would have an equal chance for an education and a decent living. He really believed in it!

Often, after long and sometimes heated arguments about the all-absorbing mess in Vietnam, he would lean back in his chair at the cabinet table, or lean over to me when we were sitting together in that tiny room by the Oval Office he used for *tête-a-têtes* and expound rhapsodically on the subject dearest to his heart. Then I could feel his overwhelming ambition for his country—an ambition, banal in its exposition yet clearly recognizable as the deeply felt drive of a strong, resourceful leader who concealed under his inurbane exterior a compelling idealism. In part, he was, I suppose, responding to a populism derived from the soil from which he sprang. But, at the same time, he was speaking the words of one who had always felt himself an outsider. He was constantly aware—particularly in the presence of his sophisticated, elegantly educated advisers—that he had acquired his education, such as it was, from the Southwest State Teachers College.

Yet much of his strength lay in his individuality and in the fact that his manners and expressions had not been honed by the debilitating polish of a more self-conscious environment. His speech gained force as an instrument of persuasion by the vividness of his metaphors, since, like all men of elemental eloquence, he spoke in images. He had, he would say, been as busy as a man with one hoe and two rattlesnakes. Or he might describe someone at a meeting as making as much noise as a crazy mule in a tin barn, or dismiss a man with the ultimate language of mistrust: "I'd never go to a water hole with him!" When we were heading into the harsher days of Vietnam his constant advice was that we should "hunker down like a jackass in a rainstorm." He had an endless repertory of anecdotes about Johnson City, Texas, which—discounting the element of epic accumulation at the hands of LBJ—appeared to have been populated by a remarkable collection of authentic American eccentrics. Some of the tales he told over and over were familiar to me from boyhood days, including the touching saga of an old German named Schmidt who was renowned far and wide for his bad humor. Though he had never before been known to smile, Schmidt one day broke into triumphant laughter. Why the unexpected mirth? "Well," he said, "I just found that old Ziegler's been payin' my wife five dollars a night to sleep with her and I can sleep with her for nothin'." Lyndon Johnson always had respect for a favorable deal.

Not only was Lyndon Johnson's language colorful, it was scatological—a habit he shared with John F. Kennedy. That sometimes created a slight problem, since I had inherited a long-established State Department practice of having a secretary take down all telephone conversations. It was a practice well understood throughout the government and eminently useful. During the course of a long conversation, I might make three or four promises: letters I would write, telephone calls I would make, memoranda I would prepare, or instructions I would give my staff. In view of the intense pace of my schedule, I had no time after completing a phone conversation to call my appropriate assistants and debrief them. Instead, I could immediately turn to my next appointment, confident that my conversation would be automatically transcribed and that my chief of staff, George Springsteen, would promptly make sure that my promises were kept. The only problem was that the secretaries who took down my conversations were gently brought up. Thus, conversations with either Presidents Kennedy or Johnson tended to be spotted with asterisks. Fortunately, the girls were not only well-bred, they were also precise; because they included the exact number of asterisks, translation required little imagination.

As a good politician, Johnson thought more in terms of people than ideas and he enjoyed gossip about people. Sometimes he would press me for comments on my colleagues, which I always tried to pass off as blandly as possible. He was neither inhibited nor charitable in his evaluation of his closest associates. One story will illustrate his attitude. He said to me one day, apropos of nothing at all, "George, you know John Connally pretty well, don't you?" "Not well, but I know him," I said. "After all, you sent him down to work with us in the Lend-Lease Administration during the war, and of course we saw one another when he was Secretary of the Navy in Kennedy's day." "Well," he said, "that John's an interesting fellow. He's got a lot goin' for him." Then he paused for a moment and continued, "You know, he'll go far. He'll go almost to the top. He'd go to the top but he lacks one thing and that could destroy him someday. He's sure as hell impressive. He can walk into a room and everybody knows he's there. He knows how to press the flesh and where the bodies are buried. He's a good politician." Then, shaking his head sadly, he repeated, "It's too bad he lacks just one thing."

"What's that?" I asked, but he was not ready yet to lose the effect.

"He's an awful quick study; you give him a memo or a brief and he can get right up and make a powerful speech about it. Sometimes he can be real eloquent. Too bad he lacks just one thing or he could go clear to the top." Again I asked what he meant, and this time he replied. "John Connally doesn't have even the tiniest trace of compassion; he can leave more dead bodies in the field with less remorse than any politician I ever knew, and that'll keep him from the top."

Another pause for effect, while his voice took on a sharp edge, "You know, I can use raw power"—drawing the words out harshly and making a tight fist—"I can use raw power as well as anyone. You've seen me do it, George. But the difference between John and me is that he *loves* it. I *hate* it!"

Perhaps he's right about Connally, I thought—although I didn't really know him well—but, as for LBJ hating to use raw power—on that point, I had grave doubts.

The War with the Press

One trait Kennedy and Johnson had in common and which, I suspect, all modern Presidents inevitably share, was an almost pathological resentment at leaks and press criticism. Kennedy had displayed that resentment early in his Administration by stopping White House subscriptions to the *New York Herald Tribune,* with the implication that it would be disloyal for anyone in the top reaches of government to read a publication so antagonistic to his policies. But that kind of petty gesture was out of character, and when he realized it was making him look ridiculous and juvenile the subscriptions were reinstated. Nevertheless, Kennedy never stopped complaining about the unfairness of the press and the inability of the bureaucracy to keep secrets.

Whenever a leak involved some speculation, discussion, or decision affecting foreign policy, President Kennedy would automatically blame it on the State Department, though we knew one junior White House minion who spouted like a fountain and we suspected that, in at least some cases, the leak came from the President himself. We were fond of repeating the hackneyed aphorism that "the United States government is the only vessel that leaks at the top," and we sometimes speculated that the intemperance of the President's denunciation of the State Department may have been a subconscious mechanism for excusing a nagging sense of culpability that he might have talked a little too freely.

If in their expressed concern over leaks, Johnson and Kennedy reacted with similar high-decibel shrieks, Johnson pushed the marker a little higher by frequently demanding that we bring in the FBI to investigate the source of some newspaper story so we could fire the culprit.[1] Here, President Johnson's odd and almost sinister relations with J. Edgar Hoover came into play. Suspicious, and sometimes vindictive, Johnson was fascinated at the thought of having at his command a man and an institution that knew so much about so many and he relished Hoover's assiduous tale bearing. Some of Hoover's stories and innuendoes were outrageous—including pornographic gossip about other heads of state and chiefs of government. I hated those preposterous canards, since they tended to influence the President's attitudes to the point of distorting policy. Once, after a particularly upsetting leak, the President arranged for Hoover to visit me and advise how we could tighten security in the State Department. As I expected, his counsel was totally fatuous. He indulged in a rambling and seemingly endless monologue so inconsequential and boring that I finally excused myself to take a pretended telephone call in my conference room, then ducked out the back way, instructing my office to apologize to Hoover and explain that I had been called away on an emergency.

The Recurrence of Congo Troubles

Early in the Johnson Administration I again became involved with the Congo—to which I had devoted so much time during the earlier Kennedy period. Responding to the strange convolutions of African politics, Moise Tshombe, the arch secessionist who had tried to lead Katanga away from the central government, now reversed course. Returning to Leopoldville from self-imposed exile in Spain at the request of President Kasavubu, he formed a provisional government of "national unity" on July 5, 1964. Unity was, however, more a hope than a reality. Rebel movements increased in violence throughout the Republic, and particularly in the eastern provinces around Stanleyville. Freed by the withdrawal of the United Nations Security Mission to maneuver as they wished, Tshombe and Mobutu, who headed the army, increased their demands for help and openly recruited white mercenaries to try to put down the swelling insurrections.

The mixed bag of rebels included rural organizers, conspirators exploiting local discontent, and finally a group of Gizenga's former associates in and about Stanleyville who had fled to Communist Brazzaville across the river. There in October 1963, they had formed a National Liberation Committee headed by Christophe Gbenye. Their insurrectionary efforts were assisted by both Moscow and Peking, because, in the Chinese ideological view, they were fighting "a war of national liberation." Besides, had Mao not said "if we can take the Congo, we can hold the whole of Africa"?[2]

Throughout the summer of 1963, I had watched the Congo with increasing uneasiness and had kept closely in touch with Belgium's Foreign Minister, Paul Henri Spaak. The rebel activities were, it appeared, expanding to the point where the Congo national army could no longer contain them. There were mounting threats to American nationals in the area—particularly missionaries, who were perennial headaches because they so often refused to leave an area when warned of danger. The danger increased enormously on August 4, 1964, when the rebels captured Stanleyville. Sentiment quickly built within the State Department for a rescue operation, particularly following many reports of butchery and brutality by the rebel *Simba* ("Lion" in Swahili) warriors. During the course of the rebellion they are said to have executed at least twenty thousand "intellectuals," "counter-revolutionaries," and "American agents."[3] These reports were embellished with gory details of the ritual disembowelment of living persons and the cannibalistic practice of eating their hearts, livers, and genitals while still warm. The fact that the *Simbas* responded largely to witchcraft and sorcery gave a Conradian edge of lunacy to the whole nightmare interlude—particularly because the Congolese Army demanded equal magic protection.

Though the Congolese themselves suffered the most from the conflict,[4] we were confronted, on the fall of Stanleyville, with the searing statistic that three thousand foreign residents of nineteen countries were now held hostage by the rebel *Simbas* and that the responsible rebel leaders were rapidly departing from Stanleyville. Among the hostages were a small number of American missionaries along with the United States consulate staff in Stanleyville, including the American Consul General, Michael Hoyt, and the Vice Consul, David Grinwis. Through the International Red Cross and the Organization of African Unity, we tried by diplomatic palaver to secure the return of the hostages, but the rebels insolently retorted that they would release them only when America had forced the central government in Leopoldville to stop trying to put down the insurrection. Since no compromise seemed possible, the Congolese Army, led by white mercenaries, started a column down the road to recapture Stanleyville.

I found this a dismal period. The rebels were constantly broadcasting that we must halt the column or our own people in Stanleyville would be murdered. Visions of a mass slaughter haunted me day and night like a *cauchemar* that grew worse on awakening. Here, as in the later case of our sailors on the De Soto Patrols in Vietnam, I felt personal responsibility for the lives of identifiable human beings. Though I argued with Secretary McNamara that we should try to impose some restraint on the advancing columns—particularly on their strafing of towns, which seemed most likely to trigger a massacre—he was resolute and undeterred.

During this period, my old friend William Atwood, then our ambassador in Kenya, was negotiating with President Jomo Kenyatta of Kenya, then chairman of the Congo Committee of the Organization of African Unity (OAU), to develop contingency plans for an air drop to rescue the hostages, while we in Washington worked with Brussels (and particularly Foreign Minister Spaak) to coordinate the effort. I had the task of persuading President Johnson to let us use American planes for the operation (code-named Dragon Rouge), although the paratroopers would be Belgian. On November 21, he authorized me to move twelve C-130s up to Kamina, only four hours away from Stanleyville. Since we wanted to synchronize the air drop with the arrival of the advancing columns, we decided on November 22 to hold up the drop for one more day to permit the column of 600 to arrive immediately after the paratroops had landed. It was twenty-four hours of agony heightened by press leaks in London that our planes were on the way. Finally, on November 24, 1964, our twelve US C-130s and 545 Belgian paratroops arrived over Stanleyville at first light (six in the morning), when the *Simbas* were still groggy. Ten C-130s commenced the airdrop, followed by the landing of planes carrying jeeps and supplies and equipped to evacuate the hostages.

The operation, conducted with superb efficiency, lasted five days. On the Monday night before it started, Dean Rusk and I arrived in dinner jackets at the Operations Center of the State Department coming directly from an embassy dinner for the German Foreign Minister. During the next few nights I slept in the State Department, awakened periodically as word trickled in on the progress of the operation. As I had been responsible for persuading the President to let us proceed, I was emotionally involved in its success; I had met the families of some of the American hostages and I could think of them as identifiable individuals whose lives depended on the outcome. If the operation had resulted in a mass killing, I would have always felt haunted: could I have avoided it? Fortunately, we saved more than two thousand foreigners in the Stanleyville and Paulis areas, although another one thousand remained in the remote bush—principally missionaries who refused to be rescued. But we did not save everyone. Almost three hundred white hostages (including about one hundred women and children whom the rebels were holding in the Victoria Hotel) were killed by bullets or spears, including two Americans, one of whom was Dr. Paul Carlson and the other, a female missionary. Carlson, a brave medical missionary, had long been on our minds, since he had been falsely charged by Gbenye with being an American spy. I had particularly wanted to save his life. Later we learned that George Clay, an NBC correspondent, had also been killed.

Two days later the Belgians pressed us to launch another airdrop 240 miles from Stanleyville, near Paulis, which was being used as a collection point for 450 hostages including seven American missionaries. The operation would have to be conducted without benefit of an advancing column. Though Vance, McCone, Rusk, and General Wheeler favored the enterprise, I had great trouble in getting the President to go along. He did not, he told me, want to "get tied in on the Congo and have another Korea or another Vietnam just because of somebody wandering around searching for Jesus Christ." "We made a mistake," he said, "first of all by running the Belgians out and taking the position we did on Tshombe and then embracing him so as to wrap the colonialist flag around us and, by acting unilaterally, have become labeled as aggressive." He resented America's having to provide transport. "Why won't the British or French send their planes?" He was not going to risk another disaster just when we already had so much on our plate. Yet, after exhausting his objections, he let us go ahead on Thursday (Thanksgiving Day) with "Dragon Noir," using a much smaller force—only seven planes and 256 men. For some poor unfortunates, however, the rescue attempt came too late: during the Stanleyville operation, the *Simbas* in Paulis had heard Gbenye's radio broadcast ordering the massacre of all hostages and had murdered twenty-two of their white captives.

Even after the two airdrops were completed, Algeria and Egypt continued to airlift large amounts of Soviet, Chinese, and Czechoslovakian arms to the *Simbas*. However, the insurrection soon began to fall apart, particularly after February 4, 1965, when the chief rebel witch doctor, Mama Onema, was captured and announced that his insurgent clients were running out of magic.

Many years later, during the 444 days that American hostages were held in Teheran, my thoughts kept returning to this incident. Although nothing seemed more ill-conceived and unrealistic than the attempted rescue mission on April 24, 1980, which left the skeletons of four helicopters and the bodies of eight Americans in the Iranian desert, I could still understand the sense of frustration and desperation that led to its launching.

Troubles in the Turbulent Caribbean

Although no crisis in the Johnson Administration carried us to the edge of world catastrophe as had the Cuban Missile Crisis, we still endured periods of tension and excitement. Against the background of a constantly escalating war in Vietnam, our attention was deflected by events in the Caribbean. The first flare-up occurred in Panama, only six weeks after President Johnson's inauguration. Though it did not last long, it briefly consumed our whole attention. I was never surprised that the people of Panama deeply resented the Americans who occupied the Canal Zone. Americans lived there on a scale of affluence contrasting shockingly with that of the Panamanians just over the fence and across the road. I had been acutely aware of this resentment since the Kennedy Administration; for, during my interlude as Under Secretary of State for Economic Affairs, I had been an ex officio member of the board of directors of the Panama Canal Company and in 1961 had attended a directors meeting in the Zone. Appalled by the shameless arrogance that prevailed in this last remaining outpost of American colonialism, I thought it only a matter of months before this small, smoldering volcano would erupt. We could not evade much longer the revision of our whole set of treaty relations with the Panamanians; the existing treaty structure was not merely an anachronism but founded on a maneuver in 1903 that verged on the fraudulent. Unhappily, a small but vocal clique in Congress felt sacredly anointed to preserve the privileged position of the Zone residents and violently waved the flag at any intrusion of equality or realism.

Eighteen months later, in September 1962, I was asked by the Department of Defense to dedicate the first high-level bridge across the Canal. Ruth and I flew to Panama on October 11 for the dedication to be held at 9:30 Friday morning. I had been told that the Panamanians were unhappy, for Congress had foolishly insisted on christening the historic span the Thatcher Ferry Bridge. Who, I asked, was Thatcher? He was, I learned, an old man of ninety who had headed the Canal's Department of Civil Administration from 1910 to 1913. The bridge, the Panamanians quite reasonably insisted, should have been named "The Bridge of the Americas," since it linked the two continents; to name it for a relic of a painful season of American imperialism was an insult. I agreed that the Congress had been guilty of a diplomatic *bêtise*, but no one had briefed me on the intensity of feeling our thoughtlessness had generated.

The next morning, at the appropriate hour, we drove to the bridge in an atmosphere of mounting tension. The band was playing the traditional tunes, but the music was not soothing anyone's savage breast. Moving to my allotted task, I boldly began my speech, but had not finished even the first paragraph when I glanced up to see a seemingly endless mob emerging over the hill just ahead of me. They were quite visibly armed with sticks and guns, and initial encounters showed they would easily push through the police lines.

I made the briefest dedicatory speech in history, clambering back into our car just as the mob surrounded and frantically began trying to overturn it. With considerable *machismo,* our driver pushed slowly through the crowd, and we finally made it back to the embassy residence. Within an hour, the mob had chiseled the bronze name plates off the bridge, eradicating all reference to the venerable bureaucrat Congress had tried to honor, while energetic Panamanian youths had scaled the huge superstructure to implant the flag of Panama.

Intervention on a Small Island

More serious than the events in Panama was our involvement in the Dominican Republic, a small country consisting of the eastern two-thirds of the island of Hispaniola.

Rafael Trujillo, who had oppressed the country for thirty-one years, was assassinated on May 30, 1961. With Trujillo's death, the Administration threw its support behind the most moderate and uncorrupted leader then apparent, Joaquin Balaguer, who had been the nominal President under Trujillo. But, on December 19, 1962, an election resulted—to everyone's surprise—in a two-to-one victory for Juan Bosch, a writer and intellectual who had been in exile ever since 1937. Though he was a rabble-rousing orator, that was the end of his leadership qualifications. I had lunch with Bosch when he came to Washington just before he took office, and I have rarely met a man so unrealistic, arrogant, and erratic. I thought him incapable of running even a small social club, much less a country in turmoil. He did not seem to me a Communist, as some were asserting, but merely a muddle-headed, anti-American pedant committed to unattainable social reforms. He might, I suspected, be easy prey to the machinations of hard-nosed apparatchiks.

In view of Bosch's instability and incapacity as a leader, relations between his government and the United States could not possibly be easy. He became embroiled in a foolish dispute with Haiti that caused us brief concern, and on September 25, 1963, a military group overthrew and exiled him. Led by Colonel Elias Wessin y Wessin, the group was backed by moderate and rightist civilians. Though in terms of principle and precedent, we regretted the coup, none of us, to my knowledge, believed that the Bosch government could have continued much longer without precipitating a national convulsion. The new junta tried to restore fiscal sanity but, in the process, increased unemployment, and discontent spread, particularly among students and intellectuals. The military were growing increasingly disenchanted with the new government's efforts to halt the graft and corruption they had long regarded as their rightful perquisite.

Thus no one was greatly surprised when, in April 1965, a small group of young colonels captured the army chief-of-staff and launched another *golpe.* The leaders of the revolt were a mixed bag, including Bosch supporters, a number of ex-Trujillo associates, some supporters of Dr. Joaquin Balaguer, and some presumed Communist elements. Still, the movement gained substantial support from the disenchanted people, particularly after some of its leaders had seized the national radio and urged the populace into the streets. But rifts developed in the rebel ranks when it became increasingly obvious that the principal instigators of the revolt were planning to recall Juan Bosch. Since he was anathema to the military, elements of the army led by Colonel Wessin launched a counter-revolution.

We had every reason to discourage Bosch's return, but we took no action to prevent his coming back—nor did we even try to keep him from constantly telephoning from American territory in Puerto Rico to incite his supporters at home to do battle. A proxy hero, he declined to return to his native land unless the United States gave him full protection, remaining instead in Puerto Rico.

Our ambassador in the Dominican Republic was Tapley Bennett, a conservative Georgian who instinctively tended to favor the established hierarchy. His basic sympathies were clearly with Colonel Wessin, whose forces appeared initially to have won. Wessin was, however, anything but a bold leader, and when a popular mass effort prevented his tanks from crossing the Duarte Bridge into the center of Santo Domingo, his forces fell back. The pro-Bosch elements seized the police stations and passed out stolen arms. Wessin's counteraction was clearly failing.

Though Ambassador Bennett had been reporting that there were Communists among the rebels (or "constitutionalists" as they were called), that was not the proximate cause for America's initial intervention. We acted to save lives. When the fighting increased, we had instructed the embassy on April 25 to advise authorities on both sides of the conflict that we planned to evacuate Americans and others wishing to leave the country and had requested a cease-fire for that purpose. On Monday, April 26, the embassy asked American civilians to assemble the next day at the Embajador Hotel as a staging point for evacuation.

In the morning of Wednesday, April 28, 1965, we were informed that the government radio, still controlled by the regular armed forces, had announced the formation of a new junta, headed by an air force colonel, Pedro Bartolome Benoit, with the avowed objective of restoring peace and preparing the country for free elections. Benoit promptly approached Ambassador Bennett and asked that we land twelve hundred marines to help restore peace, but Bennett gave him no encouragement, telegraphing Washington that he did not believe the situation yet justified such action.

But Bennett changed his mind almost immediately. While Rusk, McNamara, Mac Bundy, Bill Moyers, and I were meeting with the President in his small retreat off the Oval Office talking principally about Vietnam, someone handed the President a "critic" (highest priority) message. That message from Bennett reported that "American lives are in danger" and "the time has come" for a military rescue. The message stated, as I recall, that some four hundred foreigners, including Americans, who were awaiting evacuation in the polo grounds next to the Embajador Hotel, had now come under gunfire. There was nothing to do but react quickly. Though none of us wanted to repeat history by stationing marines in the Dominican Republic, as America had done from 1916 to 1924, we had no option. Within hours, four hundred marines were ashore without resistance and helicopters were landing on the polo field. During the balance of the day, I was kept busy calling the Latin American ambassadors to advise them of an immediate meeting of the Organization of American States, and, at 7:30 that evening, I attended a meeting in the Cabinet Room to brief the Congressional leadership, who expressed their full assent with what we had done.

Looking back, I have never questioned the wisdom of our initial landing, which was an automatic humanitarian response. What I had failed to anticipate was President Johson's increasing absorption in the Dominican problem, to the point where he assumed the direction of day-to-day policy and became, in effect, the Dominican desk officer. Meetings with him often lasted well into the evening, and J. Edgar Hoover stimulated his excitement by feeding him FBI reports of known Communists claimed to have been seen in the Dominican Republic. Since Hoover's total number was originally only fifty-three (and then raised to seventy-seven), I thought our increasing pouring in of troops was wildly disproportionate. But Johnson was fiercely determined that the Dominican Republic should not become another Cuba and was ready to use almost any means to assure that the Communists did not take over.

At his instructions, key members of the Administration engaged in a great deal of to-ing and fro-ing. Abe Fortas, whom Johnson was within three months to appoint to the Supreme Court, undertook a secret mission to Puerto Rico. Familiar with that island ever since his first involvement as Under Secretary of the Interior under President Roosevelt, he was an intimate friend of Governor Munoz-Marin, who was, in turn, a close friend and adviser of Juan Bosch. In the weeks that followed, we received many telephone calls from "Mr. Davidson" (Fortas's code name, which—for reasons I forget—was later changed to "Mr. Arnold"). My old friend John Bartlow Martin, who had been Kennedy's ambassador to the Dominican Republic, now flew to Santo Domingo to work with Ambassador Bennett and provide the President with an independent judgment; friendly with some of the rebels, he tried unsuccessfully to bring both sides together. Mac Bundy, Tom Mann, Cyrus Vance, and Jack Hood Vaughn (who had succeeded Mann as Assistant Secretary of State for Inter-American Affairs) also went to Santo Domingo, and, in June, that capital was visited by a special three-man committee of the OAS, which included Ambassador Ellsworth Bunker, our OAS ambassador. While there the committee issued a declaration urging free elections, general amnesty, and the creation of a provisional government.

Meanwhile, though the swelling influx of American troops had restored a measure of order, the killing had inevitably left a sour residue of hatred on both sides, which could not be easily dissipated. When a solution was finally worked out and elections held on June 1, 1966, it was, to my mind, almost entirely the result of a extraordinary tour de force by one of America's most brilliant negotiators, Ellsworth Bunker.

Bunker, a soft spoken Vermonter (who could, when roused, curse eloquently) is, in my view, one of the great unsung heroes of modern American diplomacy. I had first known him during my days of law practice when I represented the Cuban sugar industry, and Bunker, a successful industrialist, was the acknowledged statesman of America's sugar refining industry. In the early 1950s, he became ambassador, first to

Argentina, then to Italy, and from 1956 to 1961 to India. In the early days of the Kennedy Administration, he successfully mediated the dispute between the Dutch and the Indonesians over West Irian. By taking a house in the Virginia countryside and installing representatives of the contending nations in opposite wings, he succeeded by patient but forceful pushing, prodding, and persuading to hammer out a settlement. Later he played the same role of mediation in a dispute between Saudi Arabia and Egypt over Yemen. Soon after Lyndon Johnson became President, Ellsworth Bunker was appointed ambassador to the Organization of American States. His first task was to try to resolve the nagging frictions between the United States and Panama, producing sufficient agreement to make possible the restoration of diplomatic relations.

Bunker lived for almost a year in the Dominican Republic in the tawdry rooms of a run-down hotel with each side threatening to kill him. By extraordinary patience, skill, the sheer force of his granite will, and his obvious compassion and integrity, he finally gained the confidence of the conflicting parties; by the time his assignment was ended, he was revered by both sides as a "saint." In the end, he secured agreement for a provisional President and arranged terms for the surrender of the rebel arms. He also convinced the right-wing plotters that Washington would never tolerate another coup. But perhaps his greatest achievement was to make it plain that no matter how badly the Johnson Administration might fear a Castro-influenced government, we would never again support a military junta.

As President Johnson increasingly took over the Dominican crisis, I quietly sought to disengage. As I shall point out later, I was at that time preoccupied with a protracted effort to extricate us from Vietnam and was also dealing with such diverse matters as Cyprus, beef imports, European problems, economic problems with the Third World, and troubles in the Congo.

As I watched events unfold, I felt that the deployment of what finally aggregated twenty-five thousand marines was Texan overkill. Hard pressed in Vietnam, President Johnson was giving excessive weight to the questionable threat posed by a small number of alleged Communists dubiously reported to be in the Dominican Republic. Still, no one raised a protesting voice except Jack Hood Vaughn, who bravely challenged the President at a meeting late one evening and then left the room with an angry exchange when the President rejected his views.

Johnson's reaction could be understood only against the backdrop of Castro's subversion of Cuba which had become a nagging source of worry and mischief; it had produced the Bay of Pigs and the Missile Crisis in the Kennedy Administration. In addition, Johnson's use of excessive power and effort in the Dominican Republic reflected a wider preoccupation. We were just on the verge of committing large numbers of

American combat forces to Vietnam and the President feared that a disaster close to home might lead more Americans to challenge our adventure ten thousand miles away.

Viewed in retrospect, the exaggerated Dominican reaction did little harm. Though it stirred up liberal outrage at the time, such outrage was largely a conditioned reflex; no one could seriously argue that Bosch's return would have made anything but a bigger mess. Our intervention left few permanent scars and, quite unlike Vietnam, produced a relatively benign result. The Balaguer government that finally emerged was, in my view, the best that could have been found, and the fact that since 1965 the Dominican Republic has been relatively free from turbulence and chaos seems to me—if not the proof—at least strong evidence that the pudding was adequately cooked.

De Gaulle Throws a Spanner into NATO

The Dominican affair was a diversion from larger and more dangerous world issues. Since the greatest menace to world peace still lay in the potential expansion of Soviet power, I remained preoccupied with our transatlantic relations, including the good health of NATO. In May 1965, I had flown to London for the ministerial meeting of SEATO (including a dinner with the Queen at Buckingham Palace). France, true to form, had abstained from participating, except by sending an observer—an old friend whom I kept mischievously addressing as "Monsieur le Voyeur." Later I returned to London for the regular meeting of NATO foreign ministers, which was the one occasion that all the foreign ministers normally attended. This time, in view of the Dominican crisis, Rusk proposed that I attend the early sessions; he would arrive for the winding-up. Only technically violating our commitment to the President that one of us would be in the United States at all times, I met Dean Rusk as he arrived in London and immediately took off on his plane for Washington.

That was, I think, the last time the French foreign minister attended a NATO meeting. Because President de Gaulle was growing more and more prickly about transatlantic relations, I decided, with the President's approval, to fly to Paris for a talk with the General about both Vietnam and NATO. Since de Gaulle knew me as his most voluble critic in the American Administration and I had had a long talk with him only a year earlier, he greeted me with a friendly but sly smile. *"Ah, Monsieur Ball, c'est vous encore."* Then, with a sweeping gesture he indicated the chair on which I would sit during our interview: so placed as to give him the maximum advantage of his impressive height. His opening comment was, as always, brief and to the point: *"Monsieur Ball, je vous écoute."*

We quickly concluded a discussion of Southeast Asia, in which he reiterated his by now familiar views about the mistakes we were making, and I raised the question of the emerging problems within the Western alliance. I pointed out that many Europeans—including members of de Gaulle's own government—felt that the United States had come too late into both world wars. Our current commitments for the defense of Europe reflected our belief that an alliance could be effective only if reinforced by a combined or integrated command, common planning, and forces in being. That—and that alone—would give reality to the commitment. Thus, as we saw it, the North Atlantic Treaty and the alliance organization (NATO) were inextricably linked.

De Gaulle then came to the heart of the message he wished me to convey to the President. He stated quite emphatically that France and America must stand together against the Soviet Union, and his government did not intend to break up the alliance. In any event, there would still be a *de facto* understanding for common defense even if no signed treaty existed. But NATO as an organization was separate from the mutual defense commitment and it raised different questions. NATO had not existed at the time the treaty was signed; since then, two major changes had taken place. The first was the development of a Soviet nuclear capability. After that, no one in Europe—or even the United States—could be sure that America would launch a nuclear response in the event of an attack.

The second change had been the transformation of the Western European nations from weakness and dependency to the point where they were now reasserting their national personalities. France could no longer accept the principle of subordination—which was what integration implied—nor could it tolerate control by "foreign authority." Thus, said President de Gaulle, though France would continue to adhere to the alliance, he regarded NATO as no longer suitable; France would withdraw from it. Even the Germans, he thought, were beginning to want an alliance without subordination.

Nor, he suggested, could NATO remain in France, for his country could tolerate no foreign forces on her soil except under French command. The French government was making no proposals now—nor would it make proposals in the future. But it would, at the proper time, lay down conditions in discussions between France and the United States that would not include either Germany or the United Kingdom.

I replied that the United States was not interested in domination but in efficiency and effectiveness. We wanted to assure that the West would be fully defended. History had made it crystal clear that an integrated command was necessary to an effective common defense. The atom bomb had obviously brought about significant changes in modern warfare, and we were anxious to halt its proliferation. But, though the United States would be as disturbed as France by a German national nuclear capability, that did not mean the problem of atomic management could be disregarded. In our view, nations that had historically played a great role in world affairs could not be expected to accept forever a situation in which they had no part in their own nuclear defense. Either we permitted those nations to develop national nuclear systems or we provided some collective approach. That concern had inspired our proposal for a seaborne multilateral nuclear force, and within the next few months we would resume conversations about it. I told de Gaulle that we were prepared to discuss with France any proposed changes that might be made in the NATO organization, but if there were to be such an exchange, it should not be postponed too long—as the present organization could be impaired by unresolved questions.

De Gaulle replied that the efficiency of the alliance would be seriously impaired if some members felt subordinated to others, which was the present situation. So far as the Germans were concerned, he must express a note of precaution. We both knew that the Germans were a "great people," but, just because they were a "great people," no one could tell exactly what they would do. Obviously, Germany could not be accepted with regard to nuclear matters on the same basis as other nations. German participation in the control of atomic weapons, whether partial or direct, would certainly ruin any possible contacts with Soviet Russia or Eastern Europe. France could not forget the past.

I noted our difference in view, pointing out that in the last fifty years, German aggression had been stimulated by German isolation and by a feeling that it was not an equal member of the Western community; I felt that any discrimination or sense of grievance or inequality would play into the hands of demagogues. We should try, in dealing with Germany, to eliminate that sense of discrimination and give the Germans a feeling of equality. We should seek to forestall demands for a German national nuclear system by providing for their participation in some kind of collective nuclear arrangement. That was a concern of the United States, and we certainly hoped to discuss it further with the French government at some future date.

At the end, after thanking me, he observed that "Great powers have to choose between great difficulties. The United States is a very great power, and your choices, therefore, are exceptionally difficult."

I left the meeting impressed with the sensational news I had just heard from de Gaulle. Now, for the first time, the French government had informed us that France planned to withdraw from NATO and expel the organization from its soil. But when I reported this to Washington, few of my colleagues believed that de Gaulle would do exactly what he stated. So, on February 21, 1966, when President de Gaulle told a press conference that France was ending participation in the NATO organization, that all French ground, air, and naval forces would be withdrawn from the NATO command, and that NATO military headquarters and American bases in France would have to be removed, it created greater consternation than should have occurred.

The French action seemed to me to raise a whole set of questions. First, would NATO be badly weakened by France's departure, and where would the organization find a new home? Second, how would Germany react? That remained my abiding concern, since I was determined that we keep Germany facing firmly West and fully integrated in the alliance. I continued to be preoccupied with the implicit inequality of denying Germany a nuclear role; although I was as firm as de Gaulle in believing that Germany must never develop a national nuclear capability, it should otherwise have full equality. Third, I was concerned at the effect of the French move on an effective Western defense. Steeped in the history of the First and Second World Wars, I was aware of the catastrophe caused by the French and British failure to integrate their operations and consolidate their planning under a single command structure. (Monnet had taught me that.) Fourth, I worried about how Congress and American opinion might react to France's withdrawal. Senator Mansfield was strongly pressing for the return of American forces from Europe; anger at de Gaulle might, I feared, strengthen his hand.

In acting imperiously toward NATO, de Gaulle was exploiting the geographical position of France between Germany and the Atlantic. He implied as much when he told me with remarkable candor, "There would still be a de facto understanding for common defense, even if no signed treaty existed." The United States, in other words, would have to defend France in order to defend Germany and Western Europe. That permitted de Gaulle to play a nationalistic game with impunity, knowing that whatever he did, his country would be protected by American power. I found that mischievous and annoying; for, after all, the alliance was sufficiently fragile even without the French flaunting their sovereignty. Other nations, aware of their limited national resources, acknowledged the need to cooperate within both the European Community and the Atlantic alliance.

The Problem of Germany's Role in Europe

Germany remained for me the central point of hope and concern for European security. Not only, as de Gaulle pointed out, was it a nation with a gifted people, capable of great good or evil, but it was also subject to competing forces stemming both from history and its geopolitical position. That later became increasingly apparent with the evolution of *Ostpolitik.* The West Germans needed to establish working relations with the Soviets and Eastern Europe; only thus could they negotiate the return of their countrymen left behind when the Potsdam Conference ceded most of Upper Silesia to Poland or secure arrangements for freeing movement and communication to mitigate the agonies of separation for Germans on both sides of the Iron Curtain.

It was sensitivity to German pride that led me to seek a safe nuclear role for Germany through the Multilateral Force, though in retrospect I probably overemphasized the Germans' desire for a nuclear role and exaggerated the dangers latent in their continued exclusion from the nuclear club. Yet I do not doubt that I was right in pressing for improved relations between Bonn and Washington. Those relations had been prickly but basically firm during the long period of Adenauer's chancellorship. Now Erhard was Chancellor, and he was a different kind of man. Much milder than Adenauer, he was deeply attracted to America and, I thought, unquestionably a good friend. Still, he did not always understand American feelings.

President Johnson, on his part, prided himself on a special understanding of Germans because he had grown up in a German community in West Texas. And, since he liked Erhard both as a German and an individual, he more than once extended what he regarded as a special gesture of friendship by receiving him at his ranch on the Pedernales. That, however, created an awkward problem. The German ambassador told me privately that Erhard was embarrassed in the eyes of the German public, who interpreted the fact that he was not asked to the White House as second-class treatment. How could I explain that to LBJ? For him, the ranch was a far more glorious place than 1600 Pennsylvania Avenue. I finally did manage to get the point across gently, and on his next trip Erhard was invited to Washington rather than Texas.

Politics and Personalities

Even as late as the early decades of this century the friendship of princes, often reinforced by blood ties, was still a powerful factor in shaping the relations between nations—as one realizes on re-reading the famous correspondence between "Willy and Nicky," the German Kaiser and Russian Czar. Today the jet plane and telephone threaten once more to exaggerate the personal element, with the result that all too often the objective assessment of national interests and a larger world strategy are subverted by the complex chemistry of personalities. That injects an aleatory element that makes national decisions hard to predict and sometimes leads to unwise policy. I had seen the process at work during the Nassau Conference when John F. Kennedy had—with little appraisal of longer-range implications—offered the British a whole new generation of nuclear weapons, very largely because of his fondness for Harold Macmillan.

With Lyndon Johnson as President, the personal element played an even more powerful role. He respected de Gaulle as a leader largely because of his presumption, cunning, and imperial style. He incessantly restrained me from making critical comments, even though he could never have taken the General's constant needling from any other foreign leader. Anglo-American relations were tacitly acknowledged to be a class by themselves, but they did not flourish during the Johnson era—largely because the Labor party came in from the cold in October 1964, soon after Johnson's inauguration. LBJ had been impressed with Macmillan, even though he lacked the long personal acquaintance and family friendships that had existed between Macmillan and Kennedy. Harold Wilson, however, lacked Macmillan's consummate ability to deal on a friendly but slightly condescending basis. He wore no patrician armor, was too ordinary, too much like other politicians with whom LBJ had dealt, and Johnson took an almost instant dislike to him. On Wilson's first visit to President Johnson in Washington on December 7, 1964, relations got off to a bad start over the Prime Minister's insistence that his assistant, Marcia Williams, attend highly restricted meetings; she did not, in Johnson's view, have the rank to justify it. Then, as time wore on, Wilson's reluctance to provide a wholehearted endorsement of Johnson's Vietnam adventures and his efforts at diplomatic intervention touched the President's most hypersensitive nerve. Finally, J. Edgar Hoover made a bad situation worse by contributing scurrilous rumors about Wilson's personal character.

What Johnson wanted from foreign political leaders was unquestioning support for the policy about which he was the most uncertain: the Vietnam War. Australian Prime Minister Harold Holt most clearly won Johnson's heart when he publicly shouted, in exchanging first greetings on the White House grounds, "All the way with LBJ." Even though I knew that this rash pronouncement had assured the success of Holt's visit, the statement in that context was, I told my colleague George Springsteen, to be deplored as contributing to the delinquency of a President.

As our involvement in Vietnam lengthened, deepened, and broadened, the Administration's top foreign policy officials—and the President himself—progressively constricted their vision. The metaphor I thought most apt was that of a camera, focused sharply on a small object in the immediate foreground but with no depth of field, so that all other objects were fuzzy and obscure. Still, occasions did arise where the very fact of my colleagues' narrow preoccupation made it possible for me to undertake the management of certain dangerous situations with a relatively free hand so long as they did not directly relate to our Vietnamese agony. Included in this category were, among others, the troubles in a small country in the eastern Mediterranean, Cyprus—a bountiful and beautiful earthly paradise marred only by man's bloody-mindedness to man. My efforts to resolve the Cyprus problem consumed much of my thought and energies for a protracted period.

23. Cyprus

In my State Department office was a large lighted globe. One day in the course of a newspaper interview I pointed to it, saying "You see that globe? I'm going to get rid of the damn thing. When I spin it, I find trouble wherever it stops." It was a passing comment, and I forgot all about it until my interrogator included the comment in his column. A fortnight later I received a letter from a little girl in Kansas: "I read in the paper that you have a lighted globe you're going to get rid of. Could I have it? I'm having trouble with my geography."

A Troubled Island

I did not send the globe. Not only was it government property but I too was having trouble with geography, and particularly with a small island that has been a source of great-power conflict almost from the beginning of history. Strategically located in the eastern Mediterranean, Cyprus has had one absentee landlord after another: first Egypt, then Greece, which colonized the island, then Rome. It has been occupied successively by Richard the Lionhearted, the Templars, the Franks, the Venetians, and the Turks. In 1878, the British acquired it from Turkey in exchange for help in defending the Turks against Russia, and in 1925 the island was declared a British Crown colony.

In addition to its strategic geography, the island is tailor-made for ethnic troubles. Though it lies 40 miles off the Turkish coast and 560 miles from the Greek mainland, roughly 80 percent of its population is of Greek, and less than 20 percent of Turkish, extraction. Even before the Second World War, the mainland Greeks had joined with the Greek Cypriotes in calling for *enosis*—the union of Cyprus with Greece—but both Britain and Turkey rejected that demand. An organization known as EOKA, headed by General George Grivas, began a terror campaign in support of *enosis,* aided by Archbishop Makarios III, the head of the Orthodox Church in Cyprus and the effective leader of the island's Greek community. In March 1956, the British government exiled Makarios to the Seychelles because of his encouragement of EOKA violence, permitting him to return to Greece the following year only after he agreed to call for an end of the terror.

But terror continued until, in 1959, Britain granted independence to Cyprus within a framework of international agreements signed by Greece, Turkey, the United Kingdom, and representatives of the Greek and Turkish communities on Cyprus. Though the agreements—embodied in what became known as the London-Zurich Accords—were an impressive diplomatic tour de force, their provisions, which covered 220 pages, were too complex to be workable. The Cypriote Constitution they established provided, among other things, that the President would always be a Greek Cypriote and the Vice-President, a Turkish Cypriote—with each being able to block any significant action of the other. The same unworkable division applied to the balance of the government and the legislature.

This elaborate effort to maintain an inherently fragile balance was bound to fail, and it failed quickly. In November 1963, Archbishop Makarios, the first President of Cyprus, proposed constitutional revisions that would have destroyed most of the safeguards the Turks had fought to obtain. Warfare broke out between the Greek and Turkish communities; during Christmas week, more than three hundred people were killed.

After the United Nations Security Council had been brought into the peace-keeping process, the Cyprus problem presented the following complexities: first, it threatened to produce an armed conflict between Greece and Turkey; second, it affected the relations of the Greek and Turkish governments with the government of Cyprus; third, it involved Great Britain as one of the guarantor powers with strategic bases on the island; fourth, it affected the relationship of the government of Cyprus to the British Commonwealth, of which it was a member; fifth, it threatened the stability of one flank of our NATO defenses and consequently concerned all NATO partners; sixth, it became an active item in the parliamentary diplomacy practiced in New York; seventh, its instabilities stimulated a new relationship between the government of Cyprus and other nonaligned countries with which it had recently sought to associate itself; and eighth, Archbishop Makarios's flirtations with Moscow threatened to bring about the intrusion of the Soviet Union into the strategic eastern Mediterranean.

Each of these elements bore on the others, and one element often frustrated the effective utilization of others in the search for a solution. On December 24, 1963, the British, Greek, and Turkish governments, as the guarantor powers, appealed to Makarios and other Greek and Turkish Cypriote leaders for a cease-fire. The following day, however, Greek and Turkish forces moved out of their bases in Cyprus, and bloody battles ensued. Unable to persuade the Greek and Turkish commanders to join in three-nation truce patrols, the British undertook their own.

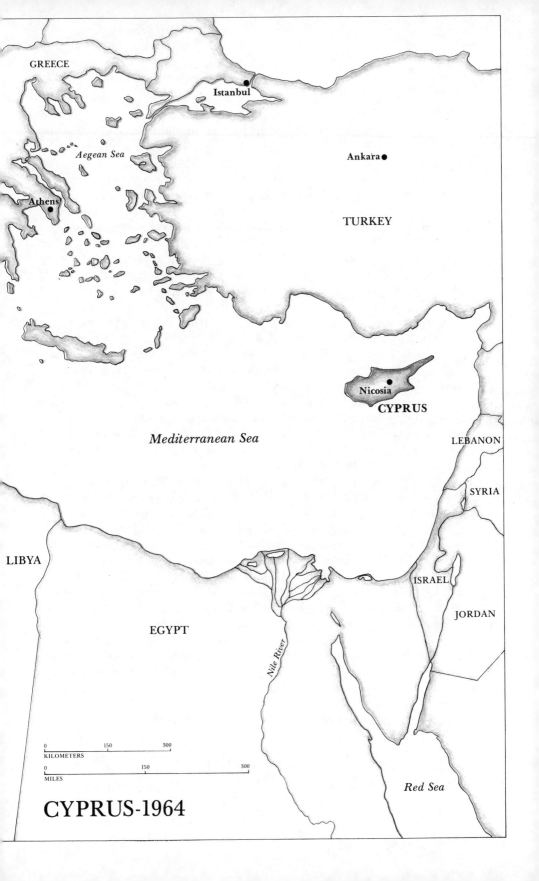

GREECE

Istanbul

Aegean Sea

Ankara

Athens

TURKEY

Nicosia

CYPRUS

Mediterranean Sea

LEBANON

SYRIA

LIBYA

ISRAEL

JORDAN

EGYPT

Nile River

0   150   300
KILOMETERS

0   150   300
MILES

CYPRUS-1964

Red Sea

Threat of Greek-Turkish War

Watching from Washington, we could see that open warfare was imminent. Since the Turkish Cypriote population was suffering the greater casualties, Turkey was on the verge of intervening. To defuse the situation, Sir Duncan Sandys, the British Secretary of State for the Commonwealth and Colonies, proposed a peace plan calling for, among other things, the establishment of a British-controlled neutral zone in Nicosia to keep the two communities apart. Though that temporarily slowed the fighting, the two communities remained at sword's point. The Turkish Cypriotes declared the constitution dead, implying that, since the two communities could not live together, partition was the only solution. Makarios demanded the abolition of the London-Zurich Accords and particularly their provisions for intervention by any of the three guarantor powers.

Cyprus was merely one more step in Britain's painful shedding of empire, and London no longer had the will or the resources to preside over such a quarrel. Thus I was not surprised when, on January 25, 1964, the British ambassador, Sir David Ormsby-Gore, called to tell me that Britain could no longer keep the peace alone and that an international force should be established on Cyprus as soon as possible. Such a force, the ambassador insisted, could be "broadly based" yet limited to detachments from NATO nations. The British needed, most of all, our diplomatic support and a United States contingent with supplies and airlift for the international force.

I stated emphatically that the United States did not want to get involved; we already had far too much on our plate. I was sick at heart at our deepening embroilment in Vietnam; at the same time, we faced mounting troubles in Panama, had an irksome involvement in the Congo, were disputing with the Soviets over Berlin, and foresaw mounting difficulties with Indonesia. But the British were adamant. They would no longer carry the Cyprus burden alone, even though involving the United Nations risked giving the Communist countries leverage in that strategically placed island. The United Nations would dither and the Turks would not wait; tired of continued outrages against Turkish Cypriotes, they would invade. Then we would have a full-scale war between two NATO allies in the eastern Mediterranean. Reports from Ankara were already indicating that the Turks considered their ultimate military intervention as almost inevitable—out of their hands and to be determined by events.

When I discussed the question with our UN ambassador, Adlai Stevenson, he responded with far more heat than I had expected. During the "troubles" he had stayed for three days in Archbishop Makarios's residence and he regarded his former host with total contempt. The Archbishop was, he said, a wicked, unreliable conniver who concealed his venality under the sanctimonious vestments of a religious leader; the only way to deal with Makarios, Stevenson assured me, was by "giving the old bastard absolute hell." In all the years I had known Adlai I had never heard him speak of anyone with such vitriol. "I have sat across the table from that pious looking replica of Jesus Christ," he said, "and if you saw him with his beard shaved and a push-cart, you would recall the old saying that there hasn't been an honest thief since Barabbas."

The United States Becomes Involved

I met with Secretary Robert McNamara at five that afternoon (January 25), and we reviewed the Cyprus problem in all its complexities. Though Bob was as unhappy as I at any broadening of our responsibilities, he was fully aware that an exploding Cyprus could not only endanger our Mediterranean position but undermine the whole southern flank of NATO. I discussed the matter later that evening with President Johnson. His reluctance came through loud and clear, but he quickly grasped the seriousness of the Cyprus problem and directed me to come up with an acceptable solution.

I told Bob McNamara that before committing ourselves to the combined force we should insist on three conditions: that the duration of the force be limited to three months, that the Turks and Greeks agree not to use their unilateral intervention rights for three months, and that they agree on a mediator who was not a representative of any of the guarantor powers but from another NATO European country. Finally, we would insist that the American contingent not exceed twelve hundred men, with the British agreeing to put in four thousand and the balance of ten thousand to come from other European nations. Meanwhile, David Bruce, our astute ambassador in London, was assuring me that we had no option but to participate; otherwise, no other country would take action, and the Turks would inevitably move. That advice was reinforced when, that same day of January 28, 1964, Turkish Prime Minister Ismet Inonu told our ambassador in Ankara, Raymond Hare, that the Turks were going to invade unless we gave them some kind of an answer by the next morning.

In their anxiety to commit us, the British leaked my three conditions to the press prematurely, and I had to deal with an outraged President. Moreover, I was annoyed that Duncan Sandys, without telling me, had on February 3 tried out our Anglo-American proposal for a NATO force on Cypriote Foreign Minister Spyros Kyprianou, who was attending the London conference. When Kyprianou reported our proposal to Nicosia, Makarios rejected it out of hand. If we were to work with the British, actions had to be carefully coordinated without the premature exposure of our thinking.

Meanwhile, violence continued in Cyprus with hostages taken by each side; on February 4, a bomb exploded in our embassy in Nicosia. Since the situation had now reached a critical flash point, we clearly needed someone on the spot not accredited to any one of the five nations actively involved. Thus, on February 8, I flew to London. At the same time, a second level of activity was under way in New York, where Stevenson was valiantly resisting the efforts of the Cypriote ambassador to the United Nations to get a UN force appointed.

At this moment the respective positions of the parties were: The Turkish Cypriotes demanded partition and the right to govern their own community; they also insisted on preserving Turkey's right to intervene under the London-Zurich Accords, since otherwise the Turkish Cypriotes might be wiped out by their Greek Cypriote neighbors, who outnumbered them four to one. The Turkish government in Ankara supported the Turkish Cypriotes, while putting special emphasis on the preservation of Turkey's right to intervene by force. The Greek community on Cyprus wanted union with Greece (*enosis*), but, at least for tactical purposes, was demanding a fully independent Cyprus run by the Greek majority. The Greek government in Athens pressed for *enosis*.

Viewed from Washington, the issues were clear enough. Cyprus was a strategically important piece of real estate at issue between two NATO partners: Greece and Turkey. We needed to keep it under NATO control. The Turks would never give up their intervention rights or be deterred from invading by the interjection of a UN force which they would regard as an instrument of Soviet or Third-World politics and subject to manipulation by Makarios.

My first and most urgent task was to coordinate our activities with the British and make sure that Duncan Sandys did not again act unilaterally. Makarios must be approached in person and not through his foreign minister, who, in his own right, had no authority.

Mission to the Center of Conflict

I had no illusions that I could easily shake Makarios out of his intransigence, but I had to try. If he finally turned us down, I planned to say to the guarantor powers: take the problem to the Security Council but understand that America will supply no component for any UN force. Though I recognized that this might trigger a Turkish invasion, I proposed to tell Makarios that, if he continued to block a solution that would eliminate Turkey's reason for intervening, we would not protect him from a Turkish move.

I made these points to Sandys when we met on February 9, 1964. I told him I was planning to go to Turkey, Greece, and Cyprus and described the strategy I would follow. He and I discussed all the solutions we could think of, including all permutations and combinations that might improve the plan's marketability. Since the President had lent me an airplane, I asked Sandys to make the tour with me, but, presumably out of a desire to limit Britain's responsibility, he declined. Later that same night I saw Cypriote Foreign Minister Kyprianou and tried to sound him out on the Archbishop's real intentions.

I went first to Turkey to meet with Prime Minister Ismet Inonu. I had looked forward to the meeting not only because of its relevance to my mission but because of the Prime Minister's history and personality. Inonu, who in his early life had been known as Ismet Pasha, was a legendary figure. Chief of staff to Kemal Ataturk during the war against the Greeks in the early 1920s, he had taken the name Inonu from a village where he won two battles. Serving as Turkey's first Prime Minister from 1923 to 1937 and then, after Ataturk's death, as its President from 1938 to 1950, he had led in transforming Turkey into a modern state. Now at eighty, once again Prime Minister, he provided stability and strength to a nation beset with troubles.

A small wiry man, Inonu's quiet voice projected force and conviction. He did not try to conceal his deep worry about the direction of events on Cyprus. We must, he insisted, move swiftly; Turkish patience was running out. Given the excited state of public opinion, any overnight flare-up of killing on the island might force the Turkish military to intervene. Turkey would, of course, have an overwhelming military advantage. Not only was it far larger and better armed than Greece, but Cyprus was outside the range of Greek fighter planes. As I expected, Inonu was as direct in his approach as Makarios was devious. So long as nothing was done to impair Turkey's right of intervention to protect the Turkish Cypriote population, the Turkish government was prepared to go along with the Anglo-American proposal for a NATO force.

If I felt reassured that Turkey had a strong and responsible government, Greece had no government at all. Prime Minister Konstantinos Karamanlis had resigned the year before, when King Paul had rejected his advice, and, since then, there had been a succession of caretaker governments. Though the caretaker Prime Minister, Ionnis Paraskevopoulos, received me courteously, he could make no commitments, saying only that the Greek government would probably approve any plan first approved by Makarios.

Meetings with His Beatitude

I arrived to find Nicosia an armed camp with barbed wire demarcating a so-called "green line" separating the Greek and Turkish communities. Access from one zone to another was restricted to designated check points. Jeeps containing British forces with tommy guns and Cypriote police roamed the area and patrolled the neutral zone that lay between the separate rolls of barbed wire.

On my first meeting with His Beatitude (as Archbishop Makarios was addressed) on February 12, I was accompanied by Joseph Sisco, the Assistant Secretary of State for International Organization Affairs; his deputy, Jack Jernagan; and Frazer Wilkins, the United States Ambassador to Cyprus. British interests were brilliantly represented by Sir Cyril Pickard, Assistant Under Secretary of State for the Commonwealth Relations Office, who was, at the time, Acting High Commissioner for Cyprus. Makarios received us on the porch of his residence, formerly the residence of the British colonial governor. Resplendent in the full regalia of his ecclesiastical office, he wore a tall black head-covering with a mantia in the rear, while about his neck was a gold chain, from which depended a large medallion known as a *panagia*. It contained a representation of Christ holding a book in his left hand while the fingers of the right hand were frozen in the gesture of giving blessing. Resting on the Archbishop's chest, the medallion symbolized a "confessor from the heart" to remind the wearer that he was always to have God in his heart. I saw few signs of that in the days that followed.

After the traditional tiresome pleasantries, the Archbishop led us to his study, where he went through an astonishing striptease, removing his gold chain, his head covering, and his robes until reduced to shirt sleeves. Newspaper pictures of the Archbishop, with his beard and clerical trappings, had given me an impression of a venerable ecclesiastic. Now I found myself facing a tough, cynical man of fifty-one, far more suited to temporal command than spiritual inspiration. (As I commented later to President Johnson, "He must be cheating about his age; no one could acquire so much guile in only fifty-one years.") Since he had spent some months in a seminary near Boston, he spoke only slightly accented English, and his conversation was marked by a whimsical, often macabre humor that both amused and appalled me. Of medium height, with eyes that peered through narrow eyelids, he seemed about to relish the fencing match in which we were to engage.

Our morning meeting was relatively calm and uneventful. As we explained our respective positions, Makarios gave nothing away. When we parted for lunch, he carefully rerobed, putting on all his paraphernalia for the photographers who assaulted us on the porch; when we returned for our afternoon meeting, he once again repeated his striptease.

I can describe the afternoon session only as "bloody." The Archbishop was unrelenting in repeating a litany he knew I would never accept. The whole matter must be submitted to the UN Security Council; and the United Nations must guarantee the political independence and territorial integrity of Cyprus. That meant, as I told my British colleague later, that Makarios's central interest was to block off Turkish intervention so that he and his Greek Cypriotes could go on happily massacring Turkish Cypriotes. Obviously we would never permit that.

Much to my delight, my British colleague, Sir Cyril Pickard, proved tough and resourceful. In the great tradition of British proconsuls, he was deeply dedicated to stopping the wanton killing and returning peace to the island. Nor did he bother with diplomatic *politesse* in expressing his contempt for the bloody-mindedness that Makarios and his government were displaying. After Pickard had denounced the Archbishop in devastating language for the outrages inflicted on the Turkish Cypriotes, I spent the next forty-five minutes telling off Makarios and his ministers. I spoke, as I telegraphed the President that night, "in a fashion remote from diplomatic exchanges," describing in lurid detail the consequences if he persisted in his cruel and reckless conduct. The Turks, I said, would inevitably invade, and neither the United States nor any other Western power would raise a finger to stop them. Though Makarios tried to conceal his discomfiture, I had the odd feeling as we left the room that, as I reported to the President, "even his beard seemed pale."

That night I conversed with the President and Secretary Rusk through the scrambled—and hence secure—teletype in the embassy, telling them that, in my view, a blow-up was exceedingly possible and that overwhelming pressure must be brought on Makarios "to frighten him sufficiently to consider some move to halt the killing."

Cyprus Anecdotes

Three or four vignettes of my Cyprus days stand out sharply in my memory. A massacre took place in Limassol on the south coast in which, as I recall, about fifty Turkish Cypriotes were killed—in some cases by bulldozers crushing their flimsy houses. As Makarios and I walked out of the meeting together on the second day, I said to him sharply that such beastly actions had to stop, that the previous night's affair was intolerable, and that he must halt the violence. With amused tolerance, he replied, "But, Mr. Secretary, the Greeks and Turks have lived together for two thousand years on this island and there have always been occasional incidents; we are quite used to this." I was furious at such a bland reply. "Your Beatitude," I said, "I've been trying for the last two days to make the simple point that this is not the Middle Ages but the latter part of the twentieth century. The world's not going to stand idly by and let you turn this beautiful little island into your private abattoir." Instead of the outburst I had expected, he said quietly, with a sad smile, "Oh, you're a hard man, Mr. Secretary, a very hard man!"

At another point in our conversation on the second day, I spoke so heatedly at his apparent indifference to bloodshed that I heard myself saying, "For Christ's sake, Your Beatitude, you can't do that!"—realizing as I spoke that it was scarcely an appropriate diplomatic reply, even to an irreligious ecclesiastic. Also on the second day, when we sat down around the table, he said, with obvious amusement, "I know you're a famous lawyer, Mr. Secretary. Mr. Spyros Kyprianou, my Foreign Minister, is also a lawyer and so is Mr. Glafkos Clerides, my Minister of Justice." Then he added with a chuckle, "I think I must be the only layman in the room."

On the third day—and final morning—the Archbishop and I had a quiet talk alone in his study. Rather whimsically, he said, "I like you, Mr. Secretary, you speak candidly and I respect that. It's too bad we couldn't have met under happier circumstances. Then, I'm sure, we could have been friends." A brief pause and then he said, "We've talked about many things and we've been frank with one another. I think it right to say that we've developed a considerable rapport. Yet there's one thing I haven't asked you and I don't know whether I should or not, but I shall anyway. Do you think I should be killed by the Turks or the Greeks? Better by the Greeks, wouldn't you think?"

"Well," I replied, "I agree that we've talked frankly to one another about many things and that we have established a rapport. But as to the matter you've just raised with me, Your Beatitude, that's your problem!"

One final incident during my stay in Cyprus sticks in my mind. Quite by accident while I was in Cyprus, British Prime Minister Sir Alec Douglas-Home, and British Foreign Secretary "Rab" Butler, were paying a working visit to President Johnson. Each night I carried on a long teletype conversation directly with them and Secretary Rusk. Late in the night of the second day, I teletyped that I wanted to make one final effort to get the Archbishop in line by offering a new variant of our proposal. After discussion back and forth in which both the President and Prime Minister took part, I received their blessing to go ahead. The next day, I played my final card but still could not budge Makarios. I sent a message around the diplomatic circuit advising of what I had done and received an angry rocket from Duncan Sandys, vehemently complaining that I had put forward a proposal that differed from those on which he and I had agreed. "I hope," he wired, "that such conduct will not be repeated." Apparently he was still smarting because I had rebuked him when he had put our proposals prematurely to Kyprianou.

I replied with a personal message that he had no basis for a sense of outrage. The proposal I made to His Beatitude was, I wrote, approved by the President of the United States and the Prime Minister of Great Britain, adding, "Should I seek higher authority?" Sandys replied promptly with a message apologizing for the "misunderstanding" and inviting me to lunch with him at his house Sunday in London. It was a pleasant lunch, and he and I have remained friends to this day.

Continued Efforts to Avoid Disaster

Convinced that only time and events could shake the Archbishop, I flew back to Ankara to see Inonu and tell the Turks that we had not given up; in going forward through UN channels we would make sure that the United Nations took no action derogating from their intervention rights under the Accords. Inonu reluctantly agreed but emphasized that if there were further serious violence on the island, Turkey would no longer stand still.

On the night of February 14, I flew to London intending to meet with my British colleagues the next morning. Because the embassy residence was filled with other visitors, my staff and I were housed in a West End hotel, the Grosvenor House. I was tired and disheartened— so deeply concerned at the danger of an imminent Greek-Turkish war that I could not sleep. After several hours of fretting over the problem, I devised one last card to be played. At three in the morning, I aroused my staff and began to dictate. By six o'clock, with a draft in shape for final typing, I decided to walk over to the chancery and get ready for the day. On the way, I bought a copy of the *Telegraph*, which had my picture on the front page. When I reached the chancery, the marine guard refused to admit me. "You claim to be the Under Secretary of State, but how do I know?" Inspired, I showed him a copy of the newspaper. It proved an adequate *laissez-passer*.

I promptly telegraphed the President advising him of my proposal, which, I said, I was putting to the British solely as an idea of my own that did not in any way represent the views of my government. Makarios, I argued, would never agree to a peace-keeping force even half-way adequate to do the job, and, "if he does agree, it will only be after the Cypriotes have exhausted all pettifogging possibilities to try to get the Security Council to nullify the Turks' rights of intervention." "The Greek Cypriotes," I wrote, "do not want a peace-keeping force; they just want to be left alone to kill Turkish Cypriotes." Meanwhile, I emphasized, the Turks would not wait for a protracted Security Council hassle.

My new plan sought to create a peace-keeping force not requiring the consent of the Makarios government. To do that, the three guarantor powers—Britain, Greece, and Turkey— should take joint action to exercise the rights of intervention provided by the London-Zurich Accords. They should move forces into Cyprus simultaneously. Those forces would be broken into small units that would be billeted together. All patrols would be organized on the pattern followed in Vienna during the four-power occupation after World War II—only this time, three, rather than four, men in a jeep—and all operations would be conducted together. The force would stay in Cyprus until an effective international force, within the framework of the United Nations, had not only been created but was actually on the ground, or until a political settlement had "been reached and translated into a viable organic document."

There were, as I saw it, a number of advantages to the scheme. It would assure the Turks that their Cypriote community was protected while the UN proceedings plodded their weary way. It would avoid any suggestion of a partition and discourage communal massacres, since members of the two communities would not have to fear the intervention of a hostile force. The three powers could answer international criticism on the ground that they were acting under the terms of the treaty.

If the British went along with my scheme, I had no doubt that Inonu would accept it. But the British wanted above all to divest themselves of responsibility for Cyprus; my scheme would reinject them into the mess. As a result, I returned to the United States without anything clearly in place to stop the war.

Falling Back on the United Nations

When I reported to the President, he agreed that the United States had gone as far as we should to try to deflect a tribal conflict. Now our only available course was to work through the United Nations. On February 15, Britain and Cyprus requested an emergency session of the Security Council, and the debate opened on February 18. For the time being, the day-to-day action shifted largely to Ambassador Adlai Stevenson, although I retained the overall direction of strategy.

There is no point in recounting the wearisome maneuvering that went on during the UN proceedings. We wanted to install a UN force as quickly as possible, while assuring that the resolution did not nullify the intervention rights of the guarantor powers, since the Turks would not stand still for that. We sought also to keep the Soviet Union as far as possible out of the action.

After masterful politicking by Stevenson and our UN mission, the Security Council, on March 5, resolved to create a peace-keeping force and provided for the appointment of a mediator. Though we hailed the resolution as avoiding the immediate danger of a blow-up, none of us saw it as more than a temporary respite. The parties most directly interested interpreted the resolution in opposite ways: Makarios regarded it as foreclosing the Turkish right to intervene; the Turks saw it as preserving their intervention rights.

Weakness of Greek Government

Meanwhile, Greek politics took a discouraging turn, when, on February 19, seventy-six-year-old George Papandreou won a landslide victory. As head of the Center Union party, he had been in the opposition for half a century; he knew how to oppose but had neither taste nor talent for positive action. A hopelessly weak leader, he found it expedient to play along with Makarios and the advocates of *enosis*. To a large extent, as I saw it, he was under the influence of his son, Andreas Papandreou, for many years a professor of economics in several American universities, who was trying to gain a foothold in Greek politics by playing closely with the Communist bloc. Oddly enough, in spite of his venomously anti-American line, many of my American academic friends still defended him as an "old boy" former member of the professors' club.

Greece was seized with a spasm of anti-British and anti-American frenzy; our embassy in Athens was subjected to mass demonstrations, our Information Office windows smashed and pictures of Lyndon Johnson burned. The President telephoned me almost plaintively to ask "Why are those Greeks burning my picture?" as though he thought it a highly personal affront. Apart from injured feelings, he worried that such incidents might alienate the Greek-American vote in the forthcoming November elections.

Threat of Turkish Action

On March 13, the Turkish government announced that unless fighting on the island ceased, it would intervene immediately, and the United Press news ticker reported that Inonu had given the interested nations twenty-four hours to reply before he attacked. Meanwhile, Canada, which offered the best hope of providing peace-keeping troops, refused to move until assured that some other country would also contribute units. We put Stockholm under great pressure, and right after lunch I reported to the President that the Swedes would announce that afternoon that they would send a force to Cyprus. The plan was to notify the Canadians, whose parliament was meeting at 2:30, so Canadian troops could be in the air within the next twelve hours.

With that assurance, the Turkish government withdrew its *démarche*. A Finnish diplomat, Sakari S. Tuomioja, was appointed UN mediator, and within a few days, the UN peace-keeping force seemed on the way toward restoring order. Meanwhile, I enlisted Dean Acheson to undertake quiet mediation, primarily between Athens and Ankara. Not only was he a brilliantly skillful negotiator but he had personal prestige in the two capitals because of his central role in formulating the Truman Doctrine when the United States first came to the defense of Greece and Turkey in 1947. I called Acheson at his home in Washington on February 27; he came to lunch the following day, and I found him willing to consider a mission that would inevitably be complex, frustrating, and of indefinite duration. He knew the high stakes involved, because he fully understood the importance of stability on NATO's southern flank.

In spite of the arrival of the UN force, fighting again broke out. On April 13, Prime Minister Papandreou of Greece mischievously announced a campaign for self-determination for Cyprus, which would, of course, mean turning the island over to the Greek Cypriotes. When the UN mediator, Ambassador Tuomioja, returned in discouragement from talks with Greek, Turkish and Cypriote leaders, Secretary-General U Thant put forward his own peace plan. He also appointed an ex-President of Ecuador, Galo-Plaza Lasso, to undertake direct negotiations with the leaders of the two communities. Using the logic-chopping for which the UN is notorious, he distinguished Galo-Plaza's duties from those of Tuomioja on the grounds that Galo-Plaza would seek to restore order while Tuomioja sought a long-term solution.

Forestalling an Imminent Invasion

On Tuesday, June 2, Ruth and I were hosts at a reception for Prime Minister Eshkol of Israel and his wife. With Secretary Rusk in New Delhi for the funeral of Prime Minister Nehru, I was Acting Secretary. That night we received a "critic" message from our ambassador in Ankara, Raymond Hare, that the Turkish Security Council had decided to invade Cyprus. Turkish forces were already deployed in the Iskenderun area with the mission of establishing a "political and military beachhead" on Cyprus. By such a show of force, the Turks hoped to negotiate a satisfactory settlement.

The news came at an extremely awkward time. I was scheduled to leave the following evening—June 4—for a meeting with President de Gaulle in Paris, then go on for a Cyprus discussion with the British on Monday ending my trip at the closing sessions of the UNCTAD Conference in Geneva. Secretary Rusk returned on the morning of June 4 and undertook to prepare a message for the President to send Inonu, which, it was agreed, I would review before departing at 7:30 that evening. When I saw Rusk before leaving for the airport, he showed me a draft on which he was still working. "That," I said, "is the most brutal diplomatic note I have ever seen." Indeed, the Secretary, aided by Assistant Secretary of State Harlan Cleveland and his deputy, Joseph Sisco, had produced the diplomatic equivalent of an atomic bomb. "I think that may stop Inonu from invading," I said, "but I don't know how we'll ever get him down off the ceiling after that." The Secretary looked at me with a sweet smile. "That'll be your problem," he said. The letter stated,

I wish to emphasize in fullest friendship and frankness that I do not consider such course of action [a Cyprus invasion] by Turkey, fraught with such far-reaching consequences, as consistent with the commitment of your government to consult fully in advance with us. . . .

Ambassador Hare has indicated that you have postponed decision for a few hours in order to obtain my views. I put it to you personally whether you really believe it is appropriate for your government, in effect, to present a unilateral decision of such consequences to an ally who has demonstrated such staunch support over the years as has the United States for Turkey. I must, therefore, urge you to accept the responsibility for complete consultation with the United States before any such action is taken.

Turkish military intervention, the letter continued, would lead to a clash with Greece. It would cause violent repercussions in the United Nations and wreck any hope of UN assistance in settling the island crisis.[1] It would "lead to the slaughter of tens of thousands of Turkish Cypriotes." The letter continued,

I hope you will understand that your NATO allies have not had a chance to consider whether they have an obligation to protect Turkey against the Soviet Union if Turkey takes a step which results in Soviet intervention, without the full consent and understanding of its NATO allies.

And unless I can have your assurance that you will not take such action without further and fullest consultation, I cannot accept your injunction to Ambassador Hare of secrecy, and I must immediately ask for emergency meetings of the NATO Council and the UN Security Council. . . .

We have considered you as a great ally with fundamental common interests. Your security and prosperity have been the deep concern of the American people, and we have expressed that concern in the most practical terms. We and you fought together to resist the ambitions of the Communist world revolution. This solidarity has meant a great deal to us, and I would hope it means a great deal to your government and your people.

We have no intention of lending any support to any solution of Cyprus which endangers the Turkish Cypriote community. We have not been able to find a final solution because this is, admittedly, one of the most complex problems on earth. But I wish to assure you that we have been deeply concerned about the interests of Turkey and the Turkish Cypriotes and will remain so.

You have your responsibilities as chief of the government of Turkey; I also have mine as President of the United States.

You may consider that what I have said is much too severe and that we are disregardful of Turkish interests in the Cyprus situation. I should like to assure you this is not the case. We have exerted ourselves privately and publicly to assure the safety of the Turkish Cypriotes and insist that a final solution of the Cyprus problem should rest on the consent of the parties most directly concerned. It is possible you feel in Ankara the United States has not been sufficiently active in your behalf. But surely you know that our policy has caused the liveliest resentment in Athens, and has led to a basic alienation between the United States and Makarios.[2]

Because this was certain to create an explosion in Ankara, I discussed with Secretary Rusk the desirability of my going straight to Ankara, but we agreed it would be awkward for me to break my appointment the next day with President de Gaulle. During the night, I telephoned to

Washington once or twice from my plane to see if there had been any second thoughts.

After a long visit with de Gaulle I went on to London for a meeting on Monday with the British Foreign Secretary during which we discussed Cyprus, among other things. Then I flew to Geneva to address the UNCTAD Conference, which was just winding up three months of meetings with nothing accomplished. After my speech on Wednesday night, Dean Rusk telephoned to tell me that the President was worried about Cyprus and thought more should be done; Rusk would call me later. I knew we had arranged for General Lemnitzer to fly to Ankara as soon as we received the news of the impending invasion and I had learned that, after receiving the President's letter, Inonu had indefinitely postponed the invasion. But I was worried about the wounded state of our relations with the Turks.

Since I had been in my hotel at the time of Rusk's first call and we thus did not have a secure line, we could not speak freely. About 4:30 A.M., the embassy called to say that the Secretary wanted to communicate with me on the chancery's scrambled teletype, which was secure. For about ninety minutes we carried on a teletype conversation. Between exchanges, I contrived a wink or two of sleep. At the end, we concluded that, in view of the Turks' anger and sense of betrayal, I should go straight away to see Inonu. Standing by was a KC-135, the tanker version of a 707, that had been fitted with what we referred to as "McNamara kits" (temporary berths that could be installed on eight hours notice). My staff somehow found the pilot and at about 6:30 he came to the telex room, where I was stretched out on a couch. I told him we were going to Athens and then on to Ankara. He looked at a map on the wall of the room and asked rather quizzically, "Just where the hell is Athens?" When I queried him further, he said he thought he could find it; he and his co-pilot did not need any further crew or supplies. We took off from Geneva at 3:45 that afternoon and I met with Prime Minister Papandreou in Athens at seven. I did not expect much to come from that session and nothing did. He lacked the force to make hard decisions and the meeting confirmed my belief that he would be of little use in solving the Cyprus headache.

Still I tried hard to force him to face the reality of Greece's predicament. Cyprus had become a major threat to the peace of the world, and Greece had considerable responsibility for what had happened. Too much time had already been wasted. Now the matter must be settled definitively. I told Papandreou that I had talked not only with the British but with General de Gaulle, had taken soundings of the opinion of most of the NATO countries, and had found everywhere "a common anxiety to see the problem resolved rapidly." I then told Papandreou of the letter President Johnson had sent to Inonu, of which Papandreou had not heard. I left little room for nuances. This time disaster had been avoided only by the President's forceful intervention and his adamant insistence that there be no war between NATO allies. But, if Greece did not show greater cooperation, we would not take such a hard line again.

Papandreou seemed old, tired, and incapable of facing reality. The time, he maintained, was not propitious for a Cyprus settlement. That, I said, was completely wrong. Greece, he maintained, needed a Cyprus solution based on *enosis*. That, I replied, was total fantasy; Turkey would never accept it and Turkey was not only larger and militarily stronger than Greece but had a major logistical advantage in any conflict over Cyprus. Papandreou then contended that the "turbulence" over Cyprus resulted only from Turkey's invasion threats. I told him that, though I had heard all that before, it simply was not true. He was, I felt sure, too well acquainted with philosophy to believe such a simplistic explanation of a complex problem of causality. He knew better than to think that in attacking the Turkish minority, the Greek Cypriotes were merely responding to a fear of external intervention.

When I pressed him to undertake talks with Inonu, he shied away. Against all the evidence, he still seemed to assume that Greece could pursue its goal of *enosis* without danger of the Turks invading Cyprus, since he apparently took it for granted that the United States would always stand ready to thwart the Turks. Though I tried to convince him that that was dangerous nonsense, he seemed too feeble to grasp a fresh idea.

Before leaving, I asked Papandreou to visit President Johnson and he accepted, but we did not discuss dates. Although I was disappointed by his obtuseness, I did find his attitude toward Makarios more realistic. The Archbishop had, I gathered, alarmed responsible Greek opinion by his "flirtations with Moscow and Khrushchev." He had, Papandreou suggested, been a nuisance during the Cyprus crisis, and he implied that the Archbishop might be excluded from any negotiations aimed at settling it, which, of course, was exactly what I had in mind. Moreover, Papandreou acknowledged that other nations besides Greece and Turkey had an interest in peaceful settlement; the "major powers," he said, "must take a hand."

Meeting with Inonu

I left Athens late that night and arrived in Ankara about two in the morning. Before going to bed, I was briefed by our ambassador, Raymond Hare. An astute and experienced professional diplomat, he reported a conversation with a high Turkish official who had said, "We understand why it may have been necessary to administer a bitter pill, but we cannot understand why it had to have a bitter coating as well."

I was to meet with Foreign Minister Feridun Cemal Erkin at 9:00 A.M.; I was not looking forward to the appointment.

I liked the foreign minister; he was an experienced diplomat who could see the problem in its larger global context, but it was his job to express the views of his government and of the Turkish people at the sudden freshet of ice water we had dumped on them. I did my best but reserved my most effective arguments for Prime Minister Inonu.

Inonu received me correctly but was far more reserved than when we had met previously. He was deeply troubled and personally hurt by the scolding he had received from the President. I reassured him regarding the warmth of America's friendship for Turkey and our desire to cooperate closely with the Turks in resolving a festering quarrel that could result in a major war. America, I told him, was not partial to the Greek side; indeed, we recognized that the Greek Cypriote majority had largely created the problem by terrorizing the Turkish Cypriotes. I made clear that we totally mistrusted Makarios. I then described in detail my talk with Papandreou and my disappointment that I had not persuaded him to stop calling for *enosis,* emphasizing the significance of what I took to be Papandreou's own increasing disenchantment with Makarios and his indication that Makarios need not be included in any negotiations. The Greek government, at long last, I said, is beginning to recognize that Makarios is an enemy of its longer-range interests.

Prime Minister Inonu replied in measured tones; my visit, I thought, had somewhat mollified him, and he seemed particularly interested in what I had just told him. America's attempt to promote a settlement based on strong principles was, he agreed, an encouraging development, but experience had shown that principles are sometimes abandoned when the time comes to translate them into concrete measures. He did, however, concede that, if I were correct in my appraisal of Papandreou's changed attitude towards Makarios, that was one of "the first rays of light in the dark situation."

After the meeting, Inonu took me aside to say that President Johnson's letter had, as he saw it, included "all the juridical thunderbolts that could be assembled. As a result, of course, he committed some errors and said some unjust things. Our foreign office will have to answer the thunderbolts." I interpreted this as reflecting Inonu's desire to warn us not to take their counter-reaction so seriously as to prejudice longer-term relations. We had unquestionably said harsh things to the Turkish government; as a matter of self-respect, they would have to say harsh things back. But we should not let that interfere with the friendship essential to both of us.

I was airborne again at 12:30, and I asked the pilot to take us nonstop to Washington, where we arrived at 5:30 that afternoon. During the entire thirteen hours, I dictated steadily to two secretaries and, by the time I arrived in Washington, I had a memorandum ready for the

President that not only gave a full report of my trip but recommended that he immediately invite first Inonu and then Papandreou to Washington. Our only hope of a settlement now lay in bringing those two leaders together, so that they could reach an understanding that did not involve Makarios. If the President worked each of them over separately, we might be able to bring that about.

I was met at Andrews Field and taken directly to the President. It was June 11, 1964, when I returned to Washington. Within a few hours, we had invited Prime Minister Inonu to visit on June 22 and Prime Minister Papandreou, on June 24.

Visits of Two Prime Ministers

The two visits took place on schedule. As I expected, the President greatly liked Prime Minister Inonu, with whom he could talk straightforwardly. If the Greek leader had shown anything like the same understanding, serious progress could have been made. But, as I had feared, the Papandreou visit came to little. Though we took the Greek Prime Minister to Mount Vernon on the President's launch, the *Sequoia,* and the President, Dean Acheson, and I all pushed him hard, he remained unresponsive. We were dealing with two old men. Though Inonu was at the time eighty-one years old and Papandreou seventy-seven, Inonu, with his brilliant past, seemed far the younger. Papandreou gave the appearance of flaccidity: a tired, slightly befuddled old man who could only repeat the banal slogans he had inherited when he took office and who seemed incapable of comprehending the larger issues.

The joint communiqué President Johnson and Prime Minister Inonu issued on June 23 had stated that the discussions proceeded from "the present binding effects of existing treaties." Now Papandreou, in a press conference, contradicted that assertion. The 1959 London-Zurich Accords were, he said, no longer valid. Greece supported independence for Cyprus and its right to self-determination. It would not negotiate directly with the Turkish government because "no one is more competent to do that than the United Nations mediator."

Acheson Tries his Hand

Although Dean Acheson had for some time been helping me review all possible settlement plans, the time had now come to bring him directly into the negotiations so we could have a strong, forceful, and resourceful representative concentrating on the problem. I, therefore, suggested to Secretary-General U Thant of the United Nations on June 26 that the Greek and Turkish representatives be asked to meet with Acheson, who, I said, was almost a legendary figure in Greece and Turkey.

As I feared, U Thant resisted the proposal on jurisdictional grounds, since it implied that the United States might be taking the diplomatic initiative away from the United Nations. If we were to have such a meeting, it should certainly not be in America. Why not Geneva? Though I expressed reluctance, I had already thought of Geneva as a fall-back.

But his next stipulation was not so easy to accept. It would be necessary, he insisted, that UN Mediator Tuomioja, rather than Acheson, ask the Greek and Turkish representatives to meet with him at Geneva. When I protested that nothing could be accomplished without the presence of American authority represented by Acheson, he conceded that Acheson could establish himself near the site of the negotiations to be consulted to the extent that any of the participants wished. Though I protested that that was not a practical arrangement, U Thant showed the kind of Burmese stubbornness I had seen on other occasions. He feared a possible Soviet charge that the United States had taken over the negotiations and did not wish to give Makarios a basis for insisting that his government be represented at the Geneva talks.

I reported to the President that we would probably have to make do with this awkward improvisation; otherwise, the Secretary-General would refuse UN sponsorship, and the Greeks would never participate. Even in the wings, Acheson was such a strong personality that he could make his views felt.

I then met with Prime Minister Inonu, who was at the moment at the United Nations. As expected, he readily agreed to having the Turkish and Greek delegates meet with Acheson in Geneva but would not commit his government to refrain from a military solution if the talks should fail. Papandreou balked as usual. He would not agree to an American representative at the Geneva meeting. As a compromise, it was agreed that Acheson should go to Geneva and set himself up "in the next room or the next building" so as to be available for consultation. Papandreou reluctantly agreed to that formula.

At my urging, President Johnson sent further letters to Papandreou and Inonu, appealing to them to try to find a solution through negotiations. Papandreou responded with a childish tirade against the United States, asserting that Johnson's letter was an "ultimatum" of the same kind Greece had received from the Nazis in 1940. Since we espoused the principle of self-determination, why not support that principle on Cyprus? It was the tantrum of an excited old man out of his depth. Though he answered with harsh, almost hysterical, words, he ended by agreeing to send a delegate to Geneva.

Dean and Alice Acheson moved to Geneva. Before leaving, Dean and I canvassed every possible solution for the Cyprus problem: proposals for partition and resettlement, federal, confederal schemes and cantonal schemes, and even what we came to call "double *enosis*." Under this last arrangement, Greek Cypriotes would all be resettled in one part of the island and Turkish Cypriotes in another, while each sector would come under the sovereignty of its respective metropolitan power. During Acheson's stay in Geneva, he evolved one proposal that came to be known as the Acheson Plan. It took account of the successful population transfers that had been carried out after the Greek-Turkish resettlements in the early 1920s. It called for the union of Cyprus with Greece, cession of the Greek Dodecanese island of Kastellorizon to Turkey, resettlement and compensation of the Turkish Cypriotes wishing to emigrate, the creation of two enclaves on Cyprus for Turkish Cypriotes who wished to remain, and the establishment of a Turkish military base on Cyprus. Neither side, however, accepted the scheme.

Meanwhile, our intelligence had reported the growing antipathy between Makarios and General George Grivas, the famous leader of EOKA. Though Grivas was, of course, a passionate advocate of *enosis*, he might, I thought, be easier to work with than Makarios, so we established an underground contact with Socrates Iliades, who was Grivas's lieutenant and director of the defense of Cyprus. Meanwhile, Grivas returned to Cyprus with a plan for *enosis* that provided protection for the Turkish Cypriotes remaining on the island and compensation for those wishing to leave. The fact that the Grivas Plan also called for the ouster of Makarios enhanced its attractiveness.

These schemes were all upset when Makarios encouraged the Greek Cypriotes to attack Turkish Cypriote villages. In retaliation, on August 7, four Turkish air force jets strafed the Cypriote town of Polis. The next day, thirty Turkish jets flew low over Greek Cypriote towns on the island's north coast. Finally, on August 9, Turkey sent sixty-four jets on another strafing and bombing foray against northwest Cyprus. The war was rapidly escalating.

In Washington, we set up a twenty-four-hour Cyprus command post, and I spent the following three nights sleeping in my office. Secretary Rusk would arrive early each morning and, in deference to his Georgian palate, we would have hominy grits for breakfast.

On Sunday, August 12, I instructed our ambassador in Athens, Henry Labouisse, to urge Papandreou to stop Makarios from further assaults on Turkish Cypriotes. We should press Papandreou to abandon "horse-trading or equivocation or passionate oratory" and act incisively to restore peace, making clear to him that Makarios was calling for military intervention by the Soviet Union and that it was "utterly essential" to keep the Russians, Egyptians, and other foreign troops out of Cyprus. At the same time, we warned Makarios that he would be publicly branded as a murderer if his units continued to harrass the Cypriote Turks. Even Moscow had apparently been shaken by the course events were following, for on that same Sunday, August 12, Khrushchev sent word to Makarios that, while he sympathized with the Cyprus government, a cease-fire would be an "important contribution." With the Soviets offering him no assistance, Makarios grumpily accepted a UN call for a cease-fire, with Turkey following suit.

Our political talks were making little progress, and on August 18, Acheson telexed me that, in his view, the chances of obtaining a quick Greek-Turkish settlement on Cyprus were "about the same as the odds on Goldwater." We should, he advised, liquidate our efforts and let him come home, though he would continue to keep in touch with Greece and Turkey to prevent Cyprus from being transformed "into a Russian Mediterranean satellite."

I urged Acheson to stay on. To "liquidate" the Geneva operations would please Makarios and make him even more intransigent. If His Beatitude ever decided that the United States had grown indifferent, he would recklessly attack the Turkish Cypriotes, and the Turks would be forced to intervene. I pointed out to Acheson that his negotiating efforts had already yielded some useful results. They had persuaded Papandreou to negotiate with Turkey and to accept a Turkish base on Cyprus; they had even got General Grivas to consider such a base. At the same time, they had eased some of Turkey's initial demands.

Since there was a six-hour difference between the United States and Geneva, I followed the practice with Acheson of talking to him around 2:00 A.M. Washington time on a scrambled teletype in the operations center at the State Department, while he sat at the other end in the consulate in Geneva. That night, after a long session of arguing over the teletype, I ended my peroration to Acheson with "*Aux armes, citoyens.*" If the Geneva enterprise must die, I contended, its burial should be conducted not "by an orthodox Archbishop but by the son of an Episcopal bishop," which, of course, meant Acheson. Acheson had tried with great skill and exceptional patience to settle a problem created by the wicked and the weak. A man of rare quality, I admired him enormously, and one of my most cherished possessions is a handwritten note commenting on something I had written. Sent two weeks before his death, it concluded with the cheering admonition: "Keep on making sense; you have the field to yourself."

End of the Crisis

In the end, the crisis momentarily subsided. Pressed by America and the United Nations and denied aid by the Soviets, Makarios's position was weakened, particularly with General Grivas challenging his hold over the island. A UN force was in place, and, for the time being, a precarious peace was maintained.

That, of course, was not the end of the Cyprus story, but we had managed to achieve a sufficient pause to permit me to turn my attention to other matters: more and more to Vietnam, which was rapidly heading toward all-out war.[3] Two distinguished journalists, Edward Weintal and Charles Bartlett, writing in 1967, appraised our accomplishment as follows:

> Thus, on most counts, the 1964 U.S. venture into crisis diplomacy can be judged a success. It prevented the establishment of a Soviet satellite in the eastern Mediterranean. It staved off a Turkish invasion of Cyprus and, perhaps, a full-scale war between Greece and Turkey, two NATO allies. The U.S. managed to preserve its firm, if somewhat cooler, relations with both Greece and Turkey, in spite of the harsh words and pressures exerted in trying to prevent conflict. It also succeeded in avoiding increased tension with the Soviet Union.
>
> And, more importantly, the entire enterprise was accomplished without commitment of American soldiers or equipment or the expenditure of American funds, except a pro rata share of UN peacekeeping costs. In this respect alone, the Cyprus incident is unique in the history of U.S. crisis diplomacy.[4]

Unhappy Sequel

During my years in the State Department, Secretary Rusk and I worked on a completely alter ego basis,[5] which meant that, when Rusk was away, he did not, as he made clear, "take the keys of his office with him." As Acting Secretary of State, I was in a position, when necessary, to move incisively, with the President's approval; Rusk established the same ground rules with my successor, Nicholas Katzenbach.

The importance of such an arrangement was disclosed in July 1974— ten years after the crisis I have just described. This time, unhappily, the United States failed to respond. Trying to run the State Department singlehandedly from an airplane, Secretary Kissinger knew nothing about Cyprus and did not bother to inform himself. As a result, he absent-mindedly let the Greek junta mount a coup in Cyprus that incited a Turkish invasion. When the Turks swarmed across the island, the Nixon Administration—under pressure from the Greek lobby—stopped arms shipments to Turkey and alienated the eastern anchor of our southern flank defense. As of this writing, 36 percent of Cyprus, including the most attractive tourist areas, remains under occupation by the Turkish army. Greece and Turkey are at sword's point and both are on uneasy terms with the United States and NATO. Makarios is dead, and the partition that might have solved Cyprus's problems has now been achieved by force and in a manner tragically unfair to the Greek Cypriotes.

The moral is clear: effective diplomacy for a great nation requires a constant high-quality institutional vigilance. That is not possible when all decisions are preempted by an individual virtuoso with a lust for travel.

The Vietnam Aberration

24. Vietnam–The Initial Error

In the day-to-day work of the State Department, Dean Rusk exercised—subject to the President's judgment—the final decision over the whole of our foreign policy. He paid particular attention to developments in the Far East, for he had devoted a large part of his military and diplomatic career to Asian affairs. As a colonel in the army during the Second World War, he had been responsible for military planning in the CBI (China-Burma-India) theater. During the early months of the Korean War, he had been the Assistant Secretary of State for Far Eastern Affairs and had effectively helped shape political-military strategy during that dismal conflict.

My own areas of experience were quite different. Except for government tours during the early New Deal days and during World War II, I had been a private lawyer, primarily concerned with European matters. Though I had favored United States intervention to rescue South Korea from invasion by a Soviet-influenced North Korea, I was appalled when our reckless push to the edge of Manchuria precipitated a massive Chinese response. General Douglas MacArthur's insistence, in April 1951, that we invade China seemed totally irresponsible, and I applauded when Truman dismissed his insubordinate general.[1]

If I had no part in the Korean War, I knew substantially more than most of my new colleagues about France's unhappy experience in Indochina and had thought it lunacy when Vice-President Nixon suggested in April 1954 that we might "put American boys in." The fact that Eisenhower disregarded this particular bit of Dulles-Nixon nonsense improved my opinion of his sagacity. General Matthew Ridgway's eloquent protests against involvement made him one of my heroes, which he has remained to this day. Through my work with the French government I had listened to innumerable French military and civilian experts discuss their nation's plans, fears, and doubts and shared vicariously in my French friends' agony over Dien Bien Phu. From that experience, I concluded—and have never ceased to believe—that we should rigorously avoid land wars in Asia.

The Laotian Operetta

Given this background, it never occurred to me in 1961 that a land war in Asia would again become America's major preoccupation, and I paid small attention to the curtain-raiser for the macabre drama of Vietnam—a piece of Graustarkian *opéra bouffe* in Laos. During the pre-inaugural interregnum, President-elect Kennedy had asked me for a memorandum on developments in that little-known land. With the help of Jeff Kitchen, then Deputy Assistant Secretary of State for Politico-Military Affairs, I had evolved a descriptive document that at least identified the players—without always defining the positions they were playing, which were, to say the least, both fluid and ambiguous. The Laotian war had its special flavor—one might almost say its charm. Proceeding with the pace and gentility of a cricket match, it was periodically interrupted so both sides could join in water festivals.

President John Kennedy, during his first months in office, spent long hours on the exotic disturbances in Laos—primarily because just before the inauguration, Eisenhower had told him that Laos was the key to all Southeast Asia. Once they had taken Laos, the Communists, he said, could bring "unbelievable pressure" on Thailand, Cambodia, and South Vietnam. If the situation reached the point where other countries could not be persuaded to act with us, we should be willing "as a last desperate hope, to intervene unilaterally."[2] Kennedy's interest in Laos was no doubt further stimulated by the natural desire of all new Presidents to show their skill at statecraft. Laos was at that time the only game in town—the only genuine shooting war, even though little actual shooting was ever heard.

To me, Laos and Vietnam were all part of the Southeast Asian drama that had begun long before. Refusing to sign the 1954 settlements that made possible the French withdrawal, Secretary John Foster Dulles had then preempted the French role. With his addiction for formalistic paper solutions, he had devised the Southeast Asia Treaty Organization (SEATO)—a so-called mutual security arrangement that included the United States, Great Britain, France, Australia, and New Zealand as well as three Asian states: Thailand, Pakistan, and the Philippines. By a supplementary protocol, the signatory states of SEATO pledged themselves to protect three nonsignatory nations: South Vietnam, Cambodia, and Laos. Through Dulles's astigmatic vision, Laos loomed large as a "bulwark against Communism" and a "bastion of freedom," and by the end of 1960, we had provided the Laotian government with nearly $300 million, of which 85 percent was to help build an army.[3]

Not much of an army was built, however, for the Laotian generals and civilian bureaucrats concentrated on stealing the new wealth. That left a Viet Minh–directed group, the Pathet Lao, to establish a firm hold on the villages and countryside. Old friendships and family played a role; the leader of the Pathet Lao, Prince Souphanouvong, was closely tied to Ho Chi Minh, while the regular government of Laos in Vientiane was headed by his half-brother, Souvanna Phouma. In October 1957, the two half-brothers negotiated the so-called Vientiane Agreements, which provided for a neutralized Laos under a coalition government— with the Pathet Lao represented in both the army and the cabinet.

That infuriated Dulles, who thought coalitions with Communists a halfway house to perdition, so he made use of his own family ties by persuading his brother, CIA Chief, Allen W. Dulles, to force out Prince Souphanouvong and replace him with a politician bearing the even more unlikely name of Phoui Sananikone. Then the CIA conjured up from France a Laotian military officer named General Phoumi Nosavan; sixteen months later, Phoumi overthrew Phoui (which could have been either a significant event or a typographical error). Five months after that, Souphanouvong escaped from jail to the North, and the Pathet Lao resumed the civil war.

Phoumi in turn was displaced by a young paratroop captain, Kong Le, who seized power and asked Prince Souvanna to form a new government that, as before, would be neutralist. Meanwhile, the Defense Department continued to whoop it up for Phoumi, who, with American encouragement, took the Royal Laotian Army to Savannakhet in September 1960, where he proclaimed a new government and denounced Souvanna. Washington promptly responded by sending him American military aid, though continuing to give economic assistance to the Souvanna government in Vientiane. Then, in December, shortly after the American elections, Phoumi marched on Vientiane. Souvanna fled to Cambodia, where he made a deal with Souphanouvong. Kong Le, prudently taking along a huge store of American supplies, joined the Pathet Lao. That ended the first act of a preposterous long-running serial that, more than anything else, resembled a Kung Fu movie.

Advent of the Kennedy Administration

After Kennedy was inaugurated, America changed its policy. By reacting with horror to a neutralist government, the Eisenhower Administration had driven the neutralists into an alliance with the Communists and provoked Soviet aid to the Pathet Lao. Under our new dispensation, neutralism would no longer be equated with evil, and we would stop trying to prop up Phoumi as the savior of a non-Communist Laos, particularly since his army was far more adept at stealing than fighting.

Every morning, at the Secretary of State's staff meeting, I listened to fearsome reports of the bloody battles on the Plaine des Jarres—a plateau on which large prehistoric stone jars had been found. But in spite of blood-curdling reports of valor, violence, and gore, that strategic terrain was largely untouched by blood. Though charming for their innocent mendacity, the fabricated communiqués quickly became boring from a monotonous lack of verisimilitude. Since Phoumi's army, though incompetent as a fighting force, was unexcelled in fast retreat, the Plaine des Jarres was soon occupied by the Pathet Lao, to whom the Soviets were now shipping more and more ammunition.

The problem faced by President Kennedy foreshadowed in miniature the predicament that would haunt his successor: how to extricate America from an overcommitment. Extrication was not recommended by the professorial warriors on the White House staff. Walt Rostow, for example, pressed for moving twenty-five thousand American troops into the Mekong Valley to deter the Pathet Lao and provide a bargaining counter for an international conference. But believing that it made no sense to tie up our armed forces in Laos, the President urged the British to reintroduce an earlier plan for an International Control Commission and to call a Geneva conference once the fighting in Laos had ended. He also warned the Soviets of the danger of a collision if they continued to support the Pathet Lao and opposed the creation of a neutral Laos. To back up that threat, we sailed the Seventh Fleet into the South China Sea, alerted combat troops in Okinawa, and moved five hundred marines with helicopters into Thailand.

I do not know what might have developed had White House attention not then been deflected by the Bay of Pigs. Though Rostow, supported by Harriman, still urged a limited commitment of American troops in the Mekong Valley, that idea fortunately lost favor at the highest level. Meanwhile, my own attitude toward Laos remained that of a skeptical eavesdropper. Preoccupied with more significant and interesting responsibilities, I did not regard Laos as an urgent problem.

Background of Vietnam

A quip current in prewar Europe was that, though the situation in Germany was serious but not hopeless, the situation in Austria was hopeless but not serious. The Laotian situation was clearly in this latter category. The situation in Vietnam was more serious, but in my view, quite as hopeless. I knew Indochina's recent history better than most. In spite of our doctrinal commitment to anticolonialism, our European ties and our anti-Communist fervor had led us to support the French against Ho Chi Minh because he was accepting help from Moscow and Peking and proclaiming Marxist principles. Then, in 1954, after the French were defeated at Dien Bien Phu, a tired French government had made peace at Geneva and extricated France from the mess.

Despite the fact that the 1954 Geneva Accords gave Ho Chi Minh control over the northern part of Vietnam above the Seventeenth Parallel, the "final declaration" of the conference explicitly stated that "the military demarcation line [was] provisional and should not in any way be interpreted as constituting a political or territorial boundary." Indeed, the Accords left the issue of the unification of Vietnam to be settled by free general elections supervised by an International Commission. Those elections were to be held before July 20, 1956.

Inevitably, the two sides interpreted those provisions to suit their own interests. To Ho Chi Minh and company, the Accords were merely a resting point in their ultimate drive to expel Western influence from the whole of Vietnam. It seems unlikely they put much faith in the contemplated election; they were prepared to wait, regroup, and ultimately take over the whole country by force or subversion. The Eisenhower Administration was determined not to let that happen. Secretary Dulles had been revolted by the armistice agreement that ceded even part of the country to the "godless Communists." Flaunting his anti-Marxist purity, he refused to look across the conference table toward Ho Chi Minh and departed, prior to the settlement, leaving Under Secretary of State Walter Bedell Smith, to sweep up as best he could.

During the following two years, the Diem regime's refusal to take even the first step in arranging the modalities for a free election was fully supported not only by Secretary Dulles but also by Senator John F. Kennedy. In June 1956, Kennedy had exhorted America to oppose the elections, as "obviously stacked and subverted in advance." Then, echoing the domino theory, in one of his more purple passages, he had emptied a whole bagfull of well-worn metaphors. Vietnam, he insisted, represented "the cornerstone of the free world in Southeast Asia, the keystone to the arch, the finger in the dike. Burma, Thailand, India, Japan, the Philippines and obviously Laos and Cambodia are among those whose security would be threatened if the red tide of Communism overflowed into Vietnam." Vietnam was, he asserted, not only "a proving ground for democracy in Asia," but "a test of American responsibility and determination in Asia" since ". . . if we are not the parents of little Vietnam, then surely we are the godparents. We presided at its birth, we gave assistance to its life, we helped to shape its future."[4]

America's Involvement Begins

By the time he became President four years later, Kennedy had tempered his language. The Viet Cong, with help from Hanoi, had achieved domination over large sections of the country, and our rhetoric was being put to the test. On October 1, 1961, Premier Diem called on the United States for a bilateral defense treaty; on October 13, he asked for United States combat troops and a substantial amount of equipment. President Kennedy responded by sending a fact-finding mission to Vietnam headed by General Maxwell Taylor and Walt Rostow, both White House advisers.

The inclusion of Rostow worried me. A friend of mine since the Second World War, he was an articulate amateur tactician. I thought him unduly fascinated by the then faddish theories about counter-insurgency and that intriguing new invention of the professors, "nation building." Still, Maxwell Taylor's presence was reassuring. Though I then knew him only slightly, I had a favorable impression of his judgment. He talked with an elegance unexpected in a soldier, and he looked exactly as a general should: clean-cut, scholarly, handsome, and resolute. In the past he had, at least ambiguously, expressed aversion to the involvement of American forces on the Asian mainland, so I hoped he might be another Matthew Ridgway. Yet, as I knew from experience with my French friends, there was something about Vietnam that seduced the toughest military minds into fantasy.

The Taylor-Rostow Report

At this time, the United States maintained in South Vietnam an advisory group of about seven hundred men (roughly the limit provided by the 1954 Geneva Accords). Now General Taylor cabled from Saigon in early November 1961 that we should introduce a military force into South Vietnam to raise national morale, perform logistical tasks "in support of military and flood relief operations," conduct combat operations necessary for self-defense and for security of the area in which it was stationed, provide emergency reserves to back up the Vietnamese armed forces "in the case of a heightened military crisis," and "act as an advance party of such additional forces as may be introduced."

Such United States troops, the general noted, might "be called upon to engage in combat to protect themselves, their working parties, and the area in which they live. As a general reserve, they might be thrown into action (with U.S. agreement) against large, formed guerrilla bands which have abandoned the forests for attacks on major targets." Contrary to the later experience of thousands of young Americans, Taylor also asserted that, "as an area for the operations of U.S. troops, SVN (South Vietnam) is not an excessively difficult or unpleasant place to operate."[5]

One of the more memorable statements in the report was that "the risks of backing into a major Asian war by way of SVN are present but

... not impressive," since, among other things, North Vietnam was "extremely vulnerable to conventional bombing." That vulnerability, according to Taylor and Rostow, was "a weakness which should be exploited diplomatically in convincing Hanoi to lay off SVN."[6] Though the initial size of our force should not exceed about eight thousand, the report emphasized that the initiative should "not be undertaken unless we are prepared to deal with any escalation the Communists might choose to impose."[7]

A Critical Meeting

On Saturday morning, November 4, 1961, I attended a meeting with General Taylor in Secretary Rusk's conference room. Secretary McNamara, Deputy Secretary of Defense Roswell Gilpatric, and a few others were also present. McNamara and Gilpatric, who were invariably prompt, arrived in advance of the general, and I talked with them about the Taylor proposals. I was, I said, appalled at the report's recommendations; we must not commit forces to South Vietnam or we would find ourselves in a protracted conflict far more serious than Korea. The Viet Cong were mean and tough, as the French had learned to their sorrow, and there was always danger of provoking Chinese intervention as we had in Korea. Moreover, I said, unlike Korea, the Vietnam problem was not one of repelling overt invasion but of mixing ourselves up in a revolutionary situation with strong anticolonialist overtones.

To my dismay, I found no sympathy for these views. Both McNamara and Gilpatric seemed preoccupied with the single question, How can the United States stop South Vietnam from a Viet Cong takeover? How did I propose to avoid it? The "falling domino" theory was a brooding omnipresence.

Conversation with the President

I was depressed by the direction affairs were taking, so at the end of a meeting on another subject the following Tuesday, November 7, I raised the question with President Kennedy. I told him that I strongly opposed the recommendations of the Rostow mission. To commit American forces to South Vietnam would, in my view, be a tragic error. Once that process started, I said, there would be no end to it. "Within five years we'll have three hundred thousand men in the paddies and jungles and never find them again. That was the French experience. Vietnam is the worst possible terrain both from a physical and political point of view." To my surprise, the President seemed quite unwilling to discuss the matter, responding with an overtone of asperity: "George, you're just crazier than hell. That just isn't going to happen."

Since then, I have pondered many times as to just what President Kennedy was trying to tell me. His statement could be interpreted two ways: either he was convinced that events would so evolve as not to require escalation, or he was determined not to permit such escalation to occur. But, why had he answered so abruptly—which was not his normal manner? Could it be that he hated to admit even to himself that he shared some of my apprehensions? I can provide no answers to those questions.

I know no more than anyone else what would have happened to our Vietnam venture had President Kennedy not been killed. Historians have speculated for years as to how the face of the world might have been changed had Good King Wenceslaus looked out on a thaw, or Alexander not caught the fever in Babylon, or what agonies America might have been saved during Reconstruction had John Wilkes Booth not fired his fatal shots. Some historians have adduced bits of evidence to show that President Kennedy had reserved in his own mind the possibility of withdrawal. But I venture no opinion. Such speculation is inherently sterile; there are no answers in the back of the book.

I left the White House in a mood of dark futility. Back in my office I said to Bob Schaetzel, then my chief of staff, "We're heading hell-bent into a mess, and there's not a Goddamn thing I can do about it. Either everybody else is crazy or I am." I was badly positioned for a fight. Political and military problems in Vietnam were not within the purview of the Under Secretary for Economic Affairs and my appointment as the Under Secretary (now known as the Deputy Secretary)—of which I was then unaware—would not formally be made until two weeks later, on November 26, 1961. For the moment, my voice carried little resonance. I saw no point in pursuing my convictions, since whatever doubts and fears President Kennedy may have had about adventuring in Vietnam, he was clearly not about to impart to me.

First Steps Down the Primrose Path

On November 8, Secretary McNamara reported to the President that he, Gilpatric, and the Joint Chiefs of Staff had reached conclusions essentially supporting the Taylor-Rostow recommendations.[8] Though McNamara conceded that the struggle might be prolonged and Hanoi and Peking might intervene, he still thought we could assume that "the maximum United States forces required on the ground in Southeast Asia" would "not exceed six divisions, or about 205,000 men."[9] Finally, he noted that, despite the fact that "the domestic political implications of accepting the objectives are also grave . . . it is our feeling that the country will respond better to a firm initial position than to courses of action that lead us in only gradually, and that in the meantime are sure to involve casualties."[10]

Dean Rusk, I knew, had serious reservations about the commitment of American combat forces. Given the nature of the struggle, he recognized that the political factor was fully as important—if not more so—than the military. But he did not want to get crosswise with McNamara. He never forgot that during a long period when Secretary of State Dean Acheson and Secretary of Defense Louis Johnson were not on speaking terms, the machinery for reaching decisions had worked creakily, and he would not let that happen. Thus, no difference of view between the Pentagon and Foggy Bottom was ever likely to surface publicly.

Moreover, both Rusk and McNamara believed that they should, without compromising their convictions, try to present the President with a common view, or, at least narrow the range of options by seeking to harmonize their opinions, thus saving the President from difficult choices. That practice could be, and in my judgment often was, overdone; on the whole, it tended to discourage expressions of doubt that might have induced greater caution. As the man ultimately responsible, the President should never be spared the necessity, often painful, of deciding between the conflicting opinions of his advisers. President Johnson would sometimes have been better served, as I saw it, had his principal cabinet members fought out their divergent views in his presence, rather than trying to compromise them in advance. The adversary process was, in our common law tradition, the best engine for adducing the truth. Presenting him with agreed recommendations or listing the available options in a memorandum did not adequately concentrate the mind; any experienced bureaucrat knew how to present such options to encourage the decision he wanted.

But compromise had become a habit, and the two Secretaries now applied it. On November 11, they submitted a joint memorandum that reflected not only their own views but also their discussions with the President. It watered down the recommendations in the original McNamara-Gilpatric–Joint-Chiefs memorandum, by distinguishing two categories of military involvement: "Units of modest size" for the direct support of the SVN military effort (such as communication equipment, helicopters, reconnaissance aircraft, naval patrols, and intelligence units) should be "introduced as speedily as possible"; but no such precipitate action was proposed for the second type of commitment: larger organized units that would "greatly increase the probabilities of Communist bloc escalation."[11]

Our Commitment to Win

Such watering-down merely slowed the process. What most disturbed me was the rejection of any turning back, the declaration of an irrevocable policy with its implication of a mind-set that could—and did—

lead to unimaginable death and disaster. It had the sound and solemnity of a religious oath: "We now take the decision to commit ourselves to the objective of preventing the fall of South Vietnam to Communism . . . in doing so, we recognize that the introduction of United States and other SEATO forces may be necessary to achieve this objective." Meanwhile, the Defense Department was directed to prepare plans "for the use of United States forces" for several purposes including dealing "with the situation if there is organized Communist military intervention."[12]

Within weeks we had sent almost seventeen hundred men to Vietnam and more were to follow.[13] That meant that the balloon was going up, and although it was not climbing as rapidly as some of my more belligerent colleagues would have liked, I had no doubt it was headed for the stratosphere. I did not have even a fragile hold on the guide ropes; the President had made that quite clear by his uncharacteristically sharp rebuff.

From my notes—and the recollections of those then working closely with me—I estimate that although my cabinet-level colleagues were becoming increasingly obsessed with Vietnam during the last eighteen months of the Kennedy Administration, I did not devote more that 5 to 10 percent of my time to that subject. I had shifted my attention to urgent problems in other areas of the world, where I could make my influence effectively felt.

The Deception of Number

There were, as was normal in any protracted struggle, brief seasons when our Vietnam *aficionados* had smiles on their faces. On his first visit to Vietnam, in 1962, Secretary McNamara reported to the President that "every quantitative measurement we have shows we are winning the war"—a comment that illustrated his instinctive fondness for assessing problems in quantitative terms. He was a superb Secretary of Defense— brilliantly skilled in planning, budgeting, devising and administering efficient procurement policies, and controlling all aspects of a great, sprawling part-military, part-civilian department. But the very quantitative discipline that he used with such effect as Secretary of Defense did not always serve him well as Secretary of War. Though he tried at the outset in 1961 to be realistic about the inherent difficulty of the struggle and the risks of its enlargement, he could not help thinking that because the resources commanded by the United States were greater than those of North Vietnam by a factor of X, we could inevitably prevail if we only applied those resources effectively—which is what our government frantically sought to do for the next ten years.

The quintessential advantage of the North Vietnamese and Viet Cong could not, however, be expressed in numbers or percentages. It was the incomparable benefit of superior *élan,* of an intensity of spirit compounded by the elemental revolutionary drives of nationalism and anticolonialism. So, with the unquantifiable omitted from the McNamara equation, the answer never came out right. As the war ground on, McNamara grew increasingly uneasy and unhappy, and I thought it largely because experience was undercutting his most deeply held premise of a quantitative rationale. In time, he began to hate the war and desperately wished for a negotiated settlement. But he could only think in terms of a settlement that conceded little and hence would inevitably be viewed by the other side as a demand for capitulation.

Inadequacy of the Diem Regime

Meanwhile, we were rapidly discovering that the tiger we were backing in Vietnam was more a Tammany tiger than a disciple of Thomas Jefferson. Kenneth Galbraith, who had visited Saigon at the President's request, had told me in unambiguous terms that Diem was an insurmountable obstacle to success, and I had had the same word from some of my press friends. Now, beginning with Diem's treatment of the Buddhist problem toward the middle of 1963, I became increasingly convinced that we had tied our nation's fortunes to a weak, third-rate bigot with little support in the countryside and not much even in Saigon.

For some time, the Diem regime had been heading toward a disruptive collision with the Buddhist clergy. During a demonstration in May, Vietnamese soldiers killed nine Buddhists; then, in protest against Diem, a monk, Quang Duc, poured gasoline over his head and burned himself to death on a crowded Saigon street while other bonzes formed a circle around him. By the end of October, there had been seven fiery bonze suicides.

The Buddhist dispute revealed with alarming clarity the degree to which Diem had succumbed to the malign spell of his brother, Ngo Dinh Nhu, and, particularly, Nhu's vicious and vindictive wife—whose talent for repulsive comments was unparalleled. "The government," she said, should "ignore the bonzes, so if they burn thirty we shall go ahead and clap our hands." Later she referred, with excruciating black humor, to the "bonze barbecue." [14]

In August, Nhu engineered a midnight raid against the Buddhist pagodas. Intelligence reports increasingly identified him and his wife with the Communists, and I thought it likely that the Nhus were deliberately trying to destroy the Saigon government to advance their own personal power. How could we hope to fight a successful war when Diem was under such poisonous influence? How could the United States continue to identify itself with a regime that behaved with such brutality and crass disregard of world sensitivities?

The Coup Telegram

All this came into sharp focus on Saturday, August 24, 1963. Weekends for Rusk and me were normally indistinguishable from weekdays; but since everything seemed quiet, U. Alexis Johnson and I left in the late afternoon for a rare golf game (I was able to play only four times in my six years in the State Department). We had time for only nine holes, and as we came up on the ninth green (where I made my only good approach shot of the day), I found Averell Harriman (then Under Secretary of State for Political Affairs) and Roger Hilsman (then the Assistant Secretary for Far Eastern Affairs) waiting for me to finish my game. The four of us drove back to my house.

Averell brought me up to the minute on the Vietnam cable traffic and showed me a proposed telegram he and Hilsman wished to send to Cabot Lodge, our new ambassador in Saigon. It was drafted in response to a telegram from Lodge reporting coup feelers from certain of Diem's top generals and was obviously explosive. As I am sure Averell expected, I declined to send it without the President's clearance. Its main theme was that our government could no longer tolerate a "situation in which power lies in the Nhus' hands."[15]

The draft telegram authorized Lodge, subject to his objections, to make clear to Diem that the United States could not accept continued brutal actions by the Nhus against the Buddhists and that the situation must be promptly redressed. At the same time, Lodge should tell the key military leaders that, unless the Nhus were removed from the scene, the United States would find it impossible to continue its assistance. Then came the key sentence: "We wish to give Diem reasonable opportunity to remove the Nhus, but if he remains obdurate, then we are prepared to accept the obvious implication that we can no longer support Diem."[16]

I did not object to the telegram except to improve the drafting. I had thought for some time that we could not retain our self-respect as a nation so long as we supinely accepted the Nhus' noxious activities. Encouraging coups, of course, ran counter to the grain of America's principles but Diem's legitimacy was dubious at best; we had in effect created him in the first place. Now the Nhus were destroying what little moral justification remained for our position in Vietnam. The decision, however, was not mine but the President's, so I telephoned him in Hyannis Port to bring him up to date and read him the relevant passages. The President on the whole seemed favorable to our proposed message, although he recognized the risk that, if a coup occurred, we might not like Diem's successor any better than Diem himself. But finally he said, "If Rusk and Gilpatric agree, George, then go ahead."

Within a few minutes, I reached Rusk in New York and told him of the proposed telegram and of my talk with the President. He was cautious but made it clear that, if the President understood the implications, he would give a green light. Soon a message arrived that Gilpatric was also in accord. To be fair to him, he was, I suspect, heavily influenced by both Rusk's and the President's approval. If they were fully prepared to accept the risks, he would support them. Richard Helms, then deputy head of the CIA (presumably speaking for his chief, John McCone, who was unreachable) expressed accord with our message. General Maxwell Taylor, who was dining at a restaurant, could not be reached, though his deputy, General Victor Krulak, gave his approval and Taylor, on seeing the telegram after it had been sent, expressed no disagreement.

In retrospect, I think we should have waited until the question could have been fully discussed in a well-prepared meeting, but since Harriman and Hilsman insisted that Lodge needed a prompt answer, I signed off on the telegram. The next day (Sunday) Lodge cabled requesting permission to go directly to the generals, without first telling Diem. It would, he argued, be unwise to ask Diem to remove the Nhus; he would not do so and our approach would alert him that something was up and give him time "to block or forestall action by the military." Instead, he proposed to tell the generals that "we are prepared to have Diem without Nhus but it is in effect up to them whether to keep him."[17] Here again I probably made at least a tactical mistake. The record would certainly have been better had we first put the issue directly to Diem, making it clear that we would withdraw our support for his regime if he did not remove the Nhus. But that, I thought, would accomplish little, since if he called our bluff—as he almost certainly would—I doubted my colleagues would ever carry through with a threat of withdrawal! At the same time, our continued support of Diem while the Nhus kept on with their repulsive activities was, in my view, impossible to contemplate. It put America in an odious position quite inconsistent with the principles on which we had based our Vietnam intervention in the first place. So I approved a telegram authorizing this change in procedures, which I cleared with Mike Forrestal, who was acting for a briefly absent Mac Bundy.

Monday, August 26, was a day of second thoughts. In particular, John McCone, back at his desk, protested that we should never have given the generals such a *laissez-passer* to undertake a coup; Secretary McNamara and Maxwell Taylor agreed. Even the President showed some misgivings that we had acted so quickly, although I thought him equally annoyed by the waffling of his top command. I held my ground, contending that the telegram was essential in view of the evil influence of the Nhus, but no one else dashed forward to accept responsibility for it.

Two days later, I left to visit Prime Minister Salazar and to see President Ayub Khan. On the same day, a telegram from Lodge, in response to the President's request for an expression of his "independent judgment," seemed to accept fully the course of action we had laid down. "We are launched on a course from which there is no respectable turning back: the overthrow of the Diem government. There is no turning back in part because U. S. prestige is already publicly committed to this end in large measure and will become more so as the facts leak out. In a more fundamental sense, there is no turning back *because there is no possibility, in my view, that the war can be won under a Diem administration. . . .*" (Italics added.) [18]

But the message in our August 24 telegram proved a damp squib. The generals got cold feet, asking their CIA contact, Colonel Lou Conein, for clearer evidence that the United States would not betray their plot. Meanwhile, Ambassador Lodge authorized the CIA to "assist in tactical planning" for the coup, although General Paul Harkins thought we should try first to persuade Diem to get rid of his brother. When Ambassador Lodge categorically rejected that idea, the President, showing deference to the political sagacity of an ex-Senator he had once defeated, came down on Lodge's side.

President Kennedy now publicly put heat on Diem, announcing on September 2, 1963, that the Diem regime would have "to take steps to bring back popular support" if the war were to be won and that success was possible only "with changes in policy and perhaps with personnel."[19] Robert Kennedy was urging that Lodge be instructed to get rid of Diem. Since, in the Washington tradition, a fact-finding mission can serve as a substitute for a policy, the President sent McNamara and General Taylor to make a first-hand appraisal of the situation. The mission returned with a report filled with the contradictions that betrayed personal uncertainty. Though optimistic about our military prospects (McNamara announced that one thousand American troops would be out by Christmas and that America would be able to terminate its major commitment by 1965), the mission's report still emphasized the unpopularity of the Diem government and recommended the continued search for "alternative leadership." Lodge, meanwhile, was authorized to use our aid program as leverage to bring about the changes he thought necessary, and this was angrily denounced by the Diem regime. The rest of the story is well known. Early in October, we learned that a coup was on again, but in view of the failure to move in August, the reaction was one of dubiety and caution. When a coup finally occurred on November 1, it was a messy affair and Diem was killed.

Because our deep involvement in Vietnam was such a ghastly error, a thousand myths have been spun to explain our failure. Nixon blamed our inability to prevent the final debacle on the United States Congress; Kissinger blamed it on Nixon and Watergate. The fiercest hawks claim we could have won had we permitted our air force to bomb everything in sight or, better yet, had sent our armies marching on Hanoi. Then there is the large club of the unreconstructed, who—seeking an excuse for preordained failure—seize on the August 24 telegram as an exculpation. Had that telegram not been sent, they contend, Diem would have remained in charge; we would have won the war; and everyone would have lived happily ever after.

Myths are made to solace those who find reality distasteful and, if some find such fantasy comforting, so be it. From the outset, I believed that we could never win the war and I do not believe for a moment that we could have won it had Diem not been overthrown. As Ambassador Lodge pointed out at the time, we could not possibly win "under a Diem Administration." The Nhus were poisonous connivers, and America could not, with any shadow of honor, have continued to support a regime that was destroying Vietnamese society by its murderous repression of the Buddhists.

Thus I would have lost no sleep over the August 24 telegram even had it triggered the coup, but the evidence suggests it had little, if anything, to do with it. When Ambassador Lodge and I testified together before a Congressional subcommittee in 1975, he made the following statement with regard to that telegram: ". . . in the Pentagon Papers they don't put in the fact that it was cancelled a week later, and they give the impression that when the actual coup did come on November 1, it was under the provisions of that telegram. . . . When the coup did come it was a thoroughly, to use Mr. Ball's phrase, a thoroughly indigenous operation, Vietnamese in origin and Vietnamese in every respect."[20]

Only a little more time was left for President Kennedy. Twenty-two days after the coup he himself was murdered, leaving the unresolved problems of Vietnam for President Johnson. We were—as was increasingly obvious—moving closer and closer to a deep involvement in the Vietnamese war. Instead of a handful of Americans in Vietnam, there were now more than 16,000. President Kennedy, though anxious to avoid any irrevocable commitments, had still made them. He had said at a press conference on July 17, 1963, "We are not going to withdraw from that effort. In my opinion, for us to withdraw from that effort would mean a collapse not only of South Vietnam, but Southeast Asia. So we are going to stay there." His acceptance of the Taylor-Rostow report had set in train a process of escalation with clear recognition that it might involve increasing troop commitments. The theoretical limit had been set at 205,000 men.

President Johnson Takes Over

President Johnson, in my own view, was as anxious as Kennedy to avoid an irreversible embroilment. At every stage, he moved reluctantly—pushed by events and the well-meant prodding of the same men who counseled President Kennedy. In proposing new escalatory measures, his inherited advisers were, in turn, responding to successive disappointments that led them to flail around frenetically in pursuit of an elusive—and, as I saw it, illusory—solution.

A determined President might at any point have overruled his advisers and accepted the costs of withdrawal, but only a leader supremely sure of himself could make that decision; Lyndon Johnson, out of his element in the Vietnam War, felt no such certainty. Not only had his long Senate experience left him untrained in the discipline of rigorous analysis and surgical decision required to break the momentum, but Far Eastern quarrels were far from his first priority. The tragedy for Lyndon Johnson—and for America—was that our ill-conceived involvement in Vietnam prevented him from applying his full energies to the realization of his vision of equality and well-being for America. Instead, he found himself committing an increasingly large portion of his time, thought, and energy to a war half a world away, for which he was wholly unprepared.

His tragedy was not unique. I remember once reading that when Woodrow Wilson was leaving Princeton en route to his inauguration, he remarked to Professor E. G. Conklin that all his life he had been preparing for the domestic problems facing our country and that "it would be the irony of fate if [his] administration had to deal chiefly with foreign affairs." That Lyndon Johnson, as Wilson before him, had to deal with foreign affairs in the intense form of a war was not only "the irony of fate" but catastrophic bad luck. He resented the whole idea of the war but was swept along by a momentum others had set in motion. In the end, the war drove him from the Presidency.

In a totally rational world, Lyndon Johnson might have devoted his early weeks in office to a critical look at all the assumptions of our Vietnam position, but he had other things to think about. Initially preoccupied with securing the passage of President Kennedy's legislative programs, he left the war largely in the hands of those who took its prosecution for granted. Meanwhile, pressures built up. South Vietnam showed itself quite unable to put down the Viet Cong insurgency, and there were increasing signs of demoralization and corruption in Saigon.

I had been present when President Johnson met with Ambassador Cabot Lodge at the time of the Kennedy funeral, and in the beginning of June 1964, they met again in Honolulu. Lodge strongly argued for the prompt beginning of a bombing offensive to bolster morale in South Vietnam; General Maxwell Taylor opposed further escalation until we had installed a government in Saigon that we could be sure would not sell us out. It was an absurdly constricted framework in which to try to resolve the major issues of the war, yet even that narrow issue was never settled, nor any clearcut decision made. The momentum of events carried us constantly forward, and, so long as no one challenged the fundamental assumptions on which our involvement rested, events, not design, would determine the future.

Refusal to Ask the Giraffe Question

Although I dislike trite metaphors, I felt as though an accelerating current were propelling us faster and faster toward a gigantic waterfall. Yet no one was questioning the navigation, only how to rev up the engines to make the ship run faster. "How?" was the obsessive question. How could we apply the vast power at our command to impose our will on the North Vietnamese and the Viet Cong? I recalled the story of a small boy at the zoo whose father had pointed out a large caged animal and announced: "See, that's a giraffe"—to which the boy had very sensibly answered: "Why?"

To ask the "giraffe" question, now that we were getting into increasingly deep trouble, was regarded as almost subversive. No one was prepared to discuss why we persisted in a war that, in my view, we could not win, in pursuit of an objective that seemed every day to have less reality. Men with minds trained to be critical within the four walls of their own disciplines—to accept no proposition without adequate proof—shed their critical habits and abjured the hard question "why." Once they caught hold of the levers of power in Washington, they all too frequently subordinated objectivity to the exhilaration of working those levers and watching things happen. The lessons of history, to my surprise, were disdained. It was useless for me to point out the meaning of the French experience; they thought that experience without relevance. Unlike the French, we were not pursuing colonialist objectives but nobly waging war to support a beleaguered people. Besides, we were not a second-class nation trying to hang on in Southeast Asia from sheer nostalgic inertia; we were a superpower—with all that that implied.

Disparate frames of reference beclouded understanding. For Hanoi's leaders, control of the whole of Vietnam was a fanatical, almost religious, objective they had relentlessly pursued for twenty years; for America, the war was a marginal affair not worth a head-on clash with Peking or Moscow, a struggle to be waged with a limited commitment of manpower and weaponry. Thus President Johnson ruled out such provocative acts as mining Haiphong Harbor, or blowing up the dikes, or bombing the city center of Hanoi, or mounting a land invasion of North Vietnam; nor did anyone even consider the use of nuclear weapons. The conflict was a limited war for limited objectives—a type of warfare for which a democracy is organically badly suited.

For me, that built-in disparity of commitment raised fundamental questions. Not only did we suffer the implicit disadvantage of waging limited war against an adversary committed to total war, there was also the question whether America, as a democratic state, could fight a limited war that lasted more than a year or so and still keep it limited. A free people would accept sustained sacrifices only if persuaded that the cause justified their deprivations. If the answer were No, we ought to withdraw; if Yes, were we not then obligated to use our full military might? That problem haunted me.

During the early months of the Johnson Administration, I was occupied with many things: Cyprus, East-West trade, the political implications of satellite communications, the Kennedy Round of trade negotiations, turbulence in Panama, wool and beef imports, political issues with Brazil, and the UNCTAD Conference. Vietnam was for me only an increasingly worrisome and distasteful affair peripheral to my principal concerns. Nonetheless, I attended meetings with the President, conducted routine business with Secretary McNamara relating to the war, and watched the recurrent Saigon coups that hatched out obscure military leaders with the political life span of June bugs who fluttered briefly in the limelight only to disappear. Each time a change occurred, I enjoyed a sweet, brief moment of hope that it would result in so much chaos as to make our withdrawal imperative.

Yet as the months passed, my conviction deepened that unless we promptly extricated ourselves, we would, sooner or later, find our country engaged in a large-scale, messy shooting war—an American version of France's *guerre sale*. Among all the top command, I found President Johnson the most reluctant to expand America's involvement. He was wary, among other things, of repeating MacArthur's error of attacking too close to the Chinese border; he did not want American boys to have to fight the Chinese hordes again. Yet the failure of our efforts in the South tended more and more to strengthen the hand of those who, in default of other tactical alternatives, were agitating for bombing attacks on the North.

"Vietnam Is Rotten Country"

At the beginning of June 1964, while considering moves that would intensify the American involvement, the President asked me to discuss Vietnam with President de Gaulle. My selection for that mission was no accident; in Lyndon Johnson's mind, the very fact that I opposed the war made me the best advocate of the Administration's position. He knew that, as long as I remained in the government, I would defend government policies, whatever they might be. The President understood and respected my commitment to that position though he liked to tease me about it. "George," he once told me, "you're like the school teacher looking for a job with a small school district in Texas. When asked by the school board whether he believed that the world was flat or round, he replied: 'Oh, I can teach it either way.' " "That's you," said the President. "You can argue like hell with me against a position, but I know outside this room you're going to support me. You can teach it flat or round."

President de Gaulle received me in the splendor of the Elysée Palace with his customary friendly greeting. I told the French President that, although both our governments wanted a viable South Vietnam, the government of Saigon seemed unable to stop the North Vietnamese and Vietcong invasion. Within a reasonable time, the United States might itself have to take action against the North, even though that might, at some point, engage the Chinese forces. Naturally we wanted a diplomatic solution, but the South was so fragile that even talk of negotiations might lead to its collapse and a quick Vietcong victory. We, however, did not believe in negotiating until our position on the battlefield was so strong that our adversaries might make the requisite concessions. Thus before serious talks, we would have to teach the Vietnamese a lesson and, in the process, persuade the Chinese also of our strength. China, as we saw it, was not unlike the Soviet Union in 1917: primitive and aggressive toward its neighbors.

De Gaulle, as I had anticipated, rejected my analysis categorically. China, he told me, was nothing like the Soviet Union in 1917; it lacked the military, industrial, and intellectual resources that Russia had even at that time. Thus, it would not become aggressive until after it had consolidated its power, which would require a long period. We were pursuing the same illusions about Vietnam that had gotten France into such trouble. It would, of course, be nice if we were right, but he knew something about Vietnam: it was a hopeless place to fight. He, therefore, felt obliged to tell me that the United States could not win, even though we commanded vastly more resources than France had been able to mobilize. The more power we committed, the more the population would turn against us. We would never succeed by force, only by negotiation.

I riposted with the established Administration line that South Vietnam would never understand a negotiating move at this time, but interpret it as a sign of American weakness. But de Gaulle did not let me get far down that course, interrupting to say that our position in Vietnam was hopeless and France would not involve itself in any way in the escalation of the fighting. We would have to go it alone. Vietnam, he said— and I shall never forget the phrase—is "rotten country." France had learned that to its sorrow.

Since de Gaulle's views supported what I had been arguing to my colleagues, I hoped they would reinforce my position, but when I returned from Europe, I found Lyndon Johnson unimpressed, or at least unwilling to listen, as he was then preoccupied with strengthening his domestic flanks. As a seasoned politician, he had concluded that if there were to be a major escalation of the war, he must make sure of having Congress behind him. Thus he would seize the earliest opportunity to obtain a Congressional mandate for a greater involvement. That opportunity came very promptly.

Tonkin Gulf Charade

During this period, I was aware that we were conducting covert military operations under the code name Operation Plan 34A. They were part of a strategy of mounting "progressively escalating pressure" on Hanoi by what President Johnson liked to call "noncommitting measures," and they included the dispatching of PT boats to bombard North Vietnamese coastal installations. During this same period (February and March 1964), the navy had begun an exercise under the code name of De Soto Patrol, which consisted of sending destroyers up the Gulf of Tonkin with the ostensible mission of collecting intelligence on such matters as radars and coastal defenses. On August 2, 1964, while the destroyer *Maddox* was heading south after completing such a mission, North Vietnamese PT boats made a run at her.

Though some of the President's advisers urged an immediate retaliatory move, the President wished for an even stronger record. So, rather than keeping our ships out of this now established danger zone, the President approved sending both the *Maddox* and the destroyer *C. Turner Joy* back into the Gulf. I was upset by this decision; the argument that we had to "show the flag" and demonstrate that we did not "intend to back down" seemed to me a hollow bravado. Thus I was disturbed but not surprised on August 4, 1964, when word came that both destroyers had been attacked. The North Vietnamese may well have thought that the De Soto Patrols were part of the 34A raids and were merely trying to defend the coast by attacking the destroyers. Moreover, there was some evidence that the commanders might have misread the radar blips; if the destroyers were in danger, it could have been because they were firing at one another. Within the next two or three days, even President Johnson began to doubt the occurrence of a second attack. With disgust he said to me at one point, "Hell, those dumb, stupid sailors were just shooting at flying fish!"

I thought we would now stop risking our destroyers, but immediately following the presumed second attack, Secretary McNamara proposed a further De Soto Patrol to show the flag and prove to Hanoi and the world that we were not intimidated. The project was briefly discussed; there was general agreement around the table; the President indicated his approval to go forward. I had said little during the discussion, but I now spoke up, "Mr. President, I urge you not to make that decision. Suppose one of those destroyers is sunk with several hundred men aboard. Inevitably, there'll be a Congressional investigation. What would your defense be? Everyone knows the De Soto Patrols have no intelligence mission that couldn't be accomplished just as well by planes or small boats at far less risk. The evidence will strongly suggest that you sent those ships up the Gulf only to provoke attack so we could retaliate. Just think what Congress and the press would do with that! They'd say you deliberately used American boys as decoy ducks and that you threw away lives just so you'd have an excuse to bomb. Mr. President, you couldn't live with that."

No one spoke for a long moment. The President seemed disconcerted and confused. Then he turned to McNamara: "We won't go ahead with it, Bob. Let's put it on the shelf."

Beginning of the Rearguard Action

The Tonkin Gulf attack—or attacks, however many there may have been—provided the President with enough leverage to extract from Congress almost unlimited authority to escalate our involvement. The Tonkin Gulf Resolution (a terrifyingly open-ended grant of power) disappointed me; I had counted on Congress to insert qualifying language, but Congress had abdicated. I did not know where we were headed, but it was clear the war was getting out of hand. So, toward the end of September 1964, I began work on a memorandum to focus attention on the "giraffe" question by challenging every major assumption underlying our Vietnam policies. Since my days were fully occupied with Cyprus, Europe, and other areas, I dictated most of it into a tape recorder at home late in the night. The subject matter was too sensitive to permit me to draw on the normal resources of the Department. Only my principal assistant, George Springsteen, and two or three secretaries were fully aware of what I was doing. I finally finished the sixty-seven-page (single-spaced) memorandum on October 5, 1964.

The paper began by noting that the political situation in Saigon was "progressively deteriorating" and there was no serious possibility of a government that could "provide a solid center around which the broad support of the Vietnamese people" could coalesce or that "could conduct military operations with sufficient effectiveness to clean up the insurgency." Thus, we had four options.

• We could continue along current lines, recognizing that at some point we should either be thrown out by a neutralist coup in Saigon or be forced to a deeper involvement "by the manifest hopelessness of the present course of action."

• We could take over the war by injecting substantial United States ground forces, but in that event "our situation would, in the world's eyes, approach that of France in the 1950s."

• We could mount an air offensive against the North to improve our bargaining position for negotiation. But though preferable to a ground force commitment, that would lead to the same result by provoking the North Vietnamese to send ground forces to the South that could be effectively countered only by United States ground forces.

• Finally, we might try to bring about a political settlement without direct US military involvement that would check, or at least delay, the extension of Communist power into South Vietnam.

We must discard the assumption that Vietnam presented the same problems that we faced in Korea. We had fought in South Korea under a United Nations mandate. Unlike the situation in South Korea, the South Vietnamese government lacked the general support of the principal elements in the country. The Korean War started only two years after Korean independence, when the people were still exhilarated by freedom: "The people of South Vietnam have been fighting for almost twenty-two years and are tired of conflict." Finally, the Korean War had begun with a massive land invasion by one hundred thousand troops across an established border; in South Vietnam, there had been no invasion, only a slow infiltration that many nations regarded as an "internal rebellion."

We urgently needed to compare the relative costs and risks of intensifying the war with the costs and risks of "a carefully devised course of action designed to lead to a political solution under the best conditions obtainable." I quoted General Taylor's statement that if the government in Saigon should "continue to crumble, air action against North Vietnam would, at best, bring a Pyrrhic victory." No one, I wrote, had yet shown that United States action against the North would create political cohesiveness in Saigon. Nor could we assume that bombing the North would persuade the Hanoi government to stop helping the Viet Cong. So long as our adversaries saw the prospect of ultimate victory, they would accept "very substantial costs from United States air action." Nor was there any reason to believe that we would be in a position to deal with the North Vietnamese more effectively after an air offensive. That was "based on a wrong assessment of the political impact of such a course worldwide and its effect on our bargaining strength."

We were misjudging not only the political consequences of bombing but also the military consequences. Sustained bombing would trigger a "major invasion of South Vietnam by North Vietnamese forces." (That was, of course, exactly what later did happen.) North Vietnam would "choose to fight the kind of war best adapted to its resources." If we were to use air power, in which we had an unquestioned advantage, the North Vietnamese would "retaliate by using ground forces, which they possess in overwhelming numbers." Our intelligence estimates were that in two months time North Vietnam could put roughly sixty thousand men across the DMZ and through the Panhandle.

Increased infiltration from North Vietnam would require substantial American ground units to defend our bases. That would put us in the position of France in the early 1950s—with all the disastrous political consequences of such a posture.

It was a mistake to assume that we could launch a military attack against North Vietnam and still "control the risk" or that we "could halt the process of escalation whenever we [felt we had] accomplished our objective or the enemy was about to respond with unexpected force." It is, I wrote—and this was perhaps the most important passage in the memorandum—"in the nature of escalation . . . that each move passes the option to the other side, while, at the same time, the party which seems to be losing will be tempted to keep raising the ante. To the extent that the response to a move can be controlled, that move is probably ineffective. If the move is effective, it may not be possible to control—or accurately anticipate—the response." I insisted that "Once on the tiger's back, we cannot be sure of picking the place to dismount."

I then came to the heart of the matter. It was a mistake to believe that we had to "stop the extension of Communist power into South Vietnam if our promises were to have any credence." Attorney General Robert Kennedy had, I noted, even gone so far as to say in Germany that "if Americans did not stop Communism in South Vietnam, how could people believe that we would stop it in Berlin?" That was not only dangerous talk but far from the truth. Our allies believed that we were "engaged in a fruitless struggle in South Vietnam" and feared that if we became too deeply involved "in a war on the land mass of Asia," we would lose interest in their problems. What we had most to fear was "a general loss of confidence in American judgment that could result if we pursued a course which many regarded as neither prudent nor necessary. . . . What we might gain by establishing the steadfastness of our commitments, we could lose by an erosion of confidence in our judgment." I then reviewed the probable reactions of each individual country of Southeast Asia to differing courses of action. I also discussed the reactions of other nations of the Third World, most of which, I thought, would favor a political solution, but would "strongly oppose an air offensive against North Vietnam."

Finally, I came back to the central point. We had originally committed ourselves to continue to help South Vietnam only "so long as the Vietnamese people wish us to help" and so long as they maintained an adequate standard of performance. Why not then serve notice on the South Vietnamese Council that we would continue the struggle only if the South Vietnamese government and people achieved unity of purpose? Such notice might conceivably "pull together the responsible elements of the country" and even lead "to the creation of a unified government." But it was far more likely that Saigon would regard it as a warning "of ultimate United States disengagement." That would, I predicted, "almost certainly accelerate existing covert probing of the possibilities of a deal with the Viet Cong elements"—which in my view would be a good thing.

I did not try to do more than outline the possibilities of settlement, offering my memorandum "not as a definitive document but as a challenge to the assumptions of our current Vietnam policy."

Reaction to Heresy

I had devoted long nights to preparing this analysis because we were at a critical turning point. We could still get out easily; we still had only a few more forces in Vietnam than at the time of President Kennedy's death; and we had not yet launched a systematic air offensive against the North. But there was an unmistakable smell of escalation in the air; the military situation in the South was fast deteriorating, the Viet Cong were extending their territorial control, and the leadership of the so-called government in Saigon was rotating among various cliques of military grafters.

My colleagues in Washington and our Saigon embassy were standing logic on its head. What we charitably referred to as a government in Saigon was falling apart, yet we had to bomb the North as a form of political therapy. That was as absurd as Candide's account of hanging admirals *pour encourager les autres.* Such a tortuous argument was the product of despair—the last resort of those who believed we could not withdraw from Vietnam without humiliation. (We seemed more concerned about "loss of face" than did the Orientals.) They still tenaciously believed that we did not dare negotiate until we had so battered the North that any settlement talks would concern only the terms of Hanoi's capitulation—which was out of the question.

When I completed the memorandum, I sent it to Secretary McNamara, Mac Bundy, and Secretary Rusk. Bob McNamara in particular seemed shocked that anyone would challenge the verities in such an abrupt and unvarnished manner and implied that I had been imprudent in putting such doubts on paper. My colleagues seemed somewhat more concerned with a possible leak than with the cogency of what I had written. We agreed, however, to meet and discuss the specific points in the memorandum, reserving two Saturdays for that purpose. But it required only one meeting, which took place on Saturday, November 7, 1964, to convince me that there was no point in carrying the argument further. My colleagues were dead set against the views I presented and uninterested in the point-by-point discussion I had hoped to provoke. They regarded me with benign tolerance; to them, my memorandum seemed merely an idiosyncratic diversion from the only relevant problem: how to win the war.

Piecemeal Attack

For a short period, I pursued the piecemeal tactic of trying to slow escalation by resisting each new escalatory project. But I could be effective only if I kept my heretical views within a limited circle. To negate any impression of dissent among the top hierarchy, President Johnson announced that he would refer to me as the "devil's advocate," thus providing an explanation for anyone outside the government who might hear that I was opposing our Vietnam policy. Though that ruse protected me, I was irked when some academic writers later implied that my long-sustained effort to extricate us from Vietnam was merely a stylized exercise by an in-house "devil's advocate." Thus are myths made. Not one of my colleagues ever had the slightest doubt about the intensity of my personal convictions. The devil, God knows, had plenty of lawyers; he was doing too well to need my services.

I hesitated for some weeks before bringing my long memorandum to the President's attention. If I were to ask him, Mac Bundy would, I knew, give it to Lyndon Johnson; he was scrupulously fair in such matters. But the President was then engaged in his election campaign and was troubled with a thousand problems. It did not seem a propitious time for a confrontation, so I decided to wait until I could get his full attention.

I was free to pick my timing. Dean Rusk had told me early in our relationship that the President was as entitled to my views as to his—a magnanimity that has haunted me ever since. In his book *The Best and the Brightest,* David Halberstam reports a member of the Administration as saying, "I cannot imagine McNamara letting Ball dissent like that if Ball were his deputy. Nor, for that matter, can I imagine George letting Rusk dissent if Ball had been Secretary and Rusk Under Secretary."[21] How can I be sure of the answer? Dean Rusk, a man of extraordinary integrity and selflessness, was quite prepared to let me urge views contrary to his, but I am by no means sure that under similar circumstances I would have been so tolerant or generous.

Somehow, word that I had filed some kind of dissent reached the ears of the columnist Joseph Alsop. On November 23, he wrote, "Ball's knowledge of Asia could be comfortably contained in a fairly small thimble." I responded in a note to him that he had inaccurately appraised my resources. "You've got the receptacle wrong. My knowledge of Asia should not be thought of as contained in a thimble but a soup plate; it is at once both wider and more shallow than you suggest." According to

Alsop, my thesis that our Vietnamese embroilment was damaging American prestige in Europe ignored the fact "that a gigantic United States failure in Vietnam will virtually give the European game to General Charles de Gaulle."

That, I thought, was about as far off base as one could get.

25. The Balloon Rises Quickly

If I were to persuade the President to halt the escalation and seek a way out of the war, I would have to convince Lyndon Johnson that no matter how much force we committed we could not win, that our deeper involvement would expose us to risks of a wider war with the possible intervention of the major Communist powers, and that the costs of extrication were less than the costs and risks of proceeding. We desperately needed to stop, look, listen, and think before the momentum of events carried us deeply into the Slough of Despond called Vietnam.

Our Changing War Aims

I was clear about my objectives but how could I achieve them? We had first justified our involvement in the war by the so-called "domino theory": if South Vietnam fell to Hanoi, all Southeast Asia would pass under the domination of North Vietnam. Since my colleagues thought Hanoi a surrogate of Moscow and Peking, a North Vietnamese triumph would dangerously extend the reach of the major Communist powers. Lyndon Johnson had flamboyantly embraced that theory as early as May 1961, when, as Vice-President, he visited Vietnam. The issue for Americans was, he had announced, "whether we are to help these countries to the best of our ability or throw in the towel in the area and pull back our defenses to San Francisco."[1]

At the time, I was neither disturbed nor impressed, writing off such hyperbole as the natural exuberance of a Texan reinforced by years in the Senate. It was not a position to be held by one with serious responsibility for policy, and when Johnson became President, the South Vietnamese army's persistent failures and our own repeated disappointments forced a tacit reappraisal. As early as the middle of 1964, the domino theory had largely vaporized under the scorching sunlight of reality.[2] But, as so often happens in international affairs, my colleagues were slow to adjust theory to reality—or, if they did, failed to put their doubts and second thoughts into words. Thus not until January 1966, would John McNaughton, McNamara's most trusted adviser on the war, spell out the new rationale that had until then evolved without explicit expression. "The reasons why we *went into* Vietnam to the present depth are varied; but they are now largely academic. Why we have not *withdrawn* is, by all odds, *one* reason . . . to preserve our reputation as a guarantor." "The present U.S. objective in Vietnam," so MacNaughton wrote, "is to avoid humiliation."[3]

Our new rationale for staying in Vietnam became, as Jonathan Schell has perceptively written, not to protect the United States from a military danger, but a "psychological domino theory." According to the original domino theory, so Schell points out, "each nation that fell to Communism would endanger its immediate neighbor." Now

according to the psychological domino theory, the ill effects of a nation's fall would not necessarily be on neighboring nations, but would be on nations all over the world which, by merely watching the spectacle, would lose confidence in the power of the United States. . . . In this thinking, Vietnam became a "test case" of the United States' will to use its power in world affairs. If the United States could not muster the "determination" to prevail in Vietnam, it was believed, then it would be showing, once and for all, that it lacked the determination to prevail in any conflict anywhere. And, since in the official view credibility was indivisible, a collapse in credibility in the sphere of limited conflict would cast doubt on the credibility of American power in other spheres of competition as well, including even the all-important nuclear sphere. Thus according to the doctrine of credibility, the United States was engaged in a global public relations struggle in which a reverse in any part of the world, no matter how small, could undermine the whole structure of American power.[4]

Schell's observations accurately describe the underlying attitude of the Johnson Administration. As was the case with so much doctrinal thought, logic was stretched too far and facile analogies accepted too uncritically. Credibility was not "indivisible"; other nations and peoples, as I constantly argued, easily distinguished between our involvement in Vietnam and our commitment to defend Berlin. The idea that the two were in any way comparable was a conceit invented at the top reaches of our government to justify what they wanted to do anyway.

Unhappily, the shift of rationale from the domino theory to the psychological domino theory committed us even more firmly to a war aim we could never achieve. If, under the original domino theory, all we sought to preserve was the integrity of neighboring states from North Vietnamese aggression, we might fall back on building a defense line in Thailand. But once the war aim was formulated in public relations terms, we were compelled to continue a struggle we could not win. By clinging dogmatically to the belief that saving "our reputation as a guarantor" meant forcing Hanoi to capitulate, we locked ourselves into a prison with no exit. The North Vietnamese would never agree to any settlement that did not offer them a virtual certainty of gaining domination of the whole of Vietnam within a reasonable time frame. That was the major point I incessantly argued with no success.

I told my colleagues they were proving George Santayana's aphorism that "fanaticism consists in redoubling your effort when you have forgotten your aim."[5] The Administration had, I contended, not so much "forgotten its aim" as discarded it for an aim that was deceptive. To fight a war at what seemed limitless cost just because we could not easily get out was quite unworthy of a great nation—particularly because, I was convinced, my colleagues greatly overestimated the costs of a carefully programmed extrication.

Rejection of a Cease-Fire in Place

Because we failed to adjust our war aims to what was now tacitly regarded as our true objective—to save our reputation—doctrine decreed that we must never agree to a cease-fire in place, which would leave North Vietnamese forces in the South. Our avowed war aim was to restore the Saigon government's sovereignty over the whole of South Vietnam and our failure to achieve it would impair our reputation as a guarantor. Nor should we agree to a coalition government that would permit the North Vietnamese apparatchiks a beachhead from which they could quickly subvert and overwhelm the softer South Vietnamese elements— a prediction that implied a vote of no confidence in the Saigon hierarchy.

Since we had now reduced our reasons for continuing to struggle in Vietnam to the simple objective of saving ourselves from humiliation— in other words, preserving our reputation—we should have concentrated on a simple question: How can we withdraw from Vietnam with the least loss of face? The indispensable first step was to free ourselves from subservience to whatever regime might at the time be in power in South Vietnam. We could never achieve terms that would satisfy the Saigon government; its war aims were rigidly defined by the desire of those in power to keep their jobs. We were constantly on the verge, as I kept pointing out, of becoming a "puppet of our puppet."

Need to Regain Freedom of Action

Our first problem was to reposition ourselves so we could negotiate bilaterally with North Vietnam to secure the return of our prisoners and the peaceful withdrawal of our forces. That required that we demonstrate what was every day more obvious: the South Vietnamese were not fulfilling their part of the bargain. The Saigon government was corrupt and without firm national roots. It could never meet the standards laid down by President Eisenhower as conditions for our aid. Once we insisted on those conditions, Saigon's rulers would most likely turn their backs on us, thus freeing us of further responsibility.

There was no time to spare; each new escalatory step was complicating the problem of ultimate extrication. On November 1, 1964, just two days before the American Presidential election, the Viet Cong launched a mortar barrage attack on American planes and facilities at Bien Hoa airfield near Saigon, killing four Americans and destroying five B-57 bombers. Instead of retaliating on election day, the President appointed an interagency working group under the chairmanship of William Bundy, the Assistant Secretary of State for Far Eastern Affairs, to develop political and military options for direct action against North Vietnam.

Working groups of seasoned bureaucrats deliberately control the outcome of a study assignment by recommending three choices, exploiting what we referred to as "the Goldilocks Principle." By including with their favored choice one "too soft" and one "too hard," they assure that the powers deciding the issue will almost invariably opt for the one "just right." In this case, Option C, the "just right" option, which both McNaughton and Bundy favored, involved gradually increasing air strikes "against infiltration centers, first in Laos and then in the DRV and then against other targets in North Vietnam" so as to "give the impression of a steady, deliberate approach . . . designed to give the United States the option at any time to proceed or not, or to escalate or not, and quicken the pace or not."[6]

Meanwhile, I had prepared a paper of my own, dated November 7, which proposed that we ask the United Kingdom to try to persuade Moscow to bring Peking and Hanoi to a conference to which the United Kingdom would, on its side, bring the United States and South Vietnam. At the same time, the United States, together with the United Kingdom and other friendly nations, would call for a cease-fire and the disarming of the Viet Cong. I was under no illusion that such a proposal would be accepted; it was intended primarily to gain time. Though everyone listened politely, the committee reviewing the working group proposals was interested in only one question—how to escalate the war until the North Vietnamese were ready to quit. I need hardly mention that I was alone in favoring the mildest of the three options.

A day or two later, I left for Europe to attend a ministerial meeting of the OECD. During my absence, the committee, influenced by General Maxwell Taylor, who was now our ambassador to Vietnam, reached a compromise recommendation for a two-phase program: thirty days of air strikes at infiltration routes, coastal raids, and some reprisal raids against the North; then a sustained air offensive in which the bombing would be gradually intensified. Ambassador Taylor hoped that he could use the promise of this bombing offensive to obtain a commitment from the South Vietnamese government to pull itself together; he feared that we might be sold out overnight by the tawdry military cabals that chased one another around the revolving door leading to control in Saigon.

When I returned from Europe, I found the President again more cautious than his advisers. Agreeing only to the first phase of the revised Bundy committee program, he conditioned the beginning of phase two on Saigon government reforms, and, of course, the placemen momentarily holding power in Saigon did promise reform. They always did, but the half-life of such promises was, as I predicted, numbered in hours. Wilfully flouting our conditions, they dissolved the High National Council and made night arrests of their political opponents, making sure that Saigon's fetid air would never be diluted by even a slight whiff of democracy. Although Ambassador Taylor gave the junta a dressing down that was, some thought, offensively brash, he still urged Washington to begin the bombing campaign. That annoyed President Johnson, who was understandably reluctant to venture further onto the Vietnamese quicksand without a firm political base in Saigon.

I have always marveled at the way ingenious men can, when they wish, turn logic upside down, and I was not surprised when my colleagues interpreted the crumbling of the South Vietnamese government, the Viet Cong's increasing success, and a series of defeats of South Vietnamese units not as proving that we should cut our losses and get out, but rather that we must promptly begin bombing to stiffen the resolve of the corrupt South Vietnamese government. It was classical bureaucratic casuistry. A faulty rationalization was improvised to obscure the painful reality that America could arrest the galloping deterioration of its position only by the surgery of extrication. Gifted dialecticians carried the charade one step further, arguing that we were principally responsible for Saigon's low morale, since Ambassador Taylor had upset Saigon's politicians by demanding that the government shape up in a manner it had no intention of doing. We must, they argued, commit our power and prestige even more intensely to stop the South Vietnamese government from falling completely apart, negotiating covertly with the Liberation Front or Hanoi, and ultimately asking us to leave. It was Catch 22 and the quintessence of black humor. Almost alone, the President seemed to recognize and reject this inversion of logic.

Bombing of North Vietnam Begins

On February 7, 1965, the Viet Cong attacked the American barracks at Pleiku. Their mortar fire killed eight Americans and wounded more than sixty. The demand for prompt retaliation was overwhelming and I realized that further frontal opposition would be not only futile but tactically unwise. I could gain nothing by antagonizing my colleagues if the President could no longer be deterred. That point became even clearer when Cyrus Vance telephoned Mac Bundy, who was then in Saigon conferring with Taylor and Westmoreland. Should we now begin the air strikes? The answer of the Saigon team was loudly affirmative.

Mac Bundy's recommendations followed the then prevailing view that we needed to bomb not in order to punish Hanoi but to pump adrenalin into the South Vietnamese. "If the United States and the Government of Vietnam join in a policy of reprisal, there will be a sharp immediate increase in optimism in the South. . . ."[7] The hope that such action would affect "the will of Hanoi . . ." was, he suggested, only a secondary objective—"an important but longer-range purpose."

Faced with a unanimous view, I saw no option but to go along, although I did try one filibustering tactic, countering McNamara's insistence on immediate bombing with the argument that we should at least postpone the action until after Kosygin, who was momentarily in Hanoi, had left the country. I was supported by Senator Mike Mansfield, the Senate majority leader, whom the President had invited to what he knew would be a critical meeting. Mansfield had developed an interest in the Far East when assigned there as a young Marine in the early 1920s and had later taught Far Eastern history; thus his voice carried special authority. Vice-President Hubert Humphrey also raised a cautionary voice against bombing during the Kosygin visit, while Ambassador Llewellyn Thompson pointed out that the Soviet Union would almost certainly think we had chosen this moment to bomb in order to humiliate Moscow.

Bob McNamara brushed these caveats aside. I was, he protested, trying to block our retaliatory raid, not merely postpone it (which, in fact, was true). There would never be a perfect moment to begin bombing; someone could always find an objection and time was of the essence. We had to show immediately that we were reacting to the Vietcong attack. It was the quintessential McNamara approach. Once he had made up his mind to go forward, he would push aside the most formidable impediment that might threaten to slow down or deflect him from his determined course. So, once again, he carried the day. Not only did the President come down on McNamara's side but he was so annoyed at Hubert Humphrey's cautionary words that the Vice-President was thereafter excluded from our meetings for many months.

Agreed Forecast

With the Administration committing itself to dangerously mounting escalation, I shifted my tactics to try to gain my colleagues' agreement to a forecast of future dangers, giving the President in early February a memorandum reflecting a collective view that would show him some of the mine fields we would be risking. I worked closely with Ambassador

Llewellyn Thompson in preparing the paper, then reviewed it with McNamara and McGeorge Bundy. (Secretary Rusk was unavailable.) The memorandum, as it finally evolved, stated that "except for the major differences in positions set forth . . . it can be taken as representing the generally agreed views of all four of us."

Reflecting our intelligence reports, the paper pointed out that as we moved the bombing line closer and closer to Hanoi, we would invite an engagement with the fifty-three Chinese MIGs that Peking had sent to defend North Vietnam. We would then be under pressure to bomb the major MIG base at Phuc Yen, near Hanoi. That would probably, at some point, induce Hanoi to send south perhaps as many as 125,000 troops. If we attacked above the Nineteenth Parallel, Peking would be under pressure to intervene with aircraft operating from Chinese bases, which would, in turn, lead to pressure to knock out offending Chinese bases. China might then move massive ground forces into North Vietnam and, subsequently, into other parts of Southeast Asia. We could halt them only by introducing five to eight United States divisions with a total troop strength of 300,000 men.

All this was, I thought, generally agreed among the four of us—McNamara, Bundy, Thompson, and me—except for certain specific points of difference:

McNamara-Bundy Position

McNamara and Bundy believe that we must pursue a course of increasing military pressure to the point where Hanoi is prepared to agree not only to stop infiltration from the North, but effectively to call off the insurgency in the South and withdraw those elements infiltrated in the past. To achieve this objective, they would accept the risks of substantial escalation, including the acceptance of ground warfare with Red China—although they believe it likely that we can achieve the desired objective without such a war. This view is shared with Maxwell Taylor.

Ball-Thompson Position

Ball and Thompson believe that—short of a crushing military defeat—Hanoi would never abandon the aggressive course it has pursued at great cost for ten years and give up all the progress it has made in the Communization of South Vietnam. For North Vietnam to call off the insurgency in South Vietnam, close the border, and withdraw the elements it has infiltrated into that country would mean that it had accepted unconditional surrender.[8]

I had hoped that by associating McNamara, Bundy, and Llewellyn Thompson in a joint effort to point out the dangers of escalation, I could shake up the President and smoke out my colleagues. But my memorandum accomplished nothing. The President met with Thompson, Bundy, and me, read the memorandum quickly, then asked me to go through it point-by-point. He thanked me and handed the memorandum back without further comment. Why he followed that uncharacteristic course I do not know.

Pressure in the Administration's boilers was rapidly building up for an intensive bombing campaign. Insistence on the precondition of a stable government in Saigon was last month's doctrine; now its most vocal proponent, Ambassador Maxwell Taylor, was recommending escalation of our air offensive as essential "to give Pulmotor treatment to a government *in extremis.*"

On Christmas Eve, the Viet Cong provided us a tailor-made excuse for such an air offensive by planting a bomb in the Brink's Hotel, a bachelor officers quarters, that killed two Americans and wounded fifty-eight. But the President was reluctant to initiate violence during the Christmas season—a sensitivity Nixon later contemptuously disdained when he launched his infamous Christmas bombing in 1972. Waiting instead until February 13, 1965, two days after the Viet Cong attacked the United States barracks at Qui Nhon, he ordered a sustained bombing campaign under the code name of "Rolling Thunder."

Discussion of October 1964 Memorandum

Since I had thoroughly conditioned the President to my opposition to the war, I thought it time for him to read the critical analysis I had prepared in October 1964. On February 24, 1965, I gave the document to Bill Moyers at lunch and he gave it to the President that afternoon. The following morning he called to say that the President had read and re-read my memorandum, had "found it fascinating and wanted to know why he had not read it before."

The following Friday, February 26, the President called a meeting to discuss my memorandum. That he had studied it was clear; he challenged specific points I had made and even remembered the page numbers where those arguments occurred. I outlined my position, and Secretary McNamara responded with a pyrotechnic display of facts and statistics to prove that I had overstated the difficulties we were now encountering, suggesting at least by nuance, that I was not only prejudiced but ill-informed. Secretary Rusk made a passionate argument about the dangers of not going forward. The meeting, though lasting a long while, ended on an inconclusive note. I had made no converts. My hope to force a systematic reexamination of our total situation had manifestly failed.

On March 8, 1965, two marine battalions were landed at Danang, and, by the end of March—after Rolling Thunder had been rolling and thundering for six weeks without perceptible results—General Westmoreland clamored for additional troop deployments. By now, even the air power zealots realized that bombing alone would not critically reduce the enemy's fighting capacity. Pressure for substantial further troop commitments mounted all through March and became irresistible when, on March 29, Viet Cong guerrillas blew up the American embassy in Saigon. At that moment I was flying to Europe to meet with the NATO Council in Paris and did not return until Sunday, April 4. I missed the key meetings on April 1 and 2 at which the President decided to increase support forces in South Vietnam by an additional eighteen to twenty thousand men.

Secretary Rusk and I saw President Johnson on the morning of April 20. Secretary McNamara, Ambassador Taylor, and the military commanders then meeting in Honolulu had, so the President told us, agreed that the enemy was spreading its control ineluctably; they now recommended that we increase the authorized ground force deployment to eighty-two thousand men, with the possibility of further increases later. I responded with an emotional plea that the President not take such a hazardous leap into space without further exploring the possibilities of settlement; I went farther than I had intended, suggesting that a settlement might then be possible. President Johnson replied, "All right, George, I'll give you until tomorrow morning to get me a settlement plan. If you can pull a rabbit out of the hat, I'm all for it!"

I drafted a long memorandum which I sent to the President later that night, suggesting moves to take advantage of what, I implied, could be a diplomatic opening. It was a deliberate stalling tactic, yet I could not let us take this tragically definitive step without employing all available tactics to slow the process.

Operation Rolling Thunder, I pointed out, had not achieved its declared purposes, and we dared no longer postpone a settlement.

1. We cannot continue to bomb the North and use napalm against the South Vietnamese villages without a progressive erosion of our world position. . . .

2. I doubt that the American people will be willing to accept substantially increased casualties if the war continues over a substantial period of time and there are no signs of active diplomacy. Distasteful as it is, we must face the hard fact that large and articulate elements in the intellectual community and other segments of United States opinion do not believe in our South Vietnamese policy. In fact, to many Americans our position appears far more ambiguous—and hence far more dubious—than in the Korean War.

Until now, the American people have gone along out of their great confidence in you and because the United States casualties have been less than a weekend's traffic accidents.

But even a doubling of the casualties would begin to make a difference.

My proposal called for the creation of a coalition government. The Saigon regime would declare a general amnesty permitting "all Viet Cong wishing to return to the North" to do so. An International Control Commission would undertake to police the cease-fire. "Once the new government was installed, the United States would withdraw."

The President read the memorandum overnight, and we met with him again at eleven o'clock the following morning. I had not, I soon realized, "pulled a rabbit out of the hat"—at least not a rabbit strong enough to fight off the hounds of war baying at its heels. Yet the next day, Bill Moyers called to say that the President had asked him to obtain a copy of my memorandum for himself. "The President," he said, "is very interested in your idea." The following day, Moyers called me again to say that, in the light of my memorandum, the President had talked with him about the need to get some people together to do nothing for three or four days but ponder the political and peaceful alternatives in Southeast Asia.

I desperately needed at least one high-level confrere on my side; how could the President be expected to adopt the heresies of an Under Secretary against the contrary views of his whole top command? But since no top-level official shared my view, I decided to seek help outside. I drafted the outline of a plan to substitute "political activity . . . for a shooting war in one after another of the provinces of South Vietnam" and enlisted the help of Dean Acheson and another old friend, Lloyd Cutler, to expand my memorandum into a detailed program for "the social and political reconstruction of South Vietnam." The program included an offer of amnesty to all Viet Cong adherents who ceased fighting, a phased schedule for establishing a constitutional government based on elections in which all peaceful citizens, including Viet Cong, could take part, the adoption of social and economic programs outlined in detail, and an announcement by the Prime Minister that foreign troops would begin withdrawing as soon as the insurgency stopped and the government had effectively extended its authority throughout the country.

My plan was so drafted as to avoid requiring the government of South Vietnam to appear to be negotiating. The government would offer the program as its own political act. As finally evolved, the proposal was set forth in some thirty-five pages covering not merely its substantive but also its procedural aspects as well as the mechanics for its execution.

I knew I would first have to sell my plan to Ambassador Taylor and Deputy Ambassador Alexis Johnson in Saigon, since only they could persuade the South Vietnamese government to adopt it. I, therefore, sent one of my personal assistants, Thomas Ehrlich, to Saigon to present the plan directly. Taylor and Johnson replied with a long list of questions. Though Johnson seemed to have some qualified interest in the proposal, Taylor was resolutely against it. I did my best to answer their detailed questions in a long telegram, dated May 25, but Ambassador Taylor was returning to Washington shortly and further discussions by telegram would obviously be futile.

The episode confirmed an opinion I had not wanted to accept. America had become a prisoner of whatever Saigon military clique was momentarily in power. Like a heroine in an eighteenth-century novel who got her way by fainting if anyone spoke crossly, each clique understood how to exploit its own weakness. If we demanded anything significant of it, it would collapse; so we never made any serious demands.

A Massive Escalation

Throughout the spring of 1965, the North Vietnamese responded to our bombing program (Operation Rolling Thunder) precisely as predicted in my original October 5 memorandum; they infiltrated regular North Vietnamese army units into the South. The Viet Cong began their summer offensive with a strong assault inflicting on the South Vietnamese Army (the ARVN) what the CIA described as a "total defeat." By the middle of June, with our military no longer believing that a gradual buildup would achieve the required results, Secretary McNamara proposed a total deployment of 395,000 personnel in South Vietnam by the end of the year. In the fall of 1961, I had predicted to President Kennedy that if he followed the recommendations of the Taylor-Rostow report, we would have 300,000 men in South Vietnam within five years. Now, within four years, we were about to exceed that figure by almost 100,000.

I sought vainly to forestall this escalation. Sensitive to President Johnson's almost obsessive determination never to lose command, I headed my memorandum of June 18, 1965, "Keeping the Power of Decision in the South Vietnam Crisis" and began it with the famous words of Ralph Waldo Emerson: "Things are in the saddle and ride mankind."

"Your most difficult continuing problem in South Vietnam," I wrote the President, "is to prevent 'things' from getting into the saddle or, in other words, finding a way to keep control of policy and prevent the momentum of events from taking over."

The best formula for maintaining freedom of decision is (a) to limit our commitments in time and magnitude and (b) to establish specific time schedules for the selection of optional courses of action on the basis of pre-established criteria.

Before we commit an endless flow of forces to South Vietnam we must have more evidence than we now have that our troops will not bog down in the jungles and rice paddies—while we slowly blow the country to pieces.

The French fought a war in Viet-Nam, and were finally defeated—after seven years of bloody struggle and when they still had 250,000 combat-hardened veterans in the field, supported by an army of 205,000 Vietnamese.

To be sure, the French were fighting a colonial war while we are fighting to stop aggression. But when we have put enough Americans on the ground in South Viet-Nam to give the appearance of a white man's war, the distinction as to our ultimate purpose will have less and less practical effect.

Ever since 1961—the beginning of our deep involvement in South Viet-Nam—we have met successive disappointments. We have tended to overestimate the effectiveness of our sophisticated weapons under jungle conditions. We have watched the progressive loss of territory to Viet Cong control. We have been unable to bring about the creation of a stable political base in Saigon.

The French, I pointed out, had much the same experience.

They quoted the same kind of statistics that guide our opinions—statistics as to the number of enemy defectors, the rate of enemy desertions, etc. They fully believed that the Vietnamese people were on their side, and their hopes received intermittent shots of adrenalin from a succession of projects for winning the war—the de Lattre de Tassigny Plan, the Salan Plan, the Navarre Plan, etc.

. . . we have not so far seen enough evidence to be sure that the South Vietnamese forces will stand up under the heightening pressure—or, in fact, that the Vietnamese people really have a strong will to fight after twenty years of struggle. We cannot be sure how far the cancer has infected the whole body politic of South Viet-Nam and whether we can do more than administer a cobalt treatment to a terminal case.

Yet the more forces we deploy in South Viet-Nam—particularly in combat roles—the harder we shall find it to extricate ourselves without unacceptable costs if the war goes badly.

I sent the memorandum through Bill Moyers to the President on Friday, June 18, and on Monday Moyers called to tell me that the President had read it over the weekend at Camp David and had discussed it with him at lunch. The President agreed in substance, Moyers said, "with most of the memorandum—one or two slight changes possibly." Moyers said that his notes reflected the following Presidential comments: "I don't think I should go over one hundred thousand but I think I should go to that number and explain it. I want George to work for the next ninety days—to work up what is going to happen after the monsoon season. I am not worried about riding off in the wrong direction. I agreed that it might build up bit by bit. I told McNamara that I would not make a decision on this and not to assume that I am willing to go overboard on this. I ain't. If there is no alternative, the fellow who has the best program is the way it will probably go."

My advocacy had by now been reduced to a Chinese water torture; all I could do was to keep on an incessant dripping of the by now familiar arguments, increasingly documented by the disappointing events of a futile war, in the hope that I might gradually wear away the resistance of my colleagues and, most of all, the President. Cato, after all, had shown the efficacy of repetition in his repeated denunciations of Carthage; if he could use that technique to start a war, I might use the same technique to stop one. So I prepared a paper, dated June 28, 1965, entitled "Cutting Our Losses in South Vietnam," which announced at the outset that it was "written on the premise that we are losing the war." We must,

I argued, "balance the risks and costs of a war fought by United States forces against the risks and costs of a carefully organized tactical withdrawal of the United States from South Vietnam or a systematic reduction of our territorial commitment to accord with the capabilities of a limited US deployment."

I then repeated my well-worn arguments for disengaging our interests from Saigon's, once more stressing President Eisenhower's prudent conditions for American aid. "Since Americans are dying in South Vietnam," my memorandum argued, "the United States has both the right and duty to demand of Saigon that it fulfill these conditions or expect our withdrawal." We should promptly make a *démarche* on General Ky and the leaders of all principal groups in Saigon that, unless within a month's time "those leaders put together a government of national union under civilian leadership," we would reconsider the extent of our commitment. "What," I continued, "would be the effect of such a notice? Either it could induce the Ky Government to adopt an extreme nationalist position and announce that it would go it alone without United States help or the Ky Government would fall in favor of a government prepared to try to find a political solution with the Viet Cong. In either event, we would expect a protracted discussion between US representatives and representatives of the various Vietnamese factions. If Ky or his successor demanded the removal of United States forces, he would be almost certainly replaced by more moderate elements, since even neutralist elements would still tend to regard our presence for a period of time as essential to prolonged bargaining with the Viet Cong and Hanoi."

If we withdrew after having demonstrated that Saigon was unprepared to perform its part of the bargain, most friendly nations would recognize that we had kept our commitments and that "our decision to force the issue of stability and responsibility was a mark of prudence and maturity." Then, under the heading *Renvoi,* I set forth my own grim assessment of the situation: "The position taken in this memorandum does not suggest that the United States should abdicate leadership in the cold war. But any prudent military commander carefully selects the terrain on which to stand and fight, and no great captain has ever been blamed for a successful tactical withdrawal. . . . [Vietnam] is clearly what General de Gaulle described to me as 'rotten country.' South Viet-Nam is . . . bled white from twenty years of war and the people are sick of it. . . . South Vietnam is a country with an army and no government. Even if we were to commit five hundred thousand men to South Vietnam we would still lose."

Appended to the memorandum was a section presenting, on a nation-by-nation basis, the effect of an American withdrawal; the presentation established, at least to my satisfaction, that those consequences would be far less harmful than had often been asserted.

The Approaching Day of Decision

The critical day of truth approached. Secretary McNamara was pressing for increasing our ground deployments to whatever force levels were needed to prove to the North Vietnamese that they "cannot win." Our forces, he recommended, should be brought within a few months to the level of forty-four battalions, on the ground that, with a greatly increased infiltration of North Vietnamese forces, the war would rapidly become a conventional type of "main force" combat, which Americans were equipped and trained to fight. I thought his "main force" prediction misconceived—the North Vietnamese were not about to accommodate us by fighting the kind of war in which we had an advantage—but I agreed with his appraisal that, if we followed his advice, "The war . . . [would] be a long one."

The war was rapidly careening out of control, and I was less and less optimistic that I could deflect the strong forces steadily gaining momentum. Nevertheless, on July 1, I sent the President a memorandum entitled "A Compromise Solution for South Vietnam." As the following excerpts make clear, it once again expressed my pessimism:

A Losing War: The South Vietnamese are losing the war to the Viet Cong. No one can assure you that we can beat the Viet Cong or even force them to the conference table on our terms no matter how many hundred thousand *white foreign* (US) troops we deploy.

No one has demonstrated that a white ground force of whatever size can win a guerrilla war—which is at the same time a civil war between Asians—in jungle terrain in the midst of a population that refuses cooperation to the white forces (and the SVN) and thus provides a great intelligence advantage to the other side.

The decision you face now, therefore, is crucial. Once large numbers of US troops are committed to direct combat they will begin to take heavy casualties in a war they are ill-equipped to fight in a non-cooperative if not downright hostile countryside.

Once we suffer large casualties we will have started a well-nigh irreversible process. Our involvement will be so great that we cannot—without national humiliation—stop short of achieving our complete objectives. *Of the two possibilities I think humiliation would be more likely than the achievement of our objectives—even after we had paid terrible costs.*

To show that the costs of a compromise solution were greatly exaggerated, I again reviewed the possible impact of a compromise settlement on each country of importance to us. I also frontally challenged McNamara's contention that we were about to enter "third phase" warfare. "Implicit in arguments for greatly augmented United States combat forces in South Vietnam is the assumption that the Viet Cong have entered—or are about to enter—their so-called "third phase" of warfare, having progressed from relatively small-scale hit-and-run operations to large unit, fixed position conventional warfare. Yet we have no basis for assuming that the Viet Cong will fight a war on our terms when they can continue to fight the kind of war they fought so well against both the French and the GVN."

Mac Bundy gave the President my memorandum, along with memoranda by his brother William Bundy and McNamara. In his transmittal note, he advised, "My hunch is you will want to listen hard to George Ball and then reject his proposal. Discussion could then move on to the narrower choice between my brother's course and McNamara's."

The Critical Decision

Thereafter, the war continued to go badly. When my colleagues and I assembled at the White House on the morning of July 21, 1965, we were given a memorandum from the Joint Chiefs of Staff. Only the prompt deployment of large bodies of American troops could, it argued, save the situation. That meant committing thousands of our young men not merely to passive defense missions but to aggressive combat roles. The war would then become unequivocally our own. There would be no turning back for months, perhaps years—not until we had suffered horrible casualties, killed thousands of Vietnamese, and raised the level of national anxiety and frustration above the threshold of hysteria.

Because of the importance of the July 21 meeting it may be useful to outline the colloquy which suggests the substance and flavor of our many long discussions.[9] It also provides some sense of the President's agonizing reluctance to go forward, his desire to explore every possible alternative, and, finally, his inability to reconcile his vaunted Texas "can-do" spirit with the shocking reality that America had painted itself into a corner with no way out except at substantial costs in terms of pride and prestige.

The President began with searching questions. Could we get more soldiers from our allies? What had altered the situation to the present point of urgency? McNamara produced a map. The Viet Cong, it showed, controlled about 25 percent of the South. United States forces would not be committed in those areas; they would be deployed "with their backs to the sea, for protection." They would conduct search and destroy operations against large-scale units.

"Why," I asked, "does anyone think that the Viet Cong will be so considerate as to confront us directly? They certainly didn't do that for the French." General Wheeler, the chairman of the Joint Chiefs of Staff, replied, "We can force them to fight by harassment."

After the others had expressed support for the proposed new escalation, the President asked whether any of us opposed it, looking directly at me. I made my usual speech, pointing out that we would be embarking on "a perilous voyage" and could not win. But, he asked, what other courses were available? We must, I replied, stop deceiving ourselves, face reality, and cut our losses. "If we get bogged down, the costs will be far greater than a planned withdrawal, while the pressures to create a larger war could become irresistible. We must stop propping up that absurd travesty of a government in Saigon. Let's let it fall apart and negotiate a withdrawal, recognizing that the country will face a probable take-over by the Communists."

The President replied, "You've pointed out the dangers but you've not really proposed an alternative."

After others had expressed similar sentiments, the President once more turned to me. "George," he asked, "do you think we have another course?" I answered, "I certainly don't agree with the course Bob McNamara's recommending." "All right," said the President, "we'll hear you out; then I can determine if any of your suggestions are sound and can be followed. I'm prepared to do that if convinced."

I could, I said, present to him only "the least bad of two courses." The course I could recommend was costly, but we could at least limit the cost to the short-term. At that point—just as I was beginning to speak—the President interrupted. "We'll have another meeting this afternoon where you can express your views in detail." Meanwhile, he wanted a further justification for the introduction of one-hundred-thousand more troops. In response to the President's concern about increased losses, General Taylor directly contradicted a view expressed earlier by Secretary McNamara that our losses in Vietnam would be proportional to the number of our men in that country. "The more men we have," the General now declared, "the greater the likelihood of smaller losses."

When we reconvened at 2:30 that afternoon, the President asked me to explain my position. I outlined why, in my view, we could not win. Even after a protracted conflict the most we could hope to achieve was "a messy conclusion" with a serious danger of intervention by the Chinese.[10] In a long war, I said, the President would lose the support of the country. I showed him a chart I had prepared showing the correlation between Korean casualties and public opinion. As our casualties during the Korean War had increased from 11,000 to 40,000, the percentage of those Americans who thought that we had been right to intervene had diminished from 56 percent in 1950 to a little more than 30 percent in 1952. Moreover, as our losses mounted, many frustrated Americans would demand that we strike at the "very jugular of North Vietnam" with all the dangers that entailed. Were it possible for us to win decisively in a year's time, friendly nations might continue to support us. But that was not in the cards.

"No great captain in history ever hesitated to make a tactical withdrawal if conditions were unfavorable to him," I argued. "We can't even find the enemy in Vietnam. We can't see him and we can't find him. He's indigenous to the country, and he always has access to much better intelligence. He knows what we're going to do but we haven't the vaguest clue as to his intentions. I have grave doubts that any Western army can successfully fight Orientals in an Asian jungle."

"That's the key question," the President remarked. "Can Westerners, deprived of accurate intelligence, successfully fight Asians in the jungles and rice paddies?"

We had, I continued, underestimated the critical conditions in South Vietnam. "What we are doing is giving cobalt treatment to a terminal cancer case. A long, protracted war will disclose our weakness, not our strength."

Since our main concern was to avoid undermining our credibility, we should shift the burden to the South Vietnamese government. We should insist on reforms that it would never undertake, which would impel it to move toward a neutralist position and ask us to leave. "I have no illusions," I said, "that after we were asked to leave South Vietnam, that country would soon come under Hanoi's control. That's implicit in our predicament." I then discussed the effect on other nations in the area.

The President then asked the question most troubling him. "Wouldn't we lose all credibility by breaking the word of three Presidents?" I replied, "We'll suffer the worst blow to our credibility when it is shown that the mightiest power on earth can't defeat a handful of miserable guerrillas."

Then, asked the President, "aren't you basically troubled by what the world would say about our pulling out?"

"If we were helping a country with a stable, viable government, it would be a vastly different story. But we're dealing with a revolving junta. How much support," I asked rhetorically, "do we really have in South Vietnam?"

The President then mentioned two of my points that particularly troubled him. One was that Westerners could never win a war in Asia; the other was that we could not successfully support a people whose government changed every month. He then asked, "What about the reaction of the Europeans? Wouldn't they be shaken in their reliance on us if we pulled out of Vietnam?"

"That idea's based on a complete misunderstanding of the way the Europeans are thinking," I said. "They don't regard what we are doing in Vietnam as in any way comparable to our involvement in Europe. Since the French pulled out of Vietnam, they can hardly blame us for doing the same thing; they cut their losses, and de Gaulle is urging us to follow suit. Having retired from their empire, the British recognize an established fact when they see one. They're not going to blame us for doing the same thing, although they might get a little mischievous pleasure from it—what the Germans call *schadenfreude*. But basically they only care about one thing. They're concerned about their own security. Troops in Berlin have real meaning; troops in Vietnam have none."

I then summarized the alternatives. "We can continue a dragged out, bitterly costly, and increasingly dangerous war, with the North Vietnamese digging in for a long term since that's their life and driving force." Or "we can face the short-term losses of pulling out. It's distasteful either way; but life's full of hard choices."

McGeorge Bundy then intervened to suggest that, while I had raised truly important questions, the course I recommended would be a "radical switch in policy without visible evidence that it should be done." "George's analysis," he said, "gives no weight to losses suffered by the other side. The world, the country, and the Vietnamese people would have alarming reactions if we got out." Dean Rusk then stated that, if the Communist world found out that we would not pursue our commitment to the end, there was no telling where they would stop their expansionism. He rejected my assessment of the situation. The Viet Cong had not established much of a position among the Vietnamese people, and he did not foresee large casualties unless the Chinese should come in. Ambassador Lodge agreed. There would, he said, be a greater threat of starting World War III if we did not go in with our forces. There were great seaports in Vietnam, and we did not have to fight on the roads.

After more talk along the same lines the meeting was adjourned.

Support from an Unexpected Quarter

The next day we met once more to hear the President's report of what the generals had told him. That meeting stands out in my memory not for anything I said—I had, after all, exhausted my persuasive arsenal—but rather because, for the first time, I found support from an unexpected quarter.

The President had asked his old friend Clark Clifford to attend and called on him to express his views. Presenting his argument with elegant precision and structure as though arguing a case before the Supreme Court, Clifford voiced strong opposition to the commitment of combat forces. He put forward the same arguments I had made the day before; in addition, he gave the President a more authoritative assessment of the probable domestic consequences Whether or not President Johnson knew in advance of the position Clifford would take I cannot say; sometimes I suspected that he staged meetings for the benefit of the rest of us. But, whatever the answer to that question, Clifford emerged as a formidable comrade on my side of the barricades.

When the meeting was over, I asked Clifford to join me in the Fish Room. I told him that ever since the fall of 1961 I had been making the same arguments he now made so eloquently, and I gave him copies of the memoranda I had submitted to the President. The next day Clifford told me that he had spent the previous evening until two in the morning carefully studying my memoranda. They were, he said, "impressive and persuasive." Throughout the last year he had come more and more to my opinion as he continued to receive reports of our deteriorating situation.

I told Clark that judging from the meeting we had just had that day with the President, his intervention had had a salutary effect. Clifford replied that he had been told through "another source" that there would have to be a great effort made if we were to block this critical escalatory step that would change the character of the war. Though he hoped that through our combined exertions we could make progress, he was not optimistic. Unfortunately, "individuals sometimes become so bound up in a certain course it is difficult to know where objectivity stops and personal involvement begins." In any event, he had tried to impress on the President that we should down-play the talk that "this was the Armageddon between Communism and the Free World."

Clark Clifford had been close to the President for many years. Perhaps his opposition might turn the balance. We had one other powerful supporter, Senate Majority Leader Mike Mansfield, who, at the President's meeting with the Congressional leadership, had weighed in along the same line we were taking. There was, he had argued, no legitimate government in South Vietnam and we owed nothing to the current cabal. We were being pushed progressively deeper into the war, and even total victory would be enormously costly. Our best hope was for a quick stalemate and negotiation; the American people would never support a war that might last three to five years. We were about to get into an anti-Communist crusade. "Remember," he had concluded prophetically, "escalation begets escalation." Finally, there was my friend Senator J. William Fulbright, who had arrived at a position similar to mine, but the President had already written him off and rejected his view of the war.

As the whole world now knows, we did not carry the day—neither Mansfield, Clifford, Fulbright, nor I—and the balloon went up farther and farther.

26. The Dusty End of a Reign of Error

As the war became progressively larger and bloodier, some of my colleagues talked with increasing wistfulness of a negotiated solution, which, in their vocabulary, meant Hanoi's capitulation. That was, I thought, quite unrealistic; the North Vietnamese would never stop fighting until they had obtained terms that would assure their takeover of the entire country. I had, therefore, only a marginal interest in efforts to open channels; they were not the answer. I did not see us achieving peace by the two techniques then being strongly urged: bombing pauses and the establishment of a multiplicity of diplomatic contacts. The battle-hardened leaders in Hanoi had no interest in mechanisms that would facilitate their crying "Uncle" in a low voice and with minimal loss of face; their interest was in forcing us to go home.

Bombing Pauses

A bombing pause, unaccompanied by significant concessions was merely pulling up a plant to see how well its roots were growing. From the middle of 1964 until the end of September 1966, when I left the State Department, there were two pauses. I supported both, not because I expected anything to come of them, but because I hoped they would break the rhythm of escalation. The first pause, which began on May 13, 1965, and lasted only until May 18, was, as I pointed out to my staff, not so much a pause as a hiccup. We told the Soviets in advance and tried to pass word to Hanoi (which rejected the receipt of our message) but we neglected to tell the American people or even the American military. The foreign minister of Hanoi denounced the pause as a "deceitful maneuver to pave the way for American escalation"—which I thought a perceptive appraisal. Peking called it a "fraud."

In spite of the failure of the first pause, Secretary McNamara continued to advocate "low-key diplomacy" to lay the groundwork for a settlement, stating that "We could, as part of a diplomatic initiative, consider introducing a 6–8 week pause in the program of bombing the North."[1] He repeated that recommendation in a memorandum to the President on November 3. On November 30, 1965, he sought to justify it as primarily a ritual gesture "before we either greatly increase our troop deployments to Vietnam or intensify our strikes against the North." It would, he argued, "lay a foundation in the mind of the American public and in world opinion for such an enlarged phase of the war, and"—he added, I thought, with no conviction—"it should give North Vietnam a face-saving chance to stop the aggression."[2] Secretary Rusk was not convinced; a pause was a serious diplomatic instrument; it could be used only once, and this was not the time to use it. President Johnson had a different concern; a pause that evoked no response would, he feared, provoke a demand for much stronger action from the American right wing—and they, he warned me, were "the Great Beast to be feared."

For several weeks the debate continued. On December 23, I left to spend Christmas at our family house in Florida. On the evening of Monday, December 28, the President telephoned me to say, "George, you wanted a pause and I'm giving you one. Now I need you to get it going. I'm sending a plane for you in the morning."

The President called me home to help plan a diplomatic extravaganza. He would send Administration personalities flying all over the world; they would tell heads of state and chiefs of government about the pause and enlist their help to bring Hanoi to the negotiating table. Averell Harriman would visit Poland and Yugoslavia, McGeorge Bundy Canada, Ambassador Foy Kohler would speak with Soviet officials, while Arthur Goldberg would call on General de Gaulle, Prime Minister Wilson, the Pope, and the Italian government.[3] My own travel assignments were modest. I was to fly to Puerto Rico to meet Senator Fulbright fresh off the eighteenth green and then to Florida to see Senators Dirksen and Mansfield.

Although President Johnson obviously enjoyed this frenetic to-ing and fro-ing (he delighted in his ability to send well-known people flying all over the world), I thought the spectacle futile and unbecoming. Still, as I was to reflect later, better a Christmas peace extravaganza than the Christmas bombing Nixon ordered in 1974. If that was part of the price we paid for a bombing pause, so be it; we at least broke the momentum of escalation, even though we would be under grave pressure to increase the pace of the war once the pause was completed.

Negotiating Gestures

The Administration constantly scanned the sky for smoke signals from Hanoi. It used disavowable envoys to try to provoke indications of willingness to talk and carried on probing operations with Iron Curtain diplomats.[4] Meanwhile, more and more of our young men were being sent to South Vietnam and casualties were rising. To borrow a phrase I had once heard Walter Lippmann use to describe his own frustrations, I felt I was "trying to swim up Niagara Falls." Not that I was idle; the President constantly pressed me for new negotiating ideas—though he really meant merely new channels and procedures. We were, as I told my colleagues, "following the traditional pattern for negotiating with a mule: just keep hitting him on the head with a two-by-four until he does what you want him to do." But that was useless with Hanoi; the mule's head was harder than the two-by-four.

On January 5, 1966, I sent the President two memoranda. One called for him to approach the heads of governments of the United Kingdom, Soviet Union, China, North Vietnam, and South Vietnam to request a secret meeting of the foreign ministers of those five countries with the United States to be held in Vienna beginning January 17, for preliminary discussions of the problem of Vietnam. The timing seemed propitious since a key member of the Soviet politburo, Alexander Shelepin, would shortly be visiting Hanoi, and we might thus arm him with specific proposals to press on the North Vietnamese. The second memorandum discussed possible ways and means of involving the United Nations in a peace effort, using either the Security Council or a special session of the General Assembly. Though I had little faith the United Nations could be useful, I still included a draft Security Council resolution.

As expected, the bombing pause evoked no response; by January, pressures were mounting to resume bombing and escalate the war. On January 20, I sent a memorandum to the President arguing that "the resumption of bombing may well frustrate the very political objectives we have in mind. There is no evidence that bombing has so far had any appreciable effect in weakening the determination of Ho Chi Minh and his colleagues. Whatever evidence there is points in the opposite direction." I recalled my experience on the Strategic Bombing Survey, pointing out that in both Europe and Japan the Survey found that "one does not break the will of the population of a police state by heavy bombing."

I followed my memorandum against bombing with a long analytical memorandum to the President. Prepared with the advice of recognized China experts Professors Allen Whiting and Fred Green, it pointed out why and how our bombing posed grave dangers of war with China. Today—with the wisdom of hindsight—it is clear that I overestimated the prospect of Chinese intervention. But President Johnson was deeply preoccupied with the China menace and the more I emphasized it, the stronger was my case for cutting our losses.

McNamara's Views

I had a distaste for ex parte Presidential approaches and whenever I wrote a memorandum to the President calling for our extrication, I showed it first to Rusk, McNamara, and Mac Bundy. Secretary McNamara and John McNaughton almost always responded by a prompt and courteous visit. Two or three times they showed me memoranda prepared by McNaughton commenting on what I had written, sometimes expressing views along the same general line while avoiding my hard conclusions. Though momentarily exhilarated by this prospect of support, I found McNamara unwilling to express those same realistic, if discouraging, views in meetings called by the President to discuss my various memoranda. Whether he privately discussed them with the President I do not know.

By May 1967, seven months after I had left the government, a draft memorandum by John McNaughton finally accepted the analysis I had been urging for the three previous years: "it now appears that no combination of actions against the North short of destruction of the regime or occupation of North Vietnamese territory will physically reduce the flow of men and materiel below the relatively small amount needed by enemy forces to continue the war in the South. . . ."[5]

First Meeting of "the Usual Suspects"

Even after my resignation in September 1966, I could not free myself from the oppressive burden of the war. It was a blight on all America—the continued killing, the dark apprehensions as we ventured more and more onto bottomless quicksand, and the hysteria in the universities that was taking an increasingly nasty turn. On November 1, 1967, at President Johnson's request, I attended a meeting at the State Department as a member of the so-called Senior Advisory Group—or, as the press called us, "the wise old men," the "elder statesmen" or, more derisively, "the usual suspects." We had dinner with Secretary Rusk and then met the following morning with the President. I made my usual plea for extrication to the usual deaf ears; the war, said the other members of the group, must be vigorously pursued. The major problem, they superciliously asserted, was how to educate American opinion. As I came out of the Cabinet Room, I said to Dean Acheson, John J. McCloy, and—if I recall properly—John Cowles of Minneapolis, "I've been watching across the table. You're like a flock of old buzzards sitting on a fence, sending the young men off to be killed. You ought to be ashamed of yourselves." I was as surprised as they—and a little embarrassed—by the intensity of my outburst.

The year 1968 caught Washington off guard with the shattering Tet offensive, which lasted for twenty-five days, from dawn on January 31 until February 24. In February, the President commissioned Dean Acheson to make an independent study of the war. Much to the President's dismay, Acheson concluded that we could not win without an unlimited commitment of forces—and that even then it might take five years. The country, Acheson told Johnson, was no longer behind the Administration, nor did Americans any longer believe what the President was telling them. Then, during the next few months, Clark Clifford, the newly appointed Secretary of Defense, accumulated mounting evidence that the war could not be won.[6] Outnumbered eight to one within the circle of advisers closest to the President, and now faced with a request from General Westmoreland for the deployment of 206,000 additional men, Clifford looked about, as I had done earlier, for outside help. The President should, he proposed, meet once again with members of the Senior Advisory Group, who would be briefed on the war and asked to express their views.

Second "Senior Advisory Group" Meeting

At 7:30 P.M. on Monday, March 25, 1968, five months after our earlier meeting, we met in the office of Secretary of State Dean Rusk: Dean

Acheson, Omar Bradley, McGeorge Bundy, Arthur Dean, Douglas Dillon, Abe Fortas, Robert Murphy, General Matthew Ridgway, Cyrus Vance, and I. After dinner we heard briefings from three government officials: Deputy Assistant Secretary of State Philip Habib, who reviewed the political situation, Major General William DePuy, who spoke of our military posture, and George Carver of the CIA, who talked about pacification and the condition of the enemy. If the North Vietnamese were to be expelled from the South and the country pacified, it would—so our briefers estimated—take at least five to ten more years. The following morning, we talked with the senior officials of the government: Dean Rusk, Clark Clifford, and others. Secretary Clifford spoke bluntly about the choices our country faced. We could either expand the war and muddle along or pursue a "reduced strategy"—cutting back on the bombing and using American troops only to defend certain populated areas.

Dean Acheson was the first of our group to acknowledge that he had changed his mind; we could not, he said, achieve our objective through military means.[7] Views were expressed around the table, and I thought to myself, "there's been a mistake in the invitation list; these can't be the same men I saw here last November." Toward noon, we went to the White House to lunch with the President in the family dining room. During lunch, General Creighton Abrams, just back from Vietnam, told us how he was training the South Vietnamese army with the object of "Vietnamizing" the war.

The President then dismissed all members of the government so as to meet alone with our group of outsiders. When we had gathered in the Cabinet Room, he asked McGeorge Bundy to summarize our collective views. Bundy mentioned particularly Dean Acheson's current opinion that we could not achieve our objectives within the limits of time and resources available. We would therefore have to change our policy drastically. Though that reflected the general view of the group he noted that Abe Fortas and Bob Murphy had dissented. Bundy then made a remark that deeply impressed me not merely for its import but its generosity: "I must tell you what I thought I would never say—that I now agree with George Ball." Bombing in the North, which Bundy had earlier favored as the way of raising the price of insurgencies around the world, staving off defeat in the South, and providing an ultimate bargaining chip was, he had now decided, doing more to erode the support of the war on the homefront than harming the North Vietnamese.

Dean Acheson announced his position in his clear, lawyerlike way. We could not stop the "belligerency" in Vietnam by any acceptable means within the time allowed to us. In view of our other problems and interests, including the dollar crisis, we should seek to disengage by midsummer. There was little support for the war in South Vietnam or in the

United States. Acheson did not think the American people would permit the war to go on for more than another year. Douglas Dillon spoke against sending additional troops and advocated stopping the bombing in an effort to move toward a negotiated settlement. He had been deeply impressed by the comments he had heard the night before that it would take five to ten years to conclude the war. General Ridgway, who had, from the first, opposed our intervention, also recommended the withdrawal of American forces, while Cyrus Vance, who, when Deputy Secretary of Defense, had always appeared to support our Vietnamese efforts, now insisted that since the war was bitterly dividing the country, it was time to seek a negotiated settlement.

I made my usual speech against the war. We could not hope to negotiate a sensible withdrawal until we stopped bombing North Vietnam. I emphasized, as I had done many times before, that the war was demoralizing our country and creating grave political divisions and that we had to get out.

There is no doubt that the unexpected negative conclusions of the "elder statesmen" profoundly shook the President. Later he grumbled to me, "Your whole group must have been brainwashed and I'm going to find out what Habib and the others told you."

No one will ever know the extent to which our advice contributed to President Johnson's decision—announced to the American people in a television speech six days after our meeting—that he would not run for President in 1968. He had, he announced, "unilaterally" ordered a halt to the air and naval bombardment of most of North Vietnam. Even that "very limited bombing of the North could come to an early end if our restraint is matched by restraint in Hanoi." Only at the end of his address did he announce his decision to withdraw from the Presidential race.

Though I knew President Johnson desperately wanted to get us out of Vietnam, he was incapable of it. His Administration had accumulated too much baggage of past statements and actions, too many fixed ideas, and too many positions it could not easily reverse. But by taking himself out of the Presidential race, Lyndon Johnson had paved the way for America's extrication, and I hoped our Vietnamese nightmare might soon be over. In spite of Hubert Humphrey's loyal and excessively exuberant support for President Johnson, I knew that he was personally revolted by the war. Once a Humphrey Administration were in place, we might then move promptly toward extrication.

Richard Nixon was in an even better position to end the war and he had everything to gain by a quick extrication. The twelve years since John Foster Dulles had first involved us in Vietnam far exceeded the short attention span of most Americans, and no one held the Republicans responsible for the current ghastly mess. By promptly negotiating an American withdrawal, Nixon could not only quiet the country but win almost universal approbation. Mendès-France had extricated France from its "dirty" Indochinese War within a month after becoming Prime Minister in 1954. That was a precedent to be pondered.

But Nixon was not, as popularly believed, a skillful politician. He was introverted, full of complexes, preoccupied with self, and insensitive to the national mood and the increasingly ominous seismic rumblings. Lacking the humanity of Humphrey and the wisdom and courage of Mendès-France, he had always been the archetypal hawk, ready at slight provocation to dispatch Americans to kill and be killed. As Vice-President in 1954, he had supported the deployment of United States troops to replace French losses and the following year had advocated that we use atomic weapons to halt Chinese moves into Vietnam. Ten years later, in 1964, he had urged retaliatory airstrikes against Laos and North Vietnam; the following year, he had opposed the Johnson Administration's efforts to start negotiations on the ground that the North Vietnamese would regard it as evidence of weakness. He had dissented in 1966, when Congressman Gerald Ford and Melvin Laird had criticized Johnson for committing the United States so deeply in Vietnam. Nixon had opposed constant calls for negotiation since those would only encourage Hanoi, and he predicted that the war would go on at least through 1971.[8] Most recently, during the Presidential campaign, he had attacked the Johnson Administration for its policy of gradualism in the use of force.

Perpetuation of a Fallacy

Nixon's central thesis was that we had failed in Vietnam because we had not used the full force at our command. To him, bombing mythology was divinely certified; like General Curtis LeMay, he seemed prepared, if necessary, to "bomb North Vietnam back to the Stone Age."

My wistful hope that the new Administration would show more wisdom than its predecessor thus had little to support it. Nixon had, as Talleyrand said of the Bourbons, "learned nothing and forgotten nothing" from Lyndon Johnson's experience and was thus doomed to repeat and even expand Johnson's mistakes. He reverted to the Johnson Administration's attitude toward the war that had prevailed in 1965— before most of my colleagues had conceded—at least to themselves— that the war could not be won.

By protracting the war and using massive air power, Nixon believed that we could wear down the enemy and ultimately achieve "peace with honor." That slogan was the tip-off; not only did the new President coopt the terminology of Lyndon Johnson, but he exaggerated and improved on it. "For the United States, this first defeat in our nation's history would result in a collapse of confidence in American leadership, not only in Asia but throughout the world."[9] And, in defending our Cambodian invasion, he said, "If, when the chips are down, the world's most powerful nation . . . acts like a pitiful, helpless giant, the forces of totalitarianism and anarchy will threaten free nations and free institutions throughout the world."[10]

For such an astute man, Henry Kissinger also seemed to have entered the government with an unrealistic view of the war. Though his old friend, Jean Sainteny, the French expert on Indochina, had told him that America was engaged in a "hopeless enterprise" in Vietnam, he rejected that advice as the product of pride and nationalism. Like my colleagues in the Johnson Administration, he gave no weight to the lessons of the French experience and he also seems to have shared Nixon's view of air power. Neither understood the limited effect of bombing against a fanatical enemy any more than had Walt Rostow or Maxwell Taylor before them.

Kissinger's initial assessment of our Vietnam prospects sounded as though he had been absent in Mars during the preceding three years. Soon after arriving in the White House in 1969, he is reported to have told a visiting group of Quaker antiwar activists that he was "quite optimistic" about the prospects of a rapid settlement. "Give us six months," he told them, "and if we haven't ended the war by then, you can come back and tear down the White House fence."[11] By dealing North Vietnam some "brutal blows" we could, he was confident, force it to make the kinds of concessions that would secure peace; he refused "to believe that a little fourth-rate power like Vietnam doesn't have a breaking point."[12] It was the McNamara quantitative approach all over again.

When he first met with a North Vietnamese representative, he "half believed," he now confesses, "that rapid progress could be made if we could convince them of our sincerity."[13] Even after he had been negotiating for some months, he showed little more sense of reality. "I had great hope for negotiations—perhaps, as events turned out, more than was warranted": a qualification that was, by any standard, astonishing understatement. "I even thought," he admits, that "a tolerable outcome could be achieved within a year."[14]

In failing to recognize that North Vietnamese obduracy far transcended the constraints of Western logic, the Nixon Administration spurned the grim lessons Americans should by then have learned. Under Nixon's guidance, America dropped twice the weight of bombs in Indochina as had been dropped during the whole of the Johnson Administration. But in the end, Hanoi conceded nothing substantial, overran South Vietnam, and emerged with everything it wanted.

The Same Old Rationale

Every new Administration feels it can improve on the performance of the past. The Nixon Administration's initial error was to accept uncritically its predecessor's rationale for staying in the war. America, it averred, had to win to preserve confidence in its promises, or, as John McNaughton had put it, to save its "reputation as a guarantor" (which was by then the trendy catchphrase). Even more important, Nixon perpetuated the Johnson Administration's fallacy of defining reputation in narrow and mechanistic terms.

On what components of reputation did America's leadership most heavily depend? Unlike the totalitarian nations, America was—at least in comparative terms—regarded as humane, fair, generous, and dedicated to showing "a decent respect to the opinions of mankind." We were not ideologically driven; we were thought not to indulge in the brutal practices of either the Soviet Union or China. All this we were putting at risk in Vietnam. Our use of napalm, flame throwers, defoliating chemicals, and heavy bombers was sending a shudder through the civilized world. Not only did we appear a great bully, there were also racial implications: would we treat a white population with the same brutality to achieve the same exiguous objective?

To preserve the respect on which our leadership depended, we needed to look at our reputation as a whole, not measure it solely by the degree of our obsessive support for an involvement most Americans— and indeed most of our allies—thought imprudent and unrelated to our strategic interests. When we engaged in increasingly indiscriminate killings in a futile attempt to achieve a marginal objective, our friends shook their heads with wonder and worry. Why were we so improvidently risking our ability to maintain our truly vital responsibilities elsewhere in the world? Why were the pragmatic Americans pursuing an *ignis fatuus?* If our judgment were no better than that, could they trust us to protect the West?

Traveling widely through the United States, as well as Europe and Asia, I grew increasingly convinced that, even more important than what other people thought of us, our effectiveness as a nation depended on the Americans' idea of America. The campuses were in flames. A whole generation of our youth was being deprived of a proper education and pushed so far into extremism as to proclaim that their country was no better—and might even be worse—than the totalitarian powers and that Ho Chi Minh was a hero compared with the evil men in Washington. Civil disruption was mounting and spreading; Kent State would incite it further. The war was destroying our coherence as a nation; if it long continued, American society would suffer organic damage. It was time to look hard at what we were doing to ourselves.

Out of mounting frustration, the Nixon Administration flailed about with neither discipline nor strategic direction—secretly bombing and then invading Cambodia, attacking in Laos, and scattering bombs all over the countryside. With the battle cry of upholding our reputation, we degraded ourselves. No friendly nation applauded our massive use of

B-52s; we invited disrespect while proclaiming that the preservation of respect was our justification for staying in the fight. The vision of the world's most powerful nation smashing up the people and meager assets of a tiny, backward country was not only unedifying, it evoked charges of colonialist, imperialist, capitalist brutality. Moreover, it damaged our own self-esteem, since, as the bombing grew more indiscriminate and desperate, our own vision of our country as strong, generous, humane, and, above all, civilized was sadly diminished.

Nixon's Illusory "Plan"

During the 1968 election campaign, Nixon had repeatedly stated that he had a "plan" to end the war. But, as Kissinger's memoirs make clear, the new Administration had at the beginning no idea where it was going. Public opposition to the war was growing more strident and violent. Secretary of Defense Laird, with his highly tuned political sensitivities, was pressing hard for the removal of American forces by phased withdrawals, and Nixon accepted that advice in the hope that, by thus reducing American casualties, we could reconcile the American people to a protracted war. Meanwhile, commanders in the field were directed to concentrate on building up South Vietnamese forces under a program called "Vietnamization" that the Johnson Administration had initiated at the beginning of 1968. The third element of the policy was the launching of an aerial offensive far more intense, reckless, and extensive than any undertaken before. The calculus of this program was tragically misconceived and callously misrepresented; it was not designed to get us out of the war but to keep us in it longer.

The plan could certainly not bring about Nixon's announced goal of a negotiated "peace with honor," for it violated the most elementary principles of negotiation. First, a government contemplating negotiations should use its most important bargaining leverage in the most effective way and at the proper moment and not give it away without a maximum concession from the other side. Second, a great power should not link its own bargaining objectives to those of a client state with irreconcilable interests.

The First Mistake: Throwing Away Our Bargaining Leverage

North Vietnam's preeminent objective was to force the United States to withdraw its troops. Once rid of America's ground forces, Hanoi's leaders were fully confident they could destroy the South Vietnamese Army (ARVN) no matter how well trained or equipped. Prior to American intervention, the ARVN had proved unable to cope with even Viet Cong elements when no North Vietnamese contingents were in the country; once we withdrew American troops, it could not possibly hold out long against Hanoi's armies, which now dominated large parts of the South. Thus, an offer to withdraw our army was the one really effective bargaining card we could play to gain even the minimal concessions needed for extrication. While we still had our full strength of 549,000 men in place, it had high value; once it was clear that we planned to withdraw forces unilaterally, that value abruptly disappeared.

When Nixon took office, our troop strength was at its maximum and unilateral withdrawals had been expressly ruled out. On December 29, 1968, less than a month before Nixon's inauguration, Secretary of Defense Clark Clifford had stated that "the level of combat is such that we are building up our troops; not cutting them down." But—astonishing as it may seem—the Nixon Administration did not even try to trade with the central resource of its bargaining position, but instead threw it away, fatuously explaining its unilateral withdrawal of troops with the same inverted logic that had so often disturbed me during the Johnson years. Rather than impairing our bargaining position, "withdrawing a number of American combat troops from Vietnam would," Nixon stated, "demonstrate to Hanoi that we were serious in seeking a diplomatic settlement."[15]

I watched these developments with increasing bafflement and despair; Nixon's feeble rationalization revealed a total failure to comprehend Hanoi's interests or intentions. The amazing *esprit* of the North Vietnamese stemmed from the conviction that time was working on their side. Aware of the tangential character of our own interest in South Vietnam, they posited their strategy on the belief that, if they only kept up fighting long enough, the United States would follow the French precedent: get tired and go home. They obviously knew all about the shrill and violent opposition to the war building in the United States, and when Nixon announced the first significant troop withdrawal, they must have concluded that the end was in sight. By announcing troop withdrawals before offering realistic concessions we destroyed any hope of an early settlement. Why should the North Vietnamese seriously negotiate when they needed only hang on and wait as we got out of the way?

Failing to understand the fanatical intensity of Hanoi's commitment, the Nixon Administration wasted the critical early days of the negotiation by demanding mutual withdrawal, which, as I had again and again pointed out, was a chimera. The North Vietnamese would never yield possession of the 25 percent of South Vietnamese territory they had gained by long years of fighting; that for them would mean capitulation. They would insist that we withdraw unilaterally while their forces remained in the field. Unhappily, when Kissinger finally recognized this obvious point, it was too late. By the time he first offered unilateral withdrawal in October 1970, twenty months had gone by; Nixon had already thrown away the negotiating value of our massive forces in Vietnam by voluntarily pulling out 150,000 men and announcing that we would withdraw another 150,000 within a year. The North Vietnamese leaders could hardly fail but recognize the obvious: the American people would never permit the President to stop or reverse course. America was tiring of the war just as France had done in 1954; Hanoi had only to dig in and wait.

Failing to Separate our Interests from Hanoi's

The second negotiating mistake of the Nixon Administration was its failure to separate our interests from those of the Saigon government. That left it in an excruciating nutcracker. The incompatibility of America's aims with those of the controlling clique in South Vietnam was obvious: America wanted to get out of the Vietnamese mess with the least harm to its reputation; while the Saigon government could survive only if we drove out the North Vietnamese, exterminated the Viet Cong, and restored its sovereignty over the whole territory of South Vietnam. When Kissinger acknowledged the reality of America's predicament and belatedly offered to withdraw unilaterally, he implicitly recognized that we would no longer try to meet Saigon's desiderata. We would never force the North Vietnamese to withdraw; we would leave them holding substantial areas of the South. But while we turned our back on Saigon's principal war aim, we still did nothing to separate our interests from those of our client. We continued to pretend schizophrenically that we were determined to achieve the very objectives we were simultaneously abandoning, hoping to placate Saigon with assurances we knew would not be kept.

While still in academic life, just prior to joining the Nixon Administration, Professor Kissinger had acknowledged the difficulties of trying to negotiate for a third party with divergent interests.[16] Nixon and Kissinger had little respect for President Thieu; as the negotiations proceeded and his demands inevitably contradicted their own increasingly urgent objectives, they made clear their disdain for him, both in their exchanges with one another and the way they treated him in the days just prior to the truce agreement. By being forced to bully and cajole Thieu, they paid the price for failing to establish America's diplomatic independence at the outset. But, as I shall point out later, it was not Nixon who paid the final price but some brave and innocent Americans.

I had—as I have recounted—persistently pointed out to Lyndon Johnson that our first step in extricating ourselves from the noisome Vietnam swamp was to demonstrate to the world that the South Vietnamese regime was failing to live up to the conditions stipulated by President Eisenhower for our continued involvement. I again spelled out that thesis in an article in the *New York Times Magazine* of December 21, 1969, and sent a copy to Henry Kissinger with a note pointing out the need to move promptly down that road.[17] Though Kissinger wrote back expressing interest, that was the end of it.

Requiring proof of acceptable performance was more than a diplomatic maneuver; it was an obligation American administrations owed the people. How could we honestly ask young Americans to risk their lives to help South Vietnam without insisting that its government make a fully effective effort? Yet the soggy Saigon regime was notoriously failing even the most elementary standards of performance. President Thieu, publicly acclaimed by the new Administration (and by its predecessor) as a heroic and charismatic figure, was, to quote Robert Shaplen (one of our most astute and experienced Far Eastern experts), "an unpopular, vacillating and conniving leader who could never pull the country together, let alone control the bickering members of his own palace guard."[18] As for the South Vietnamese army, I need only quote a description of the ARVN by another highly experienced American: "We should have asked ourselves long ago how an army can go on functioning when it is simply a business organization in which everything is for sale—from what you eat, to transfer or promotion."[19]

The Kissinger Apologia

In his memoirs, Henry Kissinger contends that the Nixon Administration could not, prior to October 1972, have secured the release of our prisoners in exchange for an American withdrawal, because until that date, Hanoi insisted on linking military and political questions, maintaining that one could not be solved without the other. "In other words," Kissinger concludes, "not even a unilateral United States withdrawal would end the war or secure the release of our prisoners." Later he comments: "Over the years we moved from position to position, from mutual to unilateral withdrawal, from residual forces to complete departure. But Hanoi never budged. We could have neither peace nor our prisoners until we achieved what Hanoi apparently no longer trusted itself to accomplish: the overthrow of our ally."[20] Later, Le Duc Tho, a North Vietnamese minister, again told him that "before any negotiations, the United States would have to set a deadline for unilateral withdrawal . . .; there was no mention of the release of our prisoners of war."[21]

I find Kissinger's conclusions quite unpersuasive. At no time did he offer merely to withdraw troops in exchange for prisoners; since he had failed to separate American interests from Saigon's, his proposals always included extraneous provisions to satisfy the South Vietnamese. Moreover—and one cannot blame him for this—even before Kissinger's first conversation with the North Vietnamese, Nixon had effectively destroyed

America's negotiating position by withdrawing large slices of our army and announcing that the process would continue. Time was working on Hanoi's side; it was getting what it wanted for nothing, so why should it offer to return our prisoners? Retaining the prisoners would increase domestic pressures on America to hasten our troop withdrawal, and meanwhile the prisoners could serve as hostages in case the United States ever halted withdrawals and tried to reverse course.

When, by October 1972, Hanoi had finally achieved what it wanted— the withdrawal of American forces—it was quite ready to agree to return the prisoners since they no longer served a useful purpose. The United States was no longer a serious obstacle to Hanoi's final seizure of the whole of Vietnam. We had only twenty-three thousand troops left in the country, and, except for the threat of continued bombing (which influenced the North Vietnamese far less than the bombing theologians believed), America was already out of the war. Unburdening itself of our prisoners and accepting a cease-fire was then all to Hanoi's advantage; it gave it a welcome opportunity to regroup, resupply, and augment its forces in South Vietnam for the final devastating push against the ARVN, now demoralized and rendered powerless by America's departure.

What Might Have Been

Our Vietnamese imbroglio was marked by the errors of judgment and missed opportunities of three administrations. For years I had watched us blunder more and more deeply into the wretched mire while we refused to face the reality of our hopeless predicament. Now once more we had missed the bus. Had we traded a unilateral withdrawal for our prisoners when we still had over a half million men in Vietnam, I have absolutely no doubt we could have gained an agreement for the return of our prisoners and a cease-fire of perhaps a year. For South Vietnam, the final outcome would have been no different from what finally occurred; its overrunning was the preordained final act of the grisly drama. For America, the difference would have been profound: we would not have lost an additional twenty thousand young American lives and would not have killed at least six-hundred-thousand Vietnamese. We would have avoided the opprobrium attached to our bombing of Laos and invasion of Cambodia and saved far more of our reputation than we finally salvaged. We would have halted the building up of a catastrophic social eruption that left a lasting scar on a whole generation of Americans. We would have kept inflation and the disruption of our economy at a manageable level.

I never had the slightest doubt that the truce agreements reached in January 1973—for which Mr. Kissinger received the Nobel Prize— assured the extinction of a separate South Vietnam. With American troops withdrawn and Hanoi's forces left occupying large areas of the South, there was no way a demoralized South Vietnam could hold out. The political protections in the agreement (the product of months of haggling) were window dressing. The cease-fire could not possibly hold. Since the agreement failed even to define the boundaries of the enclaves, each side was immediately forced to fight to protect and enlarge its own territorial holdings. Provision for an International Control Commission, which had been the occasion for endless arguement, was never more than a charade. Because the commission could report violations only by unanimous vote, its Communist members could—and did—assure the commission's impotence until, finally, the Canadian members quit in disgust. Thus events quickly demonstrated what should have been clear all along: protracted horse trading over the elaborate provisions of the agreement relating to such matters as the DMZ, elections, and so on had been shadow play. President Thieu seems to have recognized this, but he was powerless; his fate was in our hands and he had no options. At the end, he was forced to accede to the final settlement by threat and despair—and by a Nixon confidence game.

Deceptive Promises

As a result of the failure to separate our interests from Saigon's Kissinger found himself in a hopelessly compromised position. Since he had abandoned Saigon's principal war aims, he had to conceal from Thieu the promises he was secretly making to North Vietnamese Minister Le Duc Tho in Paris. He did not even show Thieu the text of the agreement he had already initialed with the North Vietnamese representatives in Paris in October 1972. When concealment proved no longer possible, Nixon bludgeoned Thieu into line against his better judgment not only by ultimata but also by promises that could never have been fulfilled.

On November 14, 1972, and January 5, 1973, Nixon sent Thieu secret letters. He wrote on November 14 that he understood Thieu's concern about "the status of North Vietnamese forces in South Vietnam" but "far more important than what we say in the agreement on this issue is what we do in the event the enemy renews its aggression. You have my absolute assurance that if Hanoi fails to abide by the terms of this agreement it is my intention to take swift and severe retaliatory action."[22]

Nixon's second letter stated, "Should you decide, as I trust you will, to go with us, you have my assurance of continued assistance in the post-settlement period and that we will respond *with full force* should the settlement be violated by North Vietnam."[23] (Italics added.)

What was meant by "full force"? Nuclear bombs? No one will ever know. To the Congress and the American people, Kissinger insisted in October and again in January that the Administration had made no "secret agreements." But what else could one call the two Nixon letters? "Peace with honor" for Richard M. Nixon had a highly special meaning; he was, in effect, saying, in the words of the prophet Jeremiah, "peace, peace, when there is no peace." Ralph Waldo Emerson had expressed it succinctly when he wrote, "the louder he talked of his honor the faster we counted the spoons." Not only were Nixon's secret promises illegal, as McGeorge Bundy has conclusively demonstrated, but they were also a gross deception of the American people.[24]

Nixon had no authority to commit the United States to send back its bombers and troops, and Congress and the American people would have rebelled at any request to give him that authority. There was no precedent for a commitment to a foreign government not hedged about by the normal language of constitutionality. Though Mr. Kissinger suggests that the President's secret promises were comparable to those the Carter Administration later gave in 1979 to reinforce the peace treaty between Israel and Egypt, McGeorge Bundy has pointed out that Carter's letters, far from being assurances of "full force," simply referred to our country's taking—"subject to United States Constitutional processes—such . . . action as it may deem appropriate."

Given the degree of Nixon's megalomania, his extravagant promises are, in retrospect, hardly surprising. He furtively gave written promises to Thieu but hid them from Congress and his countrymen. Since he also hid them from Hanoi, they had no deterrent effect.

Nixon and Kissinger knew that Hanoi had agreed to their so-called settlement only as a tactical maneuver. In his reports to Nixon during the latter part of 1972, Kissinger explicitly acknowledged that the truce they had achieved, far from offering peace, was only a pause before our further involvement in war.

On December 7, 1972, he advised Nixon from Saigon that "It is now obvious as the result of our additional exploration of Hanoi's intentions that they have not in any way abandoned their objectives or ambitions with respect to South Vietnam. What they have done is decide to modify their strategy. . . . Thus, we can anticipate no lasting peace in the wake of a consummated agreement, but merely a shift in Hanoi's modus operandi. We will probably have little chance of maintaining the agreement without evident hair-trigger U.S. readiness, which may in fact be challenged at any time, to enforce its provisions."[25]

Although Nixon lived in a world of shadows and nightmares, could he possibly have believed the country would have accepted the indefinite extension of "hair-trigger . . . readiness"? In 1968 our Senior Advisory Group had told President Johnson that the American people would not let the war continue more than another year. Now, four years later, Nixon was still promising the Vietnamese that our airmen would continue to fight and die and by the language of his secret letters, implying that our troops might even go back in. Could even he have believed that? Americans were fed up with the war to the verge of nausea; they wanted the killing stopped.

Kissinger attributes the shattering denouement to Watergate and the disintegration of the Presidency. He implies that, had Nixon not been caught *in flagrante* in impeachable crimes, he could have indefinitely used our armed forces as his personal chattel, sending our sons to kill and be killed in Vietnam without the need to consult anyone. I find that a bizarre distortion of reality. Regardless of Watergate, Americans had had almost a decade of war and were not about to let it drag on for another decade. They had washed their hands of Vietnam and would not under any circumstances approve sending our bombers to resume the carnage in a tedious, profitless, demanding, repulsive, hopeless, and ultimately meaningless struggle.[26]

I cannot believe that even Richard Nixon in his most megalomaniac phase was so insensitive as not to understand this. Then why send the letters to Thieu? My own guess is that, though he foresaw that Congress would prevent our bombers from flying, a Congressional veto would absolve him from responsibility; he could blame the final debacle on Congressional obtuseness and timidity.

All wars are brutalizing and the brutalization of our Vietnamese struggle extended even to the White House, where our casualties had become merely a cold statistic. In October 1972, Kissinger and the North Vietnamese negotiator Le Duc Tho signed an understanding intended as the basis for a final agreement. Though padded out with technical and political provisions, it was, in practical terms, nothing more than we could have obtained four years before had we then bargained from a position of maximum troop strength; nor did we later improve it. Kissinger thought it was the best achievable, and Nixon sent a message stating, "In my view the October 8 agreement was one which would certainly be in our interest" and that "we have no choice but to reach agreement along the line of the October 8 principles." Nevertheless, because we had not established negotiating independence, Nixon let Thieu—for whom any settlement meant defeat—demand so many modifications of the October draft that the North Vietnamese broke off negotiations.

Bombing to Improve Syntax

Nixon responded by launching the notorious Christmas bombing called Linebacker II. It involved sending B-52s over both Hanoi and Haiphong; the intensive attack lasted twelve days, involving 729 B-52 sorties and about 1000 fighter-bomber attack sorties. More than 20,000 tons of bombs were dropped. How many North Vietnamese casualties occurred is a matter of dispute (the North Vietnamese claimed at the time that between 1300 and 1600 people had been killed). There was no doubt that 93 American airmen were missing, with 31 reported captured, and that we lost 26 planes, including 15 B-52s.

I knew the literature of bombing, ranging back to Julio Douhet, the Italian who argued in 1921 that bombing could win wars, and I had been fascinated as an adolescent by the controversial activities of General Billy Mitchell, a bombing zealot who first showed how to destroy a battleship from the air. Yet not only had my work with the US Strategic Bombing Survey shown me the limited effectiveness of bombing, I had also long been troubled by the fact that, of all forms of warfare, it is the most impersonal. It enables warriors to kill masses of people anonymously without having to confront the results of their macabre handiwork as was required in classical battles. When we bombed Vietnam, killing not only soldiers but civilians, we could hardly justify it as responding to a real and present threat to our country or our institutions. How, then, could a humane people possibly condone Nixon's Linebacker operation, which meant death or prison for almost a hundred patriotic young Americans—as well as death for more than a thousand North Vietnamese civilians—merely to improve the syntax of an empty document that any knowledgeable person knew would be flouted by both sides? The action can be explained only as the frantic striking back of a power-obsessed leader who had come to regard himself as the sole repository of American power. Only a man too self-centered to comprehend the anguish of the human condition could give an order sending hundreds to their deaths for a trifling purpose.

Yet no one, including Henry Kissinger, has seriously contended that the agreement finally attained after Linebacker II was materially better than the understanding he signed in October 1972. The whole argument was about irrelevancies: whether a form of words might be regarded as implying something resembling a coalition government, whether the Demarcation Zone (DMZ) was a serious frontier, and other trivia. Squalid politics provides the most charitable explanation for a bloody and otherwise totally irrational act. Kissinger has suggested that Nixon rejected the agreement reached in Paris in October 1972 primarily because he wanted to stall; he could have found it politically awkward, just prior to the 1972 election, to have to defend agreements that could precipitate a row with Thieu and appear weak to his hard-line supporters. It was the final penalty for having failed to separate the interests of America from those of Saigon at the outset. It was no excuse for more killing.

The Unnecessary Tragedy

Though my active participation in the conduct of the Vietnam War ceased in 1966, I still continue to brood over it. What malign phasing of the moon drove intelligent men in two American administrations to bog us down in the longest war in our history, not because our country or its major interests were in danger, but out of a misconceived concern for "our reputation"? Were our leaders really thinking about the reputation of our nation or primarily of their own place in history? I find it revealing that Richard Nixon repeatedly plagiarized Lyndon Johnson's vainglorious boast: "I'm not going to be the first President to lose a war." May not that special phrasing tell more about the characters of the two men than about our posture as a nation? Lyndon Johnson could not face the consequences of withdrawal, because, in his oversimplified lexicon of politics, that was the equivalent of personal defeat. Though Richard Nixon had a golden opportunity to exploit Johnson's failure by a prompt settlement in 1969, his vanity and myopia prevented it.

If our Vietnam involvement taught us anything, it is that we should beware of untested assumptions, or, in other words, that we should pay far more heed to the "giraffe question": Why? Today I continue to be preoccupied with the concern that has haunted me for a decade: Will historians, assessing what has happened, quote from T. S. Eliot's *Dry Salvages* as I have for the title of this book? Will they note the poet's poignant lament: "We had the experience but missed the meaning"?[27]

We fought, so we said, for South Vietnam but it was never a country—merely an artificial slice of territory created by an improvised dividing line as a diplomatic convenience to obtain the 1954 settlement. Lacking the cohesion, drive, legitimacy, and common purpose of a nation, South Vietnam had no chance to survive against a cruel, fanatical revolutionary clique in Hanoi that responded to, and was driven by, not merely a lust for power but an atavistic anticolonialism. Still, myths have more lives than a cat. Many Americans will continue to argue that we could have beaten Hanoi had the Johnson Administration fully used the massive weight of our bombing force from the outset of the war, that we finally wrung a settlement out of the North Vietnamese only by the ferocity of our bombing, and that that settlement would have endured had Congress not cravenly denied Nixon the right to send back our bombers and troops. To those who solace themselves with such wishful thoughts I would only repeat the Duke of Wellington's famous reply when a stranger approached him on the street with the greeting, "Mr. Robinson, I believe." To that the Duke responded, "If you believe that, Sir, you can believe anything."

T. S. Eliot announced no fresh discovery when he wrote that "Humankind cannot stand too much reality." Myths are an age-old form of escape, and they rarely fade completely; people will continue to believe what they want to believe: the South could have won the Civil War if Secretary of the Treasury Memminger had adopted better financial policies or Lee had pursued a better military strategy; Napoleon need not have lost at Waterloo; Lenin would never have succeeded had Kerensky been bolder and more incisive, etcetera ad infinitum.

Lord Vansittart, the Permanent Under Secretary of the British Foreign Office, tried for years prior to 1939 to warn his colleagues of the Nazi menace, but he could not, as he put it, "induce the unwilling to accept the inevitable." My own efforts were not of the same magnitude, yet I found some comfort in that phrase, as well as a profound poignancy in Vansittart's conclusion: "There is a wonderful continuity in the Western tragedy." Our protracted involvement in the Vietnam War was an authentic tragedy—perhaps the most tragic error in American history. Not only was it bloody and unnecessary but it led us to actions that betrayed our principles as a nation. And we have not yet done with it; traces of its evil spoor still defile our economic, social, and political life.

I can only conclude, as I wrote in 1976,

we dare not let the revisionists distort the real meaning of our Vietnam adventure, or we shall have learned nothing. In spite of individual feats of devotion and valor—which this time were largely unsung—no one but a fanatic could regard our involvement in that war as a bright page in our history. We should, instead, pay heed to Churchill's famous comment to the House of Commons on April 4, 1940, following the evacuation of Dunkirk: "We must be careful not to assign to this deliverance the attributes of a victory." For, however one may try to justify it, it was a tragic defeat for America. Not in the military terms of the battlefield, but a defeat for our political authority and moral influence abroad and for our sense of mission and cohesion at home. A defeat not because our initial purposes were unworthy or our intentions anything less than honorable, but because—in frustration and false pride and our innocence of the art of extrication—we were forced to the employment of excessively brutal means to achieve an equivocal objective against a poor, small, backward country.

That is something the world will be slow to forgive, and we should be slow to forget.[28]

PART VIII

The Private Sector

27. The Decision to Resign

Once we were engaged in all-out war, diplomacy moved into the shadows. Though my civilian colleagues continued to look over the shoulders of the generals—fascinated by military tactics and the operational aspects of warfare—the day-to-day conduct of the war was largely out of their hands. To be sure, our would-be Clausewitzes still gathered in innumerable bureaucratic meetings, endlessly searching for the elusive keys to victory. But I thought the schemes they evolved more like the writhings of a decapitated chicken than rational strategy. Few any longer believed their own fantasies. The zest had gone out of the game. The war had become stylized; its tired players went through the motions, talking the familiar jargon because withdrawal was a dirty word.

My Increasing Futility

I watched all this with melancholy and a growing conviction that I could no longer play a useful part. Their single-minded concentration on the goal of pounding the North Vietnamese into capitulation was, I felt, stultifying my colleagues for whom I had not only great intellectual respect but very real affection. They seemed to be seeing the world as a pre-Cimabue painting, lacking both perspective and proportion. Where Vietnam seemed to me a tiny piece of real estate of limited strategic interest ten thousand miles away, the mental maps they used to chart our policy portrayed it as a vast menacing continent hanging over America. It was as though, following a geologic convulsion, a hostile Asia had drifted within a few miles of California and was threatening our national existence. I was reminded of the king in the musical *The King and I,* who insisted that Siam was the largest nation in the world.

As I was not an armchair military theorist and had never believed for a moment we could win, I devoted my time and attention to other areas of the world where vital American interests were genuinely involved. Even that was no longer satisfying because I found it practically impossible to interest the distracted President in any major new initiative. The war was a vampire sucking dry the Administration's vitality and setting us at odds with other friendly governments.

My job had lost its savor, and, as our involvement in the Vietnam nightmare had passed the point where I could significantly influence policy, it was time to resign. The decision was not "agonizing," to use Mr. Dulles's favorite phrase. After six intense years in the diplomatic pressure cooker, I was depleted—physically, mentally, morally, and financially. It had been a period of concentrated though (until Vietnam) highly rewarding labor; during the whole time, I had been away from the State Department (other than on negotiating trips) for only a little over thirty days out of more than two thousand—and I was tired. Dean Rusk and I worked on virtually the same schedule. Saturdays, Sundays, and even holidays were part of a gray continuum—indistinguishable except that on Saturday nights Virginia Rusk and Ruth Ball ritualistically laid out colored shirts for Dean and me to wear to work the next day. It was our means of keeping track.

Flagging spirits had produced a diminishing exuberance. A year or so before, when confronted with a challenging problem, I would have felt the adrenalin surge and urgently set about mobilizing the State Department's resources in search of a solution. Now I was inclined to greet new problems warily and wearily, indulging the squalid hope that if let alone, they might cure themselves. Nor did I have the same confidence in my judgment; I was too tired always to seek the tough-minded, difficult answer and to struggle for the support of preoccupied colleagues.

I left the Department on September 30, 1966. The following Thursday, the President and Mrs. Johnson gave a farewell party for Ruth and me, attended by all the members of the cabinet, and the next morning we flew to Milan. During a fortnight on Lake Como at the Villa Serbelloni, I began work on a book, later published as *The Discipline of Power*. Then, after ten more days at a friend's villa on the sea, we drove about in Sicily on a holiday. I needed time to clear my mind.

What deeply preoccupied me then—and still does—was how our country could have blundered into the Vietnam mess. Would we have followed a different course under a different leader? Richard Nixon compounded all of Lyndon Johnson's mistakes and added many of his own, and, in view of his consistently hawkish record, I am convinced that had he won the 1960 election, he would have got us into trouble even more quickly and deeply. But that does not resolve the fundamental enigma of Lyndon Johnson—the most conspicuous Vietnam War casualty. Though a spate of books have tried to explain Johnson's complexities, I put little stock in the armchair psychologists who analyze the psyches of political leaders with pretentious and nauseating jargon. I can give only a personal view of Johnson that is necessarily incomplete, with little conviction that my observations will add much to history.

One element that reinforced LBJ's failure to face reality in Vietnam was his sense of educational inferiority. He was overly impressed by the academic credentials of the men he had inherited from a particularly glamorous administration, sometimes expressing his sense of inferiority with, it seemed to me, a kind of silent, scornful envy, "God damn it, I made it without their advantages and now they're all working for me!" If his lack of confidence in his own intellectual sophistication made him uncritically respectful of some of their advice, it also made him vulnerable to erudite sycophancy and specious historical analogies.

On December 29, 1963, President Johnson, McGeorge Bundy, and I were breakfasting on the terrace of President Johnson's ranch on the Pedernales. Chancellor Erhard of Germany was that morning's captive audience, and, as he often did, the President began boasting of his chief advisers (without, of course, mentioning that almost all of them were part of his bequest from President Kennedy).

"No head of state," he said, "ever had such a galaxy of talent. Dean Rusk—well, he was a Rhodes Scholar, a professor, then head of the Rockefeller Foundation. Bob McNamara was a professor at Harvard [he had been, in fact, an instructor at the Harvard Business School], then he ran the Ford Motor Company. Mac Bundy, here, is my in-house Ph.D. He was Dean up at Harvard." Then—looking at me—he said as a kind of afterthought, "I'll tell you something else, Chancellor, George Ball's an intellectual, too." I let the remark go at the moment, not wishing to confuse Erhard, the prototypical German professor. But later in the morning when I was alone with the President, I said to him, "You know, at breakfast you called me an intellectual. With all due respect, Mr. President, those are fighting words where I come from, and I hope you'll never say that to me again." He laughed and slapped me on the back and said, "I know you're not one of those smart-ass eggheads."

Lyndon Johnson understood America but little of foreign countries or their history. He knew about the poor and needy and the politics of farms and cities, but not about revolution in the Asian rice paddies. Had the war not occurred, he could have been a great President; instead, he must remain an ambiguous and compromised figure. During the Kennedy Administration, he had been exposed to the problems of Southeast Asia only tangentially; President Kennedy had never brought him into his close counsels. He had strongly opposed the call for America's intervention to help the French in 1954, but, imbued with the spirit of a fighting Texan, he had consistently expressed a hard line. As Vice-President in May 1961, he had returned from Vietnam announcing that the decision we faced was vital,[1] and he went on to say that "The battle against Communism must be joined in Southeast Asia with strength and determination to achieve success there—or the United States, inevitably, must surrender the Pacific and take up our defenses on our own shores."[2]

He had liked Diem when they had met in Vietnam in 1961, and that personal impression had colored his view of the war, since he habitually thought of relations between governments in terms of personalities. Added to that was an instinctive feeling of the loyalty one politician owed another as co-members of an international self-protective association and the politician's occupational addiction to hyperbole. Thus, I shuddered deeply when in Honolulu in 1966, Johnson had embraced Ky and Thieu as "two brave leaders of the Vietnamese Republic," and, working himself up to an extravagant frenzy, had lashed out at critics of his policy, whom he described as "special pleaders who counsel retreat in Vietnam" and who belong "to a group that has always been blind to experience and deaf to hope. We cannot accept their logic that tyranny ten thousand miles away is not tyranny to concern us—or that subjugation by an armed minority in Asia is different from subjugation by an armed minority in Europe."

His reactions all too often confirmed my strong belief that American Presidents or Vice-Presidents should never be permitted outside the country without firm and experienced keepers. Freed from the constraining influence of a skeptical press and alert and well-briefed advisers, enjoying adulation and the stimulus of a foreign clime, they all too often lose focus and talk nonsense.[3]

To Lyndon Johnson, Diem was our man; we had created him and in Johnson's view, we should not have let the odious activities of his brother and sister-in-law deflect us from giving him our continued support. Thus he deplored the Kennedy Administration's encouragement of the coup as a major mistake, and I think he saw it as bad luck that he should take office just after the overthrow of Diem. By the time of his Presidency, the situation in Saigon had grown increasingly sticky, and Americans were required, every few weeks, to learn a new cast of actors with odd-sounding Oriental names. That was far too exotic for Lyndon Johnson.

Haunted by thoughts of their place in history, all Presidents dramatize themselves. Lyndon Johnson was particularly susceptible to temptation, as he demonstrated when he romanticized his hardships and struggle for his diligent Boswell, Doris Kearns.[4] Posturing and distorting facts, he sought to create a self-portrait poignantly colored with virtue, pathos, and heroism. By then, of course, he was out of power, and it was merely good fun; but I have no doubt it had affected his judgment to hear Walt Rostow compare him to Abraham Lincoln after the Wilderness Campaign or at some other dark point in the Civil War, when, bedeviled by the opposition, agonizing over the bloodshed, he still indomitably carried on the struggle. Johnson had little patience with a Tolstoyan view of history. History was heroes, and I suspect he thought of himself in the Vietnam context not so much as Abraham Lincoln but as Davy Crockett, fighting to avenge the Alamo, which—like Vietnam in 1966—had more symbolic than strategic value.

Even though Johnson was overly impressed by elegantly educated men, he might have steered a wiser Vietnam course had his erudite counsellors not all given him the same advice. As I have pointed out earlier, each of his top civilian advisers—Dean Rusk, Bob McNamara, McGeorge Bundy, and the CIA chief, John McCone—was firmly convinced, at least initially, that we could win the war. Later, even after it had become clear to at least some of them that we could not win, they were unanimous in believing that we could not afford the costs of getting out. Each had his own honorable reasons for reaching these conclusions—reasons that reflected temperament, education, and experience.

To have stood against this monolithic advice would have required a man with almost fanatical self-assurance—and that was not Lyndon Johnson, who, as I saw him, was tortured by doubts. I had sympathy for his predicament. Should he accept the urgings of a deputy adviser against the unanimous opinion of his most trusted ministers? I thought often during this period that had anyone of the top group—the Secretary of State, Secretary of Defense, or the national security adviser—joined me in promoting a withdrawal, the President might at least have held back from a massive commitment. But my colleagues were all pushing the other way and they surrounded him.

It would be unfair in this context not to mention Kenneth Galbraith, who had cautioned President Kennedy against a deep involvement. Nor should I omit reference to Arthur Goldberg, who in 1966—about a year after he had become ambassador to the United Nations—began to press for moderating policies. In the nature of things, he could be only of limited effectiveness; in spite of rhetoric to the contrary, the ambassador to the United Nations is not, nor for geographical reasons can he be, in the mainstream of policy. Besides, Goldberg marred his own advocacy by insisting to the President that he, too, had a constituency, thus implicitly threatening the President's own position, which was no way to treat a Texan. I was fully aware of the President's anger and resentment at that suggestion; Johnson spoke to me of it in scatological terms.

In addition, some officials at a slightly lower level went a long way toward concluding that the war could not be won. I would include in that list William P. Bundy, Assistant Secretary of State for Far Eastern Affairs, as well as John McNaughton, the Assistant Secretary of Defense for International Security Affairs, and Chester Cooper in the White

House. But they had all invested years of effort in the war and I could understand their reluctance to face what I considered the ultimate question: Should we let our young men continue to kill and be killed in an essentially hopeless cause or seek a way out with the least damage possible? Finally, and he was very important, there was Clark Clifford but, until 1967, he was nonofficial. Not until he had become Secretary of Defense some months after my departure could he effectively advocate shutting down the war.

Off-key with the prevailing melody, my voice seemed inevitably cacophonous and I have no inflated view as to its effectiveness. I like to think that I somewhat slowed down the escalation and I comfort myself with the unprovable speculation that without my intervention we might have lunged forward even faster into the catastrophic mess in which we finally found ourselves. Even so, I provided no more than a marginal constraint on the momentum.

In the two-dimensional portrait of Johnson frequently passed off as authentic, he is portrayed as a man intolerant of dissent. When I made my first cautionary comments and wrote my first dissenting memoranda, I was not sure how he would react. He had always treated me with warmth and courtesy; only once had he spoken with any hint of acerbity, and that was very early in our relationship—a few months after he became President. On the night of March 31, 1964, when Dean Rusk was away and I was Acting Secretary, a revolution in Brazil overthrew President Goulart, who was reported to be fleeing the country. From our point of view, almost any change would be an improvement over Goulart, who was not only bankrupting Brazil but had shown strong pro-Communist sympathies.

I was monitoring events at the State Department, and in the early hours of the morning we began to receive earnest pleas from Ambassador Lincoln Gordon in Brasilia for a message of encouragement to the new regime. Impressed by the urgency of Gordon's telegrams and after checking as much as was then possible with the Department's Latin American specialists, I authorized a telegram that, in effect, endorsed the *coup*.

The next morning, the President asked why I had acted without advising him. I told him it had been 3 A.M. and I had not wanted to waken him. "Besides," I said, "it was the right step to take and it's worked out well." To that he replied, "Don't ever do that again. I don't give a damn whether you were right or wrong. I don't care a fuck that it was three in the morning; I want to know what's being done whatever time of night it may be."

I took him literally and was right to do so. From then on, hardly a month went by that I did not wake him once or twice at two or three or four o'clock in the morning to advise him of some new occurrence. His response was always the same. "What do you propose we do, George?" I would then describe the action I intended to take—if he approved. Without exception, he would respond, "That sounds right. Go ahead," invariably adding, "and thank you very much for waking me and letting me know."

In the course of my Vietnam apostasy, I found him often my only friendly listener. After almost every meeting during which I had expressed strong—and, I thought, cogent—opposition to some new measure of escalation, or simply made a passionate argument in favor of withdrawal, the President would take me aside. Putting his arm around my shoulder and his face within three inches of mine—his curious, slightly embarrassing habit when he was trying to make a point—he would say, "George, I can't tell you how I thank you for disagreeing with me. I need you to argue with me and I like your stubbornness; keep it up. I'm grateful to you." Some of the more cynical Johnson-haters contend that I was taken in and that the President was simply trying to neutralize me, but I never doubted his sincerity—nor, I think, did any of my close colleagues. My belief that Lyndon Johnson was prepared—even eager—to read or listen to my skeptical thoughts was not based merely on my own observation. He not only discussed my views with members of his immediate staff, such as Moyers or Valenti, but almost every time I sent him a dissenting memorandum he would call me the following morning. I had, he would say, spoiled his sleep, and we must immediately get together to discuss what I had written. Then, when we met and I had made an often lengthy argument, he would begin a cross-examination: "On page seventeen you argue such-and-such, how do you defend and support that?" Or, "What do you mean by saying so-and-so on page thirty-two?"

Decision to Resign

Knowledge of my dissent from Administration policy was closely held. But I did have two old friends in the press to whom I could expose my anxieties in total confidence—Walter Lippmann and James (Scotty) Reston, of the *New York Times.* As America's involvement deepened and tensions increased, President Johnson began to chide me about my long, close friendship with Lippmann, "Tell your friend, Walter, that there's a war on," he would say. Or "Are you telling Lippmann what to write or is he telling you what to say?" Though he made the comments with a teasing smile, one could detect an overtone of malice—hostility toward Lippmann but never, I believe, toward me.

Scotty Reston understood my predicament and was, I thought, sympathetic with my decision to continue my delaying action within the four walls of the Administration so long as I was being heard. If he disapproved he did not say it. But I disappointed Lippmann. "I don't understand you," he would say. "Feeling as you do, you should resign and make your opposition public." The advice troubled me but, so long as there seemed a chance to slow the escalation, I never felt tempted to take it. Lippmann and I conducted a running argument on the question, which caused some slight cloud on our friendship. I answered him by pointing out that, throughout his long years of writing, he had disparaged protests that did not help a cause. To raise hell merely for the psychic glow and the adulation of the already persuaded—actions that did not advance what one was trying to achieve—that, I argued, was mere self-indulgence and unworthy of a serious man. What mattered was to do that which was likely to have the greatest tangible, beneficial effect.

There has long been—and there still is—a romantic vision of the hero who dramatically resigns on a point of principle and denounces his colleagues. The examples cited are mostly drawn from British precedents and reflect a fundamental distinction between Presidential and parliamentary systems. A minister is a member of the British cabinet because he has a political base in the country; if he resigns from the government, his action has substantial political repercussions. He still has clout within his party and retains the House of Commons as his forum. Except in rare cases, the head of an American department (or in my case, merely a deputy head) is little more than a hired hand of the President. I had not become the Under Secretary of State because of an independent position within the Democratic party. Were I to resign it would be a non-event—at the most a one-day wonder.

The Basis for Decision

Thus, judged by any standard of effectiveness, I did not see my resignation serving a useful purpose. I was doing, I thought, an effective job in the Department of State, looking after a number of problems that would otherwise have been neglected. Vietnam was for me always a side-issue; the more time that Secretary of State Rusk spent on Vietnam—and Vietnam increasingly absorbed his energies—the greater was my responsibility for problems in other parts of the world.

Moreover, I could always have my day in court and that was the most important consideration. The President heard me and, were I to leave, he would not hear the same views from anyone else. So why should I quit? By leaving the government and denouncing the Administration for carrying on a futile struggle, I would not make the war shorter or less futile. I could hold a press conference or two and make a few speeches, but that would be the end of it. The official leakers in the White House would let it be widely known that I had quit to avoid being fired. The President, they would whisper, had long been dissatisfied with my performance; the press would give wide currency to those off-the-record innuendoes, and most people would believe them. My dissent would be written off as disappointment or sour grapes.

How, then, should I balance the advantages of a resignation against the utility of what I was doing? I had no illusions as to my effect on events; I might slow, but I could not stop, the escalation. I could not force the President to cut our losses and retire—only events could do that—but I could certainly lay the basis for that decision. Were I to leave there would be no restraints and no alternatives.

These were some of the reasons why I did not leave early in 1966, or even in 1965 when we first committed our ground forces to combat, but by September 1966 there seemed little reason to stay longer. I would go quietly. The effectiveness of my opposition to the war while in the government—or even my ability to retain the ear of the President—had depended on Johnson's confidence that I would never betray or embarrass him. That was the condition on which I could continue to participate in discussions and have access to the intelligence information that enabled me to argue my case with some authority.

Questions of Principle

Anyone embarking on a career of opposition necessarily gives tacit hostages. I could not share the confidence of my colleagues for a sustained period, then go out and denounce them. That well-understood principle was also well-founded. If everyone disliking a governmental position felt compelled to quit and attack his colleagues, orderly government would become impossible. The fear of defection and attack from outside would lead to the suppression of dissenters and the discouragement of dissent, and that would narrow any President's vision. Finally, there was a question of style. I respected my colleagues as men of integrity, who were trying to do what they thought best for their country. Should I make their tasks more difficult by using privileged information to oppose them and thus force them to take even more obdurate positions? More than once I recalled Acheson's quiet resignation as Under Secretary of the Treasury.

Thus, in resigning in September 1966, I did not consider that I was leaving over a principle. How could I publicly attack the war without giving aid and comfort to the enemy? Men were dying in the rice paddies, pilots were risking their lives. I had an old-fashioned aversion to undercutting them. I felt deep sympathy for the young men required to fight a war in which they did not believe, but I was repelled by the hysteria and crudity of the antiwar movement and disgusted with the weakness of university administrations that failed miserably to protect the integrity of their own institutions. Simply put, I did not want to be a hero of the yippies; I had too much respect for our constitutional system to wish it to be undermined. I would not join those fatuous intellectuals who felt that issues were better settled in the streets than through established organs of government. That was the real *trahison des clercs*.

So far as I know, the issue of resignation has never been seriously addressed by anyone with more than an academic acquaintance with the problem. The books that discuss the question have, it seems to me, failed to comprehend the nuances of resignation under a Presidential system or to show much appreciation of how our government really operates. It is a subject worth more serious study. What, for example, should be the triggering event? It would be absurd for anyone in a cabinet-level position to quit whenever he found himself required to carry out a policy he did not like. Compromise is the heart of our democratic system, and even the President cannot completely impose his will on policy; he must qualify his views in ways he often finds distasteful and carry out laws of which he disapproves. Should I, for example, have resigned because I opposed President Johnson's refusal to quarrel with General de Gaulle or what our government was doing in the Dominican Republic or disliked President Kennedy's insistence on protecting the textile industry? At what point does an issue become so central and significant as to warrant a resignation? I shall leave the subject for others to discuss, noting only that it is by no means as simple and incisive as it is sometimes made to appear.

Catastrophic as it was, our involvement in Vietnam was probably inevitable. It marked the end of an uncritical globalism that reflected our postwar preeminence. We felt—and for a time with justice—that we commanded the resources and responsibility to serve as policemen to the world. But by the sixties we had, it seemed to me, reached the point where we could not forever maintain such an expansive interpretation of our commitments. On this I totally agreed with Walter Lippmann's central theme that we must reduce commitments to the dimensions of our resources.

Today I think we probably are doing this reasonably well, yet we have not overcome other consequences of Vietnam—the poisoning of the minds of some Americans toward their own government and the warped attitude of other governments toward America.

Piling Watergate on Vietnam was history's revenge for America's *hubris*.

28. The Private Sector–With East River Interlude

I spent the year 1967 traveling extensively in the Far East and Europe in connection with my investment banking activities as a partner of Lehman Brothers, but my time was not devoted exclusively to private business. In March 1967, at the request of President Johnson (who was fulfilling a promise to President Park Chung Hee), I organized a mission of American industrialists to visit Korea and explore opportunities for American direct investment in that country. With the invaluable help of Tristan E. Beplatt, an experienced banker who knew Korea well, I put together a group of some twenty chief executives of major companies. Ruth and several other wives joined the party, and we spent from March 17 through March 25 in South Korea and the Philippines. Korea, the delegation found, had much to offer American industry—an abundance of educable, low-cost labor and a government committed to free market principles and eager for foreign investment. It would be too much to suggest that our investment mission gave a major spur to Korea's phenomenal economic growth, but it did result in several substantial American investments.

I had been back in the United States only about two months when I again received a summons from the White House. This one by luck I was able to avoid. I had gone to Chicago on June 5. Early in the morning, the national security adviser, Walt Rostow, telephoned to ask, "Do you know there's a war on?" I muttered something incoherent, and he then told me that the Israelis were moving out across the desert and that the President wanted McGeorge Bundy and me in Washington that afternoon.

I explained that I had a speech to make that noon and another in the evening and it was too late to cancel those engagements, so we let the matter drop. Mac Bundy, less fortunate than I, was trapped in Washington for several weeks as executive secretary of the Special Committee of the National Security Council for the Middle East Crisis—an ExCom group roughly similar to the one we had set up for the Cuban Missile Crisis. Bundy was superbly equipped to handle the task and I was not sure where, in any event, I could have fitted in, so I was happy to have avoided that particular draft.

Coronation of the Shah

Later in the year, as guests of Prime Minister Amir Abbas Hoveida (a man of charm and wit, brutally killed by the Khomeini regime in

1979), Ruth and I attended the coronation of the Shah of Iran. The coronation ceremony was both impressive and depressing, with obtrusive contradictions and pretensions. Reflected in the mirrored walls of the Golestan Palace the Shah let one bejeweled belt drop to the floor, only to don another emblazoned with an emerald large as a hen's egg. Thereafter he crowned first himself, then the Empress. It was pure *factice*—a flamboyant attempt to give bogus legitimacy to his parvenu Pahlevi Dynasty. Any suggestion of an Islamic tradition was, we remarked to one another, rigidly avoided; the Shah was seeking not to identify his forty-year-old dynasty with Iran's rulers later than the eighth century, but to establish a continuum with the great dynasts of the days of Persia's classical glory, Cyrus and Darius. The skill and demanding labor that the jewelers Arpels of Paris lavished on fashioning the crowns seemed to me, as a Middle-Western American, an outrageous misdirection of talent and energy. Because the jewels—each derived from a different crown or ornament of some forgotten Indian mogul—were penetrated by holes bored for some prior purpose, each required its own diameter of connecting wire, and that meant months of painstaking work.

Though the garish affair was played straight it still had the atmosphere of operetta. We waited expectantly for the Empress to burst into an Offenbach aria or the Shah to shuffle smartly into a soft-shoe routine. Seated before the Peacock Throne in the Golestan Palace, dressed at eight in the morning in white tie and tails complete with medals, I felt absurd. I did not like playing a crowd scene role in a sinfully wasteful bit of Oriental satire. To complete the effect, Ruth and other female members of our diplomatic section were required to wear long-sleeved floor-length pastel dresses, while the ladies of the Royal Family were clothed in white satin, with all—including the three-year-old princess—protected from the weather by diamond and emerald tiaras. Yet even they were outdone by the Empress, who, embellished with a velvet robe embroidered with gold and seeded with pearls, patiently dragged a train twenty feet long.

What an absurd, bathetic spectacle! The son of a colonel in a Persian Cossack regiment play-acting as the emperor of a country with an average per capita income of $250 per year, proclaiming his achievements in modernizing his nation while accoutered in the raiments and symbols of ancient despotism. No wonder we talked among ourselves about the fragility of an anachronistic structure that compounded the doubtful life expectancy of an absolute monarch with wasteful display. It was, I thought, a deliberate insult to the wretchedly poor with whom the country abounded. Still, though the prodigality of Versailles had nothing on the Golestan Palace, the greatest affront was not to come until four years later. Then the Shah and his queen spent $120 million on an opulent pageant at Persepolis that enriched not Omar the Tentmaker but Pierre the Tentmaker and the other luxury merchants of Paris who handled the arrangements. A few minor heads of state showed up to keep company with Spiro Agnew, but the world was either too polite or too humorless to laugh.

The Pueblo Incident

Though firmly committed to private life, I still remained on call. On January 23 of the following year, the North Koreans seized the USS *Pueblo,* an American naval vessel engaged in electronic and communication intelligence (ELINT and COMMINT). Two days later, on January 25, President Johnson asked me to chair a committee to try to find out how this incident could have occurred and what steps should be taken to prevent future events of the same kind. The committee appointed by the President contained a number of distinguished military experts, including among others, General Mark Clark, General Lawrence Kuter, and Admiral George Anderson. We reviewed the evidence for several days, seeking to cast light on such questions as whether the *Pueblo* had, indeed, strayed into North Korean waters and why the whole affair had been so clumsily handled. Then, at the end, I drafted a report and negotiated it sentence by sentence with my committee. Greatly to my surprise, we unanimously agreed on a draft that raised serious doubts as to the exact position of the *Pueblo,* was severely critical of the planning, organization and, direction of the whole enterprise, and recommended a number of measures to avoid a similar disaster.

I sent the report to the President, who asked me to review it with Clark Clifford. Clifford and I agreed that the written document should be destroyed and I should report only orally to the President. Were we to submit a written report it would probably leak to the newspapers, and its expressions of doubt, particularly with regard to the location of the *Pueblo,* might embarrass our government in dealing with North Korea. I located all copies of the document and destroyed them so completely that I did not even keep a copy for my own files. I am quite certain that none exists anywhere.

Appointment to the United Nations

On April 24, 1968, President Johnson telephoned me while I was attending a meeting of the board of directors of the Standard Oil Company of California in San Francisco. Arthur Goldberg, he told me, had resigned as ambassador to the United Nations, and he wanted me to take the job for the balance of the year—until a new President could be sworn in. I explained that I had only just become a partner of Lehman Brothers and I could not leave my partners immediately after joining the firm. He applied his usual powers of persuasion, but I stood fast. He made me promise, however, not to give him a firm refusal but to "reflect on the matter overnight" and call him the next day.

The next morning I telephoned the President to tell him that I had talked with my partners and still felt I could not accept the proposed appointment. I had only begun to reestablish myself after six years in the government; I needed to learn a new trade and restore my finances. He replied that he understood. He regretted having to impose on me, but, he said, he wanted nothing more than peace. Because of this he had decided not to run for reelection. "I need you, George. No one else ever disagreed with me as much as you but I need you." I held my ground. I mentioned again that I had discussed the question with my partners, who felt as I did. Finally, Johnson said to me, "George, if I wanted to explain the situation to your partners, whom should I call?" I should have known then that I had lost. Not two minutes elapsed before the telephone rang again. This time it was Dean Rusk, "George, the President is not going take no for an answer. Now he's told me to call you and lean on you. You might just as well give in gracefully. You're going to the United Nations."

The next day Edwin Weisl, a partner who was close both to the chairman of my firm, Robert Lehman, and to the President, told me that the President had called him and made a strong plea. "He really needs you, George." When my other partners admonished me not to turn down the President, my negotiating posture was destroyed; I could no longer insist on my obligation to my firm. LBJ had surrounded me.

My highly qualified views of the United Nations were well known, so I was not surprised at some of the mail I received. Dean Acheson wrote me, "I always thought you were one of the brightest guys in town, but now I'm reserving a room for you at St. Elizabeth's," adding in a postscript, "This will teach you not to play poker with a Texan." John Kenneth Galbraith wrote to express his "bafflement" at my "curious career pattern."

I was annoyed to have been outmaneuvered. I needed a period of private life to restore my fortunes, and the last post I wanted was the United Nations. I recalled all too well the night Ruth and I had spent trying to persuade Adlai Stevenson to accept the UN post, and all the arguments he had made for rejecting it, which I had thought valid. But for his own peace of mind Adlai needed to stay in the public sector, I did not. For six years, I had been almost daily on the telephone giving instructions to our UN mission in New York, and, apart from Adlai Stevenson, I was, I suspect, the only American ambassador to the United Nations who knew in advance the sterility and limitations of the job.

United Nations ambassadors spend most of their time making speeches about abstractions and haggling over nuances in resolutions that have no practical effect. I have never had a taste for scholastic nitpicking, and because the United Nations has become little more than a "talking shop," the very atmosphere of the institution oppresses me. I was spoiled by too many years of active participation in critical decisions at the top reaches of the State Department.

Fortunately, I did not have to assume my new duties promptly. Under the rotational system of the Security Council, Arthur Goldberg was scheduled to be the next Council President and he wished to stay through his tenure in that office. Thus, I did not actually take over responsibility until June. Nor did Ruth and I bother to move to the embassy residence in the Waldorf-Astoria Towers. Only a few weeks earlier, we had bought a duplex apartment on the top two floors of the United Nations Plaza— a large new building almost next door to the United Nations itself. We had a spectacular view looking north up both the East and Hudson Rivers and west at the whole brilliant skyline of uptown New York, with the buildings changing colors as the afternoon sun created a shifting pattern of lights and shadows. So we used the Waldorf residence only for official entertaining.

Working on the East River

My new job was exactly as I knew it would be. Though I went to Washington every week and sat in on meetings, I was a bit player rather than a major actor. I could make noises—sometimes critical noises—off-stage, but the important roles were played by those with direct responsibility for policy and its execution.

For many years, a large part of the business of the Security Council has concerned the quarrel between Israel and the Arab states. When either side brings some new incident of outrage or violence before the Security Council, there is little to be done except paraphrase a standard speech that consists of deploring the actions of each side. Toward the end of my stay in the United Nations, those ritualistic exercises became so routine and tiresome that once, when Israel's United Nations representative called me in the early morning to request an urgent meeting of the Security Council to consider some new incident, I wearily replied that I did not think the Security Council was a "precinct police station." By the time I reached the UN mission three hours later, my comment had preceded me.

During July, when the Security Council was quiet, I paid an official visit to the Middle East, then took a brief trip to the Far East. Accompanied by Joseph Sisco, who was then Assistant Secretary of State for

International Organization Affairs, I first met with the Israeli Prime Minister Levi Eshkol, on July 15, then conferred the following day with the Defense Minister Moshe Dayan, and flew by helicopter to the kibbutz of the Deputy Prime Minister, the late Yigal Allon. I raised with Eshkol the return of the West Bank to Palestinian control. Knowing I was going to Jordan for an audience with King Hussein, he authorized me to tell the King that in return for peace, Israel would be prepared to return the West Bank with minor modifications to Jordan. But Hussein was not at the time a free agent. The Arabs had reacted to their humiliating defeat in the 1967 war with the so-called Khartoum Declaration, in which the parties had pledged "no peace with Israel, no negotiations with Israel, no recognition of Israel, and maintenance of the rights of Palestinian people in their nation." Bound by that agreement and fearing Nasser's reprisals, King Hussein was in no position to discuss a separate peace. It was an unfortunate conjunction, for had the two countries then negotiated the return of the West Bank, the festering Palestinian issue might by now be largely an historical reference.

On July 17, 1968, Sisco and I flew to Beirut. When our plane arrived, the American ambassador was waiting for me on the tarmac with his car. On the roof of the airport, fifty or more Palestinians were noisily demonstrating against United States policy in the Middle East, shouting their slogans with the same mindless repetition and narcotic rhythm that make all demonstrations sound alike, whether conducted in Arabic, Farsi or the bastardized English of this slovenly age. A press conference had been arranged in the VIP room of the terminal, where I was about to arrive in the ambassador's Cadillac. But just as I was entering the car, the ambassador's chauffeur gave me a fierce shove, and I fell face forward on the car floor. My instinctive reaction was anger; not until I had pulled myself together did I realize that the chauffeur had saved me from possible serious injury. A bottle of soda pop thrown by one of the demonstrators had missed my head but cut my wrist. Once in the car, the chauffeur drove out of the airport at a rapid pace. We stayed away long enough for the Palestinians to disperse, then returned to the press conference. Though I made every effort to conceal my wounded wrist and conducted the conference with no reference to the incident, one of the cameramen spotted the blood on my hand. The following day, the Lebanese newspapers carried large pictures of the press conference with an arrow pointing to my injury.

To avoid misunderstanding in Washington, I promptly telegraphed Secretary Rusk, reporting the incident and commenting that I was glad it had been a 7-Up bottle, since "Pepsi-Cola hits the spot." The Secretary's reply was laconic: "You can do things better with Coke."

During our brief tour in the Middle East, both Sisco and I contracted the endemic regional dysentery, and the thought of going immediately to the Far East seemed almost unbearable. But since audiences had been laid on with chiefs of government including Generalissimo Chiang Kai-shek, meetings had been arranged with foreign ministers, and dinners and lunches had been planned, cancellation or postponement was out of the question. So, wretchedly uncomfortable as we were, we endured the long flight to Tokyo, Seoul, and Taiwan.

The Czech Crisis

In August, my tour as United Nations ambassador was given a brief importance by the Czech crisis. Like everyone else, I had been exhilarated by the spirit of the evanescent "Prague Spring." But, remembering Warsaw and Budapest in 1956, I was doubtful that the Soviets could tolerate the spread of that most subversive political virus, freedom, without prescribing the only medicine the Kremlin doctors understand, force.

I knew that President Johnson had long hoped to finish his term in office by a climactic visit to Moscow, where he could try to initiate negotiations for strategic arms limitation. Such talks were needed not only for their promise of progress, but because neutral states were looking to the two great nuclear powers to agree on limiting nuclear weapons in return for their adherence to the Nuclear Non-Proliferation Treaty. At last, on August 19, the Soviets advised Washington that the President's visit could take place during the first ten days of October 1968. The White House planned to release the news on the morning of August 21.

In the evening of August 20, the Soviet ambassador advised President Johnson of the Kremlin's decision to intervene in Czechoslovakia. When I arrived at the White House the next morning—the day of the intended announcement—I found the President disappointed but in a mood of sardonic detachment. He, Dean Rusk, and I discussed the broad implications of the Soviet move and what it would mean to Soviet relations with our country. Finally, the President said to me rather abruptly, "George, the matter's now in your hands; do what you have to do." Rusk added, "that means put on your hawk's beak, go into the Security Council, and give the Russians hell."

That evening, the Council met in emergency session. Our first piece of business was to get the Czechoslovak crisis inscribed on the agenda. The USSR and Hungary opposed this procedural move. The Soviet representative, Yakov Malik, an old hard-line Stalinist, contended that there was "no basis" for a Council discussion; the USSR and its allies had moved their forces into Czechoslovakia "at the request" of the Prague government "in view of the threats created by the external and internal reaction" against the country's "socialist system" and "statehood." Thus, Moscow's intervention had been "in accordance with existing treaty obligations." The Soviet Union would not tolerate "the attempts of the imperialists to interfere" in the domestic affairs of Czechoslovakia and "in the relations between all socialist countries." I affirmed the Council's right to take up the crisis, calling the invasion "an affront to all civilized sensibilities." The Communists had sought "to impose by force a repressive political system which is plainly obnoxious to the people and leadership of Czechoslovakia," and the Soviet representative's explanation was "a feeble and futile effort at self-justification."

Once it was clear that the Soviet Union lacked the votes to block listing the item on the agenda—and could not exercise its veto on a merely procedural question—Ambassador Malik moved to withdraw his objection. I challenged this, so as to force the Council to a vote that would demonstrate the strength on our side. I was upheld by the then President of the Council, a wise and courageous Brazilian representative, Ambassador Joao Augusto de Araujo Castro.

With the steady and effective assistance of my able Danish colleague, Ambassador Otto H. Borch, we hammered out a resolution that Denmark introduced. It affirmed that the integrity of Czechoslovakia must be respected and, condemning the armed intervention by the Communist nations, called on them to withdraw.

In the colloquy that followed, I emphasized the absurdity of the Soviet position—not hard to do, since it was based on boldfaced lies. When, for example, Ambassador Yakov Malik repeatedly contended that the Soviets had been compelled to intervene for reasons of "fraternal solicitude," I replied that the fraternal solicitude they were showing toward Czechoslovakia was precisely "the kind Cain showed Abel." I answered Malik's charge that "only imperialists oppose and deplore" the Soviet government's intervention by pointing out that among such so-called imperialists were Pope Pius VI, the Rumanian and Yugoslavian Presidents, the President of Tanzania, and the leaders of the Communist parties in France and Italy. Later, when Malik protested to the President of the Council that "the distinguished United States representative should stop pounding his fist at [him]," I responded that I had not pounded my fist, I had "not even pounded my shoe."

On the first day of debate, the Council received a message from the Czechoslovak foreign minister, Jiri Hajek, demanding that "the illegal occupation of Czechoslovakia be stopped without delay," and from the Presidium of Czechoslovakia's National Assembly assailing "the occupation" of the country as a violation of international law, the Warsaw Treaty, and "the principles of equality between nations." In the ensuing debate, I was greatly aided by the British permanent representative, Lord Caradon, who spoke with a quiet strength that was perhaps more effective than my more strident rhetoric.

The next day the Canadian representative, Ambassador George

Ignatieff, introduced a resolution calling on the Secretary-General of the United Nations to send a representative to Prague "to seek the release and ensure the safety of the detained Czechoslovak leaders." Though that draft resolution was sponsored by seven nations in addition to Canada, Malik rejected it as further evidence of a plot to pave the way for British and United States "imperialists and counter-revolutionaries to lure Czechoslovakia away from its Communist allies"—an accusation that Ambassador Caradon denounced as a "contemptuous, personal insult" to the Council members. The following evening, on August 24, Foreign Minister Hajek, who had just flown from Prague, made a dramatic appearance before the Council, asserting that there was no justification for the occupation and that the invasion had not been—as the Soviet representative claimed—carried out "at the request of the Czechoslovak government." Malik's claim that the Soviets were intervening to put down counter-revolutionary activity was without basis, Hajek insisted, since the Prague regime had had the situation "firmly in hand and sufficient means existed to repel any attack upon the foundations of Socialism."

That evening, Ambassador Malik preempted the Council's proceedings by a three-hour filibuster in support of a motion that East Germany—not a member of the United Nations—be allowed to participate in the Council's deliberations. Though the proposal was defeated by a 9 to 2 vote, Malik succeeded in delaying Council action. India abstained, as it had in the earlier resolution condemning the invasion. When that action provoked an anti-government demonstration in New Delhi, Prime Minister Indira Gandhi explained that India had abstained because the resolution used the stronger term "condemns" rather than the weaker "deplores." That incident inspired me to scribble the following verse, largely for the edification of my British colleague Lord Caradon, who sat next to me at the table:

Awesome Power

Each time this august group *deplores*
It's like a feral wolf that howls.
I feel a chill in all my pores;
A fearful tremor in my bowels.

My lungs would suffocate with phlegm,
My mind recoil, my pulse race faster,
If the Council ever should *condemn*,
Since that would mean extreme disaster.
For I can't think that any nation
Could stand such deep humiliation.

Although the Czechoslovak debate was carried on before the television cameras and no doubt served the purpose of exposing Soviet brutality to the world, the diplomats on the spot indulged in rhetoric and play-acting for the consumption of their governments and hometown newspapers. Malik and I had spent a long night engaged in what the London *Economist* referred to as "savaging one another," but once the television cameras had been turned off and the meeting adjourned at three in the morning, he came around the table, pounded me on the back, and said, "Well, I certainly kept you up late, didn't I?"

For me the formalistic and artificial atmosphere of the UN proceedings grew increasingly wearying. I could not resist the feeling that I could be more useful in real life. Bored with the windy speeches that consumed most of the Security Council's proceedings, I kept myself awake by writing additional frivolous verse, which I would then toss over to Lord Caradon. Sometimes a verse would contain such scandalous references to some of our colleagues that Caradon would hastily put it face downward under a pile of papers for fear he might be seen reading it. One of my jingles inspired by Malik, the Soviet ambassador, a fat, humorless apparatchik, was this:

> REFLECTIONS ON SOVIET AMBASSADOR MALIK
> DURING THE CZECHOSLOVAKIAN CRISIS
>
> How could one ever tell Moloch from Malik,
> Since both were choleric and neither was Gallic,
> Each had a shape one could call parabolic,
> Neither engaged in pursuits apostolic;
> So their resemblance seemed more than symbolic.
>
> They differed in this: That, while both melancholic,
> They chose disparate methods to frisk and to frolic.
> Malik made speeches with words vitriolic,
> While Moloch ate children to settle his colic.

Diplomats, by training if not natural selection, develop certain defensive skills. If one is required to spend long hours in international meetings, he must learn to sleep with his eyes open, an exercise requiring a posture of meditation with the hand just shading the eyes. Though indispensable, that device can sometimes be hazardous, as was demonstrated one day during an interminable session on a Middle East outrage committed by the Arabs against the Israelis or vice versa. One of my friends on the Security Council, who shall be nameless, had received instructions from his government to abstain on the particular resolution. Just prior to the Council vote, the representative of a Middle-Eastern country who never spoke for less than two hours and never said anything useful, asked permission to address the Council; it was routinely granted. My friend quite sensibly told the young man sitting behind him to wake him when it was time to vote.

As the Middle-Eastern orator was about to conclude his first hour of impassioned irrelevance, my French colleague decided that he would try to persuade my friend to support the resolution rather than merely abstain. Walking around the table, he put his arm on my sleeping colleague's shoulder; whereupon my friend raised his hand and, in a loud, clear, voice announced with dramatic emphasis, "Mr. President, my country abstains." It was a memorable moment—in some ways, perhaps, the Security Council's finest hour.

Resignation from the United Nations

The summer of 1968 was a nightmare season for America. The country was suffering a fever of hysteria and revulsion induced by the Vietnam War; many colleges and universities had shamefully capitulated to Yahoo outrage without even the feeblest gesture of institutional self-defense. Politics were in total upheaval. I had watched the proceedings of the Democratic convention in Chicago and the ghastly mess that resulted; now, as the campaign began, I saw my poor friend Vice-President Humphrey trying futilely to make himself heard against the mindless yammering of enraged hell-raisers. I was revolted by the negation of civility and rationality and outraged that Nixon not only seemed immune from the attacks of exhibitionist hysterics, but was gaining in the polls to the point where in early September he was running seventeen points ahead.

The prospect that Nixon might be President of the United States seemed derisive. He was, I thought—and he has since shown himself to be—intellectually corrupt. So, on an official visit to Europe in August, I decided to resign from the United Nations and do what I could to help Humphrey. I did not think for a moment he could win, but at least we might deny Nixon an overwhelming victory. I called Lyndon Johnson at his Texas ranch expecting serious opposition. To deflect his counterattack, I began the conversation by saying, "Mr. President, always before when I've taken a step I've sought your permission, but this time I'm not asking you but advising you that I've made a decision as a matter of conscience." When I had finished my speech, the President responded in a sympathetic way but asked for two or three days to find a successor for me at the United Nations; otherwise, with such a rapid turnover, his Administration "would look jerky." I then called Hubert Humphrey to tell him that I was joining him and agreed to meet him in Seattle.

The Humphrey Campaign

I told the Vice-President that he must do something dramatic to halt Nixon's momentum. Most urgent was for him to stake out an independent position on Vietnam so as to deflect some of the anti-Johnson venom. At the same time, I planned to attack Nixon so outrageously as to force people to stop and think. On the day I resigned my UN job, I gave a conference in the State Department Press Room in which I announced that I was compelled by conscience to act, because Nixon "lamentably lacks" the qualities necessary for Presidential leadership. I expressed optimism that there would be "a political solution to the Vietnamese War fairly early in the term of the next President—if he is President Humphrey." But, I said, "if he is Mr. Nixon, I have no idea what he would do. . . . I don't think he has any kind of settled principles." I never spoke a truer word.

Three days later on September 29, on the CBS program "Face the Nation," I mentioned Nixon's "preposterous" choice of Governor Spiro Agnew for a running mate as an example of "cynicism and irresponsibility." I described Agnew as "a fourth-rate political hack" and suggested that the "tricky Dick" label attached to Nixon in the past might well have had some validity. As I had hoped, my comments were widely noted, and I like to think they may have helped to halt Nixon's increasing advantage at the polls. The Reverend Billy Graham, however, publicly rebuked me for questioning Nixon's integrity; he had, so he said, played golf with Nixon on many occasions and had never seen him cheat.

Humphrey on Vietnam

I thought it essential to focus attention on the inadequacies of the Republican candidates, but the campaign could not be merely negative; we needed to establish Humphrey as having an independent Vietnam position. Although Hubert Humphrey and I had frequently discussed Vietnam and I knew that his views resembled mine, he had, as Vice-President, felt compelled to support the President's policies, and he could never do anything half-heartedly.

I had innocently expected that Lyndon Johnson, having hated his own experience as Vice-President, would try to make Humphrey's ordeal more pleasant and productive, but he seemed perversely determined to make Humphrey's life as miserable as his had been. The poor Vice-President was being crushed to death by antagonistic vanities, jealousies, and political forces. He clearly did not wish to alienate the President, but he was fiercely harassed by the companions he had once led on the liberal barricades. Now, instead of attacking Nixon, they were churlishly spending their talent for invective on their old comrade, while writing quirkish dithyrambs to the higher morality of not voting. Many in their silent hearts must later have repented their contribution to Nixon's victory. At least I hope so; I shall burn no candles for them.

My first task was to try to restate Humphrey's position on the peace negotiations in terms sufficiently distinguishable from Johnson's to satisfy the more reasonable antiwar faction, without, at the same time, driving the President into outright opposition. I drafted some foggy language for a speech the Vice-President planned to make at Salt Lake City, only to find that members of his campaign staff, friends, and volunteers had also produced four or five additional drafts, each with its fervent proponents. Following the usual untidy pattern that prevails in campaign circles, nuances of language and approach were being fiercely debated. To avoid attack from Lyndon Johnson—who was at the time a far more formidable opponent than Nixon—I asked a colleague from Lehman Brothers, Harry Fitzgibbons, to fly to Paris, talk with Harriman and Vance and obtain their assurance that the key passage I had written would not prejudice the current Vietnam negotiations and that if Humphrey were attacked for making the speech, they would express that assurance publicly.

The problem was to distinguish Humphrey's position from that of Johnson by inventing a sufficiently fuzzy shibboleth. The area for maneuver was narrow. Instead of requiring enemy agreement before we stopped the bombing—which had been the Johnson position—we would have Humphrey say that he would "stop the bombing of North Vietnam as an acceptable risk for peace," then see what response might develop, "reserving the right to resume bombing if no such response was clear."

All this sounded like pettifogging, and it was; yet in a political campaign, code words and phrases are more significant than logic or substance. No one expects either the rational or relevant at the end of a Presidential race. The press, as I saw it, confused the respective roles of the players; on their score cards Humphrey was running against Johnson, while Nixon was allowed to sit sanctimoniously on the sidelines, immune from the embarrassment of searching questions. No one asked Humphrey how his views on the war differed from those of Nixon; the thrust of every inquiry was, How did Humphrey's differ from Lyndon Johnson's? That point had to be clarified in the Salt Lake City speech.

The critical language I had drafted was argued and refined and redrafted principally by men who knew little about the war but had a self-proclaimed infallibility regarding public opinion. At the end, I grew impatient and, finally, in the middle of the night, Larry O'Brien, Humphrey's campaign manager (a man with both experience and common sense) said quietly to me, "You make the final decision." I replied, "then we'll go ahead the way it's now written."

Our schedule called for the Vice-President to tape the speech at a studio in the afternoon, then immediately call the President. Once Humphrey had completed talking with Johnson, I was then to call him to explain the Vice-President's proposed statement and "get him down off the ceiling."

I waited in the hotel. Toward the the middle of the afternoon, someone called from the studio to say that the Vice-President was dissatisfied with his first taping of his speech and wished to retape it. Since he did not have time to call the President would I please do so? I should read Johnson the critical language of the speech and try to persuade him not to react in a destructive way. That was not a chore I welcomed, but I put through the call only to be told by the White House operator that the President was talking with Mr. Nixon. She would ring me as soon as the President was finished. A half-hour later she called.

I read the language to President Johnson and explained the Vice-President's intention. He listened in silence, then replied, "Well, George, nobody's better than you at explaining things to the press and I know you'll be able to persuade them that this doesn't mark any change in the Vice-President's position from the line we've all been following."

Though his reaction was not unexpected I could not leave it at that. "I'm sorry, Mr. President," I said, "but that's not quite the name of the game." I expected an angry riposte but he seemed in a relaxed mood. "Well, George, I know you'll do the best you can."

Appraisal of Humphrey

I found the whole campaign enormously depressing. Humphrey, a generous and honest man, was assailed whenever he tried to speak by the obscene gibbering and caterwauling of moronic youths who made all public discourse impossible. "I can stand it for myself," Humphrey told me, "but I can't tell you how I boil inside when a bunch of young slobs spew out their obscenities when Muriel's with me." The noxious effects of Vietnam were metastasizing—spreading through the whole fiber of our society and corrupting our institutions. My fervent wish for a Humphrey Administration stemmed primarily from my belief that he would bring the ugly war to an end. I doubted Nixon would have the sense or the character to do so—and time tragically confirmed that appraisal when he dragged it on for four more years.

I had known Hubert Humphrey a long while, and we had talked on many occasions, but I did not regard him as a close friend. He was a man of extraordinary decency—quite the most generous and compassionate man in politics. Though I had no doubt he was infinitely preferable to Nixon, I doubted he would be a distinguished President. Humphrey was, in my observation, intellectually quick, hard-working, and conscientious, but he lacked the incisiveness and ruthlessness needed of a President. He was excessively enthusiastic, too easily carried away; he could never avoid hyperbole and overstatement. His speeches were effervescent but endless, and I remember two comments current at the time. One was an observation that "Hubert never had an unexpressed thought." The other was a remark no doubt apocryphally attributed to his wife Muriel, "Just remember, Hubert, that a speech to be immortal doesn't have to be eternal."

Had Humphrey been more disciplined and self-seeking he could, during his term as Vice-President, have satisfied Johnson's wish for unquestioning support of his Vietnam position without going totally overboard in a way that made him vulnerable to his fickle liberal colleagues. But he was too exuberant for that, and they crucified him.

Later, when dying of cancer, he returned gallantly to Washington for a farewell speech, and the Senate rang with encomia. I could not help but recall Matthew Arnold's words on growing old:

> It is—last stage of all—
> When we are frozen up within, and quite
> The phantom of ourselves,
> To hear the world applaud the hollow ghost
> Which blamed the living man.

Escape to Europe

Because the country was in such a black-minded mood, I was convinced Humphrey would not win. I had endured losing campaigns before and had no taste for another sour "victory" celebration. So, to fill our minds with fresh thoughts and a brighter landscape, Ruth and I booked passage on the *France,* sailing the morning after the election. We were escaping from an American scene I thought of as the Age of Slobbism—students befouling ("trashing," as they vacuously called it) their own intellectual nests, while a few muddle-headed instructors applauded the mishandling of deans.

We had always found sea voyages diverting, and this was no exception. On our next-to-last night, a gale force wind rolled the ship to starboard for what seemed like minutes, then just as sluggishly, she righted herself and resumed course—a ship filled with broken bones and smashed furniture.

At breakfast in a shattered dining saloon I said to Arthur Sulzberger, the publisher of the *New York Times,* "My God, Punch, think what this means. Nixon's been elected for only three days and already we've been on the verge of shipwreck!"

It was a prophetic comment.

29. From Nixon to Ford to Carter

Six weeks of unplanned wandering in France and Spain immediately after the 1968 election were a comforting distraction from the confusions of an unsatisfying year. Old structures—castles, chateaus, and cathedrals—as well as the Grecos and Goyas at the Prado, restored a needed sense of continuity and perspective. Ruth and I spent Christmas with our sons in Florida, and I delayed my return to Lehman Brothers until January. I needed time to think and I was sure some of my elderly, outraged Republican partners needed a cooling off period.

To the presiding deities on Wall Street I was a pariah. I was not asked to rejoin the boards of directors of two major companies, Standard Oil of California and the Singer Corporation, on which I had sat before my tour at the United Nations, or to resume my membership on the International Advisory Board of the Upjohn Company. Shaking his head in sad bewilderment, the chairman of one of the companies explained that neither he nor his friends could understand why I had attacked Nixon with such "excessiveness." It had evoked sharp disapproval from some of the company's major shareholders. I replied that, though I regretted any awkwardness my activities may have caused him, I could not agree that I had shown excessiveness except in the restraint I had displayed. He smiled wanly, and we parted on good terms.

Twice during my days as a lawyer I had had to rebuild a professional practice after extended periods of political absence and now, as an investment banker, I once more faced that prospect. It was not a task I welcomed but it provided the occasion for travel as well as a chance to regain my financial equilibrium. I had always regarded the human comedy as absorbing theater and, freed from responsibility for helping to conduct large affairs, I was no longer inhibited in exposing my prejudices as a self-appointed critic of a muddled world. So for the next few years, I published articles in such periodicals as the *New York Times,* the *Washington Post,* the *New York Times Magazine,* the *Atlantic,* and *Foreign Affairs,* and for two and a half years wrote a foreign affairs column for *Newsweek.*[1]

I enjoyed living in New York, and I found relief in an atmosphere not soggy with politics. Each of our two sons, John and Douglas, was beginning to make his own individual mark, and Ruth and I enjoyed the variety of friendships only a metropolitan city can provide. Defined in purely personal terms, life was quite agreeable—particularly after 1973 when Peter G. Peterson took over the leadership of Lehman Brothers. A brilliant man of business with broad horizons and a relentlessly analytical mind, he not only provided a congenial professional environment but became an extremely warm and good friend. To him, Lewis Glucksman, and my other partners I owe a debt of gratitude for their indulgence of the time I spent on my vagrant interests and their tolerance of the unpopular views I frequently expressed in speeches or writing.

Though I had no ambition to become an old curmudgeon I did not like much of what I saw occurring in the world—or even in my own country. The mindless dragging on of the Vietnam War was destroying America's civility and encouraging a degradation of life—drugs, campus disorders, hippies, hysteria, pernicious egocentrism, and pervasive and ugly disarray.

Life under Nixon

Though I intensely disliked Nixon, I was still prepared to help him with policies on which we agreed. On May 13, 1971, when Senate Majority Leader Mike Mansfield seemed on the verge of securing Senate passage of legislation to withdraw American forces from Europe, Nixon called in the "elder statesmen." After a meeting that was more a pep talk than a briefing, I told him I would devote the following week to active lobbying against the Mansfield bill. During part of the time I worked out of the Vice-President's office near the Senate Chamber, a bizarre environment for a Democrat in a Republican Administration. Since I had both conviction and logic on my side, I found most Senators willing to listen. As a result, I was able to muster a number of votes against troop withdrawal.

When I returned to New York on May 19, 1971, the day of the vote, President Nixon graciously telephoned to thank me. His legislative assistants, he said, had told him that, had I not lobbied so effectively, the cause could well have been lost. Taking advantage of the opportunity, I described the lamentable state of his relations with the Senate and strongly urged that he give the matter personal attention. Though our little band of the superannuated had this time been of help, he could not use us effectively again. "A soufflé," I said, "cannot be made to rise twice." He would have to talk personally with the leaders of both houses, and I suggested that he ask Henry Kissinger to hold a series of small breakfasts. "Oh," he replied, "let me tell you, just within the family"—then, pausing awkwardly as he realized the import of his words—"I mean the international family, I can't use Henry with people on the Hill without getting Bill Rogers's nose out of joint."

"Then," I answered, "ask Bill to invite some Senators and Congressmen down in very small groups—otherwise, it won't mean anything."

That was my only direct contact with Nixon during his Presidency. Having studied his behavior beginning with his earliest days in California politics, I was not surprised by the sordid disclosures of Watergate. During the 1968 campaign, I had argued that something of the kind was inevitable and I was even more explicit on February 8, 1973—a little more than a fortnight after Nixon's second inauguration—when I spoke at the St. Stephens Club in London to a Conservative party ginger society known as the Bow Group. The audience, consisting of young members of parliament and party supporters, seemed intensely interested in

American politics, and since it was a closed meeting, I spoke with candor. During the question period following my remarks, someone asked, "How do you appraise the future course of Nixon's new Administration now that he has just achieved a second term?" I had not anticipated the question but answered impulsively; "His Administration will destroy itself by its own corruption within a few months. The chemistry is unavoidable: corruption mixed with arrogance leads to carelessness, carelessness to exposure, and exposure to disaster."

As Watergate began to reveal itself in all its squalor in the weeks that followed, I received two or three letters from young members of parliament who had been present at the meeting, asking what I knew that others did not know. "I was relying," I replied, "not on knowledge but instinct."

Not only was I on the outside during the Nixon period but my status did not change with the advent of President Ford. Though I had known and liked Gerald Ford during his days in Congress I now saw him only on diplomatic occasions. That included one memorable dinner for President Sadat when Ford's mind wandered or his tongue slipped and he toasted the people of Israel when he meant Egypt. I could not resist a silent guffaw, yet I felt a warm feeling for him, since once, in a conversation with the Shah, I had heard myself refer to Algeria instead of Iran.

The Carter Incumbency

After Jimmy Carter was elected, some of my old friends drifted back to Washington, but I felt little rapport with the new President. Prior to the 1976 campaign, I had been only vaguely aware of Carter, though after I left the government, Dean Rusk had once asked me to prepare some material for a Democratic party briefing book being put together by a young Governor of Georgia. Of all the potential candidates, I was most attracted to Edmund Muskie, but I was inhibited by my impulsive promise to Hubert Humphrey in 1968 that if he ran again, I would support him. I do not recall my first meeting with Carter, which—so I was told later—occurred on December 8, 1974, when I made a speech at one of the two meetings of the Trilateral Commission I ever attended. Jimmy Carter was in the audience; and we apparently conversed briefly afterwards. Then in October 1975, Lewis Glucksman, one of my partners, brought Carter to breakfast at Lehman Brothers.

I found the Governor eager to talk but not much interested in listening. He seemed totally enthralled by his campaign planning, describing in great detail the precise steps by which he intended to become President. I could scarcely believe he felt as self-assured as he seemed, for he appeared to have no doubt whatever that he would succeed in his quest. Yet while he was voluble about his campaign plans, he scarcely men-

tioned policies or what he hoped to do when he became President. At
the conclusion of our breakfast, he suggested that if I had any foreign
policy ideas for his campaign I should let him know, but I did not then
take him seriously as a candidate. He was, as I saw him, an attractive
young Southern politician with few apparent qualifications for the Presidency except ambition. He would, I thought, almost certainly be eliminated early in the Democratic primary race in which seventeen or
eighteen candidates were then savagely competing.

I was, therefore, quite unprepared for a telephone call I received in
January from the newspaper columnist Rowland Evans, who asked me
if I knew Jimmy Carter well.

"No," I replied. "I only met him once at breakfast last October."

"You haven't been in touch with him since?"

"No," I replied. "Not a word."

"That's funny," Evans replied. "He's just announced that you're one
of his principal foreign policy advisers."

My first reaction was annoyance, since I feared Carter's statement
might lead Humphrey to think I had betrayed him, but as I thought
about it later, I found the incident amusing. It did not, however, contribute to Carter's affection for me—particularly since Evans wrote a
needling column pointing out the discrepancy in our statements. No
doubt it was even more galling to Carter when Evans's partner questioned him about it on a national television show. Carter replied that he
had been guilty of "an inadvertence"; he had thought his staff was in
close touch with me.

After he was nominated, his staff did approach me once or twice; I
was given a speech to vet and suggested large cuts in the text, which
were almost all rejected. Later, he was gracious enough to offer me a
choice of major diplomatic assignments, which I quietly declined. I had,
I told him, been away from home too much of my life; my wife and I
had just bought a house in Princeton; and I did not want, at this point,
to live abroad. I refrained from saying what I really felt—that jet planes
and telephones and the bad habits of Presidents, National Security
Assistants and Secretaries of State had now largely restricted ambassadors to ritual and public relations. I did not wish to end my days as an
innkeeper for itinerant Congressmen.

Economic Assignment

Still I was sometimes asked to undertake an occasional special chore.
In 1978, at the instigation of my old friend Secretary of the Treasury
W. Michael Blumenthal, I was invited to join some able economists—
Robert V. Roosa, Lawrence R. Klein, the late Arthur M. Okun, and Wil-
liam G. Bowen, the president of Princeton University—to review our

major economic problems, discuss our comments and proposals with the President, and prepare a report.

Our group first met in Washington with the Secretary of the Treasury and the Chairman of the Federal Reserve Board (then William G. Miller) on September 8, 1978. Later, we had a long session with the President that began toward the middle of the afternoon and lasted until well after dinner. With the help of Bob Roosa, I had prepared a presentation showing separately, in columnar form, the nature of the domestic benefits expected from each measure we might take, the domestic trade-offs it would require, its international benefits, and its international trade-offs. As I had expected, the President, with his engineer's background, thought the presentation well-designed but he could not, he said, accept any of the trade-offs; he had been elected to help the poor, and those trade-offs would help the rich. The same moralistic attitude was exhibited by Mrs. Carter, who said to me later, when we were having drinks on the balcony, "Don't you think Jimmy is going to have to veto the tax bill? He doesn't feel right inside about it." I tried to explain, as I had to the President earlier in the afternoon, that the essence of democratic government was compromise and that the President would have to do many things with which he might not feel totally comfortable. Only by such compromises could he hope to accomplish his principal objectives.

Obviously these are brief impressions, quite inadequate on which to base a solid judgment, yet it seems clear from many bits and pieces of evidence that the intrusion of an inflexible morality quite often diminished Carter's effectiveness, since he could not reconcile it with the political process. In addition, I thought I detected one other aspect of President Carter's approach to major problems that got in the way of serious strategic thinking. When one gave him a brief or a memorandum, he would read it quickly with obvious understanding and he was impressively proficient at mastering quantitative and statistical materials. Yet, once we began to deal more profoundly with a foreign policy problem, he seemed to lack a well-developed matrix into which ideas could be fitted. In other words, he tended to see problems in a discrete form far too straitened to encompass the large framework that gave them meaning.

Imperial Megalomania

That impression was confirmed when, just as the Shah's dynasty was collapsing, the President asked me once again for advice. I had known the Shah since my days in the State Department, when I used to participate in negotiations with him. Those negotiations usually concerned, first, his importunate demand for enhanced oil sales to improve his foreign exchange revenues, and, second, his request that we sell him more and more sophisticated weapons. While we discussed the first issue with the major oil companies (which were reluctant to increase these liftings from Iran since that would incite similar pressure from Saudi Arabia), we held firm on the Shah's second demand. We did not wish to begin an arms race among the Middle Eastern countries nor did we think it useful for the Shah to waste resources on sophisticated weapons his meagerly trained forces could not use effectively. When he threatened to turn to the Soviet Union for help, we told him to go ahead; in fact, he did buy a certain amount of military hardware from France and Great Britain. In any event, we held our position so firmly that during the entire period of nineteen years from his return to power in 1953 to 1972, his total arms purchases from the United States amounted to only $1.2 billion.[2]

But all that changed in May 1972 when President Nixon and Mr. Kissinger flew from Moscow to Teheran for a meeting with the Shah. The British had announced four years earlier that they would withdraw their military presence from east of Suez, and they had, toward the end of 1971, substantially completed that withdrawal, leaving a power vacuum in the Persian Gulf. Had we followed our established practice, America would have filled that vacuum, as we had done, for example, when the British withdrew from Greece and Turkey. But, applying his so-called Nixon Doctrine, the President decided to entrust the security of the Gulf to the Shah, who would act as the protector for all Western interests. That, of course, was music to the Shah's ears, since it gave him recognition as the dominant power in the area; but, he stipulated, he would undertake the assignment only on certain conditions, of which two were particularly important.

The first was that the United States assist the Kurds in their revolt against Iraq in order to keep the Iraqis off balance. We agreed and later provided a substantial amount of money to Mustafa al-Barzani, the Kurdish leader, and sent military advisers to help the Kurdish forces.

The second condition was that we give the Iranian government unrestricted access to our most sophisticated military equipment. That was also agreed and, on returning to the United States, Kissinger, in the name of the President, directed the Secretaries of State and Defense to sell the Shah whatever he wanted, including such items as F-14 and F-15 aircraft (then still in development) and laser-guided bombs that were just being introduced to American units in Vietnam. Then, in language that drastically broke with past American practice, Kissinger directed that, regardless of the views of our government departments, they should sell the Iranian government whatever it desired; the Shah, in other words, should have the ultimate power to decide what military equipment he would acquire.

I think it clear that in anointing the Shah as the guardian of Western interests in the whole Gulf area, Nixon inadvertently encouraged the megalomania that ultimately contributed to the Shah's downfall. Permitting him free access to the whole range of advanced items in our military arsenal was like giving the keys of the world's largest liquor store to a confirmed alcoholic. As compared to the $1.2 billion of arms and equipment we had let him buy during the preceding nineteen years, he placed orders during the next seven years following the Nixon visit for $19.5 billion of our military hardware. With America recognizing him as the official guardian of the Persian Gulf, with vast amounts of imposing weapons beginning to arrive and with oil revenues beginning to mount after the price increases in 1974, the Shah felt commissioned by Allah to transform Iran into what he now boasted would become the fifth most powerful nation in the world. Overnight he sought to build a backward, religious country into a modern—though corrupt—industrial state, relying almost exclusively on Western technicians and technology. In trying to fulfill his Messianic mission, he isolated himself from his people and lost his sense of proportion, thus encouraging the destructive forces that proved his undoing.

Fall of the Shah

Ever since the latter 1960s, I had visited Iran almost every year and had made a number of close Iranian friends. I had also talked with the Shah periodically, either in Teheran or in Zurich, where he went every January for medical attention in preparation for his annual skiing vacation. During the middle 1970s, I gained the impression from my Iranian friends that the Shah's regime was becoming increasingly repressive and the secret police (the SAVAK), more brutal and unrestrained. During late evening parties in Teheran with brilliant young writers, journalists, and professional men, I listened to freely expressed predictions of chaos and disorder when and if something happened to the Shah, and my friends frankly recognized that the Shah's regime might some day be brought down. The Shah had lost touch with his nation's intellectual elite—able and Western-educated Iranians who should have formed the hard core of his support.

Yet I did not gain a sense of imminent disaster until toward the end of the decade of the seventies, when I found the atmosphere increasingly tense. I had not then fully understood the extent to which the Shah had—often through well-intended actions—disaffected almost every sector of the population. He was, as I appraised him, by no means an evil man; he had an honorable ambition for his country and worked tirelessly to fulfill it. But that ambition—stimulated by America's shortsighted encouragement—grew more and more excessive and unrealistic. In trying to carry out his grandiose plans, he alienated first one group and then another. It was not merely, as some have simplistically suggested, that he pushed modernization (which really meant Westernization) beyond the capabilities of the nation's antiquated political structure—that was only part of the problem; much more important was his lack of sensitivity to his people's needs, hopes, and aspirations, which were by no means identical with his. His weakness, selfishness, and indulgence led him to condone widespread corruption among his family and hangers-on; their obscene display of wealth and the general tone of his regime encouraged brutal abuses and repression, of which he could not have been unaware. Meanwhile, he made himself useful to a succession of United States governments—performing such unpopular chores, at our request, as selling oil to Israel. It was no wonder that American officials believed—because they found it convenient to believe—that his regime was in no danger, that it was, in the language of President Carter's New Year's toast in December 1977—a year before the Shah's downfall—"an island of stability." That characterization was, the President told the Shah, a "great tribute to the respect, admiration and love of your people for you."[3]

In retrospect, it seems clear that the revolution which was building up all through the year 1978 was not an Islamic revolt so much as a revolution of a thousand discontents, for which Islam merely provided the flag of respectability. Beginning in January 1978, I carefully followed accounts of spreading disaffection in the mosques and the demonstrations every forty days to mourn the death of mullahs killed by the Shah's police—demonstrations that resulted in further killings and, forty days later, more widespread mourning until the streets were filled with insensate mobs. But I had still not formed a clear view as to the immediacy of catastrophe until, on August 20, a fire in an Abadan movie theater killed 430 people. Since it was generally assumed to have been set by Moslem extremists opposed to the Shah's liberalization policies, it added such an impetus to the rising wave of disorder as to persuade my closest Iranian friend to move his family out of the country with no plan to return. That was a radical step for a man with so much to lose; not only was he a distinguished member of the Teheran bar, but exceptionally sophisticated in political matters and not given to intemperate or precipitate action. From then on, watching carefully for signs of increasing disintegration, I reluctantly concluded that the Shah was on the way to a great fall and that, like Humpty-Dumpty, his regime could not be put together again.

I outlined that probability and its implications for America in two or three speeches to small informal gatherings in New York during September and October 1978, and mentioned it to some of my friends in the Carter Administration—including Secretary of the Treasury Blumenthal. In November, when Secretary Blumenthal visited Iran and could appraise the situation at first hand, he was appalled by what he found—particularly the Shah's own confused and indecisive state of mind.

On returning to Washington he proposed to President Carter that I be asked to make an objective appraisal of the situation, to which the President agreed.

By then it was the eleventh hour. I was not summoned to Washington until November 30, 1978. I was given an office with the staff of the National Security Council and assigned an excellent colleague and counsellor, Captain Gary Sick of the United States Navy, an expert on the Persian Gulf then assigned to the Security Council staff. Though some had assumed that I would begin my assignment by visiting Iran, I promptly disabused them of that assumption. I had learned from our Vietnam experience how dangerous it can be when travel is substituted for thought. I could learn far more by mining the resources of Washington than by talking with a few friends and officials in Iran, while my sudden appearance in Teheran would merely provide new documentation for those attacking the Shah as subservient to America.

Muddle at the Top

In spite of Captain Sick's friendliness, insight, patience, and excellent guidance, I felt depressed by the conditions I now found—particularly the distorted role of the National Security Council (the NSC). The Council had been created during the Truman Administration in 1947 as a central mechanism to collate the views of the several departments and agencies that claimed an interest in a particular foreign policy question and to provide machinery through which the interested parties could develop coherent positions. McGeorge Bundy, as National Security Assistant during my tenure in the State Department, was the first to give substantive content to the role but he had at all times recognized the Secretary of State's primacy in foreign policy matters and had assiduously protected the State Department when others tried to make an end run to the President. During his years in the White House, Henry Kissinger had greatly expanded the NSC staff to create a miniature foreign office and had misused his role as national security adviser to try to exclude the Department from policy formulation and to cut down the Secretary of State so as to aggrandize his own power position; then, once having become Secretary, Kissinger had reduced the NSC to its earlier dimensions and mandate. Now once again, I found President Carter's National Security Assistant, Zbigniew Brzezinski, trying to emulate Kissinger's rise to prominence by inflating and manipulating the NSC. He was operating in a free-wheeling manner, calling in foreign ambassadors, telephoning or sending telegrams to foreign dignitaries outside State Department channels, and even hiring a press adviser so he could compete with the Secretary of State as the enunciator of United States foreign policy.

That Brzezinski had the President's ear and wielded significant influence seemed clear enough. He possessed the same facility as Walt Rostow for inventing abstractions that sounded deceptively global and profound—at least to Presidents not inoculated by early exposure to the practice. As Scotty Reston had said of another academic diplomat, he "delighted in flinging continents about." My father had once described that facility as "a flair for making little fishes talk like whales."

A national security adviser's influence does not depend merely on his talents as a courtier; he has the advantage of briefing the President every morning and can thus exploit the time-tested bureaucratic principle that "nothing propinks like propinquity." He is almost constantly available while, in these days of jet diplomacy, Secretaries of State tend to travel compulsively. Thus during my brief Iranian assignment, both Secretary of State Cyrus Vance and the Assistant Secretary of State for Near Eastern Affairs, Alfred L. Atherton, Jr., were away on a negotiating trip in the Middle East. Brzezinski was systematically excluding the State Department from the shaping or conduct of our Iranian policy. To assure the Department's insulation, he admonished me, immediately on my arrival, that I should not talk with the State Department's Iranian desk officer, because he "leaked"—an instruction I, of course, immediately disregarded.

Not only was the State Department being excluded from the management of our policies toward Iran, I soon found that our ambassador in Teheran, a seasoned career officer, William H. Sullivan, was being similarly bypassed. Brzezinski was forming his view of the situation, in part at least, by telephone conversations with the Iranian ambassador to the United States, Ardeshir Zahedi, who had gone back to Teheran at the request of the White House. Since, as the Shah's former son-in-law, Zahedi's power and position depended entirely on keeping the Shah on his throne, his advice to the United States was dangerously slanted.

During the next few days, I read the telegraphic traffic between Washington and our Teheran embassy and the reports prepared by the various United States intelligence agencies, interviewed everyone in government who might have insight into the situation, and talked with a number of outside experts from the universities. Then on December 12, 1979, I prepared a report for the President.

Report for the President

The Shah's regime, I wrote, "is on the verge of collapse." That "collapse is far more significant than a localized foreign policy crisis with exceptionally high stakes; it challenges the basic validity of the Nixon Doctrine." We had no one but ourselves to blame for the situation in which we were now confronted, for we made the Shah what he has become. We nurtured his love for grandiose geopolitical schemes and we supplied him the hardware to indulge his fantasies. Once we had anointed him as protector of our interests in the Persian Gulf, we became dependent on him. Now that his regime is coming apart under the pressure of imported modernization, we have so committed ourselves as to have no ready alternative.

Meanwhile, we must deal with the realities of the Shah's precarious power position and help him face it. We must make clear that, in our view, his only chance to save his dynasty (if indeed that is still possible) and retain our support is for him to transfer his power to a government responsive to the people. Only if he takes that action can Iran hope to avoid continued disaffection followed by a cumulative economic paralysis.

So long as we continued to express our unqualified support for the Shah, he would, I wrote, try to hang on to his full power and avoid the "hard decisions and . . . difficult actions required even for his own survival." He had so far given no indication that he might abdicate, yet he could not be sure of his army's loyalty were it used against the people. Though, I wrote, "the older hard-line officers in the top military command are likely to remain loyal to the Shah and if necessary to use brutal force to keep him in power," there is "growing discontent particularly among the junior officers." The worst thing that could happen would be for the Shah to try to save himself by turning his army against the people and having it disintegrate. If his troops refused to fire on their own fathers and brothers, that would mean mutiny and civil war and the Soviets could well be the largest gainer.

The problem, as I diagnosed it, was to provide a mechanism by which the Shah might transfer his powers to a democratic government that would not be automatically discredited as being his own creature. To that end I proposed that he appoint a Council of Notables, consisting of perhaps fifty individuals carefully chosen to represent all sectors of the opposition except the extreme left. (With the help of the State Department and CIA, we even prepared dossiers of more than fifty possible candidates for the Council.) The Council of Notables, as I conceived it, would not in itself be a government; instead, it would have the mandate to create a government that no one could dismiss as having been appointed by the Shah. Once created, such a broad representative government might be able to block the return of the Ayatollah Khomeini, or at least negotiate with him. I pointed out that the creation of such a council would obviously require the agreement of the military leaders. Though the Shah might remain as commander-in-chief of the armed services (though not of the secret police, SAVAK) in accordance with the 1906 Constitution, his exercise of military power would be controlled by the new government, and parliament would determine the military budget.

Speed was essential, since it was already tragically late in the day and a transfer of power was "indispensable and urgent." Any "delay or equivocation on our part in making our position clear" could "let the situation drift, create the impression that we [were] satisfied with the *status quo,* and tempt the Shah to maintain an unrealistically unyielding posture in his negotiations with the opposition." Meanwhile, it would be hard to achieve any political solution that did not have the express or implied acquiescence of the Ayatollah Khomeini. Thus we urgently needed "to open a disavowable channel of communication" with the Ayatollah or his entourage.

One of the lessons we should have learned from experience was to "avoid the catastrophic illusion that, because we support a foreign country, our vital interests are in every way congruent with the interests of that country as perceived by the government in power." We had, I pointed out, "sometimes indulged that illusion with regard to Israel." Another lesson was that "we should not—as we did with President Thieu—become the prisoner of a weakened leader out of touch with his own people."

No matter what actions we might take, we could not, I pointed out, "look forward to a tranquil future for a nation as socially, economically, and spiritually disturbed and divided as Iran." In fact, we "might well have to cope with an Iran torn by civil conflict and with the Soviet Union threatening to intervene in response to leftist elements that had managed to exploit the revolutionary turmoil." Not only would that tilt the global balance of power, but Saudi Arabia and the Gulf States would be thrown into total shock by hostile forces just across the Gulf able to interdict Gulf traffic. Meanwhile, I recommended close consultation with the Saudis to acquaint them with "the painful choices associated with security planning for the area."

Meeting with President Carter

On December 11, 1978, I sent my memorandum to the President and—on my insistence and over Brzezinski's objection—it was simultaneously distributed to key members of the National Security Council: the Acting Secretary of State, the Secretary of Defense, the Secretary of the Treasury, the chairman of the Joint Chiefs of Staff, and the head of the CIA. That group, with whom I met on the morning of December 12, greeted my report with mixed reactions. Though Acting Secretary of State Warren Christopher expressed his support, the views of most of the others tended to be either qualified or negative.

That afternoon I met with President Carter and Mr. Brzezinski. The President told me that he had carefully studied my report and, while he agreed with some of it, he did not fully accept my recommendations. He must, he said, continue to support the Shah so long as the Shah wished to remain in Iran. "I cannot tell another head of state what to do." I answered that I was not proposing that he tell another head of state what to do but rather that he play the role one good friend expected of another and "give him sound advice when he desperately needs it." "The Shah," I said, "is surrounded by sycophants, he is out of touch with his people and my impression from the telegrams is that he is eager for your advice."

But the President was not persuaded, saying, "We shall know a great deal more about this situation in a few days after Zbig has been in Teheran." At that I expressed visible surprise. To send Brzezinski to Teheran was, I said, "with all due respect, the worst idea I ever heard." Within forty-five minutes after Brzezinski's arrival at the Teheran airport the whole city would know about it. "We must remember," I said, "that the cutting edge of the revolution is anti-Western and specifically anti-American. If Brzezinski goes to Teheran, it will immoblize the Shah, since anything that he does after that will be regarded, Mr. President, as an action taken on your instructions. If the Shah abdicates, the Iranians will say that you sent one of your top advisers to force him to quit. If he stays on and uses repressive measures, it will be because Brzezinski has conveyed your order that he do so. Whatever he tells the Shah, his very presence will greatly heighten and sharpen the anti-American fury and you will be held responsible."

President Carter looked thoughtful for a moment, then replied, "I hadn't thought of it in those terms. Whom should we send?" I said, "Don't send anyone, we have a good ambassador in Teheran; I know Sullivan well, and he is a very able professional."

"But," said the President, "Sullivan doesn't have the Shah's confidence. We should send someone who has." (That comment, I thought to myself, almost certainly had its source in Zahedi's propaganda, since he himself wanted to be the only channel to the Shah.)

"I don't know about that," I replied, "but it's unimportant whether or not Sullivan has the Shah's confidence. The Shah will know that whatever your ambassador tells him comes from you. The important point is that you pass on your advice to the Shah as promptly as possible."

The conversation left me unsatisfied and depressed. The President was clearly not going to take my advice about advising the Shah to transfer his power. Nor did he authorize any contact with Khomeini. The most I had done was to block Brzezinski's projected trip, which would clearly have dramatized America's responsibility for everything that happened thereafter.

On the sixteenth, I caught a plane to Florida to stay with my family during the holidays. A day or two later, Secretary of State Vance returned from the Middle East and telephoned me. He had, he said, read my report and thought it extremely helpful. I advised him, as an old friend, that I had found a shockingly unhealthy situation in the National Security Council, with Brzezinski doing everything possible to exclude the State Department from participation in, or even knowledge of, our developing relations with Iran, communicating directly with Zahedi to the exclusion of our embassy, and using so-called back channel (CIA channel) telegrams of which the State Department was unaware. Secretary Vance was obviously upset. "He promised me he would not do that again; I must put a stop to it. I'll get back into it."

From then on, all I knew about Iranian developments came from the newspapers or the comments of friends in the Administration. The President continued to give verbal support to the Shah, thus running the risk, as I suggested, of appearing as the "orchestra leader on the *Titanic.*" Any approach to Khomeini was vetoed—presumably on Brzezinski's advice.

The Persian Gulf—The Center of Strategic Interests

I was concerned with Iran not merely—or even principally—because of its significance as an oil producer; much more important was its strategic location in relation to the East-West struggle. Soviet control would not merely provide the Soviets easy access to the subcontinent, it would give them effective control of the Persian Gulf, through which flow half the oil supplies of the non-Communist world. So long as the nations of the West remained slavishly dependent on Persian Gulf oil, the balance of power would be radically altered were the Soviets ever able to decree how many tankers could pass through the Straits of Hormuz and where the oil could go. That would, among other things, mean the end of Western solidarity; the hard-pressed nations of Western Europe, dependent on imported oil even more than the United States, would be under irresistible pressure to make their individual accommodations with Moscow.

Since Iran constituted the whole eastern littoral of the Gulf, Soviet domination would be disastrous for the fragile Arab nations across from it, whose life depended on free movement in the Gulf. Nor could we possibly defend the Gulf against Soviet expansionist ambitions unless we could develop close working relations with Saudi Arabia and the emirates and sultanates that were the Gulf's western shore.

I had first begun to worry about Middle East oil when I was working with Jean Monnet. At the end of the Second World War, Europe's economy had been largely coal-based, but, with the discovery of vast pools of cheap oil under the Arabian deserts in the early 1950s, the Europeans had been faced with the need for a totally new energy policy to reduce their reliance on mines that were rapidly becoming uneconomically deep with coal seams excessively thin. Using high-cost coal, Europe could not compete with United States industry, which was already shifting toward oil and later toward natural gas in response to market forces. I had discussed the hazards of this shift with Monnet when he was president of the High Authority of the European Coal and Steel Community and had given him a brief note on the subject. In that note I had called attention to the fact that, in betting its energy future on Middle East oil, Europe was acting on certain implicit assumptions that should be carefully examined.

The first assumption was that the oil-producing countries of the Middle East and elsewhere in the Third World would never achieve the sophistication and unity enabling them to dictate oil prices. The major international oil companies could, as I then saw it, continue for a long while to dominate Middle Eastern oil production.

The second assumption, parallel to the first, was that the oil-producing countries would have neither the will nor skill to use oil for their political objectives.

The third assumption was far more troublesome: the gamble that oil production would never be interrupted by political instability or war. The Arab world was, I noted, inherently unstable; some of its political structures were anachronisms, and I could not see most of them lasting more than a few decades.

Finally, just to be comprehensive, my note mentioned a fourth assumption: that we could keep the oil-producing areas out of the Soviet orbit.

When I gave Monnet my paper, he had his mind on other things; shifting to oil was, he thought, essential if European industry were to compete. Yet I recalled my four assumptions when oil prices began their almost vertical rise at the beginning of 1974. During my years as a director of the Standard Oil Company of California, I had learned the significance of Middle Eastern oil. In the early 1970s, an old friend from wartime days, Emilio G. Collado, then executive vice-president of what is now Exxon, showed me statistics and projections foreshadowing the financial distortions and dislocations that might be created by the expanding revenues accruing to Saudi Arabia and the smaller Gulf states as world oil demand increased. Even with oil at pre-1973 prices, Collado's projections were disturbing, and, largely inspired by my conversations with him, in 1972 I made a speech in London emphasizing the financial problems such a transfer of wealth would entail.

When oil prices thrust sharply upward following the 1973 Arab-Israeli war, my concern was multiplied by a factor whose upper limits are not yet known. The financial and economic dislocations threatened by vaulting oil prices could, in my view, be effectively managed only with the collaboration of the oil-producing states, yet the Nixon Administration was foolishly approaching the problem as a confrontation between OPEC and the West, indulging in meaningless tough talk and that windy fatuity of the copywriters, "Project Independence."

On September 17, 1974, I made a speech at a seminar in London in which I spelled out my concerns. I took as my point of departure Keynes's classic work, *The Economic Consequences of the Peace,* which I have earlier discussed in chapter 3. Keynes foresaw that reparations and war debts to America would drain central Europe of capital and set in train dangerous forces, which, in fact, later helped bring about the Second World War. Now we again faced the prospect of vast and increasing capital flows to the OPEC countries. What Keynes had called the "transfer problem" we now glibly referred to as "recycling." If we did not find a solution promptly and incisively, we might face a severe disruption in world financial markets that could once more create the conditions for serious political troubles.

Either we would respond to an enormous challenge with initiatives of comparable scale and scope or we would inevitably fall back into the old defensive, restrictive, nationalistic habits that could Balkanize our economies and precipitate depression. While we argued among ourselves, poor countries were suffering dangerous deficits and heading for financial crises.

"What we must do," I argued, "is to seek, by a combined effort of oil-producing and oil-consuming nations, to buy time for the world to adjust to the increased cost of energy," and for this I suggested the creation "of a new institution which might be established alongside the World Bank and International Monetary Fund with capital subscribed equally—50 percent by the OPEC nations and the remaining 50 percent divided among seven or eight leading non-Communist industrial powers." I elaborated the scheme, suggesting a type of debt investment the new institution might issue and techniques for dealing with currency fluctuations.

We should, I argued, stop thinking in terms of a destructive confrontation with the OPEC countries and try to see the problem as it appeared from Riyadh or Kuwait or Teheran, recognizing that, in the famous aphorism of Blaise Pascal, "What is truth on this side of the Pyrenees is error on the other side." Oil prices had, I pointed out, been held at abysmally low levels for years, and the OPEC countries had some justice in their claim that their increased oil prices were merely correcting the terms of trade.

My speech fell on deaf ears. Not only did the audience fail to respond but the Nobel prize winning economist, Professor Milton Friedman, speaking on the same platform, emphatically disagreed. "Why do you make so much of the problem?" he asked me. "Don't you realize that the OPEC cartel won't last six months? Meanwhile, no one will be hurt by the increased oil prices; they're already being offset by inflation."

Thereafter, the locusts ate the years. The American government still proceeded on the "apparent assumption," as I said in a speech two months later, "that hot air can replace petroleum as a source of energy—an ingenious thesis but with little scientific support."

Now, eight years after my London speech, we are still pettifogging, though we have made some slow progress in our thinking. The countries of the International Monetary Fund are at last planning an international mechanism to achieve the objective to which I had addressed my speech. Great nations learn slowly.

Oil as a Political Weapon

Even more ominous than the financial dislocations from vaulting oil price increases were threats to the continued availability of oil. During the Suez affair in 1956 and again in 1967, some Arab nations half-heartedly tested an oil embargo. On both occasions the United States, then still an export surplus oil producer, made up any shortfalls. Now that had changed. The West was growing increasingly dependent on Middle Eastern oil, but making no serious effort to settle the Arab-Israeli dispute, and, by the summer of 1973, a blow-up seemed inevitable. On August 14, 1973, I made a speech at the Aspen Institute in Colorado that concluded with the following dark prediction:

What is . . . likely, it seems to me, is that even the conservative and basically pro-Western Arab states such as Saudi Arabia will be forced by the pressure of the more radical Arabs to use oil as a political weapon and to threaten a freeze on expansion or a slow-down or cut-back not merely for conservation reasons but as the basis for a political ultimatum. No longer will they expend their production to satisfy growing Western demands unless the West changes its policies toward the Arab-Israeli struggle. . . .

Though I know of no easy solution to the problem, *it is essential that we face this calamitous prospect not as a remote possibility but, in my view, as almost a certainty.* It does no good to deny reality. It is something for which we should be urgently planning. (Italics added.)

Within two months, the Yom Kippur war started and the Arabs imposed an oil embargo. This time, the United States had no surplus to meet shortfalls.

Today, the dangers of a curtailment or even total blockage of the oil flow depend more than ever on the last three assumptions listed in my note to Monnet. Can we, by realistic diplomacy, resolve the Arab-Israeli dispute that may drive the Saudis and other Arab oil producers to impose another embargo? Will there be further disruptive conflicts involving oil-producing states, such as the Iran-Iraq war? Will other oil-producing states suffer a political breakdown comparable to that in Iran? Will we be able to keep the Soviet Union from spreading its tentacles around the Gulf area?

Centrality of the Palestinian Issue

After the collapse of the Second Sinai negotiations in March 1975, I urged Henry Kissinger to tackle the urgent problem of the Palestinians. We must, I argued, find the ways and means of ending the Israeli occupation of the West Bank and Gaza Strip and providing the inhabitants of those areas the opportunity to decide how and by whom they wished to be ruled. The settlement of that issue was essential to the stability of Middle East oil-producing states and particularly those in the Gulf area. I made the point in a meeting of the "elder statesmen" on March 31 and April 2, in Washington. Further progress through "step-by-step" diplomacy was, Kissinger was then inclined to concede, played out, and I urged that he shift his attention toward an overall settlement. But when he saw a chance to resume shuttling, the temptation to achieve another widely hailed triumph proved irresistible.

On November 17, 1977, I was in Tel Aviv, participating in a seminar on the Arab-Israeli conflict, when word came of President Sadat's decision to fly to Jerusalem. That night I found most of my Israeli friends euphoric; the excitement was pervasive and contagious, I was impressed by their deep yearning for peace, and could not blame them for wanting a deal with Egypt that would relieve Israel of its greatest military danger. With Egypt neutralized, the Israelis clearly had the military competence to deal with a war limited to only one front. But did that augur well for the long term?

Almost alone of the thousands in Israel that night, I was troubled by the longer-range implications of Sadat's mission. In spite of his disclaimers, his visit would almost inevitably lead, as I saw it, to a bilateral deal between Egypt and Israel. Immunizing Israel from the threat of a two-front war would relieve it of pressure to settle the Palestinian issue.

On September 8, 1978, just as the meeting at Camp David was about to begin, I discussed the problem with President Carter and was impressed with his determination that the negotiations must include an agreed plan for settling the Palestinian issue. Yet—as was foreseeable— once the Camp David talks got underway, they acquired a momentum of their own, resulting in little more than a simple bilateral deal in which we bought the sands of the Sinai for an exorbitant price from Israel, then paid Egypt a large price to take them back. The second phase dealing with the Palestinian issue was clearly an infeasible afterthought.

For almost a decade I have talked and written persistently on our need to focus on our own national interests in the Middle East, But I have made few converts. Though I have received much sympathetic mail, little is being done to arrest or deflect the strong tides of our politically warped policy. Sooner or later, the evolution of events will provide its own irrefutable documentation. That will not be a happy day for America.

30. *Over and Out*

        To celebrate my seventieth birthday in December 1979, I reread Cicero's *De Senectute,* not as I had once done, in Latin, but this time in translation. I was, after all, not preparing for an examination but performing a ritual act to celebrate my breaking the Biblical age barrier of three score years and ten, and I had been inspired to turn to Cicero by a comment in a column by Mary McGrory. "Ball has," she wrote, "reached that point in life where he is beyond ambition."

I find that a comforting thought; like Cicero, I take pleasure in the compensations of advanced years. Yet I cannot easily adjust to the role of mere innocent bystander—or at least accept that role without noisy protest—since I feel neither resigned nor complacent. Is it merely the chill of old age that induces my sense of apprehension and impatience about the world? That seems hard to accept.

Whenever during my diplomatic years some catastrophic event caught America by surprise, commentators (omniscient by their own admission) would point out why the State Department should have anticipated and prepared for the event. Sometimes, of course, they were right; when my colleagues and I looked back, we often wondered why we had not been more perceptive. Now, as a not-so-innocent bystander, I watch for trends and premonitory events that might foreshadow disaster. It is not easy. One must not merely look carefully at the current scene but also venture predictions of years to come. Though the latter exercise is implicitly hazardous, it is a risk I can afford since one comforting perquisite of old age is the freedom to speculate about the future without being available for rebuke when events refute my crystal-gazing.

The Current Mood

One should perhaps discount my more somber forebodings. Spectators who have once been players are notorious for making critical comments from the sidelines and offering grim forecasts of the outcome. Yet I am not alone in detecting a sense of unease and disenchantment pervading our bountiful land. We have never fully recovered from the anger and divisiveness of the latter 1960s, and I find increasing evidence of the baleful mark left by our Vietnam experience on almost all aspects of American life—social, economic, political—while at the same time it distorted, undercut, and diminished America's relations with other governments and peoples throughout the world.

That dismal war was not, however, the sole cause of our miseries, merely the beginning of a chain of events that has contributed to our present unhappiness. The list is familiar: Watergate, a falling dollar, relentless inflation, high interest rates, a menacing Soviet military buildup, and—most important—a succession of weak Presidents. I cannot, of course, sort out the intricate causal relations implicit in these developments not yet clearly defined. They took place during a time of major— and long overdue—social changes. Throughout the first two decades after World War II, we were, no doubt, excessively self-confident; but repeated rebuffs at the hands of poor, backward, preindustrial nations have since forced a more modest assessment of the dimensions of our nation's power. In Vietnam, we fought an irrelevant war to an inglorious conclusion; in Iran, we were forced to stand by impotently when our countrymen were kidnapped by a clerical cabal that was the negation of government. Meanwhile, for eight years we have been powerless to resist the financial decisions of a group of developing countries combining under the acronym of OPEC.

Of course, each of these incidents had a different explanation. In Vietnam, we underestimated the driving force of our adversary's fierce commitment and the marginal nature of our country's own interests. In Teheran we learned with mounting frustration that kidnappers can, by exploiting human compassion, effectively reverse power relations. In trying to cope with OPEC's mounting oil prices, all oil-consuming nations—rich and poor—yielded to the powerful leverage of collective decisions by producers who control the supply of a critical resource.

These unexpected shocks, compounded by other symbols of weakness and disorder, have revived tendencies recurrent throughout our history that most of us thought we had outgrown: anti-intellectualism, reinforced by the emergence of obscurantist religious cults, a weakness for conspiratorial interpretations of otherwise explicable developments (such as automatically crediting the Soviets with turbulence in inherently unstable countries), and a drift *not* toward isolationism (America is, I think, finally cured of that delusion) but rather toward an ignorant and absentminded unilateralism.

Unfortunately, a country preoccupied with transient minor irritations can easily be distracted from larger dangers, and it seems to me that we are now facing the world's longer-term predicaments with limited vision and a short attention span. Many of us, I sometimes fancy, are behaving like those legendary fishermen on the Seine embankment in June 1940 who were so absorbed in catching their supper that they failed to look up when the Nazi tanks rolled into Paris. Our civilization and the institutions we have inherited or created—from family to government—are suffering premonitory tremors from seismic strains and tensions. But we ignore them, largely because we find the world too complex to be understood, managed, or even fully observed, and the dangers about us too confusing and ugly to be frankly acknowledged. So we sublimate our anxieties by irascibly cultivating our own gardens, complaining about the neighbors, and worrying about how and where we can sell the produce. In the meantime, we let our once sturdy political and social structures be critically undermined by inadequate maintenance, neglect, and reckless misuse, while old and essential assumptions are left to crumble and are discarded through mindless prejudice and irrational actions.

The End of Innocence

Mankind's gravest danger is, of course, the nuclear bomb, which generations younger than mine have always known. I learned to live with the potential of nuclear death only late in life and cannot accept it as a normal and permanent aspect of our human existence. As a youth, I could never have imagined any hovering threat other than hellfire if I misbehaved, and my parents were too kind and rational to hold that threat over my head. During the first decade of the new century, in which I was born, the Western world was lighted by an ebullient optimism. With the popularization of Darwin's concept of evolution, prospects seemed bright indeed. Renan foresaw mankind gradually achieving a more perfect state through the growing dominance of reason. Herbert Spencer, interpreting Darwin, predicted that, with humankind's evolutionary adaptation, the "ultimate development of the ideal man is logically certain."

To be sure, confidence in man's perfectibility did not last long. When I was four years old, Europe was caught up in the first of two great civil wars that shook belief in the inevitability—even the possibility—of progress. After the carnage of Passchendaele, the Somme, gas warfare, and rotting bodies in the trenches, came dark prognoses. I well remember my first encounter with Spengler's *The Decline of the West* in the 1920s, and I was haunted by the despairing lamentations of Paul Valéry. As a student, I turned in disillusion from the cloying patriotism of Rupert Brooke to the bitter realism of Robert Graves, Wilfred Owen, and Siegfried Sassoon. Then the decade ended with a cataclysmic depression that raised festering doubts about Western institutions. Later I encountered a wholly new area of speculation when Aldous Huxley published his brilliant anti-utopian *Brave New World,* depicting a sterile bureaucracy perverting biology to create humanoid robots as mankind's slaves.

I could—and did—dismiss Spengler as a dyspeptic German theorist and shrug off Huxley's fantasy as grim satire; but Hitler and the Second World War conclusively ended my benign illusions. No one could overlook the shattering message of the the Nuremburg trials that man had made small, if any, progress toward perfectibility. Hitler and his scrofulous gang had shown themselves fully as depraved and brutal as the most sadistic medieval tyrants. Ghengis Khan and Attila were not, as I had assumed, merely products of a dark satanic period; rich and powerful nations could still produce monsters as leaders.

That thought gained a new malign significance with the splitting of the atom and our destructive use of that knowledge at Hiroshima and Nagasaki. Armed with the bomb, some new power-obsessed lunatic could, as Hitler had only threatened to do, slam the world's door so hard as to bring down the whole edifice. Thus, I was dismayed though not surprised, when nuclear weapons became available to the ugly, repressive, Soviet regime of Josef Stalin. No longer could we rule out the possiblity that human life might someday—even soon—perish in a pyrotechnic Armageddon.

The advent of the nuclear weapon inspired in my generation long thoughts about last things and revived the ancient anxiety that man might destroy himself if he let excessive curiosity push his exploration of nature beyond the frontiers of the forbidden. Until then, we fortunate few on this broad continent had felt protected by mighty oceans, but with the advent of nuclear weapons we faced the abhorrent reality that, though our nation was the most powerful in the world, we were now vulnerable to bombs on our cities and firesides quite as much as old Europe. That marked the end of our innocence—our exemption from the fears other men and women had always known.

Our ancestors had thought it normal to live with dragons and evil spirits, with Zeus and his thunderbolts, with Thor and his hammer. Medieval man suffered the threat of eternal damnation, and our more recent ancestors were chastened by the vision of a stern God. Though the emancipating skepticism of scientific discipline allayed the fears of divine retribution for a growing number, their respite lasted only briefly. It may be that the human psyche requires a sword of Damocles; in any event, we now used our new-found knowledge to fabricate a man-made substitute for hell—the threat of universal immolation ignited by our own willful action. We hung nuclear death like a menacing sword over mankind and we must live with the threat that it may destroy us all.

Our first reaction to our new vulnerability was irrational and demeaning. How could we have suddenly become as subject to destruction as other less favored peoples? Throughout the ugly McCarthy period, some searched for scapegoats on the vainglorious assumption that only by stealing our secrets could the Soviets have been able to build a bomb. What I found particularly repulsive in the ensuing hysteria was the realization of how little we had progressed beyond the fifteenth century; now a new form of St. Vitus' Dance afflicted even men and women I had previously regarded as intelligent. It turned friend against friend, destroying trust in human decency and producing a nation of informers.

Yet in time the fever abated; our native good sense and decency returned; and, during the national hangover that followed the McCarthy orgy, the prospect of nuclear catastrophe became, for most people, more a figure of speech than a dour possibility. If men and women live long enough on a fault line destined to produce a major earthquake, they cease, in the years between catastrophes, to think much about it—or more important—to do much about it. History, after all, is second-guessing and only future generations know the later chapters. The Malraux quotation to which Speer alluded sums up the problem vividly: "A fish is badly placed for judging what the aquarium looks like from outside."

Our adjustment to the bomb—too easily achieved—reduced the possibility of nuclear war to a misfiled datum of day-to-day existence. Those specialized men and women who continue to think and write about it concern themselves primarily with military tactics and academic speculation expressed in a vocabulary that reduces predictions of mass human slaughter to pedantic periphrasis and dessicated statistics.

The Need for a Fresh Approach

Meanwhile, scientists and engineers the world over are sedulously trying to improve man's ability to kill his fellow human beings in increasing numbers; there seems no end to it. We are prisoners of a process spinning out of our control and it takes no special perception to recognize that, unless we halt the production of ever more powerful nuclear weapons, we shall sooner or later blow one another up. Who can believe that if we endlessly pervert every scientific breakthrough to the loathsome objective of mutual murder, we shall not, sooner or later, produce a cataclysm? Yet we pretend that there is no special urgency in reaching agreements to halt the process, that we can take our time while, in the meantime, building more bombs and increasingly exotic systems to perfect our capability to wipe out civilization.

That denies rationality; I cannot accept the sense of futility and resignation implied in our current failure of realism or decision, yet we cannot, of course, solve the problem by ourselves. My negative views on unilateral disarmament are best explained by a parable I once wrote about a small community that had for centuries been troubled by disastrous floods. Finally, with great effort, the townspeople built a huge dam that kept their lands dry and fruitful for three decades. Then a new generation, unhappy because the dam was obscuring the sunset, decided to tear it down. Their reasoning was impeccable: "Since we've had no floods for thirty years, it's obvious that we no longer need such an ugly structure." So, after holding a rock festival, they blew up the dam and, as one of the young leaders remarked, "Man, was that the year of Aquarius!"

But, if we must reject unilateral nuclear disarmament as a craven abandonment of all Western values, the human race should still be able to agree on the actions needed to regain control of its destiny. In the early 1970s, the American and Soviet leaders seemed to be making slow progress toward some common rules of mutual restraint. The dialogue between East and West acquired a new civility, and we established arrangements for cooperation in a number of areas. No doubt these limited achievements inspired inflated expectations, but they did suggest that progress could be made once each side began to recognize the requirements of the other.

Just what happened to détente is not entirely clear; the current glib answers are less than fully persuasive. Nauseated by the sour taste of its Vietnam experience, America suffered a delayed overreaction to the Soviet Union's efforts to exploit situations of turbulence with low-risk, low-cost adventures. Moscow acquired an influence in Angola and Ethiopia by using Cuban surrogates, and it established a base of operations in South Yemen. But Soviet opportunism was to be expected. It was not the first time that Moscow had sought to build centers of subversion in Africa, though its previous efforts all ultimately failed. In spite of a substantial commitment of resources, the Soviets were expelled from Ghana, Guinea, and finally from the most important North African nation, Egypt. (Had we suffered a similar reversal, the cries of "who lost Egypt?" would have marred our political rhetoric for years.) Finally, the Soviets' deployment of soldiers and tanks in Afghanistan evoked from the Carter Administration cries of outrage more suggestive of a raped maiden than an experienced nation. Democracies are given to hyperbole and few bothered to note that the decision of the Soviets to commit their military forces did not alter their existing position in the country; it merely confirmed a political coup that had taken place more than a year before, while at the same time subjecting the Soviets to substantial strains and costs. Our reaction would have been far less shrill had the Soviets moved at a time when Iran was caught up in a revolutionary frenzy and the chancellories of the oil-consuming nations were concentrating their attention on the Persian Gulf.

For a variety of reasons—including the exaggeration inevitable in the media's need for drama—we have tended to build up Soviet threats while ignoring or forgetting Soviet retreats and failures. On balance, the Soviets would seem to have gained little net military or political advantage by their latest decade of adventures; their expulsion from Egypt more than offset any strategic benefits they may have gained in Angola, Ethiopia, Yemen, or Afghanistan. But what has principally upset the Western capitals—and particularly Washington—has been the formidable buildup of Soviet arms at a substantially higher rate than our own. That buildup began soon after the Cuban Missile Crisis in 1962, when the Soviet leadership was brought face-to-face with its inferior military competence in a region dominated by United States power. Thereafter, it has persistently strengthened its strategic capability, extending its military reach beyond the beaches of Eurasia by intensively building ships and aircraft.

The significance of this rapid military expansion is a central subject of dispute. The Reagan Administration has uncritically inferred an aggressive expansionist intent but the point has not been proved. The Soviets' extension of their military reach by ships and aircraft could well have been inspired by nothing more malign than a craving for recognition as a superpower on an equal footing with the United States. Or, alternatively, the Soviets may have been moved primarily by atavistic fears of invasion and what they conceived to be the implacable hostility of the United States. Throughout history, the Russians have suffered periodic invasions from the East and, twice in modern times, have been invaded from the West. Certainly history, memory, and comparative population magnitudes largely explain Moscow's commitment of a million men to guard the long frontier separating Siberia from China; for in the whole of the USSR east of the Urals (with a land area twice the size of the United States) there are only fifty-eight million people of whom thirty-seven million—or roughly two-thirds—are non-Slavic, while six or seven hundred million people live in the eastern one-third of China— an area not much larger than Argentina.

If the Soviets' buildup of a vast, costly military establishment does not by itself prove an intention to wage large-scale war, it does suggest that the Soviets will, as they have consistently done, continue to take advantage of opportunities to extend their influence just as we do, though their methods are cruder and crueler than ours and we, of course, have no territorial ambitions. Why then do they build up their military strength beyond the relatively modest forces they might require for limited operations? Perhaps it is that once having been programmed to expand Soviet forces, the bureaucratic machinery of an insensitive military-industrial complex has developed a momentum the Kremlin can no longer control. With bellicose noises from Washington and an inadequate hold over its own military sector, the Soviet civilian leaders are unable to assure the Soviet generals that the United States is not threatening Soviet interests.

I give some credence to this last explanation. During my years in the State Department, Chairman Khrushchev complained more than once that by taking a hard line, our Government undermined his ability to resist the demands of his generals. Though these were obviously self-serving complaints, they should not be wholly discounted at a time when the Reagan Administration is behaving as though we were already at war with the Soviet Union. Almost every official speech contains a condemnation of Moscow, and even the most localized tribal or religious quarrels—including squalid disputes over boundaries—are seen in terms of the East-West struggle. Our official statements are shot through with Cold War bombast; political problems are approached almost entirely in military terms and—most dangerous of all—our leaders seem on the verge of embracing the heresy most likely to destroy us: the acceptance of nuclear bombs as weapons of war and not merely instruments of deterrence. SALT II, they contend, deserved to be rejected; in spite of talk geared for public consumption, they appear reconciled to the defeatist view that we shall never be able to break the cycle of escalation—even implying doubt that such interruption is necessary; instead, they seem to argue, we must concentrate our energies on devising new and more effective means of mutual extermination.

Thus America and the Soviet Union are behaving like two boys in a schoolyard, impelled to bluster until they fight simply because neither knows how to quit without risk of being struck by the other. We should not—so our politicians and our self-proclaimed strategic experts endlessly repeat—try to bargain with the Soviets except from a position of strength, which means, in their stultifying jargon, that we must surpass Moscow in nuclear weaponry, even though the Russians are quite as determined to surpass us. One even hears again that illusory concept of "linkage." When I was a small boy running family errands to the butcher shop, the word "linkage" was used as synonymous with "baloney"; I have seen nothing since to change that view. It is certainly a misleading concept when interpreted, as our government now implies, to mean that if the Soviets should try to extend their power anywhere in the world, we should punish them by refusing to negotiate to control the arms race. What arrant nonsense! Is an effort to gain control over a mutually costly and hazardous process a favor we accord the other side? Is it something we can afford to deny the Soviets by way of a sanction? Must we inevitably go on squandering our resources to multiply our capacity for overkill until some unlucky conjunction of events leads to the weapons being fired off?

If we are to break the momentum, it seems to me, we must calm down and change our approach to the Soviet Union, and the Reagan Administration must break its addiction to language even more acrimonious than the Kremlin's own vocabulary of invective. Such strident threats, demands, and abuse can only strengthen the hard-line elements in the Soviet hierarchy and reduce the Kremlin's power to restrain its military. It is particularly dangerous at a time when the Soviet Union is about to undergo a major change of leadership, since evidence of American hostility could strengthen the position of the hard-liners in the succession.

I think it essential, therefore, that we abandon Cold War stereotypes and undertake a fresh approach. The first condition to such an approach is for our government to reject the catastrophic conclusion that nuclear warheads are usable weapons of war and that there is such a thing as winning a nuclear conflict. That is the most dangerous of all current delusions. It is based on a fantasy: the assumption that under certain unspecified circumstances we could fire off nuclear weapons in limited number and still avoid a full nuclear exchange. I do not believe that for a moment. Even one tactical nuclear weapon fired at a Soviet target would, I am confident, lead to an almost certain escalation. One of the wisest of America's military thinkers, Admiral Noel Gayler, has stated the realities succinctly: "There is," he has written, "no sensible military use for any of our nuclear forces: intercontinental, theater or tactical."[1] Their only use is for deterrence and political effect.

The second condition is to recognize that, whatever their hegemonic ambitions, the Soviet leaders are not lunatics. No doubt they will seize opportunities to try to extend Soviet authority without excessive risk, but it is equally clear that, though they crave power, they are not seeking suicide. We are far more likely to start a war by indulging false fears than by a cool appraising view; the last thing we need is for America to lead a *jihad*.

By purging our public rhetoric of the twin fallacies of limited nuclear war and a belief in a suicidal Soviet leadership, we should be able to free ourselves to talk quietly and rationally with the Kremlin leaders about the basic issue of mutual survival. Emphasizing the destructive path on which the superpowers are now engaged, we should propose a concerted step toward breaking the cycle of weapons escalation and reducing the danger to both sides—a step designed not merely to contain the pace of the arms race but drastically to reduce existing nuclear arsenals. Such an approach will obviously not evoke an immediate favorable response, but pursued quietly and lucidly over a period of time, it might calm Soviet anxieties and restore a sufficient basis of mutual confidence to permit some progress to be made.

It is not enough merely to create the conditions for straightforward talk with the Soviet Union unless we have something to say. That requires changes, not only in the methods by which we evolve new weapons systems, but in the procedures used in conducting arms control negotiations. Looking back over the history of nuclear escalation, I am dismayed to find that the United States, in almost all cases, took the first initiative in creating new weapons systems. It was we, not the Soviet Union, who

led in the development of solid fuel missiles; the creation of MRV warheads and then MIRV warheads; the improvement of accuracy that permitted counter-force and not merely counter-value weapons; and the
development of cruise missiles and submarine-launched missile systems.
In almost every case, the thrust of our new technology has made arms
control increasingly difficult. Had we sought negotiations before translating MIRV technology into operational weapons, we might well have
reached agreement with the Soviet Union not to take this step. In that
case, the Soviets' heavy missiles would have become obsolete; our land-
based Minuteman system would have remained substantially invulnera-
ble, and the problems of arms control would have been greatly simpli-
fied. Today our government is under pressure to develop an antiballistic
missile system that could be put in place when current, temporary
restrictions expire. We may soon be tempted to put missiles in outer
space despite commitments to the contrary and to develop basing systems for land-based missiles that, by making verification practically
impossible, would destroy any serious hope of stopping the arms race
this side of catastrophe.

Part of the stimulus for the development of new systems is, of course,
rivalry among our military services, which is a luxury we can no longer
afford. We have built three distinct missile systems—the so-called triad—
but, since each service insists on expanding and improving its own system, we fail to exploit the advantages of redundancy. So long as service
rivalries and service politics dominate our nuclear policies, I see no hope
of stopping the arms race.

We shall certainly not stop it if we continue to negotiate within the
pattern now established for SALT talks. Today every American concession must be carefully tailored to satisfy the ambitions of each service as
well as the scholastic speculations of nuclear strategists and the political
demands of vested interest groups in the Administration and Congress.
Realistically, there is only one way to break out of this suffocating strait-
jacket—to propose some method of across-the-board nuclear arms
reduction that will penalize each system equally.

Experience with SALT I and SALT II has amply shown that we can
never make real progress if we merely seek to trade off one item for
another. As I have pointed out in earlier chapters, America spent many
years seeking to bring about the reduction of trade barriers by that tedious
and protracted method, and the results achieved were relatively small.
It was against that background that, in 1961, I urged President Kennedy
that we seek legislative authority to make percentage cuts across the
board—the practice used in eliminating trade barriers among the member nations of the European common market. The result was the Kennedy Round of trade negotiations, which accomplished far more than
had other efforts in the past.

Our best hope of making significant progress toward controlling the nuclear arms race is to propose a similar straightforward formula. We are playing scholastic games when we try to equate our Polaris seaborne missile with a Soviet land-based missile, and it is unrealistic to think that by trying to construct such artificial equivalencies, we could achieve a significant reduction of nuclear arsenals and the maintenance of the arms competition at a lower level of intensity.

Our so-called nuclear experts insist, however, that an across-the-board cut in nuclear arms might excessively reduce some weapons systems in which we have a substantial advantage. Some of our weary trade negotiators made precisely the same argument when we first proposed across-the-board tariff cuts: it would produce trade distortions, benefit our trading partners more than ourselves, and hurt some of our industries. It is the kind of objection, narrowly focused on a statistical item-for-item approach, that in weapons negotiations ignores the larger purpose and makes serious progress impossible. Each side possesses enormous overkill capabilities, and there is no rational basis to believe that the security of either would be jeopardized by substantial across-the-board percentage reductions—phased over a period of years.

I know, of couse, that this is heresy to the professional arms negotiators who, out of exhaustion and disappointment and an uncritical acceptance of conventional wisdom, have tended to constrict their thinking to the pattern of the past. If we are ever to break the present momentum of competitive escalation, the necessary decisions will not be made by technicians but only by a major act of will at the top levels of each government.

In recent years the Kremlin's leaders have repeatedly asserted that the USSR would not be the first nation to use nuclear weapons, yet the United States has shied away from a similar "no-first-use" declaration. Since we think of ourselves as committed to peace, our posture would seem anomalous and, in principle, there should be good reason for us to make such a statement. After all, if each of the two superpowers were to renounce "first use" and mean it, nuclear weapons would cease to have any meaning either for war or deterrence. Indeed, the situation would resemble that contemplated by a statute enacted by a Western state in the early days of American railroading which provided that, if two trains met at an intersection, neither should proceed until the other had passed by.

The fact that the United States is restrained from making such a declaration goes to the heart of our predicament. The theory of flexible response on which our NATO defense has long been postulated assumes that if Europe were threatened by Soviet invasion, the United States might at some point raise the level of violence by using at least tactical nuclear weapons. That, it seems to me, points to our Western weakness for, though some nuclear theologians contend that tactical nuclear weapons could be used without triggering a major nuclear exchange, that is, to my mind, pure fantasy.

Unhappily, we cannot renounce this nuclear fantasy since the West has not prepared itself to resist Soviet aggression solely by conventional means. Thus, having sought to buy defense cheaply we now find ourselves in a trap of our own making.

Here the problem becomes fuzzy and theological, for many in the West tend to believe that only the balance of terror—the threat of mutual nuclear destruction—has enabled Europe to avoid war for almost four decades, and that if we eliminated the nuclear threat, the Soviets might risk a major expansionist adventure and plunge Europe once again into chaos.

In philosophical terms, I find that a highly disturbing thesis; it seems to suggest that mankind can restrain its own bloodlust only if threatened by hellfire and, if men no longer believe in a hell of divine fabrication, we must make and maintain one of our own creation. It is not a thesis of which humankind should be proud. What an insult to *homo sapiens!*

The End of the Nuclear Oligopoly

Even were we to succeed in reducing the arsenals of the present superpowers, we would have resolved only part of the problem. We can no longer afford to base our survival on the wishful belief that fear of reciprocal murder will prevent a nuclear collision. The assumption of a balance of terror posited on a nuclear oligopoly of the Soviets and three Western democracies is rapidly losing its factual basis. More and more nations of dubious stability and responsibility have obtained—or are about to obtain—their own nuclear arsenals: an insidious process we call, in a pallid coinage, "nuclear proliferation." Thus, we now face a danger of nuclear war that neither superpower can prevent or control, even though both might like to.

Consider the third-class powers that have already acquired nuclear weapons, or seem likely to do so in the next five years—Israel, India, Pakistan, Brazil, Argentina, South Africa, South Korea, and Taiwan, while during the coming decade, Egypt, Libya, Iran, and Iraq may be added to the list. Every day brings more imminent danger that one of those nations, in a moment of fear, panic, or revolutionary frenzy, may detonate a fatal bomb. As the list discloses, the common denominator of the nations seeking nuclear weapons is their location in areas where passions are high and conflict endemic. That is why they want the bomb, and precisely why they should not have it.

Though the current American Administration tends to blame the Soviets for all of our ills, it is Western democracies—including the United States—that have spread the ability to make nuclear weapons. For this we should feel a deep collective shame. America initiated the misguided though well-intentioned, program for scattering nuclear reactors all over the world under the beguiling slogan of "Atoms for Peace," and some Western democracies have recklessly spread nuclear knowledge and facilities out of greed and commercial advantage. The result has cast capitalism in a bad light, since, insulated from either the ambitions of private entrepreneurs or the seductions of philanthropy, the Soviets have rigorously abstained from assisting the spread of nuclear capability. Meanwhile, the problem is getting so far out of hand that only heroic measures offer hope of even slowing the process.

Instead of merely shrugging off proliferation as inevitable, we should, in concert with other nuclear-supplying powers—including the Soviet Union—take every possible initiative to halt the current trend. That requires, among other things, that we and the Soviets make substantial progress toward gaining control of our own nuclear arms race, since that is the condition on which signatory nations have agreed to comply with the Nuclear Non-Proliferation Treaty. It also means devising such initiatives as nuclear-free zones—particularly one for the Middle East, which is the center of world danger. We dare not delay such a project, as some would have us do, until the tensions and conflicts of the area have been resolved. It is precisely because those tensions and conflicts may lead to the use of nuclear weapons that we need to keep them out of the Middle East.

I look forward with cold apprehension to the day when a third-class nation involved in a local conflict fires the first nuclear weapon at a neighbor. How will other countries react if the attacked nation is allied in some manner to one or the other of the superpowers? By bombing the attacker? If a hard-pressed Israel, for example, should drop a nuclear bomb on an Arab capital, would the Soviet Union respond with a bomb on Tel Aviv? And what would we do? Any nuclear explosion anywhere would set off a wave of angry recriminations. How did the offending nation secure the fuel for the bomb? Who helped with the technology?

It is *terra incognita* for which we have no maps, but we can be sure that once some nation breaks the implicit taboo against using nuclear bombs in anger—or we or the Soviets fire off even so much as a small tactical nuclear weapon in some far-off corner of the earth—the world will never be the same again. As we Americans know from our own lunatic inability to control the gun traffic at home, fright does not conduce to rational action, particularly when there are strong, bigoted vested interests determined to exploit it.

Our Dubious Future

If we fail to gain control over the nuclear arms race and check the spread of nuclear weapons into irresponsible hands—if we do not somehow break and reverse the processes of escalation and proliferation now relentlessly at work—I doubt that we shall avoid a nuclear exchange that could menace Western civilization. Even if we do attain those objectives, other massive changes may fundamentally alter power relations to the detriment of Western influence and Western ideals.

Our Alienation from Europe

Whatever the future, I see a fragmenting of the mold that has prevailed for the last four decades, through changes not only in the West but also in the Soviet Union. Over many years, we sought to develop some common understanding with the nations of Western Europe; we tried to comprehend their problems and to seek their counsel in the shaping of common policies; but now we seem increasingly insensitive to their interests or concerns. We fail even to recognize fundamental differences in our national situations and requirements.

The Carter Administration disenchanted Europeans by failing to maintain a constant line of policy. President Reagan and his colleagues are endangering Atlantic relations by mistakenly diagnosing our reciprocal concerns. Our authority is not waning in Europe because Europeans have lost faith that we can effectively defend them but because they have lost confidence in our judgement, constancy and comprehension. They find our obsessive hectoring of Moscow not merely futile but dangerous and are disturbed that the current American government seems to view all problems as part of the East-West struggle, appears incapable of seeing East-West relations in other than military terms, and shows little if any sensitivity to their predicament.

That predicament is, of course, largely of their own making. I have described in earlier chapters the efforts to build an effective partnership among the Western industrialized nations. One of our most compelling objectives was to tie the German people tightly to the West. Unfortunately, the momentum toward unity and the building of effective institutions was halted too soon; today, a new generation of West Germans, lacking the experience of the World War and poorly instructed in either Soviet intentions or their own history, shows premonitory symptoms of disaffection. That disaffection may well get out of hand if we do not show more appreciation of Germany's special problems.

Though *détente* means for most Americans little more than increased civility in East-West discourse and less abrasive relations with Moscow, the Germans regard some measure of understanding with Moscow— some form of *détente* (or their version of it, *Ostpolitik*)—not as a luxury but as an operating necessity. Only by maintaining a dialogue with Eastern Europe can they achieve the repatriation of families from German territories incorporated in Poland by the Potsdam Treaty or mitigate the heartbreak resulting from the separation of friends and families in the two parts of a severed country. The Germans are repelled by the prospect of resuming the Cold War with poisonous fishwife squabbling substituted for a serious East-West dialogue. And that mood is more than shared by the smaller nations of Western Europe—particularly the countries of Scandinavia and Benelux.

I find little basis for optimism in observing Europe today. Too many Europeans are denying the existence of Europe even as a hope and goal and are blaming America for their own failures of will and enterprise. As nationalism reasserts itself, each country is increasingly tempted to go its own way. Washington, by conditioned reflex, misconceives and resents European doubts and hesitations. The Atlantic family is not a happy one.

Meanwhile, Europe has suffered badly from the abruptly rising oil costs and its precarious dependence on the Middle East as its principal source of energy. Initially content to let America carry the responsiblity for trying to quiet Middle East turbulence, Europeans have increasingly lost confidence in our will and ability as they watch our politicians respond more to the interests and ambitions of the Israeli government than to the United States' own interests and responsibilities. Europeans thus feel helpless and uneasy. They lack the political clout to launch effective peace initiatives of their own. Those they have tried to launch have been rebuffed by Washington.

All this is a menace to Western unity. I can think of nothing more divisive than a prolonged interruption of the oil flow from the Gulf. If it resulted from a political act of a key Arab oil-producing country, it would—quite possibly with reason—be blamed on America's biased diplomacy. If, on the other hand, European nations should ever see a threat to their oil supplies from an increase in Soviet influence in the Gulf area, some would be tempted to seek accommodation with Moscow.

The Changing Soviet Union

Our government has recently reverted to dealing with Moscow much as it did when John Foster Dulles regarded the Soviet Union as the antichrist, a demonic power seeking world domination for its secular religion. Today that view is grotesquely out of date. Moscow is no longer the central force of an evangelical world-wide movement; the gas has largely escaped from its ideological balloon. For the ordinary Soviet citizen, the Communist god is far deader than is the Christian one; ideological passion has given way to exhaustion, to the instinct to survive as best one can under an inhumane system. The result is cynicism bordering on despair. What is Communism in the Soviet Union today? It is party control and repression, while the hierarchical levels of advantage and privilege among the apparatchiks make a mockery of the Marxist faith.

These facts should help shape our dealings with Moscow. If the USSR has become merely a variant of the crude, thrusting nation we knew under the Czars, history should instruct us how to cope with it. Moreover, we should be able to deal with Moscow unhampered by doctrinal passions and rigidities that, from the beginning of time, have produced hatred and bloodshed and are at least a contributing cause of almost all of the world's current wars.*

If Soviet policy is freed from the rigidifying factor of a dogmatic creed that permits no compromise, practical politics (in other words, *Realpolitik* diplomacy) can substitute for passion, while hard-nosed considerations of reciprocal advantage can play a larger role in settling affairs with an adversary primarily motivated by mundane impulses that lack mystical underpinning—greed, jealousy, ambition, and revenge.

The fading of ideology is reflected in the progressive atrophy of Moscow's world network. Communist parties around the world no longer look to Moscow as the infallible font of dogma and authority; even in some of the older Communist parties of Western Europe there are varying degrees of restlessness. Finally, can anyone regard the Communist party in the United States as more than a Chaplinesque parody of its sinister archetype?

Even the young leaders of emerging Third World nations are no longer attracted to Communism by its doctrine so much as by its offer of a centralized system that legitimates their efforts to maintain tight central control over their new nations. Guns and tanks can often be obtained from a Soviet Union that has a vested interest in instability, while a genuflection to Marx still passes in the Third World lexicon as a gesture of anticolonialism. Because most Third World leaders identify colonialism with racial exploitation, they fail to recognize that the Soviet's Eastern European bloc is the one great surviving colonial empire.

Perhaps we could help clarify understanding by modernizing our vocabulary. To refer to the Soviet Union as a "Communist power" is wildly inaccurate. Even the Kremlin's leaders do not pretend that they have established a Communist state—that is merely their promise of caviar in the sky. They claim only that they have built a socialist half-way house toward a Communist society, and, since the road beyond does not exist even as a droshky track, they no longer seriously pretend that Com-

---

*One need mention only a few bloody conflicts in which religion is at least a major contributing element: the endless and pointless struggle in Northern Ireland; the dreary Arab-Israeli conflict; the continuing dispute between the Christian Greeks and the Muslim Turks in Cyprus; the Sunni Kurds against the Shiite Iranians; the argument between the Orthodox Ethiopians and the Muslim Somalis; the quarrel between the Christians and Muslims in Lebanon; the revolutionary violence in Iran; the communal massacres in the Asian subcontinent; and the Muslim insurgency in Mindanao in the Philippines.

munism is attainable or that they are striving to attain it. Thus, in my view, we err by speaking of the Soviet Union as a "Communist power"; not only is it wrong in substance but it attributes to the Soviet leaders a nonexistent idealism that, for the gullible, gives them a bogus respectability.

Rather than being a Communist power, the Soviet Union is a nation that by history and geographical accident fell on the Byzantine side of the cultural divide that separates it from Central and Western Europe, and it behaves very much as did the Czarist regimes that preceded it. But the influence of Byzantium has shaped it far less than the residue of genes, culture, and politics left behind by the Mongol invaders of the thirteenth to fifteenth centuries. Dostoyevsky observed: "Scratch a Russian and you'll find a Tartar," and Rosa Luxemburg noted that the early Bolsheviks were specially feared for their "Tartar-Mongolian savagery." The Stalin Terror, of which the current Soviet leaders are survivors, operated as a kind of frightful, forced, unnatural selection that preserved and emphasized those qualities the Mongols left behind: cruelty, expansionism, blind obedience, an avidity for propaganda, a pathological secrecy reinforced by an insidious spy system, deviousness, intrigue, and intolerant chauvinism. Thus it is hardly surprising that the present Soviet regime behaves as did the Muscovite empire that preceded it[2]— boorish in its habits and manner, expansionist in its hegemonic ambitions and repressive in its methods.

Threats to the Soviet Structure

Today that crude despotism faces critical problems. Controlled by an aging hierarchy, it is about to change the guard under a system incapable of assuring a succession without a power fight. Meanwhile, recent years have added further piles of evidence to confirm the lesson taught by six decades of frustration and disappointment that the Soviet economic system does not—and cannot—work efficiently. Operating a complex economy in conformity with a central plan produces a poor distribution of resources; production is constantly getting out of phase with what the country needs. It also produces shoddy goods. In fact— and this implicitly validates the advantages of the market system—the Soviets' most widely heralded production achievement is military hardware, primarily because the military constitute the only consumers with the power to reject or return inferior merchandise—or, in other words, the only effective market force in the whole Soviet system.

Besides the fading of ideology, which weakens the thrust of their expansionist drive, the Soviets face a major threat from those most insidious instruments of social and political change: demography and ethnicity. Ethnic Russians now comprise no more than 50 percent of the population of the USSR, while non-Russians are multiplying far more rapidly—especially the 40 million Muslims of Central Asia, whose rate of annual increase is several times that of the Russians. Such shifts in demography complicate the Kremlin's efforts to keep a strong hand on the fourteen non-Russian Soviet republics, with eighty distinct languages and two hundred dialects. To discourage dissension, the government has moved about one-sixth of the total Russian population (roughly 22 million in 1970) into the non-Soviet republics and transplanted a similar proportion of Moldavians and Ukrainians from their own republics into others.[3]

Czarist Russia used the slogan "For the Czar and the Orthodox faith" to justify its occupation of parts of the Ukraine and Byelorussia and to make non-Russians fight other neighbors. After the 1917 revolution, the USSR substituted the spreading of Communism for religion to sanctify its imperialist designs, while Marxist-Leninist doctrine denied the significance of national boundaries. Now with the fading appeal of that doctrine, ideology no longer serves as a binding agent to prevent the curdling of this bouillabaisse of diverse races, cultures, and histories. Instead, the Kremlin is increasingly forced back on nationalism, and since nationalism automatically incites counter-nationalisms, we can expect more and more incidents of nationalist resistance and disaffection throughout the vast reaches of the USSR—to be put down by a mass army that is itself having problems with its ethnic and nationalist elements.

If that phenomenon poses a long-range threat to the integrity of the Soviet Union, the menace is even greater in its Eastern European empire, where similar resentments are seething. With Moscow losing authority as the Vatican for an international ideology and depending once more on a chauvinistic love for "Mother Russia," such discontent can only increase. In Poland today, even the party hierarchs can no longer conceal their loss of faith while only the threat of the Red Army protects the party structure from that infectious virus—the yearning for individual freedom.

The Significance of the Soviet Union in Trouble

We instinctively applaud news that the Soviets are in trouble; our hearts lift when we watch the increasing restlessness of Poland or other Eastern European members of the Bloc. No one dedicated to freedom and democracy can do other than wish ill of a system that subjects millions of unwilling human beings to an Orwellian tyranny. So we listen wishfully to courageous Soviet dissidents who tell us that the Soviet empire must sooner or later break up, or at least change drastically; that is the fate of despotisms throughout history. Yet we know that the process of dissolution can be interrupted and retarded by the machinery of repression—Moscow's vast military force and ubiquitous secret police. We know also from Soviet conduct in Afghanistan that, if the Kremlin encounters serious trouble with its nationalist or ethnic minorities in Central Asia, it will show little squeamishness in its manner of reacting. Finally, we have learned from repeated experience that a nation cannot cruelly repress its own population without hardening the line of its foreign policy. Not only will the USSR ferociously put down dissension within its own borders but it will deal equally brutally with any serious threat to the integrity of the Warsaw Pact.

If disintegration ultimately occurs, it is thus unlikely to happen for many years. Still, looking ahead, we must be prepared for the disruption it could produce. The breaking up of the Soviet system could, among other things, force hazardous readjustments in the precarious balance of power by which world equilibrium is now maintained, and it could entail the clash of powerful forces. Threatened on the East by what I once heard General de Gaulle refer to as "the huge dustheap of peoples in China," the Soviets must feel a desperate need to use their domination of Central Europe as a glacis discouraging Western attack. If the Kremlin felt key bloc countries slipping their harness, it might well be driven to strike out blindly to the point of a dangerous collision.

Ending of the Superpower Systems

If I have learned anything from years of observing and sometimes participating in world affairs, it is that one should not assume the permanence of even those situations that appear most solid. Not only are America's ties with Europe beginning to weaken but future generations, including perhaps our own children or grandchildren, may someday witness the disintegration of both the Soviet and American world systems. What new coalescings and coalitions may then emerge are beyond imagination. For a while, the world might presumably remain broken up among regional groupings, but sooner or later one could expect the emergence of some new superpower system or systems in which China might play a significant part.

Europeans feel far more at home with speculations of this kind than do Americans. For a thousand years they have known destructive wars two or three times a century. They are accustomed to realignments among nations, the shifting of allegiances, and the reversal of alliances. They do not view the current world system as in any sense divinely ordained; nor, unlike some optimistic Americans, do they assume that the advent of nuclear weapons has meant the end of wars. Their major concern is to avoid having their countries serve as the arena for a conflict between the superpowers. As many Europeans told me after the German collapse in 1945: "We can never afford to be liberated again."

The North-South Problem

During the Kennedy Administration, many of my colleagues turned away from Dulles's compulsive concentration on the East-West struggle, in the belief that the central problem of our time was America's relations with what became romantically labeled the Third World. Though, as I have described in chapter 12, I thought that they overestimated our capacity to work miracles of instant development, the Administration's demonstration of generous concern did America honor.

Today, the pendulum has swung full cycle; the ever-widening disparity in wealth and income between the Northern and Southern Hemispheres is now regarded as a nuisance rather than a challenge, and we Americans think about it as little as possible. More than half of our economic and military aid goes to Israel and Egypt, leaving little for the rest of the world. As the head of an American delegation to an OECD meeting in 1962, I took the lead in persuading the Western democracies to set a goal of committing at least 1 percent of their gross national products to foreign economic aid; today, our own contribution is only one-fifth of 1 percent, which puts us fifteenth on the list of Western countries just below Finland. Our foreign aid, small as it is, has become largely a selective instrument for political coercion. We are tarnishing our leadership and the integrity of our promises by failing even to meet our share of contributions to multilateral aid institutions.

President Reagan's attitude might best be represented by a cartoon of the Thomas Nash genre showing a bloated billionaire descending from his limousine to tell a group of ragged urchins: "Why don't you do as I did, utilize the free market and you'll all be rich." But that it is a cruel joke. Our country did not escape Third World poverty solely because of its democratic virtues and its reliance on free enterprise and a free market; our forebears acquired the greatest area of arable land in the world, with a temperate climate and an unparalleled abundance of raw materials—land that had not been drained of its nutriment by a thousand years of primitive cultivation, ruined by erosion, or repeatedly ravaged by predatory neighbors. To ignore those facts is both arrogant and fatuous and I can think of no approach better designed to make the Third World despise us.

It distresses me that, for many Americans—particularly those ignorant of history—the disappointments of recent years have discouraged idealism. Instead of looking for new wrongs to right, new injustices to rectify, new miseries to eradicate, we have become self-centered and preoccupied with our own real or imagined troubles, concentrating on transient problems to the neglect of the future. We have turned inwards in part because we no longer feel uniquely endowed with wealth and resources; peoples in other nations have now joined that exclusive club, and are equalling or surpassing our standard of living. In addition, many have become convinced that our foreign aid has failed to achieve the transformations envisaged by our excessive expectations. Nations in which we have invested the most—such as India, Pakistan, and Indonesia—are still cursed with poverty and seem likely to remain so. Moreover, many of the poor nations are—in spite of anything we might do—doomed to fight a losing battle against demography, for a country with a high population growth rate is like Sisyphus pushing a rock up a hill. In spite of all the brave talk of flattening demographic curves, the hope that industrialization would reduce birth rates, and the efforts made to promote family planning, there is little basis for encouragement in many countries. India's population, for example, is still growing at the rate of 2.4 percent a year and that impoverished country will, by the turn of the century (less than two decades away), have a billion mouths to feed.

So far, most discussions of demography have focused largely on aggregates. Will the expanding world population exceed the availability of resources? How can we cope with the resulting political tensions when the population of many poor countries is increasing too fast to sustain standards of living even at present meager levels, while the population of the rich countries steadily declines? These problems are real enough, yet we should not concentrate narrowly on aggregate numbers but also observe the effect of high growth rates on a nation's population profile. When population grows at a rapid rate—2 or 3 percent a year—the median age moves progressively lower; in many underdeveloped nations, an increasing part of the population is under the age of twenty. At the same time, in many industrialized countries, where population growth scarcely exceeds the replacement level, the median age is steadily moving toward the upper end of the scale.

This persistently widening disparity in median ages will further complicate North-South understanding. Already, Third World delegates to international meetings are for the most part young and impatient, while spokesmen for the advanced countries are middle-aged and cautious. We are reproducing on a world scale the problem of understanding and accommodation across the wide chasm of the generation gap. It is a worrisome problem today; tomorrow it will be worse.

The lowering of the median age penalizes a poor country by increasing the percentage of its population in a nonproductive sector. In the past, an individual of productive age might have to support four others either too young or too old to work; now, in many countries he may have to support eight. There is no way most Third World economies can provide employment for a swelling wave of new entrants into the labor force. The United States cannot ignore the problem; we are on the front line. On the islands and the large continent south of our border are several Third World countries in which demographic pressures are building toward the point of explosion. The population of the United States today is 226 million, and growing at only seven-tenths of 1 percent a year; within nineteen years, the population of Latin America—where some countries have an annual growth rate of 3 percent or more—will aggregate more than 600 million. In Latin America as a whole, 60 percent of the population is under the age of twenty-five, while for Brazil and Mexico the figure is 65 percent.

With the population of Mexico still increasing at an estimated rate of 2.9 percent a year (which is an improvement over the 3.6 percent that prevailed until recently), 45 percent of the population is under the age of fifteen: the time at which youths normally try to enter the labor force. Yet even oil-rich Mexico cannot possibly create new jobs fast enough to accommodate more than a fraction of the swelling tide of young potential workers. (Last year 800,000 were looking for jobs with only 300,000 jobs available.) What will happen to this growing freshet of young men and women in the years ahead? Tiny agricultural plots cannot be subdivided below a minimum economic size, so the sons and daughters of small farmers must migrate to urban centers. Mexico City today, with a metropolitan area population estimated at 15 million, is on the way to becoming the largest city in the world.[4] But there the young find only heartbreak: no jobs, no housing, no place in an overcrowded society. What are their options? They can either join gangs outside the law (terrorist activities are already dangerously increasing) or try to gain entry to neighboring countries—which means overwhelmingly the United States.

We have seen only the first ripples of what is destined to become a tidal wave as intractable demography and the resulting lack of employment drive more and more Latin American young men and women to try to enter our country by any means possible.

Few have bothered to ponder the basic philosophical issue, which has more than one aspect. When the United States or any other nation makes a tacit social decision to stabilize its population while its neighbors—influenced by ignorance or custom or church—maintain a population growth it cannot accommodate, should we let our neighbors' social decision undercut and frustrate our own? The problem is not unlike that posed by other ecological phenomena such as acid rain, which floats on the wind without regard to national boundaries; yet, since it directly involves the fate and future of thousands of human beings, the issues are far more complex. How then do we determine the proper trade-offs between humanitarian considerations and the cold-blooded obligation of every society to protect its own integrity; between generosity and the sovereign right of every nation to design its own social policies; and between the need to keep track of illegal entrants and our commitment to individual freedom and privacy? In spite of the protests of zealous libertarians, we shall ultimately have to adopt some system of identity cards—and probably even fingerprinting. We can no longer afford the privilege of anonymity that was appropriate when Americans were conquering the empty lands beyond our wide frontier. Other civilized states have managed to live with such devices without compromising their liberties, and though it may inconvenience philanderers we shall have to come to it. We can no longer avoid such eccentricities any more than we can afford to make handguns available to every moron.

Apart from the question of illegal immigrants, I can foresee formidable social and economic problems resulting from the increasing political influence of Hispanic-Americans. In twenty years, they will become a larger ethnic minority than blacks—even though blacks are increasing so much faster than whites that, during the decade from 1970 to 1980, the percentage of white Americans in our population fell by 4.3 percent.

To mitigate the potential threat to the integrity of our political system, we should concentrate on helping and encouraging all immigrants to adapt quickly to the mores and customs of America or they will be forced into ethnic enclaves and become an indigestible lump in the American body politic. It seems to me mischievous, therefore, when a curious cabal of sociologists, social workers, psychologists, and language teachers encourages immigrants to preserve their culture and language out of a sentimental concern for "roots." The world has provided countless examples of the political fissions and irreconcilable conflicts suffered by bilingual societies; the Biblical tale of the Tower of Babel should be required reading for all statesmen.

The disruptive effect of increasingly powerful ethnic lobbies is not limited to domestic affairs. It threatens to hobble America's ability to design and administer an effective foreign policy. Already, the Israeli lobby disables us from conducting a policy toward the Middle East that advances and protects the larger interests of America and the other Western democracies; the increasing political self-consciousness of the black lobby may in time impair our ability to design a balanced and rational African policy; the Greek lobby has already prejudiced our relations with Turkey; while what remains of an Irish lobby creates at least some slight problems in our relations with Britain. The emergence of an increasingly powerful, well-organized Hispanic lobby could gravely complicate our already formidable problems in dealing with the nations of Latin America. We would gravely exacerbate the problem were we ever to commit the egregious folly of admitting Puerto Rico as the fifty-first state.

The Ordeal of Modernity

I cannot be happy with the untidiness and turmoil on the current scene, the weakening of faith in our institutions, and our anemic sense of community and common purpose. Perhaps I have lived too long, but, as I see it, the moral absolutes have disintegrated; cheating is too often accepted as the norm, and brutish criminals are no longer regarded primarily as a menace against which society must protect itself but as innocent victims of social unfairness. Moreover, we have lost our *élan;* no longer do we display the ebullience and resilience of a nation and a people confident of their own destiny—or even their desired destination. What, then, has happened?

I have pondered these questions without finding simple answers and lately I have assigned a larger role to the fading of religious conviction in many American milieus; for, in spite of the vociferous assertions of the Moral Majority, religion does not today hold the place it once did in American life. An early convert to agnosticism, in spite of a Methodist upbringing, I have all the serenity I need; yet I am still puzzled by a perplexing question: Can a nation bemused by the glitter and mystery of modern technology maintain its inner strength without some form of belief in a benign external force or presence? Can it achieve a sufficient sense of community and common purpose to provide a stable and satisfying environment for its people? Can it at the same time (and this question specifically concerns America) carry a burden of world leadership not obviously and directly related to its own security?

The answer depends in large part on how effectively people adjust to a secular environment. There is, it seems to me, ample evidence that an increasing number of Americans share Matthew Arnold's discouragement at the loss of "certitude" and feel a sense of being "on a darkling plain . . . swept by confused alarms of struggle and flight."[5] For most people, the loss of "certitude" is an irrevocable disaster, since without an abiding faith as an essential simplifier, life may be too complex and puzzling for most individuals (or even nations) to cope with. When men and women ask the giraffe question "Why?" of life's eternal mysteries and hear no easy, definitive answer, many sublimate their desire for "certitude" by escapist flights into bizarre, exotic, mystical cults, no matter how palpably fraudulent. Others indulge a furtive preoccupation with self for which psychoanalysts provide the confessional. If Marx called religion the opium of the German people, drugs are now the religion of many Americans. Only the sturdy or insensitive can accept life's inscrutability with philosophical aplomb.

Along with the fading of religious faith has come a drastic change in social *mores*—the elimination of restraints on sexual expression, the legitimization of gambling, the elevation of pornography to a folk art, the preoccupation with psychiatry (we are like monkeys picking the lice from each other's heads)—all that bespeaks a people with little belief in their own institutions or in the commonweal as a compelling abstraction.

Though we usually defend this disdain for institutions in the name of freedom, we have substituted a whole new set of taboos. Even though no society can function effectively without respect for excellence, "elite," despite its spelling, is now regarded as a four-letter word. Educational standards are manipulated and degraded to conform to rigid sociological preconceptions. We have strayed so far from our fundamental national principles as to substitute equality of condition for equality of opportunity as a central social objective. Our painting and poetry are in bondage to the iron tyranny of unintelligibility and have lost their meaning for most Americans. (Who can quote any recent poet other than Eliot or occasionally Auden?) Our literature is preoccupied with the grotesque, and we bowdlerize it not to expunge sex or violence but to conform it to a whole new set of social strictures, largely reflecting real or contrived ethnic sensitivities; indeed, we have a new *index librorum prohibitorum*, which includes such a curious *potpourri* as *Uncle Tom's Cabin*, *B'rer Rabbit*, and *The Merchant of Venice*.

Finally, as one who has always enjoyed the consistent help and support of a close and mutually affectionate family, I am most concerned by the transformation—perhaps even breakdown—of that nuclear institution. Throughout Western history, the family has provided the mechanism for the perpetuation of the race and, though the process has shown tolerance for a large element of chance, it has worked reasonably well. But, if society comes to depend merely on brief and casual matings without the traditional family responsibilities, we shall encounter serious trouble.

The New Vistas

I have few answers to the perplexing issues raised here. I am not even sure about the questions. Yet, as history has repeatedly shown, prophesy is rarely profitable; anyone who speculates about the future will almost certainly be proved wrong. "History," Paul Valéry once wrote, "is the science of what never happens twice"; and when I am in a somber mood I recall those cautionary words of Ralph Hodgson's that "the handwriting on the wall may be a forgery"—or, to put it in a contemporary idiom, it may turn out to be mere graffitti.

What most sharply marks the sad chronicle of the past two decades is the number of opportunities lost, the number of mistakes and miscalculations made—even by the most sophisticated nations and their leaders. Perhaps we have simply been enduring a protracted run of bad luck, with the statistical probability that we should do better in the decades we are now approaching.

If these observations read like the disgruntled grumblings of an old curmudgeon, I see no basis for despair or resignation; that proves nothing and helps nothing. Jean Monnet taught me that a reasoned optimism is the only acceptable working hypothesis for self-respecting men and women. Mankind has muddled through for centuries, and we have a certain facility for it. Quite likely we shall find the ways and means to continue that performance.

Certainly there is much I find exciting in present-day society and particularly the vistas opened by the new findings of science. Through the space program we have caught glimpses of an infinitely expanded universe and that should go far to cure our claustrophobia; we are literally reaching for the stars. The advancing frontiers of biological science reveal fascinating potentials for life on this planet. If I regret, as I do, not to have fifty years more to live, it is in part because I would like to know what the biologists will discover as they progressively peel the veil from a world still trying to hide its secrets. At the same time, I can easily foresee that the collision between the incessant probing of some individuals and the primordial fears of others may create an intellectual crisis beyond any we have known since the Inquisition.

The old myths reflected such fears. Aeneas, Virgil suggests, would never have suffered the hazards of the high seas had man not discovered the art of navigation. Daedalus defied gravity by inventing wings, with which his son, Icarus, flew too near the sun and was destroyed. When overly curious Pandora opened her seductive box, she released all of the world's evils. And in Hebrew myth, Adam's punishment for sampling the Tree of Knowledge was banishment from Eden. In the classical credo, fate kept mankind in its place; to expect earthly improvement was to rattle the bars separating the human from the divine. In the Middle Ages, the Church justified its opposition to scientific inquiry by the cruel assertion that original sin had destroyed all hope for man's moral improvement. Satanic curiosity might, the ecclesiastics felt, drive men to develop theories about the material world and even the universe that would challenge the Church's rigid doctrine and undercut its authority, hence its integrity as an institution. So the Inquisition burned Giordano Bruno and would have burned Galileo had he not recanted, while it frightened Descartes into suppressing his *Traité du Monde* until after his death. Only the activities of a handful of dedicated men, passionately concerned with the advancement of truth and confident of their experiments and observations, prevented a total strangulation of the effort to penetrate nature's secrets. Instead, with a courage comparable to that of today's Soviet dissidents, brave men of the sixteenth and seventeenth centuries defied both church and state in their quest for truth.

And now, once more, we hear talk of restrictions on research that echo the language of the old fears. How far should man go in his exploration of nature even though it may upset established dogmas? How far should he be permitted to venture into areas with unknowable implications? Should Galileo have been required to supply the bureaucracy of the Inquisition with an intellectual impact statement before proceeding with his studies? I should like to live long enough to see the new revelations of biology and, whenever the issue is clearly joined, to raise my voice on the side of free inquiry.

For all our current problems and anxieties, I find it a good time to be alive—a time of stimulation and challenge—and I would not have chosen any other period in which to live out my days. For seven decades, I have had the chance not only to witness the world in convulsion, but to speculate on a future well beyond my own life span.

All during my mature years, I have disciplined myself not to look back and, above all, not to let myself be disabled by remorse at my errors of omission and commission, which have been legion. But memoirs are, by definition, an essay in retrospection, and now, nearing the end of the last chapter, I find I have enjoyed writing them.

Looking ahead, however, is far more exhilarating. At an early age, I wrote off as insoluble the ultimate issues of why, by what external force or spirit, and for what purpose, I was permitted to materialize at this moment in history. Since philosophers and theologians are merely human beings with human brains, working within the same constraints, I early decided that they could find no more answers than I, so I stopped reading them. When I contemplate the future, I, therefore, limit my line of vision to what man can comprehend and do.

A Good Time to Live

That darkly prescient British diplomat Lord Vansittart, whom I have mentioned before, wrote a volume of memoirs called *The Mist Procession*. The title referred to a dream in which he had seen a long file of men and women he had known walking slowly down a road shrouded in mist then passing briefly through an open space pierced by a shaft of light. "Emerging from one obscurity," he wrote, "they passed into another." Vansittart's vision has haunted me for years as I have recalled some men and women I have valued greatly during a long life. Many of them have died—some long ago—yet I still recall with warmth and gratitude their legacy of assistance, affection, and wisdom. Their friendship was a treasure beyond price.

CODA

It is the thought of those friendships that has given me most pleasure in writing this book. Now, as I finish it, I feel a little like Tennyson's old Ulysses:

> Much have I seen and known: cities of men,
> And manners, climates, councils, governments.

And, I need hardly add:

> I am a part of all that I have met.

Though seven decades are a miniscule moment in the epic sweep of the human saga, the increasing compression of events now means that by medieval standards I have lived at least five centuries. Meanwhile, as the centrifuge of change whirls ever faster, stale cakes of custom crumble and fly violently apart. All this has meant for me a wonderfully fortunate life, even though I may not, as Justice Oliver Wendell Holmes hoped to do, leave many "fragments of my fleece on the hedges." But I have enjoyed almost every bit of it. I have been nourished by the affection of my friends and stimulated by the vitriol of my enemies. And I have been sustained by extraordinarily rich family relations: my father, who taught me what he learned not only from books but from experience, and my mother, strictly committed to her own high standards, who was still unfailingly kind and forgiving. In my own generation, I have been equally favored by my brother Stuart, who, sharing many of my interests, has been a constant source of encouragement, while my two sons, John and Douglas, have counseled and advised me and given me great comfort. Most of all, I was profoundly lucky to meet Ruth Murdoch in Paris fifty-three years ago. (It was worth going to jail for, as I have recounted in chapter 1.) We have lived together for almost half a century, and without her affectionate support I would have done far fewer things, done them less well, and life would have lacked much of its savor. Though in this book I have overused the first person singular, it has been an editorial "I"; what I claim to have done, we have done together.

What more could man want than that? I feel no sense of imminent mortality, yet, one by one, my friends are disappearing. Though I have excellent health and expect to go on presuming on my friends and annoying my enemies for at least another decade, I shall end this book of memoirs with some lines by a British civil servant, Humbert Wolfe, whose verses I read and admired in my days of adolescence.

> The high song is over. Even the echoes fail now;
> Winners and losers—they are only a theme now,
> Their victory and defeat a half-forgotten tale now;
> And even the angels are only a dream now.
>
> There is no need for blame, no cause for praise now.
> Nothing to hide, to change or to discover.
> They were men and women. They have gone their ways now,
> As men and women must. The high song is over.[6]

Notes

1. *The First Eighteen Years Are the Easiest*

1. Quoted by Paul Goodman and Frank O. Gatell, *America in the Twenties: The Beginnings of Contemporary America* (New York: Holt, Rinehart and Winston, Inc., 1972), p. 146.
2. Paul Valéry, *Oeuvres* (Paris: Librairie Gallimard, 1957), vol. I, p. 988.

2. *From Depression to War, Ploughs, and "Habbakuks"*

1. Dean Acheson, *Morning and Noon* (Boston: Houghton Mifflin Co., 1965), 2nd prtg., p. 192.
2. Arthur M. Schlesinger, Jr., *The Age of Roosevelt: The Politics of Upheaval* (Boston: Houghton Mifflin Co., 1960), pp. 505–509.
3. George Gamov, not only a brilliant scientist but also a man of wit and whimsy, later wrote several books to explain physics to the layman—*Atomic Energy in Cosmic and Human Life, One, Two Three . . . Infinity, A Star Called the Sun, Thirty Years that Shook Physics* and the *Mr. Tompkins* series, to name a few. Denied a full role in the atomic energy program because of his Russian origin, he taught for many years at George Washington University and died in 1968. I spent an evening at his house in Washington once after a trip; although we always planned to resume our acquaintance, we never got around to it in the turmoil of war time. Whatever happened to Professor Meissner, I do not know. Throughout the trip he was extremely apprehensive. He was forbidden to teach at the University of Frankfurt, and when I took a picture of him at a party in our stateroom, he begged me not to send him a print, since that could get him into further trouble. I asked about him when I was in Frankfurt at the end of the war but could discover nothing.
4. In the "Book of Habakkuk," chapter 1, verse 5, the Lord refers to a "work which you will not believe, though it be told to you." The spelling error originated, according to Lampe, with Pyke's Canadian secretary. David Lampe, *Pyke: The Unknown Genius* (London: Evans Brothers Ltd., 1959), p. 128.
5. *Ibid.*, p. 145.

3. *Lend-Lease and the Avoidance of War Debts*

1. Richard N. Gardner, *Sterling-Dollar Diplomacy: The Origins and the Prospects of Our International Economic Order* (New York: McGraw Hill, 1969), expanded edition, p. 55.
2. Eugene Staley, "The Economic Implications of Lend-Lease," *American Economic Review*, vol. 33, no. 1, pt. 2, suppl. (March 1943), p. 367.

3. John Maynard Keynes, *The Economic Consequences of the Peace* (New York: Harcourt, Brace and Howe, 1920), pp. 279–80.
4. *Press Conferences*, vol. 22, September 7, 1943, pp. 85–86.
5. Eugene Staley, *op. cit.*, p. 369.
6. Richard N. Gardner, *op. cit.*, pp. 171–72.
7. Henry L. Stimson and McGeorge Bundy, *On Active Service in Peace & War* (New York: Harper Bros., 1948), p. 188.

4. *The Bombing Survey*

1. David MacIsaac, *The United States Strategic Bombing in World War Two* (New York: Garland Publ., 1976), vol. 3, exhibit 29.
2. Solly Zuckerman, "Paris in a Railway Desert," *From Apes to Warlords: The Autobiography (1904–1946) of Solly Zuckerman* (London: Hamish Hamilton, 1978), pp. 286–305.
3. George W. Ball, "With AES in War and Politics," Edward P. Doyle, ed., *As We Knew Adlai: The Stevenson Story by Twenty-two Friends* (New York: Harper & Row, 1966), p. 142.

5. *Albert Speer on a Grade-B Movie Set*

1. Four copies of the will were sent out of the bunker. Bormann carried one but was shot before he could leave Berlin. The other copies were carried by Major Willi Johannmeier, Hitler's army adjutant; Wilhelm Zander, Bormann's personal adviser; and Heinz Lorenz, an official of the Propaganda Ministry. The pilot of a seaplane sent by Doenitz to rescue them on the Havel River panicked under Russian shelling and took off before they could board. By the time the three men reached the western sector, the war was over. Colonel Nicolaus von Below, Hitler's Luftwaffe adjutant, also left the bunker with a postscript to the will written by Hitler to be delivered to Wilhelm Keitel, but burned it during his escape. H. R. Trevor-Roper, *Last Days of Hitler* (New York: The Macmillan Company, 1962), pp. 246–49, 278–80.
2. Walter Laqueur, "Hitler's Holocaust," *Encounter*, vol. 55, no. 1 (July 1980), pp. 6–25.
3. Malraux said in his *Musée Imaginaire*, "The art which is taking over, sorting out and imposing its metamorphosis on this vast legacy of the past is by no means easy to define. It is our art of today—and obviously a fish is badly placed for judging what the aquarium looks like from outside." André Malraux, *The Voices of Silence*, Stuart Gilbert, trans. (Garden City: Doubleday & Company, Inc., 1953), p. 70.
4. The loss of Slavs is estimated to be: about 5.5 million Ukrainians (including 2.5 million POWs); 3 million Poles (including about 0.5 million in combat losses); 2 million Byelorussians (including about 0.5 million POWs). Bohdan Wytwycky, *The Other Holocaust: Many Circles of Hell* (Washington: The Novak Report, 1980).
5. H. R. Trevor-Roper, *op. cit.*, p. 302.

6. *Jean Monnet*

1. W. K. Hancock and M. M. Gowing, *British War Economy* (London: His Majesty's Stationery Office, 1949), p. 193.
2. George C. Marshall, in *Department of State Bulletin*, vol. 16 (June 15, 1947), p. 1160.

3. Czechoslovakia and Poland also accepted but were forced by the Kremlin to withdraw.
4. Quoted in W. L. Clayton, *Selected Papers of Will Clayton,* Frederick J. Dobney, ed. (Baltimore: The Johns Hopkins Press, 1971), p. 216.
5. Jean Monnet, *Memoirs,* Richard Mayne, trans. (Garden City: Doubleday & Company, Inc., 1978), p. 91.
6. Peter Calvocoressi, *Survey of International Affairs, 1951* (London: Oxford University Press, 1954), p. 113.

7. *The Parturition of Europe*

1. Jean Monnet, *Memoirs,* Richard Mayne, trans. (Garden City: Doubleday & Company, Inc., 1978), p. 303.
2. *Ibid.,* pp. 289–94, and Jean Monnet, *Mémoires* (Paris: Fayard, 1976), pp. 343–50.
3. Françoise Giroud, lecture at Princeton University, November 26, 1978.
4. Raymond Aron, "Historical Sketch of the Great Debate," Daniel Lerner and Raymond Aron, eds., *France Defeats EDC* (New York: Frederick A. Praeger, 1957), p. 10.
5. Walter Lippmann, *CBS Reports: Conversations with Walter Lippmann* (Boston: Atlantic-Little Brown, 1965), pp. 213–14.
6. Raymond Aron, *Peace and War: A Theory of International Relations,* Richard Howard and Annette Baker Fox, trans. (Garden City: Doubleday & Company, Inc., 1966), pp. 18–19.
7. George W. Ball, *The Discipline of Power: Essentials of a Modern World Structure* (Boston: Little, Brown and Company, 1968), p. 124.
8. *Ibid.,* p. 120.
9. George W. Ball, "Introduction" to Jean Monnet, *Memoirs, op. cit.,* p. 14.

8. *A Washington Lawyer*

1. John Morton Blum, ed., *The Price of Vision. The Diary of Henry A. Wallace: 1942–1946* (Boston: Houghton Mifflin Co., 1973), p. 314.
2. *Ibid.,* p. 331.
3. *Ibid.,* p. 332f.

9. *Stevenson*

1. Walter Johnson and Carol Evans, eds., *The Papers of Adlai E. Stevenson: Governor of Illinois, 1949–1953* (Boston: Little, Brown and Company, 1973), vol. 3, p. 534.
2. The March 17, 1952 handwritten letter was reconstructed by Stevenson several days later, and this phrase was added. John Bartlow Martin, *Adlai Stevenson of Illinois: The Life of Adlai E. Stevenson* (Garden City: Doubleday & Company, Inc., 1976), p. 542.
3. *The Papers of Adlai E. Stevenson,* p. 534.
4. *Ibid.,* p. 535.
5. William Costello, *The Facts About Nixon: An Unabridged Biography* (New York: Viking Press, 1960), p. 117.
6. George W. Ball, "With AES in War and Politics," Edward P. Doyle, ed., *As We Knew Adlai: The Stevenson Story by Twenty-two Friends* (New York: Harper & Row, 1966), pp. 152–53.

10. *1956 Campaign and After*

1. John Bartlow Martin, *Adlai Stevenson and the World: The Life of Adlai E. Stevenson* (New York: Doubleday & Company, Inc., 1977), pp. 311–12.
2. *Ibid.*, p. 368.
3. *Ibid.*, p. 374.
4. *Ibid.*, p. 373.
5. *Ibid.*, p. 380.
6. *Ibid.*, p. 425.

11. *French Crisis and Stevenson Again (1958–1961)*

1. Oddly enough, the harshness of the conversation is not reported in any of the books so far written—either in J. B. Martin's biography of Stevenson or A. M. Schlesinger's or Theodore C. Sorensen's account of Kennedy. Why Stevenson blew off steam to me but to no one else may have been due to momentary exasperation, for he found scatological expletives offensive.
2. John Bartlow Martin, *Adlai Stevenson and the World: The Life of Adlai E. Stevenson* (Garden City: Doubleday & Company, Inc., 1977), p. 534.
3. Arthur M. Schlesinger, Jr., *A Thousand Days: John F. Kennedy in the White House* (Boston: Houghton Mifflin Co., 1965), p. 157.

12. *Early Kennedy Years*

1. John F. Kennedy, "Algeria," *The Strategy of Peace* (New York: Harper & Brothers, 1960), p. 75.
2. *Ibid.*, p. 77.
3. John F. Kennedy, "The Missile Gap," *Ibid.*, pp. 36–37.
4. Chester Bowles, *The Conscience of a Liberal: Selected Writings and Speeches* (New York: Harper and Row, 1962), p. 85.
5. Later, as sensitivity heightened, they became known as "developing countries," though many were clearly not developing very fast, if at all. Still later, they became the "Third World."
6. My approach to figures resembles that of a woman I once sat next to at a dinner party who was telling me of her experiences mountain climbing. "How high did you climb?" I asked. "Oh," she replied, "about five hundred feet." "But that's not very high," I remarked. "Oh dear," she said, "I always get those things mixed up; it was really five hundred thousand feet."

13. *The Context of the Time and the Kennedy Program*

1. Arthur M. Schlesinger, Jr., *A Thousand Days: John F. Kennedy in the White House* (Boston: Houghton Mifflin Co., 1965), p. 309.
2. John F. Kennedy, "Inaugural Address, January 20, 1981," *Public Papers of the Presidents of the United States, 1961* (Washington: U.S. Government Printing Office, 1962), pp. 1–2.
3. David Bell, *The Cultural Contradiction of Capitalism* (New York: Basic Books, Inc., 1976), pp. 177–178.

15. *The Tradesman's Entrance to Foreign Policy*

1. There was good reason for my reluctance. For despite Prime Minister Macmillan's private emphasis on the political need for Britain to play a role in

Europe, his government publicly concentrated on the purely economic advantages of membership in the Common Market—or, more accurately, the economic disadvantages of exclusion. Britain, as an outsider, would have to sell its goods to member states over the barrier of the common external tariff, while those nations within the Community walls would enjoy the benefits of free trade.

2. To assure that trade legislation would not impede British entry, I devised a technical safeguard.

3. When he had first mentioned the word before he had used it in print, I had voiced my own distaste for confusing the American vocabulary with foreign words to express abstractions that were fuzzy in English, but I did not foresee the mystique the word would ultimately acquire for many Americans.

4. John F. Kennedy, *Public Papers of the Presidents of the United States, 1963* (Washington: U. S. Government Printing Office, 1964), pp. 460–61.

5. Robert Solomon, *The International Monetary System, 1945–1976: An Insider's View* (New York: Harper & Row, 1977), pp. 38–39.

16. *The Mystique of a Grand Design*

1. The name was, of course, grandiloquently inappropriate; what we envisaged bore no relation either to *Les Grands Desseins* of Henry IV of France or to Franklin D. Roosevelt's "great design" discussed at the Teheran Conference. But, when the columnist Joseph Kraft used the phrase as the title for a book discussing the Administration's early years, it acquired more currency than it deserved.

2. D. C. Watt, *Survey of International Affairs, 1961* (London: Oxford University Press, 1965), p. 117.

3. Diary entry for Saturday, September 10, 1966, Cecil Harmsworth King, *The Cecil King Diary, 1965–1970* (London: Jonathan Cape, 1972), p. 92.

4. Harold Macmillan, *At the End of the Day, 1961–1962* (New York: Harper & Row, 1973), p. 111.

5. D. C. Watt, *op. cit.*, pp. 147–48.

17. *Troubles in the Congo*

1. Arthur M. Schlesinger, Jr., *A Thousand Days: John F. Kennedy in the White House* (Boston: Houghton Mifflin Co., 1965), p. 554.

2. *Ibid.*

3. George Martelli, *Experiment in World Government: An Account of the United Nations Operations in the Congo, 1960–1964* (London: Johnson Publications, 1966), p. 58.

4. George Martelli described the Congo as follows: "Its geographical diversity, and the number of its tribes and languages, make it more like an empire than a colony. . . ." *Ibid.*, p. 231.

5. George W. Ball, *The Elements in Our Congo Policy,* Department of State Publication 7326, African Series 25 (Washington: Department of State, 1961), pp. 1–2.

6. Richard P. Stebbins, *The United States in World Affairs, 1961* (New York: Harper & Brothers, 1962), p. 254.

7. United Nations Document S/4426, adopted by the Security Council on August 9, 1960. Catherine Hoskyns, *The Congo: A Chronology of Events, January 1960–December 1961,* Chatham House Memoranda (Oxford: Oxford University Press, 1962), pp. 30–31.

8. Arthur M. Schlesinger, Jr., *op. cit.*, p. 576.

9. Jules Gerard-Libois, *Katanga Secession*, Rebecca Young, trans. (Madison: University of Wisconsin Press, 1966), p. 181.

18. *The General and His Thunderbolts*

1. John F. Kennedy, "Address Before the Canadian Parliament in Ottawa," *Public Papers of the Presidents of the United States, 1961* (Washington: U. S. Government Printing Office, 1962), p. 385.

2. George W. Ball, Address before the Council on Foreign Relations, New York City, January 11, 1965, manuscript pp. 14–15.

3. George W. Ball, *Discipline of Power: Essentials of a Modern World Structure* (Boston: Little, Brown and Company, 1968), pp. 84–85.

4. Piers Dixon, *Double Diploma: The Life of Sir Pierson Dixon, Don and Diplomat* (London: Hutchinson & Co., 1968), p. 302.

5. W. W. Kulski, *De Gaulle and the World, Foreign Policy of the Fifth Republic* (Syracuse: Syracuse University Press, 1966), p. 280. Also, Richard P. Stebbins, *The United States in World Affairs, 1963* (New York: Harper & Row, 1964), pp. 99–100.

19. *Ayub Khan and Salazar*

1. Salazar had come to power, therefore, through what I always thought was an amusing accident, for, in a sense, he was the beneficiary the scandal. See Murray Teigh Bloom, *The Man Who Stole Portugal* (New York: Charles Scribner's Sons, 1966).

2. Luis Vaz de Camoens, *The Lusiads,* William C. Atkinson, trans. (Harmondsworth: Penguin Books, 1952), pp. 39–40.

20. *The Cuban Missile Crisis*

1. Robert F. Kennedy, *Thirteen Days: A Memoir of the Cuban Missile Crisis* (New York: W. W. Norton, 1969), pp. 89–90.

2. In one of the earliest published accounts of the missile crisis, Roger Hilsman stated that President Kennedy raised the question of removing the obsolete and vulnerable Jupiters from Turkey soon after his inauguration, but the Berlin Crisis of 1961 deterred any action on that score. Secretary Rusk and Paul Nitze, representing the Defense Department, raised the question with the Turkish government at the NATO Ministerial Meeting in May 1962, but the Turkish Foreign Minister strongly objected on political grounds; in order not to strain our already touchy relations with Turkey, they did not pursue the matter. Hilsman adds that "In the summer of 1962, Kennedy again raised the matter with George Ball, who was Acting Secretary in Rusk's absence, and after rejecting the State Department case for further delay, he ordered, in August 1962, that steps be taken immediately to remove the American missiles from Turkey. . . . Both the State Department and the Pentagon were slow, however, and the missiles were still there." [Roger Hilsman, *To Move a Nation: The Politics of Foreign Policy in the Administration of John F. Kennedy* (Garden City: Doubleday & Company, Inc., 1967), p. 203.]

   Elie Abel in his book *The Missile Crisis* repeats the story, pointing out that Rusk and Nitze were told by the Turkish Foreign Minister, Selim Sarper, that "the Jupiters were an indispensable token of America's commitment to defend its allies." [Elie Abel, *The Missile Crisis*, (Philadelphia: J. B. Lippincott Co.,

1966), p. 190.] He then suggests that as too few Polaris submarines had yet been commissioned to replace the Jupiters, the matter was temporarily dropped. Abel further maintains that later that same summer the President asked me, as Acting Secretary of State, about the Jupiters and that when I told him it would be unwise to press the matter at that moment, "He [the President] then and there directed that the missiles must be removed, even at some political cost to the United States. Ball and Nitze talked it over with the Turkish Ambassador in Washington and once more the reaction was negative. The Ambassador warned the removal of the missiles would have a most harmful effect on public opinion in Turkey. Nothing happened, though the President, apparently, dismissed the missiles from his mind, assuming that they were about to be removed, as ordered." [*Ibid.*, pp. 190–91.]

Professor Graham Allison, currently Dean of the John F. Kennedy School of Government at Harvard, seems to have swallowed the story whole. He writes in his book, *Essence of Decision:* "Frustrated at this inaction, Kennedy had resorted to the most binding mechanism in the U.S. government for registering decisions on matters of national security—a National Security Council Action Memorandum (NASAM). In the third week of August 1962, a NASAM ordered removal of the missiles, and he personally directed George Ball (in Rusk's absence) to pay the political price and remove the missiles. Ball discussed the matter with the Turkish Ambassador in Washington and received a warning that the removal of the missiles would have most harmful effects on Turkish public opinion. So nothing happened." [Graham T. Allison, *Essence of Decision: Explaining the Cuban Missile Crisis* (Boston: Little, Brown and Co., 1971), pp. 141–142.]

It is a piquant story, suffering only the slight disadvantage of being untrue. That cynical British barrister Philip Guedalla once wrote that "history repeats itself; historians repeat one another." That was the case with the Turkish missiles. I had at all times kept the President informed regarding the state of negotiations with the Turkish government, and, while he wished the Jupiters removed, he recognized the sensitivity of the situation and particularly the uneasy state of our relations with Turkey. He was never taken by surprise; from the very beginning of the missile crisis, he knew—and showed that he knew—that the Jupiters were still in Turkey; indeed, he speculated that the Soviets might respond to an airstrike against the Cuban missile bases with a strike of their own against the Turkish Jupiters, and, in discussing the matter with Stevenson he had rejected the idea that the withdrawal of our Jupiters from Turkey be a *quid pro quo* for the Soviets' withdrawal of the Cuban missiles. Finally, the NASAM issued on August 23, 1962, did not, as Allison suggests, order the removal of the missiles; instead, it stated that "The President has directed that the following actions and studies be undertaken in the light of evidence of new bloc activity in Cuba. 1. What action can be taken to get Jupiter missiles out of Turkey? (Action: Department of Defense)." [McGeorge Bundy, National Security Action Memorandum No. 181, August 23, 1962, p. 1.]

That was hardly a command to remove the missiles. Abram Chayes, then the legal adviser to the State Department, has written in his own book on the missile crisis: "Allison's account as well as others leave the impression that the President was unaware that his earlier order had not been carried out and was angered to discover that the missiles were still in Turkey. It may well be that he was angry. But as one who had some part in the efforts to carry out those earlier orders, I cannot believe he was surprised. The delays and obstacles in withdrawing the Turkish and Italian missiles had been fully and currently reported to him. When the Cuban crisis began, he and other members of the Executive Committee were aware of the status of these weapons. Retaliation against Turkey because of the missiles there was considered a possible Soviet response to any United States action from the outset." [Abram Chayes, *The Cuban Missile Crisis: International Crises and the Role of Law* (New York: Oxford University Press, 1974), p. 96f.]

3. Barton J. Bernstein, "The Cuban Missile Crisis: Trading the Jupiters in Turkey," *Political Science Quarterly*, Spring 1980, pp. 103–4.

4. Robert F. Kennedy, *op. cit.*, p. 87.

22. *Sailing under a New Skipper*

1. An anecdote related by Nicholas deB. Katzenbach.

2. Quoted by Ernest W. Lefever, *Spear and Scepter: Army, Policy and Politics in Tropical Africa* (Washington: Brookings Inst., 1970), p. 108, from *Africa Review* (London, February 1966), p. 6.

3. M. Crawford Young, "The Congo Rebellion," *Africa Report* (April 1965), p. 11. Quoted by E. W. Lefever, *op. cit.*, p. 109.

4. It is estimated that at least fifty thousand Congolese were killed by Congolese in 1964 (Lefever, *op. cit.*, p. 110).

23. *Cyprus*

1. Summarized by Edward Weintal and Charles Bartlett, *Facing the Brink: An Intimate Study of Crisis Diplomacy* (New York: Charles Scribner's Sons, 1967), p. 23.

2. *Ibid.*, pp. 23–24.

3. During the whole time I was involved with the agonies of Cyprus, I was constantly aware of the constraints under which democratic nations must conduct diplomacy in these complex times. That was not always so; a century ago the great powers could have disposed of the Cyprus problem quickly and incisively, as they showed by their disposition of a remarkably similar affair involving a conflict between Greek and Turkish populations on another Mediterranean island—not Cyprus but Crete. In 1896 the Greek community in Crete revolted and declared for union with Greece. The Turkish government moved to reinforce its garrisons on Crete, and the Greeks sent their fleet to assist the rebels. In the gathering crisis the great powers of Europe acted promptly and effectively. They sent a fleet to assist the rebels. They landed an army and compelled the insurgents to cease firing while occupying key coastal towns. They forced Turkey—which meanwhile had overwhelmingly defeated the Greek army in Thessaly—to make peace with Greece on terms favorable to the loser. Finally, after presenting identical notes to Athens and Constantinople, the great powers decreed that Crete was neither to join Greece immediately nor to revert to the Ottoman Empire.

That settlement was imposed upon the Greek and Turkish populations of the island, as well as on the Greek and Turkish governments without seeking their consent. It was possible because the great powers of the day were quite ready to use their combined strength ruthlessly—without concern for the rights of sovereignty, the integrity of territory, or the abstract principle of self-determination.

The world of the 1960s no longer permitted such domineering intervention, nor was there any longer a Concert of Europe; on the contrary, the two strongest world powers were now in opposing camps. Moreover, in the intervening years mankind had established rules and institutions designed to discourage the direct interference by nations in one another's affairs.

Thus effective American diplomacy under today's conditions requires constant vigilance of potential trouble spots such as Cyprus. Sometimes America has shown that vigilance but more recently it has not. In November 1967, after I had left the government, another crisis occurred. Then through the skillful diplomacy of Cyrus Vance, acting as special envoy of President Johnson, war was averted for a second time.

4. Edward Weintal and Charles Bartlett, *op. cit.,* p. 36.
5. Once, in a humorous speech at a newspaper dinner in honor of Dean Rusk I said tht early in our relationship Rusk had made clear that I would be his "alter ego." I was pleased at the time and it was only later when I reflected on my childhood in Iowa and the operation farmers performed on their domestic animals that I realized what might have been implied by that designation.

24. *Vietnam—The Initial Error*

1. My enthusiasm for that war faded even more during the Stevenson campaign of 1952 when Eisenhower's sententious promise to go to Korea gained him a cheap political advantage. Stevenson had fretted throughout the campaign about the need to come forward with a rational peace initiative, and I had spent hours secretly conferring with Adrian Fisher, then the Department of State's legal adviser, trying to write a speech that would soberly analyze our Korean predicament and propose a solution through negotiated settlement. Though Adlai made that speech—a watered-down version of it—it is lost to posterity and, in a sense, never really existed. Against all advice, he chose as his forum the Brooklyn Music Hall just at the end of the 1952 campaign. It was both egregious timing and impossible geography. The Brooklyn Music Hall was traditionally regarded as the place where Democratic Presidential candidates wound up their campaigns in a purple haze of hyperbole and fustian nonsense. Not only did Adlai's high-toned discussion totally mystify a rabble that expected to be aroused, but since he drastically rewrote the speech just before he mounted the podium, there were no copies available for the press. In fact, no one will ever know just what Stevenson said since the speech was not broadcast and, in desperation, I gave the single marked-up copy to a *New York Times* correspondent who was racing to meet an overdue deadline. Since none of the speech ever appeared in print, the reporter apparently lost the race. When afterward I lamented the fact that it had been the wrong speech at the wrong time to the wrong audience, Stevenson replied, "Well, I didn't make it for that bunch of bums and hangers-on at the Brooklyn Music Hall, I made it for the American people." "You think you did," I sadly replied, "but they never knew it."
2. Arthur M. Schlesinger, Jr., *A Thousand Days: John Kennedy in the White House* (Boston: Houghton Mifflin Co., 1965), p. 163.
3. *Ibid.,* p. 325.
4. Speech before the American Friends of Vietnam. Quoted by Guenter Lewy, *America in Vietnam* (New York: Oxford University Press, 1978), pp. 12–13.
5. *The Pentagon Papers,* as published by the *New York Times* (New York: Bantam Books, Inc., 1971), p. 142.
6. *Ibid.,* p. 143.
7. *Ibid.,* p. 148.

8. *Ibid.*, p. 148–50.
9. *Ibid.*, p. 151.
10. *Ibid.*, p. 149.
11. *Ibid.*, p. 151.
12. *Ibid.*, p. 152.
13. By the time of Kennedy's death, in November 1963, there were over 16,000 American troops in Vietnam.
14. Far too little attention has been paid to the political power that has so often been exerted in the Orient by strong-minded women. Chinese history is filled with examples of women of indomitable whim—like the seventh-century concubine who overthrew the Tang Dynasty, or Tz'u-hsi, who imprisoned her nephew-emperor and ruled as dowager empress until 1908; in more modern times, there have been Madame Chiang Kai-shek, and most recently Mao's widow, Jiang Quing, an ex-actress and prostitute who led the Gang of Four that turned the Cultural Revolution into an orgy of repression and disruption.
15. *The Pentagon Papers, op. cit.*, p. 194.
16. *Ibid.*
17. *Ibid.*, p. 195.
18. *Ibid.*, p. 197.
19. *Ibid.*, p. 175.
20. United States Congress, House Committee on International Relations, Hearings before the Subcommittee on International Relations, House of Representatives, 94th Congress, First Session, July 15, 22, 23, and 24, 1975, *Reassessment of U.S. Foreign Policy* (Washington: U. S. Government Printing Office, 1975), p. 145.
21. David Halberstam, *The Best and the Brightest* (New York: Random House, 1972), p. 494.

25. *The Balloon Rises Quickly*

1. *The Pentagon Papers,* as published by the *New York Times* (New York: Bantam Books, Inc., 1971), p. 129.
2. On June 9, 1964, in answer to a question from the President, the CIA stated that "no nation in the area would quickly succumb to Communism as a result of the fall of Laos and South Vietnam." Nor, the study proceeded, would "a continuation of the spread of Communism in the area . . . be inexorable" while "any spread which did occur would take time . . . in which the total situation might change in any number of ways unfavorable to the Communist cause." *Ibid.*, p. 254.
3. *Ibid.*, pp. 491–92.
4. Jonathan Schell, *The Time of Illusion* (New York: Vintage Books, 1976), pp. 9–10.
5. George Santayana, *The Life of Reason or the Human Progress* (New York: Charles Scribner & Sons, 1905), vol. 1, p. 13.
6. *The Pentagon Papers, op. cit.*, p. 325.
7. *Ibid.*, p. 425.
8. Since I do not wish to misrepresent the position of any of my colleagues, I must note a qualification at this point. Before the four of us met with the President on February 13, 1965, Mac Bundy called to correct this statement of the views attributed to him. The burden of his qualification, my notes would indicate, is that I was incorrect in stating that he believed that we must

continue to increase military pressure "to the point where Hanoi is prepared to agree not only to stop infiltration from the North, but effectively to call off the insurgency in the South and withdraw those elements infiltrated in the past." His position—if I now properly recall his explanation—was that since "we did not know what the answer [would] be," we did not have "to follow a particular course down the road to a particular result." He was, in other words, qualifying our declared war aim of restoring South Vietnam to the *status quo ante* the Viet Cong insurgency, by opting to leave our objective unformulated and therefore flexible. Though I privately applauded his pragmatism, I could not agree that we should keep charging more deeply into the mire without clearly acknowledging where we were going and on what basis we would call a halt.

9. Based on Jack Valenti, *A Very Human President* (New York: W. W. Norton, 1975), pp. 319–40, supplemented and modified by the information from my own notes and recollections.

10. Though in the light of subsequent knowledge, I may have overstated the dangers of a possible Chinese intervention, we then knew almost nothing about what was going on in Chinese foreign policy. Governmental and party announcements repeatedly emphasized that an historic moment had arrived for the world revolution under Communist leadership, and the United States was ritualistically denounced as the major impediment. In September 1965, Marshall Lin Piao, Minister of Defense and the Deputy Premier, was to startle the Administration—and particularly upset Secretary of Defense McNamara—by publishing a long harangue announcing China's support for "wars of national liberation." That emphasized the people's struggle against United States imperialism in Vietnam and elsewhere, including areas of Asia, Africa, and Latin America. In that climate, it was normal to feel concerned at the prospects of such a move. After all, my memorandum was written only fourteen years after we had precipitated a Chinese intervention in Korea by getting too near the Chinese border, and no American could say with assurance that we might not bring down Chinese mass armies on our troops.

26. *The Dusty End of a Reign of Error*

1. *The Pentagon Papers,* as published by the *New York Times* (New York: Bantam Books, Inc., 1971), p. 470.

2. *The Pentagon Papers,* the Senator Gravel Edition. *The Defense Department History of United States Decisionmaking on Vietnam* (Boston: Beacon Press, n.d.), vol. 4, p. 623.

3. Betraying his prime interest in influencing American opinion, President Johnson told me with some pride: "That's the right touch. Send a Jew to see the Pope."

4. Janos Radvanyi, *Delusion and Reality: Gambits, Hoaxes & Diplomatic One-Upmanship in Vietnam* (South Bend, Indiana: Gateway Editions, Ltd., 1978).

5. *The Pentagon Papers, New York Times, op. cit.,* pp. 579–80.

6. Before his appointment to the Pentagon, Clifford had, as chairman of the President's Foreign Intelligence Advisory Board, toured the Pacific with General Maxwell Taylor to solicit Asian governments to send troops to assist in Vietnam. He was, he told me later, profoundly shaken by the refusal of Asian nations to offer anything more than advice and encouragement. If Vietnam's neighbors did not take the war seriously enough to help the United States, why should we carry on alone at such great cost?

7. He was later sufficiently generous to observe in my presence and that of a number of other people that "George Ball was the only one who was right all along and we made a great mistake not to follow him."

8. Allan E. Goodman, *The Lost Peace: America's Search for a Negotiated Settlement of the Vietnam War* (Stanford: Hoover Inst. Press, 1978), p. 78.

9. Tad Szulc, *The Illusion of Peace: Foreign Policy in the Nixon Years* (New York: Viking Press, 1978), p. 158.

10. *Ibid.*, p. 268.

11. Marvin Kalb and Bernard Kalb, *Kissinger* (Boston: Little, Brown and Company, 1974), p. 120.

12. Tad Szulc, *op. cit.*, p. 150.

13. Henry A. Kissinger, *The White House Years* (Boston: Little, Brown & Co., 1979), p. 279.

14. *Ibid.*, p. 207.

15. Richard Nixon, *The Memoirs of Richard Nixon* (New York: Grosset & Dunlap, 1978), p. 392.

16. Henry A. Kissinger, "The Viet Nam Negotiations," *Foreign Affairs*, vol. 47, no. 2, (Jan. 1969), pp. 211–34.

17. George W. Ball, "We Should De-escalate the Importance of Vietnam," *New York Times Magazine*, December 21, 1969.

18. Robert Shaplen, *A Turning Wheel: Three Decades of the Asian Revolution as Witnessed by a Correspondent of the New York Times* (New York: Random House, 1979), p. 13.

19. *Ibid.*, p. 12.

20. Henry A. Kissinger, *The White House Years*, pp. 281–82.

21. *Ibid.*, p. 443.

22. Henry A. Kissinger, *The White House Years*, p. 1412.

23. *Ibid.*, p. 1462.

24. McGeorge Bundy, "Vietnam, Watergate & Presidential Powers," *Foreign Affairs*, vol. 58, no. 2 (Winter 1978/80), pp. 397–407.

25. Henry A. Kissinger, *The White House Years*, p. 1435.

26. As Professor Stanley Hoffmann has written, ". . . The reintroduction of American troops was unthinkable, and airpower alone was unlikely to stop the flood forever." Indeed, as he points out, the Kissinger agreement ". . . did not save us from humiliation, and—as with so much else in the Kissinger era—consisted of what the French call *reculer pour mieux sauter*, a retreat that merely postponed the apocalypse. . . . we left the South Vietnamese to themselves, claiming to have remained loyal to our ally, yet in effect washing our hands of the country's fate, and insured that the victory of Hanoi, being a military one, would wipe out not only Thieu but all the factions caught in the middle. Yet we still claimed that we wanted to insure Saigon's survival."

Further, writes Professor Hoffmann, ". . . to keep feeding the flames (while pretending, in the last days of Saigon, that our supplies might "stabilize" the situation long enough to provide for the negotiated political accommodation we never sought to achieve when Thieu seemed in firm control) would have been . . . callous. When we decided as late as 1971, to maintain in power the cliques that relied on us, we made sure that we would have a choice only between ignominious endings." Stanley Hoffmann, *Primacy or World Order: American Foreign Policy Since the Cold War* (New York: McGraw-Hill, 1978), p. 29.

27. T. S. Eliot, "The Dry Salvages," *Four Quartets* (New York: Harcourt, Brace & Co., c. 1943), p. 24.

28. George W. Ball, *op. cit.*, pp. 82–83.

27. *The Decision to Resign*

1. *The Pentagon Papers*, as published by the *New York Times* (New York: Bantam Books, Inc., 1971), p. 129.
2. *Ibid.*, p. 128.
3. A good illustration of this is President Jimmy Carter's New Year's Eve toast to the Shah on December 31, 1977, just before the revolution, when he described Iran as an "island of stability." Flora Lewis, "Carter Will Meet Sadat in Aswan on Wednesday," *New York Times,* January 1, 1978, p. 10.
4. Doris Kearns, *Lyndon Johnson and the American Dream* (New York: Harper & Row, 1976).

29. *From Nixon to Ford to Carter*

1. My articles also appeared in *Listener, Columbia Journal of World Business, Atlantic Papers, Survey, Harper's, Saturday Review, Finance,* and many others, as well as in French, German, Italian, and Japanese periodicals.
2. J. C. Hurewitz, *The Persian Gulf: After Iran's Revolution,* Headline Series 244 (New York: Foreign Policy Association, 1979), p. 45. Professor Hurewitz also notes that: "Over the next half-dozen years, [following 1972] the Shah entered into commitments for the purchase of more than $18 billion worth of weapons, among them some of the most sophisticated systems in the inventories of the United States and its Western allies—including T-14 Tomcat fighters with Phoenix air-to-air missiles that give the fighter its 100-mile reach, P-3F Orion antisubmarine patrol planes, Chieftain tanks, Spruance-class destroyers, and the AWACS (airborne warning and control system), a plane which even major allies of the United States found too expensive. The Shah was able to do this because the United States in May 1972 had agreed to sell him virtually any conventional military hardware he wanted. That decision was taken by President Richard M. Nixon and his national security adviser, Henry A. Kissinger—at a time, it should be noted, before anyone foresaw the monumental rise in the price of crude oil that was about to take place in less than 20 months, placing in the Shah's hands more money than he could have anticipated in his wildest dreams. It proved a rash decision, which lifted all normal U.S. restraints on the transfer of the most advanced conventional weapons to Third World countries." Other authors note that between 1970 and 1973 (before the oil price increase) American military sales had already "gone from $113 million to more than $2 billion." Michael A. Ledden and William H. Lewis, "Carter and the Fall of the Shah: The Inside Story," *Washington Quarterly,* spring 1980, p. 8.
3. Flora Lewis, "Carter Will Meet Sadat in Aswan on Wednesday," *New York Times,* January 1, 1978, p. 10.

30. *Over and Out*

1. Gayler, Noel. "(II) A Way Out of the Nuclear Trap," *Washington Post,* June 23, 1981 (second in a three-part series).
2. Lenin called the prerevolutionary Russian empire "a prison of peoples" and was concerned by the Russian tendency towards imperialist behavior; in 1919 he rephrased a popular proverb into "scratch some of the Communists and you will find Great Russian chauvinists." Nevertheless, he later identified whatever was good for the "national pride" of Russians as coinciding "with the socialist interest of all other proletarians." Quoted by Albert L. Weeks,

"Russia—The 'Chosen Nation'," *Freedom at Issue,* no. 50 (March-April, 1979), p. 25.

3. In order to speed up Russification, non-Russians have been resettled from their own respective republics; e.g., since 1940 14.6 percent Moldavians and 13.4 percent Ukrainians (5 million Ukrainians) have been sent eastward, while the Russians have been dispatched to these republics. *Ibid.,* p. 26.

   This process is still active, and the 1979 census shows that from 1970, Russians in the Ukrainian SSR have increased by 15 percent (or 1.3 million), and thus now represent 21 percent of the population.

4. United Nations' estimates are quoted for Mexico City at 15 million people in 1980, and expected to reach 31 million by the year 2000. Bernard D. Nossiter, "World Population Explosion Is Slowing, U.N. Finds," *New York Times,* June 15, 1980, p. 10.

5. Matthew Arnold, "Dover Beach," *Poetical Works of Matthew Arnold* (London: Macmillan and Co., 1927), p. 227.

6. Humbert Wolfe, "The High Song," *Requiem* (New York: George H. Doran Co., 1927), p. 125.

Index